2,000 YEARS OF
CHRIST'S POWER

Switzerland

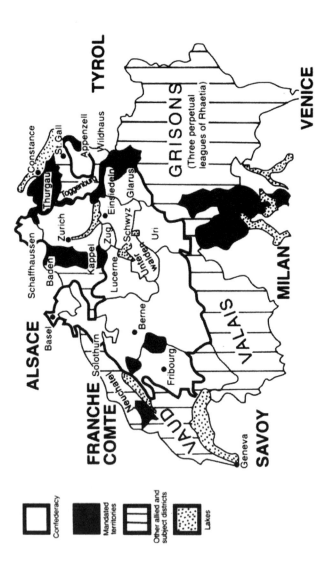

2,000 YEARS OF CHRIST'S POWER

PART THREE: RENAISSANCE AND REFORMATION

by

Dr N. R. Needham

GRACE PUBLICATIONS TRUST
7 Arlington Way
London EC1R 1XA
England
e-mail: editors@gracepublications.co.uk
www.gracepublications.co.uk

Managing Editors:
M. J. Adams
D. Crisp

First published 2004
Second impression 2010

ISBN 10: 0-946462-66-6   ISBN 13: 978-0-946462-66-7

Distributed by
EP BOOKS
Faverdale North
Darlington DL3 OPH
England

e-mail: sales@epbooks.org
www.epbooks.org

British Library Cataloguing in Publication Data available

Printed and bound in the UK by J F Print Ltd., Sparkford.

Dedication

To the Alliance of Confessing Evangelicals (ACE), who are doing so much among Lutherans and Reformed to stimulate a healthy interest in the Reformation and its ongoing lessons for today.

Western Europe

Western Europe: Key

SCOTLAND
1 Argyll
2 Ayr
3 Dundee
4 Edinburgh
5 Perth
6 St Andrews

ENGLAND
1 Berwick
2 Cambridge
3 Canterbury
4 London
5 Oxford

FRANCE
1 Angouleme
2 Meaux
3 Nantes
4 Noyon
5 Orleans
6 Paris
7 Vienne

SPAIN
1 Avila
2 Guipuzcoa
3 Manresa
4 Salamanca
5 Toledo

ITALY
1 Bologna
2 Ferara
3 Florence
4 Genoa
5 Marignano
6 Milan
7 Modena
8 Naples
9 Padua
10 Rome
11 Trent
12 Venic

SCANDI-NAVA
1 Copenhagen
2 Odense
3 Stavanger
4 Stockholm
5 Uppsala
6 Viborg

Contents

Illustrations and Maps

Acknowledgements

I wish to pay my debt of thanks to the following:

The Samuel Bill Theological College in Abak, Nigeria, whose students were the original inspiration for this work; John Appleby, who was instrumental in getting this series off the ground with Grace Publications; John Noble, who produced the indices; Joyce Bell who assisted with proof-reading; Phil Arthur and Timothy Grass, fellow Christian historians and co-workers, who each independently read through the entire first draft of this book, and made numerous valuable corrections and suggestions; Father Richard Conrad of Holy Cross Priory, Leicester, who read through and commented helpfully on an early draft of Chapter 8 on the Catholic Counter-Reformation; Father Alexis of the St Edward Brotherhood near Woking, who read through and commented helpfully on the draft of Chapter 9 on Eastern Orthodoxy; Steven Robinson of the Reformed Presbyterian Church of Ireland, presently serving as instructor of Old Testament literature at Westminster Biblical Mission's Károlyi Gáspár Institute of Theology, Miskolc, Hungary, whose knowledge of the Hungarian Reformation was an indispensable help in the writing of Chapter 6; and Alan Howe of Emmanuel Presbyterian Church, Clacton-on-Sea, England and the Alliance of Reformation Christians (ARC), who kindly translated many articles on less well-known Reformers from the German of the excellent Biographisch-Bibliographischen Kirchenlexikon, which can be accessed online at http://www.bautz.de/bbkl/; The Evangelical Library for the use of the portraits throughout this book.

A special word of thanks to my friend the Rev. Paul R. Williams of Grace Lutheran Church, Kitchener, Ontario, Canada, a walking encyclopedia on all things Lutheran (past and present), who amid a busy pastoral life kindly read through the material on Lutheranism and contributed many helpful corrections and suggestions. The Lutheran material makes up a large chunk of the volume, and without Paul's help it would have been immeasurably poorer. Paul is the Lutheran moderator of the Lutheran-Reformed discussion forum at http://groups.yahoo.com/group/Luther-Reform/, participation in which over the past 2 years has greatly enhanced and enriched my knowledge of Lutheranism.

The Eastern World

Introduction

This is the third part of a series entitled *2000 Years of Christ's Power*. Two other volumes, on the early Church fathers and the Middle Ages, precede this one. It can, however, be read by itself as an introduction to the Renaissance and the Reformation.

The Protestant Reformation is the most controversial era in the history of the Church. Its legacy of division lives on vibrantly today, with Roman Catholics, Lutherans, Reformed (Calvinists), Anglicans, and Anabaptists still worshipping in different religious communities: often suspicious of each other, more often ignorant of each other. Into the complex picture one can then add the Eastern Orthodox, peering uneasily westward over the walls of Constantinople and Moscow, and shouting in effect, "A plague on all your houses!"[1]

What I've attempted here is, in a sense, quite simple: to tell the story of the Reformation as clearly and fairly as I can. I've tried to tell it colourfully, too; there are few periods in Church history so full of human interest. As I weave my narrative, my hope is that all today's religious descendants of the amazing 16th century eruption will be able to meet and interact with the authentic voices of their epoch-making ancestors in the faith. I haven't made any attempt to tone down the divisive nature of the events of the 16th century, nor to offer any presumptuous solutions of my own to its mixed and fragmented legacy.[2] I am as enmeshed in the 16th century inheritance

---

[1] One should not, however, too readily assume that the beliefs and ethos of any of these groups have remained unchanged over the past 500 years. There may be surprises in store as you read these pages. How many modern Protestants would dream of the high view of the Blessed Virgin Mary held by the Reformers? Or how many modern Roman Catholics realise that, for a time in the 16th century, the cutting edge movement in their Church – the "Catholic Evangelicals" – believed in justification by faith, and produced a joint statement with Calvin to prove it?

[2] One cannot deny the fragmenting effect of the Reformation. On the other hand, if you have read Parts One and Two in this series, you will know that such fragmentation was not a new phenomenon. The Church had already divided long before the Reformers arrived. The Nestorians and Monophysites sepa-

as any Westerner: Reformed by theological conviction, although having a soft spot for Lutheranism. I have little sympathy with that form of "ecumenism" which relativises, and thereby trivialises, the convictions for which men and women lived and fought and died in the 16th century. That isn't to say I disapprove of deeper under-standing among the different religious traditions that claim the name of Christian; I approve heartily. But sometimes, deeper understanding will lead us to appreciate just how deeply we do differ on not a few issues, despite surprising measures of agreement on others. Papering over the cracks in the interests of some ecumenical "happy family" game, in which sincerity is more highly prized than truth, is not this writer's agenda, either as a historian or a Churchman.

I can summarise my own perspective on the Reformation by repeating something I said in my introduction to Part Two of this series:

> "As an heir of the Reformation and a Church historian, I often find myself telling people that the great spiritual and theological movement set rolling by Luther and Zwingli was in fact the best elements of Western medieval Christianity trying to correct the worst elements."

In other words, although the necessity for the Reformation may have been a tragic necessity, the Reformation itself I don't see as a tragedy (parting company, here, with the increasing tendency among Evangelicals today), but as a movement that was essentially wholesome and good.

Of course, like any wholesome and good movement in a fallen world among sinful human beings, the Reformation became mixed

---

rated from Chalcedonians in the 5th and 6th centuries; the Eastern and Western Chalcedonian Churches (Constantinople and Rome) separated in 1054; and the Waldensians, Lollards, and Hussites separated from the Western Roman Church in the period from the late 12th to the early 15th centuries. The idea that the Reformation shattered the oneness a Church that had been wonderfully united since the days of the apostles is a foolish myth.

up and tainted with a lot that wasn't quite so wholesome or quite so good. C.S.Lewis amusingly, if cuttingly, compared the 16th century quarrel between Roman Catholics and Protestants to men trying to carry on a philosophical debate amid a mob in a fairground, in a forced alliance with confidence tricksters, and under the supervision of an armed police force that kept changing sides.[3] There is rather too much truth in Lewis's caricature to leave us entirely comfortable! But perhaps it is just another way of saying that no one entirely transcends his culture. It would be an arrogant and romantic delusion of sinless perfection that thought so. And in many ways, the Protestant Reformers were profoundly people of their own times, as we are of ours. We shouldn't expect perfection of them, any more than a future generation will discover perfection in us.

We will certainly find, though, as we immerse ourselves in the Reformation era, that (as Hollywood used to claim of its films) "all human life is here". We may also find that this life – so fresh, boisterous, and daring – has much to give us today, in our own comparative jadedness and superficiality.

****

"Philip Melanchthon showed Luther a letter from Augsburg, in which he was informed that a very learned theologian, a Roman Catholic in that city, had been converted and received the gospel. Luther said: 'I like those best who do not change sides suddenly, but ponder the case with considerate discretion, compare together the writings of both parties, lay them on the gold balance, and in the fear of God search out the truth. Out of such, fit people are made, able to stand in controversy. Such a man was Saint Paul, who at first was a strict Pharisee and man of works, who stiffly and earnestly held and defended the law; but afterwards he preached Christ in the best and purest manner against the whole nation of the Jews.'"

Martin Luther, from his *Table Talk*.

---

[3]   C. S. Lewis, *English Literature in the Sixteenth Century* (London: OUP, 1973), p.37.

The Holy Roman Empire

Chapter 1.

SONGS OF SPRING:
THE RENAISSANCE.

1. What was the Renaissance?

When we hear of the Renaissance[1], perhaps what immediately springs to mind is its art, and the famous artists who flourished at that time – such as Donatello, Botticelli, Leonardo da Vinci, Raphael, Michelangelo, and Titian. Certainly there was an artistic dimension to the Renaissance. Still, this was only one facet of a more complex movement, the true nature of which is a subject of ongoing debate. Few have doubted its significance, especially (in Church history) as a forerunner of the Reformation; the 16th century saying, "Erasmus laid the egg and Luther hatched it", contains more than a grain of truth, despite the ultimate break between the prince of Renaissance humanists and the pioneer of Protestantism.[2] We will see in subsequent chapters how deeply affected the Reformers were by aspects of the Renaissance. In this chapter, however, the aim is to look more generally at the Renaissance in its own right.

We can say without much fear of contradiction that the "Renaissance" is the name historians give to a cluster of important developments within Western culture at the close of the Middle Ages. The ferment began in Italy in the second half of the 14th century and

---

[1] Pronounced "ren-ay-sonce".
[2] See section 4 for Erasmus, and Chapters 2 and 3 for Luther.

eventually spread across the whole of Western Europe, changing people's values and outlook on life (at least among the educated).

It is, however, impossible to give a single all-embracing definition of the Renaissance. Its character varied according to the times and places in which it flourished within Europe between the 14th and 16th centuries. Perhaps the closest we can get to expressing the core of the Renaissance is to say that it was movement cradled in the love of ancient Greek and Roman culture, and a desire for its rebirth in the present. (The word *renaissance* is French for "rebirth".[3]) This commitment to Europe's pre-medieval culture was rooted in a rediscovery of the literature of ancient Greece and Rome – often called "the classics" or "classical" literature. The Renaissance involved a revival of classical forms of thought, expression, and action, a revival mediated through "humane" studies – grammar, rhetoric, poetry, history, philosophy.[4] These were seen by Renaissance thinkers as the arts which transformed the raw material of the merely natural human being into the refined perfection of the cultured person: nature gives us birth, but the humane studies then recreate us and make us authentically human. In all this, a special emphasis was placed on human beings as communicators; the effective expression of thoughts and values in writing, speech, music, and visual art lay close to the heart of the Renaissance vision. The medieval Latin of the Church was particularly despised as barbaric in comparison with the beauty of classical Latin.

In the 19th century, the German thinker F. J. Niethammer coined the term *humanism* to sum up this Renaissance concept of humanity and human life. We must not confuse it with the present-day philosophy of humanism, which is anti-Christian, denying the existence of God and treating this earthly life as the only life there

---

[3]   The Renaissance of the 14th and 15th Centuries was different from the Carolingian Renaissance under Charlemagne in the 8th and 9th Centuries (see Part Two, Chapter 4). The Carolingian Renaissance did not shift people's values and outlook from heaven to earth, as the later Renaissance did.

[4]   "Humane" studies were contrasted with "divine" studies (theology).

is. In contrast to today's humanists, most of the humanists of the Renaissance were pro-Christian. Their commitment to humanity and human culture was normally part of a Christian view of the world; they saw a God-given meaning and worth in the present life, as well as in the life to come. Those who promoted this Renaissance concept of humanism regarded it as nothing less than the regeneration of true culture and therefore of true humanity, after the long medieval centuries of ignorance, superstition, and barbarism, which they scornfully called "the Dark Ages".

Central to this Renaissance critique of medieval civilisation was an adjustment of the claims this world and the next. The Christian faith taught that God had created the world "very good", but also that through the sin of Adam the world was fallen and perishing, and that humanity's final destiny lay beyond this brief life, in eternity. How then should Christians try to balance the claims of earth with the claims of heaven? In the Middle Ages, the prevailing attitude of official Western religion at its most "devout" had been one of high and holy contempt for the present life, a fixing of the mind on the four last things – death, judgment, hell, heaven – and a conviction that the only truly worthwhile use of this short-lived earthly existence was for people to prepare their souls for the eternal life to come. The perfect human beings, those who most closely conformed themselves to Christ, were therefore the monk and the nun, who renounced the present world, gave up family life and owning property, subdued the body and its passions through ascetic labours, and devoted themselves to prayer, worship, Scripture, and the attempt to become an "angel in the flesh" in anticipation of the resurrection (Luke 20:34-6).

The Renaissance changed this. It shifted people's spiritual concern back to the present life: not usually in the sense of denying the life to come, but insisting strongly that life on earth had a value, a dignity, and a beauty of its own. In the great pagan writers of Greek and Roman civilisation, there was no contempt for the world of human achievement, no monastic withdrawal from secular affairs. Even the foremost of Greek philosophers, Plato, with his profound vision of eternity, had spent his life trying to work out how to build a perfect political community on earth, where the citizens would live in harmony with eternal ideals of justice and beauty.[5] Renaissance humanists looked back on this ancient civilisation of Greece and Rome as the golden age of human culture, the perfect expression of the human spirit and its highest values; this golden age, they believed, must be reborn in the present if humankind was to fulfil its true potential. There was an awakening of interest in humanity itself and the human world, a fresh and excited optimism about the possibilities of human achievement in art, music, literature, education, science, and government. This brought with it a reaction against the monastic ideal of poverty, asceticism, and heavenly contemplation, in favour of an active and productive life in the world through "secular" pursuits (from the Latin *saecula*, meaning "this present age"). Renaissance thinkers began to glorify the secular realm of the state, politics, city life, even war, as the true sphere for human action. A new fascination for the individual human person also appeared, a new emphasis on personal self-expression and self-development, which gave rise to a flourishing of non-religious portraits and biographies (especially autobiographies).

In the culture of Greece and Rome, then, the claims of human life on earth were paramount. This contrasted keenly with the world-renouncing, heaven-aspiring attitude of medieval spirituality, and many found it liberating. Some Renaissance humanists stopped there; they simply wanted to restore the secular human-centred spirit of ancient paganism. However, the Christian humanists did not admire only the *pagan* writers of the classical age. They wanted to go back to *all* the sources of Western European civilisation, *Christian* as well as pagan. So they dug afresh into the riches of the Greek New Testament and the early Church fathers. The apostolic and patristic period became, in their eyes, a *spiritual* golden age; and again, they felt the only hope for Western Europe was that the golden age of the early Church must be reborn in the present. This

---

[5] For Plato, see Part One, Chapter 1, section 1, under the heading **Platonism**.

humanist quest for the life-giving wellsprings of culture, both pagan and Christian, found expression in the Latin phrase *ad fontes,* "back to the sources".

It was fitting that this revival of the spirit and values of ancient Greece and Rome, in their pagan and Christian aspects, should have arisen first in Italy, the ancient heartland of the Roman Empire.

2. The Italian Renaissance.

Renaissance Italy was not politically united as one nation. Five chief political communities dominated the land: Milan, Venice, Florence, Naples, and the papal states. It was in the great northern cities of Milan, Venice, and Florence that the dawn of Italian humanism took place. Trade and commerce in the age of the Crusades had made these communities prosperous and politically independent; since the 1200s, rural feudalism had been dying here, and a thriving urban culture developing.[6]

The first great Italian Renaissance figure was the poet *Francesco Petrarch* (1304-74). His parents were natives of Florence, but he grew up in southern France, in Avignon during the Avignonese captivity of the papacy.[7] The first half of Petrarch's life was to be a cause of burning shame to him. He became a Catholic priest without any sense of divine calling, lived with several mistresses, and had a number of illegitimate children. However, in 1350 Petrarch experienced a life-changing religious conversion, which he described to his friend, the illustrious Italian Renaissance writer, Giovanni Boccaccio (1313-75), like this: "I now hate that plague of sexual immorality infinitely more than I once loved it. When I remember it, it fills me with shame and horror. Jesus Christ, who set me free, knows that I speak the truth. I often prayed to Him with

---

[6]   For feudalism, see Part Two, Chapter 4, section 2.
[7]   For the Avignonese captivity, see Part Two, Chapter 10, section 1.

tears, and He has taken pity on me, given me His hand, and drawn me up to Himself."

Petrarch was a zealous admirer of the ancient pagan writers of Latin, especially Cicero, Virgil, and Seneca, and modelled his writing style on them.[8] Petrarch's own writings made him internationally famous: his Italian love-poems were works of literary genius. After his conversion his spiritual hero was Augustine of Hippo, and he never went anywhere without a copy of Augustine's *Confessions*. Since Augustine was a Platonist, Petrarch accepted Plato as the supreme philosopher. This put him in sharp conflict with scholastic theology, which had largely abandoned Plato for Aristotle.[9]

Petrarch's hostility to scholasticism was to be a typical humanist attitude. This was partly because humanism led to a renewed enthusiasm for Plato, while most scholastics tended to be Aristotelians. It was also partly because humanists thought that scholastic theology was over-complicated, too philosophical, divorced from Scripture, and expressed in barbaric medieval Latin; the schoolmen usually studied the Latin Bible of the Vulgate – humanists demanded that theologians must study Scripture in its original languages of Greek and Hebrew. There was, however, another factor which intensified the clash between scholasticism and some humanists. A significant number of humanists were, like Petrarch, admirers of Augustine. But as we saw in Part Two, Chapter 7, scholastic theology after Thomas Aquinas had (on the whole) begun to drift seriously from Augustine's views of humanity's bondage to sin and the sovereignty of God's grace in salvation. The great English schoolman William of Ockham had started a powerful trend towards a "neo-Pelagian" theology, which emphasised human free-will, effort, and worthiness as the way to secure God's

---

[8]   For Virgil and Seneca, see Part One, Chapter 1, section 1: Virgil under the heading **Traditional pagan religion**, Seneca under the heading **Stoicism**. Cicero (106-43 BC) was a Roman politician and philosopher, one of the greatest speakers and writers of Latin in the ancient world.

[9]   For Aristotle and scholasticism, see Part Two, Chapter 7, sections 2 and 3.

mercy. This gave many of those humanists who admired Augustine another strong reason to loathe scholasticism.[10]

In Petrarch, then, we see the ingredients which went into the making of Renaissance humanism, especially in its more Christian form:

(i) an attitude of contempt for the medieval period as "the Dark Ages" – Petrarch was the first man to refer to the Middle Ages by this name;

(ii) a belief in a golden age of civilisation in classical Greece and Rome, and a spiritual golden age in the days of the apostles and early Church fathers;

(iii) a new fervour for Plato which checked the commitment to Aristotle that operated in much scholastic theology, and a tendency to prefer Augustine over scholasticism in any case;

(iv) the admiration of ancient Latin authors as masters of literary style;

(v) colouring all of this, the conviction that all philosophy and theology should revolve around humanity and human life, especially the relationship between human beings and God.

If Petrarch heralded a revival of interest in ancient Latin culture, there was soon alongside it a renewal of enthusiasm for ancient Greek culture. This first sprang up in Florence, especially through a number of Greek scholars from the Byzantine Empire who fled the troubled state of Byzantium and settled in the north Italian city to teach the Greek language.[11] The most outstanding was **Manuel Chrysoloras** (1355-1415), a native of Constantinople, who lectured

---

[10] On the other hand, many humanists – notably Erasmus – were light years away from Augustine's theology of original sin and predestination, even though they admired his spirituality. Humanism could be thoroughly anti-Augustinian in this respect. Perhaps it would be better to say that humanism, through its devotion to the early Church fathers, provided a setting in which a "back to Augustine" movement could potentially flourish.

[11] The Byzantine Empire was surrounded by hostile Muslim forces that finally conquered Constantinople in 1453. See Part Two, Chapter 9.

in Greek studies in Florence University. Chrysoloras inspired a whole new generation of Italian humanists; they compared him with a sun of knowledge, illuminating all Italy. Also important was **Gemistos Plethon** (1355-1450), who gave lectures in Florence on the philosophy of Plato. The essence of Italian humanism stood revealed in Plethon's treatise *On the Difference between Plato and Aristotle*, aimed at proving how much deeper and truer Plato's teaching was than Aristotle's. Plethon got into serious trouble with his fellow Greeks for being more a pagan Platonist than a Christian.

The popularity of Greek studies in general, and Plato in particular, reached its height in 1462 in the founding of the Platonic Academy in Florence, which was dedicated to discussing and spreading Platonism. Gemistos Plethon thought up the idea of the Academy; its director was **Marsilio Ficino** (1433-99). Ficino was a Catholic priest whose theology was a rich and potent blend of Christianity with Neoplatonism; he had statues of the Virgin Mary and Plato in his study, with a lamp burning under each. Ficino translated into Latin the complete writings of Plato, Plotinus, and Pseudo-Dionysius the Areopagite,[12] while his own books, *Theologia Platonia* ("Platonic Theology", 1469-72) and *De Christiana Religione* ("Concerning the Christian Religion", 1476), argued that Platonic philosophy was the divinely inspired partner of the Christian faith, because both taught the same fundamental spiritual truths. Ficino's writings made a profound impact on other humanists such as John Colet (see section 3) and later groups like the 17th century Cambridge Platonists.[13]

Another famous member of the Platonic academy was **Giovanni Pico della Mirandola** (1463-94), a deep-thinking philosopher, student of Jewish mystical literature, and (in the last years of his life) disciple of the religious reformer Savonarola.[14] Mirandola produced one of the most celebrated of all Renaissance writings,

---

[12] For Plotinus and Neoplatonism, see Part One, Chapter 6, section 2. For Pseudo-Dionysius, see Part One, Chapter 12, section 3.

[13] Part Four will look at the Cambridge Platonists.

[14] For Savonarola, see section 5 below.

his *Oration on the Dignity of Man*. In this treatise, Mirandola maintained that God had placed humankind in the universe so that we might study, investigate, and understand everything it contains. Furthermore, human beings occupied a level of existence midway between the animals and the angels, with the capacity either to fall down to the lower level of the beasts, or to rise up to the angelic level and become like gods. Mirandola's confidence in human reason and the possibilities of human progress, within a Christian framework of belief (it was God who had given humanity these glorious powers), was typical of many Renaissance humanists. However, Mirandola himself renounced this confidence when he fell under Savonarola's influence in 1491; he turned his back on the world, gave away vast amounts of money to the poor, became a street evangelist, wrote sombre commentaries on the Psalms and Lord's Prayer, and emphasised sinful humanity's dependence on God's grace.

It was also in Italy that the Renaissance revival of interest in the early Church first blossomed. Important figures were: Ambrogio Traversari (1386-1439), a Florentine monk, head of the Camaldolese order, and one of the pioneer Renaissance students of the Hebrew language; John Bessarion (1403-72), a Byzantine archbishop who submitted to the Union of Florence and became a Catholic cardinal;[15] Leonardo Bruni (1370-1444), a Florentine politician, historian, and enthusiast for Plato; and towering above them all, ***Lorenzo Valla*** (1406-57).

Valla was a native of Rome, ordained to the priesthood in 1431, and thereafter engaged in a life of lecturing, study, and writing, financed by pope Nicholas V and king Alphonso I of Naples. Valla combined a zeal for Augustine with a pioneering study of the Greek text of the New Testament, and a highly critical attitude to some ancient Catholic traditions. His two greatest works were his *Concerning the False Credit and Eminence of the Donation of Constantine* (1440) and his *Annotations on the New Testament*. In

---

[15]   For Bessarion and the Union of Florence, see Part Two, Chapter 9, section 3.

the first of these works, Valla exposed as a forgery the so-called "Donation of Constantine", which the popes had used for 700 years to back up their exalted claims.[16] Based on this exposé, Valla argued that the papacy should renounce all political power and become a purely spiritual institution. His *Annotations on the New Testament* were not published until 1505, by Erasmus of Rotterdam (see section 4). They consisted of a critical comparison between the Greek text of the New Testament and the Latin New Testament of the Vulgate, pointing out the Vulgate's many errors. Not surprisingly, the papacy eventually condemned all Valla's writings in the aftermath of the Protestant Reformation.

Florence was the chief centre of the Italian Renaissance, but it took root in other cities too, especially in Rome itself. From the middle of the 15th century, a series of "Renaissance popes" occupied the throne of Saint Peter, and gave strong financial backing to the humanist cause. The first was pope *Nicholas V* (1447-55), Lorenzo Valla's patron, who founded the famous Vatican library in 1453, soon to house the greatest collection of books in the world. The Renaissance popes made Rome into the beating heart of Italy's artistic world; music, painting, sculpture, and architecture all flourished mightily in the Italian Renaissance, lavishly supported by the papacy.

The Renaissance particularly affected the visual arts. In the Middle Ages, most artists had limited themselves to religious subjects, but Renaissance artists painted landscapes, scenes from everyday life, individual portraits of people who were not saints or kings. They also took great care to make sure the people they depicted looked like real human beings in natural settings. They gave religious subjects the same treatment. For the first time, artists drew and painted pictures of Biblical scenes and characters, including Christ Himself, in a natural and realistic way; for example, they portrayed the Virgin Mary, not as the exalted Queen of Heaven, but as an earthly human maiden and mother. Famous Renaissance painters

---

[16] For the Donation of Constantine, see Part Two, Chapter 2, section 1.

and sculptors of Italy included the Dominican friar Fra Angelico (1400-1455), Donatello (1386-1466), Sandro Botticelli (1444-1510), Leonardo da Vinci (1452-1519), Raphael (1483-1520), Michelangelo (1475-1564), and Titian (1477-1576). The Renaissance popes promoted this artistic movement, as well as advancing the cause of humanist learning. Unfortunately, their zeal for humanism was not usually matched by a corresponding zeal for holiness; most of the Renaissance popes lived scandalously immoral lives.

3. The Renaissance in the rest of Europe.

The Renaissance reached Germany, France, England, and Spain in the closing decades of the 15th century. One of the main causes which enabled it to spread from Italy was the invention of printing by movable type. In about 1450, Johann Gutenberg (1395-1468) of Mainz set up the first European printing press; the first book he printed was the Bible. By 1500, over 200 presses were in operation throughout Europe. We can hardly overstate the cultural revolution which this brought about. Gone were the days when scribes (usually monks) had to copy out books by hand. For the first time, a publisher could make thousands of copies of a book easily and quickly, and put them into mass circulation. This meant that ideas could spread so much more swiftly.[17] It also meant that the ability to read ("literacy") became more highly valued.

Germany

In Germany, the Renaissance was more fully and explicitly Christian than in Italy. Many of the Italian humanists, although they remained within the Church, were more interested in Cicero and Plato than in the New Testament and the early Church fathers. By contrast, the German humanists created a much closer alliance between the pagan and Christian elements of Greek and Roman

---

[17] The impact of printing in the 15th century and of the internet in the 20th have often been compared.

culture. From its pagan elements they derived models of literary style, Platonic philosophy, and ideals of political citizenship. From its Christian elements, they shaped a concept of Christian spirituality which emphasised the study of the New Testament, a simple and Christ-centred faith, the abiding value of the early Church fathers, and the importance of serving God in the world rather than retreating into a monastery. (This view of the Christian life was very similar to, and undoubtedly influenced by, the *devotio moderna* – see Part Two, Chapter 10, section 6). German humanists developed these Christian concerns in conscious antagonism to scholastic theology; they scorned scholasticism as a philosophical distortion of the Christian faith, which seduced people from the simplicity of Christ into a wasteland of useless theological arguments. The German Renaissance also moved away from the scholastic tendency to interpret Scripture in an allegorical way (looking for deep, hidden theological and spiritual meanings in every statement), and placed a fresh emphasis on the old Antiochene method of "grammatico-historical" interpretation (understanding the Bible's words and statements primarily in their ordinary obvious sense).[18]

Out of this alliance of the pagan and Christian culture of ancient Greece and Rome, the German Renaissance fashioned a compelling vision for the reformation of society. German humanists hoped, through education in schools and universities, to purify people's minds of ignorance and superstition, and nurture them into godly and useful Christian citizens, glorifying God through their various abilities here on earth, as artists, politicians, teachers, merchants, craftsmen, housewives.

Another distinctive factor in the German Renaissance was its tendency towards German nationalism. German humanists looked on the Germans as the most noble people on earth. Their nationalistic feelings were inflamed by a corresponding hostility to Italians and the papacy, stemming from the medieval battles between popes and German emperors. Martin Luther was soon to exploit this

---

[18] For the grammatico-historical method of interpretation, see Part One, Chapter 9, section 1.

German nationalism to devastating effect in his own battle with the pope.

Pioneers of German humanism included the following:

Rudolf Agricola (1444-85). Agricola is sometimes called "the father of German humanism". He was actually Dutch by birth, receiving his early education in the Netherlands from the Brothers of the Common Life.[19] After studying at various German universities and sampling the culture of Renaissance Italy, he lectured on the classics in Heidelberg university (central-western Germany), promoting the teaching of Latin in German schools and universities. His treatise on education, *On the Formation of Study* (1484), greatly influenced Erasmus (see section 4). Agricola was a disciple of the religious reformer Wessel Gansfort (see section 5).

Sebastian Brant (1458-1521). Brant was a poet who stimulated the development of the German language, a follower of Joachim of Fiore,[20] and a zealous advocate of the Holy Roman Empire – he saw the emperor ***Maximilian I*** (1493-1519), rather than the papacy, as the true source of religious reform. Above all, Brant was the author of the internationally famous and popular book *Ship of Fools* (1494), written originally in German and then translated into Latin, French, and English. In this book, Brant declared that the end times were near, and condemned the sins of all classes in society, including many religious abuses in the Catholic Church, *e.g.* the corrupt lives of priests (whom he called "the devil's excrement"!) and of Franciscan and Dominican friars. He also criticised the sale of indulgences and relics for profit. The only hope Brant held out was a reformed papacy and Empire.

Conrad Celtis (1459-1508) was a poet and German nationalist, crowned by the emperor Frederick III (1440-93) in 1487 as the first German "poet laureate" (official national poet). Not really interested in theology or philosophy, Celtis's great passion in life was

---

[19]   For the Brothers of the Common Life, see Part Two, Chapter 10, section 6.
[20]   For Joachim of Fiore, see Part Two, Chapter 8, section 3.

the glory of the German people, whom he wished to unify politically into a single nation. Since he saw the papacy as Germany's supreme foe, Celtis expressed his nationalism in a violently anti-papal, anti-Italian way, especially in his *Five Books of Epigrams*. His outstanding contribution to German humanism was as a historian, carrying out brilliant ground-breaking research into various aspects of Germany's past.

Jacob Wimpfeling (1450-1528). Wimpfeling was an ardent German nationalist, many of whose writings glorified Germany as the home of true moral and cultural excellence, *e.g.* his *Epitome of Germanic Affairs* (1505), a history of the Germanic people from the 1st to the 15th Centuries. He was also a stern critic of clerical and papal corruptions – *e.g.* the sale of indulgences and Church office for profit, the ignorance and immorality of the clergy, and Rome's interference in the election of German bishops. If these abuses were not swiftly remedied, Wimpfeling warned, the Hussite heresy would break out of Bohemia and infect all Germany.[21]

Conrad Mutian (1471-1526). Mutian was a lecturer at Erfurt university (central Germany), a Neoplatonist and a committed champion of Christian humanism. He had been taught at a school run by the Brothers of the Common life at Deventer, where he absorbed a lifelong zeal for the *devotio moderna*. Mutian often criticised the moral corruption of clergy and papacy and the sort of religion that relied on rituals and relics for salvation.

Willibald Pirckheimer (1470-1530). Pirckheimer was a native of Nuremberg (central Germany). He acquired the riches of Italian Renaissance learning as a young student, and then taught Greek and Latin in his home city. Pirckheimer translated many ancient Greek writings into Latin (*e.g.* Plato and Gregory of Nazianzus[22]), wrote various historical and scientific studies of his own, and became the leader of a thriving humanist circle in Nuremberg. Nuremberg at that time was, politically and industrially, the most

---

21   For the Hussites, see Part Two, Chapter 10, section 5.
22   For Gregory of Nazianzus, see Part One, Chapter 8, section 3.

important city in Germany, and Pirckheimer was its foremost figure; he has been called the most learned layman in Germany. He was also committed to reforming Church and society. When the Protestant Reformation dawned, none were so favourable to it as the Nuremberg humanists; Pirckheimer was an early supporter of Luther, although he himself eventually decided not to leave the Catholic Church.

Johannes Reuchlin (1455-1522). Reuchlin (pronounced "roy-klin")[23] was a Greek and Latin scholar who became the first non-Jewish German academic to master the Hebrew language. He was also a student of Jewish mysticism. The humanist cry of *ad fontes* had come to include a desire to study the Old Testament in its original tongue. Reuchlin pioneered this study of Hebrew; his *Rudiments of Hebrew* (1506) was the first textbook on Hebrew grammar and vocabulary ever published. Unfortunately for himself, Reuchlin's deep Jewish learning marked him out as the man in whose career the tensions between humanism and scholasticism exploded into open warfare. In 1509, a convert from Judaism called Johann Pfefferkorn (1469-1522) persuaded the Holy Roman emperor Maximilian I to decree that all Jews must surrender all their books to the authorities. Pfefferkorn received strong backing from a Dominican friar called Jakob Hochstraten (1460-1527), who was in charge of the inquisition in Germany. Reuchlin was appalled; he spoke out in defence of Jewish literature as useful in understanding the Old Testament, and argued that friendly discussion with the Jews was better than confiscating their books, if they were ever to embrace Christianity. As a result, the inquisition accused Reuchlin of heresy and put him on trial in 1514.

German humanists rallied to Reuchlin's support. Two of them, ***Crotus Rubeanus*** (1480-1539) and ***Ulrich von Hutten*** (1488-1523), wrote a brilliant best-selling attack on Reuchlin's enemies, called *Letters of Obscure Men*, published between 1515 and 1517. Rubeanus and Hutten pretended that these letters had been written

---

[23] If you know how to pronounce a Scottish "ch" (as in "loch"), that is strictly how the "ch" in Reuchlin should be pronounced.

by Dominican friars, whom they saw as Reuchlin's greatest foes, and they made the friars say such stupid and scandalous things that the whole of educated Catholic Europe was soon laughing at them. It was a great propaganda triumph for humanism. Rubeanus was a lecturer at Erfurt university, later to become a personal friend and supporter of Martin Luther. Hutten was an odd, volatile combination of old-fashioned chivalrous knight and academic humanist scholar.[24] A fierce German nationalist, Hutten attacked papal and clerical corruptions without mercy in his various writings, in a hard-hitting popular style which increasingly alarmed the papacy. Like Rubeanus, Hutten too was to champion Luther's cause.

Despite the fact that Rubeanus and Hutten won public opinion over to Reuchlin's side, Rome finally condemned Reuchlin in 1520. But by then, the mightier storms of the Protestant Reformation had overtaken the battle between humanists and scholastics.

Christian humanism made a deeper impact on Germany than on any other nation. However, its influence spread to France, England, and Spain too.

France

In France, the central humanist figure was *Jacques Lefevre d'Étaples* (1460-1533), also known by his Latin name Faber Stapulensis. A friend and disciple of Marsilio Ficino, Lefevre combined Ficino's Neoplatonism with a zeal for studying the medieval Catholic mystics and the Bible (he translated the New Testament into French in 1523, the Psalms in 1525, and the rest of the Old Testament in 1528). Lefevre was a determined foe of scholasticism. His refusal to be bound by scholastic theology, and his insistence on the grammatico-historical method of interpreting the Bible, led Lefevre to some reformist views of what the Bible taught. In 1512, he issued a new translation of Paul's letters in Latin, with a commentary by himself, in which he denied all place

---

[24]   For chivalry and knighthood, see Part Two, Chapter 5, section 2.

to human worthiness or merit in salvation, and questioned transubstantiation. Eventually condemned for "Lutheranism" (although he never actually embraced the Reformation), Lefevre fled to Strasbourg in 1525, and ended up in the court of queen Margaret of Navarre, a friend of reform, whose daughter Jeanne d'Albret was to be a champion of French Calvinism.

A band of French humanist reformers gathered around Lefevre. The foremost was the gentle and noble-minded **William Briçonnet** (1470-1533), bishop of Meaux (east of Paris) from 1516, who led a great moral and spiritual reform movement in his diocese. From their association with Briçonnet, the other French reformers are often called "the group of Meaux". They included: **William Budé** (1467-1540), one of the outstanding Greek scholars of his day, and founder of the College de France, the most successful academic centre of French humanism; Gerard Roussel (1500-1550), chaplain to queen Margaret of Navarre; Louis de Berquin (1490-1529), one of France's earliest Protestant martyrs; and William Farel (1489-1565), who became one of the leading Protestant Reformers of French-speaking Switzerland.[25]

England

In England, William Grocyn (1446-1519) and Thomas Linacre (1460-1524) introduced humanism into Oxford University. However, the leading English humanist was *John Colet* (1467-1519). Son of the Lord Mayor of London, young Colet studied at Oxford University, then journeyed abroad in quest of more knowledge; he found what he was seeking in Italy, especially at the Platonic Academy in Florence, where he stayed from 1493 to 1496. When he arrived back in England, Colet gave lectures at Oxford university on the apostle Paul's letters, attacking scholasticism (especially Aquinas). When Colet became dean[26] of Saint Paul's Cathedral in London in 1504, he preached popular Bible-based sermons. Among his hearers were Lollards (followers of John Wyclif), who

---

[25] For William Farel, see Chapter 4, section 4.
[26] "Dean" is the title for the head of a cathedral church.

expressed warm approval of the dean's preaching.[27] Colet certainly upset many conservative Churchmen by his outspoken criticisms of contemporary religious life, *e.g.* the superstitious worship of relics and images. In fact, Colet got into such trouble that if England's new king, Henry VIII (1509-47), had not protected him, he might have ended up on trial for heresy. Colet's most enduring monument was Saint Paul's School in London, which he founded with his own money in 1509; the school offered free education for young boys, based on Christian humanist ideals of study.

Another outstanding English humanist was **Sir Thomas More** (1478-1535) of London, a Greek and Latin scholar, religious writer[28] and leading politician. More wrote the most famous of English humanist books, *Utopia* (1516), a brilliant satire in which he criticised the society of his day by contrasting it with his view of the perfect society, where no evil exists. It was a strange book for such a devout Roman Catholic as More to write; his "perfect society" tolerated all religions (unlike More himself, who became a fierce persecutor of Protestants), and the official Utopian faith allowed priests to marry and forbade images of God.

Spain

In Spain, the foremost humanist was **Francesco Ximénez de Cisneros** (1436-1517), usually called "cardinal Ximénez".[29] He was a Franciscan friar who belonged to the stricter Observant wing of the Franciscan movement.[30] In 1492, the Spanish queen Isabella appointed him her personal confessor (the priest to whom she confessed her sins), and in 1495 made him archbishop of Toledo, which meant he was the national leader of the Spanish Church.

---

[27] For Wyclif and the Lollards, see Part Two, Chapter 10, section 4, and in this volume Chapter 7, section 1.

[28] Almost all More's religious writing was done after the Reformation, in defence of the Roman Catholic Church. See Chapter 6, section 6.

[29] His name is pronounced "Him-ain-eth". Sometimes it is spelt "Jiménes".

[30] For the Observant Franciscans, see Part Two, Chapter 8, section 4, under the heading **Franciscans**.

Ximénez promoted education, scholarship and the new learning in Spain in many ways. He founded the university of Alcala in 1500 and made it the vital centre of Spanish humanism. In 1502 he gathered a team of scholars at Alcala to produce an authoritative version of the text of the Old and New Testaments; they completed the task in 1517 but did not publish it until 1522. Known as the "Complutensian Polyglot", it contained a revised Hebrew text of the Old Testament, the Greek text of the New Testament, and the Latin Vulgate, together with language aids. Ximénez and his fellow Spanish humanists were great admirers of Erasmus (see next section).

Spanish humanism was in one respect very different from its Italian, German, French, and English counterparts: it did not share their hostility to scholastic theology. Ximénez positively promoted the study of Thomas Aquinas in Spanish universities, which gave rise to a generation of Spanish theologians known as the "New Thomists". The New Thomists especially emphasised the Augustinian side of Aquinas's thought, and to that extent they were part of the Augustinian aspect of the Renaissance; but they had no intention of employing Augustinian theology as a tool for drastically reforming the medieval Church system, in the way that Martin Luther was to do.

4. Erasmus of Rotterdam.

By far the most famous, gifted, and influential of all the Christian humanists was *Desiderius Erasmus* (c.1466-1536). He was born in Rotterdam, the Netherlands, and more than any other Renaissance figure he shaped humanism into a positive programme for the reform of society. Brilliant at communicating his views in writing, he was the first thinker in history to see his own ideas become internationally famous in his own lifetime. He wrote some 226 works; two and a half million copies of them were circulated. He was called "the schoolmaster of Europe". Almost single-handedly, Erasmus created a new atmosphere in Western culture.

Desiderius Erasmus (1466-1536)

The illegitimate son of a Dutch priest, Erasmus was educated in a school run by the Brothers of the Common Life at Deventer. This early contact with the Brothers and the *devotio moderna* gave Erasmus a lifelong concern for a simple Christ-centred faith and a practical religion. He then spent some time in a monastery, but found it highly disagreeable; in fact, Erasmus came to detest everything that monasticism stood for. The great turning point in Erasmus's life was his visit to England in 1499, where he became a close friend of the leading English humanists, John Colet and Sir Thomas More. Inspired by their Christian humanist vision, Erasmus devoted himself to acquiring the new learning of the Renaissance; from now on, the Greek language, the New Testament, and the early Church fathers became the food of Erasmus's soul and the lamp of his path. He published many new editions of the writings of the fathers, helping to renew people's interest in them. Erasmus's own favourite among the fathers was Jerome, whom in many ways Erasmus took as a model for his own life – the celibate scholar, devoted to acquiring knowledge and spreading it in the cause of Christianity and reforming the lives of believers.

Erasmus wanted to use humanism as an instrument for reforming the whole of Western society. He believed that a number of things had gone seriously wrong with the religious life of Catholic Europe:

(i) Scholastic theology. Erasmus rejected the methods and conclusions of scholasticism. He thought that scholastic theologians had corrupted the Christian message by marrying it to the philosophy of Aristotle. "What has Christ to do with Aristotle?" he asked. For Erasmus, theology was not a matter of logic or philosophy, but of the New Testament and following Christ. Erasmus's hostility to scholasticism meant that its practitioners (especially monks) were always accusing him of heresy.

(ii) External religion. Erasmus kept up a constant, often cuttingly sarcastic criticism of the kind of religion that glorified external things: images, relics, ceremonies, indulgences, *etc.* True religion, he insisted, was an inward and spiritual reality; it came from the heart. Erasmus's dislike of a merely external religion meant that he placed huge emphasis on a spiritual participation in the sacraments: eating the bread of the eucharist was useless unless it was accompanied by a loving communion with Christ and one's fellow Christians. This aspect of Erasmus could easily lead his readers into a purely symbolic view of the sacramental bread and wine. Erasmus himself never took this step, although he was somewhat ambivalent and even self-contradictory on the physical presence of Christ's body in the mass: "Of the reality of the Lord's body, nothing is uncertain. Of the method of the presence, it is permitted in a certain way to be uncertain." Although Erasmus did not reject infant baptism, he did suggest that baptism could be given again once a person had reached the age of puberty and could now understand the significance of the ritual – an attitude that may have pushed some of Erasmus's disciples into Anabaptism (see Chapter 5).

(iii) The clergy, the monks, and the papacy. Erasmus attacked the immorality and ignorance of priests, monks, and popes with devastating effect. His weapon was not righteous anger, but humour: he held up corrupt Church leaders to ridicule, mocked them, and set all Western Europe laughing at them. His most famous writing in this style was his *Praise of Folly* (1509), which poured scornful laughter on contemporary abuses in Church and society; one great historian has called it "the most severe attack on the medieval Church that had, up to that time, been made". More light-hearted, although perhaps more scandalous, was Erasmus's *Julius Excluded from Heaven* (1517), which depicted pope Julius II (1503-13) being refused admission into heaven after his death. (Julius won his election to the papacy by bribes, and spent much of his reign fighting wars to expand the papal states.) *Julius Excluded* was a best seller; it went through 13 editions in four years, and was translated into English, French, and German. Erasmus never admitted writing it, but never denied it, and most of his contemporaries ascribed it to him, as do most modern scholars.

To remedy these corruptions, Erasmus proposed a threefold programme of reform, which had a moral, cultural, and Scriptural dimension:

(i) Moral reform. To Erasmus, the essence of Christianity was the Sermon on the Mount and living a pure Christlike life. Erasmus had a great longing for innocence, simplicity, and peace, and a hatred of complicated theology and ceremonial religion. He always took a very minimal attitude to doctrine, stressing the humanity of Christ as teacher and role-model. Perhaps Erasmus offered his view of the true Christian life most effectively in his *Dagger of the Christian Soldier* (1503), where he presented Christianity not as theology or ritual, but as a practical lifestyle, based on the imitation of Christ and the movement of the soul away from visible material things to unseen spiritual realities.

(ii) Cultural reform. Erasmus believed that education was the royal route to solving mankind's problems. Indeed, Erasmus created the impression that the school and the teacher, not the church and the clergyman, were the real agents for fashioning people to live excellent lives. He wanted children to be given a good humanist education in Greek, Latin, the pagan classics, and the New Testament. They would then, he hoped, grow up as enlightened Christian citizens, and the whole of society would be leavened, renewed, and Christianised by their influence.

(iii) Scriptural reform. The study of Scripture was central to Erasmus's programme of reform. Erasmus saw Scripture as the supreme source of divine wisdom for human living. If people were to understand the true message of Scripture, however, they had to study it its original languages, not the Latin of the Vulgate. (In 1505 Erasmus published Lorenzo Valla's *Annotations on the New Testament*, which showed up the errors of the Vulgate in the light of the Greek New Testament.) So Erasmus placed a strong emphasis on learning Greek. He did not stress Hebrew because he was not very interested in the Old Testament; he found it a rather crude and violent sort of book. To help the educated classes study the New

Testament in Greek, Erasmus published in 1516 his own scholarly edition of the Greek New Testament – the first ever printed edition – accompanied by a Latin translation and his own notes.[31] Erasmus also approved of the New Testament being translated into the various native tongues of the world, so that ordinary people would have the opportunity to read it (see the first quotation from Erasmus at the end of the chapter).

Christian humanism in general, and Erasmus in particular, have gained a special importance they might not otherwise have had in Church history, because in so many ways they sowed the seeds of the Protestant Reformation. As previously noted, people in the 16th century used to say, "Erasmus laid the egg and Luther hatched it." By demanding that the Bible be studied in Greek and Hebrew, through the grammatico-historical method, free from the control of scholastic theology, and by exalting the early Church fathers above the schoolmen as interpreters of the Gospel, the Christian human-ists prepared people's minds to accept that the Catholic Church of the Middle Ages had gone disastrously wrong, and needed the drastic remedy of the Reformation. The low value Erasmus placed on outward ceremonies, feeling that these were an obstacle to a true inward religion of the heart, greatly influenced the "Reformed" branch of the Reformation.[32] His ideal of imitating Christ helped to shape Anabaptist spirituality.[33]

---

[31] Erasmus's Greek New Testament, based on a small selection of manuscripts from the Byzantine textual tradition (the "authorised version" of the Eastern Greek-speaking Church), formed the basis of what became the "received text" (or "textus receptus"). The received text is often confused with the Byzantine text, but the two are actually distinct. The received text is a version of the Byzantine text, but based on a small and unrepresentative number of Byzantine manuscripts. The mainstream Byzantine text differs from the Erasmian version in a good number of places.

[32] For the Reformed faith, see Chapter 3, sections 6-8, and Chapter 4.

[33] For the Anabaptists, see Chapter 5, section 1.

5. Reformers on the eve of the Reformation.

As the 16th century approached, a variety of figures were working for the revival and reformation of Christian teaching and living in Catholic Europe. Of course, many of the Christian humanists like Erasmus were devoted to this purpose. Others, like the Italian Franciscan **Bernardino of Siena** (1380-1444), and the Swiss preacher **Johannes Geiler of Kaisersberg** (1445-1510), were not humanists, but strove to improve moral and spiritual life from the pulpit. Bernardino's sermons moved thousands to renounce the world and live in the light of eternity. Geiler's 30 year ministry in Strasbourg (then in south-western Germany, today in France) made him the outstanding preacher of his age; he not only attacked worldliness, but abuses connected with indulgences, relic-worship, simony, and the corruptions of monks, bishops, and popes. Yet Bernardino and Geiler did this without questioning the authority of the papacy or the basic teachings of traditional Catholicism. Other reformers, however, came much closer to the Protestant Reformation's rejection of the papacy and of many of the distinctive features of medieval Catholic theology. We will look at three of these "reformers on the eve of the Reformation": the German, John of Wesel; the Dutchman, Wessel Gansfort; and the Italian, Girolamo Savonarola.

John of Wesel (1400-1481)

John Ruchrath of Wesel was born at Oberwesel on the Rhine (western Germany), lectured at Basel university in Switzerland, and in 1463 was appointed a preacher in Worms Cathedral. His criticisms of the prevailing theology of the Catholic Church were many and bold. John taught that Scripture alone was the source of Christian teaching, and that popes and councils should not be followed if they contradicted Scripture. He defined the Church as the whole body of believers, not the ecclesiastical organisation headed by the papacy, denied transubstantiation, and sided with Eastern Orthodoxy on the *filioque* clause. He also rejected indulgences, because God alone could pardon sins, attacked the enforced celibacy of the clergy, and maintained that the distinction between priest and diocesan bishop was of merely human origin. With such views, it was not surprising that John entered into friendly relations with the Hussites. The Church authorities could not remain for ever silent in the face of such sweeping criticisms; in 1477, they deposed John from his office, and in 1479 the inquisition in Mainz put him on trial, accusing him of being a Hussite himself. John's frailty (he was 79 years old) proved unequal to the persuasive powers of the inquisition, and he agreed to renounce his heresies in a public statement of repentance. The authorities burnt all his writings, and sentenced him to imprisonment in the Augustinian convent in Mainz, where he died two years later.

Wessel Gansfort (1419-89)

Born at Groningen in the Netherlands, Gansfort was taught in a school at Deventer run by the Brothers of the Common Life, then went on to study in various universities before lecturing in Heidelberg and Paris. Gansfort was a pioneer humanist, expert in Greek and Hebrew; among his pupils were Rudolf Agricola and Johannes Reuchlin (see section 3). In theology Gansfort was at first a disciple of Thomas Aquinas, but later turned away from Aquinas to Augustine of Hippo as a safer guide. He went back to Groningen in about 1474 to act as spiritual director of a nunnery there, and also in the Mount Saint Agnes monastery (where Thomas a Kempis had lived). Gansfort's preaching and teaching attracted a wide circle of admirers. Like John of Wesel, he made many probing criticisms of Catholic doctrine – indeed, many of the same criticisms. He denied the infallibility both of the papacy and of ecumenical councils. He defined the Church as the entire company of believers, not the organisation headed by the papacy. He accepted transubstantiation and the sacrifice of the mass, but also maintained that Christ was present in the bread and wine for believers only. A strong Augustinian, he upheld salvation by God's sovereign grace alone, and taught a somewhat confused idea of justification by faith. He denied indulgences and the treasury of merit.

Gansfort was more fortunate than John of Wesel in escaping the attentions of the inquisition; he died peacefully in his bed. None of Gansfort's writings were printed until the Reformation had dawned, when Martin Luther (among others) issued an edition with a preface by himself.[34]

Girolamo Savonarola (1452-98)

Savonarola was a native of the Italian Renaissance city of Ferrara who in 1474 became a Dominican friar. After preaching in various Italian cities, in 1491 he was appointed prior of San Marco, a Dominican convent in Florence. His preaching in Florence was so popular that it gave him almost complete power over the city, especially after its ruling family, the Medici, fled from a French invasion force in 1494. Savonarola's popularity was not because his sermons flattered people; no one denounced sin or warned of divine judgment as sternly as this Dominican friar did. His moral reforms made the city of Florence into a sort of vast monastic community. Famously, in 1496 the citizens of Florence burned in a public fire (the "bonfire of the vanities") all their pornography, cosmetics, and things used for gambling – cards, dice, *etc.* Savonarola also carried out far-reaching political reforms, drawing up a new democratic constitution for Florence.

However, in 1495 a long and fierce quarrel broke out between Savonarola and pope *Alexander VI* (1492-1503). Alexander did not like Savonarola's claim to be a heaven-sent messenger of Christ, or the friar's involvement in politics. (Alexander was also under the influence of the Medici who wanted to regain their power in Florence.) Alexander commanded Savonarola to stop

---

[34] Luther said of Gansfort, "If I had read his books before, my enemies might have thought that Luther had borrowed everything from Gansfort, so great is the agreement between our spirits. I feel my joy and my strength increase, and have no doubt that I have taught correctly, when I find that someone who wrote at a different time, in another land, and with a different purpose, agrees so totally with my views and expresses them in almost the same words."

preaching. Savonarola refused to obey, denounced Alexander as a servant of Satan, and began preaching against the corruptions of the papal court. Alexander excommunicated Savonarola in 1497, and threatened to place Florence under an interdict unless it sent the rebel Dominican to Rome for trial. Savonarola appealed to an ecumenical council against Alexander's verdict. Savonarola's enemies in Florence, the Franciscans, suggested that they make a direct appeal to God's judgment: one of their friars and one of Savonarola's Dominicans would walk through fire; the one who survived must be in the right. Savonarola agreed, but on the day of the test in April 1498, the Franciscans raised all sorts of objections, a rain-storm put the fire out, and as night started to fall Florence's ruling council intervened and called the whole thing off. This event broke Savonarola's power. Instead of leading to his expected triumph, the trial by fire had ended up looking more like a very stupid comedy play. His popular support bled away, and the following day the city authorities arrested Savonarola, tortured him, and burnt him at the stake on 23rd May.

Savonarola was not a theological reformer like John of Wesel or Wessel Gansfort; he accepted the basic doctrines of the Catholic Church. But Luther and others regarded him as a forerunner of the Reformation for two reasons. First, Savonarola was a strong Augustinian in his understanding of God's sovereign grace in salvation. Second, he defied the papacy, and paid for his defiance with his life.

6. The mass in later medieval piety

The Protestant Reformation was a reforming of Catholic piety as well as doctrine: indeed, the two things were deeply interwoven. And one of the storm centres of the 16th century reform movement was the mass. In order to understand why the Protestant Reformers focused such attention on reforming the mass, it is useful to see how it operated in later medieval piety.[35]

The first thing that can be said is that the mass lay at the heart of later medieval piety. It was celebrated every day in the parish church, although most of the laity attended only on Sunday. For the upper classes who had their own chapels and chaplains, mass was often part of the daily routine: mass would be followed by the day's hunting. In other words, it had simply become part of the cultural scenery. Yet the lay person rarely "took communion". He usually watched as the priest alone ate and drank. Lay people generally joined in only at Easter. The mass was therefore a visual drama for the average person, an event in which he was a spectator rather than a participant. The inaccessible nature of the mass was underlined by its being in Latin, the language of the cultural elite, not understood by most people. This served to heighten the impression of the mass as a special sacred thing – part of the landscape, but a mysterious part. Having said this, it is true that there were aids to devotion in the native languages of Europe; in England, for example, there was the *Lay Folk's Mass Book*. But these could help only the literate: most people could not read. Also certain parts of the mass were felt to be too holy for translation into the common tongue, *e.g.* the words of consecration.

The medieval Church tried to compensate for popular illiteracy by the use of symbolism. All the rituals of the mass presented (at least in theory) some element of Christ's atoning death to the minds and senses of the worshippers: light and shade, different colours, visual imagery and gesture, music and quietness, were all exploited in this ceremonial proclamation of the cross. It has been said that in consequence, the suffering of Christ was more deeply impressed into the consciousness of the worshipper than at any other era in Church history. Certainly meditations on the Jesus the Man of Sorrows have a singular emotional power in the devotional literature of the late medieval Church (for example, in the writings of

---

[35] By "piety" here, I mean religious devotion as expressed in habits and practices. By "later medieval" I mean roughly the 13th-15th centuries.

Thomas a Kempis, Julian of Norwich, and William Langland's *Piers Plowman*).

The prevailing experience of the worshipper during the mass was a sense of awe and wonder. This found its focus in the wafer (the "host"[36]) which was believed to become the very flesh of Jesus Christ. Despite Thomas Aquinas's refined theory of transubstantiation, the miracle of Christ's bodily presence was probably understood in a crudely physical way by many ordinary worshippers. One of the greatest medieval temptations was to doubt that the host was truly the body of Christ (or that the wine was His blood): priests had to deal with this doubt more than perhaps any other religious difficulty. Many miracle stories about the host gained wide currency, *e.g.* in the *Dialogue of Miracles* by Caesarius of Heisterbach (1180-1240). Here is one of Caesarius's typical stories:

> "When a priest named Albero was celebrating the mass in the Church of Saint Walburgis in Hildesheim, which was his native place, a citizen who was standing behind him, and did not believe in what was being done, saw the liquid in the chalice overflow, so that it covered the whole surface of the altar, boiling over like a boiling vessel. He was very much frightened by this vision, and it hopefully brought back his faith in the sacrament. And indeed this overflowing had the appearance of human blood."

The emotion of awe towards the mass was to be an acute practical problem for the Reformers; they had grave difficulties in getting people to shake off what they regarded as a superstitious attitude to the eucharistic bread. When the German Reformer, Andreas von Carlstadt, insisted that a certain layman take the bread into his own hands, the poor man trembled so violently that he dropped it![37]

---

[36] From the Latin *hostia*, "sacrifice".
[37] Carlstadt's action here was condemned by Martin Luther as pastorally cruel and unnecessary.

The mass was seen as the meeting place of earth and heaven. There was a sense of joining in the worship that was continually being offered in the heavenly sanctuary. This was closely allied to a feeling of "solidarity with the dead". It was part of the ceremonial of the mass that the names of the faithful departed were read out to the congregation from a "bede-roll".[38] Prayer for souls in purgatory was also a routine aspect of the mass. All this helped to create a sort of human interest in what was going on.

The mass was also central in the popular perception of the Church as a vessel of God's power, a power made available to control demonic forces. Such forces were thought to operate in illness, plague, crop failure, natural disasters, sudden death: these were the powers of chaos at work, trying to overthrow the divine order of creation. To counteract them, God had made His own power available in the Church, and above all in the mass. So there was a fairly widespread interpretation of the mass as a means of releasing God's power against the demonic forces: the mass could be used to ward off bad weather or a mother's death in childbirth. The host in particular was seen as containing supernatural power in concentrated form. If a worshipper, when actually receiving the host, did not swallow it, but kept it entire in his mouth and took it away, many people felt he had obtained an object charged with magical potency. He could carry it around with him on his journeys as a charm against bad luck, or make use of it to cure illnesses. This belief was so common that the Church had to take extreme safety measures to prevent the theft of the host; the Fourth Lateran Council (1215) decreed that the communion bread and wine had to be kept locked away. Still, it is not as though the average worshipper was desperate to steal a host. It was widely held that simple attendance at mass would ensure earthly blessings, such as curing toothache, recovering stolen goods, or guaranteeing a safe journey.

The Renaissance initiated a critique of some of the more bizarre aspects of popular "mass piety". The Reformers took up this

---

[38] From the obsolete English word "bede", to offer, hence to pray.

critique with a far keener vigour, as part of a wider programme to
cleanse the Church of superstition and restore a purer apostolic
piety based on the Scriptures and the early Church fathers.

7. The witch craze

The age of the Renaissance in Western Europe in some ways
launched a tidal wave of criticism against superstitious beliefs and
practices (we have just had a glimpse of these in the previous
section). Yet strangely, the Renaissance also witnessed the birth of a
wild mania which was to sweep across Western society for the next
300 years – *the witch craze*. Fear and panic about the existence and
activities of witches gripped almost every level of society.
Governments put to death untold thousands of women and men
who were accused of practising black magic.

People today often think that the Middle Ages were the great era of
the witch craze. This is far from the case. Heresy, not witchcraft,
was the great dread of the medieval period. When the inquisition
was founded in 1215, it made no mention of witches; heretics were
its target. It was only in the 15th century that witchcraft replaced
heresy as the supreme enemy in the eyes of Church and state. Of
course, medieval thinkers had considered the subject of witchcraft.
In the 12th century, Gratian,[39] the "father of canon law", dealt with
various aspects of black magic in his writings; but Gratian regarded
most of the stories about witches (*e.g.* that they flew through the
air) as a sad delusion. So did other Church authorities.

There was growing concern about witches in the 13th and 14th
Centuries, reflected in the works of Thomas Aquinas, but it was not
until the 15th – the age of the Renaissance – that the Western
Church began to view witchcraft as a distinct cult requiring special
treatment. Whole new areas of theological study sprang up: the
varieties of witchcraft, the correct ways of detecting it, the proper

---

[39]   For Gratian, see Part Two, Chapter 7, section 3, under **Peter Abelard**.

punishments it merited. At the very dawn of the Renaissance, during the last years of the pioneer humanist Francesco Petrarch, in 1370-80, the inquisition decreed in a series of tracts that witchcraft must now be dealt with as severely as heresy. This was the first trickle. A hundred years later, in 1484, pope Innocent VIII (1484-92) published one of the most famous papal bulls, *Summis desiderantes*, which made the burning of witches into the official Catholic policy. The trickle had become a flood.

In 1486 the most influential book ever written about witchcraft appeared – the *Malleus Maleficarum* ("Hammer of the Witches"), constantly reprinted throughout the 16th and 17th Centuries. The authors were two high-ranking inquisitors from Cologne university, the Dominican friars Heinrich Kramer and Jacob Sprenger. Here was everything anyone could ever wish to know about witches and how to deal with them (and not only witches – vampires too). Stories about occultic powers and activities that a previous generation of theologians had dismissed as delusions were now embraced as horrific fact and described in lurid detail. Modern readers will need a strong stomach to read *The Witches' Hammer*! Kramer and Sprenger were particularly harsh towards women: there were ten female witches for every male one, they declared. Not surprisingly, women were the main victims of the witch craze. In the days of the early Roman Empire, people had blamed the Christians for everything that went wrong in society – "no rain, because of the Christians". Now the tables were turned – Christians blamed the witches. Bad weather, crop failures, famines, droughts, infant mortality, sterility among humans and farm animals: witches were, it was said, probably the cause of all these. Society had to destroy them for its own safety. One estimate puts the total number of (real or alleged) witches killed throughout the entire craze period as high as nine million; a less bloody estimate puts it at between 50,000 and 100,000.

The witch craze was just as fierce in countries which accepted the Protestant faith as it was in Roman Catholic lands. In Calvin's Geneva, for instance, two or three women were executed each year for witchcraft. The most notorious Protestant episodes of witch-killing, however, took place in Puritan England and Puritan America. In England, during the Civil War period, the activities of Matthew Hopkins as "Witchfinder General" provided sensational material for 20th century film-makers. In fact, Hopkins was active only from 1644 to 1647 (when he died of consumption), but along with his assistants John Sterne and Goody Phillips, he excelled all other Puritan "witchfinders" in uncovering Satan's agents, mostly in his native county of Essex. For example, in 1645 at the Summer Session of the Essex courts, 29 women were cited for witchcraft by Hopkins, of whom 19 were executed (by hanging, the normal English method of killing witches: witch-burning is largely a myth as far as English practice is concerned).

Puritan America supplies the still more infamous episode at the village of Salem in Massachusetts in 1692, where 20 people were put to death (19 by hanging, one by crushing). Fortunately some Puritan clergymen kept their nerve, and outspoken criticism by one of them, Increase Mather, helped bring the proceedings to a swift end. Five years later one of the Salem judges, Samuel Sewall, a sincere Christian man, publicly confessed to his church how deluded he had been to take part in such an outburst of public hysteria. His confession could not bring back the 20 dead, but it is one of the most moving personal statements testifying to the power of the witch craze – no medieval superstition, but one that flowered in the age of the Renaissance and Reformation.

Important people

The Church
Bernardino of Siena (1380-1444)
Pope Nicholas V (1447-55)
John of Wesel (1400-1481)
Wessel Gansfort (1419-89)
Girolamo Savonarola (1452-98)
Pope Alexander VI (1492-1503)
Geiler of Kaisersberg (1445-1510)

Political and military
Holy Roman emperor
  Maximilian I (1493-1519)

Humanist scholars [40]

The Italian Renaissance
Francesco Petrarch (1304-74)
Manuel Chrysoloras (1355-1415)
Gemistos Plethon (1355-1450)
Lorenzo Valla (1406-57)
Giovanni Pico della Mirandola (1463-94)
Marsilio Ficino (1433-99)

The German Renaissance
Rudolf Agricola (1444-85)
Sebastian Brant (1458-1521)
Johannes Reuchlin (1455-1522)
Ulrich von Hutten (1488-1523)
Conrad Mutian (1471-1526)
Willibald Pirckheimer (1470-1530)
Jacob Wimpfeling (1450-1528)
Crotus Rubeanus (1480-1539)

Elsewhere
Cardinal Ximénez (1436-1517)
John Colet (1467-1519)
William Briçonnet (1470-1533)
Sir Thomas More (1478-1535)
Jacques Lefevre d'Étaples (1460-1536)
Desiderius Erasmus (1466-1536)
William Budé (1467-1540)

On the nature of poetry
From what I know of your religious zeal, I suppose you will feel a kind of distaste for the poem which I enclose with this letter. You will regard it as totally incompatible with all your professions of religion [as a monk], and directly opposed to your entire way of

---

[40] A good number of these held positions in the Church, but it is convenient to group them all together under this heading.

thinking and living. However, do not jump to conclusions. Can there be anything more crazy than to assert an opinion on a subject that you haven't studied? The fact is, poetry is not in the slightest opposed to theology. Are you surprised by this? In fact, we can almost say that theology *is* poetry – poetry about God. To call Christ a lion [Revelation 5:5], and then a lamb [John 1:29], and then a worm [Psalm 22:6]: what is this if is not poetic? You will find thousands of examples of this sort of thing in the Scriptures, so many indeed that I cannot attempt to count them. After all, what are the parables of our Saviour in the Gospels, but language whose *sound* is alien to its *sense* – "allegories", to be technical? But allegory is the very heart and soul of all poetry…

Even the Old Testament fathers turned their hands to poetry, such as heroic song and other kinds. Moses wrote poetry, for example, and so did Job, and David, and Solomon, and Jeremiah. Even the psalms, which you are always chanting day and night, are in poetic form in the original Hebrew. I would not be guilty of any inaccuracy or anything improper if I suggested that the author of the Psalms was "the Christian's poet". In truth, the plain facts of the matter cannot help leading us to some such conclusion. Furthermore, let me remind you (since you are not disposed to take seriously anything that I say these days without authority) that Jerome himself took this view of the Psalms. Of course these holy poems, these Psalms, which sing about the blessed man, that is, about Christ – His birth, His death, His descent into Hades, His resurrection, His ascent into heaven, His coming again to judge the world – these Psalms have never been translated into another language without some loss of either the poetry or the meaning. That is inevitable. So, since a choice had to be made, it has been the meaning that has been preferred. And yet some relics of the poetic form still survive even in translation, and the separate parts we still call "verses", and quite rightly, for verses they are.

Such was the view of the ancients. Now, respecting Ambrose and Augustine and Jerome, our guides through the New Testament – it would be supremely easy to demonstrate that they too used poetic forms and rhythms. Indeed, in the case of Prudentius and Prosper and Sedulius [early Christian poets] and the rest, it is enough merely to mention their names; for we have not a single word from them in prose, while their poetic works are abundant and famous. Do not then, dear brother, disdain a practice which you see has been approved by holy men whom Christ has loved. Pay attention to the underlying meaning of the poem; and if that is wholesome and true, accept it with pleasure, no matter in what outward form it may be expressed. To applaud a feast when it is presented on plates of clay, but to scorn it when it is served on plates of gold, comes rather too close to insanity or hypocrisy.

Petrarch, from a letter to his brother Gherardo

The dignity of man

I have read, most reverent fathers, in the records of the Arabians, that when Abdallah the Saracen was questioned about what could be seen most worthy of wonder on this stage (so to speak) of the world, he replied: "There is nothing to be seen more wonderful than man." In agreement with this opinion is the saying of Hermes [an Egyptian god, Hermes Trismegistus]: "O Asclepius [god of healing], what a great miracle is man!"

Even so, when I pondered the reasons for these sayings, the various arguments put forward by many people to demonstrate the excellence of human nature did not fully convince me. For example, it has been said that man is the intermediate point of creation – the intimate acquaintance of the beings above him, and the ruler of the things beneath him; that man is the interpreter of nature, by the keenness of his senses, by the inquiring power of his reason, and by the light of his understanding; that he is set midway between the unchanging form of eternity and the fleeting forms of time; and that man is therefore (as the Persians say) the being in whom the world holds together, or rather he is the wedding-song of the world, and on David's testimony he is little lower that angels [Psalm 8:5].

These reasons are great. Yet they are not the chief ground on which man may justly claim for himself the privilege of the highest admiration. Why should we not admire even more the angels themselves, and the blessed choirs of heaven? However, it seems to me that I have finally come to understand why man is the most favoured of beings, and therefore worthy of all admiration; I have at last understood the condition which is man's destined place in the order of the universe – a condition to be envied not only by the animals, but even by the stars and by the intelligences that dwell beyond this world. Yes, the human condition is so wondrous that it surpasses belief! But why should it not be so? For it is on this basis that man is justly called and considered a great miracle, a living creature worthy of all admiration.

But now, fathers, listen to me as I explain exactly what this human condition is. In the name of your humanity, grant a gracious hearing to my work! The supreme Father, God the Architect, had already constructed this cosmic home which we see around us, this most sacred temple of divinity, according to the laws of His mysterious wisdom. He had already beautified the region beyond the stars with intelligent beings, enlivened the heavenly bodies with eternal souls, and filled the foul and filthy parts of the lower world with a host of animals of every kind. But when this work was over, the Craftsman still desired that there should be someone to think about the meaning of so great a work, someone to love its beauty, someone to wonder at its vastness.

Therefore, when everything else was finished, as Moses and *Timaeus* [one of Plato's writings] testify, He finally decided to bring forth man. But among the heavenly patterns on which God had based His creation, there was nothing left from which He could fashion a new offspring; nor in His treasure-houses was there anything left which He could bestow on his new son as an inheritance; nor among the dwellings of the universe was there any place left where man might sit to contemplate the universe. Everything was now complete; each thing had been given its place in the highest, the middle, and the lowest orders.

Yet it was not in the nature of the Father's power to fail in His last act of creation. It was not in the nature of His wisdom to hesitate in any necessary work through any lack of understanding. It was not in the nature of His unselfish love that man, who would glorify God's generosity in all other things, should have to condemn it in relation to himself. At length, the best of Makers decreed that His human creature, to whom He had been unable to give anything completely his own, should share in whatever belonged to every other being. He therefore took man, this creature without a fixed image, placed him in the middle of the world, and spoke to him thus:

"Adam, we have given you no fixed position, nor character-istics proper to yourself, nor capacities exclusive to you alone, in order that whatever position, whatever characteristic, whatever capacity you may responsibly desire, these you may have and possess according to your own desire and judgement. The nature of all other beings is limited and con-fined within the laws decreed by us. Confined by no limits, you may determine it for yourself, according to your own free will; for we have set your destiny within the power of free will. I have placed you at the centre of the world, so that from this position you may more easily look around at what-ever is in the world. We have made you neither of heaven nor of earth, neither mortal nor immortal, so that you may – as the free and wondrous fashioner of your own self – shape yourself into the form you choose. It will be in your power to sink down into the lower forms of life, which are animal; and you will have the power, according to your soul's judgement, to be reborn into the higher orders, which are divine."

From Pico della Mirandola, *Oration on the Dignity of Man*.

True worship

He who prays must speak to God as though he were in God's very presence, for the Lord is everywhere, in every place, in every person, and especially in the soul of the righteous. Therefore let us not seek God on earth, nor in heaven, nor anywhere else; let us seek Him in our own hearts, as the prophet says, "I will pay attention to what the Lord shall say to me" (Psalm 85:8). In prayer, a person may pay attention to his own words, which is a merely outward thing; or he may pay attention to the meaning of his words, which is study rather than prayer; or he may fix his thoughts on God, and this alone is true prayer. We must not consider the words or the sentences, but lift our souls above self and almost lose self in the thought of God. When the believer has attained this state, he forgets the world and worldly desires, and has a kind of foretaste of heaven's joy. The uneducated as well as the learned can just as easily rise up to this height. Indeed, it often happens that someone who recites the Psalms without particularly understanding what they mean, prays more acceptably than a scholar who can interpret them. Words are not essential to prayer. On the contrary, when a person is really caught up in a spirit of devotion, speech becomes a hindrance, and silent mental prayer should take its place. This shows the great error of those who tell us to work our way through a set number of spoken prayers. The Lord takes no joy in a multi-tude of words, but in a fervent spirit.

No doubt those whose only concern is to defend the Church's ceremonies and outward rituals will attack me for saying this. My answer is the words of the Saviour to the woman of Samaria: "Woman, believe Me, the hour is coming when you will neither on this mountain, nor in Jerusalem, worship the Father. But the hour is coming, and now is, when the true worshippers will worship the Father in spirit and truth" (John 4:21,23). This means that the Lord desires inward worship, without so many outward worship-practices. This was the custom in the early Church, when people could raise their thoughts to God without any need of being stirred up by organ music or singing. But when fervour grew cold, rituals came in like medicine to sick souls. However, in our day, Christians have become like a man who is so sick that all his natural strength has vanished, and no medicines can help him. All fervour and inward worship are dead, and outward worship-practices become ever more numerous, although they have no sanctifying power. Therefore we proclaim to the world that outward worship must give way to inward, and that rituals are nothing unless they enable the human spirit to worship truly.

From Girolamo Savonarola, *Concerning Mental Prayer*.

Utopia: Freedom of religion

For King Utopus, even at the first beginning, hearing that the inhabitants of the land were, before his coming thither, at continual dissension and strife among themselves for their religions; perceiving also that this common dissension (whilst every several sect took several parts in fighting for their country) was the only occasion of his conquest over them all; as soon as he had gotten the victory, first of all he made a decree, that it should be lawful for every man to favour and follow what religion he would, and that he might do the best he could to bring other to his opinion, so that he did it peaceably, gently, quietly, and soberly, without haste and contentious rebuking and inveighing against other. If he could not by fair and gentle speech induce them unto his opinion yet he should use no kind of violence, and refrain from displeasant and seditious words. To him that would vehemently and fervently in this cause strive and contend was decreed banishment or bondage.

This law did King Utopus make not only for the maintenance of peace, which he saw through continual contention and mortal hatred utterly extinguished; but also because he thought this decree should make or the furtherance of religion. Whereof he durst define and determine nothing unadvisedly, as doubting whether God desiring manifold and divers sorts of honour, would inspire sundry men with sundry kinds of religion. And this surely he thought a very unmeet and foolish thing, and a point of arrogant presumption, to compel all other by violence and threatenings to agree to the same that thou believest to be true. Furthermore though there be one religion which alone is true, and all other vain and superstitious, yet did he well foresee (so that the matter were handled with reason, and sober modesty) that the truth of its own power would at the last issue out and come to light. But if contention and debate in that behalf should continually be used, as the worst men be most obstinate and stubborn, and in their evil opinion most constant; he perceived that then the best and holiest religion would be trodden underfoot and destroyed by most vain superstitions, even as good corn is by thorns and weeds overgrown and choked.

Therefore all this matter he left undiscussed, and gave to every man free liberty and choice to believe what he would. Saving that he earnestly and straightly charged them, that no man should conceive so vile and base an opinion of the dignity of man's nature, as to think that the souls do die and perish with the body; or that the world runneth at all adventures governed by no divine providence. And therefore they believe that after this life vices be extremely punished and virtues bountifully rewarded. Him that is of a contrary opinion they count not in the number of men, as one that hath abased the high nature of his soul to the vileness of brute beasts' bodies, much less in the number of their citizens, whose laws and ordinances, if it were not fear, he would nothing at all esteem. For you may be sure that he will study either with craft privily to mock, or else violently to break the common laws of this country, in whom remaineth no further fear than of the laws, nor no further hope than of the body. Wherefore he that is thus minded is deprived of all honours, excluded from all offices and rejected from all common administrations in the weal public. And thus he is of all sort despised, as of an unprofitable and of a base and vile nature. Howbeit they put him to no punishment, because they be persuaded that it is in no man's power to believe what he list. No, nor they constrain him not with threatenings to dissemble his mind and show countenance contrary to his thought. For deceit and falsehood and all manner of lies, as next unto fraud, they do marvellously detest and abhor. But they suffer him not to dispute in his opinion, and that only among the common people. For else apart among the priests and men of gravity they do not only suffer, but also exhort him to dispute and argue, hoping that at the last, that madness will give place to reason.

Sir Thomas More, *Utopia, Book 2, Of the Religions of the Utopians*

The Bible for everyone

The sun itself is not more common and open to everyone than the teaching of Christ is. I utterly disagree with those who do not want the holy Scriptures to be translated into the native tongue and read by ordinary people – as if Christ's teaching were so complicated that only a few theologians could understand it! Or as if the strength of the Christian faith were found in people's ignorance of it! It may be wise to conceal the mysteries of kingly government from ordinary folk, but Christ wanted His mysteries to be proclaimed as openly as possible. I want even the lowliest woman to read the Gospels and the letters of Saint Paul. I want them to be translated into all languages, so that they can be read and understood by Scots and Irishmen, by Turks and Muslims. To make people understand what Christianity teaches is surely the first step to converting them. Perhaps many will mock the Scriptures, but some will take them to heart. I greatly desire that the farm-worker should sing parts of Scripture to himself as he follows his plough, that the weaver should hum them to the tune of his shuttle, that the traveller should banish the boredom of his journey by reading Bible stories.

From Erasmus, *The Paraclesis*

Christ our living Lord

Make Christ the only goal of your life. Dedicate to Him all your enthusiasm, all your efforts, your leisure as well as your work. And don't treat Christ as a mere word, an empty way of speaking. See Him as love, simplicity, patience and purity; see Him as everything that He has taught *us* to be. But anything that takes you away from Christ and His teaching – regard that as the devil. "If your eye is good, your whole body will be full of light" (Matthew 6:22). Set your gaze on Christ alone, so that you love nothing and desire nothing except Christ, or for Christ's sake. Do this, and everything you do, whether you sleep or wake, eat or drink or play, will increase your reward. Maybe you go to mass every day. But if you behave as though this worship were for your own selfish benefit, and have no concern for the difficulties of your brother and sister, then all you have done is take part in the sacrament in a merely outward way. The sacrifice of the mass, in a spiritual sense, means that *we* become one body with the Body of Christ, living members of His Church. If your love for things is guided by Christ alone, if you treat all your possessions as things you hold in trust for the common good of all, if you take upon yourself the difficulties and sufferings of your neighbour, then you may take part in mass very fruitfully, because now you take part in a spiritual way. But to treat religion as nothing more than outward ceremonies – this is unspeakably stupid. Such a view is a rebellion against the spirit of the Gospel, a falling back into the superstitions of Judaism. The apostle Paul never ceased trying to get the Jews to give up their confidence in outward works. Yet I feel that the great majority of Christians have sunk down again into that sickness.

Erasmus, *The Dagger of the Christian Soldier,* 4th Rule.

Pope Julius II tries to excommunicate the apostle Peter

[Julius II was pope from 1503 to 1513. He was renowned as the "warrior pope", storming Italian cities in the cause of papal independence. Erasmus's satire *Julius Excluded from Heaven* depicts Julius after his death arriving at the gate of heaven, which is guarded by the apostle Peter, the first pope according to Western Catholic teaching.]

Julius:	[Arriving at the gate of heaven] What the devil's going on here? Doors won't open, eh? Looks as if the lock's been changed, or at least tampered with.
Julius's guardian spirit:	You'd better check and see that you didn't bring the wrong key with you. You don't open this door, you know, with the same key that opens your money-box!
Julius:	I'm getting fed up. I'll pound on the door. Hey! Hey! Someone open this door at once! What's wrong? Isn't anyone there? What's keeping that doorman? I suppose he's drunk and sleeping it off.
Julius's spirit:	He judges everyone by his own standard.
Peter:	Well, it's a good thing we have a gate like iron! Otherwise this fellow (whoever he is) would have broken the doors down. Some giant or tyrant, a wrecker of cities, must have arrived. But eternal God, what a sewer I smell here! I won't open the door directly; I'll just peep through the bars of the window and see what monster this is. Who are you? What do you want?
Julius:	Unless you're just plain blind, I trust you recognise this key? That's if you don't know the golden oak [Julius's family symbol]. Can't you see my triple crown, and my robe shining all over with jewels and gold?
Peter:	I vaguely recognise the silver key – although it's the only one you have, and it's quite unlike the keys the true Shepherd of the Church,

Christ, once entrusted to me. But that arrogant crown you're wearing – how am I supposed to recognise that? No barbarian tyrant, even, has ever dared to flaunt such a thing, let alone anyone who expects to be allowed in here! As for the robe, that doesn't impress me in the slightest. I have always trampled on and despised jewels and gold like so much rubbish. But what's this? I notice that all your equipment – key, crown, and robe – bear the signs of that vile conman and imposter who had my name but not my nature, Simon [Simon Magus, who tried to buy apostolic powers with money, Acts 8:18-19], whom I humbled long ago with Christ's help.

Julius: Cut out the nonsense and open the door. Unless, that is, you'd rather have it battered down? In a word, do you see what a body of followers I have?

Peter: Well, I can see a lot of hardened bandits. But in case you didn't realise, these doors have to be stormed with different weapons.

Julius: I've had enough of all this talk. Unless you obey me right this minute, I will hurl even against *you* the thunderbolt of excommunication, with which I once terrified the mightiest kings and entire kingdoms! Behold the Bull I've already drawn up for the purpose.

Peter: What is this wretched thunderbolt, this thunder, these Bulls? What high-sounding drivel are you prating to me about, for goodness' sake? We never heard about any of these things from Christ!

Julius:	Well, you'll feel them if you don't obey.
Peter:	Perhaps you did once terrify some people with this hot air, but up here it doesn't mean a thing. Here you have to operate with truth. This citadel is won by good deeds, not evil words.

From Erasmus, *Julius Excluded from Heaven.*

How to examine a woman accused of witchcraft

A wise and zealous judge should grasp the occasion and select his way of carrying out his examination in accordance with the responses or depositions of the witnesses, or as his own prior experience or personal intelligence suggests to him. He should use the following precautions.

If he wants to discover whether the accused has a witch's power of keeping silence, let him observe whether she can weep tears when she is in his presence, or when she is being tortured. For we are taught by the writings of virtuous men who lived before us and by our own experience that this is a sure sign. Indeed, it has been found that a witch cannot weep, even if she is pressed and exhorted by grave exhortations to do so. All she can do is pretend to look tearful and daub her cheeks and eyes with spittle to make it look as if she is weeping. She must therefore be closely scrutinised by her custodians.

When he passes sentence, the judge or priest may use a method such as the following in exhorting her to genuine tears if she is innocent, or in putting a stop to false tears. He should put his hand on the head of the accused and say: I exhort you by the bitter tears that our Saviour the Lord Jesus Christ wept on the cross for the salvation of the world, and by the burning tears that the most glorious Virgin Mary, His Mother, wept in the evening over His wounds, and by all the tears which have been wept here in this world by the saints and the elect of God, from whose eyes He has now wiped away all tears, that if you are innocent you now weep tears, but if you are guilty that you shall by no means do so. In the name of the Father, the Son, and the Holy Spirit, amen.

Experience teaches that the more witches are exhorted, the less are they able to weep, however hard they try or daub their cheeks with spittle. Even so, when the judge has left, and not at the time or in the place of torture, witches may afterwards be able to weep in the presence of their gaolers.

Why is a witch unable to weep? The grace of tears, we may say, is one of the chief gifts granted to the repentant; for Saint Bernard [of Clairvaux] tells us that the tears of humble souls can reach to heaven and overcome the impossible. We cannot doubt that such tears give no joy to the devil, and that he bends every effort to stop them, to prevent a witch from finally repenting.

Someone may object that the devil in his cunning, by God's permission, might allow even a witch to weep. After all, we know that tearful sorrowing, weaving garments, and deceiving men, are all natural to women. However, since God's judgements are mysterious, if there is no other way of proving the accused guilty by valid witnesses or factual evidence, and if a strong or grave suspicion does not attach to her, she should be discharged. Still, because she has come under a slight suspicion owing to her reputation as a witch (to which the witnesses have testified), she must be required to renounce the heresy of witchcraft. We shall demonstrate this when we deal with the second way of passing sentence.

There is a second precaution that the judge and all the examiners must observe, both at this point and also throughout the whole procedure: namely, they must not let themselves be touched physically by the witch, especially on their bare arms or hands. And they must always carry with them some salt that has been conse-crated on Palm Sunday and some Blessed Herbs. These can be bound up together in Holy Wax and hung round the neck, as we demonstrated in the Second Part when we looked at remedies against illnesses and diseases that witches cause. For Consecrated Salt and Blessed Herbs have a wonderful protective power, as we know both from the testimony of witches themselves, and from the custom and practice of the Church, which exorcizes and blesses these items for this very purpose, as we see in the exorcism ceremony, when it is said, "For the banishing of all the power of the devil," *etc.*

We should not think, however, that physical contact on the joints or limbs is the only danger we must protect ourselves against. Sometimes, by God's permission, witches can with the devil's aid cast a spell on the judge by the simple sound of the words they speak, especially while they are being tortured. Experience teaches that some witches, when locked up in prison, have urgently implored their gaolers to grant them this one favour, that they should be allowed to look at the judge before he looks at them. By getting this first sight of the judge, they have been able to alter the mind of the judge or his examiners, so that they lose all their anger against the witch and do not dare to harm her in any way, but allow her to go free. One who knows and has experienced this offers this genuine testimony. O that witches were not able to do such things!

Heinrich Kramer and Jacob Sprenger, *Malleus Maleficarum*, **Part Three, Second Head, Question 15.**

Chapter 2.

MATURING SUN: MARTIN LUTHER AND THE BIRTH OF THE PROTESTANT REFORMATION.

As we saw in the last Chapter, section 3, a blaze of controversy had flared up between humanists and scholastics around the figure of Johannes Reuchlin, the famous Hebrew scholar. The inquisition put Reuchlin on trial in 1514 for his defence of Jewish literature as a source of knowledge for Christians. In the thick of this quarrel, the humanists seemed to find new allies in two remarkable men, academically well-trained pastors and preachers, one in Germany, the other in Switzerland. The German was Martin Luther, professor of Biblical studies at Wittenberg University in Saxony, north-eastern Germany; the Swiss was Ulrich Zwingli, preacher in the Great Cathedral of Zurich. Both men were part of the humanist movement (Zwingli more obviously so), and both were committed to a vision of spiritual renewal within the Catholic Church. Neither saw himself as a rebel against the Catholic faith; yet both were cast out of the Church for their programmes of renewal.

Although the lives and careers of Luther and Zwingli run in parallel in many ways, it is easier to tell their stories one at a time – we will only confuse ourselves if we keep switching back and forth between one and the other. Let us begin, then, with Luther and his programme for theological reform in Wittenberg University, but always bearing in mind that we must soon backtrack to consider the similar-yet-different renewal movement of Zwingli in Zurich.

1. Young Luther.

Martin Luther (1483-1546) was the son of a copper miner from
Eisleben in Saxony. Luther later described himself as a "tough
Saxon" of peasant blood. Soon after his birth the family moved to
Mansfeld, the centre of Germany's mining industry, where Luther's
father, Hans, eventually became joint-owner of six mining shafts
and two smelting furnaces, which raised the family's quality of life
to new heights of prosperity. It was a large family, by Western
standards of today; by 1505, Hans had four sons and four daughters,
Martin being the second son. Influenced by modern psychology,
many biographers of Luther have tried to trace all kinds of aspects
of the Reformer's adult personality to his childhood relationship
with his father. But as others have pointed out, this seems a dubious
procedure, since our knowledge of Luther's childhood comes
exclusively from his own statements (relatively few in number)
made 30 or 40 years later. Probably the most we can safely say is
that there was an emotional tension between a stern father and a
sensitive son, which may have intensified the young Luther's
spiritual insecurity and quest for the assurance of salvation.

The future Reformer grew up in a peasant society where the
everyday reality of the supernatural was taken very seriously.
Events that educated people today think of as "natural" were then
routinely ascribed to evil spirits, *e.g.* thunder and lightning. Certain
places were also felt to be the home of dark powers. Luther never
outgrew this outlook; in his maturity he said, "Many regions are
inhabited by devils. Prussia is full of them, and Lapland is full of
witches. In my native country, on the top of a high mountain called
the Pubelsberg, is a lake into which, if you throw a stone, a tempest
will arise over the whole region, because the waters are the abode
of captive demons." Luther's struggles with Satan were given a
graphic power by this demon-haunted view of the world. It was
offset, though, by a belief in supernatural forces of good – saints
and angels – and the power of God channelled through the Church.

Martin Luther (1483-1546)

Luther was educated at the town school in Mansfeld, and was then
sent at the age of 12 to a boarding school in Magdeburg, where he
spent a year before moving to a different school in Eisenach. We
know very little of these years. In 1501, aged 18, he went to the
university of Erfurt (central Germany), intending to become a
lawyer in obedience to his father's wishes. Here he studied the
trivium (grammar, rhetoric, and logic), then the quadrivium
(arithmetic, geometry, music, and astronomy): the traditional form
of medieval education.[1] Again, we know little of Luther's university life, but he was a good student; he graduated early in 1505,
coming second in a class of 17. The plan was that he should then
study for a further two years at Erfurt in order to qualify as a lawyer.

However, after only a month of legal studies, young Luther
suddenly forsook university life, renounced the world, and joined
the Augustinian order of friars in Erfurt.[2] This was in the face of
angry opposition from his father. "Have you never heard of God's
command to honour your father and mother?" Hans raged at
Martin. But something infinitely more crucial than obeying his
father had taken possession of the youthful law student: the death
of a school-friend, and a narrow escape from a bolt of lightning
during a storm, had awakened in Luther an overwhelming passion
for religion and the salvation of his own soul. It seems likely that he
had for some time been disturbed by a growing sense of his own
sinfulness, and a corresponding fear of divine judgment; the
terrifying experience of the lightning bolt very probably pushed his
mind across a boundary towards which it had already been moving
– the decision to join a religious order. (In medieval Catholic
Europe, the most popular way of increasing one's chances of
salvation was to become a monk or a nun.)

So at the age of 22, Martin Luther shook the world's dust from his
feet, took his religious vows, became an Augustinian friar, and
plunged himself into the study of theology at Erfurt University. The
teaching that reigned here was the *via moderna* of the later schoolmen,

---

[1]   See Part One, Chapter 11, section 1.
[2]   For the Augustinian friars, see Part Two, Chapter 8, section 4.

William of Ockham and Gabriel Biel, with their neo-Pelagian emphasis on natural free-will, effort, and merit in obtaining divine grace.[3] This kind of doctrine simply made Luther despair of ever finding the salvation he hungered and thirsted for. Although this young friar was very holy in the eyes of others, in his own guilt-wracked conscience he could never find any assurance that he had made himself worthy enough to deserve God's mercy. Still, Luther learned from Ockham and Biel that the believer could not trust human philosophy in matters of faith; only God could reveal the heavenly truths which humanity needed to know for its salvation – and He had treasured up these truths supremely in the Scriptures, to which even the pope was subject.

The Augustinian order soon recognised young Luther as an out-standing scholar and preacher. He was ordained to the priesthood in 1507, and in 1508 became a junior lecturer at the new university in Wittenberg, founded in 1502 by prince **Frederick the Wise** of Saxony (1486-1525). Here Luther gave lectures on the *Sentences* of Peter Lombard and the moral teaching of Aristotle.[4] At this stage, Luther's spiritual guide was **Johannes von Staupitz** (1460-1524), vicar general of the Augustinian friars in Saxony. Staupitz was professor of Biblical studies at Wittenberg University, and a fervent disciple of Augustine of Hippo and his theology of God's sover-eign, unconditional grace (a theology of salvation that was entirely opposed to the *via moderna*). A sensitive and spiritually-minded man with a clear, deep insight into other people's souls, Staupitz took Luther under his wing. He was Luther's confessor (*i.e.*, Luther made his confessions of sin to Staupitz in order to receive absolu-tion); Luther spent so long confessing, sometimes up to six hours, that Staupitz occasionally became exasperated. "God is not angry with you," Staupitz once exclaimed, "you are angry with God! Do you not know that God commands you to hope?" This was an

---

[3]   For the schoolmen and scholastic theology in general, see Part Two, Chapter 7. For William of Ockham, Gabriel Biel, and the *via moderna*, see Part Two, Chapter 7, section 3. The *via moderna* taught that if a sinner did his best according to his own natural powers, God would give him grace.

[4]   For Peter Lombard, see Part Two, Chapter 7, section 3.

accurate perception: Luther was indeed angry with the God who demanded a perfection he could never give, and who condemned him for not giving it. Staupitz tried to lead the tormented young friar to a self-abandoning trust in God's free and undeserved mercy, a mercy made visible and tangible in the wounds of the suffering Jesus. Luther testified of Staupitz, "He was my first father in this teaching, and he gave birth to me in Christ. If Staupitz had not helped me, I would have been swallowed up in hell and left there."

It was Staupitz who sent Luther off to Rome in 1511 with another friar, on important business for the Augustinian order: a decision which shows the trust that Staupitz placed in Luther. For Luther himself, the pilgrimage to "holy Rome" was profoundly disenchanting. He never forgot the cynical attitude to religion that he found there, or the obsession with money. He was later fond of repeating the Italian proverb, "If there is a hell, Rome is built over it."

Staupitz also introduced Luther to mysticism. Luther later said that the mystical teachings of Bonaventura nearly drove him mad, but he found food for his soul in the writings of Johann Tauler, and in the *German Theology* which Luther republished twice, in 1516 and 1518, with introductions written by himself.[5] It was Staupitz, too, who encouraged Luther to study for a doctorate in theology. He received his degree in 1512, and then took over from Staupitz as professor of Biblical studies in Wittenberg – Staupitz felt that in teaching others, Luther would find the answers to his own problems. Lecturing on the Psalms, Romans, Galatians, and Hebrews, Luther used the "new learning" of Renaissance humanism to interpret the Bible by the grammatico-historical method, breaking free from the methods and concerns of traditional scholastic theology.[6] Among the humanists who influenced Luther were Jacques Lefevre d'Étaples, whose commentary on the Psalms

---

[5]   For Bonaventura, see Part Two, Chapter 7, section 3; for Tauler and the **German Theology**, see Part Two, Chapter 10, section 6. The mature Luther was much cooler towards even the most evangelical of the medieval mystics.

[6]   For the grammatico-historical method, see Part One, Chapter 9, section 1.

dazzled the German professor, and Reuchlin, from whose *Rudiments of Hebrew* Luther learned the language of the Old Testament.

Like most Christian humanists, Luther had come to detest scholasticism as a betrayal of the Biblical message. He violently opposed the way that the schoolmen had blended Christianity with the philosophy of Aristotle. He had also, by this time, rejected the neo-Pelagian teachings of William of Ockham and Gabriel Biel about salvation, and followed Staupitz in becoming a disciple of Augustine of Hippo; from now to the end of his life, Luther was to be a whole-hearted believer in Augustine's doctrine of the sovereign grace of God who chooses helpless sinners for salvation by His unmerited mercy. This was the first of Luther's two great theological and spiritual breakthroughs, and it occurred around 1513. He came to understand that the apostle Paul's phrase "the righteousness of God" (Romans 1:17) does not mean the righteousness by which God *punishes* sinners, but the righteousness which He graciously *gives* to sinners as a free gift of salvation. At this early stage, however, Luther still understood God's gift of righteousness as the inner righteousness that the Holy Spirit produces in the heart (what fully developed Protestant theology would call "regeneration" and "sanctification"). Luther's second great breakthrough was when he came to understand faith as essentially personal trust in Christ rather than assent to the Church's teachings, and "the righteousness of God" as God's imputation of Christ's righteousness to the believer's account, changing the believer's legal status before God but not the believer's heart ("justification" in the sense in which Evangelical theology uses the term).[7] This second breakthrough did not happen till much later, probably in the period 1518-19.[8]

---

[7] Luther did think that the Holy Spirit changes the heart, but he came to believe that this change was not what the Bible was referring to when it spoke of "justification".

[8] See, however, the discussion in section 3.

Luther was the outstanding lecturer at Wittenberg University, but he was not alone; he had valuable co-workers in his programme of Augustinian theological renewal. Chief among them were:

Andreas Bodenstein von Carlstadt (1477-1541). Carlstadt was Wittenberg University's senior lecturer. A high-minded idealist singularly lacking in common sense, he soon went far beyond Luther and became a leading "Radical" Reformer.[9] At this early stage, however, Carlstadt was completely in harmony with Luther.

Nicholas von Amsdorf (1483-1565). Amsdorf was a famous scholastic theologian whom Luther had won over to more Augustinian views. In the wake of Luther's break with Rome, Amsdorf became a vigorous, fearless, narrow-minded Protestant Reformer, more zealously Lutheran than Luther himself.

George Spalatin (1482-1545). Spalatin was not a university lecturer, but chaplain to Luther's prince, Frederick the Wise, and a warm supporter of Luther. All Luther's dealings with Frederick were through Spalatin as intermediary. Spalatin's influence over Frederick was instrumental in persuading the Saxon prince to back Luther in his coming conflict with the papacy.

Philip Melanchthon (1497-1560). Melanchthon (pronounced "Mel-ank-thun" or "Mel-ank-tun"), who arrived at Wittenberg in 1518 at the age of 21, was the nephew of Johannes Reuchlin. He was also a brilliant young Christian humanist in his own right; he had already published some thirty books by the time he went to Wittenberg. Inspired by Erasmus's ideals for the renewal of society, Melanchthon was praised to the skies by Erasmus himself:

---

[9] For more about Carlstadt as a Radical Reformer, see next Chapter; for the Radical Reformation as a whole, see Chapter 5.

Philip Melanchthon (or Melancthon)
(1497-1560)

"Great God!" (Erasmus cried), "what expectations the young Philip Melanchthon arouses! He is only a boy, yet he has already achieved eminence in both Greek and Latin! What ability he displays in argument! How pure and elegant his words! What rare learning! How many books he has read! What tenderness and refinement in his extraordinary genius!"

Gentle, thoughtful, timid, and peace-loving, the young Melanchthon swiftly became Luther's most beloved friend and most trusted colleague. If Basil of Caesarea and Gregory of Nazianzus[10] were the "David and Jonathan" of the patristic age, the friendship between lion-hearted Luther and mild-spirited Melanchthon was the equivalent in the Reformation era. The two men were a perfect union of opposites in personality:

"I am rough, boisterous, and stormy," said Luther, "born to fight hosts of devils and monsters. My job is to remove stumps and stones, cut away thistles and thorns, clear away wild forests. Then along comes Master Philip, gently and softly, sowing and watering with joy, according to the gifts which God has abundantly granted him."

Melanchthon's main subject at Wittenberg was Greek. He did more than anyone (even Erasmus) to spread the knowledge of the Greek language in German schools and universities. He also lectured on logic, ethics, and exegesis. Later generations hailed him as the "Teacher of Germany".

Under the guidance of Luther, Carlstadt, Amsdorf, and Melanchthon, and with Spalatin and Frederick as patrons, Wittenberg University became a flourishing centre of Augustinian theology and preaching. The Protestant Reformation, the greatest religious movement since the rise of Islam, was led by a group of university professors.

---

[10] For Basil of Caesarea and Gregory of Nazianzus, see Part One, Chapter 8, section 3.

2. The 95 theses and their background.

In April 1517, Luther decided to declare open war on scholastic theology through an academic "disputation", with his 97 theses (not to be confused with the more famous 95 theses of October 1517).[11] The 97 theses, entitled *Disputation against Scholastic Theology*, attacked the neo-Pelagianism of the later schoolmen and called for a return to the theology of Augustine. To Luther's keen disappointment, the 97 theses awakened no public interest and sank without trace. However, when he resolved five months later in his 95 theses to protest against the sale of indulgences (the theses were entitled *Disputation on the Power and Efficacy of Indulgences*), the response was amazingly different. As we saw in Part Two when we looked at the theology of Thomas Aquinas (Part Two, Chapter 7, section 3), an indulgence was a certificate of pardon issued by the papacy, by which the merits of the saints in heaven were transferred to a sinner, releasing him from the "temporal penalties" of sin; the pope could even extend these pardons to souls in purgatory, hastening their passage to heaven.[12]

In 1515, pope **Leo X** (1513-21) authorised the sale of a special set of indulgences in Germany. Their purpose was to bring in cash to finance the building of Saint Peter's basilica in Rome, and the papal agent selling the indulgences was a Dominican friar called **Johann Tetzel** (1470-1519). Tetzel's indulgence preaching was an overpowering act of emotional manipulation; the Dominican promised his hearers that as soon as they bought one of his indulgences on behalf of a dead relative, God would instantly set the relative's poor suffering soul free from purgatory and admit it into the bliss of heaven. Tetzel used a little rhyme – "As soon as the coin in the money-box rings, the soul from purgatory springs!" If a person

---

[11] For disputations, see Part Two, Chapter 7, section 1.

[12] Indulgences were first extended to cover souls in purgatory by pope Sixtus IV (1471-84) in 1476. The "temporal penalties" of sin were those penalties which a sinner could "pay off" through penance on earth, or through sufferings in purgatory. They were distinguished from the "eternal penalties" which Christ's atoning death alone could deal with.

bought an indulgence for himself, Tetzel claimed, it would automatically wash away the foulest of sins, even supposing the sinner had raped the Virgin Mary. Tetzel's publicity campaign was crude, tasteless, vulgar, sensational, and contrary even to the official theology of indulgences, which taught that to be effective they had to be accompanied by repentance. By April 1517, Tetzel was preaching the indulgences in the area around Wittenberg.

Luther's anxiety about the indulgences was neither purely academic nor purely personal. Luther had by now accumulated many pastoral responsibilities in the Church. In 1512 Staupitz had made Luther "sub-prior" of the Augustinian convent in Wittenberg, in charge of the studies of all the new friars; in 1514 he had been appointed pastor of Wittenberg's parish church, the "castle church", where he preached every Sunday; and around the same time, he had become a "provincial superior" in the Augustinian order, with 11 convents under his supervision, which brought legal and financial as well as spiritual burdens. Luther was no ivory tower intellectual obsessed with his own private ideas! As Wittenberg's parish priest, he was deeply horrified that people in his own congregation were buying Tetzel's indulgences, thinking that salvation could be purchased for cash, without showing any sign of repentance for their sins. (Frederick the Wise had banned Tetzel from his own lands, but people were crossing the river Elbe into the territory of Frederick's brother, duke George, where Tetzel was active.)

So, despite the abject failure of his 97 theses in April, Luther arranged another academic disputation, this time on the topic of indulgences, wrote his 95 theses, and on October 31st 1517 announced that he was going to debate the subject in public in Wittenberg University on the following day. This was the occasion when Luther nailed up the 95 theses on the door of Wittenberg's castle church: not a dramatic gesture, but the normal way of posting a public announcement.[13] The 95 theses offered penetrating criticisms of the practice of indulgences, coloured with a display of

---

[13] October 31st is celebrated by Protestants in Continental Europe as "Reformation Day".

humanist learning, and lit up by a bright, Erasmus-like vision of Christianity as a religion of inward heart-spirituality which bears fruit in a life of love. To his astonishment, Luther found that he had loosed a storm of controversy that would grow steadily more furious and rip apart the very fabric of Western Europe.

Luther had no wish to stir up a public quarrel when he announced the disputation. He was not even criticising the official theology of indulgences, but Tetzel's grim perversion of it. Even so, within months, the whole of Germany was in uproar. Humanists translated the 95 theses from Luther's Latin into German, and printed and distributed thousands of copies throughout Germany – without Luther's approval. Luther found himself under attack from bishops, universities, monks (especially the Dominicans, who rallied to Tetzel's support), and all the upholders of scholastic theology. His assault on indulgences, however, won widespread support among three crucial groups:

(a) Humanists like Erasmus, who despised indulgences as a corruption of the spiritual religion of the New Testament. Erasmus never gave total support to Luther, but in these early days of the Reformation he sympathised strongly with much that Luther was saying. On indulgences, Erasmus said:

> "I do not condemn them, but I think it is nonsense to suppose that a person can buy his way to heaven. What a filthy trade this is, designed to fill up money-boxes, rather than to enrich people's spirituality!"[14]

(b) German nationalists, especially the German knights like Ulrich von Hutten, who saw indulgences as one of the papacy's instruments for draining away German cash to Rome.[15]

---

[14]   See previous Chapter, section 4 for Erasmus.
[15]   For Hutten, see previous Chapter, section 3, under the heading **Germany**.

(c) Many ordinary German Christians, who longed for the Church to be purified from its abuses, and needed only a leader to give a voice to their grievances and aspirations.

3. The pope and the Scriptures.

The Dominicans, and archbishop Albert of Mainz (who was profiting handsomely from the sale of the indulgences), lodged official charges against Luther in Rome. Pope Leo X, however, did not take the controversy very seriously (it was all a storm in a teacup, Leo felt: just one more quarrel between Dominicans and Augustinians). Still, Leo instructed the head of Luther's Augustinian order, Gabriel della Volta, to end the dispute; and so della Volta summoned Luther to appear before the governing body of the Augustinians which met in Heidelberg (south-western Germany) in April 1518. Here, Luther presented his "Heidelberg disputation", 40 theses in which he defended Augustine's doctrines of sin and grace, and attacked the way that the schoolmen had subjected Christian theology to Aristotle's philosophy.

The Heidelberg disputation also set out Luther's important contrast between a "theology of glory" and a "theology of the cross". By a theology of glory, he meant a theology that glorifies human achievement, whether the intellectual achievement of human philosophy in seeking to understand God, or the moral achievement of human goodness in seeking to earn its own salvation. By a theology of the cross, he meant God's rejection of human achievement, a rejection revealed in the cross of Jesus Christ; the true knowledge of God, and true salvation, are found not in the strivings of human philosophy or ethics, but only in Christ crucified. The sinner must die to his own achievements, Luther said, and despair of his own intellectual and moral ability to find God, if he is ever to receive the grace of Christ. Luther's performance at the disputation won over two young friars, Martin Bucer (1491-1551) and Johannes

Brenz (1499-1570), who were soon to become the leading Protestant Reformers of Strasbourg and Swabia.[16]

Luther as yet had no thought of breaking with the papacy. Nevertheless, with the benefit of hindsight, we can see that his theology was becoming slowly and gradually more "Protestant". In a popular pamphlet written to explain the 95 theses, he cast doubt on the divine right of the pope to be head of the Church; in the days of pope Gregory the Great, Luther said, the Church of Rome was not superior to the Eastern Church.[17] He was soon criticising even the official theology of indulgences, denying that the pope had any power to release souls from purgatory. He also started teaching that excommunication from the Catholic Church did not affect a soul's eternal salvation; no earthly power could separate a true believer from Christ's love. So if a sentence of excommunication was unjust, it severed the soul only from the outward and visible Church of the papacy, but not from the spiritual Church of the elect; and if the excommunication was deserved, sincere personal repentance before God would save the excommunicated person, even if the Catholic Church never received him back.[18] In August, pope Leo summoned Luther to appear in Rome within 60 days to answer for his errors; he also ordered Luther's prince, Frederick the Wise of Saxony, to hand Luther over to the papal legate, Thomas de Vio, otherwise known as **cardinal Cajetan** (1469-1534), a distinguished Italian theologian and disciple of Thomas Aquinas. Frederick, however, took Luther's side, and arranged a peaceful meeting between Luther and Cajetan at Augsburg in October.

Cajetan was not an extremist or a diehard defender of the old order. Indeed, in many ways he was something of a reformer himself. After the Roman-Protestant split became entrenched in the 1520s,

---

[16]   For Martin Bucer, see Chapter 3, section 5.

[17]   For Gregory the Great, see Part One, Chapter 11.

[18]   Luther's views on this point contradicted established Catholic doctrine. Thomas Aquinas had clearly taught that even an unjust sentence of excommunication deprived a soul of God's grace. See the *Supplement* to his *Summa Theologiae,* Question 21, article 4.

Cajetan recommended a policy of conciliation, advocating that the Church should accept the marriage of priests and grant the wine to the laity in holy communion. The report in which Cajetan made these proposals was felt to be so shocking that it was quickly buried in the papal archives. At this earlier stage, in 1518, Cajetan agreed with some of Luther's criticisms of indulgences, and referred to points of disagreement as "errors" rather than "heresies" on Luther's part.

However, the three meetings between the two men achieved nothing. Cajetan found that he disliked Luther personally; he thought the German friar had the eyes of a demon, continually flashing with dark light. Both men lost their tempers with each other, especially when Luther tripped up Cajetan over a misquotation the latter had made from the papal bull *Unigenitus* on the "treasury of merits". The cardinal steadily pressed Luther on the absolute authority of the papacy to interpret Scripture, ordered the German to withdraw his errors, and threatened to excommunicate him. Luther refused to submit, and Cajetan's arguments forced the Wittenberg professor for the first time to deny the infallibility of the pope. It was becoming increasingly clear to Luther that he must either abandon all his convictions and submit unconditionally to the papacy's claim to absolute authority in spiritual matters – or else stand by his views, at the price of accusing the papacy itself of being in error. At this stage, Luther still accepted that the papacy was the visible head of the Church, but maintained that the pope was subject to correction by Scripture and an ecumenical council of the whole Church. These views did not impress Cajetan, who dismissed Luther sternly: "Withdraw your errors, or do not come again into my presence!" Luther felt it prudent to flee from Augsburg on horseback, and in November he appealed to an ecumenical council to settle the dispute.[19]

---

[19] This of course stirred the embers of the 15th century conciliarist controversy, when for a time ecumenical councils had been made superior to the papacy. See Part Two, Chapter 10, section 3.

Political events gave Luther a respite for the next few months. The
Holy Roman emperor Maximilian I was dying, and both king
Francis I (1515-47) of France, and king Charles I (1516-56) of
Spain (Maximilian's grandson), were offering themselves to the
German princes as candidates to be elected as the new emperor.[20]
Pope Leo did not want either of them elected, because a German
emperor who also controlled France or Spain would be a serious
threat to the independence of the papacy in Italy. Leo's candidate
was Frederick the Wise of Saxony – Luther's prince. So Leo could
not afford to antagonise Frederick by persecuting Luther. During
this period of peace, Luther exhorted people to submit to the holy
Roman Church as (under Christ) the supreme power in heaven and
earth. But privately the thought more and more disturbed him that
the pope might be the Antichrist. Luther was convinced that what
he was teaching was the truth of Scripture. If the pope was hostile
to Scripture, then perhaps Antichrist had already come – perhaps he
was the pope! Luther here was echoing a medieval theme, when
popes had declared hostile emperors or rival popes to be Antichrist,
and dissenting movements (such as the Waldensians, Cathars,
Lollards, and Hussites) had applied Antichrist language to the
papacy itself.[21]

In June and July 1519, Luther and his colleagues Melanchthon and
Carlstadt took part in a disputation at Leipzig (eastern-central
Germany) with *Johann Eck* (1486-1543). Eck was professor of
theology at Ingolstadt University, a learned scholastic, one of the
greatest debaters of the day, and (according to contemporaries) an
arrogant bully who looked more like a butcher than a theologian.
Eck challenged Carlstadt, who held a more senior position than
Luther at Wittenberg University, to defend the doctrines its lecturers
taught; Luther and Melanchthon accompanied Carlstadt to Leipzig

---

[20] Since 1356, the crown of the Holy Roman Empire had been in the hands of
seven "electors": the princes of Saxony and Brandenburg, the count Palatine of
the Rhine, the king of Bohemia, and the prince-archbishops of Mainz, Trier,
and Cologne.

[21] For the Waldensians and Cathars, See Part Two, Chapter 8, section 3. For the
Lollards and Hussites, see Part Two, Chapter 10, sections 4 and 5.

to give him support. The proceedings opened with a dispute between Carlstadt and Eck about Augustine's doctrines of sin and grace. Carlstadt was a boring bumbler in debate, and Eck easily got the better of him.

Then Luther stepped in. He took up the subject of the papacy, setting out to prove that neither Scripture nor the early Church fathers supported the absolute supremacy of the pope. A distinguished humanist Latin scholar, Peter Mosellanus, who chaired the Leipzig disputation, has left us a vivid portrait of Luther, which captures the essence of the man with remarkable accuracy:

> "Luther is of medium size, his body thin, and so worn out by burdens of responsibility and study, that you can almost count all his bones. He is in the full maturity of his powers. His voice is clear and beautiful. His learning, and his knowledge of Scripture, are so extraordinary, that he can quote anything perfectly from memory. He understands Greek and Hebrew well enough to give his own judgment on what words and phrases mean. When he speaks, he has a rich store of subjects at his command, and a huge forest of thoughts and words at his disposal. There is nothing lofty or proud about him; he knows how to adapt himself to different people and circumstances. He is always fresh, cheerful and relaxed, with a pleasant expression on his face, no matter how hard his enemies press him –you just cannot help believing that heaven is with him in his mighty labour. However, most people criticise him for not being moderate enough when he argues against his foes; he lacks prudence, and is more cutting in speech than a theologian and reformer ought to be. During the debate he carried a bunch of flowers in his hand, and whenever the argument became heated, he looked at his flowers and smelled them."

As the argument swung back and forth, Eck cleverly cornered Luther into admitting that his views were similar to those of John Huss, whom the Council of Constance had burnt for heresy in

1415.[22] This forced Luther to acknowledge that even ecumenical councils were fallible: the Council of Constance had erred in condemning Huss. Luther now appealed to the Scriptures as the sole infallible authority. Melanchthon did not directly dispute with Eck, but suggested arguments to Luther and Carlstadt; it was Melanchthon who, at Leipzig, set forth the important Protestant view that Christians should read and judge the early Church fathers in the light of Scripture, rather than reading Scripture in the exclusive light of the fathers. This position became known by the Latin tag of "sola Scriptura" (Latin for "Scripture alone").

At this point it is crucial to understand what the Protestant Reformers did and did not mean by "Scripture alone". They *did* mean that only the canonical Scriptures possess *infallible* authority as a source of Christian teaching. All other sources, however useful or even indispensable they may be in helping Christians to understand Scripture, are subordinate to Scripture. However, they did *not* mean that a Christian could ignore or despise all other sources and authorities. Most of the Protestant Reformers most of the time continued to recognise, in one way or another, the "rule of faith" that had circulated in the Church from earliest days, best known in the West in the form of the Apostles' Creed. Although they would not have ascribed divine inspiration or infallibility to the Creed, they still saw it as a true and indispensable summary of the basic contents of Scripture, and as the necessary context for all theological interpretation of Scripture's teaching. In other words, Scripture was not some abstract authority: it was very specifically the Word of *this* God, the God who created the universe and sent His only Son to be the Saviour of sinful humanity through His cross and resurrection. Only as the Word of the true God, the Father of Jesus Christ, did Scripture have authority in the Church. The Protestant Reformers also granted a subordinate authority to the creeds of the ecumenical Councils, especially the Nicene Creed and the Creed (or Definition) of Chalcedon; these, they maintained, were providential landmarks in the life history of God's people, and had to be

---

[22]   For Huss, see Part Two, Chapter 10, section 5.

reckoned with seriously as digests of biblical truth which Christians had always received. Finally, the Protestant Reformers had no intention of rejecting the ongoing teaching ministry of the Church through its preachers and theologians. It was not infallible, but used discerningly it was an invaluable source of wisdom. Melanchthon put it like this:

> "Let pious people take note of these examples of rash opinions of every age, let them heed the voice of those who teach correctly, let them embrace with both hands and with their whole heart the prophetic and apostolic writings that have been committed to us by God, and let them attach themselves to the interpretations and testimonies of the pure Church, such as the Apostles' Creed and the Nicene Creed, that they might retain the light of the Gospel and not become involved in these raving opinions that, as I have said, follow when the light of the Gospel is extinguished. Those who read the prophetic and apostolic writings and the Creeds with pious devotion and who seek the opinion of the pure Church will easily conclude afterwards that they are aided by these human interpretations, and they will know what usefulness is afforded by correct and skilful expositions of Scripture written by pious believers and by sermons drawn from the fountains of Scripture."

The position taken by the Protestant Reformers has been described as "Tradition 1" – critical reverence for the history and traditions of the Church. The Reformers treated Christian theological tradition with deep care and respect, although they did not give it a blind or uncritical allegiance. This has been contrasted with "Tradition 2", the view held by the hardline defenders of Rome – *authoritarian* reverence for the history and traditions of the Church. These Roman Catholics elevated the theological tradition – or as the Reformers claimed, a biased reading of it – into an untouchable status. This was a kind of "all or nothing" approach. It permitted no one to subject any development of doctrine to critical scrutiny, and therefore nothing could be corrected. Reformation on this model of course became impossible: one simply had to accept everything, no matter how far it may have drifted from Scripture or the early Church fathers. Alongside Tradition 1 and Tradition 2, the 16th century also offered a third option, "Tradition 0", associated with the Radical Reformation (see Chapter 5), which had little or no respect for the Church's history or traditions: a Christian must read the Bible with fresh eyes, as if no one else had ever read it before. Modern Evangelicalism often interprets "Scripture alone" in this Tradition 0 sense, but we must recognise that this was not what the Protestant Reformers believed.

Half-way through the Leipzig disputation, Charles I of Spain was elected emperor, becoming *Charles V* (1519-56) of the Holy Roman Empire. Charles belonged to the great German family of Habsburg, the most powerful family in Europe, which had in fact occupied the Holy Roman Empire's throne since the first Habsburg emperor, Albert II (1438-40). With the far-flung lands of the Habsburgs in his possession, Charles V ruled the largest domain of any Western European king since Charlemagne[23] – Spain, southern Italy, the Netherlands, Germany, and Bohemia. He was in many ways a just and honourable ruler, but in matters of religion he remained firmly (though not fiercely) loyal to Rome. Both sides in the Luther controversy appealed to the new emperor; Charles summoned an imperial parliament or "diet" to meet at Worms (western Germany) in January 1521, where among other things Luther's case would be heard.[24]

4. Justification by faith.

It was probably in 1519 that Melanchthon's knowledge of Greek brought Luther his new understanding of what the New Testament

---

[23] For Charlemagne, see Part Two, Chapter 4, section 2.

[24] The imperial diet had been growing in importance in the Holy Roman Empire since the 15th century. In 1512 it acquired considerable power at the diet of Cologne; the Empire itself was organised into 10 "circles", each governed by two princes responsible for maintaining peace and running the imperial army.

means by "justification".[25] The doctrine of justification by faith has become uniquely associated with the Reformation. In one way, this association is correct; in another way, it can be misleading. It is correct in the sense that justification by faith (or to speak more fully and accurately, *justification by grace alone through faith alone in Christ alone*) ultimately became the doctrinal heart of Reformation theology. Any failure to grasp this would amount to a perverse misunderstanding of Protestantism. However, it can also be misleading, in two respects: (i) It took quite some time for the centrality of justification to become clear in the storms of Reformation controversy. It was certainly not the issue for which Luther was excommunicated by the papacy (see section 4). (ii) The Reformers were not only Reformers of doctrinal theology as it related to the individual's salvation. Equally important was the Reformation of worship and of Church government. Those who concentrate their attention too narrowly on the doctrine of justification often neglect these crucial dimensions of the Reformation.

Melanchthon's study of New Testament Greek convinced him that what the New Testament means by "justify" (the Greek word *dikaioo*) is "declare righteous" in a legal sense. When a judge pronounces a "not guilty" verdict on an accused person, so that the law has no more quarrel with that person, this (said Melanchthon) is what is expressed in the "justification" language of the Greek New Testament. Justification is therefore a *forensic* act – the act of a judge declaring a person "right" in the eyes of the law.

Melanchthon's interpretation involved a hugely significant development within the Western theological tradition. The understanding of justification in the Western medieval Church relied on the standard Latin translation of the Bible, the Vulgate, which rendered

---

[25] The date of Luther's "rediscovery" of justification by faith is one of the most complex issues in Luther scholarship. For the best account of the view adopted in the present book, see Lowell C. Green, *How Melanchthon Helped Luther Discover the Gospel* (Verdict Publications, Fallbrook 1980). However, this is by no means the only view; others would date Luther's acceptance of justification by faith much earlier, perhaps as early as 1514. This view has been championed *e.g.* by the great Reformation historian Heiko Oberman.

the apostle Paul's key Greek term *dikaioo* by the Latin *iustificare*. And from this sprang the difficulty. Western theologians understood (or misunderstood, as Melanchthon believed) the Latin term *iustificare* as meaning to *make* righteous, in the sense of moral transformation – the process by which a sinner is changed spiritually in his soul into a just, holy, godly person. They included a forensic dimension (the forgiveness of sins) as part of this process, but focused far more attention on the inward moral renewal of the believer.[26] In medieval theology, this moral renewal endowed the forgiven believer with a grace-given ability to acquire "merit" – qualities of personal goodness which would, when enough were acquired, entitle the believer to the rewards of heaven. Depending on how Augustinian a medieval theologian was, he would ascribe these merits either to the work of the Holy Spirit (the Augustinian view), or to the efforts of human free will (the view taken by most late medieval theologians under the influence of William of Ockham and the *via moderna*).[27]

Melanchthon, Luther, and Reformation theology broke decisively with this medieval concept of merit. The believer's acceptance to eternal life, they maintained, was not some far-off goal, grounded in the storing up of moral or spiritual qualities in the believer's life.

---

[26] In modern histories of doctrine, this view of justification is often ascribed to Augustine himself. There is indeed confusion in the way Augustine related his understanding of salvation to the Latin word for "justify". But Augustine can also be quoted in support of a more Protestant view. Certainly one of Augustine's greatest disciples, Bernard of Clairvaux, was teaching a Protestant-type concept of justification as late as the 12th century. By the time we arrive at the late 15th century, however, it seems clear that Bernard's view had all but vanished in favour of the alternative described above.

[27] The more Augustinian view was taught by Thomas Aquinas, who said that the merits of the believer acquired all their value from the fact that they were inspired by the Holy Spirit. In other words, so far from being independently human, they were fruits of divine grace. In the words of Aquinas, "If we speak of a meritorious work, to the extent that it proceeds from the grace of the Holy Spirit moving us toward eternal life, it merits eternal life by a true deserving. For the value of its merit depends on the power of the Holy Spirit moving us toward eternal life" (*Summa Theologiae*, Part Two, first part, question 114, article 3).

It was a present reality, here and now; and as far as the demands of the law were concerned, it was based on the imputation to the believer of Christ's righteousness. (Imputation means reckoning or crediting something to someone's account, and is used repeatedly in one of the great biblical passages on justification, Romans chapter 4, where "imputation" describes God's reckoning of righteousness to Abraham through his faith.) Because of the union between believers and Christ, the sins of believers were imputed to Christ, who died as their sin-bearer, so securing forgiveness; and Christ's righteousness was imputed to believers, which was the basis of their acceptance with God. John Calvin was later to give a classic definition of this cluster of concepts: "we explain justification simply as the acceptance with which God receives us into His favour as righteous men. And we say that it consists in the forgiveness of sins and the imputation of Christ's righteousness" (*Institutes* 3:11:2). Here were the two elements in the Protestant doctrine of justification – both the forgiveness of sins (negatively), and the imputation of Christ's righteousness (positively). In setting forth this understanding of justification, the Reformers claimed that they were correcting a medieval aberration by returning to a purer doctrine of grace found in the early Church fathers.[28]

Luther had been a fervent Augustinian in his theology from about 1513, so he already believed in salvation by grace alone. What Melanchthon's new understanding of justification did was enable Luther in 1519 to construct a more radically Christ-centred understanding of God's grace. Intimately related to this, just prior to his acceptance of Melanchthon's interpretation of justification, Luther's understanding of "faith" had also undergone a decisive shift. For official medieval theology, faith was essentially *a voluntary assent to the dogmas of the Church*; but Luther, based again on

---

[28] For a modern treatment of justification by faith in the early Church fathers, see Thomas Oden, *The Justification Reader* (Grand Rapids: Eerdmans, 2002). For an older but still illuminating study, see G. S. Faber, *The Primitive Doctrine of Justification* (London: Seeley and Burnside, 1839). In the later Western medieval Church, figures like Wessel Gansfort and Staupitz, had taught justification by faith before Luther and Melanchthon, but not with the same logical clarity or emotional ardour. For Gansfort, see previous Chapter, section 5.

Melanchthon's Greek expertise, was now convinced that in the New Testament, faith essentially meant *trust* (in Latin, "fiducia") – a lively personal confidence in God, that He is favourably disposed towards us for Christ's sake. Since Christ was received by this personal trusting faith, Luther contended, and since God justified the believer by imputing Christ's righteousness to his account, it followed that complete assurance of acceptance with God was possible. A sinner did not have to strive to acquire a sufficient amount of merit in order eventually to secure a place in heaven; he could know that his place there was secure through Christ's perfect work, which God freely applied to him here and now, through his faith-union with Christ, and through such faith-union alone.

One of the most serious implications of justification by faith, as Luther and Melanchthon now understood it, was that it sapped the foundations of the medieval view of the Church. According to what had become the traditional Catholic teaching, God channelled or mediated His grace through the Church's priesthood and its sacraments of baptism, holy communion, penance, and so on. For Luther, however, faith itself brought the soul into a *direct* relationship with Christ and His grace. Another redefinition was involved: "grace" in medieval theology was a created substance in the soul, a gift of God which enabled someone to perform righteous works.

For Luther and Melanchthon, by contrast, grace was *God's attitude of favour*. In effect, Luther now taught that that "grace" was God Himself – God personally present in Jesus Christ as a generous, merciful, and forgiving Saviour, embracing the sinner into a total acceptance with Himself through the sinner's reliance on His unmerited goodness. The believer could not slip into and out of this acceptance with God, needing each time to be restored by sacramental grace through an earthly priest; his trust in Christ kept him always within the sphere of God's favour, despite his many sins. Nor did this lead to a careless attitude to sin, because (said Luther) true faith by its very nature involved repentance. By receiving Christ, faith brought the Saviour Himself to live by His Spirit in the believing soul. "In faith Christ Himself is present," as Luther put it.

Christ's presence in the believer makes him holy (although not sinlessly perfect) as well as forgiven. So for Luther, the true Christian was, at one and the same time, "always a sinner, always repenting, always justified". When Luther came to this understanding of justification by the imputed righteousness of Christ through faith, he said: "I felt that I had been born again, and that I had entered paradise itself through open gates."

Perhaps the single greatest theological hallmark of the Reformation was the clear, systematic distinction it eventually made between justification (God the Father's legal declaration that the believing sinner is righteous and acceptable in His sight through Christ's imputed righteousness), and sanctification (the Holy Spirit's transforming work within the believer, by which Christ's righteousness is gradually imparted to his soul). Luther expressed the distinction thus, commenting on Acts 15:9 ("purifying the hearts of the Gentiles by faith"):

> "God purified the Gentiles, that is, He reputed them purified, because they had faith, although in reality they were still sinners... Thus the Gentiles, and we too, are pronounced righteous, although in reality we are sinners like those unclean animals. He begins to purge us in reality. But first He purifies by imputation, and then He gives the Holy Spirit, through whom we are purged more substantially. Faith purifies through the forgiveness of sins, while the Holy Spirit purifies effectively."

This distinction between justification and sanctification had by no means been neglected in previous theologians, but it was the Reformers who – in response to the religious problems they perceived in their time – brought it to the very forefront of soteriology (the doctrine of salvation), and articulated the distinction with a passion and precision that were new. Virtually all attempts at reunion between Protestants and Roman Catholics have foundered on this issue.

However, care must be taken not to exaggerate. Despite the Reformers' belief in justification by faith and their rejection of the medieval theology of merit, they did not simply consign the Middle Ages into the rubbish bin. Rather they appealed from official doctrinal formulations of the Church's theology to the faith and piety of medieval Christians. Whatever the scholastic theologians may have said, the best religious consciousness of the Middle Ages (so the Reformers argued) always knew that Christ alone had to be trusted as the fountain of all spiritual and eternal blessing. The example to which the Reformers most often appealed was Bernard of Clairvaux.[29] When Bernard lay apparently dying in the year 1125, we are told that he seemed to see himself standing before the judgment seat of God, where Satan hurled damning charges against him. But Bernard had his reply ready: "I confess myself unworthy of the glory of heaven, to which by my merits I can never attain. But my Lord possesses it by a double title: He is the only-begotten Son of the eternal Father, and He has bought it by His precious blood. This second title He has conferred on me, therefore I trust with assured confidence to obtain it through the merits of His passion".[30]

We could multiply such utterances from the godly of the Middle Ages. As the great Scottish Presbyterian theologian James Orr (1844-1913) argued, in an illuminating chapter on justification by faith in his *The Progress of Dogma*, the Reformers took their stand on this living and continuous tradition of piety that ran through the medieval Church, and adjusted the Church's doctrinal formulations to bring them into harmony with what devout and trusting souls had always known and confessed. Here was profound continuity between the Middle Ages and the Reformation.[31]

---

[29] See Part Two, Chapter 5, section 3 for an account of Bernard's life and work.

[30] I quote from the anonymous *St.Bernard, Abbott of Clairvaux*, in the Roman Catholic Notre Dame Series of *Lives of the Saints*, London 1916, pp.62-3.

[31] This is not to suggest that everyone in the medieval Church was a "devout and trusting soul". The continuity I am highlighting existed between the piety of men like (say) Anselm of Canterbury and Bernard of Clairvaux on the one side, and Martin Luther and John Calvin on the other.

5. The break with Rome.

Before the diet of Worms could meet, Luther and the papacy had finally come to a decisive break with each other. Luther had studied some of John Huss's writings and concluded that the Hussites had been in the right in their conflict with Rome, *e.g.* in their view of the Church as the spiritual body of the elect, and in their demand that the cup be given to the laity in holy communion. "We are all Hussites without knowing it," Luther declared. "Saint Paul and saint Augustine are Hussites!" He also read Lorenzo Valla's treatise which proved that the "donation of Constantine" was a fake.[32] The terrible certainty now gripped Luther that the papacy was indeed the Antichrist, the Man of Sin prophesied by the apostle Paul (2 Thessalonians 2).

For his part, pope Leo was now convinced that Luther was a dangerous heretic to whom patience and tolerance could no longer be shown. On June 15th 1520, Leo issued a papal bull entitled *Exsurge domine* ("Rise up, O Lord"), ordering Luther to submit within 60 days or be excommunicated and burnt as a heretic. The bull listed 41 of Luther's errors; these included his rejection of papal supremacy, his denial of the pope's power to excommunicate from the true spiritual Church of believers, his demand that the wine be given to the laity in communion, and his teaching that the fall of Adam had destroyed human free-will in spiritual matters. The bull did not mention justification by faith as one of Luther's errors. Therefore, strictly speaking, the Church of Rome did not excommunicate Luther for teaching justification by faith (Rome was more concerned about Luther's denial of papal authority). We should keep this in mind. It is one of the clearest indications that it took time for the doctrine of justification to become a central concern both of Protestants and of Roman Catholics.[33]

---

[32] See previous Chapter, section 2.

[33] As late as 1531, the leading Lutheran Reformer, Johannes Brenz, was still teaching the old Augustinian doctrine of justification, that God makes us internally righteous by grace. It took the intervention of Luther and Melanchthon to set him straight.

Papal agents published the bull without much difficulty in southern Germany; but in the north, people – especially university students, to whom Luther was a hero – treated Rome's representatives with open hostility. Angry crowds tore the bull to pieces in Leipzig, and threw it into the river at Erfurt. When the bull arrived in Wittenberg, Luther announced that he would burn it in public, which he did on December 10th in the presence of a large crowd of students and citizens of Wittenberg who cheered him on. The students also threw works of scholastic theology and canon law into the fire.

Between the issuing of the bull and Luther's burning it, Luther had written three treatises which together laid the foundations of the Protestant Reformation. These were his *Address to the Christian Nobility of the German Nation, The Babylonian Captivity of the Church*, and *The Freedom of a Christian*.

The *Address to the Christian Nobility of the German Nation* was published in August 1520. Popes and ecumenical councils, Luther declared, had failed to reform the Church. Therefore it was the duty of the secular rulers to step in. Luther argued that the secular rulers were Christians, and if the clergy would not reform the German Church, then the German emperor, princes, and nobles must take extraordinary emergency measures to bring about reformation and save Germany from God's wrath. Three "walls" by which the papacy had defended its power must be overthrown:

(i) The doctrine that the clergy were superior to the laity, and that the laity could not exercise any power in the Church.

Luther demolished this wall by his doctrine of "the priesthood of all believers". Every believer, Luther said, was a true priest before God by virtue of his faith and baptism. Thus all true Christians had the right to baptise, celebrate communion, expound the Scriptures, and pronounce sins forgiven; the clergyman was simply one priest chosen by the other priests (the laity) to exercise these functions within the whole priestly congregation. In effect, Luther was distinguishing between the priesthood and the ordained ministry:

all Christians were baptised into the priesthood, but only some were
ordained to the ministry of preaching and administering the
sacraments.[34] For Luther, then, clergy and laity did not have a
different spiritual status or different spiritual powers, just differing
responsibilities within Church and society.

> "If a group of earnest Christian laymen were taken prisoner
> and banished to a desert without an episcopally ordained
> priest among them," Luther argued, "and if they together
> decided to choose one of their number (whether married or
> not) and set him apart to baptise, celebrate mass, pronounce
> sins forgiven, and preach the Gospel, such a man would be
> as truly a priest as though he had been ordained by all the
> bishops and popes in the world."

Luther thus rejected the particular doctrine of apostolic succession
which had come to prevail in the Church; ordination, for Luther,
was essentially the act of a congregation which held the faith of the
apostles, not of a bishop who could trace his own ordination back
to the apostles.[35]

**(ii) The claim that the papacy was infallibly inspired by the
Holy Spirit, and therefore that the popes alone could interpret
Scripture.**

Luther attacked this claim by pointing out the scandalous lives of
many of the popes. How could such wicked men claim to possess
the Holy Spirit? He also appealed again to the priesthood of all
believers. The Holy Spirit dwelt in the whole Church, not just in the
papacy; the Creed said "I believe in the Church," not "I believe in
the pope." Therefore the ability and responsibility to interpret
Scripture belonged to all believers:

---

[34] It should be said that Luther was quite clear that no one should take it upon
himself to exercise the ministry within a congregation, unless lawfully called to
such a position.

[35] For the doctrine of apostolic succession, see Part One, Chapter 3, section 2,
under **Church organisation**.

"it is the duty of every Christian to embrace the cause of the faith, to understand and defend it, and to denounce every error."

It was contrary to a true understanding of the Church to claim that Christians should just submit to whatever the pope said. Such a claim made Scripture subject to the authority of one man, the bishop of Rome, instead of the bishop of Rome being subject to the authority of Scripture.

(iii) The papacy's claim that it alone could summon an ecumenical council of the Church.

Luther argued that the government of the Church lay in the hands of the whole Church, both laity and clergy, and not just in the pope's hands. Therefore, if the pope and his bishops refused to reform the Church, then the laity, represented by the Christian secular rulers, could and should summon a "true free council" to carry out reformation. Luther pointed out that it was not the pope who summoned the first ecumenical Council of Nicaea in 325, but a Christian layman, the emperor Constantine;[36] indeed, Christian emperors had called together the first seven ecumenical Councils. Then Luther listed some of the reform measures he thought a council should take, *e.g.* stripping the papacy of its worldly pomp and power, allowing the clergy to marry, and placing German Church affairs under a German archbishop.

The *Address to the Christian Nobility* was a popular tract, written in lively German. Thousands of copies were printed and it sold out almost immediately, requiring a second edition. Throughout the tract, Luther appealed to German national feeling against the religious tyranny of Rome, and succeeded brilliantly.

Luther's second tract, *The Babylonian Captivity of the Church*, was a more scholarly work written in Latin, published in October 1520.

---

[36] For Constantine and the Council of Nicaea, see Part One, Chapter 8, section 1.

Luther compared the Western Catholic Church to Israel exiled in Babylon. Rome's doctrine of the sacraments, he asserted, had robbed Christians of their freedom. Most of the treatise concerned holy communion. Luther attacked three Roman errors about communion which had brought Christians into spiritual bondage:

(i) The refusal to give the cup to the laity. Luther argued from Scripture that both the bread and the wine belonged to all Christians. If Christ's blood was shed for all believers, why should they not all drink the wine that signifies it?

(ii) The doctrine of transubstantiation. Luther criticised transubstantiation as a scholastic invention derived from the philosophy of Aristotle. The bread and wine, he argued, remained bread and wine in their own nature. Christ's flesh and blood were truly present in them, but without abolishing their reality as bread and wine, just as Christ's divine nature was truly present in His human nature without abolishing its human reality.

(iii) The sacrifice of the mass. This, Luther declared, was the most blasphemous bondage of all. He attacked the idea that the priest offered up Christ to God in holy communion, and thereby performed a good work which merited God's grace. Communion was not our gift to God, Luther argued, but God's gift to us. It was not a sacrifice, but a sign of our promised inheritance through Christ's death. It existed to nourish our faith in God's forgiveness, not to make God forgive us.

Luther also maintained that four of Rome's "seven sacraments" were not sacraments at all. He defined a sacrament as a divine promise of forgiveness joined to a visible sign. On this basis, Luther denied that confirmation, marriage, ordination, and extreme unction were sacraments. Only baptism and communion were Scriptural sacraments. However, Luther kept Rome's other sacrament of penance (to the extent that it involved confessing one's sins to a clergyman and the clergyman pronouncing forgiveness). He could not quite make up his mind whether it was actually a sacrament, but he certainly saw it as a beautiful way of bringing spiritual comfort to the conscience of a believer distressed by his sins.[37]

People regarded the *Babylonian Captivity* as Luther's most revolutionary writing. By attacking the official Catholic doctrine of holy communion, he was striking at the very heart of medieval Catholic worship. When Erasmus read the *Babylonian Captivity*, he said: "The breach is beyond repair." There was no possibility any longer of reconciliation between Luther and Rome.

Luther's third treatise of 1520 was *The Freedom of a Christian*, published soon after the *Babylonian Captivity* in October 1520. In contrast to the other two treatises, it was not an attack on Rome, but a positive exposition of the true meaning of the Christian life. Luther proclaimed that faith alone brought the Christian into saving union with Jesus Christ, through which all the blessings and benefits of Christ's atoning work became the believer's possession. The Christian was therefore a perfectly free person in the spiritual realm, because he was no longer enslaved to the law of works, but completely righteous and accepted in God's sight by his faith in Christ alone. Yet in the physical realm, the Christian used his freedom to be the humble servant of all through love. He did good works, not to make himself righteous before God, but to serve his neighbour freely out of selfless love, just as Christ, the exalted Lord of all, became our humble servant through love. So the Christian must be a sort of Christ to his neighbour.

---

[37] In the earlier part of the treatise Luther definitely calls penance a sacrament. But towards the end he says: "There are strictly speaking only two sacraments in the Church of God – baptism and the bread. For only in these two do we find both the divinely instituted sign and the promise of the forgiveness of sins. The sacrament of penance, which I added to these two, lacks the divinely instituted visible sign, and is (as I have said) nothing but a way and a return to baptism."

6. The Diet of Worms.

Luther's fate now depended on the new Holy Roman emperor, Charles V. Charles was a faithful adherent of the papacy who had no sympathy at all for Luther's heresies. But he was also a good politician, and knew that Luther had the backing of most of Germany. When the imperial diet met at Worms in January 1521, the pope's ambassador, ***Girolamo Aleander*** (1480-1542), argued that the Church had already excommunicated Luther – this happened on January 3rd – so there was nothing for the diet to discuss. They must simply condemn Luther and have him burnt as a heretic. However, Luther's prince, Frederick the Wise, demanded that Luther be given a free and fair hearing by the diet. Charles V finally agreed and summoned Luther to Worms with a guarantee of safe-conduct. People remembered that John Huss had gone to the Council of Constance in 1415 under a safe-conduct from the emperor Sigismund, but Sigismund had still burnt Huss at the stake. Luther courageously decided to obey the summons:

> "Even if the emperor calls me to Worms in order to kill me, or to declare me an enemy of the Empire, I shall offer to come. With Christ helping me, I shall not run away, nor shall I abandon God's Word in this struggle."

Luther was cheered all the way on his journey from Wittenberg to Worms, a popular national hero. Aleander reported back to Rome that

> "the whole of Germany is in full revolt. Nine-tenths raise the battle-cry, 'Luther!', while the other tenth care nothing for Luther but cry out, 'Death to the court of Rome!'"

The great German nationalist knight, Ulrich von Hutten, was also writing very violent pamphlets and poems in favour of Luther, and threatening to wash his hands in the blood of the pope and his cardinals. Hutten's thunderings made poor Aleander fear for his life:

"A cartoon has appeared showing Luther with a book in his hand, accompanied by Hutten in armour with a sword, under the heading *Champions of Christian Liberty*. Another picture shows Luther in front and Hutten behind, carrying a box on which are two cups and the inscription *The Ark of the True Faith*. Erasmus is in the foreground, playing king David's harp, and in the background is John Huss, whom Luther has recently proclaimed his patron saint."

Luther arrived at Worms on April 16th. On the 17th, he appeared before the diet. On a table before him lay a collection of his writings. An official of the archbishop of Triers, surnamed Eck (but no relation of the Eck who had debated with Luther at Leipzig), asked the German friar if the writings were his. Yes, Luther said. Eck asked him if he still defended them, or if he would give up his heresies. Luther asked for time to think about it. He was granted one day. The following afternoon he appeared before the diet again. Luther made a speech in German, justifying what he had written, and promised that if his opponents could prove he was mistaken from the Scriptures, he would be the first to throw his books into the fire. Then he asked permission to repeat the speech in Latin. This was refused, and Eck commanded Luther to give a straight-forward answer to a simple question: would he abandon his heretical views, which were nothing but the long-condemned errors of Wyclif and Huss? Luther replied with the most famous words in the history of Western Christianity:

"Unless I am refuted and convicted by testimonies of Scripture or by clear reason – since I believe neither the popes nor the councils by themselves, for it is clear that they have often erred and contradicted themselves – I am conquered by the holy Scriptures I have quoted, and my conscience is captive to the Word of God. I cannot and will not withdraw anything, since it is neither safe nor right to do anything against one's conscience. Here I stand. God help me. Amen."

Then Luther left, hissed by his enemies but greeted outside by a crowd of admirers, and Charles V broke up the diet amid general confusion.

7. Heretic and outlaw.

Luther had made a bad impression on the emperor and the bishops, especially by his assertion that even ecumenical councils could make mistakes. The conciliarist theory still had many supporters, and even those who agreed with Luther that the pope might be in error continued to maintain that ecumenical councils were infallible.[38] But Luther seemed to be saying that he, a single university professor, was right, and the rest of the Church was wrong. (In his darkest moments, Luther wondered whether he was guilty of this.) In reality, that was not the true situation; there were many others who agreed with Luther's teaching. And Catholic Europe had seen religious movements before Luther which had taught many of the same things that he was now proclaiming, most notably the Waldensians, the Lollards, and the Hussites. Indeed, these groups were still very active, and soon coalesced in various ways with the great new movement for reform which Luther had sparked off. So it was not really a case of one university professor against the whole Church.

However, perhaps the main point which divided Luther from his opponents was their different understanding of what exactly "the Church" was. Traditionalist Catholics defined it in terms of the outward organisation of the papacy and its clergy, who alone (by virtue of their apostolic succession) could administer the grace-giving sacraments. By contrast, Luther defined the Church as the whole body of Christian believers, who all enjoyed a direct saving relationship with Jesus Christ and His grace through faith in the gospel, as that gospel was made known in Scripture, preaching, and sacraments. Such people were indeed found within the structures of

---

[38] For the conciliarists, see Part Two, Chapter 10, section 3.

the Western Catholic Church. But Luther was now convinced he could just as easily find them outside it too – he pointed to the Eastern Orthodox. Were the Eastern Christians all damned, asked Luther, merely because they did not accept the papacy?[39]

Luther's concept of the Church was not acceptable to traditional Catholics; it was just one more of the German friar's deadly errors. Some zealous traditionalists urged the emperor Charles V to break his promise of safe-conduct and have Luther burnt as a heretic, but Charles had a high sense of personal honour, and refused to go back on his word. After several days of fruitless discussions between Luther and a committee of the diet, the emperor allowed the Reformer to leave Worms on April 26th. On May 26th, the diet officially condemned him as a heretic and outlaw (only a minority of delegates were left, most of Luther's supporters having gone home), and placed him under the ban of the Empire. This meant that anyone giving shelter or hospitality to Luther would be committing a crime.

However, issuing the ban was one thing; enforcing it was another. The Holy Roman Empire was not a centralised monarchy, but a loose federation of several hundred German states, including large domains like Luther's Saxony, the imperial cities like Strasbourg, and many small territories controlled by lesser nobles. If local German authorities chose to protect Luther, there was little Charles V could do to stop them. And Luther's own prince, Frederick the Wise, was determined to protect the popular hero. As Luther journeyed home from Worms to Wittenberg, Frederick sent a party of knights to intercept him. They carried him off to the Wartburg castle in Eisenach, where he was kept in secrecy and safety for 11 months. To disguise himself, Luther got rid of his friar's gown, dressed like a gentleman, grew long hair and a beard, and assumed the name "Sir George". When he went out of the castle for fresh air

---

[39] Thus Luther followed Wyclif and Huss in appealing over the pope's head to the Eastern Church. For relationships between Lutheranism and Eastern Orthodoxy, see Chapter 9, section 4.

and exercise, he engaged people in conversation and asked them whether anyone had discovered Luther's whereabouts yet!

Luther's stay at the Wartburg was the most creative year of his life. He translated the entire New Testament into German, finishing in February 1522 (it was published in September). Working from Erasmus's Greek New Testament, Luther produced a translation which was and still is a masterpiece of the German language. There had been other German Bibles before Luther's, but they were translated from the Latin Vulgate, and used an awkward and difficult style of German. Luther's New Testament, translated directly from the Greek, was in a lively popular style that every German could understand. Its impact transformed the religious life of Germany, and even shaped the future development of the German language. In 1534 the whole Bible in German was published, translated by Luther and his colleagues at Wittenberg University.

Meanwhile, a host of popular writers throughout Germany took up Luther's cause, writing countless tracts condemning the papacy and supporting Luther. All the chief agents of communication in Germany propagated "Lutheranism": printers, artists, students, preachers, lawyers, teachers in city schools, and merchants who could travel about spreading Lutheran ideas and books. Most of Germany was now in open revolt against the papacy, and the papacy seemed powerless to stop it.

One of the most revealing signs of what was happening in Germany took place at Luther's university in Wittenberg. At the same time that Luther began translating the New Testament in the Wartburg, a book was published in Wittenberg by his fellow professor and closest friend, Philip Melanchthon, the illustrious young humanist. His book was called *Loci Communes Rerum Theologicarum* – "Chief Points of Theological Matters". This was the first Lutheran systematic theology; Melanchthon was to revise it continually, publishing five further editions. The *Loci Communes* became the supreme textbook of theology in Lutheran universities,

the Lutheran equivalent of what Peter Lombard's *Sentences* had
been in the Middle Ages. It also showed that the young humanists
of Germany, personified in Melanchthon, were rallying to Luther's
cause: the river of Renaissance learning was flowing into the sea of
the Reformation. And it heralded the fact that the Reformers were
no longer just attacking Rome; they were starting to produce a
positive theology of their own, logically arranged and clearly
stated, as a counterpart to Rome's teaching. The protest against
Roman abuses was turning into the establishment of an alternative
Church.

Important people:

The Church
Johann Tetzel (1470-1519)
Pope Leo X (1513-21)
Johannes von Staupitz (1460-1524)
Cardinal Cajetan (1469-1534)
Andreas Bodenstein von Carlstadt
   (1477-1541)
Girolamo Aleander (1480-1542)
Johann Eck (1486-1543)
George Spalatin (1482-1545)
Martin Luther (1483-1546)
Philip Melanchthon (1497-1560)
Nicholas von Amsdorf (1483-1565)

Political and military
Frederick the Wise of
   Saxony (146-1525)
Holy Roman emperor
   Charles V (1519-50)

Staupitz on salvation

If you think we have not praised the Lord's mercy enough by
showing how He justifies us by His own righteousness, and even
enters into a marriage-union with sinners, then understand that He
does even more. He makes our sins His own! The Christian is
righteous through Christ's righteousness; likewise Christ is
unrighteous and sinful through the Christian's guilt. On hearing
this, the Jews cry out "Blasphemy!" and the Greeks "Madness!"
But the believer says, "It is so!" The Jew is insulted, the Greek

mocks, the believer rejoices. For "we preach Christ crucified, to the Jews a stumbling block, and to the Greeks foolishness, but to those who are called, both Jews and Greeks, Christ the power of God and the wisdom of God" (1 Corinthians 1:23-24). For God was pleased to conquer strength with weakness, to vanquish wisdom with foolishness, and to condemn righteousness by sin, "so that no flesh should glory in His presence" (1 Corinthians 1:29).

Now let us leave aside everything else and consider only this, whether He who is sinless by nature can be convicted as a sinner. Jesus's own confession clearly convicts Him: "My God, My God, why have You forsaken Me? Why are You so far from helping Me, involved in transgressions as I am?" (Psalm 22:1, Vulgate translation). How, O most precious Jesus, can these be Your words? Clearly I see the answer: God has placed on You the iniquity of all; You alone are the Lamb of God who bears the sins of the world...

You are mine, O Jesus, and all that You have is mine; and I am Yours, and whatever I have is Yours. Because we are one, what is Yours becomes mine, while still remaining Yours; and in the same way, what is mine becomes Yours, while still remaining mine. Therefore, I am righteous because of Your righteousness, though I am a sinner because of my own guilt. And You are a sinner because of my guilt, though You are righteous because of Your own righteousness...

As you have just seen, the sins of the Christian are transferred to Christ; they become the sins of Christ, who came not in sinful flesh but "in the likeness of sinful flesh" (Romans 8:3). Because of His likeness to sinful flesh, Christ became subject to death and suffering, and could actually suffer and actually die. Because He was unlimited, infinite, and eternal by nature, having a true claim to the very throne of God, He could carry the burden of our sins. Because of His likeness to sinful flesh, He could make satisfaction for our sins, by fasting, praying, giving charitable gifts, and offering Himself as a sacrifice to God. The Lord Jesus imposed on Himself each and every duty of repentance that belongs to the elect.

Because of His equality with God, He could condemn, bear, wipe out, and extinguish every fault and every sin. As God, Christ actually imposed penance upon Himself on behalf of all, and thus took upon Himself the sins of all mankind; as Man, He made satisfaction for all by suffering and dying.[40]

Johannes von Staupitz, *Eternal Predestination and its Execution in Time* (1516), chapters 11 and 12.

From Luther's 97 theses, *Disputation against Scholastic Theology*

5. It is false to say that the human will, left to itself, is free to choose between opposites; for it is not free, but in bondage.
6. It is false to say that the will is able by nature to obey a righteous command. I state this in opposition to Scotus and Gabriel.[41]
7. In fact, without God's grace the will produces a perverse and evil act.
17. A human being cannot by his own nature will God to be God. He would prefer to be God himself, and that God were not God.
29. The best and infallible preparation for grace, and the only thing that disposes a person towards grace, is the eternal election and predestination of God.
34. In short, human nature possesses neither a pure reason nor a good will.
39. From beginning to end, we are not masters of our actions, but their slaves. I state this in opposition to the philosophers.
40. We do not become righteous by doing righteous deeds. Rather, having been made righteous, we then do righteous deeds. I state this in opposition to the philosophers.

---

[40] Compare this quotation from Stauptiz with the quotation from Luther's **Freedom of a Christian**: they are strikingly similar.

[41] Duns Scotus (1265-1308) and Gabriel Biel (1420-95). Biel was the last great pre-Reformation representative of the neo-Pelagian *via moderna*. Luther studied Biel closely when at Erfurt University.

43. It is false to say that no one can become a theologian without Aristotle. I state this in opposition to common opinion.
71. The law of God and the human will are two enemies, which can never be reconciled apart from the grace of God
74. The law makes sin abound, because it exasperates and repels the will.
75. But the grace of God makes righteousness abound through Jesus Christ, who causes us to love the law.
76. Every work of the law appears good outwardly, but inwardly it is sin. I state this in opposition to the scholastics.
78. The will, when it turns toward the law apart from the grace of God, does so purely in its own interest alone.
88. From this it is clear that everyone's will is by nature wicked and bad.
89. Grace is necessary as a mediator to reconcile the law with the will.

From Luther's 95 theses, *Disputation on the Power and Efficacy of Indulgences*

1. When our Lord and Master Jesus Christ said, "Repent," He meant that the entire life of believers should be a life of repentance.
2. The word cannot be understood as referring to the sacrament of penance – that is, confession and satisfaction – as administered by priests.
27. It is nothing more than human talk when men preach that the soul flies out of purgatory "as soon as the coin in the money-box rings".
32. All who believe they are sure of salvation because they have papal certificates of pardon will be eternally damned, along with their teachers.
33. We must especially beware of those who say that papal pardons are "the supremely precious gift of God by which a person is reconciled to God".

36. Any Christian at all who is truly repentant receives (as is right) the full remission of his punishment and guilt, without any certificates of indulgence.

43. Christians should be taught that a person who gives to the poor or lends to the needy does a better work than if he buys pardons.

54. The Word of God suffers harm if, in the same sermon, a preacher gives to papal pardons a length of time equal to, or greater than, the time given to the Word.

62. The true treasury of the Church is the holy Gospel of the glory and the grace of God.

75. It is madness to think that papal pardons have such power that they could absolve a man even if he had done the impossible and raped the Mother of God.

81. This immoral preaching of papal pardons makes it hard even for learned men to redeem the respect owed to the pope from the slanders (or at least, from the shrewd questions) of the laity.

82. For example, "Why doesn't the pope set all the souls free from purgatory simply out of holy love and the supreme need of those souls? This would be the most righteous of reasons, seeing that he can redeem countless souls for the sake of filthy money with which to build a chapel, which is the most trivial of reasons."

Luther condemned

[Pope Leo X's bull *Exsurge domine*, published on June 15th 1520, condemned Luther for teaching the following errors, among others:]

15. They are in great error who approach holy communion relying on their own confession of sin, their consciousness of no mortal sin, their right performance of prayers and preparations. Such people eat and drink to their own judgment. But if they believe and trust that they will find grace in the sacrament, this faith alone makes them pure and worthy.

23. Excommunication is only an outward penalty. It does not deprive a person of the common spiritual prayers of the Church.

25. The Roman pope, the successor of Peter, is not the vicar of Christ over all churches in the whole world, and was not appointed to this position by Christ Himself through the blessed Peter.

30. Certain statements of John Huss, condemned by the Council of Constance, are most Christian, true, and evangelical. The universal Church could not possibly condemn them.

31. In every good work a righteous person sins.

33. To burn heretics is contrary to the will of the Spirit.

36. Free-will after Adam's sin is a mere name. When free-will does its best, it sins mortally.

37. No one can prove purgatory from the sacred and canonical Scriptures.

Luther: Justification by faith which is active in love

The third incomparable benefit of faith is that it unites the soul with Christ, just as a bride is united with her husband. By this mystery, Christ and the soul become one flesh. And if they are one flesh, and if there is between them a true marriage (in fact the most perfect of all marriages, because human marriages are only poor illustrations of this one true marriage), it follows that they share in common all that they have, the good as well as the bad. So the believing soul can boast about, and glory in, everything Christ has, as though it were her own; and everything she has, Christ claims as His. Compare the two, and see the unspeakable benefits. Christ is full of grace, life, and salvation. The soul is full of sins, death, and damnation. But let faith join them, and the sins, death, and damnation will belong to Christ, and the grace, life, and salvation will belong to the soul. For if Christ is a husband, He must take upon Himself the things that belong to His bride, and bestow upon her the things that belong to Him. If He gives her His body and His very self, how shall He not give her everything that is His? And if

He takes His bride's body, how shall He not take everything that is hers?

Here we have a delightful vision of fellowship, and more than that, of a blessed struggle, victory, salvation and redemption. Christ is God and man in one person. He has not in Himself sinned, died, or been condemned, and indeed cannot sin, die, or be condemned; His righteousness, life, and salvation are invincible, eternal, all-powerful. But by the wedding-ring of faith, He shares in the sins, death, and pains of hell which belong to His bride. In fact, He makes them His own, and acts as though they were His own, just as if He Himself had sinned; He suffered, died, and descended into hell that He might conquer them all. Now since it was Christ who did all this, death and hell could not swallow Him up; they were by necessity swallowed up by Him in a mighty contest. For His righteousness is greater than all the sins of all mankind, His life is stronger than death, His salvation is more invincible than hell. Thus the believing soul, through the pledge of faith, is free in Christ, her Husband – free from all sins, secure from death and hell, enriched with the eternal righteousness, life, and salvation of her Husband Christ. So Christ takes to Himself a glorious bride, without spot or wrinkle, cleansing her by the washing of water with the Word of life, that is, by faith in the Word of life and righteousness and salvation. Thus He marries her in faith, steadfast love, mercies, righteousness, and justice, as Hosea 2 says.

Who can fully appreciate the meaning of this royal marriage? Who can understand the glorious riches of this grace? Here, this rich and divine Husband, Christ, marries a poor wicked prostitute, redeems her from all her evil, and clothes her with His goodness. Her sins cannot destroy her now, because they are laid upon Christ and swallowed up by Him. And she has the righteousness of Christ her Husband, and may boast of it as her own, confidently displaying it alongside her sins in the face of death and hell, saying, "If I have sinned, yet my Christ in whom I believe has not sinned, and all that's His is mine, and all that's mine is His." As the bride in the

Song of Solomon says, "I am my beloved's, and my beloved is mine"...

The Christian ought to think: "Behold! Without any merit on my part, by His pure free mercy, my God has given me in Christ all the riches of justification and salvation, although I am an unworthy and condemned sinner. I no longer lack anything – except enough faith really to believe that this is so! For such a Father, why should I not freely, joyfully, with all my heart, and with an eager will, do everything that I know will be pleasing and acceptable to Him? I will therefore give myself as a sort of Christ to my neighbour, just as Christ has given Himself to me. I will do nothing in this life except what I see is necessary, profitable, and good for my neighbour, since through faith I abound in all good things in Christ."

Behold, then, how love and joy in the Lord flow from faith; and from love flows a joyful, willing, free spirit, that serves its neighbour willingly, and takes no account of gratitude or ingratitude, praise or blame, gain or loss. It does not try to put others under obligation, does not distinguish between friends and foes, does not look to gratitude or the lack of it, but spends itself and its goods freely, whether this is wasted on the unthankful or gets a reward. As the Father acts, giving all things to all people richly and freely, making the sun rise on the evil and the good, so too the child of God does all things and suffers all things with a freely giving joy, with which he delights in God through Christ, the giver of such great gifts.

Martin Luther, *The Freedom of a Christian* (October 1520)

Melanchthon on the faith that justifies

Our adversaries pretend that faith is only a knowledge of the historical events [of Christ's life], and therefore teach that it can coexist with mortal sin. Thus they say nothing concerning faith, by which Paul so frequently says that people are justified, because those who are accounted righteous before God do not live in mortal sin. But that faith which justifies is not merely a knowledge of historical events, not merely that I know the stories of Christ's birth, suffering, *etc.* (even the devils know this). No, faith means to assent to the promise of God in which, for Christ's sake, the forgiveness of sins and justification are freely offered. Faith is the assurance or the sure trust in the heart, when with my whole heart I regard the promises of God as certain and true, through which (without my merit) are offered to me the forgiveness of sins, grace, and all salvation, through Christ the Mediator. And so that no one may suppose that faith is mere knowledge, we will add further: faith means desiring and receiving the offered promise of the forgiveness of sins and of justification. Faith means that my whole heart takes to itself this treasure. It is not my doing anything [for God], not my presenting or giving anything [to God], not my work or preparation. No, faith means that my heart assures itself, and is perfectly confident concerning this: namely, that God makes a present and gift to us, and not we to Him – that He pours upon us every treasure of grace in Christ.

The difference between this faith and the righteousness of the law can be easily discerned. Faith is the worship which receives the benefits offered by God; the righteousness of the law is the worship which offers our merits to God. By faith God wishes to be worshiped in this way, that we receive from Him those things which He promises and offers. Now, Paul plainly testifies that faith means, not only a knowledge of the historical events, but such faith as assents to the promise, when he says in Romans 4:16: "Therefore it is of faith, so that the promise might be sure." For he judges that the promise cannot be received except by faith. Therefore he puts them together as things that belong to one another, connecting promise and faith. Paul fastens and binds together these two, thus: Wherever there is a promise, faith is required; and conversely, wherever faith is required, there must be a promise.

Indeed, it will be easy to decide what faith is, if we consider the [Apostles'] Creed where this article certainly stands: the forgiveness of sins. Therefore it is not enough to believe that Christ was born, suffered, was raised again, unless we add also this article, which is the purpose of the historical events: the forgiveness of sins. To this the rest must be referred, namely, that for Christ's sake, and not for the sake of our merits, forgiveness of sins is given us. For what need was there that Christ should be given for our sins, if our merits can make satisfaction for our sins? As often, therefore, as we speak of the faith that justifies, we must keep in mind that these three objects concur: the promise, grace, and the merits of Christ as the price and propitiation. The promise is received by faith; the grace excludes our merits, and signifies that the benefit is offered only through mercy; the merits of Christ are the price, because there must be a certain propitiation for our sins. Scripture frequently implores mercy, and the holy fathers [the Old Testament saints] often say that we are saved by mercy. As often, therefore, as mention is made of mercy, we must keep in mind that faith is required, which receives the promise of mercy. And, again, as often as we speak of faith, we wish an object to be understood, namely, the promised mercy. For faith justifies and saves, not on the ground that it is a worthy work in itself, but only because it receives the promised mercy.

Throughout the prophets and the psalms this worship is highly praised, although the law does not teach the free forgiveness of sins. But the fathers [the Old Testament saints] knew the promise concerning Christ, that God for Christ's sake wished to forgive sins. Therefore, since they understood that Christ would be the price for our sins, they knew that our works are not a price for so great a matter; for our works could not pay so great a debt. Accordingly, they received free mercy and forgiveness of sins by faith, just like the saints in the New Testament. Here belong those frequent repetitions concerning mercy and faith, in the psalms and the prophets, as this, Psalm 130:3: "If You, Lord, should mark iniquities, O Lord, who shall stand?" Here David confesses his sins and does not recount his merits. He adds: "But there is forgiveness with You" (verse 4). Here he comforts himself by his trust in God's mercy, and he cites the promise: "My soul waits, and in His Word I hope," (verse 5), *i.e.*, because You have promised the forgiveness of sins, I am sustained by Your promise. Therefore the fathers too were justified, not by the law but by the promise and faith.

It is amazing that our adversaries downgrade faith so much, although they see that it is everywhere praised as an eminent way of worshipping God, as in Psalm 50:15: "Call upon Me in the day of trouble: I will deliver you." Thus God wishes Himself to be known, thus He wishes Himself to be worshiped, that from Him we receive benefits, and receive them, too, because of His mercy, and not because of our merits. This is the richest consolation in all afflictions, physical or spiritual, in life or in death, as all godly people know. Such consolations our adversaries abolish when they downgrade and disparage faith, and merely teach that people deal with God by means of works and merits – that we deal with God, the great Majesty, by means of our miserable, beggarly works and merits!

Philip Melanchthon, *Apology for the Augsburg Confession* (1531), Part Three.

Luther on how to translate the Bible

[Roman Catholics criticised Luther for translating Romans 3:28 as "justified by faith alone, apart from the works of the law". The word "alone" is not in the original Greek. Luther's response shows his philosophy of translation.]

I know that in Romans 3, the word "solum" [alone] is not present in either Greek or Latin text. The papists did not have to teach me that – it is simply a fact! The letters s-o-l-a [solum in the ablative case] are not there. And these boobies stare at them like cows at a new gate, while at the same time they do not recognise that it conveys the sense of the text. If the translation is to be clear and accurate, it belongs there. I wanted to speak German, since it was German, not Latin or Greek, that I had spoken in translation. But it is the nature of our German language that in speaking about two things, one which is affirmed, the other denied, we use the word "alone" or "only" along with the word "not" or "no". For example, we say "the farmer brings only grain and no money"; or "No, I really have no money, but only grain"; "I have only eaten and not yet drunk"; "Did you only write it, and not read it over?" There are a vast number of such everyday cases. In all these phrases, this is a German usage, even though it is not the Latin or Greek usage. It is the nature of the German tongue to add "alone" in order that "not" or "no" may be clearer and more complete. To be sure, I can also say "The farmer brings grain and no money," but the words "no money" do not sound as full and clear as if I were to say, "the farmer brings only grain and no money." Here the word "only" helps the word "no" so much that it becomes a clear and complete German expression.

We do not have to ask about the literal Latin or how we are to speak German, as these [Roman Catholic] asses do. Rather we must ask the mother in the home, the children on the street, the common person in the market about this. We must be guided by their tongue, the manner of their speech, and do our translating accordingly. Then they will understand it and recognise that we are speaking German to them. For instance, Christ says: "Ex abundatia cordis os loquitur." If I am to follow these asses, they will lay the original before me literally and translate it as: "Out of the abundance of the heart the mouth speaks." Is that speaking with a German tongue? What German could understand something like that? What is this "abundance of the heart?" No German can say that; unless, of course, he was trying to say that someone was altogether too magnanimous, or too courageous. Still, even that would not yet be correct, as "abundance of the heart" is not German, not any more than "abundance of the house, "abundance of the stove" or "abundance of the bench" is German. But the mother in the home and the common man say this: "What fills the heart overflows the mouth." That is speaking with the proper German tongue of the kind I have tried for, although unfortunately not always successfully. The literal Latin is a great barrier to speaking proper German.

Again, the traitor Judas says in Matthew 26: "Ut quid perditio haec?" and in Mark 14: "Ut quid perditio iste unguenti facta est?" Consequently, for these literalist asses I would have to translate it: "Why has this loss of salve occurred?" But what kind of German is this? What German says "loss of salve occurred"? And if he does understand it at all, he would think that the salve is lost and must be looked for and found again, even though that is still obscure and uncertain. Now if that is good German why do they not come out and make us a fine, new German testament and let Luther's testament be? I think that would really bring out their talents. But a German would say "Ut quid, *etc..*" as "Why this waste?" or "Why this extravagance?" or even "it is a shame about the ointment" – these are good German expressions, in which one can understand that Magdalene had wasted the salve she poured out and had done wrong. That was what Judas meant when he thought he could have used it better.

When the angel greets Mary, he says: "Greetings to you, Mary, full of grace, the Lord is with you." Up to this point, this has simply been translated from the simple Latin; but tell me, is that good German? Since when does a German speak like that – being "full of grace"? One would have to think about a keg "full of" beer or a purse "full of" money. So I translated it: "You gracious one". This way a German can at last think about what the angel meant by his greeting. Yet the papists rant about me corrupting the angelic greeting – and I still have not used the most satisfactory German translation. What if I had used the most satisfactory German and translated the salutation: "God says hello, Mary dear" (for that is what the angel was intending to say and what he would have said if he had been German!). If I had translated it thus, I believe that these papists would have hanged themselves out of their great devotion to dear Mary and because I have destroyed the greeting.

Yet why should I be concerned about their ranting and raving? I will not stop them from translating as they want. But I too shall translate as I want and not to please them. Whoever does not like it can just ignore it and keep his criticism to himself, for I will neither look at nor listen to it. They do not have to answer for or bear responsibility for my translation. Listen: I shall say "gracious Mary" and "dear Mary", and they can say "Mary full of grace". Anyone who knows German also knows what an expressive word "dear" is: dear Mary, dear God, the dear emperor, the dear prince, the dear man, the dear child. I do not know if one can say this word "dear" in Latin or in other languages with so much depth of emotion that it pierces the heart and echoes throughout as it does in our German tongue.

From Luther's *An Open Letter on Translating* (1530).[42]

---

[42] Adapted from the translation by Dr Gary Mann of this treatise on translating, found at the Project Wittenberg website
(http://www.iclnet.org/pub/resources/text/wittenberg/wittenberg-home.html).

Chapter 3.

WARM DAYS: RENEWING THE CHURCH, 1521-31.

The 10 years between Luther's defiant stand at the diet of Worms in 1521, and the death of the Swiss Reformer Ulrich Zwingli at the battle of Kappel in 1531, were crucial for the future development of Western Christianity. On the one hand, these years witnessed the penetration of Lutheran and Zwinglian ideas into northern Europe and major parts of central Europe, a process which culminated in the creation of many new nationally-based Protestant Churches. On the other hand, these same years also saw the great rebellion against Rome solidify into three distinct forms, hostile to each other as well as to the pope: the Lutherans, the Reformed, and the Radicals.

1. The early years of the German Reformation.

The Lutheran reform movement made very swift progress throughout Germany in the years just after the diet of Worms, especially in the towns and cities. Luther's Germany had strong claims to be considered the most vibrant and progressive region of early 16th century Europe, in terms of trade, the mining industry, and the development of urban life and culture, which all contributed to great prosperity for a large and growing population. The affluent citizens of the German imperial cities proved especially enthusiastic in the "Luther movement": some 50 of the 85 cities embraced the Reformation.[1]

Luther's followers preached the gospel of justification by faith alone in Christ alone, and as people placed their religious confidence directly in Christ for salvation, the Virgin Mary and the saints soon ceased to have any place in worship as objects of religious invocation, or of veneration through images.[2] Crucially, Lutherans abandoned the exclusive use of Latin in worship, introducing services in German. One of the most basic thrusts of the Reformation was to make worship an act of the whole congregation, which it clearly could not be if Latin was the language in which worship was conducted – the vast mass of ordinary Christians could not understand Latin. It was therefore in the sphere of public worship that the Reformation produced its most revolutionary popular impact, as ancient ecclesiastical Latin was replaced, in one Protestant land after another, by the mother tongue of the people.[3] The same concern for the congregational dimensions of worship

---

[1] The "imperial cities" were towns or cities within the Holy Roman Empire which were subject to no authority except that of the emperor. They were therefore virtually self-contained states.

[2] However, it took some time for the precise Evangelical position on Mary and the saints to become clear. Luther himself, for example, continued for some years after his break with Rome to believe in Mary's immaculate conception and that believers could ask her to intercede for them. To the end of his life, Luther seems to have believed that Mary was sinless, at least from the moment that Christ was conceived in her womb. Even after Protestants had rejected the later medieval belief in Mary's immaculate conception and the practice of invoking her in prayer, virtually all the Reformers still maintained what most modern Evangelicals would regard as a "high" Mariology. For example, Mary's perpetual virginity was defended strongly by Luther, Zwingli, and Calvin, and they often referred to her with conspicuous reverence as "the blessed Virgin" or some such title. There is a book still to be written on the forgotten Mary of the Protestant Reformers.

[3] This is not to say that Lutherans simply dropped the use of Latin. Lutheran worship-services in Latin continued on into the 17th century. What Luther and other German reformers did was introduce German services alongside Latin ones. Before his German Mass of 1526, Luther produced a new Latin Mass in 1523. Eventually, though, as Latin began losing its status as the international language of education in the latter part of the 17th century (it was replaced by French), Lutheran services in Latin fell into disuse.

inspired the Reformers to encourage *vocal* participation by the people. In this regard we probably think immediately of the congregational singing of psalms and hymns, which was certainly an integral part of the new style of worship. However, it also included congregational singing (or chanting, or reciting) of the Lord's Prayer, the Apostles' or Nicene Creed, the Ten Command-ments, and perhaps a general confession of sin (the details varied from one Protestant region to another). "Prayer books" were a radical new Protestant invention, to enable the people to take part collectively in a form of worship that was both corporate and vocal.

Further, the Protestant insistence on congregational participation in worship often motivated the reintroduction of weekly celebrations of the Lord's Supper, as against the later medieval practice in which laypeople took communion only once a year. (The participatory dynamic was also the driving force behind the Protestant practice of giving the communion wine as well as the bread to the laity.) Theologically, this congregational model of Protestant worship was undergirded by the doctrine of the priesthood of all believers: the whole Christian congregation is a priestly body, and therefore its worship must be corporate and congregational in nature, rather than a performance by a professional worshipper (the "priest" in the medieval sense) watched by a passive people.

Those who embraced Luther's teaching called themselves "Evan-gelicals" (from the Greek *euaggelion*, "good news"); their enemies simply called them "Lutherans". Evangelicals themselves later adopted the name Lutheran, despite Luther's own protests:

> "Who is this Luther? My teaching is not my own, and I have not been crucified for anyone. Why should it happen to me, miserable stinking bag of maggots that I am, that the chil-dren of Christ should be called by my insignificant name? I am, and will be, no one's master. With the one Church I hold in common the teaching of Christ, who alone is our Master."

The break with the papacy also led to a reformation of Church government. Luther held that, in theory, a Christian congregation had the right to elect its own pastor (a view which, like congregational worship, flowed from the doctrine of the priesthood of all believers.) However, in the excited temper of the times, the attempt to put this theory into practice could lead to serious division and conflict, even among Evangelicals, as different factions emphasised different things – there was often a great variety of beliefs among those who had broken away from Rome. There were also immense legal and financial problems, and quarrels (sometimes violent), about who owned church funds and property, which included monasteries, nunneries, schools, hospitals, and land, as well as church buildings. So in practice, in the interests of peace and social harmony, Luther advocated that the secular rulers – the prince or the city council – should act as "emergency bishops": they should use their position of political power to reform the church locally, by appointing suitable pastors, making sure they were properly housed and paid, and administering church funds and property. Any involvement of the papacy and its agents in the appointment of clergy thus completely disappeared; state control of the Church took its place. At the same time, Lutheran princes and city councils dismantled the medieval system of independent Church courts, made all clergy subject to the justice of the civil courts, and took control of legal matters in which laypeople had previously been subject to the Church (*e.g.* marriage and the validating of wills).[4]

It was a total reversal of the victory won by the Hildebrandine reformers in the investiture controversy.[5] In the late Middle Ages, there had already been a growing tendency for the state to make inroads into the independence, power, and privileges of the Catholic Church; the Reformation brought this tendency to full strength and maturity, thus giving birth to the modern nation-state, exercising political and moral mastery over all its citizens. It must also be

---

[4] For Church courts, see Part Two, Chapter 4, section 8.
[5] For Hildebrand and the investiture controversy, see Part Two, Chapter 4, sections 4, 5 and 6.

said that taking over the vast wealth, property, land, and legal authority of the Church appealed to the greed of many German princes, and to their thirst for power. Their motives in embracing Lutheranism were not always very pure.

It is, however, important to realise that Luther himself did not think the political authorities had some automatic right to assume control of the Church. It was only because the state in Germany was represented by the *Christian* prince, and *Christian* city magistrates, that Luther made them into "emergency bishops". The secular rulers, Luther argued, were acting as baptised members of the Christian community; they were taking the task of reformation into their own hands as prominent Christian laymen, only because the papacy and its bishops had failed. In Luther's mind, this acceptance of "emergency bishop" status by the princes and city magistrates was to be a temporary measure, until the Reformation was secure against its enemies and in a settled condition. In fact, largely due to the Peasants' Revolt (see section 3), it developed into a full-scale, enduring system of state control of the Lutheran Churches. Luther had shattered the spiritual dominion of the papacy in Germany; but to escape the swelling tides of religious anarchy, the newly liber-ated German Church sought shelter in the strong arms of the state. Thus the local German prince or city council became the supreme Church authority in their own territory. Even so, for almost all practical purposes, the prince or council delegated the running of Church affairs to a special court known as a "consistory", made up of lawyers and theologians appointed by the government. The rulers of the larger Lutheran territories also divided their land up into districts, and appointed a special pastor called a "superinten-dent" to exercise spiritual oversight over all the other pastors and churches in his district.

This reconstruction of Church government was far-reaching. But the Reformation in Germany, and elsewhere, caused an even more visible change in the ordinary life of Church and society: the marginalising of monasticism in some Protestant lands and its complete disappearance in others. Monasteries had now been an integral and central part of Christian social life for over a thousand years. Under the impact of Evangelical teaching, however, most monks and nuns deserted their convents, married, and took up new positions in society. All of life's normal vocations – farmer, shopkeeper, teacher, housewife – were religious, Luther argued, when people lived them to the glory of God. Christians were to exist "in the world" as salt and light (Matthew 5:13-14), serving their neighbour sacrificially in Christlike love, not hide away from the world in the hope of keeping their own souls pure. Besides, the lifelong oath of celibacy which every monk and nun had to swear was, Luther now maintained, a dangerous violation of God's will. Celibacy was a spiritual gift from God. If people had the gift, they did not need to swear an oath; and if they did not have the gift, their oath was sinful – they must marry to safeguard their chastity. (Monks and nuns were not famed for chastity at that period.)

However, we must take care not to exaggerate. The Lutheran Reformation did not, in fact, abolish all monasteries; many of them continued to exist in Lutheran lands well into the 17th century, and monasticism did not die out in Lutheranism until the age of Pietism and Rationalism in the 18th century.[6] Despite his criticisms, Luther did believe that monasteries, as voluntary places of prayer, study, and meditation, could be a beneficial place for some people. In fact, Luther wrote in the Schmalkald Articles of 1537 (one of the official confessions of the Lutheran Church):

> "The chapters and monasteries which in former times had been founded with good intentions for the education of learned men and decent women should be restored to such purposes, in order that we may have pastors, preachers, and other ministers of the church, others who are necessary for secular government in cities and states, and also well trained girls to become mothers, housekeepers, *etc*."

A few things are worth noting in this statement. What Luther vociferously opposed was the common idea of his time that there

---

[6]   See Part Four for Pietism and Rationalism.

was something intrinsically holier about monastic life than ordinary life in the world, or that through monastic life a person could become holier before God. In fact, Luther believed that ordinary life as a husband, wife, father, mother was holier than monastic life, since the former were directly instituted by God and had His blessing upon them, while the latter (monasticism) had no divine institution. Nevertheless, Luther believed monasteries could be permitted, even encouraged, when they served to educate people for the normal vocations of the world which God had instituted. Luther went on in the Schmalkald Articles to say that "if they (monasteries) are unwilling to serve this purpose, it would be better to abandon them or tear them down rather than preserve them..."

Luther, himself a monk, abandoned the monastic life, and in 1525 married a young ex-nun of noble birth, Katherine von Bora (1499-1552); he was 42, Katherine was 26. Roman Catholic enemies darkly prophesied that Antichrist was sure to born of such an unholy union between a monk and a nun. Evangelicals mockingly replied that if sexual intercourse between a monk and nun would give birth to Antichrist, several thousand Antichrists must already have been born in the Middle Ages. In fact, Luther's marriage to Katherine proved to be very happy and holy, full of playful humour – Luther referred to her as "my lord Katie". Speaking from his own experience, Luther's verdict on married life (and on Katie) was glowingly positive:

> "Next to God's Word, there is no more precious treasure than the holy ordinance of marriage. God's highest earthly gift is a spiritually-minded, cheerful, God-fearing, home-keeping wife, with whom you can live in peace, and whom you can trust with your property, body, and life."

Luther and Katherine went on to raise a family of six.[7] Luther's example held up a new form of religious and social life in the

---

[7]   None of them was Antichrist, as far as we know.

Western world for others to copy: the lawfully married Protestant clergyman and his family.[8]

The Reformation rejection of the superiority of the celibate life, and fresh appreciation of marriage, was the continuation of a Renaissance current of thought. Renaissance humanism had already rediscovered marriage as the foundational pattern of all human relationships and the purest manifestation of love for one's neighbour: the ideal of "chaste marriage"[9] began to displace ascetic celibacy as the supreme example of human virtue. This new positive view of marriage (and corresponding critique of celibacy) was propagated by a number of important 15th century humanists, most famously Lorenzo Valla. In the early 16th century it was taken up by Erasmus, notably in his *Praise of Marriage* (1497, reprinted 1518). For Erasmus, the purpose of marriage was love and companionship, the two things being "glued together by true affections among those equal in virtue". Celibacy, Erasmus argued, was a special and extraordinary calling from God, primarily in times of persecution. Chaste marriage, he insisted, deserved equality of honour with this special celibate calling. Luther and the other Reformers enacted these new ideals in the social and ecclesiastical sphere, undergirded by their biblical studies and backed by popular disgust with the then notorious immorality of priests, monks, and nuns.

The swift growth of the Reformation throughout Germany soon made it clear that not everyone who had originally supported Luther's defiance of the papacy agreed with his programme of reform for the Church. In the early 1520s, there was a parting of the ways between Luther and a number of groups – the Radical Reformers, the older generation of humanists, the lower classes, and the princes and cities of southern Germany – which reduced

---

[8]   There was, of course, nothing new about this in the Eastern world, where the lawfully married Orthodox clergyman and his family were the norm.

[9]   Not to be confused with "celibate marriage" where husband and wife agree to live without sexual relations: fairly common in the patristic and medieval period, and still sometimes practised thereafter within the Roman Catholic and Eastern Orthodox traditions. "Chaste marriage" simply means marriage in which husband and wife are faithful to each other.

Luther's stature from religious leader of the whole German nation, to the leader of a religious party within Germany. The first of these separations was with the Radicals.

2. The dawn of the Radical Reformation.

In Wittenberg, Luther's home town, his followers undertook the task of reforming the church locally while Luther was still in hiding in the Wartburg castle. The Wittenberg Reformers included Luther's university colleagues whom we met in the previous Chapter, Philip Melanchthon, Andreas Bodenstein von Carlstadt, and Nicholas von Amsdorf. Two other lecturers who had recently joined the university, **Justas Jonas** (1493-1555) and **Johannes Bugenhagen** (1485-1558), also played their part as leading Reformers. Jonas became well-known as a Lutheran hymnwriter and translator of Luther's and Melanchthon's writings from Latin into German for the home market, and from German into Latin for the international market. Bugenhagen is sometimes known as "Pomeranus" from his birthplace in Pomerania (then the north-eastern coastland of Germany on the Baltic Sea, now in Poland). A humanist monk deeply influenced by Erasmus, Bugenhagen had in 1520 read Luther's *Babylonian Captivity of the Church* in order to write a response against it. Instead, it converted him! "The whole world may be wrong, but Luther is right," Bugenhagen concluded. He arrived in Wittenberg in 1521, and made his mark as a preacher, famous for his agonisingly long sermons,[10] and also (later) as the organiser of the Lutheran Church in Denmark and in the north German cities of Brunswick, Hamburg, and Lubeck. Another prominent Wittenberg Reformer was the flashy and adventurous **Gabriel Zwilling** (1487-1558), not a university lecturer but an Augustinian friar with a gift for rabble-rousing sermons.

---

[10]   Luther once said after listening to a long-winded sermon by Bugenhagen, "Every high priest should have his private sacrifices. Accordingly, Bugenhagen sacrifices his hearers with long sermons, for we are his victims. And today he sacrificed us in an exceptional manner."

Carlstadt and Zwilling spearheaded the Wittenberg Reformation, attacking images of Christ and the saints, condemning instrumental music in worship, offering the wine as well as the bread to the laity in communion, and trying to force laypeople to touch and handle the bread because Christ had said "Take, eat". (In the medieval Catholic mass, the laity did not touch the wafer; the priest inserted it into their mouths.) They exhorted priests and monks to abandon their vows of celibacy and get married; Carlstadt took a wife and wanted to compel all the clergy to follow his example, denouncing celibacy as a positive evil. Events span completely out of control when three preachers from Zwickau (south of Wittenberg) arrived in the city in December 1521 – Nicholas Storch, Marcus Stubner, and Thomas Dreschel. They claimed to be in direct contact with God who, they said, spoke to them in private revelations. Luther called them the "Zwickau prophets". They opposed infant baptism (and perhaps all water-baptism), and proclaimed that the end of the world would shortly take place. Carlstadt and Zwilling sided with them.

Carlstadt, Zwilling, and the Zwickau prophets were the first of the *Radical* Reformers. Historians call them "Radicals" because they departed from the Catholicism of the Middle Ages much more "radically" (in a more thoroughgoing way) than the other Reformers did, especially in rejecting infant baptism and the Church-state alliance. The more traditionally-minded Reformers like Luther, who upheld infant baptism and the connection between Church and state, are often called the *Magisterial* Reformers, because they looked to the Christian *magistrate* (the secular government – king, prince, parliament, city council) to reform the Church, or at least to help the Protestant clergy reform it.[11] This twofold distinction, however, between Magisterial and Radical Reformers, although widely accepted by historians, does an injustice to the nature of the so-called Magisterial Reformation. In terms of Church-state

---

[11]   In modern Britain, "magistrate" means a judge in a local court. In Reformation usage, it refers to any political authority, from the Holy Roman emperor downwards.

relations, there were in fact *three* distinct streams of Reformation in the 16th century:

(i)   The nationalist Reformers, who transferred the powers of the papacy to the state (king, prince, parliament, city council), in order to secure protection for Protestants against the papacy and to uphold the medieval ideal of a Christian society. This approach produced what we might call a "Protestant statism", often loosely termed "Erastianism", after the Swiss theologian Erastus (1524-83), an exponent of this view. The Lutheran and Anglican Churches would fit into this statist or Erastian pattern.

(ii) Those Reformers who remained committed to the ideal of Christianising society and culture, and therefore believed in the rightness of a Christian state, but insisted that the institutional Church must be independent of state control. This stream of Reformation life has been called the "Reformed Catholic" outlook; it was exemplified in Martin Bucer, John Calvin, and the Reformed Churches (see Chapter 4).

(iii) Those Reformers who abandoned the ideal of Christianising society and culture, rejected the notion of a Christian state, and saw the Church as an alternative society living in an irredeemably wicked and hostile world. These were the Radical Reformers.

In their own day, opponents usually called the Radicals *Anabaptists*, owing to their rejection of infant baptism; "Anabaptist" means "rebaptiser" (a term invented by the Swiss Reformer Zwingli – most Radicals were what we today would call Baptists). The Radicals did not refer to themselves as Anabaptists, because they did not accept that they were rebaptising; they held that they were baptising for the first time, since infant baptism was not valid baptism. In modern historical studies, the term Anabaptist is now usually restricted to one group within the wider Radical Reformation. (A fuller account will be found in Chapter 5.)

Under the influence of Carlstadt, Zwilling, and the Zwickau prophets, the religious life of Wittenberg became chaotic. Violence erupted. Mobs went round smashing altars, shrines, and images – chiefly statues and stained-glass windows depicting Christ and the saints, which often adorned the tombs of the upper classes. Evangelicals insulted and intimidated those who stayed loyal to Rome. The town magistrates, incapable of controlling the situation themselves, and fearing a descent into anarchy, could think of only one thing to do: they appealed to Luther to return from his secret refuge in the Wartburg castle and re-establish order. Despite the fact that he was under the ban of the Empire and his life was in danger, Luther heeded their plea and boldly journeyed back to Wittenberg, arriving on March 6th 1522, thus ending his 11 months of hiding. Then, in a series of potent sermons preached over eight days, he managed to restore peace and calm to the disturbed city.

Crucial for Luther in these sermons were two things. First, faith must always be accompanied by love; and secondly, all true reform must be truly Evangelical, growing from the freedom of the gospel, rather than from the compulsion of the law. Luther profoundly believed that no reformation could take place unless the gospel was thoroughly preached and kept central; further, the gospel must be recognised by the people in everything that was done in the name of reform. He felt that a forced law-motivated reform, such as Carlstadt and Zwilling had (in Luther's view) been promoting, would only change people's behaviour, but not their hearts. For Luther, inner spiritual reformation in the heart of the individual, setting him in a right relationship with God through personal faith in Christ, was always the great priority. Any outward religious reformation, he argued, must flow from this inner conversion, as the free and willing act of the believer. Otherwise it was worthless.

Based on this law-gospel framework, then, Luther's main message in the Wittenberg sermons was that the citizens of Wittenberg had become disastrously obsessed with mere outward matters (images, celibacy, the bread and wine of communion), and had allowed their hearts to drift away from the all-important spiritual truth of the gospel: the eternal salvation of the soul through personal faith in Jesus Christ. It deeply troubled Luther that many ordinary people, instead of finding peace with God through the gospel, were just becoming inflamed with a hate-filled hostility towards the Roman Catholic Church. This, he told the Wittenbergers bluntly, was not the fruit of the Spirit. He counselled patience to the reforming hot-heads:

> "Give people time! It took me three years of constant study, reflection, and discussion to arrive where I am now. Can the ordinary man, who has no education in such matters, be expected to move the same distance in three months? You are wrong to think that you get rid of an abuse by destroying the object which is misused. Men can go wrong with wine and women. Shall we prohibit wine and abolish women? Sun, moon, and stars have been worshipped. Shall we pluck them out of the sky? Your haste and violence reveal a lack of confidence in God. See how much He has accomplished through me. I did nothing more than pray and preach. The Word did it all. If I had wished, I could have started a riot at Worms. But while I sat still and drank beer with Melanchthon and Amsdorf, God dealt the papacy a mighty blow!"

Luther also condemned the way that the anti-Roman Catholic violence was forcing people to accept the Evangelical faith without really believing in it:

> "If I rush in and abolish the mass by force, there are many who would be compelled to agree with it, and yet not know where they stood, whether it was right or wrong, and they would say: 'I do not know if it is right or wrong, I do not know where I stand, I was compelled by force to submit to the majority.' This forcing and commanding results in a mere

mockery, an external show, a fool's game, man-made ordinances, sham saints, and hypocrites."

Luther's sermons quietened people's tempers and destroyed the influence of Carlstadt and Zwilling, who had to leave town. Suitably chastened, Carlstadt became pastor at Orlamunde, and Zwilling at Altenburg. Carlstadt eventually ended up being absorbed into the Swiss Reformation and teaching Old Testament in the university of Basel. Meanwhile, Luther restored many of the old customs of worship in Wittenberg, *e.g.* kneeling to receive the bread in communion. He was determined not to alter anything in traditional Catholic worship unless Scripture explicitly demanded it. Even then, he still would not change it until he had persuaded his congregation, by preaching and teaching, that Scripture required it. Luther felt that an Evangelical form of worship would be glorifying to God only if people embraced it freely as an act of sincere faith in His Word, not if it was forced on them by autocratic preachers or majority opinion.

Luther had defeated Carlstadt and Zwilling in Wittenberg, but the Radical element of the Reformation lived on. It found its most revolutionary spokesman in **Thomas Müntzer** (1488-1525), a young Catholic priest from Stolberg (northern Germany), trained in Christian humanism, who had initially supported Luther. Müntzer preached mighty sermons in Zwickau in 1521-22, and adopted views similar to those of the Zwickau prophets, *e.g.* rejecting infant baptism and claiming guidance from dreams and visions. He then became pastor of the church in Allstedt (central Germany), where he created the first complete worship-service in German: a fine achievement which attracted hundreds from near and far.

In his theology, Müntzer made the Bible secondary to spiritual experience, the "direct speaking" of the Holy Spirit to the heart. A church, he believed, should be made up only of those to whom God had spoken in this way. Müntzer also had an overflowing sympathy for the poor and oppressed, which made him burn with a constant, smouldering sense of outrage against the ruling classes. In

Müntzer's concept of reformation, the true churches of the Spirit-filled would be God's instruments for establishing a new society of justice and love, in which there would be no priests, nobles, princes, or private property, but perfect equality and democracy. If necessary, Müntzer taught, the elect would have to take up arms and impose this perfect society by force, slaughtering all the ungodly.

Müntzer condemned Luther as an enemy of the Holy Spirit, a mere academic who worshipped the "dead letter" of the Bible, ignored the poor, and flattered the Lutheran princes to gain their worldly favour. A genius at inventing insults, Müntzer referred to Luther as "doctor Liar", "the pope of the Lutheran Scripture-twisters", and "brother Fattened Pig". Luther for his part was horrified by Müntzer, and was just as good at inventing insults; he referred to Müntzer as "the Satan of Allstedt", and said, "Müntzer thinks he's swallowed the Holy Spirit, feathers and all." More than any other Radical Reformer, Müntzer and his activities hardened Luther against all Radicals. This was unfortunate; in the long term, most Radicals turned out not to be violent social revolutionaries like Thomas Müntzer. But Müntzer gave them all a fatally bad name, especially when he took a leading part in the Peasants' Revolt of 1524-25.

3. The Peasants' Revolt.

Germany's vast peasant population had suffered increasing social and economic hardship in the late Middle Ages. They staged violent uprisings in southern Germany in 1493, 1501, 1512, 1514, and 1517, but were overpowered each time by the princes and nobles. Their discontent was stirred up yet again by the Reformation, with its emphasis on Christian freedom and the spiritual equality of all believers, and its attack on the religious authorities for robbing Christians of their Scriptural rights. Many peasants took this one step further: they demanded political freedom and social equality, and denounced the secular authorities for robbing Christians of their human rights. In June 1524 another armed peasant uprising broke out at Stuhlingen, near the Swiss city of Schaffhausen. It was a spark which soon lit a fire of revolt that blazed across all Germany. Although historians call it the "Peasants' Revolt", it also included the working classes of the towns and cities.

The difference between this Peasants' Revolt of 1524-25 and the previous peasant rebellions was twofold: (i) the Peasants' Revolt was more widespread, engulfing the whole of Germany, north as well as south; (ii) it derived a fresh and dynamic degree of religious inspiration from the Reformation. The peasants often appealed to Luther's teaching to justify their actions, and when asked whom they would accept as a mediator in their dispute with the nobles, they responded with a single name – "Luther!" There was also a significant Radical influence on the Peasants' Revolt; several Radicals played a prominent role in it, especially Thomas Müntzer. To underline their religious commitment, many of the rebels covenanted together as "the Evangelical Brotherhood" at a mass meeting in Memmingen (southern Germany) in March 1525. Some of their demands were religious rather than political, *e.g.* they called for the right of congregations to elect their own pastors. Their social and political demands included things like returning to common ownership the forests and meadows which had been taken over by nobles, an end to being forced to work for the nobility without pay, and the creation of a better welfare service to take care of the poor. They proposed that all their demands should be tested against the Word of God, and if any were found to be unscriptural, they promised to withdraw them.

Luther at first blamed both sides in the uprising: both the nobility, whose oppressive rule had provoked the peasants into rebellion, and the peasants for taking up arms. Luther believed strongly that all armed rebellion against secular government was sinful: no matter how tyrannical a government might be, civil war was worse. He was appalled when the peasant armies began falling into excesses of violence, notably in attacking and wrecking monasteries and castles; in the central German region of Franconia alone, they destroyed 52 monasteries and 270 castles. Luther went on a preaching tour throughout Saxony in April 1525, trying to persuade the peasants to refrain from violence, but to no avail. As the rebellion grew, threatening to sweep everything before it, Luther came down conclusively on the side of the princes and nobility. In May 1525 he wrote a tract entitled *Against the Robbing and Murdering Hordes of Peasants*, in which he exhorted the German princes to slay the peasants without mercy.

The princes obeyed Luther's call only too effectively. They had at first been powerless to respond to the uprising, because almost all their fighting men were away in Italy with the emperor Charles V. However, by May 1525, the princes had managed to raise an army of professional German troops, and the slaughter began. Perhaps the most tragic episode involved Thomas Müntzer, who had put himself at the head of a peasant army of 8,000 men in Frankenhausen (central Germany). They faced an opposing army of professional soldiers, led by the great Protestant prince, Philip of Hesse.[12] Philip offered to let the peasants disperse unharmed, if they would only turn Müntzer over to him. Inspired by Müntzer's wild promises of divine protection and victory, the peasants refused. On May 15th, Philip's army attacked and annihilated the peasants. Müntzer was taken prisoner, tortured, and executed. Before he died, he recanted his Radical beliefs; one of Müntzer's last acts was to receive the Roman Catholic mass.

By November 1525 the German princes had utterly crushed all resistance to their rule, in a storm of bloodshed which must have seemed like a foretaste of hell. The troops massacred the poorly armed peasant armies; some 100,000 peasants lost their lives, leaving their wives and children completely destitute.

The Peasants' Revolt had deep and lasting effects on the Reformation:

---

[12] For more about Philip, see section 7.

(i) It marked the end of the rapid spread of Lutheranism in Germany.[13] Luther's brutal attitude in the Revolt alienated many of the lower classes. A significant number of them turned from Lutheranism to the various forms of the Radical Reformation; others simply lost any real interest in any kind of Reformation. Meanwhile, secular rulers who had not yet committed themselves to the Reformation began to think twice. If Lutheranism led to peasant uprisings, it could hardly be a good thing. Roman Catholics used this argument from now on as one of their standard weapons against the Reformation; it persuaded the princes and cities of the western territories along the borders with France and the Netherlands, and those of southern Germany (especially in Austria and Bavaria), to stay loyal to Rome. It also led to fierce persecution of Lutherans by the Roman Catholic authorities in these areas. Lutheran preachers in particular were hunted down and martyred.

(ii) The Lutheran princes became determined that they must strictly control the Reformation, as the only way to stop it turning into a popular social movement which could challenge their authority. So their status as "emergency bishops" became permanent; from now on, the princes would be the absolute rulers of the Lutheran Churches in their domains.

Luther himself encouraged the princes in this policy. The Peasants' Revolt had destroyed his trust in the ordinary German people; he felt that too many of them had diabolically perverted his gospel message of spiritual freedom through Christ into a worldly message of political freedom through armed revolution. Luther chiefly blamed Thomas Müntzer and the Radicals for this. In the period 1517-21, when Luther had stood up against the papacy at the peril of his own life, he had defended religious liberty and toleration, arguing that the state should not execute people for heresy (this was

---

[13] I emphasise the *rapid* spread. It by no means ended the territorial advance of Lutheranism. See Chapter 6, section 1.

one of the things ʃ
Exsurge domine
Luther accepted t
He still opposed
believe that *blas*
there was often a
and what was d
much when Ev
religious dissent.

ːr for in the bull
ːasants' Revolt,
ɔanish Radicals.
he did come to
leath; and since
leemed "heresy"
not protest too
d Radicals for

4. Erasmus and the older humanists.

It was also in the period 1524-25 that the older generation of Christian humanists deserted Luther. They wanted reform, but not at the cost of breaking the unity of the Catholic Church. Among those who at first supported Luther but finally refused to break with Rome were Crotus Rubeanus, Willibald Pirckheimer, and Erasmus himself.[14] Erasmus had given cautious support and encouragement to Luther when Luther had only been attacking indulgences. However, Luther's break with Rome, his violent language (*e.g.* denouncing the pope as Antichrist), and the popular disturbances that accompanied the Reformation, repelled Erasmus. He wanted to reform the Catholic Church peacefully from within, not tear it apart.

In September 1524, urged on by Roman Catholic friends, Erasmus published a book against Luther called *The Freedom of the Will*. The point at which Erasmus chose to attack the German Reformer was his Augustinian theology of sin and grace. Luther taught that the fallen human will was in helpless bondage to sin; only God by His sovereign grace could set the will free to embrace and follow Christ. Those whom God liberated, Luther maintained, had been eternally predestined to receive this salvation by God's sheer mercy, not as a result of anything in them. Erasmus rejected these

---

[14] For Rubeanus and Pirckheimer, see Chapter 1, section 3.

views in favour of a more Semi-Pelagian theology. In *The Freedom of the Will*, he argued that conversion and salvation were a shared work of human free will and divine grace; grace was essential, but free will must cooperate with it and could always at any point reject it. Luther replied to Erasmus in December 1525 with his *The Bondage of the Will*, in which he thanked Erasmus for going to the heart of the matter and criticising Luther's views of sin, grace, and predestination, instead of trivial things like indulgences and the papacy. Luther then restated his own Augustinian doctrines with vibrant energy and clarity, sometimes going well beyond Augustine.[15]

The break between Erasmus and Luther was total. The generation of humanist reformers whom Erasmus represented mostly remained within the Roman Church. Luther said of Erasmus:

> "He has done what he was destined to do; he has introduced the ancient languages in place of harmful scholastic studies. He will probably die like Moses in the land of Moab. He has done enough to uncover the evil; but to reveal the good, and lead people into the promised land, is in my opinion not his business."

Erasmus, for his part, expressed great scepticism about the spiritual fruit of the Reformation:

> "Where is your dovelike spirit? Did the apostles spread the gospel in the way you do? You cry out against the luxury of priests, the ambition of bishops, the tyranny of the pope, the prattling of scholastics, against prayers and fasts and masses. But your purpose is not so much to reform as to destroy. You

---

[15] For instance, when Luther said that God's sovereignty in itself excluded human free will, he went beyond Augustine. All Augustine ever said was that the *fall* of Adam had excluded free will in spiritual matters. Luther's view would mean that not even *before* he sinned could Adam have had free will, since God's sovereignty operated before as well as after the fall.

will uproot the wheat along with the tares! Look at these
'Evangelicals' of yours. Are they any less enslaved to luxury,
immorality, and money? The gospel is supposed to make the
drunkard sober and the cruel person kind. But I can show
you people whom your preaching has made worse than ever!
You throw images out of the churches, but what good is that
if people continue to bow down to sins in their hearts?"

Erasmus died in the Swiss Protestant city of Basel in 1536, a rather
sad and lonely figure, shunned by Roman Catholics for "hatching"
the Reformation and by Protestants for not joining it. Despite
Erasmus's break with Luther, however, many of his younger
disciples like Melanchthon and Bugenhagen in Germany, and
Zwingli and Oecolampadius in Switzerland (see section 6), were
more daring than their master, and became leading Protestant
Reformers.

5. The German Lutheran Churches.

The crushing of the Peasants' Revolt in 1525 left the princes (and,
to a much lesser degree, the great imperial cities) as the unchal-
lenged rulers of Germany. They formed political alliances, for and
against the Reformation. However, two factors prevented the
Roman Catholic champion, the emperor Charles V, from organising
effective action against the German Lutherans:

(i)   Constant wars with the French king Francis I distracted
      Charles.

(ii) The Ottoman Turks under Suleiman the Magnificent (1520-
      66), greatest of the Ottoman sultans, had invaded the
      Danube valley in Eastern Europe. Suleiman's was the
      greatest empire in the world at that time, and constantly
      threatened central Europe from its territories in Eastern
      Europe (Greece and the Balkans). Suleiman conquered
      Egypt, Syria, Iraq, North Africa, and penetrated into Eastern

Europe as far as Hungary; Charles needed German Lutheran troops to fight off the Muslim advance.

The uncertain situation prompted the imperial diet of Speyer in 1526 to pass a famous edict of religious toleration: each local German ruler should decide for himself which faith people would practise in his domain. However, the tide of battles had turned in Charles V's favour, at least temporarily, by 1529. In February that year at another diet in Speyer, the Roman Catholic delegates (including many bishops and abbots) were able to attend in great numbers under the emperor's protection, forming the majority. They outlawed any further spread of the Reformation in the Empire, and decreed that Roman Catholics must be tolerated in Lutheran lands, but Lutherans were not to be tolerated in Roman Catholic lands. The Lutheran delegates were outraged, and published a document objecting to this decree. The document was called the *Protestation*; six princes and 14 imperial cities signed it. From the Protestation, the name *Protestant* came to be applied to all adherents of the Reformation.[16]

The term "Protestant" has often been completely misunderstood as meaning simply a negative protest against Rome. Originally, however, it had a far more positive meaning; to "protest" was a transitive verb which meant to declare, to affirm, to set forth a position. (It survives in this meaning when a person "protests his innocence", or a lover "protests his love" for his beloved.) The first Protestants were not only protesting *against* medieval Catholic errors; they were also "protesting the gospel", declaring the positive truths of Scripture which medieval Rome had neglected, obscured, distorted, or denied. It is therefore incorrect that the term "Protestant" would lose its meaning if Roman Catholicism either reformed itself or ceased to exist. As long as there is a gospel, there is something to protest – to declare, affirm, and set forth to the world.

---

[16] Strictly speaking, the protestors at Speyer were not all Lutherans. A good number of the cities followed a more Swiss "Zwinglian" style of reform.

The diet of Speyer solved nothing, because Lutherans would not obey its decrees and Charles V still lacked the means to enforce them effectively. At the diet of Augsburg in June 1530, therefore, Charles changed his strategy and invited the Lutherans to set out their beliefs in writing, as a basis for discussing and resolving the religious divisions of Germany. They responded with a doctrinal statement known as the *Augsburg Confession*. Written in Latin, chiefly by Melanchthon, the Augsburg Confession was the first official Protestant confession of faith. Its doctrine, in contrast to Roman Catholicism and Radicalism, was Lutheran, but it was not specifically opposed to the outlook of Zwingli and the Swiss Reformers (see section 6). Translated into German in 1532 by Justas Jonas, the Augsburg Confession became the great doctrinal basis of all the Lutheran Churches.

However, despite the calm and moderate language of the Confession, it did nothing to reconcile Roman Catholic opinion or turn Charles V aside from his ultimate purpose of forcing German Protestants back into the Roman Church. To defend their citizens against this threat of religious persecution, the Protestant princes and cities of Germany formed themselves into the "Schmalkaldic League" in December 1531 (named after the town of Schmalkalden in Saxony, where the League was constituted). The League embraced eight princes and 11 cities, including Strasbourg and other southern cities that leaned to a more Swiss Reformed outlook.[17] The Roman Catholic princes and cities of southern Germany were already bound together by the powerful "Swabian League", which dated back to 1488 but now took on a new anti-Protestant motivation. Clearly a religious civil war was

---

[17] If one wonders how Lutherans and Reformed could enter into this political union, despite their quarrel over the Lord's Supper, an answer may be found in the Augsburg Confession. As noted above, although a Lutheran confession, it is not polemically anti-Reformed; for example, it is rather vague on the disputed issue of how Christ is present in the Supper (article 10). As a result, Reformed Protestants at that period routinely subscribed to the Augsburg Confession. John Calvin said, "There is nothing in the Augsburg Confession which is not in full accord with our teaching."

brewing in Germany; it would break out soon after Luther's death.[18]

The Augsburg Confession gave the Lutheran Churches a firm theological identity, distinguishing them from Roman Catholics and Radicals. But of course, there were other factors that went into the making of the German Lutheran Churches. The most important were:

(i) The Lutheran form of public worship. As we have seen, Luther took a very conservative attitude to forms of worship, keeping to traditional Catholic practice except where it clearly contradicted Scripture. He therefore translated the medieval Catholic liturgy into German, but did not change it very much; the main alteration was in the liturgy for the mass, where Luther did write a new order of worship which expressed a Protestant under-standing of the Lord's Supper. He retained the system of the Church "lectionary" – an ordered series of readings from the Bible which took the congregation through all the chief parts of Old and New Testaments.[19] Luther also gave a high place to holy commun-ion in worship, building into the normal Sunday morning service of German Lutheran congregations.

In 1526 Luther's new complete worship-book was finally published for use in Lutheran congregations. The normal Sunday morning service was set out as follows:

Hymn or psalm
Kyrie eleison[20]
Set prayer (written down in the liturgy)
Scripture reading chanted from the set passage for the day, from
    Acts-Revelation

---

[18] See Chapter 6, section 1.
[19] For lectionaries, see Part One, Chapter 3, section 2, under **Church worship**.
[20] The *Kyrie eleison* is a Greek prayer from the early Church, "Lord, have mercy." In the West, it took this form: "Lord, have mercy; Christ, have mercy; Lord, have mercy."

Hymn sung by choir
Scripture reading chanted from the set passage for the day, from
    the Gospels
The Apostles' Creed, sung by the whole congregation
Sermon
The Lord's Prayer in a long paraphrase
Exhortation (leading into holy communion)
The words of institution, chanted by the minister
Consecration and distribution of the bread, while a hymn is sung
Blessing and distribution of the cup, while a hymn is sung
Set prayer (written down in the liturgy)
The benediction: the Aaronic blessing (Numbers 6:24-26)

This pattern of worship was basically the same as in medieval
Catholicism, except in three areas: (i) the Lutheran service was in
German, not Latin; (ii) Luther's new communion liturgy replaced
the medieval Catholic liturgy of the mass; and (iii) Luther exalted
preaching to a central position in worship. On other matters such as
altars, candles, priestly robes, *etc.*, Luther did not really care
whether they were kept or abolished; they were *adiaphora*, things
indifferent. The Lutheran Churches of northern Germany and
Scandinavia retained them;[21] the Lutheran Churches of southern
Germany did away with them.

(ii) The Lutheran hymns, some of them (words and tunes) written
by Luther himself. These had the greatest impact of all in nourish-
ing Lutheran belief and spirituality. The first Lutheran hymnbook
was published in 1524. Luther replaced the medieval Catholic
practice of a choir singing in Latin, by what became the normal
Protestant practice of the whole congregation singing in its native
tongue. Popular melodies were used to make the singing easier, and
the hymns were full of strong Lutheran doctrinal content. More
than any other Protestant Church, the Lutherans were marked out
by their love of church music and hymn-singing. Apart from
Luther, important Lutheran hymnwriters included Melanchthon,
Lazarus Spengler (1479-1534), Paul Speratus (1484-1551), Johann

---

[21]   For the Lutheran Reformation in Scandinavia, see Chapter 6, section 1.

Walther (1496-1570) who also composed music, and Elizabeth Cruciger, wife of the Wittenberg theologian Caspar Cruciger.

(iii) The Lutheran catechisms, especially Luther's *Small Catechism* of 1529. These were for instructing church members in the basics of Lutheran belief. They revolved around the Ten Commandments, the Apostles' Creed, the Lord's Prayer, and the sacraments, and were drawn up according to a question-and-answer method: the instructor asked the questions, the learner gave the set answers which he had committed to memory. This question-and-answer pattern for catechisms was not Luther's invention; the first such catechism had been drawn up by Alcuin in the 8th century,[22] and was followed in the next 100 years by many others. However, Luther's catechisms, designed for use in both church and home, set a new standard, and blazed a trail for Protestants, Roman Catholics, and Eastern Orthodox alike to follow.

(iv) Luther's *Postils* (1527). These were sermons written by Luther on the set Scripture passages in the lectionary, to be read out from the pulpit by Lutheran pastors. Many of these men were ex-priests, not very well educated, and perhaps ignorant of all but the simplest outline of Lutheran belief. It took a very long time for the benefits of proper theological and pastoral training to reach the more remote rural areas of Lutheran lands. In this situation, Luther's *Postils* were of great value in helping pastors communicate the new faith from their pulpits.

6. Ulrich Zwingli[23] and the Swiss Reformation.

At the same time that the Reformation was taking root in Germany, a similar movement had started in Switzerland. Switzerland was a federal union (the "Swiss Confederacy") made up of 13 states or "cantons", which were in theory part of the Holy Roman Empire,

---

[22]   For Alcuin, see Part Two, Chapter Two, section 2.
[23]   Also known as "Huldrych" Zwingli.

Ulrich Zwingli
(1484-1531)

but in practice had enjoyed independence for 200 years.[24] The majority of these cantons spoke a Swiss dialect of German, although French was the dominant language in those that bordered France. Nowhere in Europe did people prize political liberty so highly as in the Swiss Confederacy: each canton was a free, self-governing republic. Together the 13 cantons formed a small country, and although their soldiers were famously brave and tough as mercenaries, the Swiss had so far played no significant part on the stage of world history. The dawn of the Reformation, however, lifted tiny Switzerland to towering heights of influence in the destiny of Western Europe and ultimately the world.

The Swiss Reformation began in Zurich, strongest of the Swiss cantons. The leading Reformer was ***Ulrich Zwingli*** (1484-1531). Born in Wildhaus (in north-eastern Switzerland), Zwingli was the son of a successful farmer and magistrate. In his youth he developed into a devoted Christian humanist, a disciple of Erasmus, and an eager student of the Bible in Greek and Hebrew and of the early Church fathers. From 1502 to 1506 he studied theology at the university of Basel, a centre of humanist learning; among its lecturers were Sebastian Brant and Johannes Reuchlin.[25] However, the teacher who had the greatest influence on the young Zwingli was ***Thomas Wyttenbach*** (1472-1526), a Christian humanist who was already moving towards a Protestant position. Wyttenbach publicly attacked indulgences some years before Luther did, exalted the authority of Scripture, and taught that salvation was by faith alone in the crucified Christ. Zwingli later testified what a deep impact Wyttenbach's views had on him. (In 1523, the elderly Wyttenbach himself introduced the Reformation into Biel in western Switzerland.)

After graduating from Basel university, Zwingli served as priest in two Swiss villages, Glarus (1506-16) and Einsiedeln (1516-18). While pastor at Glarus, Zwingli accompanied a Swiss mercenary

---

[24] The 13 cantons were Zurich, Berne, Basel, Schaffhausen, Uri, Schwyz, Unterwalden, Zug, Lucerne, Solothurn, Freibourg, Glarus, and Appenzell.

[25] See Chapter 1, section 3, under **Germany**, for Brant and Reuchlin.

army as chaplain, fighting in Italy for pope Leo X and the Holy Roman emperor Maximilian against Francis I of France. The campaign ended with a shattering defeat for the Swiss by the French at Marignano on 13th-14th September 1515 – over 10,000 Swiss lay dead on the battlefield. This effectively signalled the end of Switzerland as a major military power, and the beginning of its move towards strict neutrality in the wars of Europe. The event turned Zwingli himself decisively against the whole mercenary system.

Shortly afterwards, towards the end of his time at Glarus, Zwingli came to a clear religious conviction that the human soul should place its faith in Christ alone for salvation, not in the Virgin Mary or the saints. This revelation came to him through Erasmus:

> "In 1514 or 1515, I read a poem about the Lord Jesus, written by the profoundly learned Erasmus of Rotterdam, in which with many very beautiful words Jesus complains that people do not seek all blessing in Him, so that He might be to them a fountain of every blessing, a Saviour, a comfort, a treasure of the soul. So I thought, 'Well, if this is true, why then should we seek help from any created being?'"

Unlike Luther, then, Zwingli felt a real spiritual indebtedness to Erasmus.

Zwingli's years at Glarus and Einsiedeln were also memorable for his lapse from his priestly vow of chastity. Despite heroic efforts to subdue the flesh, and extra vows on top of his priestly one, he gave in to sexual temptation (but he never slept with a married woman, a virgin, or a nun, he insisted). This was afterwards to be a matter of deep shame to him, and no doubt helped to convince him that the enforced celibacy of the clergy was an impractical ideal. In his reforming 67 theses of 1523, thesis 29 states: "All who are called clergy commit sin when they do not protect themselves by marriage, after they have become conscious that God has not enabled them to remain chaste."

In December 1518, Zwingli was appointed preacher in the Great Cathedral of Zurich, the canton's main church. There was some opposition owing to his sexual lapse, publicised by one of the women in Einsiedeln, but this was dismissed after Zwingli made a frank confession of his fault (he was probably helped by the fact that his only rival for the post was a clergyman who had broken his vow of chastity at least six times, and had six children to prove it.)

As the new cathedral preacher, Zwingli set tradition aside by preaching his way verse-by-verse through Matthew's Gospel, rather than following the set readings for each day in the Church lectionary. His sermons offered a grammatico-historical interpretation of Matthew, free from the methods and teachings of scholasticism. Zwingli's preaching was electrifying; one hearer said that while listening to Zwingli's sermons, he felt as if he had been lifted up by the hair and suspended in space! After he had finished expounding Matthew, Zwingli preached through Acts, 1 and 2 Timothy, Galatians, and so on, until he had covered the whole of the New Testament except Revelation (which he rejected from the New Testament canon). He also preached through the Psalms every Friday in the market place. In Zurich more than anywhere else in Europe, it was Biblical preaching that gave birth to the Reformation and nourished it into strength and victory.

In September 1519, illness brought Zwingli very close to death when plague broke out in Zurich. His brother Andrew, who lived with him, did die. We have a fascinating personal record of Zwingli's own "near death" experience in a poem he wrote at the time, his so-called "plague hymn" (see end of Chapter). His full recovery animated Zwingli with the conviction that God had spared him to carry out some special mission. So he resumed his Biblical preaching, and grew steadily in popularity and influence. Zwingli's personality made his gospel attractive; he radiated happiness and confidence, sure that reason was on his side. He was certainly not as lively a writer or as profound a theologian as Luther; Zwingli's soul had neither scaled the loftiest heights nor plumbed the darkest depths of spiritual experience as Luther's had, and Zurich's

Reformer did not have so wide and creative an influence on others. However, Zwingli was just as honest and forthright as Luther in speaking out against Roman corruptions – and Zwingli's boldness never tipped over into crudely abusive anger, as Luther's often did.

Theologically, Zwingli's beliefs about the gospel overlapped largely with Luther's. He had been reading some of Luther's writings with interest since 1521, but the Swiss Reformer arrived at most of his conclusions independently of the German. He himself asserted in 1523:

> "The papists[26] say, 'You must be Lutheran, because you preach just as Luther writes.' I reply, 'I preach just as Paul writes. Why not call me Pauline?' In my view, Luther is a mighty upholder of God who has closely studied the Bible, more seriously than has been done on this earth for a thousand years. No one has been like him in the manly unshakeable courage with which he has attacked the pope. Still, I will not be called after Luther's name, for I have read little of his teaching. I will have no name except that of my captain, Christ, whose soldier I am. Yet I value Luther as highly as anyone alive."

As far as Zwingli was concerned, he had been preaching the pure gospel since 1516, from the time that Erasmus convinced him to put his trust in Christ alone for salvation. The Reformation in Zurich therefore owed little to its twin movement in Wittenberg. Rather than Luther influencing Zwingli, both men were recipients of a common influence, for they had been drinking from the same patristic source, the works of Augustine of Hippo; Zwingli was as

---

[26]   "Papist" was a term for Roman Catholics which Protestants (and Eastern Orthodox) used. It means "follower of the papacy". Another such term was "Romanist". Protestants were reluctant to use the term Roman Catholic, because it seemed to concede the belief that to be Catholic one must be Roman. Protestants claimed that *they* were the true Catholics – those who truly adhered to the faith of the apostles and the early Church fathers, which Rome had corrupted.

ardent as Luther in his belief in the absolute sovereignty of God's grace in predestination and conversion.

By 1522, Zwingli had made the first moves towards breaking openly with Rome. This came especially through his treatise *Concerning the Clarity and Certainty of the Word of God*, published in September 1522. In this work, Zwingli rejected the infallible authority of the papacy, ecumenical Councils, and Church tradition. In their place he set the Holy Spirit and holy Scripture. Christ gave the Holy Spirit to all the elect, Zwingli argued, so that a Christian gained the assurance of divine truth from the Spirit of God speaking to his mind through the Word of God. Faith must be based on God's teaching in Scripture, not on the teachings of the papacy or its traditions:

> "Even if you hear the gospel of Jesus Christ from an apostle, you will not follow it unless the heavenly Father teaches you and draws you by His Spirit. The words are clear; God's teaching clearly enlightens, teaches, and gives certainty without any intervention by mere human knowledge. If people are taught by God, they are well-taught with clarity and conviction. If they had to be taught and assured by human beings, they would be more correctly described as human-taught rather than taught by God. But you must be God-taught, not taught by human beings; that is what the Truth itself said (John 6:45), and Truth cannot lie. If you do not believe and believe firmly, leaving human vanities and submitting yourselves to God's teachings alone, you have no true faith."

Zwingli, therefore, clearly broke with the papacy in 1522. Yet Rome did nothing to stop him; it still relied on Swiss mercenaries in its struggle for political independence against French influence in Italy, and so it could not afford to antagonise Zurich by condemning Zwingli. Thus, while the papacy excommunicated Luther, it left Zwingli in peace to carry out the Swiss revolt against Rome.

Also in 1522, Zwingli started living with Anna Reinhart, a widow related to the nobility of Zurich. They could not legally marry; Western Church law insisted on the celibacy of the clergy. Zwingli and Anna, however, ignoring a Church law they did not believe in, entered into a secret and private marriage covenant with one another. They did not publicly marry until 1524, when Reformation sentiment was advanced enough in Zurich to look with favour on such an action.

In a public disputation in Zurich on January 29th 1523, Zwingli affirmed in 67 theses that salvation came exclusively through faith in Christ, good works had no merit in justifying sinners, purgatory did not exist, the Lord's Supper was not a sacrifice, and Christ alone (not the pope) was the head of the Church. The disputation was held in the presence of the Zurich city council. Zwingli believed in a careful, gradual approach to reformation, and he always made sure he had the backing of the city council for each new step he took. He accepted that Zurich was a Christian community, and that its elected Christian rulers on the city council were responsible for regulating the community's spiritual life. The outcome of the disputation was that the city council expressed approval of Zwingli's preaching, promised him protection, and instructed all the clergy of Zurich to preach from the Bible alone. The really revolutionary thing about this was that the city council, Zurich's secular government, publicly established its right to control the religious life of the city. So just as was happening in Luther's Germany, Zwingli's Zurich saw the local political authorities transferring religious authority from the papacy to themselves. Zwingli differed from Luther, however, in seeing this as normal rather than an extraordinary emergency measure. Zwingli's statist or Erastian approach to Reformation, then, was total and unqualified.

Despite their shared Augustinianism and statism, Zwingli's attitude to reforming the Church was basically different from Luther's. Luther was concerned above all with personal faith and individual salvation; his major emphasis was that the true gospel should be preached, and to this he subordinated all concern for the external forms of worship as secondary. By contrast, Zwingli had a broader vision of what he called "the rebirth of Christianity" in Church and society. Zwingli's dream was to bring all of life under the authority of God's will revealed in Scripture. This led him to a significantly divergent approach from Luther towards outward forms of worship. Luther held that traditional Catholic worship should be left as it was, unless Scripture absolutely required that it be changed; Zwingli argued that nothing should be done in worship unless God positively authorised it in the New Testament. (The Swiss Reformers published a New Testament in Swiss-German in 1524, the whole Bible in 1530.)

Zwingli's outlook produced in Switzerland a much more obvious, visible break with the traditional worship of the Middle Ages than occurred in Lutheran Germany. By April 1525, the Zurich Reformer had secured the removal from Zurich's churches of all religious pictures, statues, crucifixes, candles, altars, and relics, and the abolition of the organ, the choir, priestly robes, religious processions, and the monasteries. None of these things, Zwingli argued, were authorised by the New Testament. The campaign against images was a particularly key aspect of the Swiss Reformation, and was to be repeated across Europe wherever this style of Protestantism took off. It proved surprisingly popular (the bulk of ordinary worshippers were usually far keener than their pastors to remove or smash the images). But it also had deep roots in medieval piety; many of the reform movements within the medieval Catholic Church had been very negative about images. In the 12th century, for example, Bernard of Clairvaux, speaking for his Cistercian order of monks, had condemned pictures of saints on church walls, "attracting the gaze of the worshippers, hindering their devotions – it almost reminds me of the Jewish ritual." John Gerson, the conciliarist reformer, had been equally outspoken in the 15th century: "Is it advisable to have so great a variety of images and pictures in our churches? Do they not sometimes pervert many simple folk to idolatry?" The Swiss Reformation tapped into this medieval puritanism and gave it full-blooded expression.[27]

Zwingli also introduced the exclusive use of the native language in worship (a Swiss dialect of German), and a communion service in which the laity received the wine; the liturgy enshrined a Protestant understanding of the Lord's Supper. (In the Zurich communion service, the laity received the bread and wine sitting in their pews – a common Protestant practice today, but first pioneered by Zwingli.) Zwingli retained the liturgical form of worship, with set prayers and the congregational reciting of the Apostles' Creed. However, he did not simply translate the medieval Catholic liturgy into the native tongue as Luther did. Zwingli's was more of a genuinely new Protestant liturgy, which made use of, but did not copy, the old Catholic one. Singing was not a part of worship in Zwinglian Zurich; instead, the congregation simply read out the Psalms and the *Gloria in excelsis*[28] antiphonally (half the congregation reading one line, the other half reading the next line, and so on – Zwingli seems to have divided the lines between men and women, which implies they were seated on different sides of the church building).[29]

The normal Sunday morning worship in Zwinglian Zurich was essentially a preaching service, consisting of Bible readings, prayers, and a sermon. Zwingli was unique among the Reformers in not regarding the Lord's Supper as integral to Sunday worship; he was happy that it should be celebrated four times a year, at Christmas, Easter, Pentecost, and a local Zurich festival on

---

[27] For Bernard of Clairvaux, see Part Two, Chapter 5, section 3. For John Gerson, see Part Two, Chapter 10, section 3.

[28] The *Gloria in excelsis* is one of the earliest known patristic hymns. It can be found in full in Chapter 3 of **Part One: The Age of the Early Church Fathers**.

[29] The abolition of singing in Zurich was not because Zwingli hated music; in fact, none of the Reformers was so musically gifted as Zwingli. He loved music so much that his Roman Catholic foes used to sneer at him as "the guitar-player" and "the evangelist-on-the-flute". It was simply that Zwingli opposed musical instruments *in worship*, and felt that his congregation would understand the Psalms better by reading them out together rather than singing them.

September 11th. This infrequency of the Zwinglian Supper may be related to Zwingli's low view of what actually happened in the Supper, since for most of his reforming career he saw it as little more than an act of pious commemoration. Again, in this Zwingli was virtually alone among the Reformers; as we shall see, Luther opposed him strongly on this issue, and after Zwingli's death, Martin Bucer, John Calvin, and Peter Martyr guided the Reformed Churches into a much higher doctrine of holy communion (see next Chapter).[30]

Zwingli's communion service was rather more elaborate than the normal Sunday preaching service to which it was appended. It was structured like this:

Set prayer (written down in the liturgy)
Scripture reading: from the New Testament letters
Gloria in excelsis, recited antiphonally by congregation
Scripture reading: from the Gospels
The Apostles' Creed, recited antiphonally by congregation
Exhortation (leading into holy communion)
The Lord's Prayer, recited by congregation
Set prayer
Words of institution
Consecration and distribution of the bread and wine
Psalm, recited antiphonally by congregation
Set prayer
Benediction

---

[30] Towards the end of his life, probably under the impact of his controversy with Luther, Zwingli leaned towards a more positive view of Christ's presence in the eucharist. In his *Exposition of Faith*, written in 1530, Zwingli says: "By this commemoration, all the benefits that God has displayed in His Son are called to mind. And by the signs themselves, the bread and wine, Christ Himself is (so to speak) set before our eyes, so that not merely with the ear, but with eye and mouth we see and taste Christ, whom the soul carries within itself and in whom the soul rejoices." This still falls somewhat short of the full Reformed doctrine, but is a clear advance on a bare symbolic-memorial view.

One other important feature of the Zurich Reformation was Zwingli's commitment to theological education. Zurich had no university; but in April 1525, the city council appointed Zwingli as principal of the cathedral grammar school. Zwingli reorganised it, and the most fruitful aspect of this restructuring was the creation of a theological college for training pastors. Its curriculum was two lectures per day, delivered in Latin, Greek, and Hebrew. These lectures were focused on reading the Bile in its original languages, interpreting it, and translating it. The academic standard was high. Around 12 pastors, and 12 young men who had graduated from the grammar school, were present in the college classes at any given time. Having received their qualifications, they were regarded as having a higher status than ordinary clergy, and were known as "prophets". The college was a success, and was copied in Basel and Strasbourg.

From Zurich, the Reformation spread under Zwingli's leadership to other Swiss cantons. The cantons were divided into two basic types: (i) the four "city cantons" of Zurich, Berne, Basel, and Schaffhausen, where urban civilisation was highly developed; (ii) the other nine cantons which were more rural, centred around farm and village, and dominated by the five central "forest cantons" of Uri, Schwyz, Unterwalden, Zug, and Lucerne. By 1531, Protestantism had triumphed in all four of the city cantons, and in several other parts of Switzerland. However, the five forest cantons remained solidly Roman Catholic. As a result, the Swiss Confederacy was soon plunged into religious civil war, with tragic consequences for Zwingli, as we shall see.

Like Luther, Zwingli did not stand alone as a Reformer; he had friends and co-workers. The most significant were:

Leo Jud (1482-1542). Jud was a disciple of Zwingli's old humanist tutor Thomas Wyttenbach. He acted as Zwingli's right-hand man in Zurich, as the fervently anti-Roman preacher of Saint Peter's Church. Jud's flaming sermon against the veneration of icons in September 1523 provoked a violent popular outbreak of image-smashing. This in turn led to the "second Zurich disputation" in

October, which swung public opinion still more fully behind the Reformation. Jud also translated the Old Testament prophets and Paul's letters into Swiss-German, and wrote a Protestant catechism that enjoyed a long and fruitful history.

Oswald Myconius (1488-1552). Myconius was a humanist teacher of the classics, a personal friend of Erasmus. He taught in Zurich from 1523, and in 1532 became professor of New Testament in Basel university and the city's senior pastor. A great admirer of Zwingli from the beginning, Myconius had been instrumental in securing Zwingli as preacher for the Zurich Great Cathedral in 1518.

Johann Oecolampadius (1484-1531). Oecolampadius[31] was Switzerland's answer to Philip Melanchthon: a great Christian humanist who became a great Protestant Reformer. Oecolampadius also had a direct influence on Melanchthon's thinking about holy communion, as we shall see in the next section. A brilliant Greek and Hebrew scholar, he helped Erasmus prepare his 1516 edition of the Greek New Testament. He went on to become the chief Reformer of the city canton of Basel.

Berchtold Haller (1492-1536). Another disciple of Thomas Wyttenbach, Haller's preaching brought the city canton of Berne into the Protestant camp. Berne's adherence to the Reformation in 1528 was decisive for the future of Swiss Protestantism; it meant that the two most powerful cantons of the Swiss Confederacy – Zurich and Berne – had both committed themselves to the Protestant cause.

Zwingli had serious difficulties with a group of Radical Reformers or Anabaptists, but we will postpone their story until we reach Chapter 5.

---

[31]   Pronounced "Ekka-lam-pay-dee-us".

7. Luther, Zwingli, and the communion controversy.

By the close of the 1520s, the anti-Roman forces of reform had
flowed apart into two separate streams, the Magisterial (largely
statist at this point) and the Radical. However, it was also clear that
the Magisterial Reformers themselves had divided theologically
into two parties: the Lutherans and the Zwinglians. Once again, the
trouble was over the sacraments. Just as it was their differing
understandings of baptism that divided the Magisterial from the
Radical Reformers, so it was their differing understandings of holy
communion that split the Lutherans and the Zwinglians – or the
"Reformed", as the Swiss Reformers and their allies came to call
themselves.

Both Luther and Zwingli had indeed abandoned the later medieval
concept of the mass, and were united on the following points:

(i)   They both rejected transubstantiation and the special power
       of the priest to perform this so-called miracle.

(ii)   They both rejected the idea that the eucharist was a sacri-
       fice which had the power to secure God's grace for those
       for whom it was offered, even when they did not take part
       (*e.g.* souls in purgatory).

(iii) They both rejected the medieval Catholic practice of ador-
       ing the sacramental bread after the priest had pronounced
       the words "This is My body."

(iv)   They both demanded that the cup be given to the laity.

Despite these broad areas of agreement, Luther and Zwingli
divided over the question of how exactly Christ was present in the
eucharist. Luther held that Christ's flesh and blood were objectively
present in the bread and wine, although without converting or
abolishing their essence; the body and blood of the Saviour were,
he argued, mysteriously present "in, with, and under" the bread and

wine, and were eaten and drunk by everyone who took part in communion, whether they had faith in Christ or not. Luther felt that the words "This is My body" required that Christ's body must be objectively present in the bread. His fear was that a rejection of Christ's bodily presence in the eucharistic elements would lead to a belief in Christ's absence – or to the idea that human faith created Christ's presence, which made faith more central than the Saviour. Luther set forth his views vigorously in such books as *That These Words of Christ, "This is My Body" etc, Still Stand Firm Against the Fanatics* (1527).

Zwingli disagreed very strongly with Luther on this matter. The Swiss Reformer maintained that the word "is" in "This is My body" meant "represents" – "This represents My body." Christ's flesh and blood, Zwingli argued, were in no sense physically present in the bread and wine; His risen body was in heaven, not on earth. As for eating Christ's flesh and drinking His blood, this for Zwingli simply meant believing in Christ – a view summed up in the Latin phrase *edere credere*, "to eat is to believe". In holy communion, therefore, believers alone "ate" Christ, that is, exercised faith; any unbelievers who took part received only bread and wine. Christ was present in the Lord's Supper, Zwingli argued, not as man, but as God – not in His humanity, but in His omnipresent deity. Zwingli set forth his views in books like *A Clear Exposition of Christ's Last Supper* (1527).

The German-Swiss controversy became even more explosive and divisive when Luther tried to defend his view of Christ's presence in the bread and wine by an argument from Christology. The union between Christ's divine and human natures was so close, Luther said, that each nature communicated its properties to the other. Christ's humanity imparted to His deity the capacity for suffering and death; His deity bestowed on His humanity its "omnipresence" – the divine quality of being everywhere. Christ was therefore everywhere, not just as God, but as a man; He was omnipresent in His human nature. So it followed that His body and blood were present in the bread and wine of communion.

Zwingli passionately rejected this argument; he did not accept that Christ's two natures conferred their properties on each other. He accused Luther of reviving the ancient heresy of Eutyches, condemned by the Council of Chalcedon[32] – that is, the heresy of denying the reality of Christ's human nature, by teaching that in the incarnation His deity swallowed up and absorbed His humanity. A human body, Zwingli argued, cannot be everywhere without ceasing to be a real human body, because it is the nature of a human body to occupy a particular place. He also told Luther that if the German Reformer's view was correct, Christ's body would be present in every slice of bread, not just the bread of the eucharist. Luther's response was that while Christ's body was indeed present in every slice of bread, it was only in the eucharistic bread that it was present as a sign of God's grace (just as God is present every-where, but He is not *graciously* present everywhere: outside of the Gospel, God is present purely as Creator and Lord, with no saving benefit, no promise of forgiveness). Lutherans also felt that Zwingli's Christology was Nestorian, separating the divine and human natures so far that they ended up not being really united at all, merely placed alongside each other like two persons.[33]

The controversy between German Lutherans and Swiss Reformed became extremely bitter. Luther refused to recognise the Protestants of Switzerland as fellow Christians; they were depraved heretics to be resisted at all costs. Luther had the sort of personality that sees life in starkly black-and-white terms: something was either of God or of Satan – there could be nothing in between. And (to his critics, at least) he seemed to have an unfortunate habit of assuming that people were "of God" if they agreed with Martin Luther, and "of Satan" if they didn't. On top of this, Luther remembered that his Radical enemy, Andreas Carlstadt, held the view of communion that Zwingli was now teaching. So Luther had already learned to link this view with a Satanic attempt to undermine the Reformation from within – the religious chaos Carlstadt had unleashed in Wittenberg in 1522 haunted Luther's mind. Zwingli, then, simply

---

[32]   For Eutyches and the Council of Chalcedon, see Part One, Chapter 10, section 4.
[33]   For Nestorianism, see Part One, Chapter 10, section 3.

became a "Swiss Carlstadt" in Luther's eyes. Luther therefore condemned the Swiss Reformer in the most forthright words:

> "I cannot regard Zwingli or any of his teaching as Christian at all. He neither holds nor teaches any part of the Christian faith rightly, and is seven times more dangerous than when he was a papist."

Luther warned people to shun Zwingli's books as "the poison of the prince of hell", and even said he would rather drink blood with the papists than wine with the Zwinglians!

Luther's attitude stirred Zwingli, Oecolampadius, and the Swiss Reformers to deep anger. The Swiss wanted both religious unity and a political alliance with the German Lutherans, to deter Roman Catholic rulers from trying to reimpose Roman Catholicism by force on Protestant lands. They recognised the Lutherans as fellow Christians, and were appalled that Luther should be splitting the Reformation movement in the face of the common enemy, Rome. Oecolampadius summed up the exasperated feelings of the Swiss towards Luther:

> "Since he has lost control of himself, he believes that the greatest sin and the most unfair act in the world is to criticise him. We have here a miserable creature who smashes heaven and earth because we have told him that he too, as a man, might err, and that those who put their faith in him might miss the mark. Thus, according to him, we overthrow the entire faith! Not so, my brother; but we must not get it into our minds that the Holy Spirit is bound to Jerusalem, Rome, Wittenberg, or Basel, to yourself or to any other."

With this kind of language flying back and forth between Luther and the Swiss Reformers, it is not surprising that Roman Catholics began laughing at the Reformation as a movement doomed to self-destruction.

Efforts were made to reconcile the Germans and the Swiss, especially by *Philip of Hesse* (1508-67), the young Lutheran prince of Hesse in western Germany. Philip had sympathies with Zwingli's doctrine of communion; he also believed strongly in the need for a political alliance between German and Swiss Protestants, especially after the diet of Speyer in March 1529, where the Holy Roman emperor Charles V had cancelled religious freedoms previously granted to German Lutherans. At Philip's insistence, therefore, the Swiss and German Reformers met at Philip's castle in Marburg in October 1529, to hold a "colloquy" (conference) on the doctrine of holy communion. It was one of the greatest gatherings of Reformation theologians. The German delegation was led by Luther, Melanchthon, and Justus Jonas from Wittenberg, and three other distinguished Lutheran Reformers, Johannes Brenz of Swabia, *Andreas Osiander* (1498-1552) of Nuremberg, and *Johann Agricola* (1494-1566) of Augsburg. The Reformed delegation was led by Zwingli from Zurich, Oecolampadius from Basel, and three eminent Reformers from the south German imperial city of Strasbourg – Martin Bucer, Caspar Hedio, and Jacob Sturm (1498-1553).[34]

The colloquy achieved nothing. At its very outset, Luther took a piece of chalk and wrote on the table the words, "This is My body." He then informed Zwingli and his colleagues that he would understand these words literally, unless the Swiss could prove beyond doubt that "is" did not mean "is" but "represents". Over the four days of debate (October 1st –4th), the Swiss Reformers could not shake Luther from this position. Philip of Hesse and Zwingli were bitterly disappointed. Zwingli begged with tears in his eyes that the two parties should unite in spite of their disagreement, but Luther refused even to admit that the Swiss Reformers were Christians. As an attempt at uniting Protestants, therefore, the colloquy was a spectacular failure. However, from the Swiss standpoint, it made two gains: (i) Philip of Hesse was won over to a more Zwinglian view, which heralded the future growth of the

---

[34] For Bucer, Hedio, Sturm, and the Strassburg Reformation, see next Chapter, section 5.

Reformed faith in south-western Germany.[35] (ii) Oecolampadius had persuaded Melanchthon that the early Church fathers did not support Luther's doctrine of communion, which heralded Melanchthon's acceptance of the Reformed view as stated by Bucer, John Calvin, and Peter Martyr – an event that was to ignite consuming fires of controversy within Lutheranism after Luther's death.[36]

In the cool light of retrospect, we can see that the Luther-Zwingli controversy was basically about the relationship between signs and what they signify. For Zwingli, the signs in the eucharist were the bread and wine, and what they signified was a past event in history, the death of Christ on Calvary. With this "past reference" view of the signs, inevitably Zwingli did not see the bread and wine as conveying Christ's body and blood in the present: they simply directed faith back to the once-for-all event in history, when Christ was "crucified under Pontius Pilate". In Zwingli's mind, signs almost required the "real absence" of the things signified. For Luther, however, the signs in the eucharist were not the bread and wine, but Christ's body and blood; and what Christ's body and blood signified was the forgiveness of sin and all the saving benefits of the Gospel. Luther made statements about the bread and wine that sound rather strange to most Evangelicals today, *e.g.* that in the eucharist we can no longer speak simply of bread and wine, but must speak of "fleshbread" and "bloodwine". This was to safeguard Luther's view that Christ's body and blood, not the bread and wine, were the real "signs".

With the Zwinglian and Lutheran concepts of eucharistic signs so radically opposed, there could be little hope of mutual understanding. Later, under the impact of Martin Bucer's post-Marburg thinking, elaborated by John Calvin and Peter Martyr, a third view would develop, which saw the bread and wine as signs not only of a past event but a present reality, Christ's body and blood offered here and now as spiritual food and drink. The signs and the things

---

[35] For the spread of the Reformed faith in Germany, see Chapter 6, section 3.
[36] See the next Chapter for the Bucer-Calvin-Martyr doctrine of the eucharist.

signified were to be kept closely together in this view, but without being confused: a sign pointed not to the absence but the presence of the thing signified, even though the sign should not be *identified* with that thing.

From the frustrated efforts of the Marburg colloquy, we can date the lasting division of the Magisterial Reformation into two separate theological branches: the Lutherans (or Evangelicals, as they called themselves), and the Reformed. The Reformation movement, unwilling to accept anything but Scripture as its authority, had been unable to agree on what Scripture taught about the Supper of Christian brotherhood.[37]

8. The Swiss Reformation after Zwingli.

The religious tensions in Switzerland between the Protestant and Roman Catholic cantons had already led to one war in June 1529, just before the Marburg colloquy. The Protestants won this conflict. However, their victory proved rather fruitless, the tensions remained, and when war broke out again in October 1531, the Roman Catholic cantons inflicted a decisive defeat on the Protestants at the battle of Kappel (11th October). Zwingli fought as a private soldier on the Protestant side, and was badly wounded; when the battle was over, some Roman Catholic soldiers found him lying helpless under a pear tree, and killed him when he refused to pray to the Virgin Mary as they demanded. A second battle at Gubel on 24th October was also a resounding triumph for the Roman Catholics. The victorious Roman Catholic cantons were then able to dictate the terms of a peace treaty which put a stop to all further

---

[37] The division between Lutheran and Reformed does not quite correspond to the division between a "statist" and a "Reformed Catholic" approach to Church-state relations. Generally, Lutherans were statist, while Reformed tended to be Reformed Catholic. But the Anglican Church does not fit into this pattern, because it was Reformed in all the points of theological dispute between Reformed and Lutherans, but statist in its subordination to the English monarchy and parliament.

spread of the Reformation in Switzerland. This event permanently fixed the religious loyalties of the Swiss, with the four city cantons of Zurich, Berne, Basel, and Schaffhausen as the strongholds of Protestantism, and the five forest cantons of Uri, Schwyz, Unterwalden, Zug, and Lucerne as the guardians of Roman Catholicism.[38]

Heinrich Bullinger (1504-75), a native of Bremgarten (just outside Zurich), took Zwingli's place as the leading Reformer of Zurich. While studying at Cologne university, Bullinger had been converted to Protestantism by reading Luther and Melanchthon and comparing their teachings with the Bible and the early Church fathers. He then joined a Cistercian monastery at Kappel in 1523 as a Bible teacher, and by 1527 all the monks had become Protestants through Bullinger's expositions of Scripture. They turned the monastery into a Protestant church with Bullinger as pastor.

In 1529 he became pastor of his home village of Bremgarten, but the Roman Catholic victories at the battles of Kappel and Gubel in 1531 forced him to take refuge in Zurich. Shortly afterwards the Zurich city council chose Bullinger to succeed Zwingli as preacher in the Great Cathedral, instructing him to expound the Bible and not to meddle in politics.

Bullinger was a richly gifted preacher and theologian. His sermons were published as a textbook of systematic theology entitled *Decades*; they had a widespread influence within the Reformed Churches, especially in England where the *Decades* became the basic textbook of theology for training the Anglican clergy after 1559. Bullinger also carried out a far-reaching correspondence with the Churchmen and statesmen of Reformed Europe, exercising great personal influence – again, especially over the English, owing to the fact that Bullinger's Zurich had given shelter to many English Protestants during the persecutions of the English Roman

---

[38] Of the other four cantons, Fribourg and Solothurn were Roman Catholic, while Glarus and Appenzell were divided between the two faiths.

Heinrich Bullinger
(1504-75)

Catholic queen Mary Tudor (1553-58).[39] Bullinger's most important theological contribution was probably his development of the covenant theme. He argued that God's covenant with Abraham was the basis of "salvation history", and that Christ is the fulfilment of the Abrahamic covenant. Bullinger set this forth in such a way as to tie closely together Old and New Testaments as the unfolding of one single story, one single gracious covenant, in which the Mosaic law was only a temporary addition that served the true covenant made in Abraham and accomplished in Christ. In addition, Bullinger was the author of the Second Helvetic (Swiss) Confession, published in 1566, which became one of the most widely used confessions of faith among the Reformed Churches.

Important people:

The Church

Lutherans:
Johannes Bugenhagen (1485-1558)
Andreas Osiander (1498-1552)
Justas Jonas (1493-1555)
Johann Agricola (1494-1566)

Reformed:
Thomas Wyttenbach (1472-1526)
Johann Oecolampadius (1484-1531)
Ulrich Zwingli (1484-1531)
Berchtold Haller (1492-1536)
Leo Jud (1482-1542)
Oswald Myconius (1488-1552)
Heinrich Bullinger (1504-75)

Radicals:
Thomas Müntzer (1488-1525)
Gabriel Zwilling (1487-1558)

Political and military
Philip of Hesse (1508-67)

---

[39] For the English Reformation, see Chapter 7.

Luther against Erasmus: The necessity of dogma and assertion in Christianity

Let's take the apostle Paul as an example. How often does he require "full assurance" (Colossians 2:2, 1 Thessalonians 1:5), which is a most sure and unshakeable assertion of conscience? In Romans 10, he refers to this as "confession" – "with the mouth confession is made, resulting in salvation" (v.10). Christ says, "Whoever confesses me before men, I will confess him before My Father" (Matthew 10:32). Peter commands us to give a reason for the hope that is in us (1 Peter 3:15). What is the point of setting forth so many proofs? Nothing is so frequent and typical among Christians as making assertions. Abolish assertions, you abolish Christianity. The Holy Spirit from heaven is given to Christians so that He may glorify Christ in them, and confess Him even if it leads to death. Here we have assertion – to die for what you confess and assert. The Spirit indeed is so assertive that He intrudes Himself on the whole world and convicts it of sin (John 16:8), as though He were challenging the world to a fight. Paul tells Timothy to exhort in season and out of season (2 Timothy 4:2); and what a comedian I would think someone was, if he didn't really believe or resolutely assert those things about which he was exhorting. I think I'd pack him off to Anticyra [a Greek health resort where people were cured of mental illness].

But I'm the biggest fool of everyone for wasting all these words and all this time on something that is plainer than day. What Christian could accept that we should despise assertions? That would be a denial of all religion and godliness, asserting that religion and godliness and all dogmas are of no importance. So why do you *assert* that you find no pleasure in *assertions*, and that you prefer an undogmatic spirit to its opposite?…

If you are talking about unprofitable and uncertain doctrines, what are you saying that is new? Doesn't everyone want freedom to be sceptical about such things? In fact, doesn't every Christian freely make use of such liberty, and condemn those who become slaves of any mere opinion? Or maybe you think (as your words virtually suggest) that Christians in general are people who hold useless dogmas over which they stupidly quarrel and carry on battles of assertions. But if you are talking about essential dogmas, what more ungodly assertion could anyone make than that he wants freedom to assert nothing in such matters? The Christian will rather say this: "I delight in sceptical principles so little, that I will (as far as human weakness permits) consistently hold to and assert the sacred writings, everywhere and in every part; and I also want to be as sure as possible even about the non-essentials which Scripture does not pronounce on. For what is more miserable than uncertainty?"

From Luther's *The Bondage of the Will*.

The comfort of predestination

I frankly admit that, as far as I am concerned, I wouldn't want "free will" to be given to me, even if it could be. I don't want anything to be left in my own hands by which I might make efforts towards salvation. For I wouldn't be able to stand firm and keep my grip on salvation in the face of so many dangers and perils and attacks of demons, since one demon is stronger than all humans. No one could be saved at all on these terms. And even if there were no dangers, perils, or demons, I would still have to work without any assurance of success, fighting like a man beating the air with his fists. If I lived and worked for all eternity, my conscience would never find assurance and certainty regarding how much I had to do to satisfy God. Whatever work I had done, there would always remain an anxious doubt whether it pleased God, or whether He required something more. This is proved by the experience of all who seek to justify themselves; I learned this to my own bitter hurt over a period of many years. But now that God has taken my salvation out of my hands, and put it in His hands, making it depend on His choice not mine, and has promised to save me, not according to my own work or effort, but according to His grace and mercy, I have assurance and certainty that He is faithful and will not lie to me, and that He is too great and powerful for demons or any enemies to be able to break Him or snatch me from Him. "No one," He says, "shall snatch them out of My hand, because My Father who has given them to Me is greater than all" (John 10:28-9). So it is that if not all are saved, yet some are saved, indeed many; whereas by the power of free will none at all would be saved, but all would perish.

From Luther's *The Bondage of the Will*.

Lutherans confess their faith: The Augsburg Confession

Article 1: God.
Our Churches, with common consent, teach that the decree of the Council of Nicaea concerning the unity of the divine essence and concerning the three persons, is true and to be believed without any doubt. That is to say: there is one divine essence which is called and which is God, eternal, without body, without parts, of infinite power, wisdom, and goodness, the Maker and Preserver of all things, visible and invisible. And yet there are three persons, of the same essence and power, who also are co-eternal, the Father, the Son, and the Holy Spirit. And the term "person" they use as the fathers have used it, to signify, not a part or quality in another, but that which subsists of itself. They [Lutherans] condemn all heresies which have sprung up against this article, as the Manichaeans [Gnostics from the patristic era], who believed in two principles, one good and the other evil – also the Valentinians, Arians, Euno-mians [heretics from the patristic era], Muhammadans [Muslims], and all such. They condemn also the Samosatenes [followers of Paul of Samosata from the 3rd century], old and new, who, contend-ing that there is but one person, sophistically and impiously argue that the Word and the Holy Spirit are not distinct persons, but that "Word" signifies a spoken word, and "Spirit" signifies motion created in things.

Article 2: *Original sin.*

Since the fall of Adam, all human beings are born with sin, by the natural process of generation – that is, born without the fear of God, without faith in God, and with sinful desire. This disease or defect which we have from our very origin is truly sin, bringing condemnation and eternal death even now on those who are not born again through baptism and the Holy Spirit. Our Churches condemn the Pelagians and others who deny that this defect in our origin is sin, and who argue that mankind can be justified in God's sight by its own rational powers, thus degrading the glory of Christ's merit and blessings.

Article 3: *The Son of God.*

Also they teach that the Word, that is, the Son of God, assumed human nature in the womb of the blessed Virgin Mary, so that there are two natures, the divine and the human, inseparably enjoined in one person, one Christ, true God and true man, who was born of the Virgin Mary, truly suffered, was crucified, dead, and buried, that He might reconcile the Father to us, and be a sacrifice, not only for original guilt, but also for all the actual sins of human beings. He also descended into hell, and truly rose again on the third day. Afterwards He ascended into heaven that He might sit at the right hand of the Father, and forever reign and have dominion over all created things, and sanctify those who believe in Him, by sending the Holy Spirit into their hearts, to rule, comfort, and quicken them, and to defend them against the devil and the power of sin. The same Christ shall openly come again to judge the quick and the dead, *etc.*, according to the Apostles' Creed.

Article 4: *Justification.*

People cannot be justified in God's sight by their own strength, worthiness, or works, but are justified freely through Christ by faith, when they believe that they are accepted into grace and their sins forgiven through Christ, who made atonement for our sins by His death. God reckons this faith for righteousness in His sight.

Article 5: *The ministry.*

That we may obtain this faith, the ministry of teaching the gospel and administering the sacraments was instituted. For through the Word and sacraments, as through instruments, the Holy Spirit is given, who creates faith where and when it pleases God, in those who hear the gospel, namely, that God justifies – not for our own merits, but for Christ's sake – those who believe that they are received into grace for Christ's sake. They condemn the Anabaptists and others who think that the Holy Spirit comes to people without the external Word, through their own preparations and works.

Article 6: *The new obedience*

Also they teach that this faith is bound to bring forth good fruits, and that it is necessary to do good works commanded by God, because of God's will, but that we should not rely on those works to merit justification before God. For forgiveness of sins and justification are grasped by faith, as also the voice of Christ attests: "When you have done all these things, say: 'We are unprofitable servants'" (Luke 17:10). The same is also taught by the fathers. For Ambrose says: "It is ordained by God that he who believes in Christ is saved, freely receiving forgiveness of sins, without works, by faith alone."

Article 7: *The Church.*

One holy Church will endure for ever. The Church is the congregation of the saints, in which the gospel is rightly taught and the sacraments are rightly administered. For the true unity of the Church to exist, it is enough to agree together concerning the teaching of the gospel and the administration of the sacraments; it is not necessary that the same human traditions, rituals and ceremonies should everywhere be practised.

Article 8: *What the Church is.*

Although the Church properly is the congregation of saints and true believers, nevertheless, since in this life many hypocrites and evil persons are mingled with the true believers, it is lawful to use sacraments administered by evil men, according to the saying of Christ: "The Scribes and the Pharisees sit in Moses' seat," *etc.* (Matthew 23:2). Both the sacraments and Word are effective by reason of the institution and commandment of Christ, even if they are administered by evil men. They condemn the Donatists, and such like, who denied it to be lawful to use the ministry of evil men in the Church, and who thought the ministry of evil men to be unprofitable and of no effect.

Article 18: Free will.
The human will has a certain freedom for attaining justice in human relationships and choosing things that are subject to reason. But without the Holy Spirit, it does not have the power to attain God's righteousness or spiritual righteousness... Human nature can, in a sense, achieve outwardly good actions; it can, for example, restrain a person from theft or murder. But it cannot achieve inwardly good motives – the fear of God, confidence in God, chastity, patience, *etc.*

Article 22: Summary.
These are the chief points of our teaching, and nothing in it can be found that differs from Scripture, the Catholic Church, or the Church of Rome as we understand it from its great writers. We are not heretics. Our problem is with certain abuses which have crept into the churches without any clear authority.... The old ceremonies are to a large degree carefully preserved among us.

The Augsburg Confession (1530)

Luther's liturgy: The German mass of 1526

The mass-vestments, altars, and lights may be still be used, until they disappear of their own accord, or until it pleases us to change them. However, if anyone takes a different path in this matter, we will not interfere. Yet in the true mass, among real Christians, the altar should not remain in its present position, and the priest should always turn towards the people, as Christ undoubtedly did at the last Supper. We must await an opportune time to introduce this reform.

1. At the beginning, then, we sing a spiritual song or a psalm in German, in the first tone, as follows... [Luther here reproduces Psalm 34 and the musical line according to which each verse should be chanted.]

2. Then we sing *kyrie eleison* in the same tone, but three times, not nine times... [Luther gives musical instructions.]

3. Then the priest chants a collect [a set prayer][40] in monotone in F-fa-ut [a medieval musical term], as follows: "Almighty God, the protector of all who trust in You, without whose grace no one is able to do anything or to stand before You: Grant us richly Your mercy, so that by Your holy inspiration we may think what is right, and by Your power perform the same, for the sake of Jesus Christ our Lord. Amen."

4. Then follows the Epistle, in the eighth tone... [Luther gives musical instructions.] The priest should chant the Epistle with his face turned to the people, but the collect with his face turned to the altar.

5. After the Epistle is chanted, the whole choir sings a German hymn, "Now let us pray to the Holy Spirit," or some other hymn.

6. Then the priest chants the Gospel in the fifth tone, also with his face turned towards the people... [Luther gives musical instructions.]

7. After the Gospel the whole congregation sings the Creed in German, "In one true God we all believe."

---

[40] Collect is pronounced with the emphasis on the first syllable: *coll*-ect.

8. Then follows the sermon, on the Gospel for that Sunday or holy day. If we had ***Postils*** [printed homilies by Luther] for the entire year [which Luther did indeed complete by 1527], I think it would be best for the postil of the day to be read out of the book to the people, either in whole or in part. This is not only for the preacher's sake who can do no better, but it also acts as a safeguard against fanatics and sectarians – a practice of which we can see traces in the homilies read at matins [morning prayers]. For if there is no spiritual understanding, and the Spirit himself does not speak through the preachers (whom I do not restrict, for the Spirit can teach men how to preach better than any postils or homilies), the result will be that every man will preach what he likes, and instead of the gospel and its exposition, they will be preaching about blue ducks again![41] This is one reason why we keep the Epistles and Gospels as they are given in the ***Postils***, because there are only a few gifted preachers who can expound a whole Gospel or other book of the Bible powerfully and profitably.

9. After the sermon there follows a public paraphrase of the Lord's Prayer, with an exhortation to those who desire to come to the Sacrament, in this, or some other better fashion, as follows: "Dear friends in Christ, as we are here gathered together in the Lord's name to receive His holy testament, I exhort you, first, to lift up your hearts to God and to say with me 'Our Father' as Christ our Lord has taught us, faithfully promising that we shall be heard... [There follows a long paraphrase of the Lord's Prayer.] Next, I exhort you in Christ that with true faith you pay heed to Christ's testament, and especially that you hold fast in your hearts the Word by which Christ gives us His body and blood for the remission of sins; that you think of, and thank Him for, the infinite love which He has shown us, since by His blood He has redeemed us from God's wrath, sin, death, and hell; and then in this faith take to yourselves outwardly the bread and wine, which is His body

---

[41]   In other words, anecdotal rubbish, which Luther regarded as one of the worst features of late medieval preaching.

and blood, as an assurance and pledge of all this. In this way, in His name and as He commanded in His own Word, let us handle and receive His Testament." Whether this paraphrase and exhortation should be read in the pulpit immediately after the sermon, or at the altar, I leave free to every man's discretion... But I would ask that this paraphrase or exhortation should follow a set form of words and be formulated in a fixed manner, for the sake of ordinary people. We cannot have one preacher doing it one way today, then another doing a different way tomorrow, letting everyone parade his talents and confuse the people so that that cannot learn or remember anything. The most important thing is teaching and guiding the people. That is why we must restrict our freedom here and keep to one form of paraphrase or exhortation, especially in each particular church or congregation...

10. Then the office and consecration follows, to this tune...[Luther gives musical instructions for chanting 1 Corinthian 11:23-5.] I think it would be in accordance with the last Supper if the sacrament were distributed immediately after the consecration of the bread, and before the blessing of the cup. This is what both Luke and Paul say: "Likewise after Supper He took the cup." Meanwhile, there might be sung the *Sanctus* in German,[42] or the hymn "Let God be blessed," or the hymn of John Huss, "Jesus Christ our God and Saviour". And after this should come the blessing of the cup and its delivery, with the singing of whatever remains of the above-mentioned hymns, or of the *Agnus Dei* in German.[43] And for the sake of good order and discipline in going up to the altar, men and women should not go together, but the women after the men. Men and women should also have separate places in different parts of the church. As for

---

[42]   The *Sanctus* is Isaiah 6:1-4. It was recited or sung in the Lord's Supper from the earliest times.

[43]   The *Agnus Dei* (Latin for "Lamb of God") was an ancient eucharistic prayer: "O Lamb of God, You who take away the sins of the world, have mercy upon us; O Lamb of God, You who take away the sins of the world, have mercy upon us; O Lamb of God, You who take away the sins of the world, grant us peace."

private confession, I have written enough about that elsewhere, and my opinion can be found in the little prayer-book.

11. We do not desire to abolish the elevation of the bread and cup, but to retain it, because it fits in well with the *Sanctus* in German, and means that Christ has commanded us to think of Him.[44] Just as the sacrament is elevated physically, and yet Christ's body and blood are invisible, so through the word of the preacher He is commemorated and elevated, and in the reception of the sacrament confessed and worshipped. Yet in all this, it is a matter of faith, not of sight, for we cannot see how Christ gives His body and blood to us and still daily intercedes with God to bestow His grace upon us.

12. Then follows the collect: "We give thanks to You, Almighty God, that You have refreshed us with this health-giving gift. We beseech You in mercy to strengthen us through the same in faith towards You, and in fervent love among us all, for the sake of Jesus Christ our Lord. Amen."

13. "The Lord bless you and keep you; the Lord make His face shine upon you, and be gracious to you; the Lord lift up His countenance upon you, and give you peace" (Numbers 6:24-6).

So much for the daily worship service and for teaching the Word of God, particularly with a view to training the young and stirring the minds of the uneducated. Those who come out of mere curiosity and the desire to gape at a novelty will soon be sick and tired of the whole thing, just as they were before of worship services in Latin. For that was sung and read out in church every day, and yet the churches are deserted and empty. Already people are about to do the same with the German Service! So it is best to arrange the worship services to train the young, and those uneducated folk who may perhaps come to it. As for the rest, no law nor order, exhortation nor rebuke, that anyone can devise, is of any good to persuade them to go willingly and of their own accord to a worship service,

---

[44] The elevation was in fact abolished in Wittenberg in 1542.

they are so unwilling and reluctant. However, God takes no delight in forced service; it is futile and good-for-nothing.

From Luther's *German Mass* of 1526.

Luther on baptism and the Lord's Supper

Q. What is Baptism?

A. Baptism is not just plain water, but it is water contained within God's command and united with God's Word.

Q. Which Word of God is this?

A. The one which our Lord Christ spoke in the last chapter of Matthew: *Go into all the world, teaching all heathen nations, and baptising them in the name of the Father, of the Son, and of the Holy Spirit.*

Q. What does Baptism give? What good is it?

A. It gives the forgiveness of sins, redeems from death and the Devil, gives eternal salvation to all who believe this, just as God's words and promises declare.

Q. What are these words and promises of God?

A. Our Lord Christ spoke one of them in the last chapter of Mark: *Whoever believes and is baptised will be saved; but whoever does not believe will be damned.*

Q. How can water do such great things?

A. Water doesn't make these things happen, of course. It is God's Word, which is with and in the water. Because, without God's Word, the water is plain water and not baptism. But with God's Word it is a Baptism, a grace-filled water of life, a bath of new birth in the Holy Spirit, as Saint Paul said to Titus in the third chapter: *Through this bath of rebirth and renewal of the Holy Spirit, which He poured out on us abundantly through Jesus Christ, our Saviour, that we, justified by the same grace are made heirs according to the hope of eternal life. This is a faithful saying.*

Q. What is the meaning of such a water Baptism?

A. It means that the old Adam in us should be drowned by daily sorrow and repentance, and die with all sins and evil lusts, and, in turn, a new person daily come forth and rise from death again. He will live forever before God in righteousness and purity.[45]

Q. Where is this written?

A. St. Paul says to the Romans in chapter six: *We are buried with Christ through Baptism into death, so that, in the same way Christ is risen from the dead by the glory of the Father, thus also must we walk in a new life...*

---

[45] Some readers may find it difficult to understand how Lutherans reconciled this teaching of "baptismal regeneration" with their doctrine of justification by faith alone. Perhaps a quotation from the great Lutheran theologian Johann Gerhard (1582-1616) may shed some light: "To infants baptism is, primarily, the ordinary means of regeneration and purification from sin; secondarily, it is the seal of righteousness and the confirmation of faith. To adult believers it serves principally as a seal and testimony of the grace of God, sonship, and eternal life; but in a less principal sense, it increases renovation and the gifts of the Holy Spirit. Infants by baptism receive the first fruits of the Spirit and of faith; adults, who through the Word have already received the first fruits of faith and of the Holy Spirit, procure an increase of these gifts by baptism." In the case of infants, Lutherans argued that the very act of baptism proclaims the gospel visibly, by depicting the washing away of sins; the Holy Spirit applies this proclamation of the gospel to the baptised infant in a mysterious manner, to create a "seed of faith" in him or her. So the infant is still justified by faith in the gospel, because through baptism the Holy Spirit implants that faith.

Q. What is the Sacrament of the Altar?

A. It is the true body and blood of our Lord Jesus Christ under bread and wine for us Christians to eat and to drink, established by Christ Himself.

Q. Where is that written?

A. The holy apostles Matthew, Mark and Luke and Saint Paul write this: *Our Lord Jesus Christ, in the night on which He was betrayed, took bread, gave thanks, broke it, gave it to His disciples and said: "Take! Eat! This is My body, which is given for you. Do this to remember Me!" In the same way He also took the cup after Supper, gave thanks, gave it to them, and said: "Take and drink from it, all of you! This cup is the New Testament in my blood, which is shed for you to forgive sins. This do, as often as you drink it, to remember Me!"*

Q. What good does this eating and drinking do?

A. These words tell us: "Given for you" and "Shed for you to forgive sins." Namely, that the forgiveness of sins, life and salvation are given to us through these words in the sacrament. Because, where sins are forgiven, there is life and salvation as well.

Q. How can physical eating and drinking do such great things?

A. Of course, eating and drinking do not do these things. These words, written here, do them: "given for you" and "shed for you to forgive sins." These words, along with physical eating and drinking are the important part of the sacrament. Anyone who believes these words has what they say and what they record, namely, the forgiveness of sins.

Q. Who, then, receives such a sacrament in a worthy way?

A. Of course, fasting and other physical preparations are excellent disciplines for the body. But anyone who believes these words, "Given for you," and "Shed for you to forgive sins," is really worthy and well prepared. But whoever doubts or does not believe these words is not worthy and is unprepared, because the words, "for you" demand a heart that fully believes.

Luther's Small Catechism, sections 4 and 6.

Luther: Advice to nuns

To the free nuns, my dear sisters in Christ, written in friendship: Mercy and peace in the name of Jesus Christ our Saviour! Dear sisters, I have received both of your letters and am aware of your problems. I would have replied sooner if there had been messengers available. In addition, I have been very busy.

You are right that there are two reasons for which monastic life and vows may be forsaken. The first is where compulsion is being exercised through manmade laws and through the way life is ordered in your convent, where there is no freedom of choice, where the monastic life is thrust upon the conscience as a burden. If that is the case, it is time to run away, leaving the convent and its life behind. If this is your own situation, where you are not freely choosing the life of a nun, where your conscience is being coerced, then get in touch with your friends. Get them to help you escape! Then, if the law permits, let them look after you or supply you with the means of life. If your friends and parents refuse to help, get assistance from other good people, and don't worry about whether your parents become angry, die, or recover. For the soul's well-being and God's will are more important than everything else, as Christ says (Matthew 10:37): "Anyone who loves father or mother more than me is not worthy of me." However, if your fellow nuns do give you freedom to leave, or at least allow you freely to read and hear the Word of God, then you must remain in the convent and join them in their works, such as weaving, cooking and so forth, even though you put no confidence in it.

The second reason is the flesh. Though women are ashamed to admit it, Scripture and experience prove that among many thousands there is not one to whom God has granted the gift of remaining in pure chastity. A woman has no control over her actual nature. God has created her body to be with man, and to bear children and raise them, as the words of Genesis 1:1 clearly state. Indeed, it is plain from the members of the body fashioned by God Himself. Therefore food and drink, sleeping and waking, have all been created by God. He has also fashioned man and woman to live in the union of marriage. Therefore let no one be ashamed of how God has made and created him, not having been given the high and rare grace [the gift of chastity] to live differently.

You will fully learn, and read, and hear proper sermons about all this when you come out. I have amply dealt with these matters in the book about monastic vows, avoiding human teachings, and in sermons about married life in the Postils, where these things are proven and established as true. If you read these, you will find sufficient instruction about various things, such as confession and other matters. It is too much to write about here and not even necessary, since I am convinced that you will leave the convent, if one or both of these reasons apply to you as you have written. Once there is freedom in choosing to join a religious order, anyone who wants to can join. For example, the Council of Berne in Switzerland has opened up the most famous convent of Kînigfelden, and any young woman may freely leave, or remain, or move in, and they allow her to take away with her whatever property she brought in when she joined.

May the Lord bless you, and pray for me.

Luther's *Letter to several nuns*, 6 August 1524

An Easter hymn by Martin Luther[46]

Christ Jesus lay in death's strong bands,
For our offences given;
But now at God's right hand He stands
And brings us life from heaven!
Wherefore let us joyful be,
And sing to God right thankfully
Loud songs of hallelujah:
Hallelujah!

It was a strange and dreadful strife
When life and death contended;
The victory remained with life,
The reign of death was ended!
Holy Scripture plainly saith
That death is swallowed up by death;
His sting is lost for ever:
Hallelujah!

Here the true Paschal Lamb we see,
Whom God so freely gave us;
He died on the accursed tree
(So strong His love!) to save us.
See, His blood doth mark our door,
Faith points to it, death passes o'er,
And Satan cannot harm us:
Hallelujah!

So let us keep the festival
Whereto the Lord invites us;
Christ is Himself the joy of all,
The sun that warms and lights us.

---

[46] A tune for this may be found in the New Creation hymnbook, hymn 312, on the internet a http://www.newcreation.org.au/music/378/cmusic/301to330C.pdf The words differ slightly; as far as I am aware, the version printed above is a more accurate translation.

By His grace He doth impart
Eternal sunshine to the heart;
The night of sin is ended:
Hallelujah!

Then let us feast this Easter Day[47]
On Christ, the Bread of Heaven;
The Word of grace hath purged away
The old and evil leaven.
Christ alone our souls will feed,
He is our meat and drink indeed;
Faith lives upon no other:
Hallelujah!

Zwingli's "Plague Hymn"

1. At the beginning of illness

Help, Lord God, help,
In this trouble!
I think death is at the door.
Stand before me, Christ,
For You have conquered death.
I cry to You!
If it is Your will,
Take out this dart that wounds me,
Nor lets me enjoy an hour's rest or quiet.
However, if it is Your will
That death should take me away
In the middle of my days,
Then so be it.
Do what pleases You.
I lack nothing.
I am Your vessel
To make or to break in pieces.

---

[47] Or "this holy day" if the hymn is sung on a Sunday other than Easter Sunday.

For if You take my spirit from this earth,
It is to prevent my spirit from growing worse
And from harming the godly lives and ways of others.

2. In the midst

Comfort me, Lord God, comfort me!
The illness gets worse;
Pain and fear seize my soul and body!
Come to me, then, with Your grace,
O my only comfort!
Your grace will surely save everyone
Who sets his heart's desire
And his hope on You,
And who despises all other gain and loss.
It is all over with me;
My tongue is dumb,
It cannot speak a word.
All my senses are withered.
Therefore it is time
For You to conduct my fight from now on,
Since I am so weak
That I cannot boldly resist
The devil's deceits and treacherous hate.
Yet however the devil rages,
My spirit will constantly
Abide with You.

3. Convalescence

Healed, Lord God, healed!
I think I am already coming back.
Yes, if it pleases You
That no spark of sin
Should rule me any longer on earth,
Then my lips must speak
Your praise and Your teaching

More than ever before,
Whatever happens,
In simplicity and with no fear.
I must endure sooner or later
The punishment of death,
Perhaps with greater anguish
Than would have happened now, Lord,
When I came so close to death.
Yet by Your help
I will still joyfully bear
The spite and boasting of this world,
For the sake of Your reward
Without which nothing can be perfect.

From Zwingli's 67 theses

1. All who say that the gospel lacks validity unless confirmed by the Church are in error and slander God.
2. The sum and substance of the gospel is that our Lord Jesus Christ, the true Son of God, has revealed to us His heavenly Father's will, and by His sinless perfection He has released us from death and reconciled us to God.
3. Therefore Christ is the only way of salvation for all who were, or are, or ever shall be born.
7. He is the eternal salvation and the head of all who believe. Believers are His body, for His fleshly body has died. Nothing is of any avail apart from Him.
8. From this it follows that all who dwell in the head are members and children of God. They form the Church or communion of saints, which is the bride of Christ, the Catholic Church.
15. Our salvation lies in faith, and our damnation lies in unbelief. For all truth is clear in Christ.
18. Christ, having sacrificed Himself once and for all, is for ever a perpetual and acceptable offering for the sins of all believers. From this it follows that the mass is not a sacrifice, but a commemoration of Christ's sacrifice, and a confirmation of the salvation that Christ has given to us.

19. Christ is the only mediator between God and ourselves.
20. God will give us everything in Christ's name. Thus it follows that we need no mediator in heaven except Christ.
22. Christ is our justification. From this it follows that our works are good, if they flow from Christ; but if they flow from ourselves, they are neither right nor good.
23. Christ totally rejects the material goods and show of this world. Thus it follows that those who pile up wealth in His name shamefully abuse Him, making Him a cloak for their greed and arrogance.
38. Everything that God has allowed, or has not forbidden, is right. Thus marriage is permitted to everyone.
39. All so-called clergymen commit sin, if they do not preserve their chastity through marriage after they have received an inner conviction that God has not given them the gift of chastity.
57. The true holy Scriptures know nothing about any purgatory after this life.
58. The fate of the dead is known only to God.
59. The less God has told us about it, the less we should seek to know about it.
60. I do not reject human prayer to God to show His grace to the departed.[48] But to assign a special time for this, and to lie for the sake of material gain [a reference to the selling of indulgences for souls allegedly in purgatory], is not human but demonic.

---

[48] Probably Zwingli is referring to prayer for the *faithful* departed. He may have in mind the sort of generalised prayers found in early Church liturgies, which amount to little more than praying that God will fulfil His gospel promises by keeping the departed faithful in His grace and raising them up finally in glory. As late as the mid-17th century we find a great Protestant theologian like archbishop Ussher upholding this position. This reminds us not to read back into early Protestantism the more narrowly defined views of a later Evangelicalism.

Zwingli on the Lord's Supper

In response to the dream of Pharaoh, Joseph said, "The seven good cows are seven fertile years" (Genesis 41:26). And yet it cannot be argued that seven cows *are* seven years. Clearly the word "are" must mean "signify" or "foretell". So the meaning is, "The seven good cows you saw when you slept foretell or signify seven fertile years." Christ said, "I am the vine" (John 15:1). Yet He was not a vine, but looked upon Himself as having the characteristics of the vine. Again He said, "The seed is the Word of God" (Luke 8:11). Yet the seed is not the Word of God. Here again, "is" cannot mean "to be", but is used to mean "signify". For with these words Christ was explaining to the apostles the parable he had set forth concerning the sowing of the seed, saying, "the seed of which I speak is" – that is, signifies – "the Word of God." We can find such phrases throughout the Bible, so there is no need for me to emphasise this point any further.

Now let me examine Christ's word [at the last Supper]. Jesus took bread, and so on, with these words, "Take this and eat. This is My body which is given for you." Here I interpret "is" to mean "signifies". So, "Take this and eat. This signifies My body which is given for you." Surely, then, the words must mean, "Take and eat. For this, which I now command you to do, will signify or call back to your minds My body which is given for you." For He immediately added, "Do this as a memorial of Me." Behold the purpose for which He commanded them to eat – as a commemoration of Himself. Paul puts it like this: "Every time you eat this bread and drink this cup, you proclaim the Lord's death" (1 Corinthians 11:26). What else is Paul commanding but a public remembering of the Lord's death? This feast of our Lord, or in Paul's words the Lord's Supper, was instituted in order that we should call to mind the death which Christ endured for us. Clearly this is the sign by which those who rely on Christ's death and blood show forth their common faith with their brothers. Let the meaning of Christ's words, then, be transparently clear: this meal is a symbol by which you call back into your minds the body of God's true Son, your Lord and Master – the body that was given for you.

Zwingli, *Letter to Matthew Alber*, 16th November 1524.

Bullinger on keeping Sunday holy

[It is often said that the early Reformers were not "sabbatarians" in their view of Sunday. Certainly Lutherans were not, in theory. Yet the difference in *practice* between a sabbatarian view and an early Reformation view could be minimal, as this passage from the Swiss Reformed leader Heinrich Bullinger shows.]

Last of all, the Lord adds His own example, by which He teaches us to keep the sabbath day holy. "For," He says, "in six days the Lord made heaven and earth, the sea, and all that is in them, and rested on the seventh day, and hallowed it." The Lord our God worked for six days in creating heaven and earth, the sea, and all that is in them; and on the seventh day He rested, and ordained that day as the appointed time for us to rest. On the seventh day we must think of the works that God did in the six days; the children of God must call to mind what great blessings they have received during the week, for which they must thank and praise God, and by which they must learn about God. We must then dedicate to Him our entire body and soul, and consecrate to Him all our words and works. As on that day the Lord rested from creating but continued to preserve, so on that day we must rest from manual and bodily labours, but continue to do good works and worship God. Further, God's rest did no harm to the things He had created; nor shall the holy day, or sabbath, spent in God's service, hamper or hinder our affairs or business. For the Lord blessed the sabbath day; therefore He will bless you and your house, all your affairs and business, if He sees that you are careful to sanctify His sabbath, by doing those works that He has commanded on the sabbath day. They stray from the truth as far as heaven is wide who despise the religion and holy rest of the sabbath day, calling it an idle ease, and who labour on the sabbath day as they do on working days, under the pretence of caring for their family and necessity's sake.

All these things we must apply to ourselves and our churches. It is most certain that to Christians the spiritual sabbath is particularly entrusted above all things. We must not doubt that the good Lord's will is that even in our churches at this day, order should be kept and appointed in all things, especially in the exercises of outward religion. We know that the sabbath is ceremonial, to the extent that it is joined with sacrifices and other Jewish rites, and to the extent that it is tied to a certain time. But to the extent that on the sabbath day religion and true godliness are exercised and set forth, that a just and seemly order is kept in the church, and that the love of our neighbour is thereby preserved, in these respects the sabbath is not ceremonial but perpetual. Even today we must take thought for the comfort of our family, and instruct them in true religion and the fear of God. Our Lord Christ nowhere scattered abroad the holy congregations, but gathered them together as much as He could. Just as there should be an appointed place, so there should be a prescribed time for the outward exercise of religion, and so consequently a holy rest.

Those of the early Church, therefore, changed the sabbath day, in case they should seem to have copied the Jews and retained their order and ceremonies. Instead they made their assemblies and holy rests to be on the first day after the sabbaths, which John calls Sunday or the Lord's day, because of the Lord's glorious resurrection on that day. We do not find anywhere in the apostles' writings any mention that Sunday was commanded to be kept holy; but because we are commanded in the fourth precept of the law's first table to have a care for religion and the exercises of outward godliness, it would be against all godliness and Christian charity if we refused to keep Sunday holy, especially since the outward worship of God cannot exist without an appointed time and place of holy rest.

I reckon we should have the same attitude to those few feasts and holy days which we keep holy to Christ our Lord, in memory of His nativity or incarnation, His circumcision, His passion, the resurrection and ascension of Jesus Christ our Lord into heaven, and His sending the Holy Spirit upon His disciples. For Christian liberty is not a licentious power or a dissolving of godly Church ordinances which promote and set forth God's glory and the love of our neighbour. However, because the Lord wants holy days to be kept solemn to Himself alone, I dislike those festival days that are held in honour of mere created beings. This glory and worship is due to God alone...

If we would truly sanctify our Sunday and keep it holy, we must spend it in four things which ought to be found in the holy congregation of Christians. First, let all the godly saints assemble together in the congregation. In the assembled congregation, let the Word of God be preached; let the gospel be read, so that hearers may discern what to think concerning God, what the worshipper's duty and function is, and how we should sanctify the Lord's name. Then in the congregation let prayers and supplications be made for all the needs of all people. Let the Lord be praised for His goodness, and thanked for His inestimable benefits which He daily bestows. Then, if the time, occasion, and custom of the church requires it, let the sacraments of the church be religiously administered. For the fourth commandment requires above all that we should observe the sacraments in a holy way, and devoutly exercise them, along with all the holy, lawful, profitable, and necessary rites and ceremonies of the church. Lastly, let compassion and generosity have a place in the saints' assembly; let all learn to give charitable gifts privately, and relieve the poor daily, and do it frankly and openly whenever opportunity of time and causes of need may require. These are the duties in which the Lord's sabbath is kept holy even in the Christian Church; and even more so, if to these duties we add an earnest good-will to do no evil all the day long. This discipline must now be brought in and established by every householder in all our several houses, with as great a diligence as it was among the Jews.

Heinrich Bullinger, *Decades*, Second Decade, sermon 4.

Chapter 4.

RIPENESS TO THE CORE: JOHN CALVIN AND THE REFORMED FAITH.

1. The Reformation: losing momentum?

In the period 1521-31, as we have seen, the Reformation took deep root in Germany and Switzerland, displayed great spiritual and theological energy, and also affected many other countries (see Chapters 6 and 7). The Reformers had the initiative, while Rome staggered about, seemingly unable to make any effective response. By contrast, the period 1531-41 arguably saw the Reformation losing some of its momentum. The great reformist movement was becoming more and more confused and divided, with the lasting split between Lutherans, Reformed, and Radicals, and disagreements even within each camp. In an age which took the outward and visible unity of the Church very seriously, this break-up of Catholic Europe into warring religious factions seemed like some appalling judgment of God. Many devout Westerners who had been attracted to the Reformation felt their enthusiasm grow cold; if the price of rejecting the papacy was a descent into chaos, they were not willing to pay. On top of this, the way that the Protestant Churches of Germany and Switzerland submitted meekly to state control was deeply disturbing to some spiritually-minded Roman Catholics, who might otherwise have looked more favourably on Protestantism. It made them wonder whether, after all, the papacy was the only real guarantee of the freedom and independence of the Church.

Meanwhile, Roman Catholic persecution of Protestants made people think twice before embracing a faith that could swiftly lead them to an agonising death. The Roman Catholic civil authorities had burnt the first Lutheran martyrs at the stake at Brussels in the Netherlands in 1523, and many other Protestant martyrdoms followed, especially in Austria and Bavaria in the aftermath of the Peasants' Revolt of 1524-25 (see previous Chapter, section 3), but also across the rest of Western Europe. Roman Catholic countries banned and burnt Protestant books too; it could be a difficult as well as dangerous business just trying to find out what Luther and Zwingli were saying. Moreover, the Roman Church was beginning to revive its spiritual powers under pope Paul III (1534-49). It was looking ever more likely that Paul would summon an ecumenical Council of the Church and enact genuine reforms. Under these circumstances, why should reforming Catholics abandon their Church for the uncertainties and divisions of Protestantism?[1]

Fear of the Radical wing of the Reformation also deterred many from embracing Protestantism.[2] In 1534-35, a Radical revolution in the city of Münster, in north-western Germany, shocked the educated and ruling classes of Western Europe to the marrow. It began harmlessly enough. The humanist priest and scholar **Bernard Rothmann** (1495-1535) introduced the Reformation into Münster in 1529, winning over the vast majority by his preaching. Until 1533, indeed, it seemed that Münster was simply going the same way as most north German cities and becoming Lutheran. That same year, however, Rothmann renounced his belief in infant baptism. This brought him into conflict with the Lutheran magistrates of the city, but huge popular support for Rothmann broke the magistrates' power and placed Münster firmly in the hands of Rothmann and his Radical followers.

The news that a whole city had embraced the Radical Reformation brought Radicals flocking to Münster from all over the Holy Roman Empire, especially from the Netherlands where they were

---

[1]   See Chapter 8, **The Catholic Counter-Reformation**.
[2]   See previous Chapter, section 2, and the whole of the next Chapter.

being persecuted with the greatest severity. By February 1534, a group of Radical fanatics had usurped Rothmann's leadership of the Münster Reformation. Two remarkable Netherlanders headed the group: *Jan Mathys* (died 1534), who reputedly received direct personal guidance from dreams and visions, and claimed to be the prophet Enoch; and *Jan Beukels* of Leyden (died 1535), Mathys's most beloved disciple, a hypnotically dominating personality. Mathys and Beukels declared Münster to be the New Jerusalem. After Mathys's death in April 1534, Beukels had himself crowned king of the city, abolished private property, and ruthlessly executed opponents of his regime. The death penalty for blasphemy, adultery, disobedience to parents, theft, and begging (among other things) was imposed. In the last few months of Beukels' reign in 1535, he introduced polygamy, with the full support of Rothmann, the other preachers, and (perhaps surprisingly) the women.

We can partly explain the wild actions of Münster's Radical regime by the extreme state of mind caused by the city's military and economic situation. Throughout this entire period of Radical rule, Münster was under siege by its Roman Catholic prince-bishop, Franz von Waldeck, and his troops. Conditions inside the besieged city were increasingly desperate, and Waldeck's men killed without mercy anyone who tried to leave. Finally, after 16 months of intense misery, Münster was betrayed to the besieging army in June 1535 by a Radical – Heinrich Gresbeck – whose faith in the "New Jerusalem" had crumbled. Gresbeck showed the Roman Catholic troops how to gain entrance to the city. They slaughtered most of the inhabitants (including Rothmann). As for the few who survived, notably Beukels himself, Waldeck put them on trial and had them tortured to death with great cruelty. So the dream of the Radical New Jerusalem perished in fire and blood.

Münster was the supreme disaster for the Radical Reformation. From now on, all Roman Catholic and almost all Protestant authorities assumed that all Radicals were violent enemies of social stability and Christian morality, plotting to overthrow the established order and introduce communism and polygamy. Governments henceforth persecuted them with an unreasoning fear and a savage ferocity that were otherwise directed only at witches. The bulk of peace-loving Radicals suffered grievously for the sins of the fanatical few.[3] But the cause of Luther and Zwingli suffered as well. Men blamed the Magisterial Reformers and their revolt against Rome for having unloosed the storms of revolution which led to Münster.

Despite what could be seen as its temporary loss of momentum, however, Protestantism recovered in the 1540s in a massive way, through the extraordinary growth and consolidation of its Reformed wing. Apart from the Scandinavian countries and most of northern Germany, Lutheranism began to be supplanted in one region after another by Reformed Christianity, which became the cutting edge of the Reformation in Europe. Prior to this, we must remember that the Reformed faith was concentrated in the four city states of Switzerland (Zurich, Basel, Berne, and Schaffhausen), and in Strasbourg. By the 1560s, it had spread with startling speed and vigour across France, southern Germany, the Netherlands, England, Scotland, and large swathes of Eastern Europe, mounting a militant challenge to Roman Catholicism, creating Church structures and forms of Christian life that transformed entire cultures, and producing writings of such high spiritual and theological calibre that they have stood the test of time and are still being widely studied today.[4] This astonishing development was not the work of a single man, but undoubtedly there were five key figures who more than any others helped to articulate the Reformed vision: Ulrich Zwingli, Heinrich Bullinger, Martin Bucer, Peter Martyr, and John Calvin. We have already encountered Zwingli and Bullinger and their contributions in the previous Chapter. Let us now look at the other three.

---

[3]   On the other hand, we must not underestimate the extent to which violence appealed to considerable numbers of the Radicals. See Chapter 5.

[4]   For the geographical spread of both Lutheranism and Reformed Protestantism outside their cradle territories, see Chapter 6.

Martin Bucer
(1491-1551)

2. Martin Bucer

The Reformation in Strasbourg, one of the greatest urban centres of humanism, played a central part in shaping the distinctive outlook of the Reformed Churches; a number of leading Reformed theologians taught in the city at various times. ***Martin Bucer*** (1491-1551) was the most important of these. Born in Sélestat (then in south-western Germany, now in France), he became a Dominican friar in his youth, drank deeply of the Christian humanism of Erasmus, and devoted himself to the early Church fathers. The Heidelberg disputation in April 1518 won him over to Luther's cause.[5] In consequence, Bucer abandoned the Dominican order in 1521, and married an ex-nun, Elizabeth Silbereisen, in 1522. After the Roman Catholic Church excommunicated him for his "Lutheran" preaching in south-western Germany, he sought refuge in Strasbourg in 1523. Once in Strasbourg, Bucer swiftly took over leadership of the reform movement in the city, which had begun in 1521 with the preaching of Matthew Zell, priest of the Saint Laurence chapel in Strasbourg's cathedral. Bucer produced Strasbourg's new Protestant liturgy in 1524, and in 1530 became president of the city's "Church council".

Under Bucer's guidance, the Strasbourg Reformation steered a middle path between Zwinglian and Lutheran, but with more of a leaning towards Lutheran patterns. As we saw in the last Chapter, Bucer was present on Zwingli's side at the Marburg colloquy in 1529, where the Lutheran and Reformed branches of Protestantism finally took their separate paths. Nevertheless, after the failure of Marburg, Bucer thought his way to a more traditional doctrine of the eucharist than Zwingli had held. He argued that Christ's body and blood are "exhibited" and "offered" through the bread and wine, so that believers do truly receive Christ by faith when they eat and drink. Bucer even managed to secure agreement with Luther in 1536 in the Wittenberg Concord, which stated that Christ's body and blood are truly and objectively given "with" the

---

[5]   For the Heidelberg disputation, see Chapter 2, section 2.

bread and wine, and are received even by the unworthy.[6] The long-term future of the Wittenberg Concord, however, was nullified by Bucer's refusal to accept that *unbelievers* receive Christ's body and blood, a point that was crucial for Luther. Bucer defined the "unworthy" who receive Christ's body and blood as true believers who participate in the Supper in an unworthy way. But those who have no faith at all, Bucer said, receive only bread and wine.

Bucer's quest for harmony with Lutherans was typical of his lifelong passion for Christian unity, of which he was the out-standing advocate among 16th century Protestants. Chiefly this was unity among all forms of the Magisterial Reformation, but Bucer was also committed to dialogue with Roman Catholics. He was willing to learn even from Anabaptists, despite finding them a distasteful bunch; Strasbourg was a safe haven for Radicals until the 1530s. Bucer's "ecumenism" flowed from the way in which the Church occupied an ever more central place in his theology. He dissented from the state control of the Church that had marked the Reformation up till then; for Bucer, the Church was a divine society, quite distinct from the state, and Christ was the Church's only Lord and Head.

Bucer believed that Christ exercised this Lordship and Headship in the Church through special offices of ministry which were set down in Scripture. Bucer was not entirely clear or consistent on the number of these offices, but he mentions most often the pastor, the elder, and the deacon, sometimes adding the teacher and the evangelist. (We will look at these more fully when we consider Calvin's theology.) Through these ministries, the Holy Spirit animated the Church as Christ's body to carry out its mission, which Bucer defined as evangelism, pastoral care, and moral discipline. The Church was "a community in which the Word and sacraments, love and discipline, prevail". Discipline figured

---

6   When Calvin ministered in Strasbourg in 1538-41, he signed the Wittenberg Concord. Given that the Concord was subscribed by Luther, Bucer, and Calvin, it can claim to be the closest that Lutherans and Reformed came in the 16th century to confessional agreement on the Lord's Supper.

increasingly in Bucer's view of Church life, and he insisted that excommunication was the prerogative, not of the magistrate, but of the pastors and elders. Martin Bucer, then, lies at the fountainhead of what became the Reformed view of the Church and its govern-ment and ministries. He was not able to put much flesh on this vision in Strasbourg, but it was to be taken up and given a fairly full embodiment by Calvin in Geneva.

Bucer's theology of the Church was allied to a theology of society. Christianity was not merely a personal affair, nor even merely a Church affair, but something that God intended to pervade human life in its totality. Bucer envisaged society as a "Christian com-monwealth" in which Church and state cooperated to establish the Lordship of Christ over all society's affairs. This outlook flowed in part from Bucer's Erasmian humanism: he accepted Erasmus's ideal of the rebirth of human life and culture. As a Protestant Reformer, however, he saw this rebirth happening through the proclamation of God's Word and obedience to the divinely appointed model for Church and state. In Bucer's mind, both Church and state existed in order to serve Christ, although in different ways: the chief practical difference was that the state was empowered to use force, but the Church could use only persuasion. The Church, Bucer argued, was subject to the state in all matters where the state was responsible for community life; the state in its turn was subject to the Church, in that magistrates should consult Church leaders for their views on the moral principles which underlie social and political life. This partnership and mutual subordination of Church and state was, Bucer believed, Christ's way of permeating society with His influence, so that the whole of human life would be gradually re-ordered on the basis of service to one's neighbour.[7] Bucer's concept of the Christian commonwealth was expressed most completely in his *De Regno Christi* ("Concern-ing the Kingdom of Christ"), written in 1550 when Bucer was in England – the work was dedicated to the young English king,

---

[7] Bucer shared out the tasks of Church and state rather differently from what is common today. For instance, he made the Church, not the state, responsible for education and for poor relief.

Edward VI.[8] It was a perspective on the relationship between
Christianity and society that became a Reformed distinctive:
Lutherans tended to consign the state and all its works to the realm
of "natural law", in which pagans could be wiser and more effective than Christians.[9]

Bucer also contributed richly to the growth of biblical scholarship
and biblical preaching among Protestants. From the earliest days of
the Strasbourg Reformation, lectures on the Bible were delivered in
German to enthusiastic audiences of ordinary people. Bucer himself
lectured on the Gospels, the psalms, and the pastoral epistles; these
lectures were then published as commentaries. Most readers today
find Bucer's biblical commentaries unreadable owing to their
awkward literary style, but in the 16th century they were very highly
regarded in the Reformed world. As a good German humanist,
Bucer advocated the grammatico-historical method of biblical
interpretation, emphasising that each biblical writer should be
studied on his own terms, seeking to discover the distinguishing
features of each prophet or apostle's own individual teaching.
Alongside this, Bucer also placed a primary emphasis on the
interpretation of Scripture that the early Church fathers held; they,
Bucer believed, were the guardians in a general sense of the correct
understanding of the Bible.

Bucer's amazingly fruitful reforming career in Strasbourg came to a
sudden end in 1548, when the Holy Roman emperor Charles V,
having defeated the Protestant Schmalkaldic League on the field of
battle, enforced a religious settlement on Germany known as the
"Augsburg Interim".[10] Bucer opposed the Interim as too Roman
Catholic, and was compelled to leave Strasbourg. The English
Reformer, archbishop Cranmer, invited Bucer to settle in England;
Bucer accepted and, arriving in 1549, taught theology at

---

[8]   For the English Reformation, see Chapter 7.
[9]   Luther's dictum was that he would prefer to live under the government of a
       wise pagan than a foolish Christian. The Reformed retort has always been that
       a wise Christian is better than either.
[10]   See Chapter 8 for these events.

Cambridge university. He had significant input into Cranmer's second Book of Common Prayer. Having struggled with ill health for some time, Bucer died and was buried in England in 1551.[11]

Other leading Strasbourg Reformers were **Caspar Hedio** (1494-1552), **Wolfgang Capito** (1478-1541), and **Jacob Sturm** (1498-1553). All three men were highly educated Christian humanists who switched their loyalties from Erasmus to Luther and Zwingli. Hedio and Capito were unusual among the Magisterial Reformers in their mild and even open-minded attitude towards Radicals; Hedio resolutely opposed inflicting any punishment on them greater than banishment, while Capito welcomed Radicals into his house and held frequent friendly discussions with them. Jacob Sturm was an outstanding example of a Reformer who was not a clergyman, but a well-informed layman and politician devoted to the Protestant faith; from 1526, Sturm was Strasbourg's chief magistrate.

3. Peter Martyr

Another illustrious Reformer who taught in Strasbourg between 1543 and 1547 was **Peter Martyr** (1499-1562) – or Peter Martyr Vermigli, to give him his full name.[12] Martyr stands alongside Luther, Melanchthon, Zwingli, Bullinger, Bucer, and Calvin as a giant among the Protestant leaders of the 16th century. Born in Florence, Italy, he joined the Augustinian friars in his youth, becoming an ardent disciple of Augustine's theology, as well as a walking treasury of knowledge on the early Church fathers in general. The period 1530-42 saw him occupying several leadership posts in his Augustinian order within Italy, at Spoleto, Naples, and Lucca. Two things happened to Martyr during this time. First, he

---

[11] During the persecution of Protestants in England under queen Mary Tudor (1553-8), Bucer's body was dug up and burnt. See Chapter 7 for Cranmer and other figures in the English Reformation.

[12] Vermigli is pronounced "Vair-mee-lee". He was named after the 13th century Dominican, Peter Martyr (1200-1252).

Peter Martyr
(1499-1562)

became acquainted with the writings of the Reformers: Zwingli's *Concerning True and False Religion*, for example, and Bucer's commentaries on the Gospels and the psalms, made a deep impression on him. Second, he became part of the Catholic reforming circle of the Spanish humanist, Juan de Valdes. For a while, Martyr was content to be a Catholic Evangelical, enjoying the support of the great Catholic Evangelical leader, cardinal Gasparo Contarini.[13] The influence of Valdes, however, pushed Martyr's heart and mind further and further in the direction of Protestantism, which he was now all but teaching in the Augustinian convent at Lucca. Summoned to appear before the Augustinians' governing body on suspicion of heresy, Martyr fled from Italy in the summer of 1542, now an avowed Protestant.

Martyr settled in Strasbourg where he taught Old Testament studies for four years and became an intimate friend of Bucer. From 1547 to 1553 Martyr was in England at the invitation of archbishop Cranmer, teaching theology at Oxford and helping to reform the English Church. When the Roman Catholic Mary Tudor became queen in 1553, Martyr was placed under house arrest, but (in one of the more pleasant episodes of Mary's otherwise brutal reign) his Roman Catholic arch-enemy, Stephen Gardiner, bishop of Winchester, persuaded Mary to let Martyr return unharmed to the Continent. At first he went back to Strasbourg, but the once Reformed city was now dominated by strict Lutherans under the leadership of Johann Marbach, who regarded the Reformed as deluded sectarians little better than Anabaptists. Finally disgusted with Lutheran hostility and intolerance, Martyr left Strasbourg in 1556 to become professor of Hebrew in Zurich at the invitation of Bullinger. His last great public act before his death was to lead the Protestant delegation (along with Calvin's right hand man, Theodore Beza) at the colloquy of Poissy in 1561. This was intended to heal the religious divisions in France between Protestants and Roman Catholics, and (remarkably) it managed to draft an agreed joint statement on the eucharist. Eventually, however, the colloquy

---

[13]   For the Catholic Evangelicals, Juan de Valdes, and cardinal Contarini, see Chapter 8, section 1.

failed through the intransigence of the majority of Roman Catholic delegates.

Peter Martyr was unique among the early Reformers in combining his Protestant faith with a high regard for Aristotle. Martyr was thoroughly trained in Aristotelian logic and philosophy, and traditional Roman Catholic scholastic theologians feared him more than any other Protestant Reformer, simply because Martyr could wipe out Roman Catholics in debate with their own scholastic weapons. His immense impact on his fellow Protestants came chiefly in three ways:

(i) Martyr wrote a number of Biblical commentaries which were admired as models of Reformed exposition for the next 200 years. Most influential was his 1558 commentary on Romans.

(ii) Soon after Martyr's death, a French Reformed pastor named Robert Masson trawled through Martyr's commentaries and gathered together a mass of quotations arranged under topical headings as a systematic theology. Entitled *Loci Communes*,[14] it became one of the standard Reformed textbooks of doctrine for the next hundred years, perhaps second only to Calvin's *Institutes* in its fame and influence.

(iii) Along with Calvin, Martyr crafted the Reformed doctrine of holy communion into its final form. He did this especially in his *Defence of the Ancient and Apostolic Doctrine of the Most Holy Sacrament of the Eucharist* (1559), which was aimed against the Roman Catholic view, and his *Dialogue Concerning the Two Natures in Christ* (1561), aimed at the Lutheran doctrine. The first of these tomes has been called the greatest single work on the Lord's Supper from the entire Reformation era. Calvin said of Martyr's writings on the eucharist, "Peter Martyr brought the entire doctrine to perfection, leaving nothing more to be desired." Martyr placed the Lord's Supper in the context of union with Christ, and

---

[14] Not to be confused with Melanchthon's work of the same name.

argued that the Supper was a visible sign through which Christ and His believing people were bound together in the Holy Spirit. Although the bread and wine were nothing but symbols in themselves, they became through the Spirit "an instrument with effect, for these symbols are not only signs of Christ's body and blood, but also instruments which the Holy Spirit uses to feed us spiritually with the body and blood of the Lord." To those who asked why the sacraments were needed at all since believers had the Spirit, Martyr responded that human beings were not naked spirits but also creatures of flesh and blood. Just as the eternal Son of God did not save us from the heights of heaven but became flesh on earth, so He communicated Himself to us through visible, material forms, through the water of baptism and the bread and wine of the eucharist. The material and the spiritual belonged together:

> "We understand our union with Christ to extend not only to spirit and soul, but also to body and flesh. Whence no wonder the old [early Church] fathers said that in the Lord's Supper not only is our soul and spirit quickened by the flesh and blood of Christ, but also our body and flesh are fed from thence, so that they are restored more fit and firm to the use of good works, by which Christ is served."

Martyr, along with Calvin, staked out a distinctively Reformed understanding of the Lord's Supper which put clear blue water between it and the Roman Catholic, Lutheran, and Radical views. The Roman and Lutheran doctrines he rejected essentially on the basis that Christ's body was located physically in heaven until the second coming; the Radical view (which he interpreted as a bare "memorialism", *i.e.* that the function of the eucharist is simply to help us remember what Christ did) he rejected on the basis that it left out the Holy Spirit, who united believers to Christ and gave them a real life-giving communion in His risen and glorified humanity. Martyr also cited impressive support from the early Church fathers to back up his view; he was perhaps unsurpassed among 16th century Protestants as a student of the fathers.

John Calvin (1509-64)

4. The young Calvin, 1509-35.

Martin Bucer and Peter Martyr were theological giants by any standard, and the fact that their present day reputation is almost totally eclipsed by the more celebrated John Calvin must not blind us to their significance as founding fathers of the Reformed faith, nor impel us to give an undue prominence to Calvin. Calvin never was to Reformed Protestantism the dominating figure that Luther was to Lutheranism. Nonetheless, it remains true that if any single person among the Reformed pioneers had ultimately the most far-reaching influence on Church and world, it was surely Calvin.

John Calvin was born at Noyon in Picardy, north-eastern France, in 1509, the son of a Church lawyer attached to Noyon Cathedral. His social background was more "upper class" than Luther's, something that helps to account for the mature Calvin's rather aloof, aristocratic personality; when a Protestant refugee met Calvin after the latter had become the Reformer of Geneva, he addressed him as "brother Calvin", only to be told that the correct form of address was "Monsieur Calvin". Calvin's father Gérard intended him to enter the Roman Catholic priesthood, so the youthful Calvin prepared himself by studying at Paris university from 1523 to 1528, first at the College de la Marche, where he learned Latin from one of its greatest teachers of the day, Mathurin Cordier. Cordier must have made an impression on young Calvin; many years later, the Reformer dedicated to his old Latin teacher his commentary on 1 Thessalonians. It is worth quoting:

> "It is only right that you should come in for a share in my labours, since under your patronage, having entered on a course of study, I gained a proficiency which prepared me to be useful, in some degree, to the Church of God. When my father sent me, while yet a boy, to Paris, after I had simply tasted the first elements of the Latin tongue, providence arranged that I had, for a short time, the privilege of having you as my instructor. I was taught by you the true method of

learning, in such a way that I might be prepared afterwards to acquire a somewhat better competence... I derived so much assistance afterwards from your training, that it is with good reason that I acknowledge myself indebted to you for such progress as has since been made. And this I desired to testify to posterity, so that, if any advantage shall be added to them from my writings, they shall know that it has in some degree originated with you."

The mature Calvin's Latin was unusually pure and beautiful; we can see in his time at the College de la Marche under Cordier the beginnings of the Reformer's future brilliant style.

After his arts course, Calvin then moved to the College de Montaigu; one of his teachers here was the celebrated Scottish thinker **John Major** (1467-1550), a scholastic theologian in the *via moderna* tradition. Major was a strong conciliarist, rejecting any idea of the papacy's absolute authority; but he was also a stern critic of Luther and Zwingli, especially their sacramental theology. Historians have speculated on the nature and extent of Major's influence on Calvin. All we can really say is that he introduced the young Calvin to the *via moderna*, which made the later Protestant Calvin identify scholasticism with an anti-Augustinian view of grace and free will, and condemn it on that basis, and that Major's public opposition to Luther and Zwingli must have at least made Calvin aware of some of their doctrines. While a student in Paris, Calvin also formed a close friendship with Nicholas Cop, a zealous Christian humanist whose father was physician to the French king **Francis I** (1515-47). This friendship was to have important consequences.

In 1527, Calvin's father quarrelled with the canons of Noyon Cathedral and decided that his son should not become a priest after all, but a lawyer. So Calvin now terminated his theology studies and became a law student at Orleans and Bourges (central France). Here he also took pains to acquire the riches of the new humanist culture, learning Greek. To a far greater degree than the young

Luther, the early Calvin was a typical Christian humanist scholar. When his father died unexpectedly in 1531, this left Calvin free to abandon law and dedicate himself to Christian humanism at the College de France in Paris. The College, financed by king Francis I, was a humanist paradise; among its lecturers were Calvin's friend Nicholas Cop, and the great humanist and Greek scholar, William Budé.[15] This brought Calvin into the circle of devout scholars who looked for inspiration to France's greatest Christian humanist reformer, Jacques Lefevre d'Étaples.[16] At the College, Calvin mastered Hebrew as well as Greek, and also wrote his first book, a commentary on a moral treatise called *De Clementia* ("Concerning Mercy") by Seneca, the ancient Roman Stoic philosopher.[17] It was published in 1532, and Calvin sent a copy to Erasmus. The book clinched Calvin's reputation as a budding humanist scholar; but there was no hint in it that he had yet embraced the Protestant faith.

However, some time between 1532 and 1534, Calvin passed over (like so many others) from Christian humanism into avowed Protestantism. We do not know exactly when or how it happened. One important influence may have been a Waldensian merchant, Etienne de la Forge, in whose house in Paris Calvin lodged. De la Forge and Calvin were good friends, and the Waldensian had embraced the Reformation with enthusiasm; he used his house and his wealth to give shelter to Protestant refugees from the Netherlands. Another influence was probably Calvin's cousin, Pierre Robert Olivétan, who had embraced Protestantism in the 1520s. Olivétan translated the Bible into French in 1535, and Calvin (by then a Protestant himself) wrote the preface. At any rate, Calvin later described his conversion like this, in the preface to his commentary on the psalms:

> "Since I was more stubbornly addicted to the superstitions of
> the papacy than to be easily pulled out of that deep swamp,
> by a sudden conversion God subdued my heart (too hard-

---

[15] For Budé, see Chapter 1, section 3.
[16] For Lefevre, see Chapter 1, section 3.
[17] For Seneca, see Part One, Chapter 1, section 1, under **Stoicism**.

ened for one so young) to a teachable spirit. Thus, having gained some taste of true godliness, I burned with great zeal to make progress. Although I did not give up my former studies, I pursued them with less enthusiasm; and a year had not passed when all who desired this purer doctrine flocked to me, newcomer and beginner though I was, in order to learn it."

We cannot be sure if Calvin had become a Protestant by November 1533, but he was at least committed to some kind of reform movement which got him into serious trouble. On November 1st 1533 Calvin's friend, Nicholas Cop, gave a speech as the newly appointed rector of Paris university. Cop used the occasion to issue a humanist call for reformation in the Church, attacking scholastic theology and quoting Erasmus and Luther with approval.[18] The speech caused an uproar among traditional Catholics, and it provoked king Francis I into adopting a more repressive policy towards Protestants and their sympathisers. Cop fled to the Swiss Protestant city of Basel;[19] Calvin escaped from Paris disguised as a gardener and went into hiding in Angoulême (western France). France became an even more dangerous country for Protestant sympathisers in 1534, after the citizens of Paris woke up on the morning of October 19th and found the city covered with posters condemning the Roman Catholic mass as blasphemy and the Roman clergy as servants of Antichrist. The posters were the work of an extreme Protestant, Antoine Marcourt. The result was an outbreak of violent government persecution of French Protestants; in Paris, the authorities burnt 24 Protestants at the stake (including Calvin's Waldensian friend, Etienne de la Forge), and imprisoned and tortured many others. Now clearly a Protestant himself, Calvin followed in Nicholas Cop's footsteps and fled to Basel, arriving there in January 1535.

---

[18] Some historians have thought that Calvin wrote Cop's speech, but modern scholarship tends to reject this idea. All we can say for certain is that Calvin had a copy of the speech (or parts of it, at least) written in his own hand.

[19] Nothing more is known of Cop after this.

5. "The Institutes of the Christian Religion", 1536.

To justify his burning of Protestants, Francis I of France issued a public letter in 1535 accusing French Protestants of being political rebels intent on overthrowing the government (perhaps not surprising in the aftermath of Münster – see section 1). Calvin felt he must defend his persecuted brothers and sisters against this slander, and in March 1536 he published a short book which he had begun writing in Angoulême, called *Institutes of the Christian Religion*, prefaced by an open letter to Francis I. The letter was a masterpiece; with dignity and passion, Calvin set forth the essence of the Protestant position and vindicated French Protestants from Francis I's false accusations. From that moment, the world regarded 26 year old Calvin as the foremost champion of French Protestantism.

The book to which Calvin attached the letter, the *Institutes*, was an orderly summary of Christian doctrine and the Christian life as understood by Protestants. It was the clearest, most elegant, and best-organised presentation of Reformation theology and spirituality which had yet appeared. *Institutes* is the English form of the book's Latin title *Institutio*, which has a range of meanings – "instruction", "manual", "summary". A great success, the book sold well, and a second edition (greatly enlarged) came out in 1539. Throughout his life, Calvin continued to expand and revise the *Institutes*; the final edition was published in 1559, and it became the standard textbook of Reformed theology. The *Institutes* was a work of literary as well as theological brilliance, written in beautiful Latin and French (there were editions in both languages); the French editions had a notable impact on the future development of the French tongue.

The final 1559 edition of the *Institutes* was divided into four books. Calvin based this fourfold structure on the Apostles' Creed, with its four central assertions:

Apostles' Creed	Calvin's *Institutes*
"I believe in God the Father almighty, Creator of heaven and earth"	**Book One** – "The Knowledge of God the Creator"
"And in Jesus Christ, His only Son, our Lord"	**Book Two** – "The Knowledge of God the Redeemer in Christ"
"I believe in the Holy Spirit"	**Book Three** – "The Way we Receive the Grace of Christ"
"I believe in the holy Catholic Church"	**Book Four** – "The External Means or Aids by which God Invites us into the Society of Christ"

By setting out the *Institutes* like this, Calvin was making an important point: Protestants had not invented new doctrines of their own; they were simply rejecting the various errors that had grown up in the Western Catholic Church during the Middle Ages, and returning to the pure apostolic faith of the early Church. Calvin himself was one of the 16th century's great students of the early Church fathers; his writings overflowed with patristic quotations, especially from Augustine of Hippo.[20] Calvin also had some familiarity with the great Catholic theologians of the Middle Ages. Frequently, indeed, Calvin referred to the medieval thinkers only to criticise them, but he exempted Bernard of Clairvaux from this general condemnation, quoting the famous Cistercian monk with warm approval.[21]

The basic theology of the *Institutes* was the Reformation Gospel of salvation by God's grace alone through faith alone in Christ alone. Like Luther, Zwingli, and the other Magisterial Reformers, Calvin was a disciple of Augustine, and taught a strongly Augustinian doctrine of humanity's helpless bondage to sin, and the absolute sovereignty of God's grace in predestination and salvation. Many

---

[20] For the early Church fathers, see Part One.
[21] For Bernard, see Part Two, Chapter 5, section 3, under **The Second Crusade**.

people today associate the doctrine of predestination with Calvin in particular, as if he invented it, but this is a very serious misunderstanding of Church history. Most of the great Western theologians of the Middle Ages held a form of Augustinianism, and all the leading Protestant theologians of the Magisterial Reformation stood with Calvin in teaching the doctrine of God's sovereignty in salvation – because they had all alike drunk deeply from the fountain of Augustine's writings. Indeed, many loyal Roman Catholics in the 16th century were convinced Augustinians in their theology.[22] What divided the Protestant and Roman Catholic Augustinians was their differing views of the Church, and it was in this area that Calvin made his outstanding contribution to the Reformation.

Three main views on the Church had come to dominate the minds of those who were living through the upheavals of the Reformation:

(i) The Roman Catholic view. This defined the Church as the outward and visible organisation governed by the papacy, in which life-giving grace flowed through the sacraments administered by the Roman Catholic priesthood. The Church was separate from the state and independent of state control, but entered into partnership with the state in order to create a Christian society.

(ii) The Lutheran view. This defined the Church as the spiritual body of all who were truly united to Christ by personal faith – a body infallibly known to God alone, and thus invisible to human eyes, with Christ alone as its head. The outward and visible Church of professing Christians and their children, characterised by the preaching of the Gospel and the administration of the genuine New Testament sacraments of baptism and eucharist, was governed by the state – the Christian king, prince, or city council. The power of

---

[22] For the Roman Catholic Augustinians of the 16th century, see Chapter 8, section 1.

excommunication belonged to the Christian state, not to the Church.[23]

(iii) The Anabaptist view. This saw the Church as the visible congregational fellowship of the redeemed, made up exclusively of those who had experienced conversion, to which they testified by believers' baptism and the Lord's Supper. It was kept pure by the exercise of Church discipline, ultimately by the power of excommunication which belonged to the local congregation. The Church was separate from the state, and must never enter into any partnership with the state.

Calvin rejected all three views, but took over elements from all three in setting out his own understanding. He was not alone in his thinking here; Martin Bucer had already set forth most of what Calvin was to say. Calvin, however, said it with greater force, and moreover was able to put his and Bucer's ideal into practical effect in Geneva, something Bucer had never managed to achieve in Strasbourg. In what follows, then, although it is presented as Calvin's view, we should keep in mind that Calvin was building on foundations laid by Bucer.

Calvin agreed with Luther that the true Church was the spiritual body of all true believers, infallibly known to God alone. But he agreed with Rome that the outward visible Church (within which true believers were spiritually born and nurtured) was of supreme practical importance, and must enter into partnership with the state in order to build a Christian society – Calvin accepted the concept of the Christian state. However, he also agreed with Rome and the Anabaptists that the institutional Church was independent of the state and should not be controlled by it. And he agreed with the Anabaptists that the Church must exercise a strong internal discipline to ensure that its members were made up of those who professed the true faith and lived a Christian life. The power of

---

[23] This Lutheran view was also the Reformed view until Calvin persuaded most of the Reformed Churches to think again.

excommunication, Calvin held, belonged to the Church, not to the Christian state.

This Bucer-Calvin view of Church and state, and the relationship between them (as we noted in Chapter 3, it has been called the "Reformed Catholic" ideal), constituted a distinctive and powerful force within the Magisterial Reformation. It saved most of the Reformed Churches from becoming merely departments of state, politically controlled – the condition into which the "statist" Lutheran Churches had drifted. In Bucer's and Calvin's thought, as in Roman Catholicism, the Church once again stood forth as a divinely ordained, free, independent society, with its own God-given laws and officers. This time, however, the Church was a Protestant body, with no pope, acknowledging Christ as its only Head, submitting to Scripture alone, and teaching justification by faith alone.

Calvin's exalted view of the visible Church found further expression in the distinctive system of Church government which he taught. Calvin maintained that there were four permanent offices in the New Testament Church: pastor, teacher, elder, and deacon.

The *pastors* led the public services of worship; their chief duties were expounding the Scriptures to a congregation, administering the two Protestant sacraments of baptism and eucharist, and exercising Church discipline together with the elders. Normally there would only be one pastor, but in larger congregations Calvin was quite happy to see several pastors sharing the work.

The *teachers* (or "doctors") were responsible for instructing people in Christian doctrine – the young in schools, and those training for the ministry in theology colleges. They took no part in Church discipline.

By contrast with the teachers, the function of the *elders* was to help the pastors exercise moral discipline within congregations. All the pastors and elders of all the churches in a recognised district (*e.g.* a

city) would meet as a "consistory",[24] and together exercise a
general spiritual oversight over the affairs of all their churches. The
consistory had the ultimate power of being able to excommunicate
for heresy or sinful conduct. In Calvin's thinking, then, the oversight of the Church was in the hands of presbyters – pastors,
teachers, elders; and all the congregations of a particular region
were subject to the authority of all their pastors and elders meeting
together as a consistory. This form of Church government came to
be called *Presbyterianism*.

The fourth office of *deacons* did not share in ruling the Church by
teaching or discipline. Calvin distinguished two kinds of deacon:
the first type managed the congregation's funds; the second type
looked after the poor and sick, administering a system of Christian
social care (including medical care in hospitals).

All those nominated for any of the four offices of pastor, teacher,
elder, and deacon required the approval of a congregation before
they could assume their responsibilities within it. Calvin believed
that the most Scriptural method by which a congregation expressed
its approval of candidates for church office was by electing them
democratically.[25] As a result, lay members of Reformed Churches
were far more active, and took more responsibility in congregational affairs, than the Lutheran laity did in their state-controlled
Churches. Some historians have argued that we can trace some of
the roots of modern democracy back to Calvin's pattern of Church

---

[24] Not to be confused with the Lutheran consistory, which was a board of
government-appointed lawyers and theologians.

[25] In Calvin's Genevan Church, the teachers functioned in schools and colleges
rather than in congregations. However, in instructing young people and those
training for the pastorate, the teachers were (Calvin thought) acting in the name
of the Church, and therefore needed to be chosen and ordained by the Church.
In other Reformed Churches, teachers also functioned in congregations as
assistants to the pastor or pastors; the pastors expounded the books of the
Bible, the teachers instructed people in particular doctrines, *e.g.* from a catechism. This was the arrangement favoured by the Westminister Assembly in
17th century Britain in its *The Form of Presbyterial Church Government*.

government. Certainly Calvin had outlined a system of ecclesiastical organisation which would enable the Reformed Churches to function successfully in the most adverse conditions. He helped to raise up a whole new generation of heroic, pioneering Protestants who did not rely on state support, but could govern themselves and spread their faith even when the political authorities were fiercely hostile.

Calvin's differences with Luther over the doctrine of the Church extended to their views on holy communion. Building once again on foundations laid by Bucer, Calvin agreed with Zwingli that Christ's flesh and blood were not physically present in the bread and wine; "This is My body" meant "This signifies My body." He also agreed with Zwingli that Luther's Christology was wrong. Christ could not be everywhere in His human body, as Luther argued; the risen body of the Saviour was in one definite place, heaven, where it would remain until the second coming. However, Calvin agreed with Luther that in the eucharist there was a real reception of Christ's body and blood. Unlike Luther, Calvin understood this reception to take place through faith alone, so that only the believer partook of Christ; the unbeliever received only bread and wine. For Calvin, Christ was present in the Lord's Supper not physically in the bread and wine (as Luther said), nor in His divine nature alone (as Zwingli said), but in the power of the Holy Spirit. As the mouths of believers received the sacramental *signs* (bread and wine), the Spirit fed their souls with the *things signified* (the body and blood of the crucified and risen Christ). Apart from Bucer, the person who most helped Calvin to formulate and expound this view was the great Italian theologian Peter Martyr (see section 3).

Bucer, Calvin, and Martyr's non-Zwinglian view of the real eucharistic presence of Christ's body and blood through the Spirit became the standard Reformed doctrine. It is found in all the Reformed confessions of faith, including the 39 Articles of the Church of England (article 28), the Westminster Confession (chapter 29, section 7), and the 1689 Baptist Confession (chapter

30, section 7). Naturally, holding so positive a view of the believer's communion with Christ in the Lord's Supper, Calvin argued that the Supper was an integral part of normal Sunday worship. He wanted it to be celebrated with great frequency – "at least once a week" (*Institutes* 4:17:43). Calvin was never able to get his way on this in Geneva, owing mostly to opposition from the city magistrates, who did not want the awesome power of excommunication to receive the high profile which weekly communion would inevitably give it. However, Calvin's clearly expressed ideal was that the Lord's Supper should be celebrated whenever the local church gathered for worship.

6. Calvin the Reformer of Geneva, 1536-38.

Calvin stayed in the Swiss Reformed city of Basel for just over a year. Then he made a brief visit to Ferrara in northern Italy, where the duchess of Ferrara was encouraging humanist and Protestant reforms. Returning to Basel, Calvin made one last trip to his native town of Noyon in France to put some family business in order, then made his way to Strasbourg. As we have seen, Strasbourg was a south German imperial city which had embraced a Reformed variety of Protestantism under the Reformer Martin Bucer (see section 2). Calvin hoped to settle there and live a quiet life as a Christian scholar. However, war between the Holy Roman emperor Charles V and king Francis I of France forced Calvin to make a detour. In July 1536, he stopped overnight in the independent French-speaking city of Geneva, on the western tip of Switzerland. It has been called the most fateful detour in history.

Geneva was a strategically important city, standing on the crossroads between France, Switzerland and Italy. The Swiss Reformed canton of Berne had only just introduced the Reformation into Geneva two months previously. Geneva – not yet a member of the Swiss Confederacy – was struggling to maintain its independence from Savoy (north-western Italy), and relied heavily on Bernese support. However, Berne itself had ambitions to control Geneva;

and so, to bring Geneva more closely under Bernese influence, Berne attempted to propagate the Swiss Reformed faith among the Genevans.

The Bernese agent in this endeavour was the French Protestant Reformer, **William Farel** (1489-1565), who was like some fiery Old Testament prophet in his booming denunciations of Rome and sin, and heart-piercing demands for repentance and Reformation. Before fleeing to Switzerland from persecution in France, Farel had belonged to the reform-minded humanist circle led by Jacques Lefevre d'Étaples; as we saw, Calvin had also been linked with the same group. So Farel knew about Calvin.[26] And he knew that Calvin had recently produced that masterpiece of Reformation theology, the *Institutes*. So when Farel heard that Calvin was staying overnight in Geneva, he immediately went to see him and asked Calvin to remain in the city and help him reform its moral and religious life.

Calvin refused. He explained to Farel that he was a shy scholar who only wanted to live a peaceful and retired life among his books, reading, studying, writing. But Calvin's talk about what he wanted to do with his life did not impress Farel. He became angry and accused Calvin of putting his own desires for personal peace above the urgent spiritual needs of Geneva. Towering over the terrified Calvin, Farel called down the curse of God on the scholar's "peaceful life", if Calvin would not stay and help him. Struck with awe, seeming to hear the voice of the Lord speaking from heaven through Farel, Calvin obeyed. So began John Calvin's career as the Reformer of Geneva, which would last for (almost) the rest of his life.

Calvin and Farel wanted to make Geneva into an outstanding model of a Christian community. To lay a basis for this goal, they felt they had to secure the independence of the Church from the state, so that the Church's officers, not the city council, had the

---

[26] But had probably not previously met him: Farel left France for the more spiritually congenial soil of Swizerland as early as 1523.

power to excommunicate the unworthy. However, this attempt to introduce a strong Church discipline into Geneva met with bitter resistance. So did Calvin and Farel's desire to impose a doctrinal statement of faith on all Genevans. When the Genevan city council voted to adopt the liturgy used in Berne, Calvin and Farel saw this as the state trying to dictate to the Church how it should worship God, and they refused to accept it. As a result, in April 1538 the council banished them. Calvin's first attempt at reforming Geneva was a dismal failure.

7. Calvin in Strasbourg, 1538-41.

Farel went to Neuchatel (west of Berne), where he became pastor. Meanwhile Martin Bucer invited Calvin to settle in Strasbourg. There, Calvin found himself in the greatest international centre of the Reformed faith at that time. He acted as pastor to a large congregation of French Protestant refugees who had fled the persecution in their native land. He also lectured on theology and wrote an exposition of Romans, the first of a brilliant series of Biblical commentaries. Calvin's commentaries were perhaps even more influential than his *Institutes*; they are the only Reformation commentaries still being reprinted and widely studied today. Calvin worked closely with Bucer, learning much from him, especially in the areas of Church discipline, the ministry, and public worship (see section 9).

In August 1540, Calvin married. His attitude to marriage was resoundingly unromantic; he wrote, "I, whom you see so hostile to celibacy, have never taken a wife, and I do not know if I shall ever marry. If I did so, it would be in order to devote my time more to the Lord by being relieved from the worries of daily life." This unromantic approach was in fact fairly common in 16th century Europe; the idea that romantic love is the proper basis for marriage had not yet dawned on most minds. At any rate, Bucer took it upon himself to find a wife for Calvin. The first attempt failed, but the second succeeded, and Calvin agreed to marry a French lady,

Idelette de Bure, widow of a convert from Anabaptism to the Reformed faith. Idelette already had a son and daughter from her previous marriage; she and Calvin had one son who died in his infancy. Idelette herself, increasingly troubled with illness, died in 1549, after which Calvin consciously embraced a celibate life. Although their marriage lacked romance, it proved an affectionate union, and Calvin was emotionally stunned by Idelette's death. "Truly, mine is no common grief. I have been bereaved of the best companion of my life."

Together with Bucer, Calvin took part in a number of important conferences between Protestant and Roman Catholic theologians in 1539-41, especially the colloquy of Regensburg,[27] which tried, unsuccessfully, to heal the divisions in Western Christendom. Calvin met the Lutheran Reformer Philip Melanchthon at these conferences, and the two became close lifelong friends. After Melanchton's death, Calvin exclaimed:

> "O Philip Melanchthon! I appeal to you, who now live in God with Christ and there await us until we are gathered together with you in blessed peace. A hundred times, wearied by the battle, and overcome by trials, and resting your head on my breast, you have said, 'O would that I might die on this bosom!' I too have wished a thousand times afterwards that we had lived together."

Philip Melanchthon is the golden chain linking the two supreme figures of the Protestant Reformation, Luther and Calvin: he was the intimate personal friend of both men (Luther and Calvin themselves never met). Indeed, Melanchthon's friendship with Calvin got him into trouble with strict Lutherans, because he agreed with Calvin's doctrine of the eucharist rather than Luther's.[28] Calvin himself worked ceaselessly for union between Reformed and Lutherans, but his labours were always dashed to pieces on the rock of the Lord's Supper. Calvin did not believe that the differences

---

[27] For the colloquy of Regensburg, see Chapter 8, section 1.
[28] For the controversies within Lutheranism after Luther's death, see Part Four.

between Luther's view and the Reformed view were serious enough to justify a division among Protestants over the issue. On this point, however, Luther simply would not shift from the ground he had occupied at the Marburg colloquy in 1529, where he had refused to give Zwingli and Bucer the right hand of fellowship. "I reverence Luther, but I am ashamed of him," Calvin wrote to Melanchthon. He also complained to Bucer about Luther's "craving for victory, haughty manner, abusive language, and insolent fury". Nonetheless, Calvin's esteem for Luther as a theologian and a Reformer was almost unbounded.

> "Consider how great a man Luther is," Calvin wrote to Bullinger, "and what excellent gifts he has: the strength of mind and resolute constancy, the skill, efficiency, and theological power he has used in devoting all his energies to overthrowing the reign of Antichrist [the papacy] and to spread far and near the teaching of salvation. I have often said that even if he called me a devil, I would still regard him as an outstanding servant of God."

Luther, too, thought highly of Calvin; for example, he read Calvin's *Reply to Sadoleto* (see below), and told Bucer that it had given him "special delight". At first Luther also expressed positive and conciliatory views about Calvin's doctrine of the eucharist, but later lumped Calvin together with the other Swiss as anti-sacramental fanatics. For his part, the moderate Melanchthon, with his "Calvinian" leanings on the Lord's Supper, found himself increasingly isolated among his fellow Lutherans, most of whom preferred to follow Luther's uncompromising lead.

After years of effort, Calvin was able to unite all the Swiss Reformed Churches around an understanding of holy communion that owed more to him than to Zwingli, in a confession of faith called the Zurich Consensus (in Latin, *Consensus Tigurinus*), drawn up by Calvin and Bullinger[29] of Zurich in 1549. The

---

[29]   For Bullinger, see previous Chapter, section 8.

Consensus, while retaining all that was positive in Zwingli's doctrine of the eucharist, added on the stronger views of Calvin, Bullinger, Bucer, and Martyr on the presence and self-giving of the risen Christ to believers through the Spirit, as they ate and drank the bread and wine. It does not, however, state Calvin's doctrine as fully or robustly as other Reformed confessions, owing to Bullinger's reluctance to say that the bread and wine were "instruments" by which the Spirit communicated Christ's body and blood to believers. Bullinger preferred to say that the bread and wine were signs testifying externally to something the Spirit did internally and independently in the believer's heart, in contrast to the Bucer-Martyr-Calvin view that the bread and wine were instruments by means of which the Spirit invisibly conveyed Christ's body and blood. The Consensus compromised by calling the bread and wine "implements", which Bullinger seems to have distinguished from "instruments".

Calvin's three years in Strasbourg were the happiest of his life. This was where he felt most at home, writing and preaching and mingling with other Reformers in a pleasant atmosphere, free from bitter conflicts. Despite what ill-informed or prejudiced people have said about him, Calvin was basically a gentle, quiet, longsuffering person, who hated controversy and took part in it only when a high sense of duty compelled him – he had none of Luther's love of a good fight. If Calvin's personality seems less colourful and attractive than Luther's, the reason is partly that Calvin was a very shy and reserved man who hardly ever spoke about himself. Still, he was not a harsh or miserable individual. He was a tender husband, stricken by his wife's early death. He enjoyed many warm and enduring friendships, especially with Melanchthon and Farel. He rejoiced in the earthly gifts of God. Natural beauty, food, drink, family, friendship, art, music: these things were very good – Calvin had no doubt of that. Yet the kingly service of Jesus Christ and His Gospel was infinitely greater and more glorious. To that service, the soul of Calvin was consecrated. He expected every other believer to be as dedicated as himself.

Calvin's happy years in Strasbourg were not to last. Even in Strasbourg, Calvin could not escape from Geneva. In 1539 the distinguished Roman Catholic cardinal, Jacob Sadoleto (1477-1547), tried to win back the Genevans to Rome by writing them an open letter in which he attacked Protestants for violating the unity of the Church, and even criticised the motives and characters of Calvin and Farel. What made Sadoleto's letter attractive to wavering Protestants was the fact that Sadoleto was himself one of the foremost advocates of "Evangelical" reform within the Roman Catholic Church.[30] Stung by the personal criticisms of himself, Calvin produced a highly effective *Reply to Sadoleto* in September 1539, regarded by many as one of the most persuasive statements of Reformation principles ever written. It impressed the Genevans. In October 1540, the citizens of Geneva asked Calvin to return and resume his work there as a Reformer. A political revolution had placed in power a party friendly to Calvin. Calvin hesitated long, remembering the pathetic failure of his previous efforts at reforming Geneva. "There is no place under heaven that I am more afraid of," he wrote. "I would rather submit to a hundred other deaths, than to that cross on which I would have to perish a thousand times every day!" However, he finally yielded to the urgent and repeated invitations of the Genevans, and re-entered the city in September 1541. He went in fear and trembling: "I offer my heart a slain victim in sacrifice to the Lord." But this time he returned for good.

8. Calvin the Reformer of Geneva, 1541-64.

The invitation of the Genevans to Calvin to return to them did not mean that Calvin had an easy ride in his second period as the city's Reformer. Indeed, he struggled for many years, against all kinds of opposition, to try to make Geneva into a Christian community which he believed would embody God's will for human society. Calvin never achieved all he wanted. As previously mentioned, Calvin fervently wished the Lord's Supper to be celebrated every

---

[30] For more about Sadoleto and the "Catholic Evangelicals", see Chapter 8, section 1.

Sunday as a central part of normal Christian worship, but had to make concessions to the Genevan magistrates and accept a celebration of communion only four times a year, at Christmas, Easter, Pentecost and the first Sunday in September.[31] Again, although he won for the Genevan Church a large measure of independence from state control, he had to compromise by agreeing that the elders would be chosen by the city magistrates from among their own number. However, Calvin did finally secure in 1555 the power of Church discipline and excommunication for the consistory (pastors and elders), not the city council. This was a real triumph, since by Calvin's death in 1564 there were 18 pastors and only 12 magistrate-elders on the consistory. Calvin set out these principles of Church organisation in a document called *Ecclesiastical Ordinances of the Genevan Church*, adopted by the Genevan city council in November 1541. It taught the Presbyterian form of Church government which we looked at in section 5, modified by the compromises Calvin was forced to make with the Genevan city magistrates.

Calvin was prepared to accept these compromises because he did not simply want to reform the religious life of the Genevan Church; he wanted the entire life of the city to be brought into conformity with God's will for human living. For this, he needed the support and cooperation of the political authorities on the city council. In other words, Calvin was more than a religious reformer; he was a moral, social, and political reformer too. His great vision was not only to build up a true Christian Church in Geneva, but also to make Geneva itself into a true Christian city. Calvin therefore strove to purify the moral life of Genevan society, persuading the city council to enforce severe laws against adultery, prostitution, pornography, drunkenness, dancing, gambling, swearing, disobedience of children to parents, and so on.

---

[31] As explained in section 3, the Genevan magistrates opposed weekly communion because they wanted the Church's power of excommunication to be kept as far out of sight as possible.

However, we should not think that in Calvin's Geneva the city council tried, in a merely negative way, to stop its citizens behaving immorally. It also took strong positive measures to improve the social, economic, and cultural life of the community. For instance, the authorities created an outstanding system of free public education; they stimulated business by helping to establish a highly successful cloth and silk industry, which provided much-needed employment; they made the sale of food subject to strict health and hygiene laws; they supplied latrines free of charge for all houses that lacked them (a very real need in most 16th century European homes); they built a high-quality hospital, and a place of residence for the homeless; they set up an agency to find work for the unemployed; and they organised a noble system of social care for the poor and aged. In these and other ways, the Genevan government carried out a wide-ranging programme of social planning and reform which, alongside the moral and spiritual influence of the Genevan Church, transformed the life of the city.

Out of the purifying fire of internal conflicts, which we will look at in a moment, Calvin's Geneva eventually became a near-perfect pattern of a Reformed community. Reformed refugees from all over Western Europe (especially France) flocked to the city of Calvin; Geneva rather than Strasbourg now became the great international headquarters of Reformed Protestantism. The Reformed refugees helped Calvin to make Geneva into a model Reformed city, and at the same time the Genevan example inspired them to take the Reformed faith back to their own homelands. John Knox, the Reformer of Scotland, who pastored a congregation of English Protestant refugees in Geneva from 1556 to 1559,[32] famously referred to Calvin's Geneva in these words in a letter to a friend:

> "I could have wished, yea, and cannot cease to wish, that it might please God to guide and conduct yourself to this place; where, I neither fear nor am ashamed to say, is the most perfect school of Christ that ever was on the earth since

---

[32]   See Chapter 7, sections 6 and 7.

the days of the apostles. In other places, I confess Christ to be truly preached; but manners [behaviour] and religion to be so sincerely reformed, I have not yet seen in any other place beside."

More striking than Knox's praise was the testimony of a German Lutheran pastor, Valentine Andreae (1586-1654) of Württemberg. Andreae had all the typical Lutheran hostility to the Reformed faith, but when he visited Geneva in 1610, some 46 years after Calvin's death, he was utterly astonished by the living monument which the Genevan Reformer had left behind him:

"When I was in Geneva," Andreae wrote, "I saw something great which I will remember and desire as long as I live. There is in Geneva the perfect system of a perfect government; but the city's special beauty is a moral discipline which makes weekly investigations into the behaviour of the citizens, including their smallest transgressions. The discipline is carried out first by district inspectors, then by the elders, and finally by the magistrates, according to the nature of the sin and the moral condition of the offender. All cursing, swearing, gambling, luxury, strife, hatred, and deceit are forbidden, while greater sins are hardly even heard of. What a glorious beauty of the Christian faith shines forth in such purity of moral conduct! We must lament with tears that it is lacking and almost totally neglected among us Lutherans. Indeed, if it were not for the religious difference between me and the Genevans, I would for ever have been bound to that city by our agreement in morality, and I have ever since tried to introduce something like it into our churches. Just as outstanding as the public discipline was the home discipline of my Genevan landlord, Scarron. His house was distinguished by daily worship, reading of the Scriptures, the fear of God in word and deed, and a holy moderation in eating, drinking and manner of dress."

If this was how a hostile Lutheran reacted to Geneva, we can imagine how overwhelmed by it Reformed visitors must have been.

And yet the strange thing is that Calvin himself never held any position of public authority in Geneva, other than the simple office of pastor of Saint Peter's Church, one of the three city churches. Like the Catholic reformer of Florence, Girolamo Savonarola,[33] Calvin ruled Geneva through the persuasive power of the spoken word. He preached not only on Sundays but on three weekdays too, lectured on theology twice a week, attended the weekly meeting of the consistory every Thursday, and expounded the Bible every Friday at a special spiritual conference called the "assembly" (see next section). Calvin had no political power, and the council did not even grant him citizenship in Geneva until 1559; he reformed the city by preaching, not by force or decree. The city council would follow Calvin's reforming ideas only if Calvin's arguments convinced enough of the council members. He did not always convince them. Especially in the years 1548-55, there was bitter conflict between Calvin's supporters and opponents. His opponents dominated the city council during this period; they were mostly native Genevans from long-established families, who resented the influx of 6,000 foreign religious refugees into the small city (it had a native population of only 13,000).

Calvin's foes were led by Ami Perrin, a distinguished Genevan citizen, and were sometimes called "Perrinists". Calvin called them "Libertines" because of their opposition to the moral discipline he wished the city to embrace. A number of them led somewhat loose lives, and some held heretical views, *e.g.* denying the inspiration of Scripture, and maintaining that God and the universe were identical ("pantheism" – the view that everything is God). The Reformer had to endure many insults and even threats against his life from Ami Perrin and the Libertines, and sometimes he fell into deep depression; "I wish God would let me leave this place," he wrote in 1547. In 1549, his arch-enemy Perrin was elected chief magistrate of

---

[33]   For Savonarola, see Chapter 1, section 5.

Geneva. Yet by 1555, Calvin and his supporters had completely triumphed over the Libertine party.

Calvin's ultimate victory was partly brought about by a tragic episode involving a Spanish Radical called **Michael Servetus** (1511-53). Servetus was a physician gifted with a brilliant if erratic mind, who had shocked Roman Catholics and Protestants alike by his writings in which he denied and mocked the doctrine of the Trinity, which he called "a three-headed monster".[34] He expounded his views first in *Concerning the Errors of the Trinity* in July 1531, and at more length in his *The Restoration of Christianity* in January 1553.[35] These were among the great writings of the Rationalist branch of the Radical Reformation (see next Chapter, section 3). Servetus corresponded with Calvin in the 1540s; Calvin at first replied to his letters, trying to reason with him from the Scriptures, but he finally washed his hands of Servetus as a "desperately obstinate heretic". Arrested and condemned to death for heresy by the Roman Catholic inquisition in Vienne (southern France), Servetus escaped from prison and – for no good reason – went to Geneva in August 1553. Here someone recognised him, and the Genevan authorities arrested the notorious anti-Trinitarian.

Servetus's trial for heresy before the Genevan city council became a trial of strength between Calvin and the Libertines, who then controlled the council, with Ami Perrin as chief magistrate. Like almost all Christians in his day, Calvin accepted that the state was under moral obligation to God to punish heretics (ironically, even Servetus himself taught that Christian magistrates should put heretics to death). The crucial difference between Servetus and his Roman Catholic and Protestant opponents was that *they* believed there was no greater heresy than denying the Trinity. If the Genevan

---

[34] For more about anti-Trinitarian Anabaptists, see next Chapter.

[35] The Latin title of Servetus's *Restoration* was *Restitutio* –a deliberate reference to the *Institutio* of Calvin. Most of Servetus's *Restoration* was written as a response to Calvin's *Institutes*, correcting what Servetus believed were its many errors.

city council convicted Servetus, then, he would face the death penalty for his anti-Trinitarian faith.

The Libertines placed every possible difficulty in the way of Servetus's conviction – not out of any compassion for Servetus, but just to harass Calvin. However, they could not afford to acquit Servetus when all Western Christendom was demanding his execution. They showed their lack of principle when, after encouraging Servetus for so long by their delaying tactics, the Libertine-dominated council (by a unanimous vote) finally condemned the unfortunate Radical to death by burning. Calvin was glad that Servetus had been sentenced to death, but horrified at the cruel method of execution; he tried to get it changed to something swift and merciful, and was rebuked by his old friend William Farel for being soft. The council, however, refused to listen to Calvin, and Servetus was burnt at the stake on October 17th 1553. Farel attended Servetus pastorally in his last hours, and he died with an unshaken faith in his anti-Trinitarian convictions. His cry amid the flames was, "Jesus, Son of the eternal God, have mercy on me!" It has been pointed out that if only Servetus had said, "Jesus, the eternal Son of God, have mercy on me!" his life would have been spared.[36]

---

[36] Calvin has been denounced almost endlessly, sometimes as an unregenerate murderer, for his part in the death of Servetus. And yet, even though we might wish to reject entirely the view that heretics should be put to death, it is very difficult to understand why Calvin should be singled out for blame. Why has Zwingli not been condemned with equal severity for his part in the execution of Anabaptists? Or England's archbishop Cranmer for his part in the execution of the Radical Joan Bocher? (See Chapter 5, section 1, for Zwingli and the Anabaptists, and Chapter 7, section 3, for the death of Joan Bocher.) And so one could go on. The fact is that in the 16th century, Protestant governments, with the consent of the Reformers, did execute some people for heresy – almost always Radicals who denied the Trinity or the incarnation. The real issue here is a purely theological one, namely, whether the Bible authorises governments to put a heretic (or a blasphemer) to death. If the Bible does authorise this, as virtually all Protestants in that era believed, we can no more reproach our forefathers as unregenerate killers than we can affix that stigma to present day Christians who sincerely believe in capital punishment for murder. Further, we should keep in mind that Servetus was actually an isolated case. No one else was ever put to death for heresy in Calvin's Geneva. More particularly, no

At the time, Servetus's trial and execution greatly magnified Calvin's reputation: he had purged Europe of its most hated heretic. The other Magisterial Reformers showered the highest praise on Calvin. Peter Martyr's response was typical:

> "Regarding Servetus, I have nothing to say but that he was the devil's own son, whose evil and detestable doctrine must everywhere be banished. Nor is the magistrate who executed him to be blamed, since there could be found in Servetus no sign of repentance, and his blasphemies simply could not be tolerated."

By contrast, the Libertines had destroyed their credibility by putting so many obstacles in the path of Servetus's punishment. The Genevan elections of 1554 and 1555 went decisively in Calvin's favour. The Libertines foolishly staged a minor riot one night in May 1555; the city council responded by executing the ringleaders for treason and banishing others. Ami Perrin was sentenced to death, but fled to Berne. From that moment, Calvin was the undisputed moral and spiritual leader of Geneva until his death in 1564.

Calvin produced a great number of important writings during his second period in Geneva. He continued to revise and enlarge the *Institutes* until it reached its final form in 1559. He wrote a catechism for the Church in Geneva, the *Genevan Catechism* of 1541, which had great influence on other Reformed catechisms; divided into five sections, it dealt with faith, the Ten Commandments, the Lord's Prayer, the Word of God, and the sacraments. It differed from Luther's *Small Catechism* in putting faith first, rather than the Ten Commandments. This reflected a difference of emphasis

---

Roman Catholic ever suffered this penalty: if someone was found to be a secret believer in the old religion, he or she was merely banished from Geneva – at a time when Roman Catholic regimes were routinely burning Protestants at the stake in their thousands and tens of thousands across Europe. Setting matters in this larger historical context, it is possible to regret deeply the fate of Michael Servetus, while refusing to draw harsh personal conclusions about John Calvin.

between Calvin's theology and Luther's: Luther regarded the law of God as chiefly intended to convict unbelievers of their sin and show them their need of Christ, whereas Calvin understood the law mainly as God's plan for how believers should live to His glory.

Calvin wrote most of his commentaries during this second period in Geneva. Many of his sermons, too, were written down by a secretary as Calvin preached them, and were then published, with the result that we sometimes have both a commentary and a series of sermons by Calvin on the same books of the Bible. He produced a host of writings against the various enemies of the Reformed faith. His most important book against Rome was a commentary on the Council of Trent and its decrees, *Acts of the Council of Trent, and the Antidote* (1547). He dealt with the Radical Reformers in his *Against the Sect of the Anabaptists* (1544). He expounded the Reformed doctrine of the eucharist against the Lutherans in various tracts, notably his *On the True Partaking of Christ's Flesh and Blood* (1561). But these are only a very few of Calvin's staggeringly huge output of books and pamphlets, not to mention his letters (see section 10 below).

One other fact should be noted: Calvin's work was done against a background of chronic ill-health. He was a constant martyr to arthritis, migraine headaches, bleeding from the stomach, bowel disorders, haemorrhoids, inflamed kidneys and kidney stones, fever, muscle cramps, and gout. Yet this sick man achieved more in one lifetime than most healthy people could encompass in a hundred.

9. Calvin as a Reformer of worship.

Calvin's approach to the reform of worship in Strasbourg and Geneva was similar to that of Zwingli in Zurich. Calvin believed that nothing should be done in Christian worship unless the New Testament authorised it. So he followed Zwingli in rejecting most of the ritual of medieval Catholic worship – images, candles, priestly robes, *etc.* In one important area, however, Calvin differed from Zwingli: he was positively committed to congregational *singing*, rather than merely *reciting* Scripture as the worshippers of Zurich did. In 1539, when he was in Strasbourg, Calvin published a French song-book which contained seventeen psalms, the *Nunc dimittis* (Simeon's song, Luke 2:29-32), and the Ten Commandments and Apostles' Creed set to music. The singing of the Ten Commandments was a normal part of Sunday worship in Calvin's Strasbourg congregation, and worshippers always sang the Apostles' Creed during the Lord's Supper and the *Nunc Dimittis* at its conclusion. Calvin's Genevan liturgy of 1542 contained 39 psalms, the *Nunc dimittis*, and musical versions of the Ten Commandments, the Lord's Prayer, and the Apostles' Creed. However, especially in his second period in Geneva (1541-64), Calvin gave pride of place to the psalms in public worship. He expressed his view in the preface to the 1542 Genevan liturgy:

> "Now, what Augustine says is true, namely, that no one can sing anything worthy of God which he has not received from Him. Therefore, even after we have carefully searched everywhere, we shall not find better or more appropriate songs to this end than the songs of David, inspired by the Holy Spirit. And for this reason, when we sing them, we are assured that God puts the words in our mouth, as if He Himself were singing through us to exalt His glory."

People often think that Calvin wished Christians to sing the psalms alone in worship – the view known as "exclusive psalmody". This is not true, as we have seen; he was quite happy that other suitable things should be used: the *Nunc dimittis*, the Ten Commandments, the Apostles' Creed. But Calvin clearly thought that nothing could surpass the psalms for spiritual beauty in the Church's public praise. His view could therefore be called "predominant psalmody". Since Calvin agreed with Zwingli (and, self-consciously, the early Church fathers) in opposing the use of musical instruments in worship, Reformed Geneva sang the psalms without any instrumental accompaniment. This became the general pattern in the Reformed

Churches, in contrast to the Lutheran Churches which retained the use of the organ.

Calvin's encouragement lay behind the complete translation of the psalms into French by the poets **Clement Marot** (1497-1544) and **Theodore Beza** (1519-1605). Marot's first Genevan psalter of 1543 contained 49 French psalms, the *Nunc dimittis*, the *Ave Maria* (based on Luke 1:28 and 42), musical versions of the Ten Commandments, the Apostles' Creed, and the Lord's Prayer, and two graces to be sung at mealtimes. Marot died the following year, but Beza completed the French translation of the psalms in 1562. This final version contained all 150 psalms, the *Nunc dimittis*, and the Ten Commandments; it was used throughout the French-speaking Protestant world. The French psalms were sung to simple but lively tunes, sometimes based on popular melodies.

The greatest French Reformed composers were **Louis Bourgeois** (c.1510-61) and **Claude Goudimel** (1510-72). Bourgeois edited Calvin's Genevan psalters between 1545 and 1557 (and possibly earlier), writing many of the tunes, which musical scholars have considered the best in the collection. Goudimel produced a brilliant musical edition of the psalms in 1565 for singing in the home; he died a martyr for his Protestant faith during the Massacre of Saint Bartholomew's Day.[37] The Genevan psalter was a phenomenal success; French Reformed believers fell passionately in love with its psalms, and indeed so did some Roman Catholics for a time. Psalm 65 became the great battle psalm of French Calvinist armies during France's religious wars (see Chapter 6, section 4). The Genevan psalter achieved a similar popularity far beyond the borders of France, in all the Reformed Churches, as it was translated into German, Dutch, and English.

Based on Martin Bucer's German service, the complete form of worship in Calvin's Strasbourg congregation was structured as follows:

---

[37]   For the Massacre of Saint Bartholomew's Day, see Chapter 6, section 4.

Scripture sentence: Psalm 124:8

Opening set prayer: confession of sin (written down in the liurgy)

Scriptural words of pardon

Words of absolution

The Ten Commandments sung, with *kyrie eleison* ("Lord, have mercy" in Greek) after each Commandment (the first four-commandments were sung first, followed by a prayer for instruction in God's law and the grace to obey it; then the other six Commandments were sung)

Prayer for illumination (an example was supplied in the liturgy, but the minister could pray his own prayer)

Scripture reading

Sermon

The collection (offering)

Set prayers of intercession, followed by long paraphrase of the Lord's Prayer (all written down in the liturgy)

The Apostles' Creed or a psalm sung

Benediction: the Aaronic blessing (Numbers 6:24-26)

Contrary to Calvin's wishes, the magistrates of Strasbourg permitted the French congregation to celebrate the Lord's Supper only once a month. On communion Sundays, after the sermon, collection, and prayers of intercession, the service continued like this:

The Apostles' Creed sung by the congregation, while the minister prepares the bread and wine

Prayer of consecration

The Lord's Prayer

Words of institution

Exhortation to congregation

Communion while a psalm is sung

Set prayer

The *Nunc Dimittis* sung

Benediction: the Aaronic blessing (Numbers 6:24-26)

Modern "Calvinists", especially in Britain, may be surprised to
see the strongly liturgical nature of Calvin's order of worship,
and the high place the French Reformer gave to the Ten
Commandments, the Apostles' Creed, and the Lord's Prayer.
This simply highlights the fact that much present-day Reformed
worship in the English-speaking world is derived from 17th
century Puritanism rather than from Calvin.[38] We find another
striking feature of Calvin's Strasbourg liturgy in the "words of
absolution" spoken by the minister after the confession of sin.
This was an important element in Calvin's conception of worship. It consisted in a declaration by the minister that the sins of
the penitent congregation had been forgiven by God for Christ's
sake. This *declaration* by the minister that *God* had forgiven His
people was quite different from the Roman Catholic idea of
absolution, in which the priest actually conferred forgiveness on
the sinner. The declaration of absolution in Calvin's Strasbourg
liturgy was adopted by the English Reformers and placed in the
Anglican Book of Common Prayer.[39]

Calvin was more restricted in Geneva than he had been in
Strasbourg as a reformer of worship; he had to compromise with
the magistrates and with popular practice. The Geneva liturgy,
therefore, does not embody Calvin's ideal. However, it is still

---

[38] The English Puritans of the 17th century, especially the Independents (Congre-
      gationalists), began to oppose all liturgical prayer, including the Lord's Prayer,
      and rejected the Ten Commandments and the Apostles' Creed as suitable items
      for worship. From that time, the worship patterns of the English-speaking
      Reformed community – Presbyterian, Congregationalist, and Baptist –
      followed Puritanism rather than Calvin or the continental Reformed Churches.

[39] Calvin was quite upset when he could not persuade the Genevan Church to
      adopt a formula for absolution in its liturgy, and wrote a letter expressing the
      thinking behind his concept of Protestant absolution: "We must all acknow-
      ledge it to be very useful that after the general confession, some striking promise
      of Scripture should follow, by which sinners might be raised to hopes of
      pardon and reconciliation. I would have introduced this practice [in Geneva]
      from the beginning, but some feared that its novelty might give offence. I was
      too quick to yield to them, so that the absolution was omitted. Now it is no
      longer opportune to make any change, because the majority of our people
      begin to get up [off their knees] before we come to the end of the confession."

worth exploring because of its unique influence as the form of worship practised in the international headquarters of Reformed Protestantism. It was set out like this:

Scripture sentence: Psalm 124:8
Opening set prayer: confession of sin (written down in the liturgy)
Psalm
Prayer for illumination (an example was supplied in the liturgy, but the minister could pray his own prayer)
Scripture reading
Sermon
Set prayers of intercession, followed by long paraphrase of the Lord's Prayer (all written down in the liturgy)
The Apostles' Creed recited
Psalm
Benediction: the Aaronic blessing (Numbers 6:24-26)

On communion Sundays, after the sermon and prayers of intercession, the service continued like this:

The Apostles' Creed sung by the congregation, while the minister prepares the bread and wine
Words of institution
Exhortation to congregation
Prayer of consecration
Communion while a psalm or other Scripture passage is read out
Set prayer
Benediction: the Aaronic blessing (Numbers 6:24-26)

The Geneva liturgy was basically a stripped-down version of the fuller Strasbourg liturgy. Missing from Geneva were the Scriptural words of pardon, the declaration of absolution by the minister, the Lord's Prayer, the singing of the Ten Commandments and the *Nunc Dimittis*, and the collection.

Calvin kept the Church calendar (the "Christian year") in a simplified form: Christmas, Good Friday, Easter, Ascension Day, and Pentecost were all observed in Reformed Geneva.[40]

One final element in the way Calvin organised Geneva's religious life is worth observing. Every Friday he held a special meeting in Saint Peter's Church called the "assembly". All the pastors attended, and anyone else who wished could also take part. One of the pastors would read a Scripture passage and briefly expound it. Another would then make comments on what had been said. And then anybody was free to speak on the subject or ask a question. The "assembly" once again shows us how Calvin gave the laity the opportunity for active participation in the Church's spiritual life.

10. Calvin's achievements.

Calvin performed almost superhuman services to the cause of the Reformation. Thanks to fresh inspiration Calvin supplied, the Protestant faith in its Reformed branch became one of the great success stories of the 16th century. We can sum up Calvin's achievements as follows:

(i) He provided the Reformed Churches with a clear, deep, solid theology in the *Institutes*, shaped by his massive knowledge of the early Church fathers, and supported by his outstanding work of Bible exposition in his commentaries.

(ii) He gave the Reformed movement a pattern of Church government which mobilised the laity and enabled Reformed believers to survive, organise, and flourish despite state opposition and persecution.

---

[40] The hostility to the Church calendar one often finds among Reformed people today derives largely from Puritanism, not from Calvin.

(iii) He showed the world a city – Geneva – which embodied the Reformed faith and lived it out. The infectious power of Geneva's example inspired others to reform their communities as Calvin had reformed his.

(iv) He fashioned the Reformed faith into an international movement, with a sense of brotherhood which crossed national boundaries. From Geneva, Calvin kept up a vast correspondence with Reformed leaders throughout Europe, advising, encouraging, exhorting, rebuking. Geneva became the vital centre of a mighty international Reformed cause.

(v) He made the Reformed faith into the great Protestant "missionary" movement of the 16th century. Geneva was an international training centre for Reformed pastors, preachers, theologians and missionaries. The Genevan Academy, founded by Calvin in 1559 and headed by the psalm-translator Theodore Beza (who was also a distinguished theologian), attracted students from all over Europe. The Academy began with 162 students; within six years, the number had rocketed to more like 1,600. Although it also offered training in law and medicine, the Academy's chief purpose was to prepare men for the ministry; it sent out an ever-growing army of Reformed believers to spread the faith in other countries – particularly France, Calvin's native land, which always had a special place in his heart.

Important people:

The Church	*Political and military*
	King Francis I of France (1515-47)
Roman Catholic:	Jacob Sturm (1498-1553)
John Major (1467-1550)	

Reformed:
Wolfgang Capito (1478-1541)
Clement Marot (1497-1544)
Martin Bucer (1491-1551)

Caspar Hedio (1494-1552)
Louis Bourgeois (c.1510-61)
Peter Martyr Vermigli (1491-1562)
John Calvin (1509-64)
William Farel (1489-1565)
Claude Goudimel (1510-72)
Theodore Beza (1519-1605)

Radicals:
Jan Mathys (died 1534)
Bernard Rothmann (1495-1535)
Jan Beukels (died 1535)
Michael Servetus (1511-53)

Martin Bucer on the Church

The third controversy relates to the antiquity of the Church. Our opponents argue that the Church existed prior to Scripture, *e.g.* in Adam's time, in Noah's ark, and in the epoch of Abraham. Their argument, however, is the fallacy or false reasoning of *per accidens* [that is, in Aristotelian logic, the fallacy of presuming that what can be said about the non-essential attributes of an object can be said about the object itself].

I acknowledge that the Church was in existence prior to the written Word. Even so, the truth that had not yet been written down was still there, from the very beginning; and through this truth came faith – for faith comes from hearing the Word [Romans 10:17] which, from all eternity, has proceeded out of God's mouth. Writing was at that time lacking, but the Word which was later written down was already there. Where there is no faith, there is no Church, and where there is no Word, there is no faith. All holy people in every age have been begotten again through the Word.

Our opponents also put the authority of the Church above Scripture. Why? Because the Church gave us the books of Scripture; therefore, they argue, the Church gave authority to these books. The Church rejected the Gospels of Nicodemus and Thomas, but accepted the Gospels of Matthew, Mark, Luke, and John. They glory in this argument, but actually, it is merely a stupid and bare-faced example of the fallacy *per accidens*. Discerning the spirits and discriminating between them does not give the spirits their authority. Likewise, testing metals does not make the metals either good or bad. Or again, when citizens make a judgment about their king's decree [that it is authentic, and that it means this or that], that judgment does not bestow authority on the decree, but rather seeks to accept without a mistake the actual authority that is in the king's majesty, by being subject to his acknowledged decree. Someone hands you a crown; you test it for the correct weight, to see if it is pure gold or contains any dross; but you do not thereby create the value of the crown. A royal decree is issued to a university; the chancellor or rector examines it, to see if it is genuine or a forgery; and only then is it publicly set forth by the whole body of the university. The devil has mixed his own "sacraments" into the sacraments of Christ, and even his own books into the divine books; and the Church has sorted out the divine from the diabolical. In so doing, the Church has not given authority to the divine books, but has withdrawn authority from the others, showing that they are not divine.

May God forbid that man should confer authority on the eternal Word of God! Christ taught the ultimate authority of divine Scripture when He said, "Search the Scriptures." The Word is eternal, and thus its authority is eternal. We cannot point to any Council that gathered in order to establish the canon of Scripture; rather, the Spirit has moved the hearts of believers in every generation, persuading them to assign His authority to the canonical writings, and to reject the rest. All the Church can do is warn, instruct, plant, and water. If the human authority in the Church is as great as the claim, why can't they convince the Turks? Why don't they convert the Muslims by the exercise of this authority? Why doesn't the same authority govern over all people, not even over all Christians? No indeed. The need is for regeneration and the illumination of the mind by the Holy Spirit, in order that we may esteem the Scriptures as the pure and undefiled and eternal Word of God, from which all religious authority must derive.

Augustine says that he will rely on nothing but the Scriptures alone. In the last chapter of Luke, Christ shows from the Scriptures the truths about the Messiah which He is discussing with the Two disciples on the road to Emmaus. He does not prove these truths by a miracle, not even by His own resurrection. Therefore the Church too always derives its authority from the Scriptures, to which Christ, the Church's head, has attributed such high authority. And after Him, the apostles and martyrs of the earliest Church attributed the same authority to Scripture. The same authority is found wherever there is a succession of sound doctrine.

True, Irenaeus in writing against the Marcionites, and Tertullian in *The Prescription of Heretics*, press the authority of the Church – but only of the Church that is sound in doctrine. For this reason, they derive from the Scriptures the evidence to corroborate their arguments, as though from the surest source of proof. Besides, both Irenaeus and Tertullian recognise no apostolic tradition other than the Creed; and what is the Creed but the substance of the Scriptures? For once this substance is preserved, it preserves everything else. Ask yourself, then, as I do, whether the Roman Church retains soundness of doctrine. Then you will know if you, by the example of Irenaeus and Tertullian, can and should press that particular Church's authority.

From Martin Bucer's *Commonplaces*.

Faith, works, assurance, and final judgment

The clarity of your joy over Jesus Christ's coming can be clouded by lack of assurance of salvation. This may rise up in your soul when you hear that the last judgment will entail a thorough inspection of our works. In truth, no one (not even the best) can arrive at assurance by looking at his own works. If you fail to grasp this, instead of seeing Christ's return as a joyous event, you will see nothing but a fearful prospect of eternal death.

Let us then look more closely at this final judgment. Unbelievers do not need to be judged. They stand already condemned by their unbelief alone. Christ affirms this clearly in John's Gospel: "Everyone who does not believe is condemned already" [John 3:18]. However, because the world may wonder why some professing Christians are appointed for salvation and others for damnation, in His perfect justice our Christ will show clearly why this difference exists. He will not allow His justice to remain concealed from the world, as it was when first He lived among us. When He returns, He will make it plain to everyone. Thus He will reveal either the sincerity or the hypocrisy of those who have professed His way and His name. You must not think that this changes or cancels the repeated teaching of Scripture that we are justified by faith and not by works. The final judgment does seem to contradict this, because the verdict is based on our conduct rather than our belief. This, however, is only because Christ will put into effect the rule He taught when He was here among us, that those who are falsely dressed in sheep's clothing will finally be exposed as wolves by their works. They may have deceived the minds of other people in this world, but they can never hide from the sight of Him whose gaze penetrates all.

Christ knows very well those who profess His holy name, whether in pretence or in reality. In the presence of all humanity, He will declare their real attitude towards Him, reproving those evil works which demonstrate the falsehood of their pretended faith. For if we would be justified, it is not enough simply to believe that Christ was the Son of God, that He died, was buried, and was raised. The devil himself knows the truth of all this! It is necessary that we genuinely receive Christ's offered benefits, trusting in Him for salvation. Our assurance, then, is related to holy living. We must not just seek the forgiveness of sins, but renounce the practice of sins. We can never live comfortably with sin when true repentance is our ever-present companion. No, we work by love, and so give our neighbour a plain token of our inner character. Faith does not leave the elect empty of that fruit which Christ will declare to be so praiseworthy in believers on the last day. And faith shrinks from the lawless works which He will so sternly rebuke in the condemned.

In short, our works will not be presented in the last judgment as the basis on which we are declared righteous and holy. They will rather be presented as the outward evidence of the righteousness and holiness that we obtained as a gift through faith. The Judge will make this very plain indeed when He says to His elect, those good and godly ones, "Come, you who are blessed by My Father, inherit the kingdom that has been prepared for you since the foundation of the world" [Matthew 25:35]. We learn from this that our salvation does not depend on us but on God's choice, by which grace, the Spirit, and faith come to dwell in us. Subsequent to this, the morally commendable life referred to by Christ becomes a testimony to the world. So, my dearest brothers, I entreat you by the mercy of Jesus Christ to make progress! Let these truths be a ceaseless incentive to your efforts, so that your faith does not stand idle. Translate your faith into practice, so that it will in every way communicate to your fellow human beings the reality of your love. These are the only works that will be taken into account on the last day. No notice will be taken of how many candles you lit in church, how often you have recited the rosary, how many pilgrimages you have been on to Loreto or Jerusalem, to Saint Peter or Saint Anthony. As Paul said to the Galatians, "Faith works through love" [Galatians 5:6]. In other words, faith is an inward thing, but it must be expressed by works of love. As faith carries out these works of love, faith flourishes and even spreads to people who previously had no faith.

Peter Martyr, *A Plain Exposition of the Twelve Articles of the Christian Faith*, section 29.

The colloquy of Poissy: agreed statement on the Lord's Supper by Reformed and Roman Catholics

We confess that Jesus Christ in the Supper offers, gives, and truly exhibits to us the substance of His body and blood, by the operation of the Holy Spirit, and that we receive and eat, spiritually and by faith, that true body that was slain for us, in order that we may be bone of His bones and flesh of His flesh, and so be enlivened by Him and made to share in all that is needed for our salvation. And whereas faith, resting on the divine Word, makes to be present what it perceives, and we by this faith receive truly and effectively the true and natural body and blood of Jesus Christ by the power of the Holy Spirit, we acknowledge in this respect the presence of the body and blood themselves in the Supper.

Church government in Geneva

In the first place, there are four kinds of office instituted by our Lord for the government of His Church: first pastors, then teachers, afterwards elders, and finally deacons.

The duty of the pastors (whom Scripture variously calls supervisors, elders, and ministers) is to proclaim the Word of God, in order to instruct, admonish, exhort, and rebuke, both in public and in private. It is their duty to administer the sacraments, and to exercise brotherly discipline together with the elders and commissioners...

The proper duty of teachers is to instruct believers in sound doctrine, so that the purity of the Gospel will not be corrupted by ignorance or by ungodly opinions. Nonetheless, as things are at present, we include within "teachers" the aids and instructions necessary to preserve godly doctrine and prevent the Church from becoming a barren waste because of the lack of pastors and ministers... The order closest to the ministry and associated intimately with the government of the Church is the lecturer in theology. It seems good that this should also include the teaching of the Old and New Testaments. However, since no one can profit by such instruction unless he has first learned the languages and the humanities, and since we must train up a future generation to keep the Church from being deserted by our children, we need to establish a school for their instruction, to prepare them not only for the ministry but for political life...

The third order is the elders, that is, those commissioned or appointed to the consistory by the authorities. Their responsibility is to keep watch over everyone's life, to admonish lovingly those whom they see going astray and leading disorderly lives, and (when necessary) to report them to the body which will be designated to make brotherly corrections, acting together with the others in making these corrections. If the Church thinks it prudent, the elders may be elected as follows: two from the Little Council, four from the Council of Sixty, and six from the Council of Two Hundred[41] – honest men of commendable life, irreproachable, free from suspicion, and above all fearing God and possessing a good spiritual judgment. They should be elected from every part of the city, so that oversight can be maintained over everyone...

The fourth order of Church government is the deacons. In the ancient Church there were always two orders of deacons. One was entrusted with the duty of receiving, distributing, and keeping safe the goods of the poor, their possessions, income, and pensions, as well as the daily offerings. The other sort was to supervise and take care of the sick and administer the charity for the poor. We have maintained this custom to the present day.

The *Ecclesiastical Ordinances* of 1541

John Calvin on justification by faith

We must now discuss justification fully, bearing in mind that this is the main hinge on which religion turns, so that we give greater attention and care to it. For unless you first of all grasp what your

---

[41] The Little Council, the Council of Sixty, and the Council of Two Hundred, were the political governing bodies of Geneva.

position before God is, and the nature of the judgment He passes on you, you have no foundation on which to establish your salvation, nor one on which to build any piety toward God. But the necessity of thoroughly understanding this subject will become clearer as we examine it.

To stop us stumbling on the very threshold (which would happen if we began discussing an unknown quantity), let us first explain what these expressions mean: that man is justified in God's sight, and that he is justified by faith or works. A man is said to be justified in God's sight if he is reckoned righteous in God's judgment and has also been accepted on account of his righteousness. Indeed, since iniquity is hateful to God, no sinner can find favour in His eyes so far as he is a sinner and is reckoned as a sinner. Accordingly, wherever there is sin, there also will be the anger and retribution of God. On the other hand, a man is justified if he is regarded, not as a sinner, but as a righteous man, and for that reason stands firm before God's judgment seat while all sinners fall. If an accused but innocent person is summoned before the judgment seat of a fair judge, where he will be judged according to his innocence, he is said to be "justified" before the judge. Likewise a person is justified before God when he is removed from the number of sinners, and God testifies and affirms his righteousness.

So then, a person is justified by works if a degree of purity and holiness are found in his life which deserves a testimony of righteousness before God's throne. Such a person, by the completeness of his works, can meet and satisfy God's judgment. On the contrary, a person is justified by faith if, excluded from the righteousness of works, he grasps the righteousness of Christ through faith, and then appears in God's sight clothed in Christ's righteousness, not as a sinner but as a righteous man. Therefore, we explain justification simply as the acceptance with which God receives us into His favour as righteous people. And we say that this justification consists in the forgiveness of sins and the imputation of Christ's righteousness.

There are many clear passages of Scripture to confirm this fact. First, it cannot be denied that this is the proper and most normal meaning of the word. But because it would take too long to collect all the passages and compare them, let it be enough to call them to our readers' attention, for they will easily discover such passages from their own study. I will bring forward only a few, where this justification of which we are speaking is specifically treated. First, Luke relates that the people, having heard Christ, "justified God" (Luke 7:29), and Christ declares that "wisdom is justified by her children" (Luke 7:35). In the former passage (Luke 7:29), Luke does not mean that the people confer righteousness on God. For righteousness always remains perfect in God, even though the whole world tries to snatch it away from him. Nor does he, in Luke 7:35, intend to make the doctrine of salvation righteous, which is righteous of itself. Rather, both expressions have the same meaning – to render to God and to His teaching the praise they deserve. On the other hand, when Christ rebukes the Pharisees for justifying themselves (Luke 16:15), he does not mean that they made themselves righteous by good deeds, but that they proudly seized upon the reputation for a righteousness of which they were in reality empty.

Those skilled in the Hebrew language better understand this sense, for in Hebrew people are called "wicked" not only when they are conscious of their crime, but when they receive the judgment of condemnation For when Bathsheba says that she and Solomon "will be wicked" (1 Kings 1:21), she does not admit any sin. Rather she complains that she and her son will be put to shame, by being *counted* among the wicked and condemned. Yet from the context it plainly appears that this word, even in Latin, can only be understood relatively [referring to a relationship], rather than signifying any quality [referring to an inner attribute].

But because it is relevant to the present case, when Paul says that "Scripture foresaw that God would justify the Gentiles by faith" (Galatians 3:8), what else can you understand this to mean but that God imputes righteousness by faith? Again, when he says that God justifies the ungodly person who has faith in Christ (Romans 3:26), what can his meaning be except that sinners are freed by the blessing of faith from that condemnation which their ungodliness deserved? This appears even more clearly in his conclusion, where he cries out, "Who will accuse God's elect? It is God who justifies. Who will condemn? It is Christ who died, yes, who rose again, and now intercedes for us" (Romans 8:33-34). It is as if he had said, "Who will accuse those whom God has absolved? Who will condemn those whom Christ defends with his protection?" Therefore, "to justify" means nothing else than to acquit of guilt an accused person, as if his innocence were confirmed. Therefore, since God justifies us by the intercession of Christ, He absolves us – not by the confirmation of our own innocence – but by the imputation of righteousness, so that we who are not righteous in ourselves may be accounted righteous in Christ.

John Calvin, *Institutes of the Christian Religion,* **Book 3, chapter 11, sections 1-3.**

Calvin on the doctrine of election

Verse 4. "According as He has chosen us." The foundation and the first cause of our calling, and indeed of all the blessings we receive from God, is here defined to be His eternal election. If we ask why God has called us to enjoy the gospel, why he daily showers on us so many good things, why he opens up the gates of heaven to us, the answer is always discovered in this principle – that "He has chosen us before the creation of the world." The very time when God elected us proves that it was a gracious election; for what could we have deserved, or what merit did we possess, before the world was even created? Some people childishly try to overthrow this argument by the following sophistry: "We were chosen because we were worthy, and because God foresaw that we would be worthy." But we were all lost in Adam! Therefore there was nothing worthy to foresee in us, when God rescued us from perishing by His own election. The same argument is used in the Letter to the Romans, where Paul speaks of Jacob and Esau, and says, "For before the children were born, when neither had done any good or evil, in order that the purpose of God according to election might stand, not by works, but by Him who calls" (Romans 9:11). But though they had not yet done anything, a sophist of the Sorbonne [the theology faculty of Paris university] might reply, "God foresaw what they would do." But this objection has no force when applied to the sinful natures of human beings, in whom nothing can be found but materials for destruction.

"In Christ." This is Paul's second proof that election is gracious; for if we are chosen in Christ, it is not in ourselves. We were not chosen from some perception of anything that we deserve, but because our heavenly Father bestowed on us the privilege of adoption and introduced us into the body of Christ. In short, the mention of Christ excludes all human merit, and everything which human beings derive from their own resources. For when Paul says that we are "chosen in Christ", it follows that in ourselves we are unworthy.

"That we should be holy." This is the immediate, but not the chief purpose of election. For there is nothing absurd in supposing that the same plan may secure two objects. The purpose of building is that there should be a house. This is the immediate purpose. But its actual use as a place of dwelling is the ultimate purpose. It was necessary to mention this in passing; for we shall soon find that Paul mentions another purpose, the glory of God. But there is no contradiction here; for the glory of God is the highest end, to which our sanctification is subordinate. This leads us to conclude that holiness, purity, and every spiritual excellence that is found among human beings, are the fruit of election. So once more Paul manifestly sets aside every idea of human merit. If God had foreseen in us anything worthy of election, this would have been stated in language the very opposite of what Paul says here. Paul's words plainly mean that all our holiness and purity of life flow from the election of God. How does it come about that some people are religious, and live in the fear of God, while others surrender themselves without restraint to all kinds of wickedness? If Paul may be believed, the only reason is that the latter act out their natural disposition, while the former have been chosen for holiness. The cause, certainly, does not come after the effect. Election then does not *depend* on the righteousness of works; no, Paul here declares that election is the *cause* of the righteousness of works.

From Calvin's *Commentary on Ephesians*.

Calvin on the Lord's Supper

To sum up: the flesh and blood of Christ feed our souls in the same way that bread and wine support and sustain our bodily life. For the analogy of the sign holds true only if our souls find nourishment in Christ. This cannot happen unless Christ truly grows into oneness with us, and refreshes us by the eating of His flesh and the drinking of His blood. It may seem incredible that Christ's flesh, separated from us by such a great distance, penetrates to us, so that it becomes our food. But we must remember how far the secret power of the Holy Spirit rises high above all our senses, and how foolish it is to wish to limit His infinity by our limits. So then, let faith grasp what our mind does not understand: that the Spirit truly brings together things that are separated in space. Now, Christ also testifies and seals in the Supper that holy sharing in His flesh and blood, by which He pours His life into us, as if it penetrated into our bones and marrow. He testifies this, not by offering us a worthless and empty sign, but by manifesting in the sign the power of His Spirit to fulfil what He promises. And truly, to all who sit at that spiritual feast, He offers and exhibits the reality that is signified there, although it is received with benefit by believers alone, who accept this great generosity with true faith and thankful hearts. Likewise the apostle said, "The bread which we break is a participation in the body of Christ; the cup which we consecrate to this use by word and prayers is a participation in His blood" (1 Corinthians 10:16).

There are no grounds for anyone to object that this is a figure of speech, by which the name of the thing signified is transferred to the sign. I admit that the breaking of bread is a symbol; the broken bread is not the thing itself [Christ's flesh]. But, having admitted this, reason still leads us to accept that by exhibiting the symbol, the thing itself is also exhibited. For unless a person intends to call God a liar, he would never dare assert that God sets forth an empty symbol. Therefore, if the Lord truly signifies our sharing in His body through the breaking of bread, there ought to be no doubt that He truly exhibits and shows forth His body. And the godly certainly ought to observe this rule: whenever they see symbols appointed by the Lord, they should think and be persuaded that the truth of the thing signified is surely present too. Why should the Lord put in your hand the symbol of His body, except to assure you that you truly share in it? Truly a visible sign is given to us in order to seal an invisible gift. Therefore, when we have received the symbol of the body, let us trust no less surely that the body itself is also given to us.

Calvin, *Institutes of the Christian Religion*, Book 4, chapter 17, section 10.

The Protestant appeal to the early Church fathers

Now, if you can bear to hear a more true definition of the Church than your own, say in future that it is the community of all holy people – a community which is spread over the whole world, and exists in all ages, yet is bound together by one doctrine and the one Spirit of Christ, and nurtures and observes unity of faith and brotherly harmony. With this Church, we deny that we have any disagreement. The very opposite: we revere her as our Mother, and we desire to remain in her bosom.

But here you bring an accusation against us. You claim that everything which has been approved for fifteen hundred years or more by the unchanging consent of believers, is now being uprooted and destroyed by our self-willed audacity. I will not ask you to deal truthfully and honestly with us (though such treatment should be gladly offered by a philosopher and a Christian). I will only ask you not to descend into an prejudiced indulgence in slander, which would be extremely harmful to your reputation with serious and honest men, even if we remain silent. You know, Sadoleto – and if you dare to deny it, I will make it plain to everyone that you knew, yet cunningly and craftily disguised the fact – that our agreement with the ancient Church is far closer than yours. Further, you know that all we have attempted has been to renew the ancient form of the Church, which was at first defiled and distorted by uneducated men of indifferent character, and was afterwards scandalously mangled and almost destroyed by the Roman pope and his faction.

I will not press you so closely as to summon you back to that form of the Church which the apostles instituted (though it provides us with the only pattern of a true Church, and whoever turns aside from it in the slightest degree is in error). To indulge you so far, I beg you to set before your eyes that ancient form of the Church, such as we find it in the times and the writings of Chrysostom and Basil among the Greeks, and of Cyprian, Ambrose, and Augustine, among the Latins. Next, contemplate the wreckage of that Church as it now survives among yourselves. Surely the difference will show itself as great as the prophetic description of the difference between the celebrated Church which flourished under David and Solomon, and that which under Zedekiah and Jehoiakim had fallen into every kind of superstition, and had utterly ruined the purity of divine worship. Will you then accuse a man of being an enemy of the ancient Church, if he is zealous for the ancient piety and holiness, and dissatisfied with the state of things in a Church that has become corrupt and degenerate, and therefore attempts to improve the Church's condition and restore her to her original splendour?

From Calvin's *Letter to Cardinal Sadoleto.*

Calvin's letter to the five Protestant martyrs of Chambery

[One of the most famous examples of Calvin's correspondence was his letters to five of his theology students who, having just returned

from Geneva to their native France as evangelists, were imprisoned
and eventually put to death in the town of Chambery in 1555. This
extract is from Calvin's first letter.]

My brothers, the moment we heard about your imprisonment, I sent
a messenger over the mountains to obtain more certain information
about it, and also to find out if there was any means of helping you.
He set out last Thursday at 3 o'clock in the afternoon, and arrived
back only yesterday, late in the evening. He is about to go on a
second journey to carry our letters to you, and advise how we can
comfort you in your affliction. We have no need to tell you, at
greater length, what affection we have for you, and with what
anguish our hearts are filled by your chains. Since so many of the
brothers are praying fervently for you, I am convinced that our
heavenly Father will listen to their desires and groans. Indeed I see
from your letters how He has already begun to work in you. For if
the weakness of the flesh sometimes shows itself in hard and
difficult struggles with which you will have to contend, this is no
marvel to me, but rather a cause for magnifying God, because He
has raised you above it. The brothers Laborie and Trigalet [two of
the martyrs] have grounds of comfort, since those who are nearest
and dearest to them quietly resign themselves to the will of God.

For the rest, you have learned your lessons so well in the school of
Jesus Christ, that you have no need for long letters of exhortation.
Simply practice what you have learned. Since it has pleased the
Master to employ you in this service, continue in what you have
begun. Though the door is now closed against your edifying by
doctrine those to whom you had devoted your labour, the witness
you are about to bear will not fail to confirm them from afar. For
God will bestow on your suffering a power to echo further than the
human voice can reach. As to worldly means for your deliverance –
without being too confident, I wish we had such means, so that we
might make use of them. Indeed, we will be blameworthy if we do
not strain every nerve for that purpose. But God urges us to look
higher. Your chief task is to collect all your thoughts in order to rest
in His fatherly goodness, not doubting that He will take your bodies

as well as your souls under His protection. If the blood of His faithful followers is precious, He will effectually show it in you, since He has chosen you to be His witnesses. And if it is His will to require the sacrifice of your lives to commend His truth, this is (as you know) an offering well-pleasing in His sight. Be comforted also that in surrendering everything into His hands, you will lose nothing; for if He lovingly purposes to take us under His protection during this perishable life, then having called us away from it, He will much more show himself the faithful Guardian of our souls....

Your humble brother, whom you know, John Calvin.

Calvin's letter to the five martyrs of Chambery, 5th September 1555.

Relics of the Virgin Mary?

Their belief that the Virgin's body was not buried on earth, but was taken up to heaven, has robbed the papists of all pretext for fabricating any relics of her mortal remains, which otherwise might have been abundant enough to fill up a whole cemetery. However, in order to have at least something belonging to her, they have tried to make up for the absence of other relics by claiming to possess her hair and her milk. Her hair is displayed in several churches in Rome, and at Salvatierra in Spain, and at Magon, Saint Flour, Cluny, Nevers, and in many other towns. As for her milk, there is probably not a town, a monastery, or a nunnery, where it is not displayed in large or small quantities. In fact, if the Virgin had breast-fed babies her entire life, or been a dairy farm, she could not have produced more milk than they display as hers in various places! How they acquired all this milk they do not say. It is hardly worth adding that there is no basis in the Gospels for such foolish and blasphemous absurdities.

The Virgin's wardrobe has also produced a lavish collection of relics. There is a shirt of hers at Chartres, which has been venerated as an idol, and there is another one at Aix-la-Chapelle [Aachen]. I do not know how these things could have been acquired, for it is certain that the apostles and early Christians were not so trivial-minded as to amuse themselves by collecting such things. However, it is enough for us to consider the shape of these items of dress, in order clearly to see the audacity of those who put them on display. The shirt at Aix-la-Chapelle is a long clergyman's gown, hanging on a pole. Even if the Blessed Virgin had been a giant, she would still have felt it rather awkward to wear so large a garment. In the same church, they preserve the shoes of Saint Joseph, which (however) could only fit the foot of a little child or a dwarf. The proverb says that liars need good memories, to stop them contradicting their own sayings. This rule was manifestly not observed at Aix-la-Chapelle! Otherwise they would have taken more care that the shoes of the husband [Joseph] and the shirt of the wife [Mary] should have matched each other in size rather more suitably. And yet these relics, so empty of all semblance of truth, are piously kissed and venerated by crowds of people!

I know of only two of the Virgin's head-dresses. One is at the abbey of Saint Maximilan at Treyes, and the other is at Lisio in Italy. They may be considered quite as authentic as the Virgin's girdle at Prato and at Montserrat, and her slipper at Saint Jaqueme, and her shoe at Saint Flour. Now, those who know anything about this subject know that it was not the practice of the early Church to collect shoes and stockings (*etc.*) for relics, and that for five hundred years after the Virgin Mary's death there was never any talk of such things. These well-known facts should have been sufficient to prove the silliness of all these relics of the Virgin.

From Calvin's *Treatise on Relics.*

Chapter 5.

FLOWERS FOR THE BEES: THE RADICAL REFORMATION.

The Reformation was a complex phenomenon. The Magisterial Reformers, on whom we have thus far focused our attention, differed among themselves in their theology (Lutheran and Reformed) and in their approach to Church-state relations (what we have called "statist" and "Reformed Catholic"). However, in addition to the Magisterial Reformers, the Radicals – on whom the present Chapter will concentrate – stand forth as yet another reforming force that was quite distinct in ethos and ideology from all branches of the Magisterial Reformation.[1] If to this already intricate picture we then add the internal reformation of the Roman Catholic Church (see Chapter 7), it is not surprising that some historians have started talking about the "Reformations" of the 16th century.

This plural approach to "Reformations" is very helpful. The term "Radical Reformation" can be misleading, if we take it to mean that there was a single great entity called "the Reformation" and that the Radicals were simply one aspect of it. It is much more true to the facts to think of the Radical Reformation as *one* of the Reformations

---

[1] It would make matters clearer if we restricted the term "Protestant" to the Lutheran and Reformed Churches (and the post-Reformation Anglican Church, if one wishes to classify it as a distinct entity, although theologically it was Reformed in the 16th century). It was the Magisterial Reformers (both Lutheran and Reformed), not the Radicals, who "protested" at the Diet of Speyer in 1529, and then presented their confessions of faith at Augsburg in 1530. The Radicals were not really Protestants in any historic sense.

that was undertaken and experienced by 16th century men and women. What the present Chapter will try to do is examine the distinctive features of this Radical Reformation, in order to see what constituted its unifying characteristics, what made it differ from the other Reformations, and what its own internal diversities were.

The obvious factor that Magisterial and Radical Reformers held in common was their shared critique of certain aspects of late medieval Catholicism, and their rejection of the papacy. In the early days of Luther and Zwingli, therefore, when people were still thinking out the implications of their protest against Rome and the shape of their own positive alternative to a discredited Catholicism, it was only natural that all anti-Romanists should have seemed to be on the same side. It soon became increasingly clear, however, that this was far from the case. Luther was the first to perceive this; his swift and complete repudiation of the Zwickau prophets in 1522 (see Chapter 3) raised up a standard that served to separate the Lutheran Reformation from the Radical Reformation, which (Luther profoundly believed) had tried to hijack his own movement for a different and false agenda. Zwingli came to the same conclusion regarding the Zurich Radicals in 1523.

What, then, was the Radical agenda? The foremost modern historian of the Radical Reformation, George Huntston Williams, has argued that we can best understand the Radicals by viewing them as incarnating three tendencies – the Anabaptist, the Spiritualist, and the Rationalist (or anti-Trinitarian). This may be confusing to those who have learned to see all the Radicals as "Anabaptists"; indeed, in the 16th century, all Radicals *were* called Anabaptists by their critics. For Williams, however, the Anabaptists were one of *three* basic Radical types. These were not three separate, rigidly defined parties, but one of these tendencies would generally assume a dominant influence in the mind of a Radical or local grouping of Radicals (although the other two tendencies might also be present in a more muted form). This threefold scheme of Anabaptist, Spiritualist, and Rationalist, is now widely adopted by historians;

we will therefore use it as a way of conducting our own exploration of the Radical Reformation.

1. The Anabaptist Radicals

Among the three Radical tendencies – the Anabaptist, the Spiritualist, and the Rationalist – the Anabaptist was perhaps the most influential, and the Anabaptist Radicals stood closest to the Magisterial Reformers in their theological outlook. The birthplace of Anabaptist Radicalism is normally seen as Zwingli's Zurich, so we will begin our story there.[2]

The Swiss Brethren

Zwingli's preaching and teaching had created a definite pro-reform movement in Zurich by 1522. The same year, however, revealed that the Reformer was going to have trouble from some of his most ardent supporters. A number of them unsettled Zwingli by their outspoken and provocative anti-Catholic sentiments and behaviour. They ostentatiously broke the medieval Church's food laws (*e.g.* eating sausages during Lent[3]), disrupted Roman Catholic services of worship, and stirred up unrest over the payment of tithes and the veneration of icons and relics (there was a wave of image-smashing in September 1523).

Zwingli's attitude was ambivalent. On the one hand, he agreed with these zealots that the things they were attacking were wrong. On the other hand, he was deeply opposed to individuals taking the task of reformation into their own hands. Zurich, in Zwingli's eyes,

---

[2] I have tried to tell the story even-handedly. Most modern accounts tend to tell it from the Radical viewpoint; I have also tried to show how events must have appeared in the eyes of Zwingli and his colleagues. This does not imply any value judgment on my part.

[3] Zwingli agreed in principle that this was acceptable, but argued that in practice that Christians should refrain from breaking the traditional food laws in the interests of peace and charity, until the ignorant had been fully instructed in Christian liberty.

was a Christian city, and he was committed to a peaceful, orderly, legal approach to reforming its religious life, in which every step was sanctioned by the community through its political leaders. The way his more fervent supporters were going about the business smacked of senseless counter-productive anarchy to the methodical, community-minded Zwingli. He was particularly appalled when three of the leading Radicals – Conrad Grebel, Felix Mantz, and Simon Stumpf – approached him to sound him out on the possibility of setting up new separatist congregations which would be composed only of the truly committed. Zwingli rejected the notion emphatically; it clashed with his more medieval concept of society as a Christian body (the *Corpus Christianum*), in which all citizens were Christians by baptism and religious profession, however poorly they lived up to their religion. From Zwingli's standpoint, the Radicals were asking him to *abandon* the existing Church structures embodied in the worshipping community of Zurich, whereas Zwingli felt he had a God-given responsibility to *reform* them.

The parting of the ways came in October 1523. The recent outbreak of iconoclasm forced the Zurich city council to hold a public disputation on the whole question of icons. Zwingli dominated the proceedings; he argued convincingly that the physical veneration of icons was contrary to Scripture, and that icons should therefore be removed from churches because their presence always led in practice to idolatry. So far, the Radicals were delighted. But Zwingli believed his task was done when he had proclaimed the truth. It was not up to him, or to any private individual, to remove the icons; this must be done legally by the Christian magistrates. When the Zurich city council, therefore, failed to act against icons in the immediate aftermath of the disputation, Zwingli was not too upset. He would simply go on preaching, and external reform would inevitably follow when enough people were won over. (The city council in fact decreed the "cleansing of the churches" from icons eight months later, in June 1524). But the Radicals were left totally disenchanted. For them, Zwingli seemed to be divorcing truth from action. They could endure it no longer. A decisive psychological boundary was crossed, and from now on the Radicals turned sharply against their former leader, denouncing Zwingli as a hypocrite, a compromiser, and an apostate. "Anyone who thinks, believes, or says that Zwingli is performing his duty as a pastor," wrote Conrad Grebel, "believes and says what is ungodly."

Who were these one-time supporters of Zurich's Magisterial Reformer who now broke with him so bitterly? Their leading figure, **Conrad Grebel** (1498-1526), belonged to one of the most prominent aristocratic families of Zurich; educated at Basel and Vienna universities, steeped in Erasmian humanism, he was well versed in both Hebrew and Greek. Grebel owed his spiritual awakening to the preaching of Zwingli. **Felix Mantz** (1498-1527) was the son of one of the canons of Zurich cathedral; like Grebel, he was an accomplished humanist scholar, indebted to Zwingli for his conversion to reform. Zwingli referred to Mantz, a more eloquent speaker than Grebel, as "the Apollo of the Anabaptists".[4] Other pioneers were the fiery George Cajacob Blaurock, a converted priest; Wilhelm Roubli, another priest won over to a Zwinglian-style reform; and Simon Stumpf, an ex-monk from southern Germany, one of Zwingli's earliest supporters.

The most outstanding theologian of the group, however, was not even resident in Zurich – **Balthasar Hubmaier** (1485-1528). Although Hubmaier's career places him more in a south German context, his links with Zurich and its Anabaptists were strong. Hubmaier studied at Freiburg university, earning a doctorate in theology in 1512. He had a profound knowledge of patristic and scholastic theology, and was successively co-rector of Ingolstadt university in 1515, and parish priest at Regensburg from 1516 and at Waldshut from 1521 (Waldshut was quite close to Switzerland – hence Hubmaier's close involvement with the Zurich Radical movement). His preaching brought him popularity. Converted to Lutheranism in 1522, he passed over into Zwinglianism in 1523, convinced by Zwingli's eucharistic doctrine and more drastic ideals

---

4   Apollo was the Roman god who brought heaven's messages to mortals, and so was associated with speech and eloquence.

for reforming worship ("whatever Scripture does not authorise is forbidden"). He actually took part in the Zurich disputation on icons in 1523, standing shoulder to shoulder with Zwingli. He then returned to Waldshut and carried out a sweeping Zwinglian-style reform of worship in his parish.

It will be seen that the leaders of the Radical movement were highly educated and socially respectable men, strongly influenced by Erasmian humanism. The bulk of the Swiss Radicals may have been uneducated people – peasants, farmers, *etc.* – but their religious concerns were articulated by scholars like Grebel, Mantz, and Hubmaier, who possessed formidable intellects by any standard.

Early in 1524, Wilhelm Roubli, pastor of Zollikon and Wytikon (parishes in the canton of Zurich), began preaching against infant baptism. By August his message had borne fruit: two farmers in his Wytikon congregation refused to bring their children for baptism. Other families followed their example. The same happened in Zollikon. When the Zurich city council found out, it responded by commanding the parents to present their children for baptism. This panic reaction was counterbalanced by a more rational approach from Zwingli and his close colleagues Leo Jud and Oswald Myconius, who from October onwards engaged in private discussions with Grebel and other Radical leaders to see if they could be won over. Unfortunately the discussions were derailed when some of the Radicals resorted to physically aggressive tactics – noisily disrupting Zwinglian services of worship, vandalising the baptismal font at Zollikon. (This kind of violence was sometimes not far from the surface in rather too many of the Radicals, and it did untold damage to their cause.)

The upshot was that the council decreed a public disputation on baptism, to be held on January 17th 1525 in the Zurich town hall. Zwingli and Heinrich Bullinger[5] acted as the spokesmen for infant baptism; Grebel, Mantz, Roubli, and Blaurock argued the case for

---

[5] Bullinger became Zwingli's successor in Zurich after the latter's death in 1531. See Chapter 3, section 8.

believer's baptism. The debate lasted for two days. The council awarded victory to Zwingli and Bullinger, and enacted that those who had refused to bring their children for baptism must do so within eight days on pain of banishment. Lay preaching and private religious gatherings were forbidden.

Then followed one of the great symbolic scenes of the Radical Reformation. On January 21st 1525, some 16 or so men of Zurich made their way through the snow to the house of Felix Mantz, quite close to the cathedral. After praying together, George Blaurock asked Conrad Grebel to baptise him with true Christian baptism on profession of his faith. Grebel poured water over him while Blaurock knelt. Blaurock himself then baptised 15 others. Many more adult baptisms followed; one contemporary report stated that at least 80 were baptised in a single week in Zollikon. The newly baptised also began celebrating the Lord's Supper among themselves, outside the structure of Zurich's established church order. Having thus formed themselves into a distinct and self-conscious movement, in effect a new church, these one-time followers of Zwingli are often called the "Swiss Brethren".[6]

To Zwingli and the city council, the baptisms and eucharists of the Swiss Brethren were acts of anarchy which struck at the roots of the Zwinglian vision of Zurich as a united Christian community. Such lawless turmoil could not be tolerated – any more than a Western society today would tolerate the idea of a group of its citizens deciding to ignore state law and follow their own self-chosen legal system. Religion, for the medieval mind, was the glue that held society together. And the Magisterial Reformation was far more of a medieval than a modern phenomenon. Consequently, Zwingli saw nothing unChristian in the city council's response to the situation when it arrested a large number of the Radicals in February, including Grebel, Mantz, Blaurock, and Roubli. Once more Zwingli engaged in private discussion with his ex-disciples, but to no avail; they simply asserted their freedom to believe and

---

[6] This has nothing to do with the Brethren movement which originated in the United Kingdom and spread worldwide from the 1830s onwards.

practise as their consciences directed, whatever Zwingli or the city council might think or do. Eventually Mantz was fined, Blaurock was banished, and Grebel and Roubli departed from the city voluntarily after being given a stern warning never again to disturb the good Christian order of Zurich by their revolutionary fanaticism. (In treating the Radicals this way, of course, Zwingli and the city council were simply acting as *their* consciences directed! The appeal to conscience cuts both ways.) This exodus of the Swiss Brethren from Zurich scattered the seeds of Radicalism into the neighbouring cantons of Switzerland; many more baptisms took place in Appenzell, Basel, Berne, Constance, Saint Gall, and Schaffhausen.[7]

In May, Zwingli wrote his first theological treatise against the Radicals, entitled *Baptism, Rebaptism, and Infant Baptism*. The word he used for rebaptism was "Anabaptism", from the Greek *ana*, "again". So was born the 16th century name for those Radicals (the majority) who practised believer's baptism – the *Anabaptists*, the Rebaptisers.[8] Anabaptists themselves rejected the label, since they held infant baptism to be invalid; in their view they were not being rebaptised, but baptised for the first time. Zwingli's polemic provoked a reply from Balthasar Hubmaier, *The Christian Baptism of Believers*, a powerful piece of writing which became a classic among the Anabaptist Radicals.

Despite the banishment of the leading Swiss Brethren, Radicalism itself had not died out in Zurich. There is evidence that it even grew in strength. However, it also continued to manifest itself in highly unfortunate and bizarre ways. On one notable occasion, a procession of Radicals marched through the streets of the city, waving willow branches, chanting "Woe unto thee, Zurich!" and denouncing

---

[7]   Roubli eventually became so disillusioned by the internal problems of the Radical movement that he gave up on it altogether, and lived to a ripe old age as a conformist in Reformed Zurich and Basel.

[8]   The Rationalist wing of the Radical Reformation, exemplified in the Socianians (see section 3), also practised believers' baptism, but following Williams' schematisation I will be referring to them as Rationalists, not Anabaptists.

Zwingli as none other than the Great Red Dragon of the book of Revelation.[9]

In October, the council once more arrested Grebel, Mantz, and Blaurock for their unabated Radical activities within the canton of Zurich – from the council's standpoint, they had clearly not observed the terms of their banishment. They were imprisoned indefinitely. Another public disputation on baptism was arranged for 6th-8th November. So many people attended, it had to be held in the cathedral to accommodate them all. Zwingli, Jud, and Megander[10] faced Grebel, Mantz, and Blaurock, and the "debate" swiftly degenerated into a slanging match, each side heaping abuse on the other. In December, Balthasar Hubmaier rather quixotically turned up in Zurich, only to be promptly arrested. An ill and depressed man, he was bullied by Zwingli into signing a recantation of his Radical beliefs. However, when the day came for Hubmaier to read out his recantation in public, he instead recanted his recantation, and was promptly arrested again. After some rather ugly treatment in prison, Hubmaier recanted again and was allowed to leave Zurich. This most brilliant of the early Anabaptist thinkers ended up in Eastern Europe, in Moravia, where he is said to have (re)baptised up to 6,000 people. However, in July 1527 he was arrested by the authorities and tried in Roman Catholic Vienna. This time, he did not recant, and Hubmaier was burnt at the stake on March 10th 1528. Three days later, his wife was executed by drowning in the river Elbe.

To return to the story of the Zurich Radicals: in March 1526, the council reached the end of its patience with them, and passed an ominous decree that henceforth anyone who rebaptised another was to be put to death by drowning. Again, this had Zwingli's approval; like Calvin (and indeed like some of the Radicals themselves, notably Michael Servetus), he accepted the medieval concept that heresy was a capital crime. In November the council extended the

---

9   Since Zwingli did not believe the book of Revelation was canonical, he was no doubt not too troubled by this eyebrow-raising identification.
10 An otherwise unimportant Zwinglian Reformer.

death penalty to include anyone who attended the preaching of an Anabaptist.

The first to suffer the penalty was Felix Mantz, who thus enjoys the singular honour of being the first Radical to be executed for his religion by a Protestant state.[11] He, Grebel, and Blaurock had actually escaped from prison in March 1526, possibly with the connivance of the council which wanted nothing better than to be rid of these trouble-makers. However, Mantz and Blaurock reappeared in Zurich in October and were arrested yet again for rebaptising. This time, there would be no escape. Mantz was led out to execution on January 5th 1527; by a cruel irony, given Mantz's Anabaptist beliefs, he was put to death by drowning in the river Limmat.[12] Blaurock, not being a citizen of Zurich, was denied the privilege of being executed, and got off with merely being beaten. He made his way to the Austrian city of Innsbruck, where the Roman Catholic authorities burnt him at the stake in 1529. Conrad Grebel, in many ways the leading personality among the Zurich Radicals, eluded all forms of martyrdom by dying of the plague in the summer of 1526.

It was in the immediate aftermath of Mantz's martyrdom that one of the most historically important Radical gatherings took place, in February 1527, in Schleitheim (in the Swiss Protestant canton of Schaffhausen). The significance of the gathering lay in its promulgation of the Schleitheim Confession (see below). From the ranks

---

[11] I am excluding the Radicals like Thomas Müntzer executed in 1525 for their part in the German Peasants' Revolt (see Chapter 3, section 3). From the point of view of Müntzer and other Radicals executed for their part in the Revolt, they were indeed being put to death for their religion, since their religion was the inspiration for their violent crusade; but from the point of view of their judges, they were put to death for the act of insurrection, not the religious beliefs which lay behind it. Felix Mantz was put to death, not for acts of violence, but simply for rebaptising.

[12] Not that Mantz was the first religious martyr among the Radicals – that distinction must be awarded to Hippolytus Eberli, burnt at the stake by the Roman Catholic canton of Schwyz in May 1525. Rome had already started down the bloodstained path of executing Radicals for reasons of belief before Protestant governments decided to follow the Roman example.

of Zurich Radicals, Wilhelm Roubli was the most prominent figure in the gathering.[13] However, its dominant figure was ***Michael Sattler*** (1490-1527), from the Swiss village of Staufen, near Freiburg. Originally a Benedictine monk, Sattler abandoned his religious order in 1523 under the influence of Reformation teachings, and married. He ended up in Zurich where he threw in his lot with the Radicals, for which he was banished in November 1525. Sattler continued to promote the Anabaptist faith in southern Germany, in Horb, Rottenburg, and Strasbourg.[14] In Strasbourg he interacted with the Magisterial Reformers Martin Bucer and Wolfgang Capito, who found Sattler much more orthodox than most of the other Radicals they had encountered, and treated him sympathetically. Then in February 1527 Sattler journeyed back to Switzerland, where he effectively presided over the Radical synod which had assembled in Schleitheim.

The Schleitheim Confession (see the end of the Chapter for the main part of its text) dealt exclusively with matters of morality and Church order. In this respect, it served to highlight the crucial moral and ecclesiastical differences between the majority of Anabaptist Radicals and the Magisterial Reformation. We can summarise its teaching under the following headings: (a) believers' baptism; (b) a rigorous approach to the excommunication of the unworthy – or the "ban", as Anabaptists called it; (c) the Lord's Supper as an ordinance that belongs only to those baptised as believers; (d) the complete separation of true believers from unbelievers in all religious and political matters; (e) the high importance of the pastoral office; (f) total pacifism and non-violence, and hence the rejection of magistracy as a Christian calling, since magistrates have to use force to uphold the law; (g) the total rejection of oaths. We will look at some of these themes in more detail later. Among them all, perhaps it was the ban that became the most distinctive factor in Anabaptist church life, as we shall see.

---

[13] That is, if he was there at all; there seems to be some doubt on the matter.
[14] For Bucer and Capito, see Chapter 4, section 5.

One searches the Schleitheim Confession in vain, however, for any treatment of strictly theological issues; we find absolutely nothing in its pages about the nature of God, Christ, or salvation. It has been argued that this glaring absence of theology was due to the specific circumstances which produced the Confession – the need felt by those at Schleitheim to state their views on *controversial* points. On this basis, one might maintain that the Confession does not deal with theology because a broad agreement prevailed among the Anabaptist Radicals over theological issues.

Yet this seems less than entirely convincing. The Confession was soon being adopted as a statement of fundamental beliefs by many Anabaptist Radicals, *e.g.* the Mennonites (see below), functioning much as the Augsburg Confession did among Lutherans. There certainly *were* theological questions, very serious ones, that separated the Anabaptists from the Magisterial Reformers, and from other Radicals. Why were these not addressed in the Confession? It seems more plausible that the Confession's silence on theology was itself a symptom of the prevailing mindset among the Anabaptist Radicals. They were not primarily interested in theology, but in ethics – in the Christian life, which they understood in terms of the primacy of love and the imitation of Christ (an outlook which probably owed something to the influence of Erasmus). This very attitude set them apart sharply from Luther, Zwingli, and Calvin, who perceived Christianity primarily in terms of *dogma*. For the Magisterial Reformers, theology came first and determined everything else. For the Anabaptist Radicals, it was really lifestyle that came first, and much of their theologising arose out of their ethical and communal concerns.

What, then, was the distinctive theology of the Swiss Brethren (even if it is not found in the Schleitheim Confession)? Naturally we are tempted to rush first to their doctrine of believer's baptism, which *is* in the Confession, but there were profounder differences between the Anabaptists and Zwingli. The most fundamental was that the Anabaptists did not share Zwingli's commitment to Augustinian views of salvation. One of the characteristics of the whole

Radical Reformation was its more optimistic stance on human nature than the Magisterial Reformers held. Radicals rejected the bondage of the will, modified or even rejected the doctrine of original sin, and affirmed the freedom of all human beings to respond savingly to God's grace. A constant element in their polemic against the Magisterial Reformation was that its Augustinian theology of human depravity and sovereign grace was nothing more nor less than a license to sin. (Here we see again the practical lifestyle thrust of the Radicals: theology must be supportive of the life of obedience. Their animus against Augustinianism stemmed from their conviction that its pessimism about human nature sapped the foundations of serious moral and spiritual endeavour.)

The greatest of the early Anabaptist Radical theologians, Zwingli's one-time reforming comrade Balthasar Hubmaier, was quite forthright in condemning Augustine as a major pervertor of Christianity, and in setting out an alternative concept of salvation which made God's grace dependent on human free will for its effect. He gave classic expression to these views in his treatise *Concerning Freedom of the Will* (1527). Hubmaier basically agreed with Erasmus rather than Luther on the related issues of sin, grace, human freedom, and divine predestination (see Chapter 3, section 4).[15] Hubmaier's anti-Augustinian views proved to be typical of the Anabaptists and other Radicals, and acted as one of the widest gulfs separating them from Luther and Zwingli. In this respect, it has been argued that the Radicals were actually far more conservative than the Magisterial Reformers: it was Luther and Zwingli who broke "radically" with the Semi-Pelagian theology of the later medieval period, whereas the Radicals preserved and maintained it.

Allied to this, the Anabaptists rejected the Magisterial doctrine of forensic justification by faith alone. Although we find clear statements from Anabaptist leaders that Christ and his salvation are

---

[15]   As we've seen, Anabaptist Radicals also shared Erasmus's comparative lack of interest in theology and his emphasis on lifestyle, which comes out so clearly in the Schleitheim Confession. Erasmus was a far more formative influence on Anabaptist Radicalism than has often been acknowledged.

initially received by faith, we also find them rejecting the Magisterial Reformation's systematic distinction between justification and sanctification, and its strongly forensic definition of justification. Anabaptists perceived forensic justification (like the Augustinian view of sin and grace) as a threat to the life of obedience, a license to sin. In place of forensic justification through the objective work of Christ, they located the controlling theme of Christian faith in the new birth, conversion, and holiness. As one historian has argued, for the Magisterial Reformers the essential question was, "What must I do to be saved?"; but for the Anabaptists, it was, "How should a Christian live?" Not surprisingly, this Anabaptist distaste for forensic justification, and focussing on subjective holiness, prompted the Magisterial Reformers to see them as no better than Roman Catholics – Anabaptists were "the new monks", as Luther put it.

Another pervasive theme which made understanding difficult between Zwingli and the Swiss Brethren was their conflicting theology of the Church and its relationship to civil society. Zwingli was willing to accept as a church member anyone who professed Christianity, which in the religious culture of his day meant all the citizens of Zurich. In practice, therefore, church and civil society were simply two sides of the same coin. The Anabaptists, by contrast, saw the church as a stark alternative to civil society, and restricted church membership to those who gave evidence of their inward sincerity and commitment. They completely repudiated the medieval concept of Christendom, in which everyone born into a "Christian society" soaked up Christianity from his culture and was automatically regarded as a Christian unless he opted out through heresy or unbelief. For the Anabaptists, the Church of Jesus Christ was a radically separate community which an individual had to opt *into* by a personal act of faith. The moral purity of this community was then to be preserved by a strict and unsentimental use of the ban: the Anabaptists may have advocated religious toleration in society at large (see below), but they tended to be extremely intolerant of what they considered moral lapses among their own. Many of the most wounding internal divisions of the Anabaptists were over the extent and severity of the ban (see the section on the Mennonites).

The dichotomy between the Zwinglian and Anabaptist attitude towards Church and state was stretched to breaking point when the Anabaptists made it clear that opting *into* the Church meant opting *out* of civil society – becoming "drop-outs", as we might say today. In the eyes of the government of Zurich, this was undoubtedly the greatest crime of the Swiss Brethren. Their counter-culture revolution against the state involved the rejection of the normal responsibilities of citizenship. They refused, as we have noted from the Schleitheim Confession, to swear any oaths, taking their stand on Christ's command "Swear not at all" in the Sermon on the Mount. This not only disrupted the legal system, it laid the Brethren open to the charge of treason, because they would not take the oath of loyalty which the urban Swiss were required to swear to their city each year. Equally serious in the eyes of the magistrates (and in the eyes of most ordinary folk too, it must be said) was the pacifism of the Anabaptist Radicals. They refused all military service on principle. This was of critical significance in the Swiss context, since the cantons of Switzerland had no standing armies; every man was expected to defend his canton as part of a citizen army when called to arms by the government. This was particularly important in city-cantons like Zurich, because of their culture of intense civic pride and patriotism, the fact that they had a city to defend. To decline military service was perceived as deeply unpatriotic and criminally treacherous.

To compound matters, the Swiss Brethren went even further, entirely rejecting politics as a Christian vocation. No Christian, they argued, could be a magistrate, because magistrates had to use force to uphold the law, and this was contrary to Christ's teaching of peace. They recognised that the state was instituted by God, but maintained that it was "outside the perfection of Christ", *i.e.* it was instituted for the government of the unbelieving world, and its sword-bearing magistrates could be taken only from among unbelievers. Further, the Anabaptist Radicals denied to the state any coercive power in matters of religion. On the one hand, this meant that the state had no role in the ordering of the Church, *e.g.* in appointing pastors, or telling Christians what they must believe. (Thus far, most later Reformed Churchmen who took their cue from Bucer and Calvin would broadly agree.) On the other hand, however, the Anabaptist view also meant that the state had no right to punish heresy, blasphemy, or idolatry; and *this* was the real parting of the ways between the Radical Reformation and all other contemporary forms of Christianity, whether Protestant, Roman Catholic, or Eastern Orthodox. Radicals were fighting for what we would call "liberty of conscience" or "religious toleration". These concepts, though, had a very limited appeal to most 16th century Christians, because to the majority the Radical view seemed to de-Christianise the state. How can the state bow the knee to Christ, and enact laws on the basis of His religion, without having any right to discourage or suppress idolatrous religions which attack the very foundations of a Christian moral and political order?

To most Christians today, it will seem obvious that the Anabaptists were both right and noble in their advocacy of religious freedom. To most of their Christian contemporaries, it seemed equally obvious that this was one of the Radical Reformation's most dangerous, even blasphemously anti-Christian ideas.

The Swiss Brethren's understanding of the nature and extent of the Church came to be focused in the issue of baptism – specifically, infant baptism. Zwingli himself, in his early reforming days, had not been convinced that infant baptism was biblical. He admitted to Balthasar Hubmaier in 1523, prior to the Second Zurich Disputation, that it would be better if children were not baptised until they had been instructed in the faith. Around the same time, Zwingli had written concerning infant baptism: "I leave it untouched; I call it neither right nor wrong. If we were to baptise as Christ instituted it, then we would not baptise anyone until he reached the age of discretion." By the end of 1523, however, Zwingli had moved to a decided commitment to infant baptism, probably because he realised that its rejection undermined the concept of Zurich as a corporately Christian city, and hence to the end of government support for his reforming programme.

The Swiss Radicals took the opposite path, carrying Zwingli's initial doubts to their logical conclusion. Their rejection of infant baptism, they claimed, was the only position consistent with the principle of the sole infallible authority of Scripture. More importantly, the baptist theology of the Radicals was bound up with their view of the church as a voluntary society of penitent believers. A baby is not capable of repenting, believing the gospel, or joining himself to God's people by his own volition; therefore, no baby should be baptised, since baptism signifies repentance, faith, and church membership. The Swiss Brethren articulated a strongly ethical interpretation of baptism: it is a penitential act, a symbolic breaking with the old life of sin, and initiation into the new life of obedience in Christ. "It is," Hubmaier explained, "an outward and public testimony to the inward baptism of the Spirit." The baptised person was publicly renouncing sin, and entering into a voluntary covenant with Christ, and into Christ's covenanted community, the local church. The Anabaptists also stressed the point that had been made so cogently by Luther and Zwingli regarding the eucharist, that without faith the sacraments can confer no benefit. What benefit, then, does a baby receive from baptism?

Zwingli's response to these challenges was enormously consequential for the future of Reformed theology. The Zurich Reformer constructed a biblical defence of infant baptism by appealing to the analogy of circumcision. In the Old Testament Church, Zwingli argued, the offspring of covenant members were themselves born into the covenant community, and received circumcision as the initiating sign of this membership. Since the coming of Christ in the flesh, baptism has replaced circumcision; therefore the children of covenant-parents are now to receive baptism as the initiating sign of their New Covenant membership. Romans chapter 4 was Zwingli's proof-text for all this, with its theology of Abraham's circumcision as a "sign and seal" of covenant righteousness. To the fires, then, of the Zwingli-Anabaptist controversy, we can trace (at least in part) the origins of Reformed "covenant theology", which is still today the mainstream Reformed paedobaptist understanding of Church and sacraments. As for the Radical challenge that a baby lacks faith and repentance, Zwingli countered this by arguing that the parents accept the baptismal obligation on the child's behalf, promising to bring him up as a faithful, penitent Christian. (The Lutheran response to Anabaptism was significantly different at this point: Luther argued that baptism, as God's visible Word, actually creates a seed of faith in the baptised infant.)

Pilgram Marpeck

The Swiss Brethren were the first major Anabaptist grouping. Others followed, with significantly different beliefs and practices. One of the most important early Anabaptist leaders outside of Switzerland was *Pilgram Marpeck* (1495-1556). Born in Ratten-berg (then in Tyrol, now in Austria), Marpeck journeyed in the 1520s from medieval Catholicism, through Lutheranism, to Ana-baptism. From 1528 to 1531 he was in the relatively tolerant Protestant city of Strasbourg, where he fought hard to keep the local Anabaptists on an even keel, attracted as many were to the Spiritualist wing of Radicalism, or to the apocalyptic wing that wanted to set up God's kingdom by revolutionary violence (as in the Münster regime of Jan Beukels). These were both siren voices which Marpeck vigorously denounced. Unfortunately he also engaged in a running theological battle with Martin Bucer, Stras-bourg's leading Magisterial Reformer. The Reformed city council eventually ran out of its tolerance reserves and ordered Marpeck to leave Strasbourg, which he did in December 1531. Marpeck spent the rest of his life trying to unify the more evangelically minded and pacifist Anabaptists of southern Germany. He wrote prolifi-cally, and in his own lifetime his influence rivalled that of Menno Simons (see below). Marpeck, however, left no distinctive group of "Marpeckites" to transmit his legacy much beyond the 17th century.

Marpeck's distinctive theology included some idiosyncracies. For example, he taught a somewhat peculiar doctrine of the Trinity.

Marpeck strongly upheld the correct "order" within the Trinity as being Father-Spirit-Son, and so insisted on calling the Spirit the second person of the Godhead, and the Son the third. In fact, he preferred not to speak about the "Son" at all, but about the "Word" or "Logos", thus rejuvenating the older pre-Nicene language and concept. Regarding the incarnation, Marpeck was ambivalent about the "heavenly flesh" Christology which had attained such popularity among many Anabaptists (see the sections on Melchior Hoffman and Menno Simons for a full description); he argued that it was of no theological or practical consequence whether Christ's flesh was heavenly or earthly. Marpeck's rejection of infant baptism was bound up with his view of the universal scope of Christ's work. The incarnate Word, he maintained, has universally washed away the stain of original sin from all humanity, so that infants possess an "inherited grace" which gives them "creaturely innocence" before God. How could an innocent child require baptism for the remission of sins? For Marpeck, human beings become sinful in God's sight only when they personally sin at a mature age. Not surprisingly, some – including the great Spiritualist Radical, Caspar Schwenckfeld – accused Marpeck of Pelagianism.

Marpeck's ecumenical efforts among the Anabaptists were rooted in his aversion to all extremes. He rejected what he felt was the works-righteousness of the Swiss Brethren, the loveless use of the ban (excommunication) among the Mennonites, and the social communism of the Hutterites. As often happens, a moderate opposition to perceived extremes made Marpeck a suspect figure among those he criticised, thus negating his attempts at brotherly unity.

Melchior Hoffman

In some ways it is difficult to say whether we should consider *Melchior Hoffman* (1495-1543) an Anabaptist or a Spiritualist; the difficulty simply spotlights how fluid and flexible these definitions are. Nonetheless, Hoffman's extreme emphasis on the Spirit speaking through a church hierarchy rather than directly in each individual's heart places him more in the Anabaptist area of the Radical spectrum.

Hoffman was born at Schwäbisch Hall in south-western Germany. In 1523 he became a Lutheran and a lay preacher in Livonia, a Baltic state controlled by the Teutonic Knights. His Lutheranism, however, was blended with Spiritualism even at this early stage; he claimed to be a prophet (possibly Enoch or Elijah: he was not yet sure which), maintained that he could discern a special spiritual meaning in Scripture, defined the Church as a democratic community of the Spirit-filled, and used his special insight to prophesy the second coming for 1533. He also rejected Luther's doctrine of the eucharist in favour of a Zwinglian understanding. A violent figure, Hoffman led image-smashing riots. By 1526 he had alienated both friends and foes of reform and was thrown out of Livonia. He spent the next three years in Sweden and Denmark, dominated by visions of the second coming, until expelled in 1529 after a public clash with the Lutheran Reformer Bugenhagen over the Lord's Supper. He went to Strasbourg, at that time something of a safe haven for Radicals.

The next three years, 1530-33, were Hoffman's most productive. He toured the Netherlands, where his preaching won multitudes of disciples, so much so that Hoffman is often called "the father of Dutch Anabaptism". Ominously, one of his converts was Jan Beukels, soon to be king of the disastrous Radical "New Jerusalem" in Münster.[16] Hoffman's abundantly fruitful years in the Netherlands ended in 1533 when another Radical, claiming to be a prophet, foretold that Hoffman must go back to Strasbourg and be imprisoned, and that after six months in prison Christ would return, and Hoffman would lead the Radicals in a triumphal procession across the world. Hoffman duly went back to Strasbourg and was imprisoned, but Christ did not return and he stayed in prison for the rest of his life, dying 10 years later.

---

[16] See previous Chapter, section 1.

Hoffman's theology was in most ways typical of the Radical movement. He rejected original sin, predestination, and justification by faith. He strongly affirmed the "heavenly flesh" Christology: indeed he was one of the first to do so, and it was sometimes called simply the "Melchiorite" heresy by its critics. Alongside this, Hoffman held that divine truth and guidance came from a special class of enlightened people, whom he divided into apostolic messengers and prophets. The apostolic messengers were sinlessly perfect, and alone possessed the authority to discern infallibly between God's will and error. The prophets functioned under the apostolic messengers and received God's Word in dreams and visions. Perhaps unsurprisingly, Hoffman was an apostolic messenger, eventually claiming to be Elijah, one of the two witnesses of Revelation 11.

After Hoffman's imprisonment and the Münster tragedy of 1534-5, those who particularly revered Hoffman (the "Melchiorites") tended to move away from any belief in apostolic messengers and prophets into a more Bible-based Anabaptism.

The Hutterites

Jacob Hutter (died 1536) was, like Pilgram Marpeck, an Austrian Anabaptist. Unlike Marpeck, he left behind an organised body of disciples. Born in Moos, Hutter became involved in the Anabaptist movement through the Swiss Brethren after their expulsion from Zurich. When George Blaurock was martyred at the hands of the Roman Catholic authorities of Innsbruck in 1529, Hutter stepped into a position of leadership over the Tyrolese Anabaptists.

Hutter became convinced he had a special apostolic mission from God to establish the true Church. His letters reveal this exalted awareness of his own apostleship:

> "Jacob, servant of God and apostle of all His elect saints everywhere far and wide in the land of Moravia, called in the powerful grace and unutterable mercy of God, elected and

made worthy of this without any merit of my own, but rather
by reason of His overwhelming faithfulness and generosity,
who has counted me faithful and made me worthy as His
servant of the new and eternal covenant, which He first
established and made with Abraham and his seed for ever,
and has given and entrusted to me His divine eternal Word...
evidenced in powerful miracles and signs in me, whom He
has established as watchman, shepherd, and guardian over
His holy people, His elect, holy, Christian congregation,
which is the bride and spouse, the beloved and gracious
partner of our dear Lord Jesus Christ..."

Hutter's apostleship was accepted by many Anabaptist refugees in
Moravia, where he exercised his ministry among them from 1533-
35. His unique contribution to the emerging Hutterite movement
was his belief that the true Church must practice communism, *i.e.*
there should be no private property: all goods and assets were to be
jointly owned by the congregation. Obviously this required the
establishment of Hutterite communes in which this egalitarian
socio-economic order could be practised. These were set up in
Moravia, under the protection of sympathetic members of the
Moravian nobility. However, disaster struck in 1535, when king
Ferdinand of Austria, a Roman Catholic, expelled all Anabaptists
from Moravia, and put a price on Hutter's head. Hutter fled back to
Tyrol but was captured together with his wife. Ferdinand's men
inflicted the most horrific tortures on the apostle of Christian
communism; he was scourged, half frozen in iced water, and then
set on fire after being drenched in brandy. Eventually he was burnt
at the stake in February 1536. His wife was executed two years
later.

The Hutterite movement lived on under the leadership of **Peter
Riedemann** (1506-56), originally from Silesia (see section 3 and
Caspar Schwenckfeld for a description of Silesia). Arrested in the
Lutheran principality of Hesse in 1540, Riedemann was imprisoned
in Wolkersdorf castle – in decent conditions, owing to prince Philip
of Hesse's reluctance to persecute on religious grounds. From here

he wrote, in 1540, his great theological work, the *Rechenschaft* ("Account"), which the Hutterites adopted as a sort of confession of faith. Divided into two sections, part one of the *Rechenschaft* was based loosely on the Apostles' Creed. Conspicuous by its absence was the doctrine of justification by faith; Riedemann conceived the Christian life wholly in terms of sanctification. He defined the Church not only as a worshipping community but also a socio-economic unit. The ethical purity of the Church received an overwhelming emphasis from Riedemann, a purity to be secured by the strict use of the ban.

While Riedemann was in prison in Hesse, a new Hutterite leader emerged in the figure of **Leonard Lanzenstiel** (died 1565). A Bavarian by birth, Lanzenstiel had by 1529 become an Anabaptist, and in 1542 took over the leadership of the Moravian Hutterites. The opposite of an egomaniac, Lanzenstiel persuaded the Hutterites that they needed Riedemann; and so they wrote a letter of appeal to him, to which Riedemann finally responded by escaping from his easy captivity (Philip of Hesse was probably glad to see him go) and joining Lanzenstiel in Moravia. Under their joint leadership, the Hutterite communes prospered both economically and numeri-cally. In 1545, however, Ferdinand of Austria ordered their expul-sion yet again. Not all the Moravian nobility obeyed; some were prepared to defy their king and shelter the Hutterites. But in 1547, Bohemia (where Moravia was situated) joined the Schmalkaldic League of German Protestants in battle against the Holy Roman Emperor, Charles V (Ferdinand's brother).

The League's defeat by Charles left Bohemia at the mercy of Ferdinand, and he persecuted the Hutterites ruthlessly; they were reduced to a scattered band of refugees, hiding in underground tunnels. By 1553, however, the Moravian nobility had reasserted their local right of rule against Ferdinand, and allowed the Hutterites to establish three colonies. The golden age of the Hutterites had dawned. The Hutterites interpreted their freshly acquired territory in Bohemia and Moravia as a new "holy land", the geographical centre of God's purposes of salvation. All who would live according to God must come join them. In the 1560s and 1570s, under the leadership of the Tyrolese **Peter Walpot** (1521-78), it is estimated that the Hutterite communes reached a membership of 30,000 baptised adults.

Perhaps this is the point at which to satisfy our curiosity about how people lived in the Hutterite communes. From one viewpoint, these were very similar to the monastic communities of the patristic and medieval periods. The striking difference, though, was that the Hutterite communities claimed to be the Church of Christ on earth, outside of which there was no salvation, and they were composed of families, not celibates. All property was vested in the commune, not the individual, and the affairs of the commune were governed by Hutterite elders. The sharing of goods was not a primarily a socio-political ideal, but one manifestation of a deeper philosophy of Christian love: it was impossible to practise authentic love, the Hutterites maintained, unless private property with its divisive sense of "mine!" and "yours!" was abandoned. The communes were economically self-supporting through various trades and industries, *e.g.* farming, weaving, carpentry, building. Here the Hutterites did not practise a strict separation from the world, but sold their skills and products; as the official Hutterite chronicle says, "There were not a few carpenters and builders who made many millhouses, breweries, and other buildings for the [Moravian] lords, noblemen, burghers, and other people."

There was also a profound stress on submission and obedience within the commune, of wives to husbands, and the whole commune to its elders. Marriage was subordinated to the primary interests of the commune: husbands and wives referred to each other as "marital brother" and "marital sister" (*i.e.* the communal brother-sister relationship was paramount), and men were separated from their wives and children during the communal mealtime. The Hutterite children, from the age of two, lived together in school-communities, where they received an excellent basic education, as well as being thoroughly catechised in Hutterite doctrine and practice. Illiteracy was virtually unknown among the Hutterites.

Later the children were taught a trade. Education ceased after adolescence, however; the Hutterites felt that university-type learning was not conducive to true piety.

Many dark days lay ahead for the Hutterites in the kaleidoscope of European religion and politics. But a firm foundation had been laid by Riedemann, Lanzenstiel, and Walpot, and today the Hutterites (or Hutterian Brethren) still exist mainly in America and Canada.

Menno Simons and the Mennonites

The single most influential group of Anabaptists proved to be the Mennonites. Their name derives from the greatest Anabaptist of the Reformation era, indeed one of the greatest religious leaders of the 16th century – *Menno Simons* (1496-1561). Born at Witmarsum in the Netherlands, Menno's religious journey started off within Roman Catholicism when he was ordained to the priesthood in 1524, serving first at Pingjum, then from 1531 in his native Witmarsum. His doubts, however, began early; from 1525 he had serious problems over transubstantiation, and from 1529 over infant baptism. He had soon abandoned both, but concealed his new beliefs and continued in the Roman Catholic priesthood. He was later to reproach himself bitterly for this hypocrisy.

The crisis for Menno came when his brother Peter, together with many other Anabaptists, became caught up in the revolutionary enthusiasm of the Münster episode. While the brutal Radical regime of Jan Beukels of Leyden ruled in the north German city, and the New Jerusalem seemed to be at hand, 300 Dutch Anabaptists (including Peter Simons) took up arms and seized a monastery near Bolsward in March 1535. They were besieged there by government forces for eight days, and eventually all 300 Anabaptists were killed. Menno was devastated. Although he believed that his brother and the other Anabaptists were profoundly wrong to

Menno Simons (1496-1561)

resort to violence, he admired their willingness to act out their faith and die for it. It contrasted unbearably with his own hypocrisy: secretly an Anabaptist, outwardly a Roman Catholic priest.

And so the mask came off. For the next year, Menno tried to enact an evangelical reform in his parish. He also wrote a treatise against the Münsterites, *The Blasphemy of Jan of Leyden*, where Menno advocated pacifism as the proper Christian attitude. However, even this stance as a reforming priest did not satisfy Menno's conscience, and after a year he abandoned his clerical profession entirely to become an itinerant Anabaptist evangelist. Menno soon found himself among a small company of seven or eight Anabaptists in Groningen, who asked him to become their pastor. He agreed, and was ordained in 1537.

Menno spent the rest of his life as a hunted man; in the aftermath of the Münster fiasco, all Anabaptists were perceived as revolutionary anarchists by the governments of Europe. Menno had to preach by night to secret gatherings, baptising people in streams and lakes. And yet his success in planting churches and ordaining pastors for them was phenomenal. It becomes even more amazing when we consider that Menno's wife and three children accompanied him in his hazardous travels, and that for much of his life he seems to have been a cripple (the earliest known portraits of Menno depict him on crutches). Although Menno was Dutch, he actually spent only a few years of his ministry in his native Netherlands; most of it was carried out in northern Germany, in East Frisia, Cologne, Holstein, and the Baltic coast.

Almost single-handed, Menno saved Dutch and north German Anabaptism from the fanaticism that had manifested itself at Münster, and from disintegrating into a wasteland of warring sects. His polemic against the violent Münsterite wing of the movement was vigorous, merciless, and unceasing. Even after Münster itself had fallen, many Dutch and north German Anabaptists were still entranced by the vision of establishing God's kingdom by force of arms. Organised by John of Batenburg, they formed into mobile guerilla squads, the *Zwaardgeesten* ("sword-minded"), who spread terror across the countryside, destroying church buildings and killing anyone who stood in their path. Batenburg himself was eventually caught and executed, but the violence continued. Menno was instrumental, by his preaching, writing, and personal example, in turning the Anabaptist tide against the *Zwaardgeesten*, and reclaiming the movement for pacifism. Perhaps this was Menno's greatest achievement, to convert Dutch and north German Anabaptism from a movement of revolutionary anarchism to a Church of peace-loving martyrs.

Out of the crucible of this transformation came, in 1562, the first edition of what would later be called *The Martyrs' Mirror* (known originally as *The Offering of the Lord*). A product of the Dutch Mennonites, this volume nourished Mennonite piety for generations; it chronicled in moving detail the martyrdoms of the peaceful Anabaptists. The account of Michael Sattler's martyrdom, quoted at the end of this Chapter, comes from here.

Menno also fought hard and largely successfully to purify the Dutch and north German Anabaptists from the Spiritualist wing of Radicalism, with its reliance on new private revelations. Menno's chief opponent here was **David Joris** (died 1556). Joris claimed to be a prophet standing in succession to Jan Beukels of Münster; he exalted the "inward Word" of personal revelation over the outward word of Scripture. His cult of inner spirituality led him to reject all external forms of religion, including believers' baptism. Perhaps conveniently, this enabled Joris to conform to the Reformed Church of Basel from 1544 onwards (after all, what did external conformity matter?), while at the same time secretly printing and distributing books, tracts, and letters in which he advocated his extreme spiritualising views.

Menno's literary warfare with Joris was fierce. Menno was uncompromising in his rejection of the appeal to private revelations:

"Are you claiming that the teaching of Christ and of His apostles was imperfect, and that your teachers are now bringing forth the perfect doctrine? I respond that teaching and believing such things is the most horrible blasphemy!"

And again:

"My brothers, I declare the truth to you and do not lie: I am no Enoch, no Elijah; I am not someone who sees visions. I am not a prophet who can teach and prophesy anything, other than what is written in the Word of God as understood through the Spirit... I have no visions, I have no angelic inspirations. In fact I do not even desire them, in case I should be deceived. The Word of Christ alone: that is enough for me!"

Menno's crusade against private revelations gave a strongly biblical flavour to the Mennonite Anabaptists. Whatever else they might be, they were determined to be people of the Scriptures, not people of dreams and visions.

Most of Menno's characteristic theology appears in his most influential writing, *The Foundation of Christian Doctrine* (1540), which became the Mennonite equivalent of Calvin's *Institutes*. Some of it is simply a restatement of traditional Christian teaching: the Trinity, Christ as God and man, and so forth. In what ways, however, did Menno's theology depart from that of his Roman Catholic and Protestant contemporaries and pursue a distinctively Anabaptist outlook?

In the first instance, Menno clearly rejected the doctrine of original sin as classically understood in the Western Church. The atoning death of Christ, which Menno held was universal in extent, had put all human beings in a state of acceptance with God, until they reached the age of discretion and deliberately sinned. Only then did God impute guilt. Prior to this, all children were "like Adam and Eve before the fall, innocent and blameless". Since infants were guiltless, they did not need baptism for the remission of sins. Menno's denial of original guilt was therefore basic to his denial of infant baptism. He did, however, believe that every infant had a seed of corruption in his or her soul which would in course of time manifest itself in sinful actions.

Menno endorsed the "heavenly flesh" Christology that was widely held among the Radicals. In order to preserve Christ from any taint of sin, or even the possibility of sin, Menno felt he must deny that Christ took flesh from Mary. The Saviour's flesh was a special heavenly creation which was then implanted in Mary's womb; but Christ did not receive His human nature from the Virgin. The difference between Menno's view and the traditional view is that for the latter, Christ became flesh *of* Mary, whereas for Menno, Christ became flesh *in* Mary. Menno's heavenly flesh Christology was to be a constant source of stormy conflict between himself and Magisterial Protestants.

Menno's doctrine of salvation recapitulated many of the themes we have already encountered among the Anabaptists. He completely rejected the Augustinian view of grace: Zwingli's doctrine of predestination he condemned as "an abomination of abominations". For Menno, human free will, in the sense of an ultimately self-generated choice to cooperate with God's grace, was essential. The Lutheran and Reformed understanding of human bondage to sin and divine election to salvation he regarded as sheer excuses for wickedness. For the same reason, Menno also repudiated the doctrine of forensic justification by faith alone. This he felt was a threat to the urgency and seriousness of the new life of obedience in Christ. Menno poured his withering scorn on Lutherans:

> "The Lutherans teach and believe that faith alone saves, without any contribution from works. They emphasise this doctrine so much, it looks as if works were totally unnecessary – in fact, as if faith by its nature could not tolerate any work standing beside it… They start up a psalm, 'The chain is broken, now we are free, praise the Lord!' while the beer and the wine come running out of their drunken mouths and

noses. Anyone who can simply recite this off by heart, no matter how sinfully he lives, is regarded as a good evangelical man and a brother!"

Menno's doctrine of Scripture occupied a more complex position between Roman Catholicism and Protestantism. On the one side, he stood with Rome in accepting the apocrypha as divinely inspired and canonical. On the other side, he strongly endorsed the supreme and final authority of Scripture ("sola Scriptura"), refusing to let this be undercut by any appeal to tradition (or to private revelations, as we have seen in his campaign against David Joris). Even here, though, there were differences between Menno's version of sola Scriptura and the version articulated by the Protestant Reformers. First, Menno severely downplayed the significance and authority of the Old Testament. For Menno, and the Anabaptists generally, sola Scriptura tended to mean "the New Testament alone". This was because Menno stressed the discontinuity between the two testaments to the point where it became a virtual dichotomy, with the New supplanting the Old. This enabled Menno to offer a far simpler and clearer justification of Anabaptist ethics (pacifism, the rejection of the Christian state and of oaths, *etc.*) and ecclesiology (the rejection of infant baptism), since traditional Christianity often appealed to the Old Testament to vindicate these practices.

Second, Menno's concept of sola Scriptura disallowed *any* appeal to tradition. This was not the stance of the Protestant Reformers. As we have seen, they habitually appealed to the early Church fathers, not as infallible authorities, but as witnesses to the true interpretation of Scripture; and they saw themselves as standing in line with the Trinitarian and Christological formulations of the patristic era, especially the ecumenical Councils and Creeds of Nicaea, Constantinople, Ephesus, and Chalcedon. In other words, the Protestant Reformers operated within a framework of deference to the early Church, and a concept of the *subordinate* authority of the Church's creedal tradition.[17] Menno, by contrast, refused to

---

[17] See Chapter 2, section 2.

concede any role to tradition as a subordinate authority. He self-consciously tried to cut Scripture loose from all prior Church reflection on its meaning, so that Scriptural truth might stand unaided and shine simply by its own light. This meant that when controversies over the Trinity broke out within Anabaptism, Menno's Scripture principle ruled out any use of the extra-Scriptural language of Nicaea and the Cappadocian fathers ("homoousios", "eternal generation", and so forth).[18]

It was in the 1540s that the term "Mennonite" was first applied to those Anabaptists who looked to Menno for leadership. This happened in the German state of East Frisia, where from 1544 Menno was active. Countess Anna of Oldenburg, a remarkably tolerant ruler, was permitting Protestants and Anabaptists of almost all varieties to live and worship in her lands. Her chief religious advisor was the Polish Reformed leader Jan Laski (see Chapter 6, section 4, under **Poland**), who superintended all the Protestant churches in Anna's lands. Laski and Menno met and discussed theology at some length. Although Laski disagreed profoundly with Menno's views on baptism and the incarnation (he published a refutation of Menno's "heavenly flesh" Christology), the Polish reformer nonetheless used his influence to protect the Mennonites from persecution. In a decree of Anna's published in 1545, Laski was responsible for describing the peaceful Anabaptists of East Frisia as "Mennonites", using the label to distinguish them from violent revolutionary Anabaptists of the Münster type. Mennonites were to be granted toleration: Münsterites were not.

The latter years of Menno's ministry were clouded by internal disputes among the Mennonites over the practice of "shunning". All Anabaptists agreed on the use of the ban (excommunication), though with varying degrees of rigour; Mennonites were distin-guished by adding to the ban a further discipline of shunning the banned individual. This meant that no social contact was permitted with him or her. Menno at first had some reservations about this,

---

[18] The Cappadocian fathers: the 4th century theologians Basil of Caesarea, Gregory of Nyssa, and Gregory of Nazianzus. See Part One, Chapter 8, section 3.

but he was eventually won over to a strict position: if a husband or wife was banned, the marital partner must break off all marital duties – and would be banned himself/herself for refusing to do so. The controversy spilled out of the Mennonite ranks to affect other the major Anabaptist groups. In 1557, the Mennonites banned all the Swiss Brethren, Hutterites, and disciples of Pilgram Marpeck, because of – their weak view of the ban! Divisions were intensified when the Mennonites went further by denying the validity of the baptism practised by these other Anabaptist bodies. Tragically, this kind of disharmony among the Anabaptists magnified the perception that they were a warring wasteland of sects who could be spiritually discounted by their Roman Catholic, Lutheran, and Reformed opponents.

2. The Spiritualist Radicals.

The second of the impulses within the Radical Reformation which we will be considering was the Spiritualist impulse. It is worth reminding ourselves, as we said at the outset, that the three Radical impulses – Anabaptist, Spiritualist, and Rationalist – were not completely separate; they often mingled among the same groups or the same individual. However, it has become customary to characterise Radicals by the impulse that predominated. The Spiritualists, then, were those Radicals in whom the Spiritualist impulse gained the upper hand.

What was this Spiritualist impulse? Basically it was a subordinating of all external authorities – Scripture, tradition, the Church – to the living voice of God speaking directly in the individual's own heart. For the Spiritualists, inward personal experience became the supreme factor in their understanding of God and practice of Christianity.

Their governing emphasis on the direct speaking of the Spirit to the individual in the heart meant that the Spiritualists were the least organised group among the Radicals. We can best appreciate their story by looking at their three outstanding individuals: Hans Denck, Sebastian Franck, and Caspar Schwenckfeld. If we had not already looked at him in Chapter 3, Thomas Müntzer would have featured here; and in fact, he does make a dramatic appearance in the life of our first key figure. David Joris was also an important Spiritualist whom we have already encountered when we looked at Menno Simons.

Hans Denck

One of the earliest influential Spiritualists was *Hans Denck* (1500-1527), nicknamed "the pope of the Anabaptists" by his critics.[19] Born at Heybach in Bavaria, Denck studied at Ingolstadt university, where he acquired Latin, Hebrew, and Greek. Soon after he settled in the Swiss canton of Basel, drawn by the scholarly brilliance of Oecolampadius. It was on the strength of Oecolampadius's recommendation that in 1523 Denck was appointed rector of the school attached to Saint Sebald's Church in Lutheran-leaning Nuremberg. At this point Denck's theological loyalties were Lutheran, but in Nuremberg he fell under the sway of the pioneer Radicals Thomas Müntzer and Andreas Carlstadt, who happened to be in the city. The encounter pushed Denck decisively into the Radical camp. Not long after, he was hauled up before the city council for spreading unorthodox views (Denck had been attacking the Lutheran belief in justification by faith alone, and some of his followers were denying the deity of Christ). The council asked him to produce a written confession of faith; he did so, and in his confession Denck exalted the "inner Word" over the external Word of Scripture. By the "inner Word", Denck meant Christ dwelling and speaking in the depths of the individual's own being. Unimpressed, the Nuremberg council banished Denck from the city.

Denck went to the Swiss Roman Catholic canton of Schwyz, where the authorities imprisoned him for attacking infant baptism and purgatory, and (ominously) for asserting the universal salvation of

---

[19] We must remember that in the 16th century, all Radicals were called "Anabaptists".

all fallen spirits, including Satan. This universalist strain was not uncommon among the Radicals, especially the Spiritualists. Released from jail, between September 1525 and October 1526 Denck acted as sole leader of the Anabaptist congregation in Augsburg. Here he published some of his most important writings. These included a vigorous anti-Augustinian defence of free will, entitled *Whether God is the Cause of Evil*, which echoed Erasmus's treatise on the same topic; and *Who Truly Loves the Truth*. This latter revealed how far Denck had gone in his Spiritualism: he collected a multitude of what he argued were contradictions in the Bible, and used them to prove that Christian unity could not be based on Scripture, but must rather be grounded in the Holy Spirit who points us to the "inner Word". Challenged to a public debate by the leading Lutheran reformer of Augsburg, Urbanus Rhegius, Denck declined, left the city, and ended up in Strasbourg. Unfortunately he got involved in turbulent conflict with Strasbourg's chief Magisterial Reformer, Martin Bucer, who found Denck's theology so abhorrent that he had the Radical banished.

We next meet Denck in Worms. Here he wrote several works, including *Of the True Love*, which had an abiding influence among Radicals. In August he returned to Augsburg to take part in the important "Martyrs' Synod",[20] where he debated with **John Hut** (died 1527), another leading Spiritualist. Hut had been deeply influenced by Denck (indeed, Denck had baptised him in 1526), but also by Thomas Müntzer. Hut had been with Müntzer's army in the Peasants' Revolt at Frankenhausen, but left the battle early and so escaped Müntzer's fate. The Spiritualist side of Hut can be seen in his concept of "the Gospel of All Creation": the inner Word is universally present in human hearts, and all who respond (whatever their religion) become God's elect friends. However, Hut combined Denck's Spiritualism with Müntzer's apocalyptic visions. One of the main points of dispute at the Martyrs' Synod was Hut's formulation of "the Seven Decrees of Scripture", which among other things liberated the believer from the rule of the state, and predicted

---

[20] It was given this name because within five years almost all the participants had been martyred for their faith.

that the second coming would take place at Pentecost in 1528. Denck was unhappy with these notions. Hut never lived to see the failure of his date-setting, since he was arrested and died, probably as a result of torture, in December 1527.

After the synod, Denck became totally disillusioned with the way the whole Radical movement was working in practice, especially its divisive sectarian nature. He returned to the Reformed city of Basel, wrote a recantation of his Radical errors, and threw himself on the mercy of his one-time mentor, Oecolampadius, who ensured his safety. Although Denck now conformed to the Swiss Reformed Church, this was perhaps less an act of sincere Reformed Church-manship, than the weary conformism of a disenchanted Spiritualist to whom outward forms were still ultimately irrelevant.

Denck died soon after his recantation. Despite his final disillusion-ment, he remains a key figure in the development of early Spiritual-ist Radicalism.

Sebastian Franck

The second key figure among the Spiritualists was *Sebastian Franck* (1499-1542). Born at Donauworth (southern Germany, near Munich), he studied theology at Heidelberg from 1518 and may have seen Luther in action at the Heidelberg disputation in April.[21] Soon after, Franck entered the Roman Catholic priesthood, but by 1524 he had broken with Rome and was preaching Luther-anism in the village church of Buchenbach (just north of Donau-worth). There he experienced (but played no part in) the turmoil of the Peasants' Revolt, and moved on to become a chaplain in nearby Gustenfelden. Franck's demand in Gustenfelden that open sinners be excommunicated was opposed by the local magistrates, which prompted him to quit the ministry entirely and become a printer. From this point Franck moved over into the Radical camp. In Nuremberg he printed a Spiritualist manifesto, which tells us how

---

[21]   See Chapter 2, section 2.

his thinking had developed: Spiritualists will abolish audible praying, preaching, the sacraments, and the ministry. The true Church, Franck argued, was a purely invisible body with no external means of grace.

From 1529 Franck was in Strasbourg, and it was here that he printed his most influential work, his *Chronicles, Book of Time and Historical Bible*, which proved very popular among Radicals – it went through 16 German editions in the 16th century. Divided into three parts, part one is Franck's narrative of world history from creation up to the coming of Christ. Part two is his history of the emperors from Augustus to Charles V. Part three is itself sectioned into three parts. The first is a history of the popes from the apostle Peter to Clement VII (1523-34). The second is a history of Church councils. The third is a history of heresy (that is, what the Church of Rome considered heresy). Here Franck stated his Spiritualist credentials in an uncompromising way, criticising the Anabaptist branch of the Radical Reformation: the Anabaptists, according to Franck, had merely put suffering in the place of good works. They were legalists who worshipped the bare letter of Scripture and were wedded to a schismatic separatist mentality.

What about Franck's own positive beliefs? They are outlined in a letter to fellow Radical John Campanus (1500-1575), sent from Strasbourg on 4th February 1531. Franck accepted the heavenly flesh Christology so common among Radicals, embraced a Sabellian view of the Trinity, and denied the existence of any visible historical Church:

> "I believe that the outward Church of Christ, including all its gifts and sacraments, because of the breaking in of Antichrist right after the death of the apostles, went up into heaven and lies concealed in the Spirit and in truth. I am thus quite certain that for 1400 years now there has existed no gathered church nor any sacrament."

Franck's invisible spiritual Church included all good pagans and Muslims who responded to the universal inner Word. He was less kind to the early Church fathers:

> "Foolish Ambrose, Augustine, Jerome, Gregory – of whom not one even knew the Lord, so help me God, nor was sent by God to teach. Rather they were all apostles of Antichrist."

Franck was also scathing about Lutherans, especially the doctrine of justification by faith alone. He condemned this as a license to sin:

> "The freedom taught by Lutheranism is a deception and a pretence. It does not build God's house but demolishes it. The people become more perverted. It teaches 'faith, faith!' but thereby makes people deaf and devoid of works."

For Franck, the only significance of faith was as the means to inward spiritual and ethical renewal: faith brought a person into contact with the inner Word, which was secretly present in everyone, and through this contact a believer was "deified", which Franck seems to have understood as some kind of sharing in the divine essence.

Franck was expelled from Strasbourg in 1531 at the instigation of Martin Bucer, who was horrified by Franck's *Chronicles*. After some wanderings Franck ended up from 1533 in Ulm, near his old haunts in southern Germany. Here he resumed some literary activity, but by 1535 he was in trouble with the Ulm magistrates and had to give an undertaking not to publish any more of his own writings. He simply had them published elsewhere, *e.g.* his *The Book with Seven Seals* (1539), in which Franck listed what he believed were the contradictions of Scripture, which God had deliberately placed there in order to point away from the deadness of the written Word to the life-giving inner Word. Franck could be remarkably outspoken about the comparative uselessness of Scripture, especially the Old Testament, claiming at one point that

Plato and Plotinus "had spoken to him more clearly than Moses did".[22] Eventually even Ulm could not endure Franck, and he was expelled in 1539. He re-settled in Basel (the great Swiss Reformed city proving remarkably tolerant), where he helped edit in 1541 a new Latin and Greek New Testament. He died in 1542.

As befits someone who did not believe in a visible Church, Franck left behind him no organised body of followers, but his writings had a far-reaching impact on the Radical Reformation.

Caspar Schwenckfeld

Our third and final key figure is Caspar Schwenckfeld (1489-1561), certainly the most intellectually brilliant of the Spiritualists, and the only one who left a body of devoted disciples who still exist today. Born at Ossig in Silesia (in modern Poland: Silesia covered territory found today in western Poland), Schwenckfeld belonged to a distinguished aristocratic family, and after university studies he entered the diplomatic service of the powerful Silesian duke Frederick II of Liegnitz. Severe deafness ended his career in 1523, but Schwenckfeld's path had already turned towards spiritual things through an inner experience of awakening that he had in 1518 or 1519. Luther's writings also prompted him to study the Bible and the early Church fathers, and by 1521 he had become a Lutheran lay evangelist in his spare time. Success crowned his efforts; many leading Silesians were converted, including duke Frederick.

By 1524, however, Schwenckfeld had parted company with Luther. In June of that year he wrote an *Admonition* to all Silesian preachers, criticising a number of basic aspects of Luther's theology, such as justification by faith alone, the denial of free will, and the disparagement of good works. The break with Luther became even wider in 1525 when Schwenckfeld found himself disagreeing with Luther's doctrine of the eucharist. Schwenckfeld could not accept any physical mingling of Christ's glorified flesh with the

---

22 Plato (427-347 BC) and Plotinus (205-70), two of the greatest non-Christian philosophers in Greek and Roman history.

communion bread. In response to Luther's favourite text, "This is My body," Schwenckfeld came up with a novel interpretation, arguing that it should really be read in reverse order; what Christ meant was "My body is this" – *i.e.*, "My body is spiritual food, even as the bread you have just eaten is physical food." Schwenckfeld visited Luther at Wittenberg in November 1525 to discuss the issue, but Luther reacted strongly, classifying Schwenckfeld as the "third man" (along with Carlstadt and Zwingli) at the head of an anti-sacramental sect. Luther was to become very abusive about Schwenckfeld, describing him as "possessed by the devil", but Schwenckfeld would always speak with gratitude about Luther and the part the Wittenberg Reformer had played in his own spiritual pilgrimage.

As a result of the eucharistic controversy among the Reformers, Schwenckfeld now advocated (from 1526) that all celebrations of the Lord's Supper should be suspended until harmony had been reached. This suspension (in German, "stillstand") was observed by Schwenckfeld's disciples until 1877!

Schwenckfeld's view that feeding on Christ was a purely inward and spiritual event was closely linked with his understanding of Christ's human nature. For Schwenckfeld, there could be no real union or communion between Christ's humanity and created matter. Christ's humanity, he argued, was "uncreaturely", not part of creation at all. (This was yet another variety of the "heavenly flesh" Christology.) Schwenckfeld put it like this:

> "I recognise nothing of creation or creatureliness in Christ, but rather a new divine birth and natural sonship of God. Therefore I cannot consider the man Christ, with His body and blood, to be a creation or a creature."

Furthermore, throughout Christ's life on earth, His "uncreaturely" humanity underwent a process of being "divinised", made progressively more divine; the process was completed by His resurrection and ascension into heaven, so that now Christ's humanity has been "equalised" with His deity. Despite his protests, it is difficult to see that Schwenckfeld had not, in effect, abolished Christ's human nature by transforming it into the essence of divinity. Our contact with this glorified, divinised humanity of Christ, he maintained, can happen only in a spiritual way, as we ourselves are reborn and recreated, so that we share in the divine humanity of Christ. Schwenckfeld's whole understanding of salvation became focused on this transformation of the believer into a divinised being; he no longer had any use for forensic ideas like justification.

Schwenckfeld's disagreement with Luther led to his exile from Silesia in 1529. The region was drawing close to the Lutheran rulers of Germany, and Schwenckfeld had become an embarrassment. To save his patron duke Frederick any trouble, Schwenckfeld left voluntarily and went (like so many Radical wanderers) to Strasbourg. Welcomed by Martin Bucer, for two years he lodged in the house of another leading Strasbourg Reformer, Wolfgang Capito, where he gave lectures on the epistles of Peter. Trouble brewed, however, when Schwenckfeld refused to join any of the churches in Strasbourg. He argued that he had Christ within him and that this sufficed: why should he join a church? He caused further problems when he damned all sides in the infant baptism controversy. Basically Schwenckfeld saw all water baptism as irrelevant. While preferring believer's baptism, he refused to support the adult baptism of those already baptised in infancy. His practical indifference to baptism and church membership were symptoms of Schwenckfeld's growing alienation from all external forms of Christian life. He applied this even to Scripture: faith, he argued, did not come from hearing the written Word, but from the direct personal indwelling of Christ in the heart. Scripture, after all, was as external as baptism and eucharist, and as useless in producing true spirituality. At best Scripture could bear witness to how a Christian should outwardly live. By 1533 Bucer had had enough of Schwenckfeld's Spiritualism, and the Strasbourg city council asked him to leave.

Schwenckfeld spent the rest of his life in the Ulm region, but often in hiding. His writings were published anonymously; the greatest was his *Great Confession of the Glory of Christ* in 1541, which defended his Christology. From this book his disciples called themselves "Confessors of the Glory of Christ". These disciples were not organized into churches, but rather withdrew from all churches and met privately in homes; they practised nothing beyond prayer meetings and mutual exhortation, having no ministry, no sacraments, and no formal worship.

When Schwenckfeld died in 1561, his followers buried him secretly. They then had an uncertain existence, subjected to persecution whenever they were discovered, but they remained intensely loyal to Schwenckfeld's memory and principles. By the early 18th century the "Schwenckfelders" had come together as a small but tight-knit group in Silesia, who found a refuge from Roman Catholic persecution by fleeing across the Silesian borders into Saxony. There they enjoyed religious freedom on the land owned by a tolerant German Protestant noble, count Nicolas von Zinzendorf.[23] Still harried by the Roman Catholics of Silesia, however, who demanded that Zinzendorf hand them back, the Schwenckfelders emigrated to America in six stages, between 1731 and 1737, settling in Philadelphia, where they continue to this day, although they are now organised as churches and celebrate the Lord's Supper.

3. The Rationalist Radicals

The third of the impulses within the Radical Reformation which demands our attention was the Rationalist impulse. Again we should recollect that the three Radical impulses – Anabaptist, Spiritualist, and Rationalist – were often combined among the same groups or within the same individual. The Rationalists were those Radicals in whom the Rationalist impulse proved strongest.

---

[23] The famous Pietist and Moravian. The story of the Pietists and Moravians belongs to a later volume.

There were perhaps two main theological aspects to Rationalism. First, it subordinated everything in Christianity, including Scripture, to a concept of reason – "right reason", as it was often called – insisting that this reason supplied the one true principle of interpretation, and that nothing which conflicted with it should be believed. Second, based on this principle, Rationalists uniformly rejected the doctrines of the Trinity and the incarnation as contrary to reason.

The Rationalist branch of the Radical Reformation had Italian roots. The notable exception is Michael Servetus, who was Spanish (see previous Chapter, section 8). Apart from Servetus, however, all of Rationalism's first generation of leaders were Italians. This alerts us to the fact that Italy in the first part of the 16th century was quite open to reforming influences of various kinds; Italy was, after all, the heartland of the Renaissance, with all of its many-sided challenges to late medieval Catholicism. The Italian Radicals were themselves clearly men of the Renaissance, who had been deeply influenced by Erasmian humanism. Coupled with this, however, they took a robustly intellectual rather than experiential attitude to religion, so much so that they have been criticised for not really having any genuinely religious instinct at all. For the Italian Radicals, Christianity was a matter of thinking things out and behaving morally. Their front rank figures included *Benardino Ochino* (1487-1564), *Matteo Gribaldi* (1506-64), *Giovanni Gentile* (1520-66), *Coelius Sucundus Curio* (1503-69), *Camillo Renato* (active 1540-70), *Francis Stancaro* (1501-74), and *Giorgio Biandrata* (1515-88). By and large, they were individualists who left no organised bodies of disciples; they began as Protestants, passed over into anti-Trinitarianism, and then usually spent the rest of their lives as unwanted wanderers, hounded by Protestants and Roman Catholics alike for their denial of the fundamental doctrine of the Church's ancient creeds.

We may look at Bernardino Ochino as a fascinating case study. A native of Siena in northern Italy, he began as a Franciscan friar, later joining the new Capuchin order of which he became vicar-general in 1538.[24] Falling in with the Catholic Evangelical circle of Juan de Valdes, Ochino imbibed reforming ideals that increasingly loosened his loyalties to Rome. He finally fled from Italy in 1542 to evade a summons to Rome, went to Calvin's Geneva, and there became pastor to its Italian congregation. From 1547 to 1553 Ochino lived and worked in the England of the Protestant king Edward VI, but returned to Switzerland in 1553 as pastor to the Italian church in Zurich from 1555. Ochino's Protestantism was now beginning to slide across into Rationalism; this was partly through the influence of another Radical, Laelius Socinus, about whom we will hear more shortly. The two men had a big impact on each other. Ochino became an increasing embarrassment to the Swiss Reformed Churches, denouncing the execution of Servetus, propagating a purely symbolic view of the eucharist, and finally in 1563 publishing *Thirty Dialogues* in which he seemed to defend polygamy and deny the orthodox doctrine of the Trinity. He may also have rejected predestination – historians argue about this. At any rate, Zurich banished him, and Ochino spent what was left of his life wandering in Eastern Europe, dying of the plague in Moravia in 1564.

Ochino's life reveals how the Rationalist impulse of Radicalism could penetrate deep into the Reformed community and carry off one of its illustrious teachers. Ochino travelled the whole route from Roman Catholic, through Catholic Evangelical, Calvinist, and finally anti-Trinitarian Rationalist.

Socinianism

The most significant and enduring form of Rationalism, however, was from the outset a systematic denial of almost all the basic tenets of Reformation Protestantism, and indeed of historic Catholic Christianity. This was Socinianism, and to this we now turn. It derived its name from **Laelius Socinus** (1525-62) and his more

---

[24] For the Capuchins, see Chapter 8, section 4.

influential nephew **Faustus Socinus** (1539-1604). These are the more well-known Latin versions of their names; they were by birth Italians, and their actual Italian names were Lelio and Fausto Sozzini. Laelius was from a renowned family of lawyers in Siena, who by the 1540s had embraced a Protestant faith. Indeed in 1550-51 he was in Wittenberg, enjoying the friendship of Melanchthon. He then settled in Reformed Switzerland, spending time in Basel and Geneva before putting down roots in Zurich (where he met Ochino – see above). We do not know when Laelius made the transition into Rationalism, largely because he kept his views to himself, but the execution of Servetus in 1553 seems to have concentrated his mind on the doctrine of the Trinity, and from that point he certainly appears to have secretly abandoned his belief in the traditional theology and Christology of the historic Church. He died young, aged only 37, in 1562, which perhaps prevented him from stepping out openly as a Rationalist and presenting a mature theology to the world.

Although Laelius never made his ideas public, he did commit them to writing, and this is where his more famous nephew Faustus enters the picture. Shortly before Laelius's death, the entire Socinus family in Siena had attracted the attentions of the inquisition; one of them was arrested, and the others fled. Faustus made his way to Geneva and then to Lyons in France. He visited Zurich on Laelius's death to collect his uncle's papers, mostly on religious subjects, and these probably formed the basis for his own thinking. He wrote a treatise of his own that same year in which he denied the deity of Christ and questioned the immortality of the soul. From 1563 to 1575, however, Faustus was back in Italy, in the republic of Florence, where he conformed outwardly to Roman Catholicism and was employed by Isabella de Medici, daughter of the grand duke of Tuscany. After Isabella's death, he relocated to the Swiss Reformed city of Basel for several years.

While he was living in Basel, Socinus published his first great religious treatise, his *De Iesu Christo Servatore* ("Concerning Jesus Christ the Saviour"), written as a response to the French Reformed pastor Covetus, who in correspondence with Socinus had set forth the standard Protestant view of the atonement and justification by faith. Socinus's treatise revealed his Rationalism in full flow. God was not bound in justice to punish sin, he argued, but could cancel the punishment by a simple act of will. Christ therefore did not die in order to satisfy divine justice, since forgiveness is freely given. What was Christ's role in salvation? Not to purchase or merit salvation by obedience or substitutionary death, according to Socinus, but simply to teach human beings the way of salvation. Christ revealed that we can be saved by faith and keeping God's commands. Socinus used the language of "justification by faith", but put a completely different meaning into it from what the Reformers taught. In Socinus's view, people were justified by faith because faith meant believing the truth of Christ's message and living in harmony with it; and such faith made a person actually righteous in character, his remaining sins being freely forgiven by God. Christ's death Socinus interpreted as a martyrdom in which Christ gave His life to seal the truth of His doctrines.

The resurrection was far more important to Socinus than the death of Christ. By raising Him from the dead, God had appointed Christ the King of His people, delegating to Him the power of conferring eternal life on obedient believers. For Socinus, eternal life meant physical immortality, which was God's gift to believers alone – unbelievers would not be raised.[25] Further, while Christ was not God by nature, His resurrection and ascension had made him into an "adopted God", given divine dignity by the Father (who alone was God by nature) so that the Father now ruled the universe in partnership with the exalted Man, Christ Jesus.

No doubt Reformed Switzerland was an unsafe place after the publication of this treatise, and Socinus departed that same year, first for Transylvania, then in 1579 for Poland. Rationalism was flourishing in both kingdoms. In Transylvania, the Italian Radical Giorgio Biandrata had found favour and power as the court

---

[25] In other words, to use modern terminology, Socinus was an annihilationist.

physician to king **John II Sigismund Zapolya** (1540–71). Biandrata won over to the Rationalist cause **Francis David** (1510–79), the leader of Transylvania's Reformed Church. With king John Sigismund's support, Biandrata and David organised a large anti-Trinitarian Church (or as we would say, a Unitarian Church, although the word was not used until 1600, and not applied to the Church until 1638). The Transylvanian Unitarians called themselves "the Church of the Kolozsvar Confession", after the place where their strength was concentrated.

Under the guidance of Biandrata, David, and John Sigismund (the only Unitarian king known to history), Unitarianism enjoyed a golden age in Transylvania, winning the allegiance of almost the entire ruling class. By the end of the 16th century, there were over 400 Unitarian congregations in Transylvania. Further, in 1571, the last year of his reign, John Sigismund granted legal rights to the Unitarian Church, so that it became one of the four officially recognised religions of Transylvania, alongside the Roman Catholics, Lutherans, and Reformed. From that time, all princes of Transylvania had to swear in their coronation oath to uphold the legal rights of the four recognised religions. This was just as well, since it acted as a brake on the strongly anti-Unitarian outlook of John Sigismund's successor, Stephen Bathory – prince of Transylvania (1571–75) and king of Poland (1575–86). Stephen was a Roman Catholic, who did everything he could within the law and the constitution to harass the Unitarians. For example, although the Reformed were forbidden to try to convert Roman Catholics or Lutherans, they were given full permission to evangelise the Unitarians. (This rubbed salt in the Unitarian wound, since the Unitarians were renegades from the Reformed Church.)

In addition to Stephen's hostility, there were internal troubles among the Transylvanian Unitarians. Biandrata and David had quarrelled fiercely over the place of Christ in Unitarian worship. David maintained that since Christ was only a human being and not God, He ought not to be worshipped; Biandrata took the opposite view, and argued that it was appropriate to address worship to

Christ despite His human status. Deeply impressed by Socinus's recent *Concerning Jesus Christ the Saviour*, Biandrata invited him to come to Transylvania and curb David's influence by refuting him. Socinus stayed in David's house from autumn 1578 to spring 1579, conducting a sort of running debate on the worship of Christ, with a constant flow of Unitarian ministers also taking part. Socinus deployed all his intellectual powers to argue that since Christ had been exalted to participate in God's kingly rule over the universe, Christ was rightly held to be God by adoption, and it was right for Christians to pray to Him. David remained unconvinced, but Socinus won the debate and the Unitarians of Transylvania rejected both David and his theology. He died in disgrace, a prisoner in Deva castle, charged by king Stephen with introducing religious innovations not covered by the 1571 legal guarantees of liberty.

Despite Socinus' lasting contribution to the Unitarian Transylvanians in this debate, his real sphere of influence was to be Poland, where he went in early 1579. Poland too had a blossoming Unitarian movement, an offshoot (as in Transylvania) from the Polish Reformed Church – indeed the Polish Unitarians were confusingly called the Minor Reformed Church. Biandrata had been instrumental in the founding of the Polish Unitarian movement in the 1560s before he moved to Transylvania. When Socinus arrived in 1579, he found vibrant Unitarian centres of influence in Vilna and Rakow, protected by the great noble, Jan Sieninski. Rakow in particular became something of a Radical paradise, with all forms of the Radical Reformation flourishing there in a climate of complete religious toleration. Socinus applied to join a Unitarian congregation; but one of the conditions of membership was believer's baptism, and Socinus declined to submit. In his theology, water baptism was unnecessary for those who had been raised Christian: it was proper only for people who converted from another religion, such as Judaism or Islam.

Socinus continued to worship with the Unitarians, despite his inability to join them, and gradually attained an unparalleled influence over them, through his sheer intellectual prowess and personal charm, aided by his marrying into the Polish nobility which gave him high standing among the Unitarian ruling class. By the time the Polish Unitarians held their 1588 synod at Brest, Socinus had been accepted as their great theologian and leader, to the extent that they were soon being called "Socinians". When Socinus died in 1604, the Socinians had some 300 congregations in Poland, an academy whose educational excellence attracted students from all over Europe, and a thriving printing press that flooded the market with Socinian books. The only significant point on which the Socinians did not follow Socinus was the issue of baptism; after his death, they fully embraced believer's baptism by immersion.

The most famous confessional statement to emerge from Socinianism was the *Racovian Catechism*. Based on Socinus's unfinished *Very Brief Instruction in the Christian Religion*, it was first printed in 1605 in Polish, with a Latin edition for international consumption in 1609.

In the eyes of the Magisterial Reformers, Socinianism became the arch-demon among the various forms of the Radical Reformation. There were never that many Socinians in Europe (Poland was, after all, only one country[26]), yet Lutheran and Reformed theologians devoted time and energy and ink to the refutation of Socinianism, out of all proportion to its numerical strength. This was perhaps because Socinus had touched a raw nerve: with unequalled intellectual sharpness and subtlety, he had subjected Reformation theology to a critique which, if successful, would leave in ruins every single distinctive doctrine the Reformers had stood for, and other doctrines the Reformers shared in common with Rome. The persons of the Trinity, the nature of God,[27] the immortality of the soul, original sin, the incarnation, the atonement, predestination, justification by

---

[26] The Socinians were eventually banished from Poland by the Jesuits in 1658.

[27] Socinus denied not only God's essential retributive justice but also God's foreknowledge of the future, something that Lutherans and Reformed always considered to be one of his gravest errors.

faith, the supreme authority of Scripture, the sacraments as means of grace, the eternal punishment of the wicked – all were rejected by Socinus or radically reinterpreted to mean something quite different to what the Reformers believed. On Scripture, for example, Socinus denied its inerrancy (even the apostles could make some mistakes), and placed it beneath "right reason" as the ultimate authority: Scripture must be understood only in a sense that is compatible with what our human reason dictates. Of course, this is why Socinus's branch of the Reformation is called "Rationalist". Still, it struck at the vitals of the Protestant Reformation. The Reformers had fought to give the Bible back to the people in their own language; Socinus had said, "Thank you very much," and – through a rationalist system of interpretation – turned the Bible against the Reformers on almost every point.

Important people

The Church

Anabaptists
Conrad Grebel (1498-1526)
Michael Sattler (1490-1527)
Felix Mantz (1498-1527)
Balthasar Hubmaier (1481-1528)
Jacob Hutter (died 1536)
Melchior Hoffman (1495-1543)
Pilgram Marpeck (1495-1556)
Peter Riedemann (1506-56)
Menno Simons (1496-1561).
Leonard Lanzenstiel (died 1565)
Peter Walpot (1521-78)

Spiritualists
Hans Denck (1500-1527)
John Hut (1500-1527)
Sebastian Franck (1499-1542)
David Joris (died 1556)
Caspar Schwenckfeld (1489-1561)
Rationalists
Laelius Socinus (1525-62)

Political and military
John II Sigismund Zapolya of
Hungary (1540–71)

Benardino Ochino (1487-1564)
Matteo Gribaldi (1506-64)
Giovanni Gentile (1520-66)
Coelius Sucundus Curio (1503-69)
Camillo Renato (active 1540-70)
Francis Stancaro (1501-74)
Francis David (1510-79)
Giorgio Biandrata (1515-88)
Faustus Socinus (1539-1604)

Anabaptism: The Schleitheim Confession

To all who love God and all the children of light, who are dispersed everywhere, wherever they may have been placed by God our Father, wherever they may be assembled in unity of spirit in one God and Father of us all: joy, peace, and mercy to you from our Father, through the atoning blood of Christ Jesus, together with the gifts of one Spirit, who is sent by the Father to all believers to give strength and comfort and constancy in all affliction until the end, amen. Grace and peace of heart be with you all. Amen.

Beloved brothers and sisters in the Lord: first and principally, we are always anxious for your comfort and the assurance of your conscience which was at one time confused, so that you might not always be separated from us as strangers and almost completely cut off, but that you might turn to the true implanted members of Christ, who have been armed through patience and self-knowledge, so that you may thus be united with us again in the strength of a godly Christian spirit and zeal for God.

It is clear with what abundant cunning the devil has turned us aside, so that he might destroy and crush the work of God, which His mercy and grace has partially begun in us. But Christ, the true Shepherd of our souls, who has begun this work in us, will direct and teach it to the end, to His glory and our salvation, amen.

Dear brothers and sisters, we who have gathered together in the Lord at Schleitheim on the Randen[28] declare, in points and articles, to all who love God, that as far as we are concerned, we have been united in heart to stand firm in the Lord as obedient children of God, His sons and daughters. We have been and shall be separated from the world in all that we do and in all that we abstain from. Praise and glory be to God alone, we have not been contradicted by any of our brothers, but are perfectly at peace. We have sensed in this the unity of the Father, and of Christ whom we share in common, both present with us in their Spirit. For the Lord is a Lord of peace and not of dissension, as Paul says (1 Cor.14:33). So that you may understand the points in which this occurred, you should mark and understand what follows.

A very great offence has been brought in by some false brothers among us, on account of which several have turned away from the faith. They think that they practise and follow the freedom of the Spirit and of Christ. But they have fallen short of the truth, and to their own condemnation they are given over to fleshly lust and license. They have reckoned that faith and love may do everything and allow everything, and that nothing can harm or condemn them, since they are "believers".

Note well, members of God in Christ Jesus, that this is not the way that faith in the heavenly Father through Jesus Christ is formed. Faith produces and bears no such fruits as these false brothers and sisters practise and teach. Shield yourselves and be warned against such people, for they are not serving our Father, but their father, the devil. But it is not so in your case; for those who belong to Christ have crucified their flesh with all its lusts and desires (Gal. 5:24). You understand what I am saying, and you know the brothers whom we mean. Separate yourselves from them, for they are depraved. Pray to the Lord that they may have the knowledge that leads to repentance, and pray for us that we may have constancy to

---

[28] Hills overlooking Schleitheim.

endure along the path on we have entered, to the glory of God and of Christ His Son. Amen.

The articles which we discussed and on which we were of one mind are these:

1. Baptism;
2. TheBan;
3. Breaking of Bread;
4. Separation from the Abomination;
5. Pastors in the Church;
6. The Sword; and
7. The Oath.

1. Concerning baptism.

Baptism is to be given to all those who have learned repentance and reformation of life, and who truly believe that their sins are removed by Christ, and to all those who live according to Jesus Christ's resurrection, and wish to be buried with Him in death, so that they may be resurrected with Him, and to all those who with this intention request baptism from us and demand it for themselves. This rules out all infant baptism, which is the greatest and chief abomination of the pope. In this you have the basis and testimony of the apostles. We wish to hold this simply, yet resolutely and with assurance.

2. We are agreed as follows on the ban.

The ban [excommunication] is to be used towards all those who have yielded themselves to the Lord to live according to His commandments, and towards all those who are baptised into the one body of Christ and who are named brothers or sisters, and yet who sometimes stumble and fall into error and sin, being unwittingly overtaken in a fault. Such people are to be warned twice in private, but the third time openly disciplined or banned according to the command of Christ. Matt. 18. But this is to be done before the breaking of bread, according to the Spirit's command, so that we may break and eat one bread, with one mind and in one love, and may drink of one cup.

3. In the breaking of bread, we are of one mind and are agreed.

All those who wish to break one bread in remembrance of the broken body of Christ, and all who wish to drink of one drink as a remembrance of the shed blood of Christ, are first to be united by baptism into the one body of Christ which is the church of God, whose Head is Christ. For as Paul points out, we cannot drink the cup of the Lord and the cup of the devil at the same time. In other words, all those who share in the dead works of darkness have no fellowship with the light. Therefore all who follow the devil and the world have no fellowship with those who are called out of the world to belong to God. All who live in evil have no fellowship with the good.

Therefore the matter is and must be as follows: Whoever has not been called by the one God to the one faith, to the one baptism, to the one Spirit, to the one body, with all the children of God's Church, cannot be made into one bread with them. But this is what must be done if a person is truly to break bread in accordance with the command of Christ.

4. We are agreed on separation.

A separation is to be made from the evil and wickedness which the devil planted in the world. It must be made in this manner, that we simply will not have fellowship with the wicked, and we will not join with them in the multitude of their abominations. The matter stands thus: since all who do not live in the obedience of faith, and have not united themselves with God so that they desire to do His will, are a great abomination to God, it is not possible for anything to grow or proceed from them except abominable things. For truly there are only two classes of people, the good and the bad, the believing and the unbelieving, darkness and light, the world and those who have come out of the world, God's temple and idols, Christ and Belial; and neither can have fellowship with the other.

To us, then, the Lord's command is clear, when He calls upon us to be separate from evil people, so that in this way He will be our God and we shall be His sons and daughters. He further exhorts us to depart from Babylon and worldly Egypt, so that we may not share in the pain and suffering which the Lord will bring upon them. From this we ought to learn that everything which is not united with our God and our Christ cannot be other than an abomination which we should shun and flee from. By this we mean all Catholic and Protestant works, church services, meetings and church attendance, public houses, civic affairs, the oaths sworn by unbelievers, and other things of that kind. These things are highly esteemed by the world, and yet are carried on in naked contradiction to God's command, in accordance with all the unrighteousness that is in the world. From all these things we must be separated, and have no fellowship with them, for they are nothing but an abomination; they are what cause us to be hated by our Messiah Jesus, who has set us free from the slavery of the flesh and equipped us for the service of God through the Spirit whom He has given us. Therefore we will also undoubtedly renounce the unChristian, devilish weapons of force – such as the sword, armour, and so forth, and all their use, either on behalf of friends or against one's enemies – by reason of Christ's command, "Do not resist the evil man."

5. We are agreed as follows concerning pastors in the church of God.

As Paul has specified, the pastor in the church of God is to be one who has a totally good reputation among those who are outside the faith. His task shall be to read [the Scriptures in public], to admonish and teach, to warn, to discipline, to ban in the church, to lead in prayer for the advancement of all the brothers and sisters, to lift up the [communion] bread when it is to be broken, and in all things to look after the body of Christ, in order that it may be built up and cultivated, that the mouth of the slanderer may be stopped. Moreover he shall be supported by the church which has elected him, in whatever his needs may be, so that he who serves the gospel may live by the gospel, as the Lord has ordained. But if a pastor does anything that requires him to be disciplined, he shall not be dealt with except on the testimony of two or three witnesses. And when they sin, they shall be disciplined in the presence of all, in order that the others may fear. But if through the cross this pastor is banished or called away to the Lord, another is to be ordained in his place in the same hour, so that God's little flock and people may not be destroyed.

6. We are agreed as follows concerning the sword.

God has ordained the sword outside the perfection of Christ [among non-Christians]. It punishes and puts to death the wicked, and guards and protects the good. Under the law [the Old Testament], the sword was ordained for the punishment of the wicked and for their death, and the same sword is now ordained to be used by worldly magistrates. In the perfection of Christ, however, the only discipline is the ban, used to warn and to excommunicate the one who has sinned, but without putting the flesh to death – simply the warning and the command to sin no more.

Now it will be asked by many who do not recognise this as Christ's will for us, whether a Christian may or should employ the sword against the wicked to defend and protect the good, or for the sake of love. Our unanimous reply is as follows: Christ teaches and commands us to learn of Him, for He is meek and humble in heart, and thus we shall find rest for our souls. Also Christ says to the ungodly woman who was taken in adultery, not that she should be stoned according to the law of His Father (and yet He says, "As the Father has commanded me, thus I do"), but in mercy and forgiveness and warning, that she must sin no more. This also ought to be our attitude in its entirety, according to the rule of the ban.

Second, it will be asked concerning the sword, whether a Christian may pass sentence in worldly disputes and discord, such as unbelievers have with one another. This is our unanimous answer. Christ did not wish to decide or pass judgment between brother and brother in the case of the inheritance, but refused to do so. Therefore we should do likewise.

Third, it will be asked concerning the sword, Shall a Christian be a magistrate if he is elected as such? The answer is as follows: They wished to make Christ king, but He fled and did not view it as the will of His Father. Thus we shall do as He did, and follow Him, and thus we shall not walk in darkness. For He Himself says, "He who wishes to come after Me, let him deny himself and take up his cross and follow Me." Also He Himself forbids the use of force by the sword, saying, "The worldly princes lord it over them, *etc.*, but not so shall it be with you." Further, Paul says, "Those whom God foreknew, He also predestined to be conformed to the image of His Son, *etc.*" Also Peter says, "Christ has suffered (not ruled) and left us an example, that you should follow His steps."

Finally, it is not appropriate for a Christian to serve as a magistrate for these reasons: The magistracy of government is according to the flesh, but the Christian's government is according to the Spirit. Their houses and dwelling remain in this world, but the Christian's are in heaven. Their citizenship is in this world, but the Christian's citizenship is in heaven. The weapons of their conflict and war are carnal and against the flesh only, but the Christian's weapons are spiritual, against the fortification of the devil. The worldlings are armed with steel and iron, but Christians are armed with the armour of God, with truth, righteousness, peace, faith, salvation and the Word of God. In short, as the mind of God is towards us, so shall the mind of the members of Christ's body be through Him in all things, so that there may be no division in the body through which it would be destroyed. For every kingdom divided against itself will be destroyed. Now since Christ is as Scripture says of Him, His members must also be the same, that His body may remain complete and united to its own cultivation and upbuilding.

7. We are agreed as follows concerning the oath.

The oath is a confirmation among those who are quarreling or making promises. In the Law it is commanded to be performed in God's Name, but only in truth, not falsely. Christ, who teaches the perfection of the Law, prohibits all swearing to His followers, whether true or false –neither by heaven, nor by the earth, nor by Jerusalem, nor by our head –and that for the reason He shortly thereafter gives, For you are not able to make one hair white or black. So you see it is for this reason that all swearing is forbidden: we cannot fulfil that which we promise when we swear, for we cannot change even the very least thing on us.

Now there are some who do not give credence to the simple command of God, but object with this question: Well now, did not God swear to Abraham by Himself, since He was God, when He promised him that He would be with him and that He would be his God if he would keep His commandments, –why then should I not also swear when I promise to someone? Answer: Hear what the Scripture says: God, since He wished more abundantly to show unto the heirs the immutability of His counsel, inserted an oath, that by two immutable things in which it is impossible for God to lie we might have a strong consolation. Observe the meaning of this Scripture: What God forbids you to do, He has power to do, for everything is possible for Him. God swore an oath to Abraham, says the Scripture, so that He might show that His counsel is immutable. That is, no one can withstand nor thwart His will; therefore He can keep His oath. But we can do nothing, as is said above by Christ, to keep or perform our oaths: therefore we shall not swear at all.

Then others further say as follows: It is not forbidden of God to swear in the New Testament, when it is actually commanded in the Old, but it is forbidden only to swear by heaven, earth, Jerusalem and our head. Answer: Hear the Scripture, He who swears by heaven swears by God's throne and by Him who sitteth thereon. Observe: it is forbidden to swear by heaven, which is only the throne of God: how much more is it forbidden to swear by God Himself! Ye fools and blind, which is greater, the throne or Him that sitteth thereon?

Further some say, Because evil is now in the world, and because man needs God for the establishment of the truth, so did the apostles Peter and Paul also swear. Answer: Peter and Paul only testify of that which God promised to Abraham with the oath. They themselves promise nothing, as the example indicates clearly. Testifying and swearing are two different things. For when a person swears he is in the first place promising future things, as Christ was promised to Abraham. Whom we a long time afterwards received. But when a person bears testimony he is testifying about the present, whether it is good or evil, as Simeon spoke to Mary about Christ and testified, Behold this child is set for the fall and rising of many in Israel, and for a sign which shall be spoken against.

Christ also taught us along the same line when He said, Let your communication be Yea, yea; Nay, nay; for whatsoever is more than these cometh of evil. He says, Your speech or word shall be yea and nay. However, when one does not wish to understand, he remains closed to the meaning. Christ is simply Yea and Nay, and all those who seek Him simply will understand His Word. Amen.

The martyrdom of Michael Sattler

On the day of his departure from this world, after a lengthy trial, the charges against him being numerous, Michael Sattler asked that they be read to him again, and that he should be allowed another hearing. The court officer, as the appointed governor, opposed this and would not allow it. Michael Sattler then asked permission to speak. The judges consulted, then responded that if his opponents would allow it, the judges would agree. Then the town clerk of Ensisheim, as the appointed prosecutor, said: "Prudent, esteemed, and wise sirs, he has boasted of possessing the Holy Spirit. Now, if his boast is true, it seems unnecessary to grant his request; for if he has the Holy Spirit, as he boasts, the Spirit will merely tell him what has been done here." Michael Sattler replied: "Servants of God, I hope my request will be granted; for I do not yet know the charges against me." The town clerk responded: "Prudent, esteemed, and wise sirs, though we are not obliged to do this, yet in order to give him satisfaction, we will grant his request, so that no one may think injustice is done to him on account of his heresy, or that we wish to wrong him. So let the charges be read to him."

Charges or counts against Michael Sattler:

First, he and his disciples have acted contrary to the law of the emperor.

Second, he has taught, maintained, and believed that the body and blood of Christ are not present in the sacrament.

Third, he has taught and believed that infant baptism does not bring salvation.

Fourth, they have rejected the sacrament of extreme unction.

Fifth, they have scorned and denounced the Mother of God and the saints.

Sixth, he has maintained that people should not swear oaths before the authorities.

Seventh, he has started up a new and unheard-of practice respecting the Lord's Supper, putting the bread and wine on a plate, and then eating and drinking them.

Eighth, he has deserted his religious order, and married a wife.

Ninth, he has said that if the Turks invade the country, people must offer no resistance to them; and if it were right to take part in war, he would rather fight against the Christians than against the Turks! It is certainly a matter of great significance, to set the greatest enemies of our holy faith [Muslims] against us.

Then Michael Sattler asked permission to consult his brothers and sisters, which was granted him. Having spoken with them for a short time, he began his intrepid answer thus:

"Regarding the charges against me and my brothers and sisters, hear this short answer:

"**First**, we do not admit that we have acted contrary to the imperial law. For this law forbids anyone to follow the *Lutheran* doctrine and delusion, bidding us adhere only to the gospel and the Word of God. But this we have kept; for I am not conscious that we have acted contrary to the gospel and the Word of God. I appeal to the words of Christ.

"**Second**, we admit that the actual body of Christ the Lord is not present in the sacrament. For Scripture says that Christ ascended into heaven and sits at the right hand of His heavenly Father, from where He shall come to judge the living and the dead. From this it follows that He is in heaven, and not in the bread, so that He may not be eaten physically. Mark 16:19; Acts 1:9; Col. 3:1; Acts 10:42; 2 Tim. 4:1.

"**Third**, regarding baptism we say that infant baptism is of no use for salvation. Scripture says that we obtain life by faith alone. Again, 'He who believes and is baptised shall be saved.' Peter likewise says, 'There is also an antitype which now saves us – baptism (not the removal of the filth of the flesh, but the answer of a good conscience toward God), through the resurrection of Jesus Christ.' Romans 1:17; Mark 16:16; 1 Pet. 3:21.

"**Fourth**, we have not denied the oil [as used in the Roman Catholic sacrament of extreme unction]; for God created oil, and what God has made is good and not to be rejected. However, we do not believe that the pope, bishops, monks, and priests can make the oil any better than it is; for the pope never made anything good. The letter of James does not speak of the pope's oil. Gen. 1:11; 1 Tim. 4:4; James 5:14.

"**Fifth**, we have not condemned the Mother of God and the saints. The Mother of Christ is to be called blessed among all women; for to her was granted the grace of giving birth to the Saviour of the entire world. But the Scriptures know nothing of her being a mediator and advocate; for together with us she must await the judgment. Paul said to Timothy: Christ is our mediator and advocate with God. As for the saints, we say that we believers now alive are the saints; which I prove by the letters of Paul to the Romans, Corinthians, Ephesians, and in other places where he always writes: 'To the beloved saints'. Hence we believers are 'the saints'; but those who have died in faith we regard as 'the blessed'. Luke 1:28; Matthew 1:21; 1 Tim. 2:5; 1 Cor. 1:2; Eph. 1:1; Rev. 14:13.

"**Sixth**, we maintain that we must not swear oaths before the authorities. For the Lord says: 'Do not swear at all; but let your words be, Yes, yes, or No, no.' Matt. 5:34; James 5:12.

"**Seventh**, when God called me to bear witness to His Word, and I read Paul, and considered the unChristian and dangerous state in which I lived [celibacy], and when I saw the ostentation, arrogance, usury, and great fornication of the monks and priests, I went and took a wife to myself, according to the command of God. For Paul prophesies about this to Timothy: 'In the last days, men will forbid people to marry, and command them to abstain from foods which God created to be received with thanksgiving.' 1 Cor. 7:2; 1 Tim. 4:3.

"**Eighth**, if the Turks invade, we ought not to resist them, for it is written: 'You shall not kill.' We should not defend ourselves against the Turks, or anyone else who persecutes us. We should simply ask God with earnest prayer that He will repulse and resist them. As for what I said, that if war were right, I would rather fight against the so-called Christians, who persecute, arrest, and kill godly Christians, than against the Turks – it was for this reason. The Turk is a genuine Turk. He knows nothing of the Christian faith, and is a Turk in a fleshly sense. But you, who claim to be Christians, and boast of possessing Christ, persecute the godly witnesses of Christ. So you are Turks in a spiritual sense.

"In conclusion: Servants of God, I admonish you to consider the purpose for which God has appointed you, to punish the wicked, and to defend and protect the godly. Since we have not acted contrary to God and the gospel, you will find that neither I nor my brothers and sisters have offended in word or deed against any authority. Therefore, servants of God, if you have not heard or read the Word of God, send for the most learned men, whatever their language, and for the holy books of the Bible, and let them discuss the Word of God with us. If they prove from the holy Scriptures that we are in error and in the wrong, we will gladly withdraw and recant and also willingly suffer the sentence and punishment for what we have been charged with. But if no error is proven against us, I hope to God that you yourselves will be

converted, and accept instruction." Wisd. 6:4;[29] Acts 25:8;
Rom. 13:4; Acts 25:11.

After this speech, the judges laughed and conferred. Then the town
clerk of Ensisheim said: "O you notorious, desperate scoundrel and
monk, shall we hold a disputation with you? The hangman is the
one who will dispute with you, I assure you!"

Michael said: "God's will be done."

The town clerk said: "It would be better if you had never been
born."

Michael replied: "God knows what is good."

Town Clerk: "You chief of heretics, you have seduced the godly. If
only they would now renounce their error and accept grace."

Michael: "Grace comes from God alone."

One of the other prisoners said: "We must not depart from the
truth."

Town Clerk: "You desperate scoundrel and chief of heretics, I tell
you that if we didn't have a hangman here, I would hang you
myself, and reckon I had performed a service for God."

Michael: "God will judge righteously."

Then the town clerk said a few words to Michael in Latin (we do
not know what). Michael Sattler answered him "*Judica*" [pass
judgement!].

---

[29]   A reference to the apocryphal book of Wisdom. As we saw, many Radicals
accepted the apocrypha as part of Scripture.

The town clerk then exhorted the judges: "He will not stop talking like this today. Therefore, my lord judge, pronounce the sentence; I will commit it to the law."

The judge asked Michael Sattler whether he also committed it to the law.

He replied: "Servants of God, I am not sent to sit in judgment on God's Word; we are sent to bear witness to it. Thus we cannot consent to any law, since we have no command from God concerning it. But if we cannot be released from the law, we are ready (as long as we have breath within us) to suffer for God's Word, whatever sufferings may be imposed upon us all for the sake of faith in Christ Jesus our Saviour, unless we are persuaded to the contrary from the Scriptures."

The town clerk said: "The hangman will convince you; he will dispute with you, chief of heretics."

Michael: "I appeal to the Scriptures."

Then the judges stood up and went into another room, where they remained for an hour and a half and decided on the sentence. Matt. 6:10; John 16:2; I Cor. 4:5; John 1:8; Job 27:3; Acts 25:11.

Meanwhile, some people in the room treated Michael Sattler very harshly, heaping abuse upon him. One of them said: "What do you think will happen to you and the others, whom you have seduced?" He then picked up a sword which lay on the table, saying: "See, this will be the weapon by which they will dispute with you!" But Michael did not answer a single word for himself, but willingly endured it all. One of the prisoners said: "We must not cast pearls before swine." Matt. 27:14; 7:6. On being asked why he had not remained a leader in his monastery, Michael replied: "According to the flesh I was a leader; but what I am now is better." He spoke this fearlessly but did not say more than what is recorded here.

The judges then returned to the room, and the sentence was read. It was as follows: "In the case of the governor appointed by his majesty the emperor versus Michael Sattler, judgment is passed: Michael Sattler shall be delivered to the executioner, who shall lead him to the place of execution, and cut out his tongue, and then throw him on a wagon, and then tear his body twice with red-hot tongs. After he has been taken outside the gates, he shall be pinched five times with the tongs."

After this had been carried out, Michael was burnt to ashes as a heretic. His brothers were executed by the sword, and the sisters were drowned. Michael's wife too, after being subjected to many appeals, warnings, and threats, against which she remained very steadfast, was drowned a few days later. This happened on the 21st day of May, AD 1527.

From *The Martyrs' Mirror*, a collection of stories of Anabaptist martyrdoms

The Spiritualists: The invisible Church

Since the all-knowing Holy Spirit foreknew that all these external ceremonies would sink beneath the Antichrist and degenerate through abuse, He gladly gave up these signs to Satan, and instead nourished, gave to drink, baptised, and gathered believers with the Spirit and with truth, in such a way that no loss of truth would happen even though all outward matters might pass away. Thus, just as the Spirit of God is the only teacher of the New Covenant, so He alone baptises, He alone dispenses all things (in the Spirit and in truth). Just as the Church is now a purely spiritual thing, so too is all law, promise, reward, spirit, bread, wine, sword, kingdom, life: all in the Spirit and no longer external. So the one Spirit alone baptises with fire and with the Spirit – baptises all believers and all who obey the inner Word, wherever they are in the world. God has no favourites; He is he same to the Greeks and to the barbarians and the Turks, the same to lord and servant, so long as they keep the light which has shone on them, giving an eternal radiance to their hearts.

In short, my dear brother Campanus, to sum up openly in order that you may grasp it, I assert against all Church authorities that all external things and ceremonies, which were observed in the apostolic Church, have been abolished; they are not to be restored, even though many are trying to bring back the sacraments out of their decay, without having any authority or calling to do so. The Church will remain dispersed among the pagans until the end of the world. Only the second coming of Christ will finally destroy and remove Antichrist and his Church. Christ will gather together the scattered and always hidden Israel from the four corners of the world. It is therefore my view that no ordinance of these [apostolic] Churches should be restored which were once held in high regard in the Church.

This idea of restoration has been energetically spread by the wolves, the teachers of unwisdom, the foolish imitators of the apostles, the antichrists. But as for those who understood the truth of the matter, their writings and teachings have been banned as ungodly heresies and rubbish. Instead, people look up to foolish Ambrose, Augustine, Jerome, Gregory – of whom not one even knew the Lord, so help me God, nor was sent by God to teach. Rather they were all apostles of Antichrist, and still are. I am a liar if all their books don't prove this, since they are self-contradictory and utterly unlike the apostles. Not one of them seems to have been a Christian, to judge by their books, unless maybe on their death-beds they felt differently in their hearts, were taught better by God, and repented of their wasted work. They teach nothing aright concerning Christian faith. In fact, they did not know and did not teach what God is, or law, Gospel, faith, baptism, Supper, true righteousness, Scripture, the Church, and its law. They muddle up Old Testament with New (as their disciples today are still doing). When they can find nothing to support their opinion, they go running to the Old Testament, and from that empty sheath they prove war, oaths, government, the power of the magistrate, tithes, priesthood – and then praise it all and foist it on Christ without His approval. Just as the popes got all this from the Old Testament, so today many so-called Evangelicals think they have gloriously escaped the pope's and the devil's snare; nut all they have accomplished with their sweat and labour is merely this, that they have confused and swapped the priesthood of the pope for the kingdom of Moses!

From Sebastian Franck's *Letter to Campanus*.

The anti-Trinitarians: Socinianism

Q. Inasmuch as you have said that those things have been revealed by Jesus Christ, concerning the will of God as it properly relates to those who shall obtain eternal life, I would entreat you to declare those things to me concerning Jesus Christ which are needful to be known.

A. I am content. First, therefore, you must know that those things partly concern the Essence, partly the Office of Jesus Christ.

Q. What are the things that concern his Essence or Person?

A. Only that he is a true man by nature, as the holy Scriptures frequently testifies concerning this matter, and namely, I Tim. 2.5, "There is one Mediator between God and men, the man Christ Jesus." And I Cor. 15.21, "Since by man came death, by man also came the resurrection from the dead." And indeed such a person God promised beforehand by the prophets, and such a person the Apostles' Creed, acknowledged by all Christians, confesses Jesus Christ to be.

Q. Is the Lord Jesus then a mere man?

A. By no means. For he was conceived of the Holy Spirit, and born of the Virgin Mary, and therefore is from his very conception and birth the Son of God, as we read in Luke 1.35, where the Angel speaks thus to the Virgin Mary, "The Holy Spirit shall come upon you, and the power of the Highest shall overshadow you, therefore also that holy thing begotten shall be called the Son of God." I shall omit other causes, which you shall afterwards discover in the Person of Jesus Christ, most evidently showing that the Lord Jesus ought by no means to be reputed a mere man.

Q. You said a little before that the Lord Jesus is a man by nature. Has he not also a divine nature?

A. Not at all; for that is repugnant not only to sound reason, but also to the holy Scriptures.

Q. Show me how it is repugnant to sound Reason.

A. First, because two substances imbued with opposite properties cannot combine into one Person, and such properties are mortality and immortality; to have beginning, and to be without beginning; to be mutable, and immutable. Again, two Natures, each of which is apt to constitute an individual person, cannot be crowded together into one Person. For instead of one, there must of necessity arise two persons, and consequently become two Christs, whom all men without controversy acknowledge to be one, and his Person one.

Q. But when they allege that Christ is so constituted of a divine and human Nature, as a man is of a body and soul, what answer must we make to them?

A. That in this case there is a wide difference; for they say that the two natures in Christ are so united that Christ is both God and Man. Whereas the soul and body in a man are so conjoined, as that a man is neither soul nor body. For neither does the soul nor the body individually constitute a Person. But as the divine Nature does by itself constitute a Person, so must the human nature by itself necessarily also constitute a Person.

Q. Show how it is also repugnant to the Scripture that Christ should have a divine Nature.

A. First, because the Scripture proposes to us but one God by nature, whom we formerly demonstrated to be the Father of Christ. Secondly, the same Scripture witnesses that Jesus Christ is a man by nature, as was formerly shown. Thirdly, because whatever divine excellency Christ has, the Scripture testifies that he has it by a gift of the Father. John 3.35. John 5.19, 20, 21, 22, 23, 26, 27, John 10.25. John 13.3. John 14.10., Acts 2.26, Rev. 2.26, 27.2, Pet. 1.17. Finally, the Scripture most evidently shows that Jesus Christ perpetually ascribes all his divine acts, not to himself, or any divine nature of his own, but to the Father. Therefore who does not see that such a divine nature as our adversaries imagine in Christ would have been altogether idle, and of no use?

Q. I perceive that Christ hath not a divine nature, but is a true man. Now tell me of what avail to salvation will this knowledge be?

A. From the knowledge of this, that Christ is a true man, a sure and well grounded confirmation of our hope follows, which by the contrary opinion is exceedingly shaken, and almost taken away.

Q. How so?

A. Because from the adverse opinion it follows that Christ is not a true man. For since they deny that there is in Christ a human person, they with one and the same labour deny him to be a true man; for he cannot be a true man, who lacks the person of a man. But if Christ had not been a true man, he could not die, and consequently not rise again from the dead, whereby our hope which rests on the resurrection of Christ, as on a firm basis and foundation, may be easily shaken, and well nigh thrown down. But that opinion which acknowledges Christ to be a true man (who conversing in the world, was obedient to the Father, even unto death) asserts and clearly determines that Christ died, and was by God raised from the dead, and imbued with immortality. In a wonderful manner, this supports and bolsters our hope concerning eternal life. For it sets before our eyes the very image of that thing, assuring us thereby, as it were with a pledge, that although we are mortal and die, we shall nonetheless in due time rise from death, to come into the society of the same blessed immortality of which Christ is made partaker, if we tread in his steps.

From the *Racovian Catechism*

Chapter 6.

THE WINNOWING WIND: EUROPE DIVIDED.

We have explored how the Reformation came to birth in Germany and Switzerland, under the leadership of spiritual giants like Martin Luther, Philip Melanchthon, Ulrich Zwingli, Heinrich Bullinger, Martin Bucer, Peter Martyr, and John Calvin. In this Chapter, we will see much of the rest of Western Europe feeling the Protestant wind and throwing off the yoke of papal Rome, with enduring effects on the politics and culture of nations to this very day. We will begin, however, by looking at the important religious and political developments in Germany after 1531.

1. Germany: Lutheranism from the Schmalkaldic League to the Peace of Augsburg

Lutheranism continued to grow in Germany after the Protestation of Speyer (1529) and the formation of the Schmalkaldic League (1531).[1] Two of the greatest gains were the politically weighty territories of Wurttemberg and ducal Saxony. Wurttemberg embraced Lutheranism in 1534 and became an enduring stronghold of the Lutheran faith. Ducal Saxony, however, requires a longer word of explanation, since (confusingly) there were two Saxonies in Germany at the time. The Saxony we have thus far encountered was "electoral Saxony", whose prince was one of the seven electors

---

[1]   See Chapter 3, section 5.

of the Holy Roman empire. The other Saxony, "ducal Saxony", lay alongside electoral Saxony; it was smaller and had no rights in the election of the emperor. The two Saxonies had become detached in 1485 for reasons of family inheritance, separating into two different lines, the Albertine (electoral) and Ernestine (ducal). Until 1539 ducal Saxony had been ruled by duke George, a reactionary Roman Catholic who often appears in Luther's writings and conversation as an incarnation of anti-gospel hostility. But George died in 1539 and was succeeded by his brother Henry; and Henry was a devout Lutheran, who reformed ducal Saxony's Church with his people's general approval. Henry died only two years later in 1541 and was succeeded by his young and politically smart son *Maurice* (1541-53), who figures largely in the following narrative. Further territorial advances of Lutheranism meant that Brunswick, the last remaining Roman Catholic district of northern Germany, went over to the Reformation in 1542, and from 1544 the Palatinate (one of southern Germany's most important regions) began welcoming Protestant preachers.

However, this relentless geographical progress was severely offset by one of the great moral scandals of the 16th century. It involved Philip of Hesse, in many ways the captain and champion of the Schmalkaldic League.[2] Despite his early and sincere acceptance of Protestantism, Philip led a troubled sex life. His wife Christina, owing to her serious health and behavioural problems ("She is neither beautiful nor affectionate; she smells and she drinks," was Philip's verdict), had become repellent to him, and his keenly sensual nature found satisfaction in a series of affairs. These left Philip utterly stricken in conscience, so that between 1526 and 1539 he took part in the Lord's Supper only once!

In 1539, Philip thought he could see a way out of his dilemma: his affections had been captivated by a 17 year old court beauty, Margaret von der Saale, whose mother consented to Philip's proposal that he should take Margaret as a second wife (there were

---

[2]   For Philip's earlier career, see Chapter 3.

no grounds for a divorce from Christina). Unwilling to commit bigamy without the backing of his theologians, Philip consulted Martin Bucer of Strasbourg on the matter, and seems to have bullied Bucer – who in any case had liberal views on marriage and divorce – into accepting the idea, and Bucer then took the case to Luther and Melanchthon, who also consented. Luther's opinion was decisive. Although critics have accused him of pandering to Philip's lust, merely to retain the prince's political loyalty to Protestantism, Luther was not one to be moved by such considerations; he was genuinely concerned as a pastor to find a solution to Philip's moral quandary, and he sincerely believed that bigamy could in some circumstances be justified (*e.g.* from the example of the Old Testament patriarchs). So, fatefully, in December 1539, Luther gave his consent, and Philip secretly married Margaret von der Saale, with Melanchthon and Bucer as witnesses.

Unfortunately it is hard to keep a second wife hidden, and the scandal soon broke. Christian Europe was appalled; the Roman Catholic foes of the Reformation nodded their heads in gleeful anger – see, this is exactly what we said would happen: reject the pope, accept Luther's "faith alone" heresy, and you get moral anarchy! Luther then compounded the scandal by advising Philip to cover up the whole business by telling "a good strong lie", in case it hurt weaker consciences, but Philip refused and told the truth. It was a gift to the Holy Roman emperor, Charles V, at his wits' end about Germany's collapse into Protestantism. Bigamy was a death penalty offence under Empire law, and to save himself Philip had to make a total submission to Charles, promising that he would make no foreign alliances either personally or as representative of the Schmalkaldic League. This spelt diplomatic isolation for the League, severely undermining its effectiveness.

When the last great hope for Protestant-Catholic unity, the colloquy of Regensburg, fell to pieces in 1541, Charles V finally resolved on the use of force to bring Germany back into the one true Church of

Rome.[3] His secret weapon in this plot was the fact that not all German Protestant princes were members of the Schmalkaldic League. Charles hoped to disengage them completely from the League and win them to his side. He found his most willing ally in young Maurice of ducal Saxony. Although Maurice was a Lutheran, he did not allow his religion to interfere with his political ambitions; he coveted the electoral status that belonged to the other Saxony, plus a good share of its land. Charles promised him these in return for his support in the coming war. But other pieces of the jigsaw also needed to be put in place, especially France and the papacy. Continual wars with France had been a key factor in preventing Charles from acting against the Schmalkaldic League; Charles now at last secured French neutrality. The other thorn in Charles' side was the pope. No pope wanted a powerful Holy Roman emperor, since that could easily destroy the papacy's independence; to that extent, the popes found the German Protestants a useful counterweight to Charles' imperial schemes. However, in June 1546, Charles finally struck a deal with pope Paul III during the opening stage of the Council of Trent (see next Chapter), according to which papal troops would help Charles conquer Protestant Germany for the Church.

The Schmalkaldic League woke up rather late in the day to what was happening, and mobilised its forces in July 1546. The long delayed war had come. But the League found itself stabbed in the back by Maurice of ducal Saxony, who invaded electoral Saxony on behalf of the emperor. Meanwhile Charles went on the rampage in southern Germany, taking one Protestant city after another. To his surprise, with the exception of Augsburg the cities refused to bow to the knee to Rome but remained defiantly Protestant in faith. Charles had not reckoned on this depth of popular adherence to the Reformation.

In April 1547, Charles' Spanish troops completely shattered the forces of the Schmalkaldic League at Muhlberg. Elector John

---

[3]   For Regensburg, see Chapter 8, section 1.

Frederick of Saxony was captured and sentenced to death, but Charles then commuted this to imprisonment at the imperial pleasure. Philip of Hesse surrendered to Charles and joined John Frederick in captivity for as long as Charles saw fit. Maurice of ducal Saxony was rewarded for his treachery with a good chunk of electoral Saxony and the title of "elector". Northern Germany, the heartland of Lutheranism, lay prostrate at the emperor's feet. Yet not all resistance was crushed: the great Lutheran city of Magdeburg, which Charles had promised to Maurice of Saxony, defied the imperial victory and was placed under siege.

Where was Luther when the German Reformation needed him most? He was far from the scene of strife. Luther had died in February 1546, five months before the fighting broke out. Melanchthon described the event in a moving address to the students of Wittenberg, quoted at the end of the Chapter. Whether for good or ill (or both), Luther's mighty work was done. One of the true giants of history was dead; smaller men were left to pick the bones of his legacy. To his credit, Charles V did not abuse his conquest of Germany to dishonour his enemy's mortal remains. Standing by Luther's grave, Charles was exhorted by fanatical Roman Catholics to dig up and burn the arch-heretic's body. Charles cut off such demands curtly: "I do not quarrel with the dead."

Charles' triumph over Protestant Germany was purely military. To his dismay, the emperor found that force of arms could do nothing to reconquer the souls of German Protestants for Rome. He made his grand attempt at the diet of Augsburg in May 1548, where he persuaded Germany's politicians to enact the "Augsburg Interim". This was meant to be a temporary religious settlement until the Council of Trent had devised something more permanent. The Interim was a mainly Roman Catholic statement, which decreed the traditional seven sacraments, transubstantiation, and the sacrifice of the mass, acknowledged papal supremacy by divine right, retained most of the medieval Catholic rituals, but also allowed Lutheran clergymen to marry, and the wine to be given to the laity in holy communion. It also tried to fudge the differences over justification by faith in this way: "to the extent that love is added to faith and hope, to that extent we are truly justified by inherent righteousness. For this righteousness is made up of faith, hope, and love, so that if you would subtract any of these from righteousness, you would clearly leave it incomplete."

Charles imposed the Interim on the cities under his control; the most eminent of these was Strasbourg, and its chief Reformer, Martin Bucer, went into exile in England rather than submit. On the borders of Switzerland, the great city of Constance refused the Interim; Charles' army expelled some 400 pastors and teachers from its lands and enforced the new religious settlement. Yet despite these strong-arm tactics, the Interim met with almost universal passive resistance by the Protestant inhabitants of the occupied cities. They scorned to worship in churches where it operated; they condemned and mocked it in a flood of hostile poems, pamphlets, and songs. To make matters worse for Charles, his Spanish troops were exciting fierce resentment among all Germans, both Protestants and Roman Catholics, who saw their beloved Germany being subjected to military occupation by a foreign power. Meanwhile, the siege of Magdeburg went on and on, with no end in sight; the city's heroic defiance fired Protestant spirits with a new enthusiasm across Germany.

Charles' victory was unravelling before his eyes. And unknown to Charles, a new threat was about to turn his victory into the ashes of a humiliating defeat that broke the emperor's will. The threat was Maurice of Saxony. Maurice was not prepared to see Charles erect a powerful imperial monarchy in Germany which would destroy the independence of the princes. Further, Maurice was desperate to win back the esteem of the other Protestant lords of Germany, who despised him for his treachery in the late war which had brought such persecution upon their faith. As a reward for his services, Maurice's own lands had been spared the rigours of the Augsburg Interim, but only in the shape of a different Interim, the "Leipzig Interim", a modification of Augsburg by Melanchthon. The Leipzig

Interim clearly taught justification by faith, but still imposed various medieval rites and ceremonies which Melanchthon excused on the grounds that they were "things indifferent" (*adiaphora*, to use the technical term). This ignited a blazing controversy between Melanchthon and the Lutherans of defiant Magdeburg, led by Nicolas von Amsdorf and Flacius Illyricus, who protested that, in the context of a religious settlement that endangered the gospel, it was a sin to submit even to things indifferent.

Maurice was determined to undo this state of affairs and reunite the Protestants of Germany under his own banner. The key was Magdeburg. Maurice could not let Charles capture it: that would weaken Maurice's power. But he could not capture it himself either: he would be execrated by all Protestants if he conquered this symbol of Protestant heroism. So, with great political astuteness, he took personal charge of the siege, but did not press it, and told the other Protestant princes that it was all a sham. After much devious manoeuvring, Maurice banded together in May 1551 with a few other princes to form the League of Torgau. Its professed aim was to protect the power of the princes from imperial tyranny, and to liberate Philip of Hesse from captivity. The latter was a deep embarrassment to Maurice; he was married to Philip's daughter, and had pledged his honour that Philip would come to no grief in the war of 1546-7, a pledge that Charles was trampling on by keeping Philip a prisoner. Then in November, Maurice put an end to the siege of Magdeburg, but did not disband the army. Charles should have seen that mischief was afoot, but mysteriously did nothing.

In January 1552 Maurice made a treaty with the French king Henry II; in March, Henry invaded the western borderlands of Germany, claiming several French-speaking districts, while Maurice publicly renounced his allegiance to Charles because (he claimed) of the emperor's failure to release Philip of Hesse. Maurice's forces then liberated Germany from imperial rule, and Charles was sent fleeing ignominiously from Innsbruck, escaping capture by only a few hours. Maurice's counter-strike was a complete success, sealed by the Treaty of Passau in July. Philip of Hesse and elector John Frederick of Saxony were set free, and Protestants were guaranteed equal religious rights with Roman Catholics until a general council of the Church could settle affairs in a more abiding way.

Charles V was a broken man after Maurice's coup, and he handed German affairs over to his brother Ferdinand, who – though a Roman Catholic – was far more tolerant and sympathetic to Protestants than Charles. In June 1553 Maurice was killed in battle with a renegade Protestant prince, Albert Alcibiades of Brandenburg, but this did not alter the new balance of power in Germany, and matters were finally resolved at a new diet in Augsburg which met from February to September 1555. The comprehensive settlement was called the Peace of Augsburg, and was a milestone in the history of religious toleration. It stipulated the "territorial principle", that a region was to follow the faith of its ruler (prince, city council): a principle summed up in the Latin phrase *cuius regio, eius religio* ("whose region, his religion"). If anyone in a particular region disagreed with his ruler's religion, he was allowed to move to a different region, with guaranteed rights to a fair sale of his property. In any city where both Lutherans and Roman Catholics were represented, each was to be tolerated. No prince or city council was permitted to offer any inducements to the inhabitants of other regions to change their faith.[4]

The one grave defect in the Peace of Augsburg was that it recognised only two religions, Lutheranism and Roman Catholicism. It gave no recognition to the Reformed faith; and in the 17th century, this omission was ultimately to wreck the 1555 settlement. Of course, Anabaptists were not granted toleration either. Even so, for the next 60 years the Peace of Augsburg brought a degree of religious stability and freedom to Germany which it had not known since the heady days of 1517-21.

---

[4]   See the end of the Chapter for the text of the Peace.

2. The Reformation in the Scandinavian countries.

Denmark, Norway, Sweden, Finland, and Iceland were all linked
by a common cultural history. These were the lands of the Norsemen (or Vikings) who had inflicted such devastation on Europe in
the 9th and 10th Centuries, but had by the 11th century abandoned
paganism for the Christian faith.[5] Now in the 16th century they all
likewise abandoned the papacy for the Protestant faith.

Denmark

The nations of Denmark, Norway, Sweden, and Iceland had been
politically united under the Danish monarchy since 1397 in the
"Union of Kalmar". But the monarchy was weak. In 1521 the
Danish king *Christian II* (1513-23) tried to introduce Lutheranism
in Denmark in order to magnify his own authority as governor of a
state-controlled Church. Christian was a strange man: a cultured
Erasmian humanist who was sympathetic to the common people,
but cruel, crafty, and treacherous. His attempt at reforming
Denmark failed due to the opposition of the powerful Scandinavian
bishops and nobility, who toppled the detested Christian from
power. They replaced him with his uncle *Frederick I* (1523-33).
Christian fled to the Netherlands, where he entered into an alliance
with the Holy Roman emperor, Charles V; Charles would supply
Christian with ships and money to reconquer Denmark, if Christian
would re-convert to Roman Catholicism and impose it on the
Danes as the one true faith. Christian agreed, renouncing his
Protestant errors before a papal legate. As a prelude to conquering
Denmark, he invaded Norway in 1531; the Norwegian Catholic
archbishop, bishops, and many nobles swore allegiance to Christian, but his army was thwarted at the siege of Akershus. Danish
forces captured him, and the unlucky ex-king, who had first
embraced and then abandoned Protestantism to advance his own
power, spent most of the rest of his life in prison (he died in 1559).

---

[5]   For the Norsemen or Vikings, see Part Two, Chapter 4, section 1.

While Christian II was conspiring with the Holy Roman emperor to vanquish Denmark under a papal banner, his uncle Frederick, the new Danish monarch, was presiding over a genuine spiritual Reformation in his kingdom. Frederick was quite open to Protestant influences, especially through his son Christian, a zealous Lutheran, who as duke of north Schleswig (in Germany) had thoroughly Lutheranised his lands. A man ahead of his times in his respect for freedom of conscience, Frederick adopted a gentle approach to reform; he tolerated both Roman Catholics and Lutherans, and protected the popular Lutheran preacher, **Hans Tausen** (1494-1561), nicknamed the "Danish Luther". Tausen, the son of a poor farmer, had become a monk in his youth, and while studying in Löwen and Cologne discovered Luther's writings. This led him to embrace Reformation teaching, and in 1523 he went in secret to Wittenberg to drink from the fountainhead. After returning to Denmark in 1524 Tausen's Lutheran convictions were all too obvious, and he was thrown out of his monastery in Antvorskop and barred from the whole of Sjaelland and Fyn (two regions comprising the bulk of Denmark). Taking refuge in a monastery in Viborg in the west, from there he spread the Lutheran gospel like wildfire. Arrested on the orders of bishop Fries in 1526 and expelled from his monastic order (the order of Saint John), Tausen at this point found favour with king Frederick, who made him a royal chaplain so that Tausen could work unmolested as the king's servant. Tausen's friend Sadolin founded a Protestant theological college for him at Viborg that same year, financed by king Frederick.

The pace of reform now quickened. At the diets of Odense in 1526 and 1527, Frederick broke Denmark's ecclesiastical ties with Rome, decreeing that the Danish archbishop (rather than the pope) should from now on consecrate Danish bishops, and that Danish clerical taxes should be paid to the Danish monarchy, not the papacy. In 1529 the New Testament in Danish appeared, translated by the Lutheran **Christian Pederson** (1480-1554), one of Denmark's greatest humanists. Pederson had been interested in reformist ideals from as early as 1515, when he published a collection of sermons in Danish on the Church lectionary's set texts from the gospels and epistles, with edifying lessons attached from everyday life or from legends. This was the greatest work that had been published in Danish to that point; Pederson deliberately wrote it for people who could not understand Latin, convinced that God's Word was equally holy in any language. This conviction now bore its richest fruit in his Danish New Testament. In 1550 the complete Danish Bible appeared, most of it Pederson's work. His 1529 New Testament was energetically promoted by Tausen, who that year had moved from Viborg to the Saint Nicholas Church in Copenhagen, where he introduced hymn-singing in Danish. At the landmark diet of Copenhagen in 1530, Tausen and other leading Danish Lutherans triumphantly defended 43 Protestant theses against a disheartened Roman Catholic opposition.

By the time king Frederick died in 1533, two rival Churches faced each other in Denmark, one Roman, one Lutheran. In what they saw as their last chance of recovering their power, the Roman Catholic bishops opposed the succession of Frederick's strongly Lutheran son *Christian III* (1533-59). The great north German city of Lubeck, supported by many of the Danish peasants and towns, threw its military weight behind a campaign to restore the deposed Roman Catholic monarch, Christian II, to the Danish throne. Tausen was officially banished from Copenhagen by the forces of reaction, but popular support enabled him to defy the ban. Most of the Danish nobility backed Frederick's Lutheran son, Christian III, electing him king of Denmark in July 1534. A civil war followed; by 1536, king Christian had crushed his foes. The country, how-ever, was now tottering on the brink of national bankruptcy. Christian decided to solve the problem at a single bold stroke by destroying the Roman Catholic Church in Denmark, now widely detested by Danes for its part in inflaming the civil war. He confis-cated all the land and property of the old Church, outlawed its bishops, and asked the German Reformers for help in creating a new Danish Lutheran Church. Luther sent his colleague Johannes Bugenhagen,[6] who in 1539 (together with Tausen) produced a

---

[6]   For Bugenhagen, see Chapter 3, section

Protestant system of Church organisation for Denmark, sanctioned by the diet of Odense. Bugenhagen placed the control of the Church in the hands of the Danish monarchy, acting through consistory courts and royally appointed Church administrators. The new Lutheran Denmark was fully born.

Norway

It took several generations for Lutheranism to gain any popular support in Norway. The Danish monarch, Christian III, imposed the new faith on the Norwegian people in 1536 by royal decree, at the same time stripping Norway of its political liberties. The Danes did little to foster any effective Lutheran preaching and teaching in Norway; no Bible or Protestant catechism was published in the Norwegian tongue. Nor did any great popular Reformation leader appear in Norway. Among the few committed native Reformers, the most effective was probably Jorgen Erikkson, Lutheran bishop of Stavanger from 1571 to 1604, but he was not of the same mighty stature as a Martin Luther or a Hans Tausen. On the other hand, the Roman Catholic Church in Norway seems to have been uniquely dead. It made no real attempt to resist the gradual inroads of the new faith, and eventually faded away through lack of interest.

Iceland

The Icelandic Church was divided into a northern and southern province, Holar and Skálholt, each with its own bishop. The fortunes of the Reformation differed widely in the two provinces. In Skálholt, Lutheranism won many followers, under the leadership of Jon and **Gissur Einarsson** (died 1548) and **Odd Gottskalksson** (died 1556). Gottskalksson, converted to the Lutheran faith while in Norway, translated the New Testament into Icelandic; published in Denmark in 1540, it was the first printed book in Iceland's native language. A complete Icelandic Bible followed in 1584. Gissur Einarsson drank deeply of Lutheranism at the fountainhead in Wittenberg. He vigorously promoted the new faith in Iceland, first as assistant to bishop Palsson of Skálholt from 1538. After the

bishop's death, king Christian III of Denmark imposed Bugenhagen's system of Lutheran Church organisation on Iceland in 1541,
and Einarsson became the Lutheran superintendent of Skálholt.

While Lutheranism was springing up in the southern province of
Skálholt, Roman Catholicism reigned supreme in the northern
province, Holar. The champion of Rome's cause was Holar's
bishop, Jon Arason (died 1550). Arason was more like one of the
old Norse warriors than a Christian bishop; fond of the sword, he
was quite happy to smash the skulls of Protestants and personal
foes alike. He was also a notable Icelandic poet. The foremost
Protestant evangelist of the north was Olaf Hjaltason, whom
Arason deposed from the priesthood. King Christian III eventually
declared Arason an outlaw, which merely inspired the Viking-
bishop to stir up an armed revolt against Christian in 1550; the
revolt received pledges of support from the papacy and the Holy
Roman emperor Charles V. Arason succeeded in toppling and
expelling the Danish governor of Iceland, but his rebellion
collapsed when one of the bishop's old personal enemies ambushed
and murdered him in November 1550. From then on, under
Hjaltason's leadership, Lutheranism spread across the north of
Iceland as well as the south.

Sweden

The Swedish Reformation was linked with a patriotic struggle for
national independence against Danish rule. In 1521 the Swedes
rebelled against the hated tyranny of king Christian II of Denmark
(two years before the Danes themselves decided to get rid of him).
The leader of the Swedish revolt was *Gustavus Vasa*, who by 1523
had secured Sweden's independence and, the same year, was
elected king (1523-60). Gustavus was himself a convinced Protestant, having embraced the Lutheran faith while in exile from
Sweden in the north German city of Lubeck. Meanwhile, the two
Petersson brothers, *Olaf* (1493-1552) and *Lars* (1499-1573), had
unleashed Lutheranism on Sweden in 1519 by their soul-stirring
evangelism. Both men had studied theology at Wittenberg, and

from 1524 king Gustavus gave them his backing. Gustavus's chief royal advisor **Lars Anderson** (1480-1552) was a zealous Lutheran, converted by the preaching of the Petersson brothers.

Olaf Petersson did more than any other Swede to popularise the Reformation. After returning from Wittenberg he became deacon in Strängnäs, where the dean of the cathedral chapter protected him against harassment for his anti-Roman Catholic stance, especially towards the mass. Eventually Olaf's bishop, Hans Brask, decided to take action against him in 1523, but it was at this point that king Gustavus Vasa stepped in and gave Olaf his support. In 1524 Gustavus appointed Olaf as secretary to the Stockholm municipal authority, and also opened the door for him to preach at the city church. Olaf's preaching made such an impact that the Reformation quickly spread beyond Stockholm, particularly in the towns. Olaf began work on translating the New Testament into Swedish in 1525, finishing it in 1526. A complete Swedish Bible appeared in 1541. These landmark events cradled the beginnings of a national Swedish language. Olaf also published in 1526 a catechism entitled *A Helpful Instruction Manual*. The same fruitful year he produced the first Swedish Protestant hymnbook. In 1531 came his Swedish Lutheran liturgy. Olaf was also something of a social reformer, working hard to reform the justice system, *e.g.* by the abolition of torture.

King Gustavus relied on Lutheran support in his conflict with a party of rebellious nobles led by the archbishop of Uppsala, who was in league with the papacy. Like Denmark, Sweden faced national bankruptcy; and at the diet of Vasteras in 1527, Gustavus gave the Swedes an ultimatum: either the Swedish Catholic Church must supply his financial needs out of its huge wealth, or he would resign and leave the country. Since it was only Gustavus's authority that was holding the country together, this was rather like the police force in a crime-ridden town threatening to go on strike. The Church gave in, Gustavus confiscated most of its property, and the diet enacted a measure which legalised Lutheran preaching. In 1531, Lars Petersson became archbishop of Uppsala. Apart from

England, Sweden was the only Protestant country whose Reformation preserved the apostolic succession of bishops from the Middle Ages; its first Lutheran bishops were consecrated by their Catholic predecessors.

King Gustavus's relationship with his Reformers went through a stormy period in 1539-44. The old Church-state conflict which had so often shaken medieval Europe now set Gustavus at odds with Olaf Petersson and Lars Anderson, who wanted a larger measure of independence for the Swedish Church than Gustavus was willing to allow. Olaf in addition did not hold back from criticising the king in his sermons. The quarrel became so bitter that at one stage (January 1540) Gustavus had Petersson and Anderson tried for treason and sentenced to death! The king relented, however, partly because of the huge popular support the two Reformers enjoyed, and pardoned them. It seems Gustavus realised that Rome was a greater menace to his throne than Petersson and Anderson could ever be. The second diet of Vasteras in 1544 outlawed Roman Catholicism, declared Lutheranism the national faith of Sweden, and at the same time made the Swedish monarchy hereditary in the family of Gustavus.

Lutheranism was slow in winning the enthusiastic allegiance of the whole Swedish nation, and the Swedish Church underwent a reaction back towards Roman Catholicism in the reign of John III (1568-92). John married a Polish Roman Catholic princess, and their son became king Sigismund III of Poland in 1587. When John died in 1592, this meant that the Polish and Roman Catholic king Sigismund was the rightful heir to the Swedish throne. Lutheran and nationalist forces in Sweden could not stomach this for long; led by Sigismund's Lutheran uncle Charles, his regent in Sweden, they rose up in rebellion and defeated Sigismund in the battle of Stangebro (southern Sweden) in 1598. The Swedish diet then deposed him in 1599; and eventually, in 1604, Sigismund's uncle accepted the crown of Sweden as king Charles IX. Sweden and Poland remained at war (on and off) for the next 60 years. By the end of this struggle, the whole of Sweden had become deeply and solidly Lutheran.

Finland

King Gustavus of Sweden introduced the Lutheran Reformation into Finland too, which at that time was under Swedish sovereignty. **Peter Sarkilax** (died 1530) and **Michael Agricola** (1512-57) had been preaching Lutheranism in Finland since 1523, protected by Finland's sole bishop, **Martyn Skytte** of Abo (1480-1550). Skytte, a Dominican, was a disciple of Erasmus, a Biblical humanist committed to reform; he spent part of his earlier life in Sweden, where he enjoyed the patronage of king Gustavus Vasa, who made him vicar-general of the Swedish Dominicans. Then in 1528, without the pope's approval, Gustavus appointed Skytte bishop of Abo. Thereafter he was a key figure in the Finnish Reformation, working hard to frame it on a conservative model which kept everything Skytte believed was of value in the medieval Church.

Of the other Finnish Reformers, Sarkilax was a more fiery Lutheran than Skytte. Having studied theology at Wittenberg from 1517-23, he was instrumental in winning over to Protestantism Michael Agricola, Finland's greatest Reformer. In character, Agricola was a combination of Skytte and Sarkilax, a sort of Finnish Melanchthon: a man of immense learning and deep gentleness, Agricola's approach was to let the Protestant faith seep gradually into the Finnish Church by a programme of slow but sure reform, avoiding open controversy. His translation of the New Testament into Finnish (completed in 1548) had an enormous impact on the development of the Finnish language – he has been called "the father of Finnish literature". Agricola also produced a handbook of worship for Finnish Lutheran pastors, the *Biblical Prayer Book* (1544), and a Finnish Lutheran communion liturgy (1549). He became bishop of Abo in 1554. King Gustavus of Sweden was not as tolerant as Agricola; he took harsh measures to destroy the Roman Catholic Church in Finland. Between them, Gustavus and Agricola moulded the national Finnish faith into a sturdy Lutheranism, but with an Eastern Orthodox minority in the region of Karelia (south-eastern Finland).

3. The Reformed faith in Germany

Although Lutheranism was the prevailing form of Protestantism in Germany, the second half of the 16th century saw the growth of the Reformed faith in the land of Luther. The great German city of Strasbourg, of course, had been more Reformed than Lutheran since the 1520s. However, it had swung over into the Lutheran camp after Holy Roman emperor Charles V's victory over the Schmalkaldic League in 1547, which had resulted in the exile of Strasbourg's Reformed leaders, Martin Bucer and Peter Martyr, who fled to England.

The new heartland of the Reformed faith in Germany was an important south-western state called the Rhenish Palatinate, whose prince was one of the seven electors of Germany (responsible for electing the emperor). Its territory included the great university city of Heidelberg. Initially the Palatinate had tolerated both Lutheran and Reformed Protestantism, but this led to increasing quarrels between the two parties, especially when the local Lutheran leader, Tilemann Hesshus, an uncompromising foe of all things Reformed, established forms of ritual for Lutheran worship which seemed indistinguishable from Roman Catholic superstition to the Reformed. Things came to a head in 1559 with the accession of a new prince, *Frederick III* (1559-76). Frederick, one of the most sincere and godly Protestant rulers of the 16th century, made an intense study of the issues dividing Lutherans from Reformed, and was inclined to the Reformed side of the argument. To settle the matter he held a five day disputation in June 1560, which finally convinced Frederick that the Reformed were in the right. So began the new Reformed history of the Palatinate.

Frederick invited Peter Martyr to become Heidelberg's professor of theology, but Martyr declined on grounds of old age, recommending instead one of his German students, ***Zacharias Ursinus*** (1534-83). Ursinus, a disciple of Melanchthon as well as Martyr, took up the position in 1561. His closest colleague was ***Caspar Olevianus*** (1536-87), pastor of Saint Peter's Church in Heidelberg. Ursinus and Olevianus achieved a kind of immortality in the Reformed Churches as the joint authors of the Heidelberg Catechism, first published in 1563.[7] Marked by a moderate but lucid expression of Reformed theology and a warm evangelical spirit, the Heidelberg Catechism became arguably the most important of all Reformed confessions, gaining acceptance across the entire Reformed world, especially in Germany and the Dutch Republic.[8] Meanwhile, Ursinus, Olevianus, and other Reformed theologians, helped prince Frederick to organise the Reformed Church in the Palatinate as a Presbyterian body, with the Church (not the state) having control of its own internal discipline.

This grand experiment of a German Reformed Church came to a temporary halt in 1576 with Frederick's death. His son Louis VI, who was a staunch Lutheran, succeeded him and expelled no fewer than 600 Reformed theologians and pastors from the Palatinate, reconverting it into a Lutheran state. Louis, however, died in 1583, and since his son was only nine years old, Louis' brother John Casimir ruled in his name, and John was Reformed. He expelled the Lutherans and made the Palatinate a Reformed land once more. The effect of John Casimir's action was enduring, in that from then onwards there would always be a German Reformed Church in the Palatinate, despite the varying religious policies and loyalties of its princes.

---

[7]   At least, the co-authorship of the Catechism is traditionally ascribed to them. They were certainly both involved.

[8]   The Dutch Reformed Church officially incorporated the Heidelberg Catechism into its confessions of faith at the Synod of Dort in 1618-19, an international Reformed council that met to counter the rise of Arminianism in the Dutch Republic. This meant that together with the Belgic Confession and the Canons of Dort, Heidelberg constituted one of the "Three Forms of Unity" in the Dutch Reformed tradition.

Perhaps inspired by what Frederick had done in the Palatinate, in the closing decades of the 16th century and on into the 17th other German territories embraced the Reformed faith, either totally or by extending toleration to Reformed believers – Nassau, Bremen, Wesel, Julich, Cleves, Berg, Anhalt, Hesse, and Brandenburg, among others. Protestant Germany would henceforth have a strong Reformed presence alongside its original Lutheranism. The fact that the Reformed faith was not recognised by the Peace of Augsburg (see section 1) did not check its spread, but did stoke up political problems which in 1618 would finally explode that Peace.[9]

4. The Reformation in France.

As we saw in Chapter 4 on Calvin, Protestantism penetrated into France in the 1520s and 1530s, but was opposed by the French king Francis I who persecuted Protestants, especially after the affair of the anti-mass posters in October 1534. Indeed, persecution was probably fiercer in France than any other major country where Protestants managed to establish themselves. Despite the persecution, the number of French Protestants grew steadily, particularly in the 1540s and 1550s, as France began to feel the fresh influence of Calvin and Geneva. French Protestantism became decisively Reformed rather than Lutheran under Calvin's guidance. Between 1555 and 1562, Geneva trained and supplied at least 88 pastors for French Reformed congregations (in other words, Geneva was sending into France an average of 11 pastors per year). The French government actually protested to Geneva in 1561 against this influx of preachers who (the government claimed) were stirring up political discontent.

Because of the persecution, for years the French Reformed congregations had to meet in secret – in private houses, in the depths of forests, or in remote country fields. Some congregations required all their members to swear an oath never to reveal the names of

---

[9]   In the 30 Years' War of 1618-48. See Part Four.

other members. The pastors wore disguises and assumed false names; if their identity became known in one place, they moved to another. The influence of the Reformed faith on French society also grew in other ways. Sometimes a Roman Catholic priest would embrace a Reformed outlook but continue as a priest, and gradually introduce his new views to sympathetic members of his flock.

The turning point in the fortunes of French Calvinism came in the 1550s, when a number of great French nobles began to favour the Reformed faith. The most important were prince **Louis of Condé** (1530-69), the acting head of the powerful Bourbon family, and **Gaspard de Coligny** (1519-72), admiral of France and head of the illustrious Chatillon family. These two chieftains of the French Reformed faith made a striking contrast to one another. Condé was all fire and fury, a hot-blooded young aristocrat whose reckless boldness sent the Calvinists of France tumbling into deep political trouble just as often as it inspired them to heroic heights. The older Coligny, however, was a calmer, humbler man, more rock than fire, who rose up to true greatness of character only when the odds were against him and his cause seemed doomed – "never more dangerous than when defeated", as his enemies said. Both men were to die for their faith, but it is Coligny whom the world remembers as a glorious Christian martyr.

By the 1560s, historians estimate that up to half the French nobility had become Reformed. Protected by these rich and powerful nobles in the lands they owned, the French Reformed congregations began to meet and worship openly, often defended against Roman Catholic violence by the armed guards of the nobles. In 1559 the Reformed congregations held their first national assembly in Paris, which set up a nation-wide organisation for the French Reformed Church. At local level, each congregation was governed by its pastor and elders. Above the congregation was a district assembly, then above that a provincial synod, and at the top a national synod. The 1559 assembly also approved a confession of faith, drafted by Calvin and revised by the assembly, the French (or Gallican) Confession, which became the official creed of French Protestants.

Admiral Gaspard de Coligny (1519-72)

By 1561, admiral Coligny reckoned that there were 2,150 Reformed congregations in France; in places where they formed the majority, the Reformed took over Roman Catholic church buildings and used them for worship. Some of the Reformed congregations were huge: the one in Rouen (northern France) had 10,000 members, four pastors, and 27 elders. It was also at this time that people started calling French Calvinists *Huguenots* (pronounced "Hu-ga-noze"). No one knows for certain what the name means or how it originated. One possibility is that it came from the German word *Eidgenossen*, "Confederates", *i.e.* those admitted to the Swiss Confederacy; in Geneva the term was adapted into the French form *Eigenotz*.

The French monarchy began to lose its ability to persecute effectively in 1559, when king Henry II (1547-59) died. His son Francis II was only 16, sick, and died a year later. Francis's brother became king – Charles IX, aged 10. Charles's mother, the Italian **Catherine de Medici** (1519-89), ruled in his name. But real power had passed from the weakened throne to the great nobles of France, who were divided into two factions: the Guises, led by duke Francis of Guise and his brother the cardinal of Lorraine, who were Roman Catholics of the most intolerant type; and the Bourbons, led by Louis of Condé and admiral Coligny, who were Huguenots. This tense and brittle balance of power prompted Catherine de Medici to issue a royal edict in January 1562, which granted a limited degree of official religious toleration to the Huguenots. Some Huguenots felt it was now only a matter of time before the whole of France became Protestant. This fair prospect, however, was destroyed by the outbreak of a religious civil war between Roman Catholics and Huguenots which tore France apart for the next 40 years.

The incident which provoked the religious civil wars in France happened in 1562, when duke Francis of Guise, on the way to Paris, attacked a Huguenot church at the town of Vassy. 63 Huguenots were killed. This was followed by similar massacres in other places where Roman Catholics were in the majority. After the massacre of Vassy, Coligny was awoken one night by the weeping

of his wife, Charlotte de Laval, who said to her husband: "Sir, I
have on my heart and conscience all our people's blood that has
been shed. This blood and your wife cry to God in heaven and in
this bed against you, to warn you that you will be guilty of
murdering those whom you do not prevent from being murdered."
Moved by such reasoning, the Huguenots, especially the nobility,
decided it was their duty to take up arms in protection of their
families and fellow believers. So began a long and bloody series of
civil wars which almost destroyed France. Atrocities were committed by both camps; one Huguenot leader commented ruefully of his
own side, "We fought the first war like angels, the second like men,
the third like devils."

The greatest of the atrocities happened in 1572, and has gone down
in history as one of the worst crimes against humanity ever perpe-
trated. A temporary peace between Huguenots and Roman Catholics had been made in 1570, during which the young king Charles
IX fell almost completely under the influence of the great Huguenot chieftain, admiral Coligny, whose policy was to unite the
Protestants and Roman Catholics of France in a war against
France's traditional enemy, Spain. Charles' mother, Catherine de
Medici, opposed Coligny, partly through jealousy of his influence
over her son, partly through fear that war with Spain would be
disastrous. She therefore plotted the murder of Coligny, aided by
duke Henry of Guise who blamed Coligny for the assassination of
his father Francis by a Huguenot fanatic in 1563.

In August 1572, Huguenot and Roman Catholic nobles flocked to
Paris to witness the marriage of the Huguenot prince Henry of
Navarre to the Roman Catholic princess Margaret, Charles IX's
sister. This marriage was meant to signify the new religious peace.
But four days afterwards, on August 22nd, Coligny was shot by an
assassin employed by Catherine. Coligny survived, and Catherine
panicked. Fearing that the Huguenots gathered in Paris might take
revenge, she and the Guise nobility planned a general massacre of
all Huguenots. On August 24th, which was Saint Bartholemew's
day in the Church calendar, the massacre was carried out in Paris

and other major cities. Coligny and many other Huguenots were slaughtered. The total number of those killed is uncertain; a conservative estimate favoured by modern historians is that some 20,000 Huguenots may have been put to death across the whole of France. The incident has gone down in history as "the Massacre of Saint Bartholomew's Day".

The result of the massacre was renewed civil war between Roman Catholics and the surviving Huguenots. The Huguenots were now led by ***Henry of Navarre*** (1553-1610), one of Reformation Europe's most colourful leaders, a highly skilful general, an inspiring leader, and a man of overflowing generosity, incapable of cruelty or vindictiveness . Unfortunately his overflowing generosity extended to his affections for the opposite sex, and his endless sexual adventures were the despair of Huguenot pastors. (On the eve of one battle, Henry was forced to kneel before his army and express his contrition for having seduced the daughter of a local Huguenot.) Still, from a military and political point view Henry of Navarre was the Huguenots' greatest weapon. Meanwhile, the more extreme Roman Catholics, led by Henry of Guise, formed themselves into the Catholic League, and were supported by the Spanish king Philip II. The Catholic League were quite happy to see France become a Spanish province if that would secure the extermination of the Huguenots. The excesses of the Saint Bartholemew's day massacre, however, had alienated many moderate Roman Catholics, who broke away from Catherine and Henry of Guise to form a new grouping known as the "Politique" party (pronounced "pollit-eek"). The Politiques were determined to secure peace with the Huguenots and destroy the growing influence of Spain over French affairs. This division in the ranks of their enemies greatly helped the Huguenots, and a Huguenot-Politique alliance became ever more effective against the Catholic League. The Huguenot heartlands in and around Languedoc became a virtually independent state.

During the course of these wars, the political thinking of both Roman Catholics and Huguenots became radicalised. Some began seriously questioning and challenging the traditional institution of monarchy in favour of more representative forms of government. Among the Huguenots, the most influential of these thinkers was **Philip Duplessis Mornay** (1549-1623), a soldier and diplomat of such dominating brilliance that he was nicknamed "the Huguenot pope". Horrified by the Saint Bartholomew's Day massacre, from which he had escaped by a hair's breadth, Mornay wrote a political treatise entitled *A Defence of Liberty against Tyrants*, finally published in 1579. He argued that a king's authority was not unlimited; he was bound to observe the laws of God and of his country. If a king trampled on these laws, he must be opposed and called to account. Monarchy was merely one political institution among others; it existed for the benefit of the people, not its own advantage, and the people were loosed from obligation to obey a king who tyrannised over their lives, rights, and property. However, this right of resistance, Mornay argued, was not lodged in the people as a whole or in any private citizen, but in the lesser authorities that operated under the king: the nobility, the gentry, the parliaments and councils of the realm. They alone could legitimately curb a tyrant's actions or depose him.[10] Although Mornay's political philosophy did not come into its own in France until the French Revolution 200 years later, it had a profound influence on British history, where the idea of a limited, constitutional monarchy, held in check by a representative parliament, was fully vindicated in the 17th century.

To return to our narrative of the French wars, king Charles IX died in 1574 and was succeeded by his brother Henry III (1574-89). Henry III was childless, and when his brother died in 1584, it meant that the heir to the throne was now Henry of Navarre, the Huguenot leader. By this time the Catholic League, led by Henry of Guise, had virtually taken over the government of France. In a desperate bid to restore his own authority, Henry III had Guise assassinated in 1588. It failed to break the League's power and cost

---

10   Mornay's view had already been stated, although only in a brief paragraph, by Calvin, *Institutes* 4:20:31. But Calvin offered nothing like Mornay's detailed political philosophy.

Henry III his life, when he was assassinated in 1589 by a fanatical Catholic League monk, in revenge for Guise's death. This meant that Henry of Navarre, the Huguenot chief, became France's lawful king as Henry IV. But the Catholic League refused to acknowledge him. Philip II of Spain now sent Spanish troops into France to help the Catholic League. After several years of war (1590-92), Henry IV managed to establish his power across most of France, except in the one place that really counted – Paris, the great capital city, still controlled by the League. To win over Roman Catholics who would not accept a Protestant king, Henry abandoned Protestantism in 1593 and joined the Church of Rome: an act that deeply disappointed many of his Huguenot followers like Mornay, but which others of them understood. The strategy certainly worked. The power of the Catholic League melted away, as more and more Roman Catholics declared their loyalty to Henry. Several more years of fighting were needed to crush the Guise nobility entirely and drive out the Spanish, but by 1598 France once more had peace throughout its borders.

Henry IV proved loyal to his old Huguenot friends. In April 1598 he issued the Edict of Nantes. It secured freedom of worship for Huguenots wherever it had existed in 1597, with the exception of Paris and a few other cities; it allowed the Huguenots to hold four fortified towns of La Rochelle, Montauban, Cognac, and La Charité; it guaranteed their right to bring up their children in their own faith; and it made all positions of public responsibility open to Huguenots. The Edict of Nantes was a landmark in the history of religious liberty. For the first time one of the great historic Christian states of Europe had committed itself to the official acceptance of two faiths.[11] This enabled the French Reformed Church to embark on a golden age of freedom and theological vitality. Their colleges in Saumur, Sedan, Montauban and elsewhere prospered. However, Huguenot fortunes began to worsen from 1628 onwards, as French

---

[11] Hungary had already done this in 1557: see section 5. But France was a far older, far more powerful nation, and the French example was correspondingly far more significant.

Catholicism became ever more aggressive and intolerant under Jesuit influence.[12]

5. The Reformation in the Netherlands.

The Netherlands in the 16th century was a group of 17 provinces whose economy and prosperity were based on trade and manufacture. The inhabitants of the Netherlands were called the "Dutch". They were in theory under the sovereignty of the Habsburg family, represented in this period by king **Philip II** of Spain (1556-98), son of the Holy Roman emperor Charles V; and Philip was the most powerful and most zealously intolerant Roman Catholic ruler in Europe. However, the Netherlands were exposed to strong Protestant influences on every side: Lutheran Germany to the south, Lutheran Scandinavia in the north, the French Reformed churches in the south-west, and English Protestantism in the north-west.

The earliest Protestants in the Netherlands were Lutherans. Indeed, Europe's first Lutheran martyrs were two Dutch Augustinian monks, Henry Voes and John Esch, burnt to death for their faith in July 1523 at Antwerp. The Lutheran monks died with courage and joy:

> "As they were led to the stake, they cried with a loud voice that they were Christians; and when they were fastened to it, and the fire was kindled, they recited the twelve articles of the Apostles' Creed, and after that the hymn *Te deum laudamus*, which each of them sang verse by verse alternately, until the flames deprived them of both voice and life."

Among the Dutch lower classes, the impetus of Lutheranism soon gave way to the Radical Reformation in all its varieties. Then in the 1550s, under the inspiration of Calvin's Geneva, the Reformed faith became the rising Protestant force in the Netherlands, especially in

---

[12] For the Jesuits, see Chapter 8, section 2.

the southern manufacturing provinces. The leading Reformed preacher and organiser of the Dutch Reformed movement was *Guy de Bres* (1522-67). A native of Mons whose personal study of the Scriptures persuaded him of the truth of the Reformation gospel, Bres spent several years in Protestant England from 1548 to 1552, as part of a congregation of Dutch Reformed refugees who had fled from Spanish persecution. However, from 1552 to 1561 he was back in the Netherlands, preaching, teaching, and church-planting – all of which he had to do under cover, owing to government hostility. He also tried to restrain the more militant Dutch Calvinists from anti-Catholic violence and open rebellion against the civil authorities. Bres' enduring literary monument was the Belgic Confession, which he wrote in 1561; addressed to king Philip of Spain, it was a defence of the Reformed Protestants of the Netherlands as true Catholic Christians, not strange sectarians. Together with the Heidelberg Catechism and the Canons of Dort, the Belgic Confession became one of the "Three Forms of Unity" in the Dutch Reformed Church.[13] Bres did not labour alone: one of his greatest co-workers was the popular preacher *Peregrine de la Grange* (died 1567). Quite a colourful and dashing character, Grange would gallop on horseback into a forest glade where Dutch Protestants had secretly gathered to hear him preach, and fire his pistol to signify that the service had started.

By the 1560s there were several large Dutch Reformed congregations in the Netherlands, including one of 15,000 at Antwerp (the financial capital of Western Europe), and one of 20,000 at Tournai. Philip of Spain, however, was not prepared to tolerate such a spectacular growth of heresy in his dominions, and from 1560 Spanish persecution of Dutch Protestants became ever more brutal. One point in favour of the Reformed faith was that the Dutch merchants and nobility were opposed to Philip's repressive policy, even though most of them were still Roman Catholics. Their antagonism to Philip was for two basic reasons: (i) his policy of religious persecution damaged Dutch trade and commerce; (ii) it

---

[13] See footnote 8.

outraged Dutch patriotic feeling that the Netherlands were increasingly controlled from far-off Spain.

The clash of convictions between Roman Catholicism and the Reformed faith finally provided the spark which ignited one of the 16th century's most heroic conflicts. In 1566, the simmering tension between the two religions in the southern provinces erupted into violence, and Reformed congregations, albeit against the wishes of their pastors, went on a six-week rampage, destroying Roman Catholic church buildings and images, although no one was killed. Philip II's patience (such as it was) finally snapped, and he took harsh military reprisals. The Netherlands would from now on have to get used to seeing its towns and cities seized and occupied by Spanish troops, whose conduct was often barbarous in the extreme. In 1567 Philip sent his greatest general, Ferdinand Alvarez, the duke of Alba (1508-82), to take charge of these operations. Alba set about the business with shocking savagery, working through a special court, "The Council of Blood", which earned an enduring infamy in the annals of human carnage. By 1571, the Council had executed some 6,000 people. The victims of the Spanish holocaust included not only Guy de Bres and Peregrine de la Grange (hanged together in May 1567) and their fellow Calvinists (especially women, who proved outstandingly devoted to the new faith), but also moderate Roman Catholics who opposed Philip's policies. It was a dark night of the soul for the Netherlands: the ruling and educated classes were laid waste, trade was decimated, the prisons overflowed, every city and town was lit up with sufferers burning at the stake, and a tide of terrified refugees flooded into England and Germany.

The dangerous role of leading the resistance to Spain fell to one of Reformation Europe's most brilliant soldiers and statesmen, prince William of Orange, known as *William the Silent* (1533-84) from his habit of keeping his own counsel. William was also one of the most personally attractive figures of our period: a man of immense humanity, whose single-minded devotion to liberating his country in a long and bloody war never hardened or narrowed his tolerant and sympathetic nature. Few leaders in history have inspired such affection in their people; the oppressed Netherlanders were soon referring to him as "Father William". Initially a moderate Catholic, William embraced the Reformed faith in 1573.[14] Beginning in 1568, he spearheaded a series of military campaigns to free the Netherlands from Spanish tyranny, calling on his fellow country-men "to restore the entire fatherland to its old liberty and prosperity out of the clutches of the Spanish wolves and vultures". William's most zealous supporters were Calvinists, and during the progress of the epic struggle the cause of the Reformed faith became increasingly identified with the patriotic crusade against Spain. Reformed Protestantism was now strongest in the northern provinces, which declared their independence of Spain by forming the Union of Utrecht in 1579. Thousands of southern Calvinists migrated northwards to join their comrades in arms. The conflict had by this time become intensely religious in nature, and the Roman Catholics of the southern provinces acquiesced in Spanish leadership in the war against the Reformed north.

Crucial to the success of William's contest with Spain was his use of the sea. We are accustomed to modern guerrilla warfare in which fighters "take to the hills" to carry on a struggle; William's men "took to the seas" and struck at Spain from their ships. The Nether-lands were honeycombed with sea inlets and dotted with islands, and William and his "Sea Beggars" exploited this to excellent effect; in the process they almost accidentally founded the Dutch navy, which in the 17th century would be one of the best in the world. In this earlier period they were more of a gang of pirates, who left a trail of anti-Spanish and anti-Catholic blood and destruction wherever they went. They also had something of an

---

[14] In fact William had been raised a Lutheran as son of the count of Nassau-Dillenberg (north-western Germany), but the complexities of family life in the aristocracy had meant that he left home at the age of 11 to take up an inheri-tance (bequeathed to him by his elder cousin) in the Netherlands as Prince of Orange, and he had thereafter conformed to Roman Catholicism until 1573.

international flavour as French and English Protestants often joined them in their exploits against the common foe, Philip of Spain.[15]

The Netherlands were thus torn apart into two separate nations. The northern Reformed regions became an independent republic known as the United Provinces (Holland was the largest and most influential of these provinces), often called the Dutch Republic; the Roman Catholic south remained under Spanish sovereignty (present day Belgium). As the battle was waged, the Dutch Reformed Church became a deeply rooted and vital aspect of life in the United Provinces. It was organised like the French Reformed Church, with government by consistory, local synod, and national synod. Its theological training centre was the university of Leyden, founded by William the Silent in 1575, and soon famous throughout Europe for teaching theology and science. The United Provinces' Reformed theologians became internationally celebrated for their scholarship and intellectual acuteness. The Dutch Reformed Church fought long and hard for independence from state control; its freedom varied from one province to another.

Perhaps surprisingly, the United Provinces proved to be an international centre of religious toleration, despite the general Reformed view that heresy should be punished by the magistrate. This tolerance was due largely to William the Silent, who never tired of telling his Reformed supporters how odious it would be if they persecuted others as Rome had persecuted them. In William's Dutch Republic, then, Roman Catholics were granted the legal right of residence and employment, although still forbidden to worship in public or hold political office. William also extended toleration in 1577 to the Anabaptists: the first official recognition of their freedom to worship which they had received in any independent nation-state. Religious refugees from all over Europe fled to the United Provinces as a haven of liberty.

---

[15] The origin of the name "Beggars" for the Dutch rebels is unclear. Sometimes it is traced to Charles Berlaymont, a member of the Council of Blood.

William the Silent was assassinated in 1584 when the war for Dutch independence had not yet been won. As the news of his death became known, we have it on good record that children wept in the streets over the loss of "Father William". His son Maurice (1567-1625), however, carried on the struggle against Spain, and was soon acknowledged as Europe's greatest soldier. He was ably assisted by the politician Jan van Oldenbarneveldt (1547-1619). Maurice and Oldenbarneveldt succeeded in maintaining the United Provinces' freedom against all Spanish attempts at reconquest, and in 1607 a war-weary Spain effectively recognised Dutch independence by suspending hostilities and in 1609 signing a truce. A new, prosperous, and powerful Reformed nation – the Dutch Republic – had been created.

6. The Reformation in Eastern Europe.

The great non-Orthodox nations of Eastern Europe – Bohemia, Poland, and Hungary – were affected by the Reformation in varying degrees.

Bohemia

The land of John Huss and the Hussites[16] responded to Protestantism in a rather complicated way. Bohemia was right next to Saxony, and Lutheran influence streamed freely across the borders; lack of any centralised government in Bohemia made it difficult for Rome to organise effective persecution. Lutheranism, however, had only a limited appeal to Bohemians, who were Slavic by race and traditionally hostile to all things German. And Hussites could always say they didn't need Luther because they had already had Huss. Despite this anti-German Hussite nationalism, the Utraquist branch of the Hussites slowly absorbed more and more Lutheran theology. The Utraquists had remained within the Catholic Church

---

[16]   For the Hussites, see Part Two, Chapter 10, section 5.

at the time of the Hussite wars in the 15th century, but this gradual drift into Lutheranism now put them gravely at odds with Rome.

The other more radical branch of the Hussites, the United Bohemian Brotherhood, gave a much warmer welcome to the new faith. Their leader, the eloquent *John Augusta* (1500-1575), positively sparkled with enthusiasm for Luther. Augusta was bishop of the Brotherhood from 1532, and that same year he published a Brotherhood confession of faith for which Luther himself wrote a preface. In 1536 Augusta actually visited Wittenberg, and Luther helped to get a heavily revised confession of faith printed in 1538. Luther's enthusiasm for the Brotherhood was strongly expressed in 1542, when he told Augusta that the Bohemian Brotherhood were to be the apostles to the Bohemians, as Luther and his co-workers were apostles to the Germans. Under Augusta's guidance, the Brotherhood pursued dreams of union with the Utraquists, so as to create a single Bohemian Hussite Church, but these dreams came to nothing. The Utraquist leader, Mistopol, opposed Augusta; and when the Small Council took over leadership of the Bohemian Brotherhood (see below), they renounced Augusta's union plans.

In the 1540s, the Reformed faith took off in Bohemia, especially among the nobility and the Brotherhood. Its Swiss rather than German origins gave it an edge over Lutheranism for the traditionally anti-German Bohemians. John Augusta carried on a friendly correspondence with Calvin and Martin Bucer. As well as breathing fresh impulses into the Brotherhood, Calvinism proved attractive enough for a Bohemian Reformed Church to come into being, led by sons of the Bohemian nobility who had studied theology in Reformed centres of influence such as Geneva, Strasbourg, Heidelberg, and Leyden.

The (short-lived) military victory of the Holy Roman emperor Charles V over the Lutheran princes of Germany in 1547 (see section 1) brought tribulation to the Bohemians. Charles's brother Ferdinand was king of Bohemia, and became emperor in 1556. He imposed a much stronger centralised government on the nation, and punished its Protestants for their refusal to fight the German Lutherans in the recent war. His wrath fell with special force on John Augusta, the Brotherhood leader, who had championed the anti-war cause. Ferdinand threw Augusta into prison, where he remained for 17 years, under constant pressure to renounce his Protestant faith. During Augusta's long imprisonment, leadership of the Brotherhood passed to a Small Council, which disowned Augusta because of his alleged ambition to rule the Brotherhood like an autocrat (although when Augusta was finally released from prison, he was received back into the Brotherhood). The Small Council now became the Brotherhood's supreme governing body. Meanwhile, Ferdinand's repressive measures all but extinguished the Bohemian Brotherhood in Bohemia itself; vast numbers emigrated to Moravia, and the Small Council had its base there. Another Hussite, the Moravian *George Israel* (1505-88), led many of the Brotherhood into exile in Poland (see below), where they were warmly received by the Polish aristocracy. Israel became the dominant figure in the whole Brotherhood in the latter years of his life.

Religious liberty returned under Ferdinand's successor, the tolerant emperor Maximilian II (1564-76). All four of Bohemia's Protestant groups – Lutherans, Reformed, Utraquists, and Brotherhood – drew up a united Protestant confession of faith, the "Bohemian Confession", and presented it to Maximilian in 1575; he received it graciously and promised freedom to all Bohemian Protestants. Maximilian's son, emperor Rudolf II (1576-1612), however, who became king of Bohemia one year before assuming the imperial crown, was a devout and inflexible Roman Catholic who did everything in his power to promote the aggressive new Catholicism of the Counter-Reformation. Although the Bohemian nobility finally forced him in 1609 to concede religious freedom to Protestants, the long struggle was an omen of far worse things to come for Bohemia in the Thirty Years War (1618 onwards).[17]

---

[17]　See Part Four.

Hungary

Constant warfare with the Ottoman Turks produced great internal disorder in Hungary. The Hungarian army was wiped out by the Turks in 1526 at the battle of Mohacs; the Hungarian king Louis II was killed. Hungary split apart into three regions: Turkish Hungary, ruled by the Ottoman Empire of Suleiman the Magnificent (1520-66); Transylvania, ruled by Louis II's son John Zapolya (governor of Transylvania 1511-1526, king of Hungary 1526-1540), who acknowledged Turkish overlordship;[18] and north-western Hungary, ruled by the German prince Ferdinand of Habsburg.

Hungary was ethnically a mixture of Germanic Saxons, Magyars, and Szeklers.[19] This was to have a crucial effect on the fortunes of Protestantism. Lutheranism entered the country in 1523, and swept everything before it, aided by Erasmian humanism which had already predisposed educated minds to reformist ideas. One of the great Hungarian Lutheran Reformers was **Johannes Honterus** (1498-1549), a Transylvanian Saxon based in Kronstadt (present-day Brasov in Romania), a major centre of trade and industry. Honterus, an accomplished humanist scholar, founded Kronstadt's first printing press and used it to publish both humanist and Protestant works from the 1530s onwards. The Lutheran Reformation in Kronstadt became the model and inspiration for the rest of Saxon Transylvania, with the full backing of Luther and Melanchthon in Wittenberg. In spring 1544 Honterus's reforming career was crowned by his election as Kronstadt's "Evangelical (*i.e.*, Lutheran) City Pastor". Luther called Honterus the "Evangelist of the Lord", and Melanchthon praised him as "a man of great erudition and virtue who is in charge of the study of Christian doctrine in the town of Kronstadt in Transylvania."

---

[18] Transylvania is now part of Romania.
[19] The Szeklers were a large ethnic group in Transylvania, who claimed to be descended from the Huns.

Another prominent Lutheran was *Mátyás Biró Dévai* (1500-1545).[20] Ordained to the Roman Catholic priesthood in 1527, Dévai became castle chaplain in Bödökö. Drawn to the Reformation, however, he moved to Wittenberg to sit at Luther's feet. Returning to Hungary in 1531, he spread Lutheranism in Ofen and Kaschau, but was strongly opposed by the bishop of Erlau, and ended up in prison for three years. Released in 1534, Dévai found greater success in Sárvár, under the protection of the local prince, Thomas Nádasdy. Here he established a printing press to promote education and thus stimulate Reformation through literacy (yet another instance of the typical combination of humanism and Protestantism we have so often encountered). Dévai wrote an elementary Hungarian grammar, and translated Luther's children's prayers into Hungarian from Luther's *Small Catechism*; Dévai's colleague, the humanist scholar János Sylvester, published a translation of the New Testament into Hungarian in 1541. That same year, however, the Ottoman Turks invaded, forcing Dévai to flee, first to Wittenberg, then to Basel. In Basel he was won over from Lutheranism to the Swiss Reformed pattern of Protestantism, and spent the last 18 months of his life back in Hungary in 1544-5, propagating the Reformed faith.

Lutheranism, then, enjoyed massive success in Hungary. Indeed, by the 1550s there were only a tiny handful of Hungarian nobles who remained Roman Catholic. The triumph of Protestantism was so complete that, in 1556-7, the property of the old Church was legally taken over by Protestants by decree of the country's diet (parliament). The Lutheran complexion of Hungarian Protestantism during this first phase is also shown by the huge popularity of Wittenberg as a theological college, where Hungarian students flocked to train for the ministry. Although Roman Catholicism seemed to have died the death in Hungary, the diet of Torda in 1557 nonetheless extended freedom of worship to Protestants and Roman Catholics in equal measure – the first time that a European country had enacted legal toleration for both religions.

---

[20] Biró was his family name. Dévai comes from his birthplace Déva.

Despite these successful beginnings, however, the Hungarian Reformation was soon slipping into a state of crisis. The first reason for this was the growth of the Reformed faith in Hungary. We have already seen signs of this in the late conversion of the Lutheran Reformer Dévai to the Reformed faith in 1544-5. The first effective Hungarian champion of the Reformed faith, however, was **Martin Kálmáncsehi** (died 1557), pastor of a congregation in Debreczen, more a disciple of Heinrich Bullinger of Zurich than of Calvin.[21] Still more influential was **Peter Melius** (1536-72),[22] who (like Dévai) started off as a Lutheran, studying at Wittenberg in 1556-7, but when he entered the ministry in Debreczen in 1558 promoted the Reformed faith with the utmost vigour. Elected to the bishopric of Debreczen in 1561, Melius was the chief author of the Hungarian Reformed Confession of Faith (confusingly for modern Evangelicals, called the "Catholic Confession"), printed that same year. During almost fifteen years of ministry, Melius took part in numerous synods, appeared in public disputations before John Sigismund Zapolya (1540–71), king of Hungary and prince of Transylvania,[23] and wrote sermons, Bible translations, songs, and many other religious works – and also the first book on herbs in Hungarian, thus earning a place in medical history. Through Melius, Debreczen became a stronghold of Hungarian Reformed Protestantism, which is why he was often called the "Hungarian Calvin", and Debreczen the "Hungarian Geneva".

From Debreczen, the Reformed faith flowed east into Transylvania. Indeed, Transylvania, the original heartland of Hungarian Lutheranism, proved especially fertile territory for Calvinism among the Magyars and Szeklers, although not the Saxons who remained Lutheran. This ethnic division repeated itself across the country: faced with this choice between the Lutheran and Reformed version

---

[21]   For Bullinger, see Chapter 3, section 8.

[22]   Sometimes called Peter Juhász. Juhász was his family name, meaning "shepherd"; he translated it into Greek, Melius, presumably because this was what all good humanist scholars did in those days.

[23]   The son of John I Zapolya, and grandson of king Sigismund I of Poland after whom he was also named.

of Protestantism, the Hungarian Saxons stayed Lutheran, whereas the Magyars and Szeklers embraced Calvinism. In the case of the dominant Magyar nobility, this was at least in part owing to their traditional patriotic dislike of all things Germanic; the Swiss Reformed faith was more attractive to their nationalism. The conflict between Lutherans and Reformed, especially over the Lord's Supper, in what had been a harmonious Hungarian Protestant Church, eventually split the two factions apart in the 1560s into two separate Churches. Lutherans and Reformed continued to spend much of their time and energy fighting each other, which made a united Protestant front almost impossible. The Hungarian Reformed Church signified its allegiance to international Calvinism by adopting the Heidelberg Catechism as one of its confessional standards; but it differed from almost all other Reformed Churches in retaining an episcopal form of government, apparently rather indifferent to the Presbyterian zeal which motivated other Reformed Protestants – an indication in the eyes of some historians that the Hungarian Reformed faith always had an element of incoherence and superficiality about it.[24]

Other factors were at work to prevent the early victories of Protestantism from maturing into a solid Hungarian Protestant nation. Alongside the quarrelling Lutherans and Reformed, the anti-Trinitarian Rationalist wing of the Radical Reformation also took deep root in Hungary, finally consolidating its strength and membership at the outset of the 17th century as the Hungarian Unitarian Church.[25] This fragmented still further the ranks of those who had once been united as reformers against Rome. More ominously, from 1572 to 1608, Hungary was ruled by king Rudolf II, whom we met under the previous heading – the intolerant Roman Catholic, who was also king of Bohemia and Holy Roman emperor. Rudolf harnessed all the machinery of the Hungarian state to harass Protestants, curtail their freedoms, and advance the cause of Counter-Reformation Catholicism. And then finally, Hungarian

---

[24] The same thing has been said about the Reformed English Church, which also combined Reformed doctrine with Episcopal government. See section 6.

[25] See previous Chapter, section 3.

Protestantism failed to produce a single great leader (either in its Lutheran or Reformed branch) who could capture the imagination and affections of his country and shape its destiny. There were a few significant figures like Johannes Honterus and Mátyás Dévai among the Lutherans, and Peter Melius, the Reformed bishop of Debreczen; but these men were not of the commanding national stature of a Luther, a Zwingli, a Calvin, Denmark's Hans Tausen, or Sweden's Petersson brothers.

Hungary therefore squandered its opportunities through disunity and lack of leadership. By the time it entered the 17th century, the initiative had passed back to the Rome of the Counter-Reformation; beginning with Rudolf II, the Hungarian monarchy fell under the sway of the Jesuits, and dark days were ahead for Hungarian Protestants.

Poland

The German state of East Prussia, which was under Polish sovereignty, became Lutheran in the early years of the Reformation. Lutheran ideas and literature flowed over from East Prussia into Poland. The Polish king Sigismund I (1506-48) tried to suppress Lutheranism in Poland itself, but without any great success, owing to the weakness of the Polish monarchy. In the 1540s Calvinism began to attract Polish priests and nobles; the new king *Sigismund II* (1548-72) exchanged letters with Calvin and studied Calvin's *Institutes* admiringly. Calvin went so far as to draw up a scheme of Church reform for Poland, presenting it to Sigismund in 1554; in this scheme, the Polish Church was to keep its outward structure of bishops headed by an archbishop, but would teach Reformed doctrine and practise Reformed worship. Sigismund's chancellor, Nicholas Radziwill (1515-65), was a Calvinist and supported the scheme, but Sigismund could not quite bring himself to take the plunge and "Calvinise" his kingdom. Indeed, he eventually decided to stay loyal to Rome, welcoming the Jesuits into Poland in 1565. Despite this religious commitment, Sigismund was a tolerant man, and did not persecute Protestants. With such generally favourable conditions, the Reformed of "Lesser Poland" (in the Polish south, around Krakow) organised themselves into a Polish Reformed Church in the 1550s.

The chief Calvinist Reformer of Poland was ***Jan Laski*** (1499-1560) – priest, disciple of Erasmus, and nephew of the Polish archbishop.[26] Converted to the Protestant faith around 1538, Laski pastored a congregation in Emden, the Netherlands, from 1540. In 1543 he became superintendent of all the Protestant churches in the lands owned by countess Anna of Oldenburg (a German state on the extreme northern tip of the Netherlands). Anna was a tolerant woman who allowed all kinds of Protestants and Anabaptists to flourish in her domain. Laski himself proved to be one of the most broad-minded and peace-loving of the Reformers; a Calvinist himself, he worked ceaselessly for Protestant unity. In 1550 he went to the England of king Edward VI (see below), where he pastored a congregation of Protestant refugees from the Netherlands, France, and Germany. Returning to his native Poland in 1556, Laski tried to bring together Polish Lutherans, Calvinists, and Hussites (immigrants from Bohemia) into a single Church, but failed due to the determination of the Lutherans to remain a separate body with their own Lutheran theology and practice. Calvinists and Hussites did not actually unite, but did enter into close friendly relations. Laski also cooperated with other scholars in translating the Bible into Polish.

Despite Laski's work, the Jesuits destroyed Polish Protestantism almost completely during the reign of the Polish king Sigismund III (1587-1632).[27]

---

[26] Often called John à Lasco in English sources.

[27] This section deals only with Magisterial Protestantism. For the far more significant anti-Trinitarian Radical movement in Poland, see previous Chapter, section 3.

Important people

The Church
Germany
Zacharias Ursinus (1534-83)
Caspar Olevianus (1536-87)

Denmark
Christian Pederson (1480-1554)
Hans Tausen (1494-1561)

Iceland
Gissur Einarsson (died 1548)
Odd Gottskalksson (died 1556)

Sweden
Olaf Petersson (1493-1552)
Lars Petersson (1499-1573)

Finland
Peter Sarkilax (died 1530)
Martyn Skytte (died 1550)
Michael Agricola (1512-57)

The Netherlands
Guy de Bres (1522-67)
Peregrine de la Grange (died 1567)

Bohemia
John Augusta (1500-1575)
George Israel (1505-88)

Hungary
Matthias Biró Dévai (1500-1545)
Johannes Honterus (1498-1549)

Political and military
Germany
Maurice of Saxony (1541-53)
Frederick III of the Palatinate
    (1559-76)

Denmark
Christian II (1513-23)
Frederick I (1523-33)
Christian III (1533-59)

Sweden
Lars Anderson (1480-1552)
King Gustavus Vasa (1523-60)

France
Louis of Condé (1530-69)
Gaspard de Coligny (1519-72)
Catherine de Medici (1519-89)
Henry of Navarre, king Henry
    IV (1589-1610)
Philip Duplessis-Mornay
    (1549-1623)

The Netherlands
William the Silent (1533-84)

Spain
Philip II (1556-98)

Poland
Sigismund II (1548-72)

Martin Kálmáncsehi (died 1557)
Peter Melius (1536-72)

Poland
Jan Laski (1499-1560)

Melanchthon's announcement of the death of Luther

Dear students: as you know, we are engaged in a grammatical exposition of the letter to the Romans, which contains the true doctrine about God's Son, revealed to us by God at this time by His remarkable goodness, through our reverend father and beloved teacher, Doctor Martin Luther. But sad news has come here today, making my pain so great that I do not know if I can carry on with this lecture. As advised by the other lords, I will tell you what follows, so that you will know how it really happened, and not believe the false rumour that spreads and not spread untrue tales yourselves.

On Wednesday February 17th, just before supper, the doctor [Luther] started to suffer from his regular complaint, pressure of liquid at the stomach's opening, from which he had suffered earlier at various times. Afterwards he had some pain again. In the midst of this suffering he wished to be taken to the neighbouring room; there he lay for nearly two hours as the pain grew worse. Doctor [Justas] Jonas was sleeping in the same room, so Doctor Martin called him and woke him up with the request to get up and instruct the tutor of his children, Ambrosius, to heat the room. But when he had gone, count Albert of Mansfeld and his wife came in, and many others whose names are not mentioned in this letter for reasons of haste. Just before four o'clock the next day, February 18th, he felt the end of his life had come, and committed himself to God with the following prayer [see next quotation]…

After he had spoken this prayer a number of times, God called him to everlasting rest and joy, where he will rejoice in communion with Father, Son, and Holy Spirit, and all the prophets and apostles.

Alas! The charioteer and chariot of Israel has died, he who guided the Church in this last age of the world. The doctrine of forgiveness of sins and faith in God's Son was not grasped through human wisdom; no, it was revealed by God through this man whom we perceived had been stirred up by God. So let us treasure his memory and the teaching he communicated. Let us be humble and ponder the huge disasters and weighty changes that will proceed after this death!

Luther's dying prayer

"My heavenly Father, God and Father of our Lord Jesus Christ! I thank you, God of all comfort, that You have revealed Your beloved Son to me, even Jesus Christ whom I believed, preached, and confessed, loved and praised, yet whom the wicked pope and all the godless condemn, persecute, and blaspheme. O my dear Lord Jesus Christ, I pray to You and commit my soul to You. O heavenly Father, though I must leave this body and depart from this life, I truly know that I will be with You for ever, and no one will snatch me out of Your hands." And in Latin he said: "For God so loved the world that He gave His only-begotten Son, so that whoever believes in Him will not perish but have eternal life." He also spoke the words of Psalm 68: "Our God is a God of salvation! To God the Lord belongs escape from death." Then he quickly said three times over, "Father, into Your hands I commit my spirit. You have redeemed me, O God of truth."

Melanchthon's funeral sermon for Luther

Some well-intentioned people have criticised Luther for being harsher than he ought. I will not deny this, but I call to mind what Erasmus frequently said: "Because of the great evil of our most corrupt age, God sent us a harsh physician." Also I will not deny that Luther was sometimes quite extreme. But no human being is completely free of the errors that accompany our natural weakness.

Such was Luther as we knew him. What more shall I say of his splendid character? I was often with him when he prayed weeping for the Church. Almost every day he gave some time to reciting the Psalms, which he took into his intercessions with mourning and tears. Contrary to what many think, he did not overlook the wider good of the community, nor did he fall short in taking the opinions of others into account... Let us imitate his virtues as far as we can in our inferior character: his fear of God, his faithfulness and diligence in his calling, his purity in carrying out his spiritual responsibilities, his blameless walk and life, the discernment and care with which he shunned seditious counsel, and finally his zeal to acquire new knowledge.

The Peace of Augsburg

To bring into the holy Empire of the German nation peace between the imperial Roman majesty and the electors, princes, and states: his imperial Roman majesty and the electors, princes, *etc.*, shall offer no violence or harm to any state of the Empire for the sake of the Augsburg Confession, but permit them to enjoy their religious faith, worship, and ceremonies in peace, as well as their property and other rights and privileges. Let total religious peace be achieved only by Christian methods of friendly accord, or under threat of the penalty of the imperial ban [for violating the terms of the Peace]. Likewise the states that embrace the Augsburg Confession must permit all the states and princes who adhere to the old faith to live in complete peace in the enjoyment of all their property, rights, and privileges... No state shall attempt to persuade the citizens of other states to forsake their faith, nor protect them against their own government... If any of our citizens, adhering to the old faith or to the Augsburg Confession, wish to leave their homes, with their wives and children, and settle in another place, they must not be hampered in selling their goods, after due payment of the local taxes, nor must their honour be abused.

French Huguenot political theory

Necessity demands that kings were appointed for the people's sake. For it cannot be that everyone else was made for the pleasure of a few hundred kings (who are manifestly more foolish and evil than many of the others); rather, the few hundred kings were made for the use and service of the rest. Reason requires that a person should be ranked higher than others only in terms of his proper function. For example, when a ship sails, her owner appoints a pilot over her, who sits at the helm, and makes sure that the ship holds to her course, and does not run into a dangerous reef. When the pilot does his duty, the mariners obey him; indeed, even the ship's owner obeys him. Still, the pilot is a servant of the ship, just as much as the lowest mariners. The pilot differs only in this, that he serves in a higher place than they do. In the political community, which is often compared with a ship, the king occupies the place of a pilot; the general body of the people are the owners of the vessel, who obey the pilot, as long as he cares for the public good; but this pilot neither is nor should be reckoned as anything other than a servant of the public. It is the same case as a judge or a general in war, who differs little from other officers except that he is bound to carry heavier burdens and expose himself to greater dangers. So what a king gains by force of arms, such as frontier territories in wars with the enemy, or what he gains by forfeit or by confiscation, he gains it for the kingdom, not for himself; he gains it for his people, who make up the kingdom, even as a servant gains things for his master. No one may pledge or oblige themselves to him without reference to the authority derived from the people. Further, there are vast multitudes of people who live without a king, but we cannot imagine a king without people…

Now what we say about the people in general should be understood (as set forth under the second question) as referring to those who in every kingdom or city lawfully represent the body of the people, and who are normally called (or ought to be called) the officers of the "kingdom" or "crown", not officers of the king… The officers of the kingdom receive their authority from the people in the parliament of the different classes of the realm (or at least this is how in ancient times they were accustomed to receive their authority); and they cannot be stripped of authority except by the parliament.

Philip Duplessis-Mornay, *A Defence of Liberty against Tyrants***, question 3.**

Popular Calvinism in the Netherlands

Long live the Beggars!

Joyfully, joyfully beat the drum,
O beat it with joy, O beat it with joy:
Joyfully, joyfully beat the drum,
"Long live the Beggars!" is our battle-cry.[28]

The Spanish inquisition,
Without any intermission,
The Spanish inquisition has drunk up our blood:
The Spanish inquisition,
O may God's just decision
Blast the Spanish inquisition and all its brood!

Long live the Beggars!
If Christ's Word you'll cherish,
Long live the Beggars!
Be bold of heart and hand;
Long live the Beggars!
God will not see you perish:
Long live the Beggars,
O noble Christian band!

---

[28] The "Sea Beggars" was the popular name for William the Silent and his anti-Spanish resistance forces.

To the duke of Alba [29]

Our devil, who does in Brussels dwell,
Cursed be your name in earth and hell;
Your kingdom speedily pass away,
Which has blasted and blighted us many a day;
And may your will nevermore be done,
In heaven above or under the sun.
You take away our daily bread;
Our wives and children lie starving or dead.
No one's trespasses you forgive;
Revenge is the food on which you live.
You lead all people into temptation;
To evil you have delivered this nation.

Our Father in heaven, to You we pray:
Soon send this hellish devil away,
And with him, his Council false and bloody
Who make murder and pillage their daily study;
And all his savage war-dogs of Spain,
Send them back to the devil, their father, again! Amen.

The Heidelberg Catechism

Question 1. What is your only comfort in life and death?

Answer. That I with body and soul, both in life and death, am not my own, but belong to my faithful Saviour Jesus Christ; who, with His precious blood, has fully satisfied for all my sins, and delivered me from all the power of the devil; and so preserves me that without the will of my heavenly Father, not a hair can fall from my head; yes, that all things must be subservient to my salvation, and therefore, by His Holy Spirit, He also assures me of eternal life, and makes me sincerely willing and ready, henceforth, to live for Him.

---

[29] Alba was Philip of Spain's military governor of the Netherlands. The poem is a bitter parody of the Lord's Prayer.

Question 2. How many things are necessary for you to know, that you, enjoying this comfort, may live and die happily?

Answer. Three; the first, how great my sins and miseries are; the second, how I may be delivered from all my sins and miseries; the third, how I shall express my gratitude to God for such deliverance.

Question 3. Where do you learn of your misery?

Answer. Out of the law of God.

Question 4. What does the law of God require of us?

Answer. Christ teaches us that briefly, Matt. 22:37-40, "You shall love the Lord your God with all your heart, with all your soul, and with all your mind, and with all your strength. This is the first and the great commandment; and the second is like it, You shall love your neighbour as yourself. On these two commandments hang all the law and the prophets."

Question 5. Can you keep all these things perfectly?

Answer. In no way; for I am prone by nature to hate God and my neighbour.

Question 6. Did God then create man so wicked and perverse?

Answer. By no means; but God created man good, and after His own image, in true righteousness and holiness, that he might rightly know God his Creator, heartily love Him, and live with Him in eternal happiness to glorify and praise Him.

Question 7. From where then does this depravity of human nature proceed?

Answer. From the fall and disobedience of our first parents, Adam and Eve, in Paradise; hence our nature is become so corrupt, that we are all conceived and born in sin.

Question 8. Are we then so corrupt that we are wholly incapable of doing any good, and inclined to all wickedness?

Answer. Indeed we are, unless we are regenerated by the Spirit of God…

Question 31. Why is He called Christ, that is, anointed?

Answer. Because He is ordained by God the Father, and anointed with the Holy Spirit, to be our chief Prophet and Teacher, who has fully revealed to us the secret counsel and will of God concerning our redemption; and to be our only High Priest, who by the one sacrifice of His body, has redeemed us, and makes continual intercession with the Father for us; and also to be our eternal King, who governs us by His word and Spirit, and who defends and preserves us in that salvation He has purchased for us.

Question 32. But why are you called a Christian?

Answer. Because I am a member of Christ by faith, and thus am partaker of His anointing; that so I may confess His name, and present myself as a living sacrifice of thankfulness to Him: and also that with a free and good conscience I may fight against sin and Satan in this life: and afterwards reign with Him eternally, over all creation.

Question 33. Why is Christ called the only-begotten Son of God, since we are also the children of God?

Answer. Because Christ alone is the eternal and natural Son of God; but we are children adopted of God, by grace, for Christ's sake.

Question 34. Why do you call Him "our Lord"?

Answer. Because He has redeemed us, both soul and body, from all our sins, not with gold or silver, but with His precious blood, and has delivered us from all the power of the devil; and thus has made us His own property…

Question 37. What do you understand by the words, "He suffered"?

Answer. That He, all the time that He lived on earth, but especially at the end of his life, sustained in body and soul, the wrath of God against the sins of all mankind: so that by His passion, as the only propitiatory sacrifice, He might redeem our body and soul from everlasting damnation, and obtain for us the favour of God, righteousness, and eternal life.

Question 38. Why did He suffer under Pontius Pilate, as judge?

Answer. That He, being innocent, and yet condemned by a temporal judge, might thereby free us from the severe judgment of God to which we were exposed.

Question 39. Is there anything more in His being crucified, than if He had died some other death?

Answer. Yes; for thereby I am assured, that He took upon Him the curse which lay upon me; for the death of the cross was accursed of God.

Question 40. Why was it necessary for Christ to humble Himself even to death?

Answer. Because with respect to the justice and truth of God, satisfaction for our sins could be made in no other way, than by the death of the Son of God.

Question 41. Why was He also "buried"?

Answer. Thereby to prove that He was really dead.

Question 42. Since then Christ died for us, why must we also die?

Answer. Our death is not a satisfaction for our sins, but only an abolishing of sin, and a passage into eternal life.

Question 43. What further benefit do we receive from the sacrifice and death of Christ on the cross?

Answer. That by virtue of His death, our old man is crucified, dead and buried with Him; so that the corrupt inclinations of the flesh may no more reign in us, but that we may offer ourselves to him as a sacrifice of thanksgiving.

Chapter 7.

SWEET KERNEL: THE ENGLISH AND SCOTTISH REFORMATIONS.

As an Englishman who has spent most of his adult life in Scotland, I may be pardoned for describing the English and Scottish Reformations as the "sweet kernel" of our story. Patriotism has its claims. It is also a reasonably safe assumption that most readers of this book will feel a similar special interest in the origins of that Anglo-Scottish Protestantism which has, since its beginnings, had so wide and deep an impact on our world, notably on America. These facts (I hope) justify me in devoting an entire chapter to a subject that is, in any case, both fascinating and richly instructive in its own right.

1. The English Reformation: dawn

The English Reformation has generated more argument among historians than any of Europe's other Protestant Reformations. Some have seen England's Reformation as essentially a political experience, an act of state. Others have argued that while there is some truth in this, it is not the whole truth: there was, after all, a real battle being waged for the minds and hearts of the English people. It is best to embrace both points of view, and to think of the Reformation in England taking two forms which developed alongside each other, sometimes in harmony, sometimes in conflict. On the one hand, there was a political Reformation in which the English monarchy, first under king Henry VIII (1509-47), threw off its loyalty to Rome. On the other hand, there was a popular Reformation in which a spiritual war was carried on for possession of the soul of England.

The spiritual Reformation began first, as Lutheran books and ideas began to penetrate England, especially the capital city London. There was already a thriving Lollard underground movement in London, and the disciples of John Wyclif eagerly seized on the new Lutheran revolt against Rome and made it their own.[1] Indeed, a significant Lollard revival seems to have been gathering pace in the decades just before the arrival of Protestantism in England; we can see this from the increase in numbers of those arrested and executed for Lollardy. Of those Lollards who suffered the final penalty, three or four were burnt at the stake in Berkshire in the early 1500s; five were burnt in Kent in 1511-12; two were burnt in London in 1517; seven were burnt in Coventry in 1519; and six were burnt in Lincoln in 1521. Hundreds more were arrested in this brief 20 year period, who escaped death either by renouncing their beliefs (perhaps only to take them up again), or by managing to persuade less hardline magistrates of their orthodoxy. Lollards were certainly no passive movement; they made new if rather crude English translations of parts of Scripture and actively distributed their own religious literature. A leading London Lollard in this connection was "old father Hacker" (John Hacker), who spread Lollard writings until he was caught in 1521.

This Lollard underground provided a ready-made welcome for Protestant literature, especially new English translations of the Bible. Various examples of progress from Lollardy to Lutheranism have been discovered by modern scholars: two of old father Hacker's fellow-workers, John Stacey and Lawrence Maxwell, prominent guildsmen,[2] both became Lutherans in the 1520s and distributed Lutheran books. Probably old Lollardy and new

---

[1] For John Wyclif and the Lollards, see Part Two, Chapter 10, section 4.
[2] A guild was a sort of medieval trade union: an organised body of merchants or craftsmen who drew up and enforced rules and regulations for their sphere of activity.

Protestantism began to merge together from around the time that William Tyndale's English New Testament began circulating in 1525-6 (see below for Tyndale). The English Church authorities clearly tended to see all heresy in terms of Lollardy; in 1523, bishop Tunstall of London wrote to Erasmus, "It is no question of pernicious novelty; it is only that new arms are being added to the great crowd of Wycliffite heresies." The English Protestants also latched onto Lollardy to give themselves a native spiritual ancestry. Between 1530 and 1547, at least nine old Lollard works were reprinted by the Protestant press.

Humanists at Cambridge university also felt attracted to Luther; a group met regularly in the White Horse Inn to discuss the German Reformer's ideas (the group was nicknamed "Little Germany"). Among this group were the leaders of the first generation of England's Protestants: Robert Barnes, Thomas Bilney, Thomas Cranmer, John Frith, and Hugh Latimer, all of whom were eventually burnt as martyrs for the Protestant faith, and Edward Fox (1496-1538) and Nicholas Shaxton (1485-1556) who escaped martyrdom by different routes.[3] The move from humanism to Protestantism found a bridge in Erasmus's New Testament (1516); Bilney was won over to justification by faith by studying Paul's letters in this edition. As early as 1520, the vice-chancellor of Cambridge ordered a mass burning of Lutheran books.

In 1526 the authorities cracked down on the Cambridge group, singling out Bilney, Barnes, and Latimer for exemplary punishment. *Thomas Bilney* (1495-1531) was a curious "Protestant": a young priest immersed in Erasmian humanism, who believed in

---

[3] Fox escaped by dying of natural causes while bishop of Hereford. Shaxton's fate was more tragic. After a great career as a Protestant Reformer, he fell under Henry VIII's wrath in 1546 and was condemned to death for false teaching on the sacraments. Shaxton saved his life by renouncing his Protestantism. For the rest of his life, even during the reign of the Protestant king Edward VI, Shaxton was a committed Roman Catholic, and during Mary Tudor's reign, when Roman Catholicism was restored in England, he acted as a judge at trials of Protestants, passing death sentences on them for heresy. Shaxton died while Mary was still queen.

justification by faith and violently denounced images, pilgrimages, the adoration of Mary, and praying to saints, he nonetheless adhered to transubstantiation and the supremacy of the pope. Crumbling under the pressure of his trial he publicly renounced his Protestant beliefs in 1527, but was consumed with guilt for having done so, and seems then to have deliberately courted martyrdom by a course of unauthorised evangelistic preaching and distributing William Tyndale's English New Testament. Bilney was arrested in 1531 and made up for his previous lapse by dying at the stake. **Robert Barnes** (1495-1540), the second victim, was an eminent young scholar, head of the Augustinian monastery at Cambridge which he turned into a centre of humanist studies. He preached Erasmian humanism until Bilney converted him to justification by faith in 1523. Outspoken in his attacks on Church corruption in general and cardinal Wolsey in particular,[4] Barnes was forced to do public penance and was put under house arrest. Escaping to Luther's Wittenberg in 1528, where he wrote a number of Protestant works, he returned to England in 1535 under the protection of Thomas Cromwell (see below), to die a martyr at the stake just after Cromwell's fall from power. Barnes is the only known example of an English Reformer whose views were practically pure Lutheran. **Hugh Latimer** (1485-1555), the third victim, will figure more prominently in the narrative later; for now, it is enough to note that like Barnes he, too, was converted by Bilney, and alone of the three men managed to survive his trial unscathed, dismissed by Wolsey with liberty to preach throughout all England.

The greatest of the early English Protestants was not a member of the Cambridge group – **William Tyndale** (1495-1536). Tyndale was a priest and university-trained linguist (educated at Oxford), whose religious views were at an advanced stage before 1522, under Erasmus's influence; it is not known when he passed over into

---

[4]   Thomas Wolsey (1475-1530) was the virtual head of the English Church in the first part of Henry VIII's reign. He was archbishop of York from 1514, but his special position as the pope's representative (legate) from 1518 gave him superiority over the archbishop of Canterbury, William Warham.

avowed Protestantism. He early conceived it to be his mission to translate the Bible into English from the original Greek and Hebrew, and to give it to the common people as the surest way of overthrowing Roman error. A contemporary of Tyndale records the famous incident that stiffened Tyndale's commitment to his mission:

> "Master Tyndale happened to be in the company of a learned man, and in communing and disputing with him drove him to that issue that the learned man said, we were better without God's law than the pope's: Master Tyndale, hearing that, answered him, 'I defy the pope and all his laws,' and said, 'If God spare my life ere many years, I will cause a boy that driveth the plough shall know more of the scripture than thou dost.'"

Tyndale began his life's work in London in 1523; the Protestant merchant, Humphrey Monmouth, acted as his patron. Opposed, however, by the English Church authorities, Tyndale sailed to the Continent and lived the rest of his life an exile in Germany and the Netherlands. His English New Testament was first published in 1525 at Worms, and thousands of copies were smuggled into England. This complete English translation soon superseded the old Lollard hand-written fragments.

Tyndale's translation was a masterpiece. Working from Erasmus's Greek text, the Latin Vulgate, and Luther's German version, Tyndale produced a fresh and original rendering of the New Testament, which formed the basis of virtually all English New Testaments until the 20th century, including the Authorised or King James Version. The subsequent flowering of the English language into its full glory (most famously in Shakespeare) in the reign of Elizabeth I owed much to the inspiration of Tyndale's New Testament; it would not be going too far to call him the father of modern English. The English bishops of his own day, however, instantly condemned Tyndale's work as subversive, and seized and burnt as many copies of his New Testament as they could. Subversive it

William Tyndale 1495-1536

was: Tyndale translated "church" as "congregation", "priest" as "senior" (later "elder"), "do penance" as "repent", "confess" as "acknowledge", thus ridding the Bible of terms that had acquired a distinctly medieval Catholic flavour. Tyndale managed to translate the Pentateuch, Jonah, and Joshua − 2 Chronicles into English too, before his death.

Tyndale's theological writings are the most important of any produced by the English Reformers in Henry VIII's reign. Three notable works were *The Parable of the Wicked Mammon* (1528), a lyrical exposition of justification by faith, heavily reliant on Luther; *The Obedience of a Christian Man* (1528), which glorifies the doctrine of the absolute authority of kings, soon to be enacted by Henry VIII; and *The Practice of Prelates* (1530), a vitriolic condemnation of the English Church establishment as morally and spiritually corrupt. Tyndale also conducted a literary duel with Sir Thomas More, England's greatest humanist and an increasingly intolerant foe of the Reformation. We learn from More that Tyndale was "a hell-hound in the kennel of the devil", "a new Judas", "worse than Sodom and Gomorrah", "an idolater and devil-worshipper", and "a beast out of whose brutish beastly mouth cometh a filthy foam": remarkable enough when we remember that Tyndale's unpardonable sin was simply translating the New Testament into English. Ironically, both More and Tyndale died for their faith, and both at the hands of the same monarch – More was executed for treason in July 1535 for opposing Henry VIII's break with Rome, and an English Catholic spy in the pay of Henry's government betrayed Tyndale in Antwerp, the Netherlands, in May 1535. Tyndale was strangled and burnt at the stake at Vilvoorde castle near Brussels in October 1536. His famous last words were, "Lord, open the king of England's eyes!"

Tyndale's English New Testament was smuggled into England and distributed by a secret Protestant society with Lollard connections, known as "the Christian Brethren".[5] This was an organised body

---

[5]   Nothing to do with the present day Christian group "the Brethren".

with its own accounts and auditors; prominent among the Brethren were wealthy merchants like William Petit, Richard Hilles, and Tyndale's patron Humphrey Monmouth. They also financed, smuggled, and distributed English translations of the writings of the Continental Reformers, and books by native English Reformers. Like Tyndale's New Testament, these had to be printed abroad, since no printing press in Catholic England would produce heretical works. Most of the English Protestant literature was published in Cologne, Strasbourg, or Basel, sold at the big book fairs in Frankfurt, smuggled up the river Rhine in barges (the route was patrolled by the inquisition), and shipped to England in bales of cloth from Antwerp or Hamburg to London, Bristol, or Lynn. Here it was unloaded, picked up by distribution agents, and taken to likely buyers in the cities, universities, and monasteries. This activity was coordinated from the English merchants' house at Antwerp. German Lutheran merchants resident in England were also involved: two of them were forced to renounce their errors with Robert Barnes in 1526.

Three other early English Protestant writers worthy of a brief glance here are Simon Fish, John Frith, and John Bale. *Simon Fish* (1500-1531), a London lawyer and distributor of Tyndale's New Testament, was responsible for the famous *Supplication of the Beggars* (1529). This was a full-blooded expression of the anti-clerical nationalism which had such a widespread influence in the English parliament of that time, and which would contribute so strongly to England's break with Rome. Fish rejected the authority of the papacy, denied that the clergy had any power other than the purely spiritual one of teaching, and affirmed the absolute political supremacy of the king. Fish's book may have influenced Henry VIII himself. *John Frith* (1503-31), perhaps the most brilliant of the young Cambridge humanists, worked for a time with Tyndale on the Continent, and wrote some outstanding theological and devotional works. He is particularly important for his advocacy of breadth and tolerance in doctrinal matters, and for being the first known English Reformer to reject Luther's eucharistic views (having been present at the Marburg colloquy[6]) in favour of a more Reformed "spiritual presence" of Christ in the Supper. Frith was also the first definitely Protestant English author to be burnt for heresy. *John Bale* (1495-1563), ex-monk and client of Thomas Cromwell, was the most savage and prolific of the English anti-Roman writers, as well as probably the most learned man in England. His most striking work was his drama *King John*, performed in 1538, an allegory of the struggle between Henry VIII / Protestantism and Rome.

2. Henry VIII and England's quarrel with Rome

The political Reformation began when the English king *Henry VIII* (1509-47) wanted to divorce his wife Catherine of Aragon because of her failure to give him a male heir to the throne. Catherine was not childless: she had given Henry a daughter, Mary Tudor. At that time, however, it was not thought safe or proper for a woman to sit on the English throne; a male heir was considered indispensable to the peace of the realm. There was a real fear that without a son to succeed Henry, England might plunge back into the civil wars from which it had only just emerged under Henry's father, Henry VII (1485-1509) (the "Wars of the Roses"). Henry began to brood on the possibility that his marriage was cursed by God, owing to Catherine having been the wife of Henry's brother Arthur before Henry married her on Arthur's death. Did the Old Testament not pronounce a curse of childlessness on a man who married his brother's wife?[7] But to set Catherine aside, Henry needed to have the marriage dissolved by the pope, Clement VII (1523-34). The problem was that Clement was in the power of the Holy Roman emperor Charles V, especially after Charles' mutinous troops had sacked Rome during an Italian campaign in 1527. Charles was Catherine's nephew; the emperor refused to allow his aunt to be treated shamefully by Henry; and so Clement refused to

---

6   For the Marburg colloquy, see Chapter 3, section
7   "And if a man shall take his brother's wife, it is an unclean thing: he has uncovered his brother's nakedness; they shall be childless," Leviticus 20:21.

dissolve the marriage. This drove Henry closer and closer to the idea of breaking the connection between the English Church and the papacy, so that he could secure his divorce within an autonomous English Church.

Henry's divorce proceedings fell into three stages. First he tried to obtain his divorce by exerting diplomatic persuasion on pope Clement through Henry's chief minister, cardinal Wolsey, a policy which lasted till 1529. Wolsey's failure to achieve his royal master's wishes brought about his own downfall. Next from 1529 to 1531, Henry tried to secure his divorce by putting pressure on Clement through the English clergy. Henry progressively tightened his grip on the English Church, and so prompted the clergy to appeal to the pope to grant his divorce for their own relief. When this too failed, Henry played his most drastic card, and from 1532 to 1534 moved towards divorce by enacting schism.

The schism – the separation of the English Church from papal jurisdiction – took place through the Reformation Parliament, which Henry summoned in 1529. The Anglican[8] separation from Rome was thus not an act of the monarch alone (as is often mistakenly thought), but of the monarch acting in concert with parliament. First the English Church lost its legislative independence in 1532 through the "Submission of the Clergy", which stripped the Church of its right to make laws without the consent of the laity in parliament. Next (also in 1532) it lost its financial independence: parliament passed an act diverting "first fruits and annates" (clerical taxes) from Rome to the English crown. Initially this was a conditional measure, pending the success of Henry's divorce; but the

---

[8]   The term "Anglican" does not necessarily imply an English Church independent of Rome. It is just another way of describing the English national Church: "Anglicanus" is Latin for "English". Similarly in Scotland, the Latin term "Scotican" was used to describe the Scottish national Church. In post-Reformation times, however, "Anglican" acquired the meaning of "the English national Church as reformed in the 16th century", and eventually in the 19th century the term "Anglicanism" was coined. To avoid misunderstanding, I will apply the term Anglican to the English national Church only after its break with Rome.

following year it was made permanent through the Act in Restraint of Annates. This was accompanied by the Dispensations Act which stopped all payments to Rome. Finally the Church lost its judicial independence: in 1533 parliament passed the Act in Restraint of Appeals (to Rome) which deprived the papacy of any right to judge English cases in either Church or state. This act contains a famous assertion that "England is an empire" – that is, as the term was understood in the 16th century, a self-sufficient sovereign state whose king owes allegiance to no other power on earth.[9] Finally in 1534 came the Act of Supremacy: Henry was declared the head of the Church of England.

Almost all the bishops and clergy submitted to Henry's and parliament's ecclesiastical revolution. The handful who remained loyal to Rome were executed. The victims, as we have seen, included Sir Thomas More, a devout believer in papal supremacy.

Although Henry VIII had broken the English Church's ties with Rome, he did little to change its doctrine. Having replaced the pope as head of the Church of England, Henry had no wish to adopt a full-blown Lutheran or Zwinglian theology. He struck down obstinate Roman Catholics and provocative Protestants with equal severity. Nevertheless, Protestantism did make some progress in the period 1530-40, largely through the influence of two Thomases, Cranmer and Cromwell. ***Thomas Cranmer*** (1489-1556), a gentle humanist scholar from Aslockton in Nottinghamshire, was a cautious thinker who was moving slowly in the direction of Protestantism. He supported Henry's case for divorce; he had become one of Henry's favourites when he suggested that the universities of Europe should be canvassed for their opinion on whether Henry's marriage should be dissolved on the grounds of Catherine having been his brother's wife. The mixed response lent some credibility to Henry's case: the European academic establishment, including Roman Catholic universities, failed to give anything like united support to pope Clement's opposition to the

---

9   And that is all it meant in the 16th century. It had no overtones of "imperialism" – invading and conquering other nations.

divorce.[10] Cranmer became perhaps the only man Henry ever trusted, and Henry rewarded him by making him archbishop of Canterbury in 1533. Cranmer pronounced Henry's marriage to Catherine void because it violated Leviticus 20:21, and Henry's marriage to Anne Boleyn, a lady of the court, was declared lawful in June 1533 (Henry had already married her in secret). Pope Clement excommunicated Henry, who appealed to an ecumenical Council. In September Anne gave birth, but not to the desired male heir; her child was a daughter, Elizabeth, the future queen.

Thomas Cromwell (1485-1540)[11] became Henry's prime minister from 1534, as a reward for having successfully guided through parliament the legislative revolution which had made the "English empire" independent of the papacy. Cromwell had strong personal leanings towards Protestantism, and encouraged Protestants as far as he could, despite Henry's traditional Catholic beliefs. In 1536-40 Cromwell oversaw the suppression ("dissolution") of the monasteries throughout England. As a prelude to this, Cromwell and his civil servants compiled a comprehensive register of the English Church's wealth, the *Valor Ecclesiasticus*, which revealed that the income of the monasteries was three or four times greater than that of the crown. As the monasteries were suppressed over the four year period, most of the monks were given a pension or a parish appointment, while their property was taken over by the monarchy and sold to the English nobility. This was nothing less than an economic revolution, a redistribution of land and wealth on a scale unsurpassed in English history.

The disappearance of monasticism was also a severe psychological blow against medieval Catholicism. In northern England it was a critical element in provoking "the Pilgrimage of Grace" in 1536-7, a popular uprising against Henry VIII which the king suppressed

---

[10]   Many Roman Catholic universities upheld Henry's case, while the Protestant universities of Germany supported pope Clement!

[11]   Not to be confused with his more famous namesake, Oliver Cromwell, the 17th century Puritan soldier and statesman. Oliver was the great-grandson of Thomas's sister (who retained the Cromwell name after her marriage).

with great savagery. Profound economic and religious grievances against the government were mixed together in the rebellion. But we should not minimise the religious element. It demonstrates that the "old religion" was still capable of inspiring great loyalty in the hearts of ordinary English people. The Reformation in England was not a conflict between sincere, vibrant Protestants and a dead Church which nobody loved. Each side could appeal to deep wellsprings of popular support. Even within Henry VIII's court there was a constant struggle between conservative and reformist groups, with the balance of power tipping now one way, now another.

Cromwell was also instrumental in promoting the English Bible. He and Cranmer prevailed on the Anglican clergy to petition Henry for an official English translation of Scripture. In 1535, **Miles Coverdale** (1488-1569), who had stepped into the martyred Tyndale's place, published the first complete English Bible (probably at Zurich) with an unauthorised dedication to Henry. In 1537, Henry sanctioned a London printing of Coverdale's Bible; the same year he issued by royal licence a different translation by John Rogers (another Cambridge humanist), known as "Matthew's Bible". In 1538 Cromwell, acting as Henry's vicegerent, commanded every parish church in England to obtain an English Bible, for all to read (or have read to them). In 1539 the long awaited official version appeared, the "Great Bible", Coverdale's masterpiece. The driving force behind the Great Bible was Cromwell, who helped finance it personally. It was illustrated by a picture of Henry delivering the Word to Cranmer and Cromwell, with Christ surveying the scene favourably. Political factors brought about Cromwell's downfall and execution in 1540, but he had done much to move England in a more Protestant direction.

The English Bible and its effects were part of the wider progress of Protestantism in the period 1530-47. The 1530s, the decade of the Reformation parliament, Cromwell, and the dissolution of the monasteries, saw a more general growth of Protestant views, spread by sympathetic clergy and laypeople, protected to a considerable extent by powerful figures like Cromwell. London became notorious for Protestant "heresy" – indeed, England's capital city would always be the stronghold of English Protestantism; but the rest of southern England was being impacted too. This was the decade of the evangelical bishops, of whom there were seven: Thomas Cranmer of Canterbury (1533 onwards), Thomas Goodrich of Ely (1534 onwards); John Hilsey of Rochester (1535-38); Edward Fox of Hereford (1535-38); Hugh Latimer of Worcester (1535-39); Nicholas Shaxton of Salisbury (1535-39); and William Barlow of Saint David's (1536 onwards). Cranmer worked mostly behind the scenes. Goodrich and Fox were more political figures than pastors, but did much for reform in this capacity. Hilsey became infamous in Roman Catholic eyes for his iconoclasm, especially his exposure of such time-honoured frauds as the Blood of Hailes and the Rood of Boxley.[12] Nicholas Shaxton, William Barlow, and Hugh Latimer were zealous evangelical preachers. Latimer proved particularly effective in his diocese of Worcester, preaching in his uniquely homely and hard-hitting style (he has been called the greatest preacher of 16th century England) and encouraging the destruction of images and relics.

The greatest phenomenon of the 1530s and 1540s, however, was the huge growth of lay Bible reading. Ordinary people were discussing the Bible in ale-houses. The illiterate learned to read so that they could study Scripture. Women dared to argue with priests

---

[12]   The Blood of Hailes was (allegedly) a sample of Christ's blood kept at Hailes abbey (Gloucestershire) in a special vessel mounted in a case. The vessel was designed with a thick opaque crystal on one side and a transparent crystal on the other. The "blood" could be seen only when a concealed monk turned the vessel with the transparent side towards the onlooker. The monks claimed that the blood was miraculously visible only to those whose sins God had pardoned, and by a strange coincidence God seemed to pardon those who gave rich gifts to the abbey. The Rood of Boxley was a crucifix at Boxley abbey (Kent) which "miraculously" nodded, winked, and bent its body if a visitor's offering was adequate, but turned away if it was too small. The movements of the crucifix were controlled by hidden wires pulled by a monk. Hilsey had the crucifix removed and taken to Henry VIII's court, where its movements provoked great laughter and scorn for a religion that could stoop to such deceptions.

about what the Bible taught. By 1537, Edward Fox could say to his fellow bishops: "Make not yourselves the laughing-stock of the world; light is sprung up and is scattering all the clouds. The lay people know the Scriptures better than many of us." Some qualifications are needed: this picture applies mainly to southern England and mainly the cities; and devotion to Scripture is not in itself equivalent to Protestantism – there is evidence that points to some people using the Bible in a merely negative way, to criticise the priestly establishment. In fact the chief fruit which the Bible bore among the English people at this period was to open up a yawning credibility gap between the Christianity of the New Testament and that of the contemporary Church. In the acid words of the Protestant propagandist Jerome Barlow, an ex-friar from Greenwich:

"Might men the Scripture in English read,
We secular people should then see indeed
What Christ and the apostles' lives were."

By Henry's death in 1547, Protestantism was firmly established in southern England, especially in London. Much of it was the product of the spiritual Reformation which had been going on alongside Henry's political Reformation and owed little to the king's break with Rome. English Protestantism was also unique in being neither fully Lutheran nor fully Reformed; it developed an individual character of its own, marked by an intense love of the Bible, an emphasis on vital personal godliness, and a swelling English nationalism which saw England as God's chosen nation, always at the forefront of His purposes in history, especially His quarrel with the Roman Antichrist. Henry VIII, however, never embraced Protestantism himself, remaining a traditional Catholic in most of his beliefs (apart from his rejection of the papacy), and he continued to inflict periodic persecution on outspoken Protestants as well as on stubborn supporters of the pope. Things turned especially bleak for Protestants in 1539 when Henry decreed a new test of orthodoxy, the "Six Articles", which reaffirmed transubstantiation, a celibate priesthood, and other medieval dogmas. Latimer

Nicholas Ridley (1503-55)

and Shaxton resigned their bishoprics in protest; Cranmer publicly opposed the articles in the House of Lords but survived.[13]

3. Edward VI: The young Josiah

The spiritual and political Reformations came into close harmony in the reign of *Edward VI* (1547-53), Henry VIII's young son by his third wife Jane Seymour. Henry – perhaps sensing the direction the English mind was taking – had ensured that Edward had been raised by Protestant tutors, and the youthful new monarch was sincerely and ardently devoted to the Protestant faith. Archbishop Cranmer too had by now fully accepted Protestantism. Since Edward was only nine when he became king, two nobles ruled on his behalf: first the Duke of Somerset (1547-49), a moderate but honest Protestant, then the Duke of Northumberland (1549-53), a more militant Protestant but also a reckless self-interested adventurer.

Under Somerset and Northumberland, Cranmer and other leading Reformers progressively transformed the Anglican Church into a fully Protestant body. Among Cranmer's most effective co-workers were three men destined to share his high place in the annals of England's Reformation. There was Hugh Latimer, Henry VIII's bishop of Worcester, now a court preacher and itinerant evangelist, who had lost none of his riveting power in the pulpit. Then there was *Nicholas Ridley* (1503-55), bishop of Rochester from 1547 and of London from 1550, perhaps the greatest professional theologian among the English Reformers, and a man of steel who flinched at nothing to promote the Protestant cause. Like Cranmer, Ridley had moved slowly towards Protestantism in Henry VIII's reign; unusually, the decisive influence on him was the newly

---

[13] Cranmer is often depicted as a cowardly time-server, but the facts do not bear out this interpretation. A cowardly time-server would not have dared publicly to oppose a tyrant like Henry VIII. Cranmer's remarkable ability to survive the twists and turns of Henry VIII's policies and moods was due more to Henry's huge personal esteem for Cranmer, whom Henry seems to have felt was the only man who sincerely loved him.

rediscovered treatise on the Lord's Supper by the 9th century theologian Ratramnus, which convinced Ridley in the early 1540s that transubstantiation was not the ancient doctrine of the Church.[14] Finally there was ***John Hooper*** (died 1555), bishop of Gloucester from 1551. Hooper had been in exile in the Reformed cities of Strasbourg, Basel, and Zurich since 1539, and had a more thoroughly Swiss Reformed outlook than most of the English Reformers. He is often seen as a forerunner of Puritanism in his dedication to purifying the Church of England of all that savoured of Roman Catholicism in worship (notably the special "vestments" worn by the clergy since early medieval times – Hooper had to be brutally bullied into wearing them at his episcopal ordination in 1551), and in his commitment to educating his people in a biblical and Protestant faith.

Adding to the increasingly Protestant complexion of England was an influx of distinguished Protestant refugees from Continental Europe, which had become an unfriendly place for committed Protestants after the military victories of Holy Roman emperor Charles V over the German Protestant princes.[15] It was significant for the future of English Protestantism that no Lutheran theologians took refuge in England, although Cranmer did invite Melanchthon. Leading Reformed Churchmen, however, such as Martin Bucer, Peter Martyr, and Jan Laski, did settle and work in England during Edward VI's reign, helping to inject a strong dose of the Reformed ethos into English Protestantism. Martin Bucer in particular worked with Cranmer in preparing the second edition of the Book of Common Prayer (see below); Cranmer included many of Bucer's suggestions in the final text.

Edward VI's Church combined a Lutheran attitude to Church government (state control through king, parliament, and royally appointed bishops), with a Reformed perspective on other doctrinal issues, notably the Reformed view of the Lord's Supper. This was set out in the second edition of the Book of Common Prayer in

---

14   For Ratramnus see Part Two, Chapter 2, section 4.
15   See previous Chapter, section 1.

1552 (see below) and in an aggressively Protestant confession of faith, the 42 Articles, promulgated as the Anglican Creed in 1553. Less militant was a *Book of Homilies* published in 1547; these, like Luther's *Postils*, were intended as popular summaries of official Church doctrine to be read out from the pulpit by clergy unable to preach.[16] Originally produced under Henry VIII, the *Homilies* embodied a mild, conservative Protestantism which in some ways did little more than set forth England's official religion as it was in Henry's day (perhaps "Henrician" religion at its most Protestant-leaning). Even so, homily number three on "the salvation of all mankind" by Cranmer was fairly clearly a Protestant treatise on justification by faith. In 1549, the marriage of the clergy was made legal.

It was, however, in the realm of public worship that the deepest impact was made. Negatively, there was a massive wave of government-sponsored iconoclasm, with images of the saints being removed from churches or destroyed, and church walls being whitewashed to cover over pictures. Stone altars were also replaced by wooden tables. More positively, Cranmer produced a service book for use in worship called the Book of Common Prayer, which was gradually to win the overwhelming affection of generations of Anglican worshippers (after 400 years, it has been widely abandoned within Anglicanism only since the 1960s). The first Prayer Book was issued in 1549: a cautious work, it did not go much beyond making English the language of worship and granting the wine as well as the bread to the laity in communion. The second Prayer Book of 1552 was a much more thoroughly Protestant liturgy, in which a Reformed view of the eucharist was clearly set forth. Cranmer's Prayer Books were not in essence original creations, but largely compilations, adaptations, and translations into English of existing historic liturgies. Cranmer's genius as a translator, however, is universally recognised, and the English language has never been put to a more noble spiritual use than in Cranmer's rich and measured Prayer Book prose. Cranmer also structured the

---

[16]   For Luther's *Postils*, see Chapter 3, section 5.

Prayer Books to incorporate the older practice of the early Church, lost in the Middle Ages, of vocal participation by the laity in the service of worship. No liturgy from the Reformation era has more spoken responses by the congregation. As well as expressing the Protestant "quest for the early Church", this participatory model of worship was also Cranmer's way of building Luther's fundamental insight about the priesthood of all believers into the very form of the service.

No Roman Catholic was put to death for his religion during the reign of Edward VI, and indeed some parts of England remained hotbeds of open loyalty to the old religion.[17] This was especially true of Oxford, where the great majority of teachers and students in the university were convinced and committed Roman Catholics. The Italian Reformer, Peter Martyr, who lectured on theology at Oxford, was given a very rough ride, although even his most ardent foes had to admire his scholarship and his brilliance in debate.

Under Edward VI, the economic aspect of the Reformation was also completed. Henry had suppressed the monasteries; the Edwardian government suppressed "chantry chapels", where mass was celebrated for the souls of the departed. This was a revolutionary measure: there were over 4,000 chantries in England. Their disappearance made a huge psychological as well as economic impact. The precious metals used in adorning the chantries were melted down and sold off to enrich the monarchy (although Cranmer protested – he thought the money rightfully belonged to the Church).

---

[17] However, two Radicals, Joan Bocher and George van Parris, were executed for Trinitarian and Christological heresies. Joan Bocher, sometimes called Joan of Kent, held practically all the Anabaptist peculiarities (the heavenly flesh of Christ, the sinless perfection of the believer, and so forth), and perhaps outraged 16th century feelings about the role of women by giving freelance theological lectures in London in which she taught her views. Her lectures became an embarrassing focus for Radical activity in Protestant London. Cranmer took a leading part in Joan's condemnation. George van Parris was a Dutch Rationalist Radical who denied the deity of Christ.

4. Bloody Mary: Rome triumphant

After a brief but landmark-setting reign of only six years, king Edward died of tuberculosis in 1553, and his older sister Mary I (1553-58), Henry VIII's daughter by Catherine of Aragon, became queen. The terms of the succession were set out in Henry's will as ratified by parliament. Mary was known to be a zealous Roman Catholic. Fearing what she might do, the Duke of Northumberland and others hatched a Protestant plot in Edward's dying days to exclude Mary from the throne, strongly supported by Edward himself; the royal candidate chosen by the plotters was Jane Grey, the daughter-in-law of Northumberland – she was fourth in line to the English throne. Ridley championed the scheme boldly, Cranmer cooperated reluctantly (bullied into it by the dying Edward). However, the plot failed. Most of England – including many Protestants – rallied to Mary Tudor as the legitimate claimant. Northumberland was captured and executed, along with the unfortunate Jane Grey who had been queen for nine days. Northumberland converted to Roman Catholicism in a vain attempt to win Mary's favour, but Jane died a convinced Protestant.[18]

Mary had initially given no indication that she would persecute Protestants, which was no doubt why so many of them had supported her claim to the throne. She was not long in power, however, before she set about undoing the Reformation with a vengeance. Acting in concert with a parliament which contained some elements hostile to her (the nobility and gentry would not return any of the wealth and property they had acquired from the suppression of the monasteries and chantries), Mary brought the Anglican Church back under the authority of the papacy, and restored traditional Roman Catholic worship in Latin.[19] She also married king Philip of Spain, the most deadly foe of Protestantism

---

[18] Northumberland was executed immediately. Lady Jane was put to death only after Sir Thomas Wyatt's rebellion (see later in this section).

[19] When parliament passed the act restoring the Latin mass, the great majority (350) voted in favour, but a diehard Protestant minority of 80 dared to vote against.

in all Europe. Many English Protestants fled abroad: most found
refuge in Germany and Switzerland. Protestants who stayed behind
in England were now arrested and tried for heresy. Throughout all
this, Mary's archbishop of Canterbury was ironically Reginald
Pole, a "Catholic Evangelical" who had much in common with the
theology of the Reformers; but Pole seems to have blinded himself
to the horrible reality of the persecution in his idealistic enthusiasm
for the renewal of the Roman Catholic faith in England.[20]

In 1555, the executions began; between 1555 and 1558, some 300
English Protestants were burnt at the stake, and another 100 died of
maltreatment in prison. England had never known such a concentrated burst of religious persecution in its entire history. Most of the
martyrs were obscure, ordinary men and women, whose often
joyful and triumphant deaths revealed an unsuspected depth of
grass-roots Protestant faith. Some of England's famous Protestant
leaders, however, were also burnt, including Cranmer, Ridley,
Latimer, and Hooper. Ridley and Latimer were burnt together at
Oxford, and Latimer made the most oft-quoted remark of the
English Reformation as they were led to the stake: "Be of good
comfort, Master Ridley, and play the man; for we shall this day
light such a candle, by God's grace, in England, as I trust shall
never be put out."

Cranmer's martyrdom made an even greater impression. He had
been subjected to unceasing psychological pressure in prison to
renounce Protestantism, and had eventually succumbed (driven
partly by his extreme, almost abject reverence for monarchy: how
could he defy his lawful sovereign?). Despite his submission, Mary
decided to make an example of Cranmer and burn him anyway, as
the foremost figure of the Anglican Reformation (and perhaps as
the man who had declared her mother's marriage to Henry VIII
unlawful back in 1535, thus stigmatising Mary as a bastard). At the
place of execution in Oxford, however, Cranmer unexpectedly
refused to read out his recantation, and stunned everyone by

---

[20]   For more about Pole, see Chapter 8, section 1.

vigorously reaffirming his Protestant faith, blaming himself for his cowardice in ever having renounced it, and denouncing the pope as Antichrist. As the flames rose around him at the stake, the old archbishop held out the hand which had signed the document of recantation, so that it was the first part of his body to be burnt away. By this final act in death, Cranmer may have done more to sanctify the Protestant cause in English eyes than anything he had accomplished in his life.

The martyrdoms were soon afterwards chronicled in great detail by **John Foxe** (1516-87), in his "Book of Martyrs" (its real title is *Actes and Monuments of these latter and perilous times touching matters of the Church*). Foxe, a native of Boston in Lincolnshire and an early convert to Protestantism, had fled to Continental Europe in 1554 to escape the persecution under Mary. From the safety of Reformed Basel, he not only watched the drama that was unfolding in England but was supplied with a constant flow of information by contacts there. Almost immediately after Mary's death, in 1559 he published his account of the martyrdoms, in Latin; in 1563, an enlarged edition in English was published. As well as chronicling the Protestant martyrdoms under Mary, Foxe's *Actes and Monuments* weaves them into a larger story of all Christian martyrdoms from the early Church onwards, in which the great persecutor of the Church is always Rome, first pagan Rome and then papal Rome. In Foxe's account of this age-long conflict, England emerged as the central theatre of God's purposes. It is safe to say that no work of propaganda was ever more successful. Historians (especially Roman Catholic ones) have energetically disputed the accuracy of some of Foxe's accounts and the trustworthiness of his methods; but there can be no doubt that the *Actes and Monuments* is built around a core of fact which tapped into and expressed the feelings and experiences of English men and women at that soul-stirring time. It was a runaway success, and in 1571 the Anglican "convocation" (clerical governing body) ordered that copies of the *Actes and Monuments* should be lodged in all cathedrals for the public to read. The book was also put on display in many Anglican parish churches. Foxe had ensured that for centuries the majority of England's inhabitants would look on Roman Catholicism as an inherently cruel and intolerant religion that was hostile to the lives and liberties of the English people.

Even before Foxe's *Actes and Monuments* was published, the burnings themselves caused a great revulsion of feeling among most Englishmen, earning Mary the nickname "bloody Mary". Mary's marriage to Philip of Spain was also deeply unpopular: it seemed to put England under Spanish domination. There were plots to topple Mary and replace her with her Protestant sister Elizabeth, daughter of Henry VIII by his second wife Anne Boleyn; indeed, even before the burnings began, there was a serious rebellion against Mary as early as 1554 in Kent, led by Sir Thomas Wyatt, an anti-Spanish English nationalist and Protestant sympathiser. Mary managed to crush Wyatt's uprising, but English feeling continued to be inflamed against Mary's Spanish marriage. The steady stream of Protestant blood from 1555 onwards intensified this feeling, although paradoxically the Spanish were opposed to Mary's policy of burning Protestants – they could see only too clearly how counterproductive it was. By the time Mary died in November 1558 (followed by archbishop Pole a few hours later), there had begun to develop in much of England a widespread hatred of Roman Catholicism, as a foreign religion which murdered brave and honest Englishmen and women.

Meanwhile, all was not well among the English Protestant exiles on the Continent. Serious division occurred over the vexed matter of worship. The English refugees adopted two different approaches to this question. Some, like the congregations in Zurich and Strasbourg, worshipped according to the Anglican Book of Common Prayer. Others, like the congregation in Geneva, adopted a Continental Reformed liturgy. The English congregation in Frankfurt, however, split over the issue in 1554-55. Their pastor, John Knox (the future Scottish Reformer who had during Edward VI's reign been living and working in England), wanted the congregation to worship according to a more Continental form of liturgy. So Knox and a number of others drew up such a liturgy, but it met with disfavour from too many in the congregation. A vocal party who eventually found a leader in **Richard Cox** (1500-1581) agitated for the Book of Common Prayer. (This has, of course, gone down in history as "Knox versus Cox".) Cox was an important figure: the dean of Westminster and hardline Protestant chancellor of Oxford university under Edward VI, he was an intimate colleague of Cranmer, and had worked with him on the two Prayer Books. Arrested by Mary Tudor and charged with treason, Cox managed to escape to the Continent, eventually to Frankfurt. Torn by liturgical controversy, the Frankfurt church at first adopted what has been called the "Liturgy of Compromise", a halfway house between the Anglican Prayer Book and the more Continental Reformed liturgy. This did not permanently satisfy the Anglican party, especially not when the aggressively outspoken Cox arrived. The Coxians renewed the campaign for the Book of Common Prayer, won the day, and dismissed Knox from the pastorate. Knox was then expelled from Frankfurt by its magistrates when Cox pointed out to them that Knox had, in one of his writings, compared the German emperor Charles V to the wicked Roman emperor Nero.[21]

The Frankfurt dispute was in many ways summed up by some remarks exchanged by Cox and Knox. Arguing for the Anglican Prayer Book, Cox said: "We would have the face of an English Church." Knox replied: "The Lord grant that we may have the face of Christ's Church." The Coxians were determined to uphold the Book of Common Prayer, partly out of loyalty to the English Reformation and those who were now suffering for it under Mary, partly out of genuine love for Cranmer's liturgy. The Knoxians, by contrast, sat light to such factors, and considered the Reformation in England as only just begun – everything was still open to further revision in the light of Scripture and what they believed was a purer Protestantism. To them Cranmer's Prayer Book was, in Knox's

---

[21] This is an extremely condensed and simplified account of a very complicated controversy. See the sections below on the Scottish Reformation for a fuller account of Knox.

words, full of "impure superstitions".[22] This division over the form
of worship was an ominous foreshadowing of conflicts soon to
come in the newly Protestant Anglican Church of Queen Elizabeth I.

5. "It is the Lord's doing and marvellous in our eyes": The Elizabethan settlement[23]

Mary's death in November 1558 brought the 25 year old Elizabeth
to the throne amid great popular rejoicing. Elizabeth was a Protestant; the English Protestant exiles flocked home, and the Anglican
Church's ties with Rome were once again broken. This time, the
breach was to be permanent.[24] Many of the Protestant exiles found
themselves in positions of leadership in the Anglican Church. One
exception was Elizabeth's new archbishop of Canterbury, Matthew
Parker (1504-75), not a returning exile but a learned Protestant
scholar who had remained in England during Mary's reign, living
in hourly fear of arrest and martyrdom. Fifteen of the other bishoprics, however, were given to Protestants like Cox who had kept the
English Reformation heritage alive on the Continent in the dark
days of Mary.

The "Elizabethan settlement" of religion, as it is usually called, can
be summed up as follows.

It was a *parliamentary* settlement, embodied in legal acts and
statutes. Elizabeth had no alternative but to work through parliament (as of course her father Henry VIII had), since the bishops

---

[22] However, Knox's concept of "impure superstition" is sometimes hard to
      follow. For example he objected to the Prayer Book's "O Lord, open Thou our
      lips, and our mouth shall show forth Thy praise" solely on the grounds that this
      prayer was not found in the Bible but was translated out of the Roman liturgy.

[23] The quotation from Psalm 118:23 is said to have been young Elizabeth's
      response on being told of Mary's death and her own new status as queen of
      England.

[24] At least, permanent up to the time of writing. In today's ecumenical climate, it
      is always possible that the Anglican Church might enter into some kind of
      reunion with Rome.

appointed under Mary were steadfast Roman Catholics, and the English Church's governing body, convocation, proved uncooperative. Elizabeth's first parliament met in January 1559; it was dominated by a well-organised body of Protestant activists, who overthrew Mary's religious regime and made England once more a legally and constitutionally Protestant country.[25] The Act of Supremacy recognised the monarch as the "supreme governor" of the Church of England; all foreign jurisdiction, especially that of the pope, was abolished; all officials were required to take an oath acknowledging Elizabeth's sovereignty in both Church and state. The Act of Uniformity reintroduced Cranmer's 1552 Book of Common Prayer as the Anglican form of worship, with some relatively minor revisions. Severe penalties for dissent were threatened. The chief alterations from the 1552 Prayer Book were the omission of the so-called "Black Rubric" (originally inserted at John Knox's insistence) which had explained that kneeling at communion was not an act of worship towards the bread and wine; the omission from the litany of a prayer against the pope;[26] a combining of the 1549 and 1552 Prayer Book formula for administering communion;[27] and the restoration of priestly vestments (special garments worn by the medieval clergy) in the "Ornaments Rubric". This last element was to prove very divisive and sparked off the first great post-1559 religious controversy in Anglicanism,

---

[25] One modern historian of the period estimates that in Elizabeth's first parliament, out of the 404 MPs, something like 100 were convinced Protestants. Led by two returned exiles, Sir Francis Knollys and Sir Francis Cooke, they seized the initiative and controlled the proceedings.

[26] "From all sedition and privy conspiracy, from the tyranny of the Bishop of Rome and all his detestable enormities, from all false doctrine and heresy, from hardness of heart, and contempt of Thy word and commandment, good Lord, deliver us." The phrase "from the tyranny of the Bishop of Rome and all his detestable enormities" was left out of the 1559 Prayer Book.

[27] The 1559 formula said: "The body of our Lord Jesu Christ, which was given for thee, preserve thy body and soul into everlasting life: and take and eat this in remembrance that Christ died for thee, feed on Him in thine heart by faith, with thanksgiving. The blood of our Lord Jesu Christ, which was shed for thee, preserve thy body and soul into everlasting life: and drink this in remembrance that Christ's blood was shed for thee, and be thankful." The first part of each sentence comes from 1549, the second part of each sentence from 1552.

with many Protestant clergy objecting to vestments as a relic of
Rome. This controversy provided the context for the emerging
Puritan movement.[28]

The Elizabethan settlement was also a *royal* settlement. It could not
have happened apart from Elizabeth, and it could not have survived
without her. As Anglican apologist Richard Hooker was later to say,
"By the goodness of almighty God and His servant Elizabeth, we
are." Church and crown were integrally united. Article 37 of the
Anglican 39 Articles stated: "The queen's Majesty hath the chief
power in this realm of England and other her dominions, unto
whom the chief government of all estates of this realm, whether
they be ecclesiastical or civil, in all causes doth appertain, and is
not nor ought to be subject to any foreign jurisdiction." Royal
control of the Church was exercised through convocation (summoned by the queen), through parliament, and through royal
injunctions.

It was a *compromise* settlement. Elizabeth framed the English
Church to be as inclusive of as many of her subjects as possible:
Roman Catholics, "Henricians" (those who were happy with Henry
VIII's idea of Anglicanism – "Catholic without the pope"), conservative Protestants, and proto-Puritans. As far as Elizabeth was
concerned, English people could believe as they pleased in the
privacy of their own minds, as long as outwardly they worshipped
according to the Book of Common Prayer. The form of worship,
rather than a strictly enforced theology, was the real bond of union
in Elizabethan Anglicanism. Despite this comprehensive approach,
several hundred Roman Catholic clergy from Mary's reign refused
to conform (including all but one of Mary's bishops), and a tiny but
resolute minority of Roman Catholic laity also refused to accept the
Elizabethan settlement. They could be fined for non-attendance at
their local Anglican parish church, but little more was done to
harass them until, in 1570, pope Pius IV excommunicated Elizabeth
and released all English Catholics from their duty to accept her as
queen. From that moment, every English Catholic was a real or

---

[28] See Part Four for Puritanism.

potential traitor, and Elizabeth's government took a much harsher line against them. But the history of English Roman Catholicism as a small dissident movement outside of the national mainstream had already begun in 1559.

Although Elizabeth was not herself a very committed Protestant in a theological sense, most of her supporters and advisors were. And so the Elizabethan Church did become theologically Protestant, indeed Reformed, as the Edwardian Church had been. A slightly edited, somewhat toned down version of Edward's 42 Articles was promulgated as the 39 Articles in 1563 in Latin, and then in English in 1571. They are Reformed rather than Lutheran on the Lord's Supper, but Lutheran rather than Reformed on Church-state relations. The *Book of Homilies* too was reissued, and a *Second Book of Homilies* was published, in its final form in 1571.

Probably no one at first expected the Elizabethan settlement to be final or beyond the possibility of further reform. It became increasingly clear, however, that this was precisely how Elizabeth herself regarded it; and Elizabeth was as imperious as her father Henry VIII had been. And so English Protestants in turn became increasingly divided. On the one side stood those who were willing to accept the settlement, despite reservations about its imperfections (such as priestly vestments, poor theological training for pastors, lack of competent preachers in many parts of the country, lingering Roman Catholic sentiment among many ordinary people which Elizabeth was content not to touch). On the other side stood those who were determined to challenge the settlement in the name of a more perfect Reformation that would address the issues mentioned above, and other Reformed concerns too, like the Anglican form of government by royally appointed bishops (those who contested the settlement preferred Presbyterianism). This was not a simplistic black-and-white division into two clear-cut parties, more two ends of a spectrum with many shades of opinion. Those who tended towards the "further reform" end of the spectrum were soon being nicknamed "Puritans"; but their story belongs to Part Four of this series.

6. The Scottish Reformation: origins

The Reformation in Scotland was perhaps uniquely influenced by international diplomacy. At the heart of Scottish foreign policy stood the country's relations with France and England, in which Scotland became something of a battleground for French and English interests. England was usually allied with France's great enemy, the Habsburgs, who ruled Spain, the Netherlands, and the Holy Roman Empire. France was therefore in danger of being encircled on all sides; and so to break the hostile circle, the French looked to Scotland for help. The Scots were willing to ally themselves with France against England because of the old English claim to the Scottish throne, deeply resented in Scotland. This diplomatic context is crucial to understanding the story of the Scottish Reformation.

Protestantism first appeared in Scotland in the 1520s through merchants trading between Scotland and the Netherlands, who brought with them Lutheran books and William Tyndale's English New Testament. The Scottish ports became hotbeds of religious discussion; Edinburgh and Saint Andrews were notable centres where the new ideas circulated. The official anxiety over this was demonstrated in July 1525 when the Scottish parliament passed an act prohibiting the import of Lutheran books. The same year, a royal warrant was sent to the sheriffs of Aberdeen, instructing them to conduct an inquiry into "sundry strangers and others [who] were possessed of Luther's books and favoured his errors", and to confiscate their goods.

The first outstanding Scottish teacher of Protestantism was a Catholic priest named **Patrick Hamilton** (1504-28), a member of the great Hamilton family, one of Scotland's most powerful aristocratic houses. Hamilton fell under the influence first of Erasmus, then Luther, while at university, and actually spent some time in Luther's Wittenberg. In February 1528, he was arrested for preaching Lutheran doctrine, and tried for heresy before archbishop James Beaton of Saint Andrews, Scotland's chief clergyman.

Convicted and condemned, Hamilton was burnt at the stake on Feb 29th, a mere 24 years old. It seemed like a waste, but the sacrifice bore unexpected fruit; as John Knox commented, "Almost within the whole realm there was none found who began not to inquire: wherefore was Master Patrick Hamilton burned?" Scottish Protestants immediately began appealing to the noble and heroic example of Christ's martyr Patrick Hamilton.

The English king Henry VIII's breach with Rome in 1534 had an immediate effect on Scotland. It meant that the young Scottish monarch James V, who had assumed personal government in 1528, was lobbied by Henry to follow the English example, and by Francis I of France to remain loyal to the papacy. The French policy was handled by **David Beaton** (c.1494-1546), nephew of archbishop James Beaton. David Beaton arranged James V's marriage to **Mary of Guise** (1516-60) in 1538. Mary was the daughter of the Duke of Guise, one of France's mightiest nobles. The marriage strengthened the Franco-Scottish alliance, and Mary of Guise was to play a pivotal role in the unfolding drama of the Scottish Reformation. The same year (1538) Beaton was made cardinal, and 1539 succeeded his uncle as archbishop of Saint Andrews. He became the dominant figure in James V's government.

Beaton's policy was twofold: maintain the Franco-Scottish alliance, and suppress Protestant heresy, which he identified with English influence. Protestantism was certainly growing in Scotland in this period. Beaton is reported to have drawn up a list of 360 members of the nobility and gentry who were heretics and whose property the king might confiscate. There was a flurry of prosecutions for heresy in the 1530s and early 1540s, especially in Dundee, Perth, Stirling, and Edinburgh. To judge by these prosecutions, Lutheranism seems to have had a wide-ranging appeal: ordinary townspeople, members of the nobility, university students, priests, and monks were all involved. Perhaps in panic, parliament passed a new series of severe acts in March 1541 aimed at suppressing Protestantism and upholding the old Church. Among other things it was decreed that no one must question papal authority on pain of death.

John Knox (1514-72)

But in 1542 matters suddenly lurched in an unforeseen direction. War with England broke out. Beaton had gone to Europe to organise an anti-English alliance, but Henry VIII struck first, and the Scots were resoundingly beaten at the battle of Solway Moss. The Scottish king James V died soon after, his death hastened by a deep depression at his army's catastrophic defeat. Just before he died, his wife Mary of Guise bore him a daughter – the future Mary queen of Scots.

This crisis briefly precipitated a pro-Reformation government into power in Scotland, led by *James Hamilton* (1516-75), the earl of Arran. Cardinal Beaton was arrested. Arran's government permitted the reading of the Bible in English – very soon, John Knox declared, William Tyndale's English New Testament could be seen "lying almost upon every gentleman's table". Protestant preachers frequented government circles, and the militant Protestants of Dundee sacked the monasteries while Arran pretended not to notice. Arran's Protestant stance, however, provoked a Roman Catholic backlash; in 1543 Beaton recovered his power, and although Arran remained governor, policy was reversed back into a pro-French, pro-Rome direction.

At this time Scotland's second great Reformer appeared, *George Wishart* (1513-46). Wishart was a schoolmaster in Montrose, where he taught New Testament Greek. Threatened with heresy proceedings by the bishop of Brechin, he fled to England. Returning to Scotland probably in 1543 while Arran's government was still pro-reform, Wishart preached in Dundee, Ayrshire, and East Lothian. His preaching attracted large crowds and made a profound spiritual impression. In East Lothian he was for the first time accompanied by a priest named *John Knox* (1514-72) who acted as his bodyguard. Wishart's theology signalled a transition phase in Scottish Protestantism from its original Lutheranism to a more Reformed standpoint; as in so many other countries, by the 1540s the initial Lutheran impulse began to be supplanted in Scotland by the alternative Reformed concept of reformation. Wishart himself translated into English the Swiss Confession of 1536, which took the Reformed view of the Lord's Supper.

In early 1546, however, with cardinal Beaton firmly back in control, Wishart was arrested and tried for heresy. The trial took place in Saint Andrews Cathedral before an invited audience of the nobility and clergy: Beaton intended it to be a great show-piece occasion where the old Church would triumph over the new heresy. Unfortunately things did not go according to plan. Wishart's bold performance, appealing to the Scriptures as his authority, began to create a sympathetic response, so when the time arrived for the verdict against him to be pronounced, Beaton prudently cleared the cathedral. Wishart was condemned and burnt at the stake on March 1st 1546. The effect of his death was mixed. On the one hand, it meant the loss of the first Scottish Protestant leader who had the capacity to command a wide following; it would be another ten years before John Knox stepped into this vacuum. On the other hand, Wishart's martyrdom burned itself into the minds and memories of Protestants and their sympathisers, stiffening their conviction that the old Church was a corrupt tool of Satan which had to be overthrown if Scotland was to enjoy spiritual freedom.

The unsettled and increasingly polarised state of religious opinion in Scotland was dramatically illustrated a few weeks later. In the early morning of May 29th, a party of extreme Protestants led by several high ranking Scots (including John Leslie, son of the earl of Rothes, and William Kirkcaldy of Grange, one of the most sincere of Scotland's Protestants, a natural born leader), broke into cardinal Beaton's castle in Saint Andrews. It was a strange and awful scene, as one of the Protestants, James Melville, calmly assured a terrified Beaton that they had nothing against him personally, but were simply instruments of God who were bringing justice upon him for the murder of God's holy servant George Wishart. Having explained this, Melville encouraged Beaton to repent, and then ran him through with his sword. "I am a priest, I am a priest!" the dying cardinal cried. "Fie, fie, all is gone!" The conspirators proceeded to take over the castle, and were soon joined by other Protestants fleeing there as a stronghold from persecution. The refugees included John Knox and the great court poet Sir David Lindsay, although neither had been privy to the assassination of Beaton.

Arran put the castle under a year-long siege, during which Knox was set apart by the defenders as their pastor and preacher. Eventually the Protestants were bombed into submission by a French fleet and taken as captives to France, where Knox became a galley slave in the French navy.

At this point we should step back and pick up the threads of Knox's life story, which becomes increasingly intertwined with the Scottish Reformation and finally identified with it. What Luther was to Germany, and Calvin to Geneva, John Knox was to be to Scotland.

7. Scotland's trumpet: John Knox

Knox was born in (roughly) 1514 at Haddington, studied at Saint Andrews university, and was ordained to the priesthood by the bishop of Dunblane in 1536. Unable to find a parish, he practised as a lawyer. We are not sure exactly when Knox was converted to Protestantism, but it may have been in 1543 through the preaching of Thomas Guillaume, an ex-Dominican friar who had become chaplain to the earl of Arran. Knox then, as we have seen, attached himself to Wishart. After Wishart's martyrdom and the Saint Andrews castle siege, Knox spent 19 months as a French galley slave, a gruelling experience during which he was sometimes so ill that his friends despaired of his life. However, Knox kept up their spirits with the intrepid and audacious quality of his faith; when, early on, their Roman Catholic captors tried to force the Protestant galley slaves to worship the Roman way, Knox took the image of the Virgin Mary that they thrust into his face to kiss, and calmly threw it overboard. That was the end of any attempt to impose Roman Catholic worship on the Protestant prisoners. He also emboldened his fellow captives by making confident predictions that God would liberate him to preach again in Scotland: Knox always had a touch of the "charismatic prophet" about him.[29] After

---

[29] Some of the later "cessationist" ideas should not be read back into the Reformation era. While the Reformers were quite clearly not modern

19 months, the prediction was fulfilled as Knox gained his freedom, by what means we are unsure.

Knox made use of his new liberty to settle in the Protestant England of Edward VI. As well as being a prudent move which guaranteed his freedom from persecution, Knox's settling in England also revealed his lifelong sense of deep kinship with English Protestants. He became pastor of the Anglican church in Berwick, and in 1551 was appointed chaplain to king Edward. He was also offered the bishopric of Rochester, but declined it for unknown reasons. Clearly Knox was a figure of no mean stature in Edward's England. Further, his outspoken opposition to kneeling to receive communion created a big enough stir to force archbishop Cranmer to insert the "Black Rubric" into the 1552 Prayer Book, which explained that kneeling was not an act of worship towards the bread and wine.

When the Roman Catholic Mary Tudor became queen of England in 1553, Knox fled to the Continent, one of the tide of Protestant refugees. Initially he pastored the English congregation in Frankfurt, where (as we saw in the previous section) he became embroiled in controversy with Richard Cox over the Book of Common Prayer. Driven out of Frankfurt, Knox ended up as co-pastor of the English refugee congregation in Calvin's Geneva, alongside Christopher Goodman, who had been professor of divinity at Oxford university under Edward VI. Knox looked on his time as co-pastor of the English church in Geneva as the happiest period of his life. The fellowship had 186 members, and worshipped according to a Continental-style Reformed liturgy which had been drawn up by Knox and others. The Knoxian liturgy in Geneva was to have a long life; it was used in private services by many English Puritans during Elizabeth I's reign, and it became the official liturgy of the Scottish Reformed Church in 1560.

---

charismatics, they were also not so suspicious of the supernatural as some modern anti-charismatic Evangelicals have perhaps been.

It was as pastor in Geneva that Knox wrote his most revolutionary writings. First came his *The First Blast of the Trumpet Against the Monstrous Regiment of Women* in 1558. By "regiment" Knox meant "government", and by "monstrous" he meant "unnatural". Female rule, he argued, contradicted both the law of nature and God's revealed law in Scripture, and female rulers must be deposed. The treatise was aimed chiefly against Mary Tudor, "that horrible monster Jezebel of England", whose regime Protestants had good reason to consider monstrous. Unfortunately, soon after the book's publication, Mary Tudor died and was succeeded by a female Protestant sovereign, Elizabeth. Knox's book alienated Elizabeth badly, and made Protestant Anglo-Scottish relations more difficult than they should have been. The book also outraged the majority of Protestants, who thought its conclusions extreme and subversive of good order in society. Would civil war and anarchy not follow in any land ruled by a queen, if Knox's view gained a hearing? This was Calvin's opinion; indeed, Calvin was so opposed to the *First Blast of the Trumpet* that he had its sale in Geneva banned. English Protestants too were bitter, perhaps especially because their hopes were pinned on the death of monstrous Mary Tudor and the accession of Protestant Elizabeth as a godly queen; Knox complained that "my *First Blast* hath blown from me all my friends in England." So Knox's first political treatise was not a great success.

Next came Knox's *The Appellation* (also in 1558). In this work, Knox appealed to the Scottish nobility to enact reformation, and to the Scottish common people to put pressure on the government in favour of Protestantism. The nobility, Knox maintained, had the right to depose an idolatrous monarch; the common people had the right to establish their own Reformed Church if the government would not establish one. Knox's thinking was dominated by the question of how the true believer confronted idolatry and persecution by idolatrous governments. The mainstream Protestant position held that Christians must refuse religious obedience to idolatrous governments, and peacefully suffer the consequences. However, a number of radical Protestants were questioning this – notably the

English refugees John Ponet (who had been Edward VI's bishop of Winchester) and Christopher Goodman (Knox's co-pastor). They argued that Christians could move beyond passive resistance to righteous rebellion and forcibly topple an idolatrous government. Knox took this more radical approach. This too proved distasteful to many Protestants, but in fact Knox's basic position in the *Appellation* was acted on by the Huguenots, the Dutch Sea Beggars, and eventually by Scottish Covenanters and English Puritans in the British Civil Wars of the 17th century. It was akin to Calvin's view that a monarch's authority was not absolute, but must be held in check by the lesser political authorities (such as parliaments) whose duty it was to call a wicked ruler to account for his or her misdeeds.[30]

Knox returned to Scotland May 1559 at the urgent request of its Protestant leaders. But what had been happening in his native land since his departure for the French galleys in 1547?

Mary of Guise, widow of James V and the mother of the 12 year old queen Mary Stuart, had assumed the regency of Scotland in 1554. At first she was tolerant of Protestants, because she wanted to win them over to her anti-English, pro-French policy. But there was growing resentment among many Scots at the way Scotland seemed to be becoming a mere French province, especially after young Mary Stuart was married to prince Francis of France, the heir to the French throne, in April 1558. This fear of French domination fed into the religious conflict. The government of France was militantly Roman Catholic; and so anti-French and anti-Roman Catholic feeling easily coalesced. Or to put this in positive terms, the cause of Scottish nationalism became increasingly identified with the cause of Protestantism in Scotland.

Popular Protestantism was kept alive in this period by various means, notably the *Good and Godly Ballads*. These were compiled largely by the brothers James (1495-1553) and ***John Wedderburn***

---

[30] For the Huguenots and Sea Beggars, see the previous Chapter, sections 4 and 5. The Puritans and the English Civil War will be covered in Part Four.

(1508-56), although others probably contributed. John Wedderburn seems to have been the most prominent figure involved. A priest from Dundee, he fled from a heresy charge in 1539, taking refuge in Protestant Germany, where he became an ardent disciple of Luther and Melanchthon. In 1542, during the brief pro-Protestant period of Arran, he returned to Scotland, but when Cardinal Beaton regained power, Wedderburn fled to England, where he died in 1556. The *Good and Godly Ballads* were mostly satirical anti-Roman-Catholic pieces set to well-known song tunes. They were remarkably effective at communicating Protestant doctrine and promoting a satirical contempt for Roman Catholicism.[31]

Within this religious and political context, the Protestant members of the Scottish nobility were become increasingly radicalised in their determination to secure a Protestant government for their country. On 3rd December 1557, the leaders of the Protestant nobility banded together by signing a covenant, in which they pledged themselves to renounce Roman Catholicism as "the Congregation of Satan", and to promote a positive reform of worship, calling for Sunday worship according to the Anglican Book of Common Prayer, and freedom of Protestant preaching in private. The Protestant nobles called themselves "the Lords of the Congregation of Jesus Christ". This practice of covenanting or banding together was partly an old Scottish custom, but probably in this instance it owed somewhat more to the biblical Old Testament notion of a covenant between God and Israel.

In early 1558, under the protection of the Lords of the Congregation, Scottish Protestants began openly appointing Protestant preachers, who often led worship according to the English Prayer Book. In 1558 and 1559, there were outbreaks of iconoclasm, each more devastating than its predecessor. Clearly the upsurge in popular Scottish Protestantism was reaching crisis point. Persecution

---

[31]   As well as the satirical songs, the *Good and Godly Ballads* also contained a catechism, dealing with the 10 Commandments, the Creed, the Lord's Prayer and the sacraments; 16 spiritual songs based on Bible passages; and 20 of the psalms.

fanned the flames. The last Protestant martyr to be burnt in Scotland was Walter Milne, an obscure schoolteacher aged 82, burnt at
the stake at Saint Andrews in April 1558. This was perceived as an
act of cruelty and proved utterly counter-productive; John Knox
commented that out of the ashes of Walter Milne sprang "thousands
of his opinion and religion in Scotland". In July 1558 Mary of
Guise summoned Protestant preachers to account for their activities. This provoked a show of force by the Protestant gentry of
western Scotland, who turned out bearing arms to shield their
preachers from danger. Mary panicked and cancelled the summons.

It was at this point that Knox returned from Geneva. He preached
with overwhelming effect in Dundee and Perth. The two cities
openly declared themselves to be Protestant communities. So did
the town of Ayr. Knox's sermon in Perth resulted in an image-
smashing riot; Knox condemned the action as the work of the
"rascal multitude", but seems to have privately approved of the
religious fervour which lay behind the outbreak.

A new covenant was now drawn up in Perth by the Lords of the
Congregation for the defence of Protestantism. Mary of Guise
mobilised her forces (an army of 8,000) to take decisive action, but
this merely sparked off a Protestant counter-mobilisation: Protestants gathered in force in Perth to protect their preachers. The Lords
of the Congregation received a great morale boost when they were
joined by Arran, the ex-governor who had presided over the brief
Indian summer of Protestantism in 1543. From this point, Arran
became the nominal head of the Lords of the Congregation.[32] They
opened negotiations with England, Protestant since Elizabeth's
accession in November 1558, and received an English grant of
£3,000 (not much in today's terms, but a considerable fortune in the
16th century). For a time, the military situation hung doubtfully and
dangerously in the balance; only Knox's phenomenal preaching
kept alive the courage and constancy of the Scottish Protestant army.

---

[32] Textbooks often refer to Arran as "Chatelherault" from this point in the
narrative. He became duke of Chatelherault in France in 1548. I have continued
to call him "Arran" for consistency.

But then in January 1560 the entire situation was suddenly transformed. An English Protestant fleet appeared in the Firth of Forth (just off Edinburgh) and cut the French supply lines. This event tipped the scales of war back to the Lords of the Congregation. They signed the Treaty of Berwick with Elizabeth in February, and in April an English Protestant army arrived on Scottish soil. The balance of power now lay decisively with the Protestant forces, and the French army was put under siege in Leith, by land and sea. In June Mary of Guise died; the French army immediately surrendered. On July 6th, the Treaty of Edinburgh between England and France brought about the withdrawal of both French and English troops from Scotland.

8. The Reformation parliament

The immediate aftermath of the Treaty of Edinburgh was the "Reformation Parliament" of July and August 1560. In terms of Scotland's religious history and cultural identity, this was the most important parliament in the country's history.[33] On 17th August, the parliament approved a new Reformed confession of faith for the national Church. This was the Scots Confession, drawn up by John Knox and five other leading Reformed men – John Willock, John Winram, John Spottiswoode, John Row, and John Douglas – the six Johns! It is clearly a Reformed confession: the new Protestant Church of Scotland was to be a Reformed, not a Lutheran body. Most obviously, the Confession embraces the Reformed view of the Lord's Supper. Yet one of its most striking features is the strength and richness of its eucharistic teaching: it emphasises the real sacramental eating and drinking of Christ's flesh and blood by the faithful. Divided into 25 articles, the first 12 are largely non-controversial, an exposition of classical creedal Christianity, rooted in the apostles' and Nicene Creed, and Creed of Chalcedon, although with some elements of Reformed theology (such as article

---

[33] The Scottish parliament at that time was an upper class body, made up of the aristocracy, gentry, and high-ranking clergy. They mostly sat by right, rather than by election.

eight on election). The other 13 are distinctively Protestant, affirming the supreme authority of Scripture and other such basic Reformational convictions. Two unusual elements in the Confession have often been noted. One is the way it highlights "salvation history", the outworking of God's purposes in space and time from Adam onwards – this receives as much emphasis as systematic theology does in the Confession's approach. The other is its profound stress on ecclesiology: a dominant theme is the conflict between the true and false Church, and the importance of recognising and belonging to the true Church.

On 24th August, parliament outlawed the Roman Catholic mass with penalties for its celebration, acknowledged the Reformed preachers as alone competent to administer the sacraments, and abolished all papal jurisdiction over Scotland. There was hardly any resistance in parliament to these Protestant measures: the tide of public opinion among the educated and ruling classes in Scotland had clearly turned in a decisively Protestant direction. Mary queen of Scots (who was still in France at this point, married to the French king Francis II) refused to ratify the legislation, but it was finally approved in the first parliament of James VI's reign in 1567.

Two other great documents of the Scottish Reformation were the Book of Common Order and First Book of Discipline.

The Book of Common Order was Knox's answer to the vexed question of worship. Since 1556 Scottish Protestants had been organising their own congregations. Prior to 1560, they had used the English Book of Common Prayer – brought to Scotland by Scottish preachers who had (like Knox) served in the English Reformed Church under Edward VI but fled after Mary Tudor's accession in 1553. Since the official triumph of Scottish Protestantism was due to English intervention, it might be thought that uniformity of worship would prevail in the two kingdoms, with the Scottish Reformed Church worshipping according to the manner of the English. Why did this not happen?

There were two chief reasons. First, Elizabeth's Book of Common Prayer was not quite so radically Protestant as Edward VI's second one (see section 5). Second, while in exile on the Continent, Knox had developed a preference for Calvin's Geneva liturgy, which was simpler and more streamlined than the Anglican Prayer Book (see section 4). It is Knox's English version of the Geneva liturgy that is known the Book of Common Order (or more commonly, "Knox's liturgy"). It was printed in Edinburgh 1562, and authorised by the General Assembly (the Presbyterian governing body of the Scottish Reformed Church) that same year. The Book of Common Order was to remain the official liturgy of Scottish Protestantism until it was replaced by the Westminster Directory of Public Worship in 1645.

An outline of the service runs like this:

Confession of sin
Prayer for pardon
Metrical psalm
Prayer for illumination
Scripture reading
Sermon
Offering for the poor
Long prayer concluded by Lord's Prayer
Apostles' Creed
Metrical psalm
Benediction

The Lord's Supper was in theory to be observed once a month, but in practice was less frequent.

The other great document, the First Book of Discipline, was a comprehensive blueprint for a Protestant society. It outlined a Presbyterian form of Church polity, which included the popular election of ministers by congregations, elders who were to assist ministers in the exercise of moral discipline, and deacons who were to take charge of the finances of the Church. Where the disorganized state of the times meant there was no minister in a congregation,

the First Book of Discipline established the appointment of "readers" who were to conduct services from the Book of Common
Order; "exhorters" who could deliver sermons but not administer
the sacraments; and "superintendents" who were spiritually to
oversee large areas of the country and be accountable to the
General Assembly.[34] The First Book of Discipline also set out a

---

[34] There has been much debate over the nature of the superintendent. The modern
     historian Gordon Donaldson has argued that the superintendents were basically
     identical in office and function with the bishops of the Anglican Church. If so,
     the Scottish Reformed Church of 1560 was an Episcopalian, not a Presbyterian
     body. Naturally this claim is contentious (especially to Scottish Presbyterians).
     What does the First Book of Discipline say about the superintendents? The
     section on superintendents (section 5) justifies their existence on the basis that
     there are so few ministers, and that if the best of them became ministers in the
     important towns (as most of them had been), this would leave much of the rest
     of the country devoid of an effective Protestant ministry. Therefore a godly
     man should be appointed to take care of the spiritual wellbeing of each of the
     ten provinces into which the country was divided. These provinces roughly
     matched the old medieval Catholic dioceses, and indeed the First Book of
     Discipline calls them "dioceses", but some changes were made: there were no
     longer dioceses for Caithness, Dunblane, Galloway, Moray, and the Isles, but
     there were new dioceses for Edinburgh, Jedburgh, and Dumfries. This measure
     is said to be "most expedient for this time". The superintendents were to
     examine the conduct of ministers, the state of churches, the spiritual condition
     of the people, the welfare of the poor, and the education of the young. If a
     vacant congregation failed to elect a minister, after 40 days the superintendent
     and his council of advisors were themselves to present a nominee to the
     congregation, although it was still the final choice of the congregation to accept
     or reject the nominee. But above all, the superintendent was to preach unceas-
     ingly – this was his primary vocation. In fact only five superintendents were
     actually appointed, for Lothian, Fife, Glasgow, Angus, and Argyll and the
     Isles.
       So, were the superintendents bishops? There were certain differences.
     First, the medieval idea of apostolic succession was quite absent, and in that
     sense the Reformed Church of 1560 cannot be said to be Episcopalian in the
     classical sense of the term. Second, it does seem clear that the Scottish Re-
     formers established the office of superintendent as an expedient because of the
     unsettled condition of the times. There is no suggestion that the system of
     superintendents was the permanent ideal entertained by Knox and the other
     Reformers. And third, it is plain that the office of superintendent was regarded
     in the First Book of Discipline as being of human, not divine institution. On
     these three counts, it would be difficult if not impossible to sustain the thesis
     that the 1560 settlement was Episcopalian. On the other hand, the superinten-

program of poor relief on a scale unknown in Western Europe until the coming of the welfare state. A massive educational program was likewise drafted; every parish was to have a school as well as a church. All of this was to be financed by the wealth of the old Church.

Such was Knox's dream. But it failed to take flesh. The democratic tone of the First Book of Discipline made the nobility uneasy, and most of them preferred to seize the old Church's assets for themselves rather than for Knox's utopian program. Knox was deeply disillusioned; "the belly has no ears" was his verdict on the covetousness of the nobles. Most ministers in the new Reformed Church would have to subsist on a pittance for pay; the educational vision was put into practice only in a very modified form.

The triumph of Protestantism in Scotland through the Reformation Parliament had a profound impact both on Scottish identity and on Anglo-Scottish relationships. Traditionally, England had been the "Old Enemy" of Scotland since the 13th century, and Scots had in some senses defined themselves as those who existed in this context of hostilities with the English. The Reformation changed all this. The victory of the Protestant faith over Roman Catholicism in both England and Scotland – and with English help in Scotland – forged a new psychological bond between the two nations. Especially when the forces of the Catholic Counter-Reformation began their concerted effort to win back the territory lost to Protestantism, Scotland and England found themselves drawn even closer together through the shared self-interest of wanting to survive as Protestant nations against the spiritual and political fight-back of the papacy. In both Scotland and England, a deep-rooted anti-Catholic feeling became ingrained into the national psyche. Not surprisingly, then, Protestant Scotland became a pro-English country. This helped

---

dents clearly did function as bishops in exercising spiritual oversight over the ministers of the new Church. A strict Presbyterian would not accept that there is any office above that of parish minister, and to that extent it is undeniable that the 1560 settlement had some Episcopalian elements.

pave the way for the union between their monarchies in 1603, and their parliaments in 1707.[35]

How far did Protestantism triumph in 1560 at the grass roots level in Scotland? The Scottish capital, Edinburgh, is an interesting case study. When the city had been offered a referendum on its religious loyalties in 1559, the Protestants of Edinburgh rejected the idea: God's truth must not be made subject to human votes. This may suggest they were not confident of winning the referendum! After the political triumph of the Reformation in 1560, Edinburgh remained collectively unsure of its religious position. At the Easter communion service of 1561, only 1,200 adults out of Edinburgh's 12,500 attended the new Protestant service. Nevertheless there was no vocal opposition. The majority of Edinburgh's inhabitants seem to have had no real commitment to either side in the religious dispute. It has been argued that this may well have been a typical attitude in many of the towns and cities of Scotland (apart from Perth and Dundee, which were hotbeds of Protestant fervour). By the opening decades of the 17th century, however, the Reformed Church had largely succeeded in evangelising and Protestantising the Scottish Lowlands, where the Reformation took deep popular root.

Not so in the Scottish Highlands. The only part of the Highlands where Protestantism found strong support was in Argyll-shire, owing to the personal commitment to the Reformation by the earls of Argyll, the Campbells. When the Lords of the Congregation signed their first covenant in 1557, the first signature on the list was that of the earl of Argyll. But Argyll and the Campbell clan were unusual among the Highland nobility, and Protestantism made very little popular impact outside Campbell territory in the 16th century. This does not mean the Reformed Church made no efforts at establishing itself in the Highlands; Protestant parish ministers were certainly planted in the region. However, there was a huge practical problem in the language barrier, since Gaelic was the common

---

[35] Scotland regained its own parliament in 1999, but the Anglo-Scottish Westminster parliament still retains important powers over Scotland, *e.g.* in relation to defence, foreign affairs, national security, and employment.

tongue of the Highland people, whereas very few Protestant ministers spoke anything other than English. Still, even here the situation was not wholly barren. The first ever book to printed in the Gaelic language (in either Scotland or Ireland) was the Book of Common Order. It was translated by *John Carswell* (d.1572), the superintendent of Argyll from 1560, and bishop of the Isles from 1565; it was published in 1567. This was a landmark in the history of Gaelic culture: a Protestant liturgy marked the arrival of Gaelic as a printed and published language. On the debit side, Carswell's zeal for conveying the Reformation into a Gaelic cultural framework had a limited effect, in that he owed his influence to his patron, the earl of Argyll – so his real sphere of influence was the southern part of Argyll-shire. Most of the Highlands remained Roman Catholic in sentiment, with large doses of pre-Christian folk paganism mixed in.

9. Mary queen of Scots

On December 11th 1560, king Francis II of France died. His widow, *Mary* (born 1542; reigned 1560–67; died 1587), Scotland's lawful queen, was 18 – and a Roman Catholic. It seemed likely that Mary would return to Scotland. She immediately became the focus of Roman Catholic discontent; Scottish Roman Catholics expected her to overthrow the Reformation settlement. So in early 1561 Lesley, a prominent Roman Catholic clergyman from Aberdeen, visited Mary in France and promised that if she came to Aberdeen, the powerful Roman Catholic earl of Huntly would raise an army of 20,000 to enable her to crush the Protestants and enter Edinburgh in triumph. On the other hand, many Scottish Protestants also entertained hopes of Mary. Her half-brother, *James Stewart* (1531-70), soon to be earl of Moray, representing the Protestant party, also visited her. Stewart was an unusual politician, a man of such awesome purity and integrity in his private life that some found him repellent, seeing in him a cold austerity that somehow always managed to coincide with ambitious worldly aims in his public life. But there could be no doubting his loyalty to the Reformation, and he stood high in Knox's esteem. Stewart probably promised Mary that the Protestants of Scotland would support her claim to the English throne (Mary was the grand-daughter of Margaret Tudor, who was the daughter of king Henry VII of England – this made her the rightful queen of England in the eyes of English Roman Catholics who refused to acknowledge any Protestant sovereign). The Protestant party, then, would uphold Mary's claim by trying to persuade Elizabeth to recognise Mary as her successor. On this basis, Protestants hoped that if Mary came to Scotland she would drop the Franco-Scottish alliance for an Anglo-Scottish one, which in turn might persuade Mary to embrace Protestantism.

Mary arrived in Scotland by sea in August 1561 and set up court in Holyrood palace. She was young, beautiful, charming, spirited, highly intelligent and well educated in the learning of the French Renaissance. These qualities won her widespread popularity, and few men (even devout Protestant men) could resist her attractions, with the notable exception of John Knox who viewed her simply and exclusively as an enemy of the Reformation. Despite Mary's Roman Catholicism, she chose to commit herself to the pro-English Protestant party whose figurehead was James Stewart, but whose most effective leader was William Maitland of Lethington. However opposed they were to her faith, Stewart and Maitland were staunch advocates of her claim to the English throne. Mary elevated Stewart to the rank of earl of Moray, by which title he is commonly known to history.[36] She undertook a successful publicity tour of Scotland masterminded by Moray, and accompanied him on his military campaign against the Roman Catholic earl of Huntly – Huntly's forces were annihilated, thus dealing a body blow to the Roman Catholic cause in Scotland. So far, the working alliance between Mary and the Protestant party seemed to be effective.

But there were problems. After Mary established herself in Edinburgh, she arranged for the Roman Catholic mass to be celebrated in Holyrood. A Protestant mob marched on the palace, and only the

---

[36] Moray is pronounced, and sometimes spelt, as "Murray".

personal intervention of Moray stopped them breaking in. A gulf quickly opened up between the Protestant nobility and the common people. The queen's privy council, composed entirely of Protestant nobles, were determined to secure for Mary the freedom to practise her faith. The common people, led by Knox, regarded the mass as idolatry (the ultimate evil, in Knox's view), and were convinced that a Christian state should not tolerate idolatry: it would bring God's judgment on the land. Knox, who was now minister of Saint Giles cathedral in Edinburgh, affirmed in a sermon that one mass was more dreadful than an invasion of Scotland by 10,000 Roman Catholic troops intent on suppressing the Protestant faith. But Knox not only objected to the idolatry; he also interpreted the privy council's lenient attitude as a weakening of Protestant resolve and the first step on the slippery slope back to the revival of Roman Catholicism. Knox's attitude led to a rupture with Moray, who until then had been Knox's most devoted ally among the nobility – they did not speak to each other for 18 months!

Relations between Knox and Mary herself were obviously very strained. Even before Mary returned to Scotland, she declared that Knox was the most dangerous man in the country which was not big enough to hold both of them. For his part, Knox never ceased to regard Mary as the niece of the Guise nobility in France, who were chiefly responsible for the persecution of French Protestants. Mary had an exalted conception of her royal authority and the obedience owed her by her subjects, even in matters of religion; Knox held equally exalted views of the duty of a Christian preacher to proclaim God's Word without fear or favour, even to monarchs. Mary did not worship at Saint Giles, but Knox's utterances were reported to her, and she was infuriated – he condemned the frivolity of her court, denounced the mass, and worst of all, called on the Protestant nobility to resist her proposed marriage to the Roman Catholic prince Don Carlos, the son of Philip II of Spain. As a result of these utterances, Knox was summoned into her presence four times to account for himself. Knox got the better of the queen in these famous exchanges, on one occasion reducing her to hysterical tears by his forthright no-nonsense commitment to a

Protestant Scotland in which the idolatry of the mass could have no place.

Soon after the fourth interview, Mary lost all patience with Knox and put him on trial for treason. This was because Knox had circulated a letter to Protestant friends, urging them to gather in Edinburgh on the day fixed for the trial of two members of Knox's congregation who had been arrested for entering Mary's chapel at Holyrood. Knox's treason trial took place before the privy council, where to Mary's disgust he was unanimously acquitted.

Mary's downfall, however, was brought about not by Knox but by her own actions. It began in 1565 when she fell in love with the young Henry Stewart, lord Darnley, a Roman Catholic, marrying him according to Roman Catholic ceremonial in July. This alienated even the moderate Protestant nobles; they saw the marriage as the first step towards the destruction of their power and of Protestantism in Scotland. Mary aimed a pre-emptive strike at Moray, summoning him to court, believing that he was plotting to kidnap Darnley; Moray refused to obey the summons, and was joined by Arran and other leading Protestant nobles, intent on protecting their freedom. Mary declared them rebels and marched on them at the head of an army. After a rather inglorious run-around, Moray and his friends fled across the borders into England. Mary seemed to have triumphed: yet profound tragedy followed. Mary's marriage to Darnley was not a success, and she fell increasingly under the sway of her Italian counsellor, David Rizzio. Darnley became insane with jealousy, and in March 1566 he took part in a Protestant plot to eliminate Rizzio. A band of men, including Darnley, broke into Holyrood palace and into the queen's supper room where she and Rizzio were dining. Rizzio was dragged away and stabbed to death.

This event destroyed Mary's loyalty to Darnley. She now cast her affections on the Protestant earl of Bothwell, James Hepburn, a married man. A year after Rizzio's murder, on Feb 8th 1567, Darnley himself was strangled by murderers in Kirk o'Field, a church just outside the walls of Edinburgh, and the church was blown up. Bothwell was universally believed to be the man behind Darnley's murder. A few months later, Bothwell kidnapped Mary and took her to Dunbar castle. Bothwell's divorce from his wife was then hurried through the courts, and he and Mary were married in Holyrood on May 15th according to a Protestant marriage ceremony.

This act left Mary totally isolated. The Protestant nobility were already hostile to her; and by marrying a Protestant, she had lost the support of Roman Catholics. In the absence of Moray, another leading Protestant noble, James Douglas, the earl of Morton, raised a Protestant army and trapped Mary's smaller force at Carberry Hill, where they demanded that she hand over Bothwell for trial on the charge of Darnley's murder. Mary contrived the escape of Bothwell to Norway, and then surrendered to Morton. She was imprisoned in Lochleven castle and forced to abdicate on July 24th in favour of her newborn son, James VI. Moray became the regent of Scotland. Mary was kept prisoner at Lochleven for a year. In May 1568 she was liberated by followers, but her army was defeated by regent Moray at the battle of Langside on May 13th. Mary fled to England, expecting to be received as a honoured guest; but Elizabeth could not afford to be generous when English Roman Catholics regarded Catholic Mary, not Protestant Elizabeth, as the rightful English queen. So Elizabeth had Mary imprisoned. Even in prison Mary was a danger; one Roman Catholic plot after another was formed to topple Elizabeth and replace her with Mary. Eventually, in 1587, when the Babington Plot was exposed, in which Mary was implicated in a conspiracy to assassinate Elizabeth, the English queen's patience was at an end, and Mary was executed.

After Mary's flight to England, there remained a "queen's party" in Scotland working for her restoration. The queen's party was led by Maitland and Kirkcaldy of Grange; the opposing party, the king's party, more committed to Protestantism, was led by Knox's friend, regent Moray. The conflict came to a head in 1570 when Moray was assassinated in Linlithgow by one of the pro-Mary Hamiltons.

Civil war broke out. Eventually the king's party triumphed, led by the earl of Morton. He accomplished the final destruction of the queen's party in 1573, when with the aid of English artillery and engineers, he captured Edinburgh castle, the last stronghold of the queen's party. From then until 1580 Morton ruled Scotland with a strong hand; peace and Protestantism were secure under his government.

Meanwhile Knox's epic life had drawn to a close. He died on November 24th 1572 and was buried in the grounds of Saint Giles church. Morton's epitaph, spoken at the funeral, was fitting: "There lies one who neither feared nor flattered any flesh."

Important people

The Church

England
Thomas Bilney (1495-1531)
Simon Fish (1500-1531)
John Frith (1503-31)
William Tyndale (1495-1536)
Robert Barnes (1495-1540)
Hugh Latimer (1485-1555)
Nicholas Ridley (1503-55)
John Hooper (died 1555)
Thomas Cranmer (1489-1556)
John Bale (1495-1563)
Miles Coverdale (1488-1569)
Richard Cox (1500-1581)
John Foxe (1516-87)

Scotland
Patrick Hamilton (1504-28)
David Beaton (1494-1546)

Political and military

England
Henry VIII (1509-47)
Thomas Cromwell (1485-1540)
Edward VI (1547-53)
Mary I (1553-8)
Elizabeth I (1558-1603)

Scotland
Mary of Guise (1516-60)
James Stewart, earl of Moray
   (1531-70)
James Hamilton, earl of Arran
   (1516-75)
Mary queen of Scots (born 1542;
   reigned 1560-67; died 1587)

George Wishart (1513-46)
John Wedderburn (1508-56)
John Carswell (d.1572)
John Knox (1514-72)

William Tyndale: The meaning of the Gospel

Evangelion (that we call the gospel) is a Greek word; and signifieth good, merry, glad and joyful tidings, that maketh a man's heart glad, and maketh him sing, dance, and leap for joy: as when David had killed Goliah the giant, came glad tidings unto the Jews, that their fearful and cruel enemy was slain, and they delivered out of all danger: for gladness whereof, they sung, danced, and were joyful. In like manner is the Evangelion of God (which we call gospel; and the New Testament) joyful tidings; and, as some say, a good hearing published by the apostles throughout all the world, of Christ the right David; how that he hath fought with sin, with death, and the devil, and overcome them: whereby all men that were in bondage to sin, wounded with death, overcome of the devil, are, without their own merits or deservings, loosed, justified, restored to life and saved, brought to liberty and reconciled unto the favour of God, and set at one with him again: which tidings as many as believe laud, praise, and thank God; are glad, sing and dance for joy.

This Evangelion or gospel (that is to say, such joyful tidings) is called the New Testament; because that as a man, when he shall die, appointeth his goods to be dealt and distributed after his death among them which he nameth to be his heirs; even so Christ before his death commanded and appointed that such Evangelion, gospel, or tidings should be declared throughout all the world, and therewith to give unto all that repent, and believe, all his goods: that is to say, his life, wherewith he swallowed and devoured up death; his righteousness, wherewith he banished sin; his salvation, wherewith he overcame eternal damnation. Now can the wretched man (that knoweth himself to be wrapped in sin, and in danger to death and hell) hear no more joyous a thing, than such glad and comfortable tidings of Christ; so that he cannot but be glad, and laugh from the laugh from the low bottom of his heart, if he believe that the tidings are true.

To strengthen such faith withal, God promised this his Evangelion in the Old Testament by the prophets, as Paul saith, (Romans 1), how that he was chosen out to preach God's Evangelion, which he before had promised by the prophets in the Scriptures, that treat of his Son which was born of the seed of David. In Genesis 3 God saith to the serpent, "I will put hatred between thee and the woman, between thy seed and her seed; that self seed shall tread thy head under foot." Christ is this woman's seed: he it is that hath trodden under foot the devil's head, that is to say, sin, death, hell, and all his power. For without this seed can no man avoid sin, death, hell, and everlasting damnation.

Again, (Genesis 22), God promised Abraham, saying, "In thy seed shall all the generations of the earth be blessed." Christ is that seed of Abraham, saith Saint Paul (Galatians 3). He hath blessed all the world through the gospel. For where Christ is not, there remaineth the curse, that fell on Adam as soon as he had sinned, so that they are in bondage under Damnation of sin, death, and hell. Against this curse, blesseth now the gospel all the world inasmuch as it crieth openly, unto all that knowledge their sins and repent, saying, whosoever believeth on the seed of Abraham shall be blessed; that is, he shall be delivered from sin, death, and hell, and shall henceforth continue righteous and saved for ever; as Christ himself saith in the eleventh of John, "He that believeth on me, shall never more die."

"The law" (saith the gospel of John in the first chapter) "was given by Moses: but grace and verity by Jesus Christ." The law (whose minister is Moses) was given to bring us unto the knowledge of ourselves, that we might thereby feel and perceive what we are, of nature. The law condemneth us and all our deeds; and is called of Paul (in 2 Corinthians 3) the ministration of death. For it killeth our consciences, and driveth us to desperation; inasmuch as it requireth of us that which is impossible for our nature to do. It requireth of us the deeds of an whole man. It requireth perfect love, from the low bottom and ground of the heart, as well in all things which we suffer, as in the things which we do. But, saith John in the same place, "grace and verity is given us in Christ:" so that, when the law hath passed upon us, and condemned us to death (which is his nature to do), then we have in Christ grace, that is to say, favour, promises of life, of mercy, of pardon, freely, by the merits of Christ; and in Christ have we verity and truth, in that God for his sake fulfilleth all his promises to them that believe.

Therefore is the Gospel the ministration of life. Paul calleth it, in the fore-rehearsed place of the 2 Corinthians 3 the ministration of the Spirit and of righteousness. In the gospel, when we believe the promises, we receive the spirit of life; and are justified, in the blood of Christ, from all things whereof the law condemned us. And we receive love unto the law, and power to fulfill it, and grow therein daily. Of Christ it is written, in the fore-rehearsed John 1. This is he of whose abundance, or fullness, all we have received grace for grace, or favour for favour. That is to say, For the favour that God hath to his Son Christ, he giveth unto us his favour and good-will, and all gifts of his grace, as a father to his sons. As affirmeth Paul, saying, "Which loved us in his Beloved before the creation of the world." So that Christ bringeth the love of God unto us, and not our own holy works. Christ is made Lord over all, and is called in scripture God's mercy-stool: whosoever therefore flieth to Christ, can neither hear nor receive of God any other thing save mercy.

William Tyndale, from *A Pathway into the Holy Scripture*

Hugh Latimer: Who is the best bishop in England?

And now I would ask a strange question: who is the most diligent-est bishop and prelate in all England, that passeth all the rest in doing his office? I can tell, for I know him who it is; I know him well. But now I think I see you listening and hearkening that I should name him. There is one that passeth all the other, and is the most diligent prelate and preacher in all England. And will ye know who it is? I will tell you: it is the devil. He is the most diligent preacher of all other; he is never out of his diocese; he is never from his cure; ye shall never find him unoccupied; he is ever in his parish; he keepeth residence at all times; ye shall never find him out of the way, call for him when you will he is ever at home; the diligentest preacher in all the realm; he is ever at his plough: no lording nor loitering can hinder him; he is ever applying his business, ye shall never find him idle, I warrant you. And his office is to hinder religion, to maintain superstition, to set up idolatry, to teach all kind of popery. He is ready as he can be wished for to set forth his plough; to devise as many ways as can be to deface and obscure God's glory.

Where the devil is resident, and hath his plough going, there away with books, and up with candles; away with bibles, and up with beads; away with the light of the gospel, and up with the light of candles, yea, at noon-days. Where the devil is resident, that he may prevail, up with all superstition and idolatry; censing, painting of images, candles, palms, ashes, holy water, and new service of men's inventing; as though man could invent a better way to honour God with than God himself hath appointed. Down with Christ's cross, up with purgatory pickpurse, up with him, the popish purgatory, I mean. Away with clothing the naked, the poor and impotent; up with decking of images, and gay garnishing of stocks and stones: up with man's traditions and his laws, down with God's traditions and his most holy word. Down with the old honour due to God, and up with the new god's honour. Let all things be done in Latin: there must be nothing but Latin, not so much as *Memento, homo, quod cinis es, et in cinerem reverteris*: "Remember, man, that thou art ashes, and into ashes thou shalt return:" which be the words that the minister speaketh unto the ignorant people, when he giveth them ashes upon Ash-Wednesday; but it must be spoken in Latin: God's word may in no wise be translated into English.

Hugh Latimer, from a sermon preached at Saint Paul's, London, in 1548

The martyrdom of archbishop Cranmer

[This extract from John Foxe's *Actes and Monuments* begins with Cranmer's speech prior to his execution.]

"And now forasmuch as I am come to the end of my life, where-upon hangeth all my life past, and all my life to come, either to live with my Master Christ for ever in joy, or else to be in pain for ever with wicked devils in hell, and I see before mine eyes presently either heaven ready to receive me, or else hell ready to swallow me up: I shall therefore declare unto you my very faith how I believe, without any colour of dissimulation; for now is no time to dissemble, whatsoever I have said or written in times past." He then recited the creed, and added; "I believe every article of the Catholic faith, every word and sentence taught by our Saviour Christ, His apostles and prophets, in the New and Old Testament."

"And now I come to the great thing which so much troubleth my conscience, more than any thing that ever I did or said in my whole life, and that is the setting abroad of a writing contrary to the truth; which now I here renounce and refuse, as things written with my hand contrary to the truth which I thought in my heart, and written for fear of death, and to save my life if it might be; and that is, all such bills and papers which I have written or signed with my hand since my degradation, wherein I have written many things untrue. And forasmuch as my hand hath offended, writing contrary to my heart, therefore my hand shall first be punished; for when I come to the fire, it shall be first burned. As for the pope, I refuse him, as Christ's enemy and antichrist, with all his false doctrine. As for the sacrament, I believe as I have taught in my book against the bishop of Winchester, which my book teacheth so true a doctrine of the sacrament, that it shall stand at the last day before the judgment of God, where the papistical doctrine contrary thereto shall be ashamed to shew her face."

Here the standers-by were all astonished and amazed, and looked upon one another, whose expectation he had so notably deceived.

Some began to admonish him of his recantation, and to accuse him
of falsehood. Briefly, it was a world to see the doctors beguiled of
so great a hope; for they looked for a glorious victory by this man's
retractation. As soon as they heard these things they began to rage,
fret, and fume: and so much the more, because they could not
revenge their grief; for they could no longer threaten or hurt him.
For the most miserable man in the world can die but once; whereas
of necessity he must needs die that day. And so when they could do
nothing else to him, yet lest they should say nothing, they ceased
not to object unto him his falsehood and dissimulation. To this he
replied:

"Ah, my masters, do not you take it so. Always since I lived
hitherto, I have been a hater of falsehood, and a lover of simplicity,
and never before this time have I dissembled." In saying this he
wept bitterly. And when he began to speak more of the sacrament
and of the papacy, some of them began to cry out and bawl,
especially Cole, who cried out, "Stop the heretic's mouth and take
him away!"…

When he came to the place where the holy bishops and martyrs of
God, Latimer and Ridley, were burnt before him for a confession of
the truth, kneeling down he prayed to God; and not long tarrying in
his prayers, putting off his garments to his shirt, he prepared
himself to death. His shirt was made long, down to his feet, which
were bare; likewise his head, when both his caps were off, was so
bare that one hair could not be seen upon it. His beard was so long
and thick, that it covered his face, and his reverend countenance
moved the hearts both of his friends and enemies. Then the Spanish
friars, John and Richard, began to exhort him, and play their parts
with him afresh; but Cranmer, with steadfast purpose, abiding in
the profession of his doctrine, gave his hand to certain old men and
others that stood by, bidding them farewell. When he had thought
to have done so likewise to Mr. Ely, the latter drew back his hand
and refused, saying, it was not lawful to salute heretics, and
especially such an one as falsely returned to the opinions he had
forsworn. And if he had known before that he would have done so,

he would never have used his company so familiarly, and chid those serjeants and citizens who had not refused to give him their hands. This Mr. Ely was a student in divinity, and had been lately made a priest, being then one of the fellows in Brasenose college.

Then was an iron chain tied about Cranmer, whom when they perceived to be more steadfast than that he could be moved from his sentence, they commanded the fire to be set unto him. And when the wood was kindled and the fire began to burn near him, stretching out his arm, he put his right hand into the flame, which he held so steadfast and unmovable, (saving that once with the same hand he wiped his face,) that all men might see his hand burned before his body was touched. His body did so abide the burning of the flame with such constancy and steadfastness, that standing always in one place without moving his body, he seemed to move no more than the stake to which he was bound; his eyes were lifted up into heaven, and oftentimes he repeated "his unworthy right hand," so long as his voice would suffer him; and using often the words of Stephen, "Lord Jesus, receive my spirit," in the greatness of the flames he gave up the ghost, in the sixty-seventh year of his age.

From Foxe's *Actes and Monuments (Book of Martyrs)*

The 1559 Book of Common Prayer: The Morning Service

[I have omitted the Scripture passages, noting in square brackets what they were. I have modernised the spelling but kept the old verb endings and punctuation. The passages in italics were spoken by the congregation, or by congregation and priest together. Note: this order of service is somewhat different from what is found in most copies of the Book of Common Prayer, as it was revised in 1662.]

At the beginning both of Morning Prayer, and likewise of Evening Prayer, the Minister shall read with a loud voice, some one of these sentences of the Scriptures that follow. And then he shall say that, which is written after the said sentences.

[Scripture verses on repentance and forgiveness follow.]

> Dearly beloved brethren, the Scripture moveth us in sundry places, to acknowledge and confess our manifold sins and wickedness, and that we should not dissemble nor cloak them before the face of almighty God our heavenly Father, but confess them with an humble, lowly, penitent and obedient heart to the end that we may obtain forgiveness of the same by His infinite goodness and mercy. And although we ought at all times humbly to knowledge our sins before God, yet ought we most chiefly so to do, when we assemble and meet together, to render thanks for the great benefits that we have received at His hands, to set forth His most worthy praise, to hear His most holy word, and to ask those things which be requisite and necessary, as well for the body as the soul. Wherefore I pray and beseech you, as many as be here present, to accompany me with a pure heart and humble voice, unto the throne of the heavenly grace, saying after me.

A general confession, to be said of the whole congregation after the minister, kneeling.

> *Almighty and most merciful Father, we have erred and strayed from Thy ways, like lost sheep. We have followed too much the devices and desires of our own hearts. We have offended against Thy holy laws: We have left undone those things which we ought to have done, and we have done those things which we ought not to have done, and there is no health in us, but Thou, O Lord, have mercy upon us miserable offenders. Spare Thou them O God, which confess their faults. Restore Thou them that be penitent, according to Thy promises declared unto mankind, in Christ Jesu our Lord. And grant, O most merciful Father, for His sake, that we may hereafter live a godly, righteous, and sober life, to the glory of Thy holy name. Amen.*

The absolution to be pronounced by the Minister alone.

Almighty God, the Father of our Lord Jesus Christ, which desireth not the death of a sinner, but rather that he may turn from his wickedness and live: and hath given power and commandment to His Ministers, to declare and pronounce to His people being penitent, the absolution and remission of their sins: He pardoneth and absolveth all them which truly repent, and unfeignedly believe His holy gospel. Wherefore we beseech Him to grant us true repentance and His Holy Spirit, that those things may please Him, which we do at this present, and that the rest of our life hereafter may be pure and holy so that at the last we may come to His eternal joy, through Jesus Christ our Lord.

The people shall answer.

Amen.

Then shall the Minister begin the Lord's Prayer with a loud voice.

Our Father, which art in heaven, hallowed be Thy name. Thy kingdom come. Thy will be done in earth as it is in heaven. Give us this day our daily bread. And forgive us our trespasses, as we forgive them that trespass against us. And lead us not into temptation. But deliver us from evil. Amen.

Then likewise he shall say: O Lord, open Thou our lips.
Answer. *And our mouth shall show forth Thy praise*
Priest. O God, make speed to save us.
Answer. *Lord, make haste to help us.*
Priest. Glory be to the Father, and to the Son and to the holy Ghost.
As it was in the beginning, is now and ever shall be: world without end. Amen.

Praise ye the Lord

Then shall be said or sung, this Psalm following.

[Psalm 95 follows.]

Then shall follow certain Psalms in order, as they been appointed in a table made for that purpose, except there be proper Psalms appointed for that day, and at the end of every Psalm throughout the year, and likewise in the end of Benedictus [Luke 1:68-79], Benedicite ["Bless the Lord" – the Song of the Three Children, from the Septuagint version of Daniel], Magnificat [Luke 1:46-55], and Nunc Dimittis [Luke 2:29-32], shall be repeated:

Glory be to the Father, and to the Son, *etc.*

Then shall be read two lessons distinctly with a loud voice, that the people may hear. The first of the Old Testament, the second of the New, like as they be appointed by the Calendar, except there be proper Lessons, assigned for that day: the Minister that readeth the Lesson, standing and turning him so as he may best be heard of all such as be present. And before every lesson, the Minister shall say thus. The first, second, third, or fourth chapter of Genesis or Exodus, Matthew, Mark, or other like, as is appointed in the Calendar, And in the end of every chapter, he shall say,

Here endeth such a Chapter of such a Book.

And (to the end the people may the better hear) in such places where they do sing, there shall the lessons be sung in a plain tune after the manner of distinct reading: and likewise the Epistle and gospel.

After the first lesson shall follow, Te deum laudamus in English daily through the whole year.

[The Te Deum follows]

Or this canticle, Benedicite omnia opera Domini domino.

[The Benedicite follows]

And after the second lesson shall be used and said Benedictus, in English, as followeth

[The Benedictus follows]

Or the C. Psalm, Jubilate.

[Psalm 100 follows]

Then shall be said the Creed, by the Minister and the people, standing.

> *I believe in God the Father almighty maker of heaven and earth. And in Jesus Christ His only Son our Lord, which was conceived by the Holy Ghost, born of the Virgin Mary. Suffered under Pontius Pilate, was crucified dead and buried, He descended into Hell. The third day He rose again from the dead. He ascended into heaven, and sitteth on the right hand of God the Father almighty. From thence He shall come to judge the quick and the dead. I believe in the holy Ghost. The holy Catholic Church. The communion of saints. The forgiveness of sins. The resurrection of the body. And the life everlasting. Amen.*

And after that, these prayers following, as well at Evening prayer as at Morning prayer: all devoutly kneeling. The Minister first pronouncing with a loud voice.

The Lord be with you.
Answer. *And with thy spirit.*
The Minister. Let us pray.
Lord have mercy upon us.
Christ have mercy upon us.
Lord have mercy upon us.

Then the Minister, Clerks, and people, shall say the Lords prayer in English, with a loud voice.

Our Father which, etc.

Then the Minister; standing up shall say: O Lord, show Thy mercy upon us.

Answer. *And grant us Thy salvation.*

Priest. O Lord save the queen.

Answer. *And mercifully hear us when we call upon Thee.*

Priest. Endue Thy ministers with righteousness.

Answer. *And make Thy chosen people joyful.*

Priest. O Lord save Thy people.

Answer. *And bless Thine inheritance.*

Priest. Give peace in our time, O Lord.

Answer. *Because there is none other that fighteth for us, but only Thou, O God.*

Priest. O God make clean our hearts within us.

Answer. *And take not Thy Holy Spirit from us.*

Then shall follow three Collects. The first of the day, which shall be the same that is appointed at the Communion, the second for peace, the third for Grace to live well. And the two last Collects shall never alter, but daily be said at Morning prayer, throughout all the year, followeth.

The second Collect for Peace.

O God, which art author of peace, and lover of concord, in knowledge of whom standeth our eternal life, whose service is perfect freedom; defend us Thy humble servants in all assaults of our enemies that we surely trusting in Thy defence, may not fear the power of any adversaries: through the might of Jesu Christ our Lord, Amen.

The third Collect for Grace.

O Lord our heavenly Father, almighty and everlasting God, which hast safely brought us to the beginning of this day: defend us in the same with Thy mighty power, and grant that this day we fall into no sin, neither run into any kind of danger: but that all our doings may be ordered by Thy governance, to do always that is righteous in Thy sight: through Jesus Christ our Lord. Amen.[37]

The martyrdom of George Wishart

When the fire and the gallows were made ready at the west part of the Castle, near to the Priory, my Lord Cardinal [Beaton], dreading that Master George should have been taken away by his friends, commanded his men to bend all the ordnance [guns] of the Castle against the place of execution, and commanded all his gunners to be ready, and stand behind their guns, until such time as he was burned. All this being done, they bound Master George's hands behind his back, and led him forth from the Castle with their soldiers, to the place of their cruel and wicked execution. As he came forth from the Castle gate, there met him certain beggars asking for his alms [gifts of money for the poor], for God's sake. To these he answered, "I want [lack] my hands, wherewith I was wont to give you alms. But may the merciful Lord, who feedeth all men, vouchsafe of His benignity and abundant grace to give you necessaries, both for your bodies and souls." Then met him two false fiends – I should say, Friars – saying, "Master George, pray to our

---

[37] There is no set place for a sermon in the Prayer Book. This is not because the Anglican Reformers did not believe in preaching. However, not every priest was authorised to preach. Under the Elizabethan settlement, one of Elizabeth's royal injunctions laid it down that the bishop of a diocese had to "license" a priest to preach. Licensed clergy had to preach at least once a month, and on at least four Sundays a year they had to preach on the royal supremacy (the doctrine that the queen was "supreme governor" of the Church of England). Clergy who were not licensed to preach were commanded to read to their congregation one of the homilies from the Books of Homilies.

Lady that she may be a mediatrix[38] for you to her Son." To them he answered meekly, "Cease: tempt me not, my brethren." After this he was led to the fire, with a rope about his neck, and a chain of iron about his middle.

When he came to the fire he sat down upon his knees, and rose again; and thrice he said these words, "O Thou Saviour of the world, have mercy upon me: Father of Heaven, I commend my spirit into Thy holy hands." When he had made this prayer, he turned him to the people, and said these words: "I beseech you, Christian brethren and sisters, that ye be not offended at the Word of God because of the affliction and torments which ye see already prepared for me. I exhort you that ye love the Word of God, your salvation, and suffer patiently and with a comfortable heart, for the Word's sake, which is your undoubted salvation and everlasting comfort... Do not fear them that slay the body, and afterwards have no power to slay the soul. Some have said of me that I taught that the soul of man should sleep until the last day; but I know surely that this night, before six o'clock, my soul shall sup with my Saviour, for whom I suffer thus."

Then Master George prayed for them that accused him, saying, "I beseech Thee, Father of Heaven, to forgive them that have of any ignorance, or else of any evil mind, forged lies upon me; I forgive them with all mine heart; I beseech Christ to forgive them that have condemned me to death this day, ignorantly." And last of all, he said to the people on this manner, "I beseech you, brethren and sisters, to exhort your prelates to the learning of the Word of God, that they at least may be ashamed to do evil and learn to do good; and if they will not convert themselves from their wicked error, there shall hastily come upon them the wrath of God, and that they shall not eschew [escape]."

Many faithful words said he in the meantime, taking no heed or care of the cruel torments which were then prepared for him. Then,

---

[38] Mediatrix is Latin for a female mediator. The title is applied to the Virgin Mary in Roman Catholic theology.

last of all, the hangman that was his tormentor, sat down upon his knees, and said, "Sir, I pray you, forgive me, for I am not guilty of your death." To whom he answered, "Come hither to me." When he was come to him, he kissed his cheek, and said, "Lo! Here is a token that I forgive thee. My heart, do thine office." And then by and by he was put upon the gibbet, and hanged, and there burned to powder. When the people beheld the great tormenting of that innocent [man], they could not refrain from piteous mourning and complaining of the innocent lamb's slaughter.

John Knox, *History of the Reformation in Scotland*, Book First.

The Good and Godly Ballads

[Some examples of verses from this popular and influential collection of Scottish Protestant songs:]

The pope, that pagan full of pride

The pope, that pagan full of pride,
    He hath us blinded long,
For where the blind the blind doth guide
    No wonder both go wrong.
Like prince and king he led the reign
    Of all iniquity:
Hay trix, trim go trix,
    Under the greenwood tree.

I come from heaven to tell

I come from heaven to tell
The best nowells that ever befell:
To you their tidings true I bring,
And I will of them say and sing.
My soul and life, stand up and see
Who lies there in a crib of tree:

What babe is that, so good and fair?
It is Christ, God's Son and heir.

A song of the cross

Come here, saith God's Son to me,
Sinners that heavy laden be,
   I will your silly souls refresh:
Come young and old, both man and wife,
I will give you eternal life,
   Though troubled here sore be your flesh.

A song of the Evangel

Be blithe, all Christian men, and sing,
   Dance and make mirth with all your might:
Christ hath us shown great comforting,
   Wherefore we may rejoice of right;
A work to wonder that is wrought,
Christ with His blood full dear us brought,
   And for our sake to death was put.

Of our belief

We trust in God alonely,[39]
Full of all might and majesty,
Maker of heaven and earth so broad,
Which hath Himself our Father made:
And we His sonnes are indeed,
He will keep us in all our need,
Both soul and body to defend,
That no mischance shall us offend;
He taketh care both day and night,
To save us through His godly might
From Satan's subtlety and sleight.

---

[39] "Alonely" is pronounced as a four syllable word, a-lone-a-lee.

The Scots Confession

Chapter 18 –The Notes by Which the True Kirk Shall Be Determined From The False, and Who Shall Be Judge of Doctrine

[Note: the word "kirk" is the old Scottish word for "church".[40]]

Since Satan has laboured from the beginning to adorn his pestilent synagogue with the title of the Kirk of God, and has incited cruel murderers to persecute, trouble, and molest the true Kirk and its members, as Cain did to Abel, Ishmael to Isaac, Esau to Jacob, and the whole priesthood of the Jews to Christ Jesus Himself and His apostles after Him. So it is essential that the true Kirk be distinguished from the filthy synagogues by clear and perfect notes, lest we, being deceived, receive and embrace, to our own condemnation, the one for the other. The notes, signs, and assured tokens whereby the spotless bride of Christ is known from the horrible harlot, the false Kirk, we state, are neither antiquity, usurped title, lineal succession, appointed place, nor the numbers of men approving an error. For Cain was before Abel and Seth in age and title; Jerusalem had precedence above all other parts of the earth, for in it were priests lineally descended from Aaron, and greater numbers followed the scribes, pharisees, and priests, than unfeignedly believed and followed Christ Jesus and his doctrine... and yet no man of judgment, we suppose, will hold that any of the forenamed were the Kirk of God.

The notes of the true Kirk, therefore, we believe, confess, and avow to be: first, the true preaching of the Word of God, in which God has revealed Himself to us, as the writings of the prophets and apostles declare; secondly, the right administration of the sacraments of Christ Jesus, with which must be associated the Word and promise of God to seal and confirm them in our hearts; and lastly, ecclesiastical discipline uprightly ministered, as God's Word prescribes, whereby vice is repressed and virtue

---

[40] In fact, it is the old Middle English word for church too.

nourished. Then wherever these notes are seen and continue for any time, be the number complete or not, there, beyond any doubt, is the true Kirk of Christ, who, according to his promise, is in its midst. This is not that universal Kirk of which we have spoken before, but particular Kirks, such as were in Corinth, Galatia, Ephesus, and other places where the ministry was planted by Paul and which he himself called Kirks of God. Such Kirks, we the inhabitants of the realm of Scotland confessing Christ Jesus, do claim to have in our cities, towns, and reformed districts because of the doctrine taught in our Kirks, contained in the written Word of God, that is, the Old and New Testaments, in those books which were originally reckoned as canonical. We affirm that in these all things necessary to be believed for the salvation of man are sufficiently expressed. The interpretation of Scripture, we confess, does not belong to any private or public person, nor yet to any Kirk for pre-eminence or precedence, personal or local, which it has above others, but pertains to the Spirit of God by whom the Scriptures were written.

When controversy arises about the right understanding of any passage or sentence of Scripture, or for the reformation of any abuse within the Kirk of God, we ought not so much to ask what men have said or done before us, as what the Holy Ghost uniformly speaks within the body of the Scriptures and what Christ Jesus himself did and commanded. For it is agreed by all that the Spirit of God, who is the Spirit of unity, cannot contradict Himself. So if the interpretation or opinion of any theologian, Kirk, or council, is contrary to the plain Word of God written in any other passage of the Scripture, it is most certain that this is not the true understanding and meaning of the Holy Ghost, although councils, realms, and nations have approved and received it. We dare not receive or admit any interpretation which is contrary to any principal point of our faith, or to any other plain text of Scripture, or to the rule of love.

Chapter 21 – The Sacraments

As the fathers under the law, besides the reality of the sacrifices, had two chief sacraments, that is, circumcision and the passover, and those who rejected these were not reckoned among God's people; so do we acknowledge and confess that now in the time of the gospel we have two chief sacraments, which alone were instituted by the Lord Jesus and commanded to be used by all who will be counted members of his body, that is, baptism and the supper or table of the Lord Jesus, also called the communion of His body and blood. These sacraments, both of the Old Testament and of the New, were instituted by God not only to make a visible distinction between His people and those who were without the covenant, but also to exercise the faith of His children and, by participation of these sacraments, to seal in their hearts the assurance of His promise, and of that most blessed conjunction, union, and society, which the chosen have with their Head, Christ Jesus.

And so we utterly condemn the vanity of those who affirm the sacraments to be nothing else than naked and bare signs. No, we assuredly believe that by baptism we are engrafted into Christ Jesus, to be made partakers of His righteousness, by which our sins are covered and remitted, and also that in the supper rightly used, Christ Jesus is so joined with us that he becomes the very nourishment and food for our souls. Not that we imagine any transubstantiation of bread into Christ's body, and of wine into His natural blood, as the Romanists have perniciously taught and wrongly believed; but this union and conjunction which we have with the body and blood of Christ Jesus in the right use of the sacraments is wrought by means of the Holy Ghost, who by true faith carries us above all things that are visible, carnal, and earthly, and makes us feed upon the body and blood of Christ Jesus, once broken and shed for us but now in heaven, and appearing for us in the presence of his Father. Notwithstanding the distance between his glorified body in heaven and mortal men on earth, yet we must assuredly believe that the bread which we break is the communion of Christ's body and the cup which we bless the communion of his blood.

Thus we confess and believe without doubt that the faithful, in the right use of the Lord's table, do so eat the body and drink the blood of the Lord Jesus that He remains in them and they in him; they are so made flesh of His flesh and bone of His bone that as the eternal Godhood has given life and immortality to the flesh of Christ Jesus, which by nature was corruptible and mortal, so the eating and drinking of the flesh and blood of Christ Jesus does the same for us. We grant that this is neither given to us merely at the time nor by the power and virtue of the sacrament alone, but we affirm that the faithful, in the right use of the Lord's Table, have such union with Christ Jesus as the natural man cannot apprehend. Further we affirm that although the faithful, hindered by negligence and human weakness, do not profit as much as they ought in the actual moment of the Supper, yet afterwards it shall bring forth fruit, being living seed sown in good ground; for the Holy Spirit, who can never be separated from the right institution of the Lord Jesus, will not deprive the faithful of the fruit of that mystical action. Yet all this, we say again, comes of that true faith which apprehends Christ Jesus, who alone makes the sacrament effective in us.

Therefore, if anyone slanders us by saying that we affirm or believe the sacraments to be symbols and nothing more, they are libellous and speak against the plain facts. On the other hand we readily admit that we make a distinction between Christ Jesus in His eternal substance and the elements of the sacramental signs. So we neither worship the elements, in place of that which they signify, nor yet do we despise them or undervalue them, but we use them with great reverence, examining ourselves diligently before we participate, since we are assured by the mouth of the apostle that "whoever shall eat this bread, and drink this cup of the Lord, unworthily, shall be guilty of the body and blood of the Lord."

Chapter 8.

GATHERING SWALLOWS: THE CATHOLIC COUNTER REFORMATION.

How did the Roman Catholic Church respond to the challenge of the Reformers? It took almost 40 years before any clear and committed response became the official Roman policy. There were many conflicting opinions among those who stayed loyal to Rome. Even the most traditionally-minded Catholics soon realised that simply persecuting Protestants would not solve the problems and abuses in the Church to which the Reformers had pointed. In this Chapter, we will see how Rome's ultimate response to the Reformation took shape, and how it affected both the Roman Catholic Church and the religious history of Europe.

1. The Catholic Evangelicals.

One Roman Catholic response to the Reformation was to agree with much that Luther, Zwingli, and the other Reformers said, and yet to regret their break with the papacy. Those who responded in this way worked in the period 1521-41 to reform the Church of Rome from within, towards a more Biblical theology and practice, and thus to win back the Protestants into the one true Church. These Roman Reformers are usually called the *Catholic Evangelicals*.

We have already met one of these Catholic Evangelicals – Johannes von Staupitz (1460-1524), the young Luther's spiritual guide.[1] Staupitz agreed with almost everything Luther said, but after much agonising he eventually decided not to follow his brilliant pupil in breaking with the papacy. The two men drifted painfully apart, and in April 1524, eight months before his death, Staupitz wrote his last letter to his spiritual son, Martin Luther. He admitted that Luther had achieved a great deal of good: "We owe so much to you, Martin. You have taken us out of the pig-sty into the pastures of life." But Staupitz went on to criticise the Reformer:

> "Having been your forerunner in the holy Evangelical doctrine, I trust that my humble exhortations may have some influence with you. My love for you is unchanged, but you seem to me to condemn many outward things which do not affect a sinner's justification. Why do you hate monasticism so much, when many monks have lived holy lives? There is nothing that men cannot abuse. I beg you to remember the weak, my dear friend. Do not condemn things which are not important, and which can be sincerely held, although you must of course speak out on matters of faith."

Luther responded with great sadness to Staupitz's decision to remain in the Church of Rome:

> "I am afraid that you hesitate between Christ and the pope, though they are utterly opposed. You seem to me to be a very different Staupitz from the one who used to preach grace and the cross."

In December 1524 Staupitz died, still within the Church of Rome – an Evangelical, but a Catholic one. Rome was not very

---

[1]   For Staupitz, see Chapter 2, section 1.

grateful for his loyalty; it placed all Staupitz's writings on the "index of forbidden books" in 1563.[2]

Staupitz lived and died in Germany, but the great majority of Catholic Evangelicals were based in the Italian cities – Florence, Venice, Padua, Naples, Modena, even Rome itself. Most of them were upper class laypeople, deeply indebted to Erasmus and Christian humanism, often students of Paul's letters, and linked with each other by a network of personal friendships. Women were particularly prominent in the group. The main theological influence on them was Augustine of Hippo; they believed strongly in salvation by grace alone, rooted in divine predestination. They also read Protestant writings with sympathy, and accepted justification by faith. Their foremost leader, cardinal Gasparo Contarini, had this to say on justification:

> "By faith we have a twofold righteousness: first, an inward righteousness of our own, and the love and grace by which we are made partakers of the divine nature; second, the righteousness of Christ, given and imputed to us. We ought to trust in Christ's righteousness bestowed on us, and not in our own inward holiness and grace. For our own righteousness is incomplete and imperfect, and it cannot stop us offending and constantly sinning in many things. But the righteousness of Christ given to us is a true and perfect righteousness; it is altogether pleasing in God's sight. We must therefore rest only upon this, and believe that we are justified before God on account of Christ's righteousness alone."

The chief difference between Catholic Evangelicals and Protestants was that the Catholic Evangelicals combined their views on salvation by grace alone with a continuing belief in the papacy as the divinely ordained head of the visible Church, and in transubstantiation

---

[2]   The index of forbidden books was an official catalogue of morally or doctrinally unsound books that no Roman Catholic was allowed to read without special permission. It was first drawn up by pope Paul IV in 1557. See section 6.

as the only true doctrine of the eucharist. Their ideal was a reformed Evangelical Church of Rome. The Catholic Evangelicals
could be as bold as the Protestants in condemning abuses in the
Church; they expressed their criticisms most forcefully in 1537, in
the report of a reform commission set up by pope Paul III (1534-
49). The report was entitled *Consilium de Emendanda Ecclesia*
("Consultation on Reforming the Church"). It was so forthright in
its condemnation of the existing state of the Roman Church that
the pope refused to publish it. However, copies of the report
"leaked" out and were printed unofficially – especially by Protestants, who claimed that it justified all the criticisms they had made
of Rome. It was so embarrassing that the Roman inquisition finally
placed it on the index of forbidden books!

Leading figures among the Catholic Evangelicals included the
following:

Gasparo Contarini (1483-1542), their greatest champion. A native
of Venice, Contarini was a humanist and politician who had
experienced an agonising search for salvation, resulting in a
conversion experience in 1511, which reminds us of the spiritual
struggles of the young Luther. Unlike Luther, Contarini's humanism
and Augustinian theology were blended with a high regard for the
scholastic theology of Thomas Aquinas. A layman of outstanding
godliness, pope Paul III made him a Roman Catholic cardinal in
1535, and bishop of Belluno (north-eastern Italy) in 1536. He
approved of many aspects of Luther's and Calvin's theology, but
feared that their rejection of the papacy would plunge Western
Europe into religious and political chaos. Contarini was one of
those responsible for the *Consilium de Emendanda Ecclesia*.

Juan de Valdes (1500-1541), a Spanish humanist who fled from
persecution in Spain and settled in Naples (south-western Italy).
Strongly influenced by both Erasmus and Luther, Valdes's home in
Naples became a flourishing centre of the Catholic Evangelical
movement; he hosted meetings every Sunday for Bible study,
prayer and discussion of theology. Valdes placed great emphasis on

personal experience of Christ, dismissing as mere opinion any faith that was based only on the Church's teaching or on reason. Some of Valdes's disciples became outright Protestants, most notably Peter Martyr of Florence.[3]

Albert Pighius (1490-1542), a Dutch theologian from Kampen. In some ways we can hardly think of Pighius as a Catholic Evangelical; he was anti-Augustinian in his concept of original sin and predestination, opposing Luther and Calvin strongly on these issues. He also wrote in defence of papal infallibility and of Roman Catholic tradition as a source of truth alongside Scripture. However, he embraced an understanding of justification which was virtually identical with the Reformation view, influenced in this by Johann Gropper (see below). Although Pighius is remembered (if at all) by Protestants today as someone scolded by Calvin for his non-Augustinian views of sin, grace, and free-will, a previous generation was kinder: John Owen, the prince of Puritan divines, quoted Pighius at great length in his classic treatise *The Doctrine of Justification by Faith* as a Roman Catholic witness to Protestant truth.

Jacob Sadoleto (1477-1547), Italian humanist and Biblical scholar, bishop of Carpentras in south-eastern France from 1517. He was made a cardinal by pope Paul III in 1536, and was one of the authors of the *Consilium de Emendanda Ecclesia*. A disciple of Erasmus, Sadoleto joined Pighius in being unusual among Catholic Evangelicals, not holding to an Augustinian view of sin and grace; theologians attacked his commentary on Romans (1535) for teaching a form of Pelagianism. Repelled by Luther's abusive anti-Catholic language, Sadoleto greatly admired Melanchthon and Bucer, and always opposed violent action against Protestants; he even sheltered some Waldensians fleeing from persecution in 1545. However, Sadoleto is best known to Protestants as the author of an open letter to the citizens of Geneva, written in 1539, in which he

---

[3] For Peter Martyr, see Chapter 4, section 3.

tried to persuade them to return to the Church of Rome – a letter which inspired Calvin's more famous reply.[4]

Gregorio Cortese (1483-1548), an Italian Benedictine monk who had a great knowledge of the early Church fathers and studied the writings of Luther with sympathy. From 1532 to 1537 he was abbot of a Benedictine monastery in Venice, where he became an intimate member of Contarini's reforming group. A firm believer in the papacy, Cortese was none the less outspoken in condemning its corruptions; he was one of those who produced the *Consilium de Emendanda Ecclesia*. Pope Paul III made him a cardinal in 1542.

Reginald Pole (1500-1558), an English noble (son of the countess of Salisbury), humanist scholar and close friend of Erasmus, Contarini, and Sir Thomas More.[5] He fled from England in 1532 to escape the wrath of the English king Henry VIII (1509-47), which Pole knew would fall on him if he refused to support Henry's break with the papacy. He wrote a book against Henry in 1536, entitled *Pro Ecclesiasticae Unitatis Defensione* ("In Defence of the Church's Unity"), in which Pole attacked his monarch for making himself head of the English Church. Henry responded by condemning Pole to death and executing his mother. Pope Paul III appointed Pole a cardinal and a member of the reform commission which produced the *Consilium de Emendanda Ecclesia*. He was also one of the three papal legates who presided over the first stage of the Council of Trent (see section 3).[6]

Johann Gropper (1503-59), a German theologian from Soest in Westphalia, and a disciple of Erasmus. He held various positions in the Church, and became involved in the Catholic reforming efforts of the archbishop of Cologne, Hermann of Wied. It was, however,

---

[4]   See Chapter 4, section 7.

[5]   For Sir Thomas More, see Chapter 1, section 3, under **England**, and previous Chapter, section 1.

[6]   Pole's career as England's last Roman Catholic archbishop of Canterbury under queen Mary Tudor (1553-58) has been told in the previous Chapter , section 4.

Gropper's *Enchiridion* (1538) which made him famous. This was a handbook of doctrine written against the Reformer; for instance, it taught that Scripture can be understood only from apostolic and patristic tradition, and that the Church has authority to decide things not set down in Scripture or by Councils, and defended the seven sacraments, transubstantiation, the invocation of saints, and the authority of the pope. Yet at the same time, the *Enchiridion* compromised deeply with the Reformation's theology of justification. Gropper's view is usually called "double justice" (or "twofold righteousness"). He held that Christ's righteousness was inwardly imparted to believers, who then did good works; but because sin remained in believers, spoiling their best performance, they could never perfectly meet God's requirement. Therefore, when believers stood before God in judgment, He would graciously impute to their account just so much of Christ's forensic righteousness as would cover the gap in their performance. The final justification of believers was therefore a combination of Christ's imparted righteousness, the good works that flow from this, and Christ's imputed righteousness which makes up what is lacking. Based on this concept, Gropper cooperated extensively with Martin Bucer, prior to the Regensburg colloquy (see below), in producing a joint statement on justification which became known as the *Regensburg Book*. Despite his sympathy with the Reformation view of justification, Gropper remained firmly committed to the Roman Catholic Church as God's visible society; when archbishop Hermann of Cologne became a Lutheran, Gropper was instrumental in having him deposed and excommunicated in 1546 and in restoring Roman Catholicism in Cologne with the help of the Jesuits. Nevertheless, his *Enchiridion* was placed on Rome's index of forbidden books after the Council of Trent.

Girolamo Seripando (1493-1563), of Apulia (south-eastern Italy), a distinguished Hebrew and Greek scholar who lectured in theology at Bologna university (northern Italy), and in 1539 became head of the Augustinian order of friars – the order to which Luther had belonged. Seripando held strongly Augustinian views on humanity's bondage to sin and God's sovereign grace in salvation, and a

broadly Lutheran concept of justification by faith which he set forth
with great eloquence at the Council of Trent (see section 3).

Giovanni Morone (1509-80) of Milan, bishop of Modena (northern
Italy) from 1529, a close friend of Contarini. Morone consistently
worked for better relations between Rome and the Reformers. Pope
Paul IV (1555-59), who was violently opposed to the Reformation,
had Morone imprisoned from 1557 to 1559 for his Protestant-
leaning views on justification by faith and praying to the saints.
Restored to favour after Paul IV's death, Morone presided as pope
Pius IV's legate over the Council of Trent in 1562-63 (see section 3).

The most popular writing to emerge from the Catholic Evangelical
camp was *The Benefits of Christ's Death*, published in Venice in
1543. Historians are not sure who wrote it; the author was probably
a Benedictine monk, ***Benedetto de Mantova*** (died 1546), a disciple
of Valdes who had belonged to Gregorio Cortese's monastery in
Venice before moving to Sicily. Highly recommended by Pole and
Morone, the book was hugely popular among Italian Catholics,
selling 40,000 copies by 1549. It taught a strongly Augustinian
theology alongside a Protestant view of justification by faith. In
fact, large parts of the *Benefits* were simply a translation into Italian
of the 1539 edition of Calvin's *Institutes*! It is difficult to think that
Pole and Morone did not know this; and if they knew it, they were
indirectly recommending Calvin as a spiritual guide. The inquisition eventually placed the *Benefits* on the index of forbidden books.

The influence of the Catholic Evangelicals on the papacy reached
its height in the period 1539-41. In these three years, leading
Roman Catholic and Protestant theologians held a series of meetings, under the authority of the Holy Roman emperor Charles V
and backed by pope Paul III, with the aim of restoring the shattered
unity of the Church in Western Europe. Catholic Evangelicals
dominated the Roman delegates at these meetings. This Roman-
Protestant dialogue came closest to success in 1541 at the colloquy
of Regensburg (sometimes called "Ratisbon", in Bavaria, south-
eastern Germany). Contarini presided over the colloquy; Gropper

and Pighius were among the Roman Catholics, and Calvin, Melanchthon, and Bucer among the Protestants. The two sides managed to produce a common statement on original sin and justification by faith.[7] Calvin wrote to William Farel:

> "To our delight, they agreed with us without difficulty on original sin. Then followed a discussion about free-will, which was settled according to the opinion of Augustine. In these two points the Catholic delegates do not differ from us. Regarding justification, there were sharper arguments. In the end a formula was drawn up, with corrections agreed on by both sides, which you will certainly accept. When you read the copy of the formula which I include with this letter, you will be amazed, I know, that our opponents came so far over to our views. They have retained the whole truth of our doctrine! There is nothing in the formula which is not found in our writings. I know you will desire an even clearer explanation, and I agree with you on this. But truly, if you think about the men with whom we have reached this agreement, you will realise how much has been achieved."

However, after these hopeful beginnings, the colloquy broke down completely over the doctrine of the eucharist. The Catholic Evangelicals insisted on transubstantiation; the Protestants refused to tolerate it, on the basis that it would lead to the idolatrous worship of the communion bread as Christ's actual body.

The Catholic Evangelicals continued to enjoy a significant degree of popular success, as the sale of *The Benefits of Christ's Death* showed, but the failure of the colloquy of Regensburg marked the end of their official influence in the papal court. Regensburg seemed to prove that nothing was to be gained by the policy of reconciliation with Protestants. Many leading Roman Churchmen rejected the joint Roman-Protestant statement on justification by faith as a vile Lutheran heresy; paradoxically, some Protestants, including Luther, rejected it as a compromise with Rome! Pope

---

[7]   See the end of the Chapter for the agreed statement on justification by faith.

Paul III removed Contarini from all positions of influence, and the great Catholic Evangelical leader died a year later. As a result of the Catholic Evangelical failure, Augustinian theology fell into disfavour in Rome. The way was clear for a policy of reforming the Church, not in order to win back the Protestants, but in order to make the Church an effective instrument for their extermination.

2. Ignatius Loyola and the Jesuits.

A completely different idea of a reformed Roman Church came from Spain. Spain was the most intensely Roman Catholic nation in Europe; Roman Catholicism and Spanish nationalism had fused together into one single passionate outlook, through the long centuries of Catholic-Muslim warfare by which Spanish Catholics eventually reconquered the whole of Spain from Islamic control in 1492.[8] Christian humanism, which elsewhere in Western Europe helped pave the way for the Reformation, had been purified of its "Protestant" tendencies in Spain by the great archbishop of Toledo, cardinal Francisco Ximénez. Under Ximénez' guidance, humanism became a tool for reforming moral and educational standards within the Spanish Catholic Church, but leaving its traditional theology and spirituality unchanged.[9] Not surprisingly, then, Spain was the one Western European country where the Reformation made almost no impact. There was a tiny handful of Spanish Protestants, but they were swamped by the overwhelming Catholicism of Spain's national character, as undergirded by the Catholic-reformist ideals of Ximénez and others which seemed to make the drastic cure of Protestantism unnecessary in healing the Church's corruptions.

One Spanish Protestant who deserves to be briefly mentioned is **Cassiodoro de Reina** (1520-94).[10] Reina was the Spanish equivalent of William Tyndale. A monk who devoted himself to Bible study, he led a Protestant movement in his monastery, and had to

---

[8]   For the Christian-Muslim warfare in Spain, see Part Two, Chapter 1, section 3.
[9]   For cardinal Ximénez and Christian humanism in Spain, see Chapter 1, section 3.
[10] In Latin, Reginaldus Gonsalvius Montanus.

flee from the inquisition to Geneva, then to Frankfurt. In 1559 he moved to London in the newly Protestant England of Elizabeth I, where he became preacher to a Spanish congregation, and began his translation of the Bible into Spanish. His country's government, fearing the subversive potential of Reina's work, engineered his departure in 1563 on false charges of homosexual behaviour, then illegal. Reina lived in fear of his life on the Continent (king Philip II of Spain had put a price on his head), living in various cities – Antwerp, Frankfurt, Basel. It was in Basel that his completed translation of Scripture was published in 1569; suppressed in Spain by the inquisition, hardly any original copies have survived. Thereafter, Reina was a Lutheran pastor in Antwerp and Frankfurt. Despite its suppression in Spain, Reina's translation, revised by Cipriano de Valera in 1602, formed the basis for all Spanish Protestant Bibles from that time until well on into the 20th century.

Reina, however, unlike Tyndale in England or Luther in Germany, remained outside the mainstream of his country's religious and cultural development. Occupying centre stage in Spain was the Catholic Reformation. And the Spanish concept of reforming the Roman Church was the exact opposite of the Catholic Evangelical one: cleanse the Church of its corruptions and abuses, so that it can become a mighty disciplined army under the leadership of the pope, consecrated to the utter destruction of Protestantism. This view of Catholic Reformation has often been described as the "Counter-Reformation" – that is, aimed against the Protestant Reformation.[11]

The man through whom this Spanish vision of Catholic reform flowed into the Roman Church was ***Ignatius Loyola*** (1491-1556).

---

[11] I have used the phrase "Catholic Counter-Reformation". Older textbooks prefer "Counter-Reformation", newer ones "Catholic Reformation". This latter description is allied to a belief on the part of many (especially Roman Catholic) historians that a reformation of some kind would have happened within the Roman Church even if Luther and the Protestant movement had never arisen. My own view is that whatever might have happened if Luther had not existed, it can hardly be denied that the actual reformation within Roman Catholicism was profoundly shaped by Rome's responses to Protestantism.

If Luther gave birth to Protestantism, Loyola was the spiritual father of Counter-Reformation Catholicism. A native of the mountain province of Guipuzcoa, in the Basque region of northern Spain where the armies of Islam had never conquered, Loyola belonged to an ancient branch of the Spanish nobility, the Recaldes, direct descendants of the Visigoths.[12] The Recaldes family had a strong military tradition, and so it was as a soldier that the young and well-educated Loyola began his remarkable life, in the service of the Spanish kings Ferdinand II of Aragon (1479-1516) and his son Charles I (1516-56) – this was the Charles who became Holy Roman emperor in 1521. At this stage in his development, Loyola was obsessed with the great medieval tales of knighthood and chivalry;[13] his burning ambition was to become a famous knight. However, it was not to be. In 1521, one of Loyola's legs was shattered and crippled in a war between Spain and France, and his military career came to an abrupt end.

As he lay at home recovering from his injury, Loyola's thoughts turned to religion. Instead of reading stories of medieval knights, he began to read lives of the saints. But the book that made the deepest impression on him was *The Life of our Lord Jesus Christ* by the 14th century German writer, Ludolph of Saxony (1300-1378), a Carthusian monk.[14] This book was the most detailed biography of Christ that had been written in the Middle Ages; it included comments on the different Gospel passages by the early Church fathers and medieval theologians, together with prayers and practical teaching based on each passage. Reading Ludolph's *Life of Christ* proved to be the turning point of the young Loyola's life.

---

[12]   For the Visigoths, see Part One, Chapter 11, section 1.
[13]   For knighthood and chivalry, see Part Two, Chapter 5, section 2.
[14]   For the Carthusians, see Part Two, Chapter 4, section 3, footnote 10. Ludolph of Saxony had a great influence on Thomas a Kempis, for whom see Part Two, Chapter 10, section 6. Loyola became a great admirer of a Kempis, recommending his *The Imitation of Christ* with great enthusiasm.

Ignatius Loyola (1491-1556)

He renounced his worldly ambitions, and vowed that from now on, he would only ever be a spiritual knight in the heavenly service of the Lord Jesus Christ and His mother, the blessed Virgin Mary. He gave away his knightly costume, put on a hermit's garb, and went to the Dominican convent in Manresa, north-eastern Spain. Here, between March 1522 and February 1523, Loyola devoted himself to prayer and harsh ascetic self-discipline. He also received a series of supernatural visions which entitle him to a place among the Roman Catholic mystics, and which inspired him to produce one of the most influential religious books ever written: the *Spiritual Exercises*. This became the training manual of the religious order Loyola founded, the Jesuits (see below).

As its title suggests, the *Spiritual Exercises* presented a set of exercises in prayer and meditation, spread over four weeks. Divided into four parts, part one of the *Exercises* dealt with sin and hell; part two focused on the kingdom of Christ, His royal claims on the soul, and the main events of His earthly life; part three was about the sufferings and death of Christ; and part four considered His resurrection and heavenly glory. No spiritual handbook before the *Spiritual Exercises* had placed such a powerful emphasis on the use of the imagination in training the soul. Loyola wanted those who used the *Exercises* to experience personally all the realities he was describing: the flames of hell, the cries of the damned, Gabriel's annunciation to the Virgin Mary, Christ in the garden of Gethsemane – the believer was to imagine that he was actually there, seeing every sight, hearing every sound, smelling every odour, touching and tasting and feeling all the details with all his senses. Loyola also gave advice on how a person was to involve his body in taking the *Spiritual Exercises*. Some parts of the *Exercises* were to be practised standing, other parts walking about, others sitting down or lying on the floor; some should be undertaken after meals, others during fasts, some at daytime, others in the night, and so on. People who went through the *Exercises* in this way testified to the utterly overpowering impact it made on their imaginations and emotions: they were never the same again.

The purpose of the *Spiritual Exercises* was to bring the soul into total obedience to Christ through total submission to the Roman Church as His one true Church, His Bride, outside of which there was no grace, no Christ, and no salvation. Here was the very heart of Loyola's personality and faith. He believed passionately in the infallibility of the Church of Rome, its exclusive possession of grace through its priesthood and sacraments, and the absolute truth of its traditional scholastic theology. In Loyola's mind, faith meant an unquestioning acceptance of all Rome's teachings; there was no room for criticism, and all dissent was damnable heresy. The *Exercises* ended with "Rules for Thinking in Harmony with the Church", which contained the following famous statement:

> "Setting aside all personal judgment of our own, we must keep our minds prepared and ready to obey in all things the true Bride of Christ our Lord, which is our holy mother, the Catholic Church.... To make perfectly sure of our orthodoxy, if the Catholic Church proclaims something to be black which appears to be white, we must accept that it is black. For we believe that there is one and the same Spirit in Christ our Lord the Husband, and in the Church His Bride. This Spirit governs and guides our souls to salvation; the same Spirit and the same Lord who gave the Ten Commandments guides and rules our holy mother the Church."

Not surprisingly, Loyola did not intend individuals to undertake the *Spiritual Exercises* on their own. He required people to practise the *Exercises* only under the close supervision of a Jesuit spiritual director, someone who had gone through the *Exercises* himself, and who was himself guided by Loyola's *Directory*. This was a companion volume which gave detailed instructions to spiritual directors on how to lead souls through the *Spiritual Exercises*.

Loyola studied in various Spanish universities in 1524-28, and then in Paris in 1528-35. This means that Loyola was a student in Paris at the same time as John Calvin, although there is no record that the two spiritual giants ever met. During his time in Paris, Loyola collected a group of six disciples, who in 1534 bound themselves together by an oath to go to the Holy Land and work for Christ among the Muslims there. Among the six were Loyola's two fellow Spaniards, ***Diego Laynez*** (1512-65), who became the leader of the Jesuits after Loyola's death, and Francis Xavier (1506-52), who was to be the greatest of the early Jesuit missionaries.[15] Loyola and his six disciples gathered in Venice in 1537, intending to sail to the Holy Land, but a war between the Venetians and the Turks prevented them. So they journeyed instead to Rome, where they became a band of mendicant preachers. In 1539 they started calling themselves "the Society of Jesus", a name Loyola claimed had been revealed to him by Jesus Himself in a vision. The word "Society" has a military flavour; a modern equivalent would be something like "the Regiment of Jesus". More popularly, people were soon calling them *Jesuits* (the word was first used in Germany as a nickname, and it caught on). In 1540 pope Paul III gave the Society official recognition as a new religious order, and Loyola was elected its first leader or "general".

The rules of the Society, known as the "Constitutions", were drawn up by Loyola, who believed they were given to him by divine revelation. The Jesuit Constitutions organised the Society along military lines, reflecting Loyola's own background. At the top was the "general" (sometimes referred to as the "black pope" by enemies of the Jesuits), who exercised absolute authority over the rest of the Society. He appointed all the lesser leaders. Under the general were the "provincials", who governed different regional branches of the Society (*e.g.* in France or Spain); under the provincials were the "rectors" who controlled local Jesuit groups in towns and cities. Loyola laid down strict conditions about who could join; they had to be healthy, physically beautiful, intelligent, good at

---

[15]   For more about Xavier, see section 7 below.

public speaking, and free from the least suspicion of heresy. Loyola wanted none but the best for his special order of spiritual knights. Within the Society, there were four grades:

(a) **The *novices*.** These were men who had only just joined; they had to undergo two years of initial training, instead of the one year that was normal in other religious orders. The training included taking the *Spiritual Exercises*.

(b) **The *scholastics*.** After two years as a novice, the aspiring Jesuit spent five years studying and another five years teaching junior Society classes.

(c) **The *coadjutors*.** This grade ran the wider teaching, preaching, and missionary work of the Society. The general chose the rectors from this group.

(d) **The *professed of the four vows*.** These were the highest members of the Society, who alone acted as its governing body. The general chose the provincials from this grade. They were always a small group; when Loyola died, only 43 out of some thousand Jesuits belonged to this highest class. The "four vows" referred to the religious vows that members of the Society had to swear. Ordinary Jesuits only took the three vows that were normal in any religious order, the vows of poverty, celibacy, and obedience to superiors. The fourth vow was unique to the Society of Jesus, found in no other religious order, and sworn only by the Society's governing élite – a vow of going without delay wherever the pope might send them. This vow created a special relationship between the Jesuits and the papacy; over the next three centuries, Jesuits would be the most zealous advocates of the absolute supremacy of the pope over Church and state.

Loyola laid a powerful stress on education as one of the main tasks of the Society, and in 1551 he founded in Rome the first Jesuit college, which became a model for all the others. By the 17th century some 400 Jesuit schools and colleges had been established across Western Europe; they were amazingly popular, charging no fees, and using the best educational methods then in existence, with a novel emphasis on physical games and drama. The Society's schools were particularly successful in training a whole new generation of devout and committed Roman Catholics; Jesuits concentrated on educating the sons of Roman Catholic kings and nobles, so that Jesuit teaching and Jesuit ideals would mould the souls of future Roman Catholic rulers. "Give me a child before he is seven," the Jesuits boasted, "and he will remain a Catholic for the rest of his life." As for the content of Jesuit teaching, the Society's Constitutions named Aristotle as the supreme guide in philosophy, and Thomas Aquinas in theology. Because of the blossoming growth and success of the Society, this helped to make Aquinas into the most widely studied theologian in the Roman Catholic Church, a position previously held by Peter Lombard. However, Loyola did state that on some points Aquinas's views were not binding, especially the great Italian schoolman's denial of the immaculate conception of the Virgin Mary.[16]

At first the Society of Jesus was concerned mainly with teaching orthodox Roman Catholic theology within the Church, *e.g.* to children in schools and to the illiterate, and also with missionary work among Muslims and other unevangelised peoples. However, in the 1550s, the destruction of Protestantism became another chief purpose of the Society. Jesuit theologians dedicated themselves to studying, mastering, and overthrowing the works of the Protestant Reformers. They soon became Rome's mightiest weapon in the war against the Reformation; Protestants feared and hated the Society of Jesus more than any other Roman Catholic body. The papacy sent Jesuit priests into every Roman Catholic nation which had been affected by Protestantism, to win their peoples back to a full allegiance to Rome, usually with great success. They also went secretly into Protestant nations, to strengthen persecuted Roman Catholic minorities in their faith; Protestant governments put many Jesuits to death, especially in England.

---

[16]   For Peter Lombard and Thomas Aquinas, see Part Two, Chapter 7, section 3.

As a striking example of a Jesuit triumph, we can look at the work of **Peter Canisius** (1521-97) in southern Germany. Despite Roman Catholic persecution of Protestants, the Reformation still had many followers at grass-roots level in Austria, Bavaria and the smaller German territories that bordered on Switzerland; Rome continued to fear that the whole of Germany might embrace Protestantism. Canisius, a native of the Netherlands and one of Loyola's favourite disciples, turned the spiritual tide in southern Germany decisively back towards Roman Catholicism. Roman Catholics sometimes call him "the second apostle of Germany".[17] Beginning in 1549, Canisius worked tirelessly in Austria and Bavaria, preaching, teaching, founding Jesuit schools and colleges, training a new generation of devout and well-educated Roman Catholic priests. His supreme achievement was his German Catholic *Catechism*, first published in 1555. Canisius created a Roman Catholic copy of the Lutheran system of catechising; it was highly effective – some 130 editions of his *Catechism* were published. Canisius's vigorous labours almost wiped out Protestantism in Austria and Bavaria, and raised up a strong Jesuit-led Roman Catholic influence in Hussite Bohemia.

By Loyola's death in 1556, the Society of Jesus had 936 members in the various grades of the order. The Society had taken root and flourished swiftly in Italy, Spain and Portugal; it grew more slowly in France and southern Germany. Beyond question, the astonishing discipline, dedication and energy of this "regiment of Jesus" proved to be the single most powerful force in reviving the fortunes of traditional Roman Catholicism. Sweeping aside the Catholic Evangelicals, Loyola's spiritual knights taught and spread a new, fiercely anti-Protestant expression of Roman Catholic theology and spirituality throughout Europe. With one hand, they dealt staggering blows to the Reformation; with the other, they founded orphanages, schools, centres for the care of the poor, houses for reforming prostitutes, and societies for ransoming Christian captives from Muslims. Jesuits soon stood on the front line of Roman Catholicism

---

[17]   The "first apostle" of Germany was Boniface. See Part Two, Chapter 2, section 1.

at every level, as preachers, educators, chaplains, spiritual guides, and theologians.

Yet at the same time, there was serious opposition to the Jesuits from *within* the Roman Catholic Church. Roman Catholic monarchs were sometimes afraid of the Society's far-flung and powerful international organisation. Many Roman Catholic bishops, and the other religious orders – notably the Dominicans and Franciscans – were jealous of the special favour the Jesuits enjoyed from the papacy. Augustinian theologians (mostly Dominicans) within the Roman Church disliked Jesuit theology, which had very quickly become marked by a deep hostility to Augustine's doctrines of sin and grace; and many Roman Catholic moral teachers tried to combat what they believed were the Jesuits' low and easy-going views of morality. (For more about the Jesuits, see section 7 on Roman Catholic missions.)

3. The Council of Trent.

Alongside the Society of Jesus, the Council of Trent was the second great instrument of the Counter-Reformation. Trent was supposed to be the ecumenical council of the whole Western Church for which Luther had called before his break with Rome, and which others had been demanding for years. When it finally met, it was no longer an ecumenical council of the whole Western Catholic Church, because half of Western Europe had abandoned Rome and the papacy. Trent was a council, not of the *Western* Catholic Church, but of the *Roman* Catholic Church.

The main pressure for convening an ecumenical council came from the Holy Roman emperor, Charles V. Pope Paul III (1534-49) was reluctant to call a council together, fearing that it would create more problems for the papacy than it solved – *e.g.* by resurrecting the conciliar movement,[18] or being forced by Charles V into

---

[18]   For conciliarism, see Part Two, Chapter 10, section 3.

compromising with the Reformers. However, Paul III finally yielded to the emperor's urgent insistence and summoned the council, which met in December 1545 in Trent, northern Italy. One of the most serious problems in assembling the council was the perpetual quarrel between Charles V and the French king, Francis I, the West's two most powerful monarchs. Each wanted to influence the council; neither wanted the other to influence it. It was very difficult to find a meeting place which would satisfy both parties. In the end, Paul III chose Trent, which was within the frontiers of the Holy Roman Empire, in the imperial region of Tyrol (now the extreme north-east of Italy). This deeply offended Francis I, and only a few French delegates bothered to turn up at the Council. It was dominated by Italians, but with a strong Spanish contingent too. It met in three stages: (i) 1545-47; (ii) 1551-52; (iii) 1562-63. From a Protestant point of view, the period of time covered by Trent stretched from the death of Luther to the death of Calvin.

There were tensions in the Council between the Italians and the Spanish. The Italian delegates were "papalists" – strong supporters of papal supremacy. The Spanish, however, were "imperialists" – that is, they were more loyal to the emperor Charles V (who was king of Spain) than to the papacy, and tended towards conciliarism, upholding the supremacy of the Council over the pope. On the other hand, the cause of the Catholic Evangelicals was not yet dead, and they were mostly Italians; they found an influential spokesman in the head of the Augustinian order, Girolamo Seripando (see section 1), who argued for justification by faith at the Council's first session. The Spanish, however, had no sympathy for such dangerous flirtations with Lutheranism, and the great Spanish Jesuit, Diego Laynez, one of Ignatius Loyola's original six disciples, effectively opposed Seripando. There were other differences too about particular doctrines and the way they should be expressed.

Stage one: 1545-47

The first point to be discussed was the order of proceedings: should doctrinal or practical reform be dealt with first? The Council eventually finally decided to look at both matters at the same time. Still, the central significance of the first meeting lay in a number of important theological decisions the Council made in response to the challenges of the Protestant Reformation. These and all the decisions of Trent were reached by a process of discussion and debate, sometimes heated argument; we must not think that all the delegates had the same theology or identical views of reform. To illustrate the way in which the Council came to its decisions, let us look briefly at its first session, where the doctrine of "Scripture and tradition" was considered.

The subject was opened up by one of the papal legates, del Monte, who argued that God's revelation was contained equally in Scripture and in Church traditions. Most of the bishops violently opposed him; they insisted that the only tradition they were willing to discuss was *apostolic* tradition – teachings and customs that could be traced directly back to the apostles, rather than those which had grown up in the Church since the 2nd century. This was agreed. Then followed several weeks of argument about the nature of apostolic tradition and its relationship with Scripture. The Council was divided into three parties:

(a) those who held that apostolic tradition was equal with Scripture as a source of revelation;

(b) those who believed that tradition was secondary to Scripture, and that Scripture contained everything that people needed to know for their salvation;

(c) those who agreed with the second group that Scripture contained all saving truth, but maintained that apostolic tradition was the inspired and infallible *interpreter* of Scripture.

The committee responsible for drafting the Council's decree on Scripture and tradition had to produce something that these three parties could all approve. Their first attempt failed miserably; they drafted a statement which said that divine truth was contained partly in Scripture, partly in apostolic tradition, and that both Scripture and tradition must be accepted with an equal faith. The draft was shot down in flames, especially by group (b); one of their spokesmen, Bonuti, declared that "*all* evangelical truth is in Scripture, therefore not partly." After further weeks of debate, and sometimes uproar,[19] the delegates finally voted to approve the following decree:

> "Following the example of the orthodox fathers, the Council receives and venerates with the same sense of loyalty and reverence all the books of the Old and New Testaments (for God alone is the author of both), together with all traditions concerning faith and morality, as coming from the mouth of Christ, or being inspired by the Holy Spirit, and preserved in continuous succession in the Catholic Church."

Here was a decree which even group (b), with their emphasis on the supremacy of Scripture, could accept. If we wonder how they could accept it, it was for two important reasons. First, the drafters of the decree had dropped the demand that tradition *in general* be given an equal place with Scripture; the final decree said specifically "traditions *concerning faith and morals*". In other words, traditions concerning customs of worship (*e.g.* turning to the east when praying) were not made equal with Scripture. The only traditions which the decree sanctioned were *doctrinal* traditions involving questions of belief and morality. This satisfied group (b), whose members had been outraged by the idea that Catholics should give equal reverence to the Gospel of John and the practice of turning to the east in prayer. Second, the drafters of the decree got rid of the controversial statement that divine revelation was contained "partly" in Scripture, "partly" in tradition; the final decree simply said that God's truth was to be found in Scripture and tradition. This allowed group (b) to continue believing that *all* truths

---

[19] A member of group (b), Nacchianti, caused uproar when he told the delegates, "I cannot suffer that this Council should receive traditions and the holy Scriptures with an equal acceptance of faith. To speak my mind, this is ungodly!"

concerning salvation could be found in Scripture, even if some of them were *also* in tradition.

This very condensed account of how the Council of Trent arrived at its decree on Scripture and tradition shows that there was a rainbow-variety of positions, and much debate, within the Roman Catholic Church about its theology and its response to the Reformation.

The Council then went on to debate and approve decrees which stated that the Roman Church was the only body capable of interpreting divine revelation, that the Latin Vulgate was the supreme and authoritative text of Scripture (more so even than the Hebrew and Greek originals), and that the apocrypha was divinely inspired and part of the Old Testament canon.[20]

The Council next set forth its decree on the doctrine of justification, which denied that it was by faith alone; but it explained "justification" in a way that no Protestant would have understood the term:

> "Justification itself... is not only forgiveness of sins, but also the sanctification and renewal of the inward man, through the voluntary reception of the grace and gifts by which an unrighteous person becomes righteous, and an enemy becomes a friend, so that he may be an heir according to the hope of eternal life... For although no one can be righteous unless the merits of our Lord Jesus Christ's passion are communicated to him, yet this is done in this justification of the ungodly, when by the merit of that same most holy passion, the love of God is poured forth, by the Holy Spirit, in the hearts of those who are justified, and is inherent in them. Thus, in this justification, together with the forgiveness of sins, a person receives, through Jesus Christ in whom he is ingrafted, faith, hope, and love, all these infused at the same time. For faith, unless hope and love are added to it, does not

---

20   For the Vulgate and the apocrypha, see Part One, Chapter 9, section 2.

unite a person perfectly with Christ, nor makes a person a living member of His body."

For Trent, then, justification involved not only the non-imputation of sin ("not the remission of sins only"), but the actual personal transformation of the sinner into an inwardly and spiritually holy person, through the infusion of faith, hope, and love into the soul by the Holy Spirit.

Trent also asserted that, "the sole formal cause is the righteousness of God, not that by which He Himself is righteous, but that by which He makes us righteous, that is, the righteousness with which we are endowed by Him, by which we are renewed in the spirit of our mind. Thus we are not only reputed [declared], but are truly called righteous, and are righteous, receiving righteousness within us, each one according to his own measure, which the Holy Spirit distributes to every one as He wills, and according to each one's personal disposition and co-operation." The section ended with the statement that believers, having received this inner righteousness in the new birth, must "preserve it pure and spotless.... so that they may wear it before the judgment seat of our Lord Jesus Christ, and may have eternal life".

Trent also passed a series of anathemas against what it deemed Protestant errors about justification. However, these anathemas were aimed at straw men; Trent constantly (perhaps wilfully) misinterpreted Protestants as teaching that there was nothing more to salvation than a naked remission of sins. The most awesome anathema was in canon 11: "If anyone says that human beings are justified either by the sole imputation of Christ's justice, or by the sole remission of sins, to the exclusion of grace and the love which is poured forth in their hearts by the Holy Spirit and is inherent in them, or even that the grace by which we are justified is only the favour of God, let him be anathema." Since by "justified" Trent meant the whole process of salvation, this anathema condemned only those who would claim forensic justification in the absence of sanctification.

From a Protestant standpoint, the fundamental error of Trent on justification was its insistence that when Scripture used the word "justification" it meant *both* justification *and* sanctification – a denial of the forensic nature of justification, so important to Protestant theology. Also Protestants rejected Trent's view that salvation was based on the believer's inherent infused righteousness rather than in the imputation of Christ's righteousness, so that sinners were declared righteous because God had made them inwardly righteous.[21] Finally Trent's teaching that faith does not make a person a living member of Christ, unless hope and love are added, meant either a denial of justification by faith alone (in favour of justification by faith, hope, and love), or else a definition of "faith" which made it into a bare and fruitless mental assent which must be spiritually enlivened by hope and love (which no Protestant would have understood "faith" to be).[22]

Trent's decree on justification also contained a passage which some Protestants have interpreted as the official rejection of Augustinian theology by the Roman Catholic Church. The passage is found in chapter 5 of the decree:

> "The Council furthermore declares that in adults, the begin-
> ning of this justification is to be derived from the prevenient
> grace of God, through Jesus Christ, that is to say, from His
> calling which is addressed to them without any merits exist-
> ing on their part. Thus those who by sins were alienated from
> God are disposed, through His quickening and assisting
> grace, to convert themselves to their own justification, by
> freely assenting to and co-operating with that grace. This
> happens in such a way that, while God touches the human
> heart by the illumination of the Holy Spirit, a person is not

---

[21] As even modern Roman Catholics have pointed out, there is nothing very wonderful about God *declaring* righteous those who *are* personally righteous. In Scripture, justification is amazing because God declares the *ungodly* righteous.

[22] In other words, Trent separated out some of the essential ingredients of Protestant "faith" and made them into different virtues, "hope" and "love", leaving "faith" as little more than intellectual belief in the truth.

utterly passive when he receives that inspiration, since he is also able to reject it; yet he is not able, by his own free will, without the grace of God, to move himself to righteousness in His sight. Thus, when it is said in the sacred writings, 'Turn to Me, and I will turn to you' [Zechariah 1:3], we are reminded of our liberty; and when we answer; 'Convert us, O Lord, to You, and we shall be converted' [Lamentations 5:21], we confess that the grace of God precedes us."

Some of this passage seems to contradict Augustine's view that the first work of grace in a sinner does not require his cooperation, since he is at that point spiritually dead. However, the language in this passage is so ambiguous and capable of subtle interpretations that it would be hard to pin it down to a rigidly anti-Augustinian meaning.[23] This is especially the case when we know that there were many staunch Augustinians at the Council (all the Dominicans, for a start, who upheld Thomas Aquinas's doctrine that the omnipotent God was the only cause of conversion). It was not until the Jansenist controversy in the second half of the 17th century that Rome gave something like a kiss of death to Augustinianism.[24]

The Holy Roman emperor, Charles V, had hoped the Council would work towards restoring the unity of the Western Church. Things did not seem to be moving in that direction. When the Council delegates started discussing the sacraments, and seemed intent on framing anti-Protestant decrees, Charles lost his temper completely. Pope Paul III transferred the Council from Trent to Bologna, within the papal states where Paul could control the Council more effectively. But the imperialist Spanish delegates refused to leave Trent. The resulting political complications prompted Paul III to adjourn the Council in September 1549.

---

[23] For example, when the passage says that "a person is not utterly passive" in the experience of regenerating grace "since he is also able to reject it", an Augustinian could say, "Quite right. The human will is able to resist grace. The very fact that many resist shows that the will has this ability. But in the case of the elect, God brings it about that their wills won't resist. "

[24] See Part Four for Jansenism.

Stage two: 1551-52

Paul III died shortly after adjourning the Council. In May 1551, pope Julius III (1550-55) reconvened it. Emperor Charles V forced Julius to allow Lutheran delegates to attend, but they wanted to discuss all the decisions made during stage one, something the Roman delegates refused to countenance. Eventually both sides lost patience with each other, and the Lutherans walked out in March 1552. The Council then focused its attention on the sacraments, passing decrees which made any realistic hope of reconciliation with the Protestants impossible. The delegates reaffirmed with great emphasis the traditional later-medieval theology of the sacraments, declaring them to be seven in number: baptism, mass, confirmation, penance, marriage, ordination, and extreme unction. They set forth the doctrine of transubstantiation in uncompromising language. They stated the sacrificial nature of the mass. They affirmed that the cup should be withheld from the laity. And they gave strong expression to the priesthood of the clergy which virtually denied the Protestant understanding of the priesthood of all believers.

This sitting of the Council came to an ignominious end: the assembled delegates fled in panic when the emperor Charles V was humiliated on the battlefield by the Lutheran prince Maurice of Saxony.[25] Fearing for their own safety, the Council members dispersed. They were not to reconvene for ten years.

Stage three: 1562-3

Pope Pius IV (1559-65) judged the time right in January 1562 for the Council to reassemble. There were, however, serious internal difficulties. The new emperor Ferdinand I (1558-64) was far less hostile to Protestants than his elder brother Charles V had been, and he pursued a moderate agenda at the Council. Ferdinand wanted the communion cup to be given to the laity, priests to be allowed to marry, hymns to be sung in worship in the people's native tongue,

---

[25] See Chapter 6, section 1.

the liturgy to be purged of all dubious elements (such as legendary saints), and a stripping down of the papacy's power in favour of ecumenical Councils (the old conciliarist scheme). In this he had the backing of almost all German Roman Catholics and the French bishops. He was, however, opposed both by Pius IV (who could always count on the Italian delegates) and by the Spanish delegates who were ultra-conservative on most issues (except conciliarism).

Pius IV was nothing if not a diplomatic genius. He got around Ferdinand and his supporters by making sure the Council was treated as a continuation of the one first begun in 1545, which meant that all further discussion had to be on the basis of decisions already taken (*e.g.* the withholding of the cup from the laity). Further, Pius insisted that "proxies" were not allowed – delegates had to be present in person; and this meant that the Council was numerically dominated by the papally compliant Italians, who could be present without much difficulty, whereas the French and Spanish had to risk travelling great distances through possibly hazardous terrain. Finally Pius ensured that only papal legates could actually propose resolutions to the Council.

As a result of these manoeuvres, Pius was able to guide the Council to the conclusions he wished. It passed anti-Protestant decrees on the invocation of saints, the veneration of relics, purgatory, requiem masses, and indulgences. The most contentious issue proved to be conflicting views of the authority of bishops in relation to the pope. Many bishops held that their position came directly from Christ, and was not mediated to them through the pope – a kind of "episcopalian" theory. The papacy and its supporters, however, maintained that the pope alone has his position directly from Christ, and that all other bishops derive their position from the pope – a view known as "curialism", after the curia, the name for the papal court. Pius IV wanted the Council to reject the episcopalian view outright, but feeling in support of it was so strong that, despite all his efforts, the best Pius could do was persuade the Council by a five vote majority (71 to 66) to remit the whole question back to the curia for further consideration. Ultimately, though, this proved to be a decisive victory for curialism in the long term. From Trent onwards, there was a slow, creeping growth of curial views of the papacy throughout the Roman Catholic Church, paving the way at length for the First Vatican Council of 1869-71, at which the pope was declared to be infallible when defining any matter of "faith or morals".

One other vitally important decision taken at this final stage of the Council was a decree to establish in every diocese a seminary for the training of priests. The cry for an educated ministry had been close to the heart of the Protestant Reformation; the Roman Catholic Church now took this on board. It would be much harder from now on for critics to claim that the Roman Catholic clergy were ignorant.

The Council was dissolved on December 4th 1563, and the collected decrees from all three stages were given official papal sanction on 24 January 1564 by Pius IV. This was not quite the end of the Council's work, since before dissolving it set up a commission to reform the way that the mass was celebrated. In 1570 the commission finished its work and published the Roman Missal (the liturgical textbook for the mass), whose use was made binding throughout the Church; it remained unchanged until the reform movements of the 1960s which resulted in Roman Catholics abandoning Latin and adopting the congregation's native language for worship.

The Council of Trent was the single greatest landmark of the Catholic Counter-Reformation. It replaced confusion with clarity, and rectified many of the practical abuses in the Church's life – Roman Catholic bishops and priests would no longer be an easy target for Protestant condemnation, at least as far as their moral integrity and education were concerned. For the next 400 years, Trent's formulation of Roman Catholic doctrine would be the standard to which Roman Catholics rallied, and against which all alternative visions of Christianity (especially Protestantism, but Eastern Orthodoxy too) would be measured – and found wanting.

Quite fittingly, then, the Latin name for Trent (Tridentum) became attached to the whole teaching and ethos of the Roman Catholic Church after Trent: *Tridentine* Catholicism. This was to be the type of Catholicism that dominated Rome until the Second Vatican Council of 1962-5.

4. The papacy

The papacy itself had been one of the chief causes of scandal in the Church prior to the Reformation. Erasmus and other humanists had attacked the worldly, immoral popes of the Renaissance with merciless mockery; Luther and the early Reformers had denounced the papacy as the Antichrist. If the Roman Catholic Church was to survive, the papacy itself had to be reformed.

The first signs of renewal came under pope *Paul III* (1534-49). In some ways still a Renaissance pope devoted to art and architecture and opulent feasting, he nonetheless strongly supported the reformist cause within the Roman Catholic Church. In pursuit of this, he promoted Catholic reformers like Contarini to positions of influence, gave official recognition to the Jesuits, and summoned the first meeting of the Council of Trent. He also reorganised the inquisition, making it a more efficient instrument for the discovery and suppression of heresy. The inquisition had, by the 16th century, become largely ineffective outside of Spain; Paul reconstituted it in 1542, and no one was beyond its power, especially in Italy and Spain. Paul's concern for the Church was further demonstrated by his appointment in 1536 of the reform commission, dominated by Catholic Evangelicals, which in 1537 produced the fairly shattering *Consilium de Emendanda Ecclesia*. As we saw, this report was so outspoken in its criticism of abuses that Paul III refused to publish it: he wanted reform, but this kind of damning indictment would, he felt, merely play into the hands of the Protestants. Ultimately, although Paul III did not achieve any spectacular success in his reforming actions, he did set the Church on the path to reform, and everything that happened thereafter flowed from this initial impetus.

Paul III's successor, Julius III (1550-55), fell back into the scandalous ways of the Renaissance popes. He was interested less in genuine reform (despite reconvening the Council of Trent), and more in feasts, hunting, plays, art, and in a 15 year old boy called Innocenzo with whom he was infatuated. Probably the less said about Julius the better. He was followed by Marcellus II, a man of opposite type, a zealous reformer, who died after a reign of only 22 days.

The next pope *Paul IV* (1555-59) carried on the reformist thrust that his short-lived predecessor had begun. Paul IV, one of the Catholic Counter-Reformation's larger-than-life figures, was Giovanni Pietro Caraffa, born in Naples in 1476. Caraffa was originally a Catholic Evangelical, but by the 1550s he had entirely abandoned any sympathy for Luther and become convinced that the Church's survival depended on wiping out the Protestants. As pope Paul IV, Caraffa proved a zealous Catholic reformer, a man of unimpeachable personal morals (no infatuations with teenage boys!), and a fierce enemy of the Protestant Reformation. He did not, however, reconvene Trent, owing to his hostility to councils, which stemmed from his exalted view of his own authority as pope. His papal reign was little short of a tyranny. He waged war on all forms of corruption in the city of Rome, from petty criminals and prostitutes to Catholic Evangelicals and heretics; he lavished time and energy on strengthening the inquisition; and in 1557 (then again in revised form in 1559) he issued the first official Roman "index of forbidden books", which included all the works of Erasmus and all translations of the Bible into any of Europe's native tongues. Paul IV's fanatical and violent intolerance of everything that did not measure up to his standards made him hugely unpopular, and on his death the population of Rome rose up in revolt, smashed Paul's statue, and sacked the offices of the inquisition.

Pius IV (1559-65) was not a great man in any sense, but he turned out to be a great pope, because by brilliant diplomacy he guided the last stage of the Council of Trent to a triumphant conclusion (see section 3). Apart from this monumental achievement, Pius – a mild, easy-going, jovial native of Milan – is also remembered as the pope who made his nephew **Charles Borromeo** (1538-84) a cardinal and archbishop of Milan. Borromeo went on to become one of the spiritual heroes of the Catholic Counter-Reformation: a model bishop of blameless life who devoted himself to reforming his diocese, and founding seminaries, schools, orphanages, and homes for deserted wives.

Pius V (1566-72) was more like Paul IV. A devotee of the inquisition, a grim persecutor of Protestants, witches, homosexuals, and all deviants, he was also a man of extreme ascetic morality. It has been said that he made Rome into one vast monastery. The papacy has never since seriously wandered from this puritanical ethos. Among his other successes he reformed the entire fiscal system of the curia to a high standard of probity and efficiency. In European secular history he is best remembered for his masterminding a military alliance with Venice and Spain which inflicted a decisive defeat on the Ottoman Empire at the naval battle of Lepanto in 1571: a devastating blow to Muslim morale from which it never really recovered. In England he is best remembered as the pope who excommunicated queen Elizabeth I and called upon all loyal English Catholics to disown her – an act which brought great suffering on the English Catholic community, now perceived as potential traitors by Elizabeth's government.

With Paul IV, Pius IV, and Pius V, the papacy was once more in the hands of dedicated Churchmen. Protestants despised their doctrines, but they could no longer accuse the popes of scandalous immorality. And Roman Catholics once more had popes they could honestly respect, who rescued the moral prestige of the papacy from the all-time low into which it had sunk on the eve of the Reformation.

5. The revival in the religious orders

One of the features of the Catholic Counter-Reformation was a blossoming of new religious orders. The greatest of these, the Jesuits, we have already considered. But they were by no means alone. In this section we will look at the other main religious orders that sprang up in the 16th century, and made their contribution to the renewal of Roman Catholicism.

The Oratory of Divine Love

This was a small, intimate group which flourished in Rome in the period 1517-27. It had begun in Genoa around 1500 as a "holy club" for both clergy and laity, but by 1517 it had moved to Rome where it attained its height of influence. There were never more than 50 or 60 people involved, but among them we find some of the leading lights of the Catholic Evangelicals – Contarini, Sadoleto, Morone – and also Giovanni Pietro Caraffa, later to become pope Paul IV (see section 4). The Oratory of Divine Love[26] was cradled in Christian humanism and had a rather quiet, inward-looking temper. Its members believed that the best way to reform the Church was to reform the lives of individual Catholics, and they began with themselves. They were devoted to prayer, confession, mutual exhortation, attendance at mass, and doing charitable works. Although the Oratory of Divine Love never became an official religious order, remaining more informal, it was the first of the new religious associations that were to flower forth in the 16th century, and it provided a fertile atmosphere for the later careers of its more illustrious members. (Note: the Oratory of Divine Love must not be confused with the Oratorians – see below).

The Theatines

The Theatine order was an offshoot of the Oratory of Divine Love. Two members of the Oratory, Caraffa and **Gaetano Thiene** (died

---

[26] An oratory is a chapel where mass may be celebrated.

1547), founded the new order in 1524 at Theate in northern Italy (where Caraffa was bishop – he resigned from his bishopric to join the order). Thiene was a son of the Italian aristocracy who had entered the priesthood; a theologian, philosopher, and expert in Church law, he abandoned a well-paid job in the curia to dedicate his life to the new order. In its ethos, the Theatines were very similar to the Oratory of Divine Love, combining it with a rigorous rule of poverty which forbade even begging for money (this meant they tended draw into their ranks people of independent wealth). Thiene intended the Theatines to be a school for forming new Church leaders, and many Theatines did indeed become bishops. Although (like its parent body, the Oratory) a small body, the Theatines exercised an influence out of all proportion to their numbers, and a contemporary nickname for anyone of strict morality became "Theatine".

The Capuchins

The Capuchins were a reformed branch of the Observant Franciscans, founded in 1528 by **Matteo de Bascio** (1495-1552), from Umbria, the region of northern Italy where Saint Francis had been born. As an Observant Franciscan, Bascio felt an ever stronger identification with Francis, which inspired him to start his own movement within the Observants in 1525. It also produced the new movement's name: Bascio believed that Francis had worn a certain kind of hood, a pointed cowl, which in Italian is *cappuccino* – hence Capuchin, from the hoods of the new order.[27] Initially Bascio had hoped to reform the Observants from within, but opposition led to the movement becoming separate in 1528. The Capuchins were marked out by their extreme asceticism (*e.g.* walking barefoot, sleeping on planks), a violent and theatrical style of preaching, and the radical simplicity and plainness of their church interiors. Apart from the Jesuits, no other order of the Catholic Counter-

---

[27] For most of us, *cappuccino* means espresso coffee topped with steamed milk or cream. This is because in Italy the colour of the coffee was thought to resemble the colour of a Capuchin friar's gown, and so was nicknamed cappuccino coffee. This worldwide fame was no doubt of a type not anticipated by Bascio.

Reformation was so dedicated to preaching and evangelism, and the Capuchins did much to bind the loyalties of the Italian masses to Rome. However, the order underwent a crisis that almost ended its existence in 1542, when its then leader (vicar general), Bernadino Ochino, defected to Protestantism.[28] The Capuchins weathered this storm, recovered, and became one of the great religious orders of the 16th and 17th centuries, especially active in charitable work, preaching, overseas missions, and as chaplains to Roman Catholic political and military leaders.

The Barnabites

The founder of the Barnabites was *Antonio Maria Zaccaria* (1502-39) of Cremona (northern Italy), a doctor who entered the priesthood in 1528. Passionately committed to ministering to prisoners and the sick, it was nonetheless his preaching that proved Zaccaria's greatest gift. So he moved from Cremona to nearby Milan, one of northern Italy's principal cities, where in 1530 he founded the new order. It was given official recognition by pope Clement VII in 1533, and Paul III in 1535 granted them exemption from episcopal authority. The order's real name was the "Clerks Regular of Saint Paul": their rule obliged them to study Paul's letters. They became known, however, as "Barnabites" after their church of San Barnaba in Milan, their headquarters from 1545. They soon spread across Italy, France, Bohemia, and the Roman Catholic regions of Germany, aiming (in the words of their rule) to "regenerate and revive the love of the divine worship, and a truly Christian way of life by frequent preaching and the faithful administration of the sacraments."

The Somaschi

The Somaschi were founded by *Girolamo Emiliani* (1481-1537), nicknamed "Miani", a native of Venice. Originally a loose-living soldier, two remarkable deliverances from imprisonment and illness turned his mind to religion, and he entered the priesthood in 1518,

---

[28] See Chapter 5, section 3.

devoting himself to caring for the poor, the sick, and orphans. It is not certain when he founded the Somaschi – some time between 1528 and 1532. It was at first a close-knit little community based in Somascha (hence the group's name), an obscure village near Milan. Miani's rule for the community specified ministry to the poor, sick, and orphans as its chief work, after Miani's own pattern. After Miani's death in 1537, the community faced a doubtful future; they amalgamated with the Theatines in 1547-55, but at length pope Pius V recognised them as a distinct order in 1568. It spread thereafter into Switzerland, France, and Austria, and became famous for its youth education facilities.

The Ursulines

This was an order for women founded by *Angela de Merici* (1474-1540). Born at Desenzano in northern Italy, she was a model of piety from her childhood. As the 16th century dawned, she conceived it as her mission in life to educate young girls in the Catholic faith, and founded a school in Desenzano for this purpose. The Ursuline order, however, did not come into existence until 1535, in Brescia (near Desenzano); named after Angela's patron saint, Ursula, it began as a community of twelve virgin women, dedicated to the education of young girls. Historically, this was the first female "teaching order" to be set up. It received papal recognition from Paul III in 1544, and in 1572 the Ursulines became a full monastic order. They spread throughout Italy, France, and the Roman Catholic parts of Germany, and were soon found in the Americas and the far East too as part of the Counter-Reformation missionary movement. Using educational methods that majored on rewards rather than punishments and were concerned equally with the physical and mental well-being of pupils, the Ursulines enjoyed huge success in training a whole new generation of girls to be virtuous, pious, capable Roman Catholic wives and mothers.

The Oratorians

Not to be confused with the Oratory of Divine Love, the Oratorians were founded by *Philip Neri* (1515-95), one of the greatest saints

of the Catholic Counter-Reformation. Neri was a native of Florence. After a good humanist education, he began to feel some
special divine calling which inspired him to cut himself off from his
family and live in Rome, where for 17 years (1533-50) he lived as a
layman who nonetheless gave his time and energy to works of
charity and exhorting everyone he met to love and serve God. In
1548, he formed the "Confraternity of the Most Holy Trinity", a
group devoted to prayer, religious discussion, and caring for
Rome's pilgrims and sick people. In 1551 Neri finally entered the
priesthood, joining a team of priests at the Church of Saint Girolamo in Rome. He held informal meetings in his room, and these
evolved into the "spiritual exercises" that formed the Oratorians'
ethos. The exercises included open dialogue based on the reading
of particular books (such as mystical writings and lives of the
saints), and the singing of hymns to a high musical standard.[29] Neri
had an oratory built atop the Church of Saint Girolamo, and it
seems that the group took its eventual name from this. From 1564
there was another community under Neri's direction at the Church
of Saint Giovanni in Florence. In 1575 pope Gregory XIII gave
official recognition to the movement as "the Congregation of the
Oratory".

The Oratorians were at the opposite end of the spectrum from the
Jesuits in character. Where Ignatius Loyola emphasised structure,
discipline, and obedience, Neri extolled the virtues of individual
freedom and personal self-direction. He infused his own personality
into the Oratorians: Neri was a remarkably cheerful man, with a
great sense of fun, who believed that the truest spiritual development must emerge freely from within the individual rather than be
imposed by external constraints. So he discouraged the taking of
vows, and insisted on the independence of each Oratorian community. Of all the saints of the Catholic Counter-Reformation, he
deserves the nickname that he acquired, "the lovable saint". Not
that this made him any less opposed to the Protestant Reformation;
but he opposed it with his own weapons of gentleness, affection,
and humour.

---

[29] This gave rise to the musical form known as the "oratorio".

6. The new spirituality

The Catholic Counter-Reformation witnessed a new upsurge of spirituality within Roman Catholicism. Some of the figures involved we have already considered, such as Ignatius Loyola, whose *Spiritual Exercises* had such a profound influence. Other figures, however, were just as influential in their own way, even though they founded no new religious order. Most of them were Spanish; and among the greatest were two of the 16th century's most colourful and fascinating characters, Teresa of Avila and John of the Cross.

Teresa of Avila

Teresa of Avila (1515-82) – full name Teresa de Cepeda y Ahumada – was born at Avila in Castile. After being educated by Augustinian nuns, she entered the Carmelite convent in Avila (the break with her family she described as a "death"). She soon fell seriously ill, and the medical treatment worsened her condition; although Teresa recovered to a degree, she was never really well again. Despite her monastic life, it took a long time for Teresa to become single-minded in consecration to God. This happened in a landmark experience in 1555 while she was praying in front of a statue of Christ's scourging. From that point onwards, Teresa was a new person, not least because of the intense spiritual feelings she underwent, which involved visions and voices. The most famous of these came in 1560, when she records how an angel appeared to her and pierced her heart with a flaming spear, which produced an ecstasy of divine love. The occasion is celebrated in Bernini's great statue, *Ecstasy of Saint Teresa*, in the Cornero Chapel in Rome. We should not, however, think that Teresa made a cult of these experiences. Indeed, she warned against any such form of spirituality: true piety, she insisted, lay not in "shedding tears, in feeling those spiritual pleasures and that sweetness which are normally so much desired, but in serving God in righteousness, strength of soul, and humbleness".

After Teresa's awakening, she began to hanker after a more strict observance of the Carmelite rule. This desire bore fruit in 1562 when she founded the new convent of Saint Joseph in Avila. Eventually Teresa founded 17 new convents, both for nuns and for friars, and their more rigorous observance of the Carmelite rule earned them the name of "Discalced Carmelites" ("discalced" means "barefoot"). The Carmelite establishment did not take kindly to this reforming activity, and Teresa and her co-workers (the most famous being John of the Cross – see below) often suffered harassment and sometimes violent persecution. At one point, only the personal intervention of king Philip II of Spain saved Teresa and her plans from the abusive maltreatment of Spain's papal nuncio.[30] Teresa and her movement weathered the storms, and the Discalced Carmelites eventually both survived and flourished as a reformed branch of the Carmelite order.

Teresa's wider impact came through her writings. These have become classics of mysticism: *The Way of Perfection*, *The Interior Castle*, and her *Life*, an autobiography that has been compared to Augustine's *Confessions* for its intimate and captivating revelation of a soul's pilgrimage. Teresa tells her own story, and teaches her wisdom, in a manner that combines an exalted spiritual penetration with a disarming down-to-earth informality and practical sense. She was the first to give a detailed analytical account of the different stages of prayer, and in particular to describe spiritual states in between meditation and ecstasy. True prayer, she taught, was possible only when a person totally renounced and forgot all thoughts of self, because God can fill only a soul that has emptied itself of created things. The prayer of the heart was more important than the prayer of the lips; and through silent inner prayer, the soul could be united with God in love – the state of "spiritual marriage". The greatest single influence on Teresa's mysticism was probably Augustine, especially the *Confessions*, but she also relied much on her confessor, **Domingo Banez** (1528-1604), a prominent Domini-can theologian who taught at Salamanca university. Banez was

---

[30] A nuncio is an ambassador of the pope to a particular country. His duty is to deal with relations between the papacy and the country's secular government.

noted for his outspoken defence of the Augustinian theology of Thomas Aquinas on grace and free will against the more Semi-Pelagian views of the Jesuits.

John of the Cross

Teresa's greatest disciple was Juan de Yepez y Alvarez, better known as *John of the Cross* (1542-91). Born in Hontoveros, after a childhood spent in poverty he studied in a Jesuit college at Medina, but joined the Carmelites in 1563. He met Teresa in 1567, and from then onwards was co-founder with her of the Discalced Carmelites. The forces of reaction in the Carmelite order that disliked the new movement vented their fury with special ferocity on John; he was imprisoned from December 1577 to August 1578 and tortured cruelly (flogged so often that his clotted blood glued his clothing to his flesh). Yet it was during this period that John started writing the *Spiritual Canticle*, one of his mystical masterpieces. His escape from prison in 1578 has been ascribed to a miraculous providence. He unscrewed the lock on his cell door, sneaked past the guard, and climbed down from a high window with a rope made of blanket strips. All he had with him was the poetry he had written. Without the slightest idea where he was, he followed a dog which led him to a convent, and the nuns hid him in their hospital from his pursuers.

Further experiences of persecution lay ahead, but by the time of his death John's personal qualities had conquered the hearts even of his enemies. His writings – *The Ascent of Mount Carmel*, *The Dark Night of the Soul*, *The Living Flame of Love*, *The Spiritual Canticle*, and a collection of *Poems* – were literary as well as spiritual classics. John was well trained in the theology of Thomas Aquinas, and his discussions of the life of the spirit showed a rare blend of logical and doctrinal clarity with passionate feeling, imagination, and verbal melody. His spiritual poems rank with the greatest Spanish poetry. Theologically the two master influences that stood out on John's pages were the Bible and Aquinas's *Summa Theologiae*: the first he knew by heart and could extol in an almost Protestant fashion ("If we are guided by divine Scripture, we shall not be liable to err, for He who speaks in it is the Holy Spirit"), the second he knew more intimately than most professional Thomist theologians have done.

John's spiritual teaching was similar to Teresa's, but presented differently, with more intellectual acuteness and more poetry. The way to perfect union with God, John said, lay first through "active purification", which involved a renouncing not only of sin but of self, so that a person drank up humiliation like water, and then through "passive purification", in which God alone worked to complete the process in chosen souls by means of trials, especially inward ones (described by John very grimly – "the understanding is in darkness, the will barren, memory without remembrance, the affections of the soul lost in grief and anguish"). As if to make up for this bleak portrait of the "dark night of the soul", John depicted the state of perfected union with God in words that haunt and enchant. The centre of the soul was, in this state, like a crystal struck by a beam of sunlight; it was drenched in light, wounded by God's beauty with a wound that brought ecstatic joy, burning with divine love.

John's works were first published after his death in 1619 at Alcala, but in an imperfect form. A proper scholarly edition was finally published in 1912-14.

Other figures in the new spirituality

Both Teresa and John were living proofs that a mystic could at the same time be a practical person of action who achieved much in the world. They were not, however, alone in pioneering the new spirituality. *John of Avila* (1499-1569) was another influential figure. A native of Almodovar del Campo in southern Spain, he is best known as the "apostle of Andalusia". Originally intending to be a missionary in America, the archbishop of Toledo persuaded him instead to be a home missionary in Andalusia, the southern-most region of Spain. John's work here lasted from 1529 to 1554, with one year as a prisoner of the inquisition (1532-3) under suspicion of being unbalanced in his mysticism and his severity towards the rich on behalf of the poor. John attracted a wide circle of admirers, including Teresa of Avila and Luis of Granada (see below). His greatest written work was his *Hear, O Daughter*, which went through various authorised and unauthorised editions; its apparently Protestant-leaning emphasis on confident trust in God's mercy through the merits of Christ caused one edition to be placed on the index of forbidden books in 1559. Still, this treatise (written in the first instance as spiritual counsel for a young nun), together with John's letters, found many appreciative readers in the 16th and 17th centuries.

Luis of Granada (1504-88) was a Spanish Dominican who after 1550 spent almost all his time in Portugal, where he held high office among the Portuguese Dominicans and acquired a great reputation as a spiritual guide. His masterpieces were the *Book on Prayer and Meditation*, and the *Guide for Sinners*, where he set forth a spirituality based partly on Savonarola and Erasmus, stressing the inner life of grace and strongly downplaying the role of external rites. Luis wrote the most eloquent Spanish, which gave his spiritual writings a huge and probably unparalleled circulation; but the *Book on Prayer and Meditation* and the *Guide for Sinners* both ended up on the index of forbidden books in 1559. Later editions, revised to met the concerns of the inquisition, ensured the continued circulation of his works, which were translated into Italian, French, and English.

Luis de Leon (1528-91) was another important influence; born at Belmonte in Aragon (north-eastern Spain), he joined the Augustinian order when he was 14 and became professor of theology at Salamanca university in 1560. Here he clashed with the authorities over the status of the Vulgate: Leon, a humanist scholar of the highest calibre, refused to treat the Vulgate as the sole authoritative text of Scripture, insisting on his right to consult the Hebrew and the Septuagint as well. This seemed to fly in the face of the Council of Trent's decree on the supremacy of the Vulgate, and Leon ended up in the prisons of the inquisition for four years. Eventually acquitted, he resumed his university lectures with a defiant, "As I was saying the other day..." His abiding fame rests on his theological and devotional writings.

A friend and admirer of Teresa of Avila, Leon wrote her life and produced an edition of her works, but also composed his own brilliant mystical poems which have secured his permanent place in both the spiritual history of the Catholic Counter-Reformation and the literary history of Spain. The most celebrated of these were *The Prophecy of Tagus*, *The Life of the Fields*, *The Serene Night*, and *Hymn on the Ascension*. On the basis of such poems, the most famous of all Spanish authors, Cervantes, declared that Leon was "a genius who astounds the world and who, in ecstasy, might rob us of our senses".[31] Leon's prose has been almost equally praised as among the most beautiful that 16th century Spain has to offer; in English translation it is best known in his work *The Names of Christ*. His *The Perfect Home* was a long-cherished work on the virtues of a Christian wife.

Through these and other leaders, the new spirituality spread far and wide within Counter-Reformation Catholicism, well beyond the borders of their native Spain. It was introduced into France, for example, in the following generation by great figures like Francis de Sales (1567-1622), Pierre de Berulle (1575-1629), and Vincent de Paul (1580-1660).[32]

7. Roman Catholic expansion outside Europe

The 16th century witnessed a vast expansion of Roman Catholicism outside Europe owing to the colonial empires so rapidly built by the two great powers of Iberia – Spain and Portugal – in the Americas, Africa, and India. In 1492 the West Indies were discovered by **Christopher Columbus** (1451-1506), an Italian mariner in the service of the Spanish monarchy. Altogether Columbus made four

---

[31]   Miguel Cervantes (1547-1616) was the author of *Don Quixote*.
[32]   Their story will be told more fully in Part Four.

voyages (1492-93, 1493-96, 1498-1500, and 1502-04), which opened up the Americas for exploration and colonisation by Spain and Portugal, and later by other European powers such as England, France, the Dutch Republic, and Denmark. In the period covered by this book, the coast of north America was discovered in 1497 by *John Cabot* (dates of birth and death historically unknown), another Italian but this time in the service of the English king, Henry VII. America was named after *Amerigo Vespucci* (1451-1512), yet another Italian, whose explorations and reports of the American coast made the new continent widely known in Europe.[33]

Also in 1497, the Portuguese mariner *Vasco da Gama* (1469-1524) discovered the sea route to India and the East by sailing round the Cape of Good Hope (the extreme southern tip of Africa), which at a stroke made obsolete the whole complicated business of over-land caravans to convey Eastern goods to the West. To ward off conflict between Spanish and Portuguese forces, in 1493 pope Alexander VI officially divided up the New World between the two nations, an arrangement modified in the treaty of Tordesillas in 1494. Spain received Mexico, Peru, and the West Indies, settlements in Columbia and Panama, and outposts in California and Chile; Portugal received Brazil, West Africa, Mozambique, India, and Ceylon, parts of the Persian Gulf, and the Malay archipelago south of China (the Philippines, however, were conquered by the Spanish in 1564 and named after king Philip II of Spain). Mass colonisation followed this parcelling out of these regions.

The Spanish and Portuguese arrived in the Americas as conquering armies first, with the missionaries coming afterwards in their wake. For the indigenous inhabitants, it was little short of a disaster. The Iberian armies ("conquistadores", conquerors) were half pirates bent on plunder, half crusaders intent on destroying the paganism of the natives and imposing Roman Catholic Christianity as the one true faith. We should not underestimate this crusading ardour: it was as real as the religious enthusiasm that had taken the medieval

---

[33] North America had been discovered by Vikings from Greenland in the late 10th – early 11th centuries, but no permanent Viking colonies were established.

Crusaders into the Holy Land to wage war against Islam in the name of Christ. With astonishing speed, the European invaders overthrew America's Aztec and Inca empires in the early decades of the 16th century. The Spanish general Hernando Cortés destroyed the Aztec empire in Mexico in 1519-21; Francisco Pizzaro, another Spaniard, vanquished the Inca empire in Peru in 1532.

After this abrupt and ruthless conquest, the land was flooded by Dominican and Franciscan missionaries, who shepherded the native Americans into Roman Catholic Christianity through mass baptisms, while the Spanish "crusader" troops destroyed their pagan idols and temples. It certainly resulted in the Christianising of the indigenous people and their culture, but often only at surface level. The old pagan ways persisted, dressed up in a Christian guise. Still, there was a genuine seriousness in Spain about bringing Christianity to the native Americans. The Spanish monarchy's grant of land to colonists in Florida was fairly typical:

> "Whereas our chief intent in the discovery of new lands is that the inhabitants and natives, who are without the light or knowledge of faith, may be brought to understand the truth of our holy Catholic faith, that they may come to a knowledge of it, and become Christians and be saved, and this is the chief motive that you are to have and hold in this affair, and to this end it is right that religious persons should accompany you, by these grants I empower you to carry to the specified land the religious persons whom you may judge necessary, and the vestments and other things required for the observance of divine worship; and I command that whatever you shall thus spend in transporting the religious persons, as well as in maintaining them and giving them what is necessary, and in their support, and for the vestments and other articles required for divine worship, shall be paid entirely from the rents and profits which in any manner shall belong to us in the specified land."

However, despite these idealistic words, a huge practical problem was the social and political oppression to which the native Americans were subjected by their Spanish masters. Wherever Spain conquered, the natives in particular districts were given into the power of a colonist, who had the right to tax them and demand their labour, in return for which he was obligated to protect them and Christianise them. The system produced great injustice, and the native Americans often rebelled, massacring the Dominican and Franciscan missionaries. This of course provoked savage reprisals and even harsher oppression. The Spanish settlers regarded the natives as inferior beings, fit only to be ruled by the superior Spanish Christians: a view devoutly upheld by many Spanish theologians. Many of the missionaries collaborated in this "white supremacist" attitude. Some, however, did not. The Dominican **Antonio de Montesinos** protested vigorously on behalf of the native Americans:

> "Tell me, by what right or by what justice do you keep these Indians[34] in such brutal and horrible bondage? By what right do you wage such hateful wars on these people, who lived gently and peacefully in their own lands, where you have wiped out infinite numbers of them with unprecedented murders and devastation? Why do you keep them so burdened and exhausted, not giving them enough food, not looking after them when they are ill? By your extreme demands for work, they become ill and die, or rather, you kill them by your lust to dig up and acquire gold on a daily basis. What care do you take to give them religious instruction so that they come to know their God and Creator, or that they be baptised, hear mass, or observe holy days and Sundays? Are they not human beings? Do they not have rational souls? Is it not your duty to love them as you love yourselves?"

Montesinos spoke thus in a sermon preached in Santo Domingo (the Spanish colony on the West Indian island of Hispaniola) on

---

[34] The native Americans were called Indians because Columbus and the first explorers mistakenly believed that America was India.

Christmas day in 1511. The sermon provoked outrage among the colonists, although Montesinos's Dominican superiors refused to take any action against him, and Montesinos ended up back in Spain defending himself before king Ferdinand. Ferdinand passed the matter to a special council, which conceded that native Americans were by nature free, not slaves, but decreed that nothing should in practice be done to disturb the existing state of affairs in the colony. Disillusioned, Montesinos returned to South America and devoted himself to (successful) evangelism on the island of Puerto Rico, east of Hispaniola. He was the first Christian champion of the rights of the native Americans.

More famous and more effective was **Bartholomew de Las Casas** (1474-1566), a priest who joined the Dominican order because he approved of the stand taken by men like Montesinos. Las Casas devoted his life to campaigning for just treatment of native Americans. He argued strongly against any use of compulsion in evangelism; non-Christian kingdoms had to be respected as legitimate, not seen as mere booty for Christian crusaders, and the only true method of conversion was by peaceful preaching and persuasion and the attractive example of holy living. One fruit of Las Casas's struggle was a guarantee in 1542 that the Spanish and the native Americans were to be given equality under the law as fellow human beings. Strangely, in spite of Las Casas's enlightened attitude to the native Americans, he did not extend the embrace of human brotherhood to the black Africans shipped to America as slaves.[35]

In the East, the Jesuits spearheaded the missionary thrust. The trailblazer was **Francis Xavier** (1506-52), a Spanish noble of charming manners and appealing simplicity of character, Ignatius Loyola's intimate friend.[36] Xavier headed East to India in 1541, at the request of king John III of Portugal. Arriving in Goa (the centre

---

[35] The importation of black African slaves to America began in 1510-11.

[36] Usually pronounced "Zavier", although if his Spanish birth is to count for anything, it should be pronounced "Hab-ee-air".

Francis Xavier (1506-52)

of Portuguese operations) on the eastern coast of India in 1542, Xavier dedicated the next 10 years to preaching in India, Malaysia,[37] Maluku,[38] and Japan. An impulsive man who leapt from one project to the next, Xavier then conceived it as his great mission to evangelise in China, but died before he could penetrate the country. He left behind him a host of converts (through mass-baptisms on what many would now regard as the slenderest evidence of conversion), but more important, the infectious example of a heroic life freely spent in missionary enterprise. In Roman Catholicism, Xavier is seen as the greatest missionary since the apostles. His work in Japan certainly paved the way for the phenomenal expansion of Roman Catholic Christianity in that land in the latter half of the 16th century. Many Jesuits would follow in Xavier's Eastern footsteps, with results which were to transform Christian missionary thinking and ignite fierce controversy: but we must leave that story for Part Four.

8. Effects of the Catholic Counter-Reformation

We can summarise the effects of the reform movement with Roman Catholicism as follows:

(i) The triumph of the papacy. The Catholic Reformation strengthened the papacy against its internal enemies, both conciliarists (who gave highest place to an ecumenical Council) and imperialists (who looked to the Holy Roman emperor). The popes had managed the Council of Trent masterfully. It also restored the public reputation of the papacy from the depths of scandal in which it had been mired as the 16th century began its course. The popes were once again grand, impressive spiritual figures, worthy successors to the apostle Peter in the eyes of the Roman Catholic faithful,

---

[37] Then called Malaya.
[38] Then called the Moluccas.

with something of the aura of Hildebrand and Innocent III about them.[39]

(ii) The definition of doctrine. The Council of Trent had authoritatively clarified the teaching of Rome: Roman Catholic theologians now had a standard of doctrine to use, promote, and defend against Protestants. A new sense of theological self-confidence returned to Roman Catholicism after the initial upheavals and tormenting uncertainties in which Rome had wallowed after 1517.

(iii) The flourishing of spirituality. Roman Catholicism was once again producing great saints and masters of the spiritual life – Ignatius Loyola, Philip Neri, Teresa of Avila, John of the Cross. With such holy men and women abounding, no committed Roman Catholic doubted that his Church was the home of a divine sanctity, God's true Spirit-indwelt Church on earth.

(iv) The recovery of zeal. A fresh enthusiasm returned to the Roman Catholic Church. The moribund institution of the early 16th century, which had so disgusted even its friends, was now on fire with a heroic zeal to recreate its spiritual empire in Europe, and to spread Christianity into the newly discovered or newly colonised lands of America, Africa, and the far East. Morale had been mightily reborn among a once dispirited army, and nothing seemed impossible.

In the first shock-waves of the Protestant Reformation, the question had been: can Rome survive? As a result of the Catholic Counter-Reformation, a new question arose: can Protestantism survive?

---

[39]   See Part Two for Hildebrand and Innocent III, the two greatest popes of the Middle Ages.

Important people

The Church   *Others*

Popes   John Cabot (dates unknown)
Paul III (1534-49)   Christopher Columbus (1451-1506)
Paul IV (1555-59)   Amerigo Vespucci (1451-1512)
Pius IV (1559-65)   Vasco da Gama (1469-1524)
Pius V (1566-72)

Catholic Evangelicals
Juan de Valdes (1500-1541)
Gasparo Contarini (1483-1542)
Albert Pighius (1490-1542)
Benedetto de Mantova (died 1546)
Jacob Sadoleto (1477-1547)
Gregorio Cortese (1483-1548)
Reginald Pole (1500-1558)
Johann Gropper (1503-59)
Girolamo Seripando (1493-1563)
Giovanni Morone (1509-80)

The new religious orders
Girolamo Emiliani (1481-1537)
Antonio Maria Zaccaria (1502-39)
Angela de Merici (1474-1540)
Gaetano Thiene (died 1547)
Matteo de Bascio (1495-1552)
Ignatius Loyola (1491-1556)
Diego Laynez (1512-65)
Philip Neri (1515-95)
Peter Canisius (1521-97)

The new spirituality
John of Avila (1499-1569)
Luis of Granada (1504-88)
Teresa of Avila (1515-82)

Luis de Leon (1528-91)
John of the Cross (1542-91)

The overseas missionaries
Antonio de Montesinos[40]
Francis Xavier (1506-52)
Bartholomew de Las Casas (1474-1566)

Others
Cassiodoro de Reina (1520-94)
Charles Borromeo (1538-84)
Domingo Banez (1528-1604)

The Regensburg Colloquy: The joint statement on justification

1. No Christian should doubt that after the fall of our first parent all human beings are, as the apostle says [Ephesians 2:3], born children of wrath and enemies of God and thereby are in death and slavery to sin.

2. Likewise, no Christian should question that nobody can be reconciled with God, nor set free from slavery to sin, except by Christ the one Mediator between God and human beings, by whose grace, as the apostle said to the Romans [6:17f], we are not only reconciled to God and set free from slavery to sin, but also made sharers in the divine nature [2 Peter 1:4] and children of God.

3. Likewise, it is quite clear that adults do not obtain these blessings of Christ, except by the prevenient movement of the Holy Spirit, by which their mind and will are moved to hate sin. For, as Saint Augustine says, it is impossible to begin a new life if we do not repent of the former one. Likewise, in the last chapter of Luke [24:27], Christ commands that repentance and forgiveness of sin should be preached in his name. Also, John the

---

40   His dates of birth and death are historically unknown.

Baptist, sent to prepare the way of the Lord, preached repentance, saying: "Repent, for the kingdom of heaven is drawing near" [Matthew 3:2]. Next, the human mind is moved toward God by the Holy Spirit through Christ, and this movement is through faith. Through this [faith], the human mind believes with certainty and without doubt all that God has transmitted, and also with full certainty and without doubt assents to the promises made to us by God who, as stated in the psalm [144:13], is faithful in all His words. From there a person acquires confidence on account of God's promise, by which he has pledged that He will remit sins freely and that He will adopt as children those who believe in Christ, those (I say) who repent of their former life. By this faith, a person is lifted up to God by the Holy Spirit, and so he receives the Holy Spirit, remission of sins, imputation of righteousness, and countless other gifts.

4. So it is a reliable and sound doctrine that the sinner is justified by living and efficacious faith, for through it we are pleasing and acceptable to God on account of Christ. And living faith is what we call the movement of the Holy Spirit, by which those who truly repent of their old life are lifted up to God and truly appropriate the mercy promised in Christ, so that they now truly recognise that they have received the remission of sins and reconciliation on account of the merits of Christ, through the free goodness of God, and cry out to God: "Abba, Father." But this happens to no one unless also at the same time love is infused which heals the will so that the healed will may begin to fulfil the law, just as Saint Augustine said. So living faith is that which both appropriates mercy in Christ, believing that the righteousness which is in Christ is freely imputed to it, and at the same time receives the promise of the Holy Spirit and love. Therefore the faith that truly justifies is that faith which is effectual through love. Nevertheless it remains true, that it is by this faith that we are justified (that is, accepted and reconciled to God), inasmuch as it appropriates the mercy and righteousness which are imputed to us on account of Christ and His merit, not

on account of the worthiness or perfection of the righteousness imparted to us in Christ.

5. The one who is justified receives righteousness, and through Christ also has inherent righteousness, as the apostle says: "you are washed, you are sanctified, you are justified," *etc.* [1 Corinthians 6:11]. This is why the holy fathers [of the early Church] made use of "to be justified" even to mean "to receive inherent righteousness". Nevertheless the faithful soul depends not on this, but only on the righteousness of Christ given to us as a gift, without which there is and can be no righteousness at all. And so by faith we are justified or reckoned to be righteous, that is, we are accepted through His merits and not on account of our own worthiness or works. And on account of the righteousness inherent within us we are said to be righteous, because the works which we perform are righteous, according to the saying of John: "whoever does what is right is righteous" [1 John 3:7].

6. Fear of God, patience, humility, and other virtues ought always to grow in the regenerate, because this renewal is imperfect and enormous weakness remains in them. Nevertheless it should be taught that those who truly repent may always hold with most certain faith that they are pleasing to God on account of Christ the Mediator. For it is Christ who is the propitiator, the High Priest, and the One who prays for us, the One the Father gave to us and all good things with Him.

7. Seeing that in our weakness there is no perfect certainty and that there are many weak and fearful consciences, which often struggle against great doubt, nobody should be excluded from the grace of Christ on account of such weakness. Such people should be earnestly encouraged boldly to set the promises of Christ against these doubts and by diligent intercession to pray that faith may be increased, according to the saying: "Lord, increase our faith" [Luke 17:5].

8. Likewise, every Christian should learn that this grace and this
   regeneration have not been given to us so that we might remain
   idle in that stage of our renewal which we at first obtained, but
   so that we may grow in everything into Him who is the Head.
   Therefore the people must be taught to devote effort to this
   growth which indeed happens through good works, both internal and external, which are commanded and commended by
   God. To these works God has, in many passages from the
   Gospels, clearly and manifestly promised a reward on account
   of Christ – good things in this life, as much for the body as for
   the soul (as much as seems right to divine providence) and, after
   this life, in heaven. Therefore, although the inheritance of eternal
   life is due to the regenerate on account of the promise as soon as
   they are reborn in Christ, nevertheless God also renders a
   reward to good works, not according to the substance of the
   works, but to the extent that they are performed in faith and
   proceed from the Holy Spirit who dwells in us, free choice con-
   curring as a partial agent.

9. The joy of those who have performed more and better works
   will be greater and more abundant on account of the increase in
   faith and love in which they have grown through exercises of
   that kind.

10. Now those who say that we are justified by faith alone should at
    the same time teach the doctrine of repentance, of the fear of
    God, of the judgment of God, and of good works, so that all the
    chief points of the preaching may remain firm, as Christ said:
    "preaching repentance and the remission of sins in My name"
    [Luke 24:47]. And that is to prevent this way of speaking ["faith
    alone"] from being understood other than has been previously
    mentioned.[41]

---

[41] I have taken this translation almost entirely from Tony Lane, with his kind
permission. See A.N.S.Lane, *Justification by Faith in Catholic-Protestant
Dialogue: An Evangelical Assessment* (T&T.Clark, 2002).

The Council of Trent on Justification

Chapter 3: **Those who are justified through Christ.**
But even though He died for all, yet all do not receive the benefit of His death, but only those to whom the merit of His passion is communicated. For truly human beings, if they were not born the children of Adam's seed, would not be born unjust, since by that Adamic ancestry they contract unrighteousness as their own when they are conceived. So also, if they were not born again in Christ, they never would be justified, since in that new birth there is bestowed upon them, through the merit of His passion, the grace by which they are made righteous. For this benefit the apostle exhorts us always "to give thanks to the Father, who has made us worthy to share in the condition of the saints in light, and has delivered us from the power of darkness, and translated us into the Kingdom of the Son of His love, in whom we have redemption, the remission of sins" [Colossians 1:12-14].

Chapter 4: **A description of the justification of the ungodly, and of how it is accomplished under the law of grace.**
By these words, a description of the justification of the ungodly is indicated, as a transferral from that state in which humanity is born a child of the first Adam, to the state of grace, and of the adoption of the sons of God, through the second Adam, Jesus Christ our Saviour. And this transferral, since the time the gospel was first announced, cannot be effected without the washing of regeneration, or the desire for it, as it is written: "Unless a man is born again of water and the Holy Spirit, he cannot enter into the Kingdom of God" [John 3:5].

Chapter 5: **On the necessity, in adults, of preparation for justification, and the origin of this justification.**
The Council furthermore declares that in adults, the beginning of this justification is to be derived from the prevenient grace of God, through Jesus Christ, that is to say, from His calling which is addressed to them without any merits existing on their part. Thus those who by sins were alienated from God are disposed, through

His quickening and assisting grace, to convert themselves to their own justification, by freely assenting to and co-operating with that grace. This happens in such a way that, while God touches the human heart by the illumination of the Holy Spirit, a person is not utterly passive when he receives that inspiration, since he is also able to reject it; yet he is not able, by his own free will, without the grace of God, to move himself to righteousness in His sight. Thus, when it is said in the sacred writings, 'Turn to Me, and I will turn to you' [Zechariah 1:3], we are reminded of our liberty; and when we answer; 'Convert us, O Lord, to You, and we shall be converted' [Lamentations 5:21], we confess that the grace of God precedes us.

Chapter 6: The manner of preparation.
Now adults are disposed to this righteousness in the following way: They are stirred up and assisted by divine grace, they conceive faith by hearing, and they are freely moved towards God, believing those things to be true which God has revealed and promised. They especially believe this, that God justifies the ungodly by His grace, through the redemption that is in Christ Jesus. They understand themselves to be sinners, and turn themselves through the fear of divine justice (which gives them a profitable shock) to consider the mercy of God. They are raised to hope, trusting that God will be propitious to them for Christ's sake, and they begin to love Him as the fountain of all righteousness. They are therefore turned against sin by a certain hatred and detestation, that is, by that penitence which must be practised before baptism. Lastly, they resolve to receive baptism, to begin a new life, and to keep the commandments of God.

Concerning this disposition it is written: "He who comes to God must believe that He is, and is a rewarder of those who seek Him" [Hebrews 11:6]; and, "Be of good cheer, son, your sins are forgiven" [Matthew 9:2]; and, "The fear of the Lord drives out sin" [Ecclesiasticus 1:27]; and, "Do penance, and be baptised every one of you in the name of Jesus Christ, for the remission of your sins, and you shall receive the gift of the Holy Spirit" [Acts 2:38]; and, "Going, therefore, teach all nations, baptising them in the name of the Father, and of the Son, and of the Holy Spirit" [Matthew 28:19]; finally, "Direct your hearts to the Lord" [1 Samuel 7:3].

Chapter 7: **What the justification of the ungodly is, and what its causes are.**
This disposition, or preparation, is followed by justification itself, which is not only forgiveness of sins, but also the sanctification and renewal of the inward man, through the voluntary reception of the grace and gifts by which an unrighteous person becomes righteous, and an enemy becomes a friend, so that he may be an heir according to the hope of eternal life.

Of this justification the causes are these: The final cause indeed is the glory of God and of Jesus Christ, and eternal life. The efficient cause is the merciful God who washes and sanctifies gratuitously, sealing and anointing with the Holy Spirit of promise, the pledge of our inheritance. The meritorious cause is His most beloved only-begotten, our Lord Jesus Christ, who, when we were enemies, because of the great love with which He loved us, merited justification for us by His most holy passion on the wood of the cross, and made satisfaction for us to God the Father. The instrumental cause is the sacrament of baptism, which is the sacrament of faith; without this faith no one was ever justified. Lastly, the sole formal cause is the righteousness of God, not that by which He Himself is righteous, but that by which He makes us righteous, that is, the righteousness with which we are endowed by Him, by which we are renewed in the spirit of our mind. Thus we are not only reputed, but are truly called righteous, and are righteous, receiving righteousness within us, each one according to his own measure, which the Holy Spirit distributes to every one as He wills, and according to each one's personal disposition and co-operation. For although no one can be righteous, unless the merits of our Lord Jesus Christ's passion are communicated to him, yet this is done in this justification of the ungodly, when by the merit of that same most holy Passion, the love of God is poured forth, by the Holy Spirit, in the hearts of those who are justified, and is inherent in them.

Thus, in this justification, together with the forgiveness of sins, a
person receives, through Jesus Christ in whom he is ingrafted, faith,
hope, and love, all these infused at the same time. For faith, unless
hope and love are added to it, does not unite a person perfectly with
Christ, nor makes a person a living member of His body. For which
reason it is most truly said, "Faith without works is dead" [James
2:17] and profitless; and, "In Christ Jesus neither circumcision, nor
uncircumcision, are of any avail, but faith which works through
love" [Galatians 5:6, 6:15]. Before the sacrament of Baptism,
catechumens ask the Church for this faith, in conformity with a
tradition of the apostles, when they ask for the faith which bestows
eternal life, which faith cannot bestow without hope and love. Thus
they also immediately hear that word of Christ: "If you wish to
enter into life, keep the commandments" [Matthew 19:17]. Therefore, when receiving true and Christian righteousness, immediately
on being born again they are commanded to preserve it pure and
spotless, as the best robe given them through Jesus Christ in place
of the robe which Adam, by his disobedience, lost for himself and
for us, so that they may wear it before the judgment seat of our
Lord Jesus Christ, and have eternal life.

**Chapter 8: In what manner it is to be understood that the
ungodly person is freely justified by faith.**
When the apostle says that a person is freely justified by faith, those
words are to be understood in the sense which the perpetual consent
of the Catholic Church has held and expressed, namely, that we are
said to be justified by faith because faith is the beginning of human
salvation, the foundation and the root of all justification, without
which it is impossible to please God and to come into the fellowship of His sons. But we are said to be justified freely, because none
of those things which precede justification – whether faith or work
– merit the actual grace of justification. For, "If it is by grace, it is
no longer by works, otherwise" [as the same apostle says] "grace is
no longer grace" [Romans 11:6].

Chapter 9: **Against the vain confidence of heretics.**

Although it is necessary to believe that sins are forgiven, and were only ever forgiven, freely by the mercy of God for Christ's sake, yet it must not be said that sins are forgiven, or have been forgiven, to anyone who boasts of his confidence and certainty of the forgiveness of his sins, and rests on that alone. For this confidence may exist, indeed it does in our day exist, among heretics and schismatics, and this vain confidence, which is alien to all godliness, is preached with great vehemence in opposition to the Catholic Church. Again, it must not be asserted that those who are truly justified must, without any doubt whatever, settle within themselves that they are justified, and that no one is absolved from sins and justified, except the one who believes for certain that he is absolved and justified. Nor must it be said that absolution and justification are brought about by this faith alone, as though a person who does not have this belief were doubtful of the promises of God, and of the efficacy of Christ's death and resurrection. For just as no godly person ought to doubt the mercy of God, the merit of Christ, and the virtue and efficacy of the sacraments, even so each person, when he considers himself, and his own weakness and indisposition, may fear and be anxious about his own grace, since no one can know that he has obtained God's grace with a certainty of faith which cannot be subject to error.

> The decrees of the Council of Trent, Session 6 [1547], Decree on Justification

The Spiritual Exercises of Ignatius Loyola

Second week: The summons of the earthly king helps us to contemplate the life of the eternal King.

Prayer. The preparatory prayer will be the usual one.

First Preliminary. The first preliminary is a picture, visualising the place. Here it will be to see with the eyes of imagination the synagogues, towns, and villages through which Christ our Lord went preaching.

Second Preliminary. The second is to ask for the grace which I want. Here it will be to ask our Lord to give me grace that I may not be deaf to His summons, but ready and zealous to carry out His holy will.

First Heading. The first heading is to imagine a human king chosen by God our Lord, one whom all Christian princes and people honour and obey.

Second Heading. The second is to imagine this king addressing all his people thus: "It is my purpose to subdue to myself all the land of unbelievers. Therefore, whoever wishes to come with me must be content to eat as I eat, and to drink and dress and so forth as I do. He must also work as I do during the day and keep watch as I do during the night, and so forth, so that afterwards he may share with me in the victory, as he has shared with me in the hardships."

Third Heading. The third is to think about the response that loyal subjects ought to make to a king so generous and so kind. Also think about how, if anyone refused the appeal of such a king, he would deserve to be denounced by the whole world, and be counted a gutless knight without honour.

The second part of this exercise consists in applying this parable of the earthly king to Christ our Lord, in harmony with the three headings.

First Heading. Regarding the first heading, if we take seriously such a summons by an earthly king to his subjects, how much more seriously must we take it when Christ our Lord, the eternal King, challenges the entire world, and to each individual in particular calls and says: "It is My purpose to subdue all the world and all enemies, and in this way to enter into the glory of My Father. Therefore, whoever wishes to come with Me must labour with Me, so that following Me in the hardships, he may also follow Me in the glory."

Second Heading. The second is to grasp that all those who have understanding and reason will offer themselves completely to this labour.

Third Heading. The third is this, that those who wish to be more devoted and to distinguish themselves in full service to their eternal King and universal Lord, will not be satisfied merely to offer their persons to the labour. Acting against their own sensuality and against their fleshly and worldly affection, they will offer things of greater value and importance, saying:

> "Eternal Lord of all things, in the presence of Your infinite goodness, and in the presence of Your glorious Mother and of all the saints of Your heavenly Court, by Your grace and assistance I make this offering: I wish and desire, and it is my deliberate resolution, if only it works for Your greater service and praise, to imitate You in enduring all injuries, all abuse, and all poverty of spirit and of body too, if Your most holy majesty is willing to choose and accept me into such a life and state."

First Note. This exercise should be carried out twice in the day; namely, in the morning on getting up, and an hour before dinner or the evening meal.

Second Note. For the second week and thereafter, it will be very helpful to read at various times from the *Imitation of Christ* or the Gospels, and from lives of the saints.

Ignatius Loyola, *The Spiritual Exercises*, sections 91-100.

The castle of the soul

I was praying to our Lord today, asking Him to speak through me, but I could not find a thing to say. I had no idea how to begin carrying out the duty laid upon me by my monastic obedience.[42] However, a thought came to me which I will now write down, so that I have some basis on which to build. I began to think about the soul as though it were a castle: a castle built from a single diamond or from a very clear crystal. There are many rooms in this castle, just as there are many mansions in heaven. Now if we think about this carefully, sisters, the soul of a righteous person is indeed a paradise, in which God finds His delight (as He tells us). What do you think a room will be like, when it is the delight of a King so powerful, so wise, so pure, so full of all goodness? I cannot find anything with which to compare a soul's great beauty and its great capabilities. No matter how sharp our intellects may be, they will no more be able to grasp the soul than grasp God; for He created us in His image and likeness, as He Himself says. Now since this is so, it is a waste of time to weary ourselves in trying to understand the beauty of this castle. For though it is God's creation, and is as different from God as a created thing from the Creator, His Majesty nonetheless says it is made in His image; and this means that we can scarcely have any idea of the soul's great worth and beauty.

If through our own fault we do not understand ourselves, or do not know who we are, this is very pitiful, and a cause of great shame. Would it not be a token of terrible ignorance, my daughters, if you asked someone who he was, and he could not say – if he had no idea who his father and mother were, or what country he came from? That would great idiocy. But our own is indescribably worse, if we do not try to find out what we are: if we only know that we are living in these bodies, and have some vague idea (because we have heard about it, and because the Christian faith tells us so) that we have souls. We hardly ever think about what good qualities there may be in our souls, or Who has taken up residence within them, or what value our souls possess. So we concern ourselves

---

[42] Teresa is referring to her duty of instructing the nuns under her care.

very little with conscientiously preserving the soul's beauty. Our feelings are all focused on the rough setting of the diamond, the outer wall of the castle – in other words, on our bodies.

Now then, imagine that this castle houses many mansions: some above, others below, others at the sides. In the centre and hub of them all is the foremost mansion, where the most hidden things pass between God and the soul. Ponder this illustration very carefully; perhaps God will condescend to use it to reveal to you something of the favours which He graciously grants to souls, and of the different kinds of favour, so far as I understand such things. For there are so many divine favours that nobody can possibly understand them all, especially not someone as senseless as I. If the Lord grants you these favours, it will be a great comfort to you to know that such things are possible. But if you never receive any, you can still praise His great goodness. It does us no harm to think of the things stored up for us in heaven, and of the joys of the saints, but rather moves us to rejoice and to labour towards those joys ourselves. Likewise, it will do us no harm to discover that in this our state of earthly exile, God in all His greatness can have fellowship with such stinking worms as we are. Indeed, this makes us love Him for His unbounded goodness and mercy!

If you find it unpleasant to realise that God can grant such favours to other people during this our exile, but not to you, you must surely be very lacking in humility and in love of your brother or sister. How can we help rejoicing that God should grant these favours to one of our brothers or sisters, since this in no way prevents Him granting them also to ourselves? Indeed, how can we not rejoice that His Majesty should give an understanding of His greatness to anyone at all? Sometimes our Lord does this simply to reveal His power, as He said of the blind man to whom He gave his sight, when the apostles asked Him if the man was suffering for his own sins or the sins of his parents. He grants these favours, then, not because those who receive them are more holy than those who don't, but in order that His greatness may be made known. We see this in the case of Saint Paul and Mary Magdalen. He does it so that we may see Him at work in His creatures, and praise Him for it.

Teresa of Avila, *The Interior Castle*, First Mansion, section 1.

The sin of pride

A secret pride often comes to those who are starting out on the spiritual path. They become satisfied with themselves and what they are doing. They begin to think of themselves as rich, because of their spiritual fervour and their exertions in godliness. (Even so, it is still the true nature of holiness to produce humility.) Because of the imperfection in these spiritual beginners, they feel a need to speak about spiritual things in the presence of others, and even to teach where they ought to be learning. This is owing to their conceit. They condemn in their hearts those who do not have the spiritual devotion which they themselves are aspiring to. Sometimes they even speak like the pharisee who praised God for his good works and scorned the tax collector.

The devil often works in such people to get them to behave in these ways more and more, so that their pride and arrogance grow. For the devil knows that spiritual activities carried out in this spirit are not only worthless but a breeding ground for sins. These people can sink into such evil that they think no one else except themselves is good! So whenever the opportunity arises they condemn and denigrate others by word and by deed, seeing the speck of sawdust in their brother's eye but ignoring the plank sticking out of their own eye. They strain out someone else's gnat and swallow their own camel.

Sometimes, when their spiritual overseers – perhaps their monastic superiors, or their priestly confessors – do not approve of their attitude or conduct, they assume it is because they are being misunderstood. Their only concern is to win applause and be highly regarded. Because their overseers don't approve or don't agree with them, they conclude that the overseers themselves must be unspiritual. So they crave and seek another, one who better suits their taste. Their aim is to speak about spiritual things with someone who will praise them. They shun like death those who point out their errors and try to guide them to a safer path. Indeed, they may even feel a rankling resentment against such people. And so, having too high a view of themselves, they naturally expect almost everything and accomplish almost nothing. They wish sometimes to show others how great their own spirituality and godliness are, to demonstrate it to the eyes and ears of others with gestures and sighs and so on. Sometimes they experience spiritual ecstasies in public instead of in solitude. The devil gives them a helping hand in these experiences. They are so delighted to get noticed, and they yearn for this recognition more and more.

John of the Cross, *The Dark Night of the Soul*, Book One, chapter 2.

The methods of the inquisition: a Spanish agent's report

In obedience to Don Francis d'Alua, in Montpelier – a French town – I kept company with a number of Lutherans who have close contacts with Spain. My purpose was to find out if they ship their literature to Spain, or know of heretics living there. To gain this information in an opportune way, without drawing attention to myself, I pretended to be a heretic myself. I let them believe that I wanted to get some books, such as the writings of John Calvin and Theodore Beza, and take them to Spain. I said I was afraid of the Spanish inquisition, so I did not dare to buy the books in Spain. If they wished as believers to help me in this matter, I would take back some books of their religion with me. Then I said I would send the books to several ladies and other friends who had fervently asked for them. A bookseller and a merchant agreed to bring the books in secret to Barcelona, to the home of one of their friends there who shared their faith.

I had to use a thousand deceptions to get hold of this information. At length, Don Francis gave me permission to purchase a number of the heretical books, and the merchant agreed to take them to Barcelona. To save money he will send them in the middle of Lent to the house of one of their friends. He gave me a letter of introduction. Don Francis, I assume, has already told you the other details. He permitted me to proceed to Barcelona to expose this false movement. I discovered the names of all the merchant's friends, for he told me that they shared his faith. I am staying here and awaiting the books in order to promote the affair in service to God and your majesty.

True evangelism: Christ's way is not violent

Divine providence sets forth only one single way of teaching a living faith to everyone, everywhere, at all times: it is the way that wins over the mind with reasons, and wins over the will with mildness and invitation. This way has to be applied to all the people of earth, making no distinction on account of sects, errors, evil itself...

Divine wisdom and providence lie behind this way and method, fashioned by Christ and commanded by Him in preaching and teaching His gospel and faith to all without distinction, everywhere, in all times, from the time of His ascension into heaven until He returns in judgment. This way and method wins over the mind with reasons, and the will with mildness and invitation. So divine providence and wisdom lie behind this way of teaching people a living faith, winning over their minds and wills...

It is by means of spiritual weapons that we must bring into being, draw together, establish, and preserve a Christian people. This is the way Christ desired, and still desires, to draw together, establish, increase, and preserve the people over whom He desired to exercise a spiritual dominion, so that they would become His people by faith, hope, and love, the virtues that belong only to a free soul. He conquers by spiritual arms, by means of a gospel message that overflows with light, gentleness, kindness, by means of the sacraments, by means of the Holy Spirit's actual and habitual grace...

The contrary way, obviously, would be if a group charged with preaching the gospel to pagans, or to send preachers to them, decided they could carry out their task more quickly and effectively if they subjugated the pagans (whether they liked it or not) to Christian political power. The Christians could then preach to the pagans without any problem once they had conquered them physically. And of course the Christians would not then force the pagans to believe, but appeal to their minds and woo them gently – once the pagans' instruments of political strength had been removed by conquest.

But no pagan in possession of his senses, especially a pagan ruler, is going to surrender political power to a Christian people or a Christian king. War would be inevitable. And war brings cannon fire, ambushes, lawless and indiscriminate coastal raids, violence, insurrections, scandals, corpses, massacre, murder, looting, parents and children torn apart, slavery, the desolation of states and king-doms, of nobles and local rulers, the destruction of cities, towns, countless human beings...

What pagan would want to hear about our faith and our Church, if we have inflicted frightful injury by the brutal burden of war – the savage, intolerable waste of war?... It would be perfectly reason-able for such pagans to be eternally hard-hearted, unrelenting, hostile, unteachable, and utterly opposed to listening to anything called "Christianity", and to be foes to that name for time to come.

From Bartholomew de Las Casas, *The Only Way*

Jesuit missionary work: Francis Xavier in India

I announce the Ten Commandments, which the people repeat. Then together we all say: "Jesus Christ, Son of God, give us the grace to love You above all things." After asking for this grace, we then say the Our Father together, and then in harmony we cry out, "Holy Mary, mother of Jesus Christ, acquire grace for us from the Son so that we may be able to keep the First Commandment!" Next we say

the Hail Mary, and then we carry on in the same way through all
the other nine of the Commandments. Just as we recited twelve Our
Fathers and Hail Marys in honour of the twelve articles of the
Creed, likewise we say ten Our Fathers and Hail Marys in honour
of the Ten Commandments, and ask God to grant us grace to live
up to them...

As I go about my business, visiting the Christian villages, I pass by
many pagodas [pagan temples]. In one of them lived more than two
hundred bragmanes [an ancient name originally applied to the
Indians living around the river Ganges]. They came out to meet me
and we discussed many issues, during which I asked them this
question: "What do your gods and idols, whom you worship,
command you to do in order to be saved?" They argued a lot about
which of them should give me a reply. The task alighted on their
oldest member, in his eighties, who said he would answer if I
would first tell him what demands the Christian God made on His
followers. I saw that his words were malicious, so I refused a
response until he had answered my question. This exposed his
ignorance. He replied that the gods gave two commandments for all
who wished to enter their heaven; the first was not to kill cows but
to worship the gods themselves as they were manifest in the cows,
and the second was to give charitable gifts to the bragmanes who
served the pagodas. When I heard this, sadness overwhelmed me
that the devil should exercise such power over our fellow human
beings, drawing to himself the worship that belongs only to God.
So I leapt up, told the bragmanes to sit down, and then with a loud
voice I recited to them the Creed and the Commandments in their
own language, pausing a short time after each commandment. Then
I gave an exhortation (still in their language) about heaven and hell,
explaining who would end up in which place. When my sermon
was over, the bragmanes all got up and warmly embraced me,
saying that the God of the Christians was really the true God,
because His Commandments were so much in harmony with all
that sound reason taught.

Francis Xavier, letter dated 15th January 1544.

Chapter 9.

THOU HAST THY MUSIC TOO: THE EASTERN ORTHODOX WORLD.

It is all too easy, when studying the Reformation, to forget the parallel world of Eastern Orthodoxy. This is partly because there was nothing comparable to the Protestant Reformation, or the Catholic Counter-Reformation, in Eastern Europe; Orthodoxy's story in our period is far less dramatic and earth-shaking. It is also partly because Protestants and Roman Catholics have become accustomed to asking of any person or country or movement in the 16th century, "Was it pro-Reformation or pro-Rome?" To this question, the Eastern Orthodox answer is, "Neither," and this has robbed it of much of its interest for many Westerners. However, if we are to understand the Eastern world of the "Reformation era", we have to stop asking those biased theological questions, and indeed to stop thinking of it as the "Reformation era". That is a useful way of describing Western Europe at that time. It is not even a remotely useful way of describing Eastern Europe. It was a different world: one that we must learn to see and appreciate in its own unique terms.

1. Greek Orthodoxy under the Ottoman Turks

As we saw in Part Two, the Byzantine Empire finally fell to the Ottoman Turks in 1453. Constantinople, the great Christian city built by the first Christian emperor of Rome, Constantine the Great, was now under the yoke of Islam. A thousand years of Byzantine civilisation were at an end. How did Greek Orthodoxy survive the Islamic conquest?[1]

The sultan (king) of the Ottoman empire at this juncture was ***Mehmet II*** (1451-81), sometimes called "Mehmet the Conqueror".[2] A young man of only 23 when he overthrew Byzantium, Mehmet combined ferocity in warfare with a genuine desire to live at peace with Christians once he had conquered them. As was the case in other ancient Christian territory under Muslim domination, the Christians of Byzantium were treated as a single ethnic unit, a *milet*, and bound to a condition of *dhimma* (treaty) which turned them into a body of protected but second-class citizens within the Islamic Empire. Again as in other Eastern Christian lands, the local patriarch was made responsible for the Christian population. Mehmet's first problem, however, was that Constantinople had no patriarch! The previous patriarch, Gregory Mamas, had fled to Italy in 1451, leaving the patriarchal throne vacant. Exercising the usual despotic power of Eastern kings, Mehmet decided to fill the vacancy with a man of his own choice, George Scholarius, who on entering the monastic life had taken the name Gennadius – which meant that, as patriarch, he was now ***Gennadius II*** (born 1405; reigned 1454-56, 1463, and 1464-65; died 1472). However, it took Mehmet a little time to track Gennadius down: after the conquest of Constantinople, he had been taken into slavery by a Muslim, who was so astounded by the Christian's cultured brilliance that the master was heaping unheard-of honours on the slave. Mehmet found Gennadius, ransomed him, and had him installed as new patriarch.

It was an excellent choice. Gennadius was respected by both Christians and Muslims alike. He was the greatest intellectual in Constantinople, admired by ordinary Orthodox people for his

---

[1] I say *Greek* Orthodoxy because the other great ethnic and linguistic branch of Orthodoxy – Slavic Orthodoxy – remained largely free of Islamic domination, in the form of the Russian Orthodox Church. See section 2.

[2] Mehmet is short for Muhammad, so he is sometimes called Muhammad II.

outspoken opposition to the Union of Florence in 1439, when most of the political and spiritual leaders of Byzantium had signed their Church away to the papacy. In fact, Gennadius had at first supported the Union, but was then thoroughly converted to rejecting it by Mark of Ephesus, its foremost opponent.[3] Mark had died in 1444, leaving Gennadius as the champion of Orthodoxy against Rome. This endeared him not only to his own people, but also to Mehmet II, who counted on Gennadius' hostility to the papacy as a guarantee that the new patriarch would not try to enlist Western support against Ottoman rule. In this, Mehmet was fully justified; Gennadius could tolerate submission to the authority of the sultan, but never to the pope.

Gennadius, then, was enthroned as patriarch of Constantinople in January 1454. Mehmet granted him freedom from taxation, liberty of movement, security against being deposed (except by the holy synod, the assembled body of metropolitan bishops within the territory of the patriarchate), and the authority to pass on these rights to the next patriarch. Mehmet also signed a document promising that no more churches would be converted into mosques – as Hagia Sophia, the Church of the Holy Wisdom, Constantinople's chief church, had been in the wake of the Muslim conquest. Unfortunately this document later perished in a fire, and subsequent sultans broke the promise. Since Hagia Sophia was now a mosque, and the other great Byzantine church, the Church of the Holy Apostles, was in a Muslim-dominated area, Gennadius relocated to the Phanar quarter of the city; the new patriarchal church was the Church of the Pammacaristos.

In one way, the Islamic conquest worked to the advantage of the patriarchs of Constantinople. During the 16th century, the Ottoman Empire swallowed up Syria and Egypt, thus taking control of the other three historic Eastern patriarchates of Antioch, Jerusalem, and Alexandria. Owing to the centralised nature of Ottoman government, with the sultan as absolute monarch, it was natural for the

---

[3]   For Mark of Ephesus and the Union of Florence, see Part Two, Chapter 9, section 4.

sultans to want to deal with only one representative of their Christian subjects. As a result, the sultans made the patriarch of Constantinople the intermediary between themselves and all the Greek Orthodox peoples of the Empire, so that the patriarchs of Antioch, Jerusalem, and Alexandria could approach the sultans only through the patriarch of Constantinople. When any of these fell vacant, the sultans simply asked the patriarch of Constantinople to recommend a suitable man for the post. This gave the Constantinople patriarchate unprecedented power over Antioch, Jerusalem, and Alexandria.

Having secured a trustworthy patriarch of Constantinople, Mehmet appointed Gennadius "ethnarch" (pronounced "eth-nark") of all the Greek Orthodox Christians, laity as well as clergy. In other words, Gennadius was to be the official head of the whole "ethnos" (race) of Orthodox Greeks. From now on, the patriarchs of Constantinople would have to be responsible for both the spiritual and secular welfare of their fellow believers: any legal matter that had a religious aspect – marriage, divorce, wills, the care of minors – were now dealt with in the patriarch's courts. Although in one way this was yet another expansion of the patriarch's role and power, in another it was a heavy burden that consumed time and energy which had previously been devoted to spiritual affairs. A far more problematic long-term effect of this consolidation of all Greek Orthodox as an "ethnos" under the patriarch was that it led to an increasing loss of the psychological boundaries between what it meant to be Orthodox and what it meant to be Greek. Hellenism – Greek culture and nationality – became ever more identified with Orthodoxy, and vice versa. This confusion between religion and ethnic culture remains within the Greek Orthodox world to this very day: a fact lamented by a good number of Greek Orthodox spiritual leaders.

Despite the theoretical protected status ("dhimmitude"[4]) of the Greek Orthodox under the Ottoman yoke, they were subject to

---

4   "Dhimmitude" comes from *dhimmi*, an Arabic word meaning "protected". Muslims applied the term *dhimmi* to native non-Muslim populations who surrendered by a treaty (*dhimma*) to Muslim rule.

severe disadvantages which, over time, produced a collective sense of deep ethnic and religious humiliation. No church could be built without Muslim permission, which normally was not granted. No existing church could be repaired without permission. Christians had to wear special clothes marking them out as Christians and (therefore) second-class citizens. No Christian, except the patriarch of Constantinople, could ride on a horse. Any dispute between a Christian and a Muslim had to be settled in an Islamic court, with little or no chance of justice for the Christian. Any overt criticism of Islam was punishable by death. Any Christian who became a Muslim, even against his or her will as a young child or a slave, was automatically liable to the death penalty if he or she turned back to Christianity. (This law was sometimes exploited by unscrupulous Muslims to bring about the death of Christian enemies, simply by claiming that the Christian had expressed a wish to become a Muslim and by producing false witnesses to back up the claim. Many Christian martyrs in the Ottoman Empire went to their deaths by this route.) The Christian population was systematically decimated and demoralised by the Ottoman practice of *devshirme*, "child-gathering": young Christian boys would be taken away from their families, forcibly converted to Islam, and made into soldiers in the sultan's "Janissary" bands, a feared elite body of notoriously brutal troops.[5] To add to the heartache of Christians, their girls were exposed to a similar hazard, often taken away by force to be made part of the harem of a local Muslim dignitary.

Although relationships started off well between the sultans and the patriarchs, with Mehmet's warm and sincere regard for Gennadius, this proved a false dawn. After Gennadius's departure in 1456 (he resigned, fed up with the burdens of office, although Mehmet summoned him back twice in 1463 and 1464-65), things went downhill rapidly. The patriarchate became a mere prize that was bought and sold to enrich the treasury of the sultans and the power-lust of Christians desperate to be patriarch. The sorry process began in 1466, when Symeon of Trebizond paid 2,000 gold pieces to the

---

5   "Janissary" is Turkish for "recruits".

sultan's officials who then commanded the holy synod to depose the resident patriarch, Mark, and install Symeon. Sultan Mehmet's mother, Mara (a Christian), then stepped in, paying Mehmet a further 2,000 gold pieces on behalf of her personal favourite, Dionysius, who was then appointed patriarch. Symeon, however, was determined not to let the prize slip through his fingers; he fought back, in 1471 paying another 2,000 gold pieces as a bribe for the coveted office. Dionysius was duly deposed and Symeon installed. Alas, in 1474 a certain Raphael managed to get himself appointed on an extravagant promise to pay Mehmet 2,000 gold pieces every year! Raphael had difficulty in meeting his financial obligations, and Mehmet threw him out of office in 1477, appointing one Maximus. But Symeon had still not given up, and a few months after the deaths of both Mehmet and Maximus, he bought his way back to the patriarchal throne.

This brief narrative demonstrates the moral degradation which overtook the patriarchate after Gennadius. The bribe money became institutionalised as the *peshkesh*, and even holy men had to pay up if they were to exercise the responsibilities of being patriarch. It was a blight on the patriarchal office, and one that the Orthodox themselves had brought about, in the greed of their less worthy men to be enthroned in Constantinople. As well as degrading the internal life of the Church, it made the sultans very cynical about the integrity of their Christian subjects. Memhet had esteemed Gennadius highly; he looked with derisive contempt on the good man's successors. Sometimes a sultan ordered the holy synod to elect a Christian he happened to like. Sometimes a patriarch who had proved thoroughly acceptable to ordinary Orthodox people was deposed – not necessarily by the sultan, but even by the patriarch's own officials. For another complication was the immense power these officials came to exercise if they belonged to the Greek nobility. They were quite capable of engineering the downfall of a patriarch if he crossed them.

The Islamic conquest inflicted a grave wound on the culture and education of the Greek clergy. A steep decline in standards set in, to such an extent that Western visitors to the Greek East were soon commenting with horror on the sheer ignorance of Orthodox village priests. The Muslim triumph had ended the life of Constantinople's great university; the patriarch's own academy had to step into the breach, not very adequately. All it did was train clergy in strictly religious matters. All other subjects were dropped, with the exception of philosophy at a very elementary level. A sizeable amount of the patriarch's resources had to be channelled into secular concerns, now that he was ethnarch, leaving too little for the upbuilding of the Church, including the education of its priests. The standard education for a Greek Orthodox priest under the Ottoman yoke was to go to a monastery as a boy, to learn how to read and write (but see below), and to memorise a number of religious texts. He received no theological education.

If an Ottoman Greek really wanted a good education of any kind, he generally left the Empire altogether, and went to Venice in northern Italy. (This was easy enough to do, if a Greek could afford it; the sultans raised no objections.) Venice had a Greek colony, initially of merchants, which had been greatly enlarged by Greek refugees fleeing the Muslim onslaught. By the mid 1400s, Venice had become a vibrant hub of Greek culture. In addition, the powerful city-state of Venice was an outstanding centre of religious toleration; it would not permit the inquisition to operate within its territory, except under strict government control that robbed it of almost all its power. The Orthodox could live and worship in Venice without molestation by intolerant Catholics. They could also study at Padua university, which was within Venice's territory, and was the most free and independent-spirited university in Western Europe, untroubled (thanks to Venice) by interference from papacy and inquisition. Padua boasted a thriving department of Greek studies.

The fact, however, that Greek Orthodox subjects of the Ottoman Empire could normally secure a sound education only by temporarily emigrating to Venice reveals the crisis that had afflicted Orthodoxy within the Empire. The only places in the East where Greek

culture survived in a healthy form were the Ionian islands, which
were under Venetian not Ottoman control, and among the great
Greek noble families in Constantinople, called the "Phanariots" from
their living in the Phanar quarter of the city. Beyond these narrow
confines, not only did high educational levels decay among the
Greek Orthodox, but illiteracy became ever more widespread. The
simple ability to read was increasingly lost, even in monasteries and
(especially) nunneries. This in time developed, in some quarters,
into a positive Orthodox "cult" of ignorance and illiteracy; many
monks began to frown on all learning, as thought it were incompatible with the highest spiritual life. Even a friendly witness, an
Orthodox metropolitan of Thessalonica in the 16th century, complained: "not one monk in the diocese knows ancient Greek or
understands the Church prayers." In consequence, a great number
of the monastic libraries, which were treasuries of patristic and
medieval knowledge and wisdom, fell into scandalous neglect.
Monks would use the pages from priceless manuscripts to wrap up
their food! This was a far cry from the glory days of Byzantium,
when spirituality and learning had walked hand in hand.

Some progress was made in the latter half of the 16th century, with
Greeks trained in Padua university nurturing a reform of the
patriarchal academy in Constantinople. Philosophy at last began to
be taught in a full-orbed way. Then in 1593, patriarch Jeremias II
enacted a thorough-going reformation of the academy, so that it
now offered courses in literature and science, as well as theology
and philosophy. But this takes us across the frontiers of this volume
into the 17th century.

It would be wrong, however, to conclude this section on anything
other than a positive note. If the Islamic conquest was in many
ways a catastrophe for Greek Orthodoxy, both in terms of the
political and religious oppression it suffered, and its own internal
decline (loss of probity in the patriarchate, the corrosion of culture
and education), yet in another way the light of Orthodoxy shone all
the brighter. There was a constant stream of martyrs who bore a
faithful blood-witness to their triune God rather than bow the knee

to Allah. These martyrdoms generally came about in one of three ways: a Christian who converted to Islam would rediscover his or her ancestral faith, renounce Islam, and proclaim himself or herself a Christian once more, knowing full well that the penalty was death (usually a horrific death); or a Christian would be falsely accused of having converted to Islam, so that the Islamic court gave him or her the choice of accepting the faith of Muhammad or suffering the punishment of an (alleged) apostate; or sometimes a Christian would be spiritually overcome with a burning desire to bear witness to Christ at the cost of his life. Orthodox leaders tried to discourage this last avenue to the glory of martyrdom, pointing out that the would-be martyr might not be able to endure the tortures that would be inflicted; but if he or she persisted in the thirst for a martyr's crown, and gave evidence of being a sincere Christian in full possession of his or her senses, then a priest or monk would give his blessing and promise to pray for the confessor's coming ordeal.

Pious Greek Orthodox believers gathered together the heroic tales of the "new martyrs of the Turkish yoke", and they became the Greek equivalent of John Foxe's *Book of Martyrs* among English-speaking Protestants, or *The Martyrs' Mirror* among the Anabaptists. There is indeed little in the Greek accounts to distinguish them from the Protestant or Anabaptist martyrdoms, except that the Greek martyrs were facing the power of Islam rather than an intolerant Christianity, and were put to death not for affirming justification by faith or believers' baptism or for denying transubstantiation, but for affirming the Trinity and the deity of Christ and for denying that Muhammad was a true prophet. Still, just as the blood of the Protestant and Anabaptist martyrs fertilised the piety of their co-religionists in the West, so the blood of the Greek Orthodox martyrs was the seed of the Church in the East. No matter how oppressed they were by Islam, and no matter what disarray spoiled the inner life of their Church, the Greek martyrs who died under the Ottoman yoke bore testimony to the continuing spiritual strength of an Orthodox faith that was still capable of inspiring ordinary, obscure men and women (even children) to the heights of loyalty and love towards Christ the God-Man, and whose sacrifice would itself inspire generations of believers to come. (See the end of the Chapter for an account of some of the martyrdoms.)

2. Greek Orthodox theology

There were not many outstanding Greek Orthodox theologians in this period. All we can do is give a brief account of the few whose writings or influence gave them distinction.

Gennadius

The greatest Greek theologian of our period was undoubtedly Gennadius. In some ways, he was a very odd thinker. As we have seen, he led the Orthodox opposition to union with Rome, inheriting the mantle of Mark of Ephesus – that was why Mehmet II had chosen him as his new patriarch. Yet no previous Orthodox theologian had been so profoundly influenced by Western Latin thought. Not only had Gennadius immersed himself in the study of Augustine of Hippo, Duns Scotus, and other Western medieval theologians, notably those belonging to the Franciscan order; he also went one better and virtually took Thomas Aquinas, most brilliant of the Latin scholastic theologians, as his supreme guide.[6] "I doubt whether Thomas has any more fervent disciple than me," he wrote.

One factor which drew Gennadius to Aquinas was their shared reverence for Aristotle. The great Greek philosopher had been "discovered" by the Latin West in the 12th and 13th centuries, but he had never been lost in the East, where he and Plato were exploited in roughly equal measure by Orthodox theology. At any rate, Aquinas's Christian Aristotelianism seemed a thing of beauty to Gennadius. He translated into Greek some of Aquinas's treatises, and wrote a summary of the contents of Aquinas's masterpieces, the *Summa Contra Gentiles* and books one and two of the *Summa*

---

6   For Aquinas, see Part Two, Chapter 7, section 3.

Theologiae. The only areas where Gennadius would not endorse Aquinas were the *filioque* clause, predestination, and the Latin thinker's alienation from the crucial Eastern distinction between God's essence and His energies.[7] Here Gennadius reiterated the traditional Eastern views: he affirmed against Aquinas the *filioque* clause; he rejected Aquinas's Augustinianism by making predestination to salvation conditional on God's foreknowledge of human choices; and he followed Gregory Palamas in distinguishing between the divine essence and the divine energies. For the rest, he forgave Aquinas these blind spots and almost doted on him.

Partly this was because of Gennadius's own highly intellectual personality. He had a mind of the first magnitude; he could not tolerate ignorance or sloppy thinking; and he found in Aquinas a man after his own heart, learned, logical, clear, thoughtful. Along with this seemed to go a good deal of intellectual vanity on Gennadius's part. "No one of all the men now living anywhere knows as much about sacred theology as I do," he blithely wrote!

Gennadius produced a huge number of works on almost every topic, but the most interesting is perhaps his treatise on the *filioque* clause, first published in 1444, with two further revised editions. On the one hand, he argues firmly against the Western view that the Spirit proceeds from the Son as well as from the Father, contending that this would introduce two principles of origin into the Trinity. The Father is the source of the Son and of the Spirit, while Himself having no source; the Father, therefore, is the principle of unity within the Godhead. On the other hand, he was sceptical about erecting into a dogma the Eastern formula that the Spirit proceeds "from the Father alone", even though it had been championed by Photius the Great back in the 9th century.[8] Gennadius here revealed

---

[7]   The *filioque* clause was the added phrase in the Latin version of the Nicene Creed which made it say that the Holy Spirit proceeds from the Father *and from the Son*. It was one of the major causes of East-West division. For the Eastern view of God's essence and energies, most fully taught by Gregory Palamas, see Part Two, Chapter 9, section 3.

[8]   See Part Two, Chapter 3, section 4.

the full force of Eastern conservatism: the Nicene Creed clearly said that the Spirit proceeds "from the Father", but not "from the Father alone". Gennadius opposed the West for adding to the Creed the words "and from the Son"; he did not want to fall into the same trap by adding the word "alone". So he concentrated his energies on a purely negative refutation of the West. Its *filioque* theology was a perilous speculation lacking all creedal authority. As for the Eastern opinion that the Creed must be understood as meaning that the Spirit does not proceed from the Son, but only from the Father, Gennadius said:

> "We do not canonise it; we do not proclaim it publicly, but only in private conversation, for we cannot proclaim that which does not have the acceptance of the universal Church. We must hold fast to the traditional doctrine accepted by all and confess simply that the Holy Spirit proceeds from the Father. To hold anything else is dangerous."

One other work of Gennadius that merits attention is the *Confession of Faith* he wrote at the request of Mehmet II to explain what Greek Christians believed. In fact it contained little or nothing that was distinctively Orthodox, being more of an exercise in "mere Christianity". It dealt with the Trinity, the incarnation, the atonement, the resurrection, and final judgment. He also wrote treatises on providence, predestination, and the origin and nature of the soul (he held that God infused the soul into the embryo on the 40th day after conception).

Manuel of Corinth

Manuel of Corinth (died 1551) was famed in his day for his comprehensive statement of Eastern Orthodox teaching and practice in opposition to Roman Catholicism, although he was also a great hymn-writer and canon lawyer. His magnum opus was a work written against a Dominican theologian named Francis, in which Manuel highlighted the following issues as dividing Orthodoxy from Rome: the *filioque* clause, purgatory, the authority of the papacy, the mode of baptism, the kind of bread used in the eucharist, and divorce.

The last three points may need some explanation. Regarding baptism, the East practised triple immersion, dipping the candidate three times, once for each person of the Trinity; Rome generally practised baptism by affusion, pouring or sprinkling water once on the candidate's head. Regarding the eucharistic bread, the East used leavened bread, while Rome used unleavened. The Roman argument was that unleavened bread had been used in the Last Supper; the Eastern response was to accuse Rome of lapsing into Judaism, maintaining rather that the resurrection of Christ made the use of leaven necessary (leaven is what makes bread rise). Regarding divorce, Rome was totally opposed to it, whereas the East allowed divorce for various reasons (*e.g.* adultery, the husband's impotence, one spouse plotting against the other's life). In fact this issue threw into sharp relief the different approach to morality taken by Rome and by Orthodoxy. The Roman approach thought in terms of absolute moral principles which had to be intelligently applied to numerous situations; the Eastern approach thought more in terms of what was best for the people concerned in any given situation. This of course led to far greater flexibility in the East, which could argue (for instance) that it would be better for a husband and wife who implacably hated each other to separate. This would be a sin against marriage, but it would be an even greater sin for them to stay together and grow in hatred. To Rome (and many Protestants, especially in the Reformed tradition), the Eastern approach seemed woefully anarchic and tending to sheer moral relativism; to the East, the Roman approach seemed harshly rigid and legalistic.

Manuel also wrote an attack on the great Renaissance Platonist, Gemistos Plethon, for remaking Christianity in the image of pagan Platonism,[9] and an interesting treatise on the death of Christ. In this latter, Manuel argued that Christ's human body was deified from the moment of conception, but that the effects of this fleshly

---

9   For Plethon, see Chapter 1, section 2.

deification were suspended in order to permit His body to undergo suffering and death for our salvation. In the resurrection, the full effects of deification flowed into Christ's risen body.[10]

Pachomius of Rhus

Pachomius (died 1553) was a monk in the Saint George monastery on the Ionian island of Zante. His was probably the most cultivated mind among Greek theologians in our period, fully versed in the Scriptures and the early Church fathers. He was deeply concerned over the problem of declining educational standards in the Greek world (see section 1); ignorance, he argued in his treatise _On the Usefulness of Holy Scripture_, was the curse of religion, a curse that had now infected the Greek Orthodox world. It had to be remedied by the dedicated study of Scripture, where the prophetic and apostolic witness to Christ was treasured up. Allied to the problem of ignorance was, in Pachomius's opinion, the disarray that had crept into Greek monasticism. He strongly opposed the increasing abandonment of cenobitic (community) life in favour of a kind of freelance monasticism where the monk was a law unto himself. This chaotic freedom was the enemy of all discipline. Since the monasteries were the life-giving heart of Orthodoxy, Pachomius saw no hope for the future unless true cenobitic discipline was restored. To aid in this work, he collected testimonies from Basil of Caesarea, Gregory the Great, the rule of Athanasius of Trebizond, and others, in order to demonstrate from revered sources the nature and value of monastic community life.

Pachomius also became involved in a stimulating controversy about the proper use of Greek in contemporary theology. At that time, there was one form of Greek – Byzantine or Koine Greek – spoken as a universal language among Greeks, but alongside this there were also various local dialects of Greek. Some theological

---

[10] "Deification" is the normal Orthodox way of understanding salvation. It refers to human nature's participation in the "energies" of God, that is, in the power and activity that eternally stream forth from the divine essence like light from the sun.

writers had started authoring works in their local dialect. Pachomius contested this practice vehemently, arguing in favour of Byzantine Greek as the only appropriate language for theology. He made two major points in this regard. First, Byzantine was the only form of Greek universally understood throughout the Greek world; the use of local dialects would destroy the universal character of Greek theology. Second, Byzantine Greek had over the centuries evolved a highly refined, clear, technical language for theology; there was simply no equivalent in the local dialects. To use the latter would shipwreck theology by launching it adrift in primitive, untested languages, incapable of expressing the truth with the beauty and precision of Byzantine Greek. Pachomius had real grounds for this latter concern in the writings of Joannes Kartanos (see below), whose dabbling in written theology in his local dialect had produced a mish-mash of doctrinal confusion. The debate about theology and language, of course, raised general issues that are still fought over today.

Joannes Kartanos

Joannes Kartanos (dates unknown) was a native of the Ionian island of Corfu, who became a priest-monk and an official of bishop Athanasius of Naupactos. As we just saw, he provoked the wrath of Pachomius of Rhus by writing theology in his local Greek dialect rather than in Byzantine or Koine Greek. The work in which he did this was entitled *Anthos* ("Flower"), which offered an outline of Christianity's basic teachings, a summary of biblical history, the ethics of the New Testament, and an exposition of the Lord's Prayer. Kartanos believed that the bulk of ordinary Greek people could no longer understand the technical language of Byzantine Greek; it was essential to communicate the faith to them in their own everyday language. Unfortunately it seems that his attempt suffered badly from his clumsy use of dialect and his relatively weak grasp of theology. Pachomius accused him of teaching pantheism, the view that God and the universe are identical. This was probably an uncharitable interpretation. We know little else about Kartanos, but his *Anthos* appears to have made a considerable impact on its target audience.

3. Greek Orthodoxy and Roman Catholicism

In Part Two, we saw the stormy relationship between Eastern Orthodoxy and Western Catholicism after the Great Schism of 1054, a tale of mutual misunderstandings, bitter recriminations, reunions engineered by Byzantine emperors but repudiated by the mass of the Orthodox faithful, and the disastrous conquests of Orthodox lands by the Crusaders, culminating in the seizure and looting of Constantinople itself in the Fourth Crusade in 1204. This stormy relationship continued in our period.

Not all of Greek Orthodox territory was under Ottoman control. Some of it was controlled by the Catholic West: the islands of Naxos, Chios, Rhodes, Cyprus, Crete, and the Ionian islands (Zante, Ithaca, Cephalonia, Corfu). Here the situation of the native Orthodox inhabitants was paradoxically different to that of their compatriots in the Ottoman Empire. The Greeks on these Western-held islands were forced to submit to the Catholic Church (they did, grudgingly), but were otherwise left alone. So while Ottoman Greeks had relative religious liberty under Islam but were degraded to second-class citizens politically, the Greeks on the islands lost their religious liberty (albeit not their Christianity) but retained their civil privileges. However, some Greeks on the Western-held islands were subjected to considerable annoyance by their Catholic masters, for example through taxation. It was not an ideal life.

By far the most harmonious Orthodox-Catholic relationships were in the Ionian islands, controlled by liberal Venice. Here the two religious communities not only lived side by side in peace; they even practised intermarriage, and sometimes went to the lengths of taking holy communion in one another's churches.

As the Roman Catholic Church became increasingly caught up in the ferment of the Counter-Reformation in the 16th century, a new disturbing element was added to Orthodox-Catholic relations: the Jesuits.[11] Ignatius Loyola's "shock troops" were active in the Ottoman Empire within a few years of the founding of the Society of Jesus, entering as priests and spiritual advisors to Roman Catholic merchants and ambassadors. They had a threefold aim: to win over individual Orthodox to the Roman faith, to promote a Romanising movement within Orthodoxy, and to prevent Protestantism from spreading into Orthodox territory. The story of this Jesuit-led Catholic penetration into the Orthodox East really gathered pace at the end of the 16th century and on into the 17th, and so lies outside the timeframe of this volume; but it began earlier, and needs to be noticed here. The Jesuits seemed indeed destined for great early success, finding as they did a staunch friend and ally in bishop Metrophanes of Caesarea, who became patriarch of Constantinople in 1565. However, Metrophanes was so obviously pro-Rome that the holy synod lost all confidence in him and deposed him in 1572. Orthodoxy was never to be an easy conquest for the Catholic Counter-Reformation.

One of Rome's most successful strategies in winning over Orthodox clergy either to Roman Catholicism itself, or to a Romanising form of Orthodoxy, was the founding of the College of Saint Athanasius in Rome in 1577. The College was established by pope Gregory XIII for the express purpose of offering a high quality education to Greeks from territories currently or in the recent past controlled by an Italian power. The College was state of the art in its educational methods and facilities; it attracted Greek boys and young men in considerable numbers. The Jesuits who were active in the Ottoman Empire persuaded high-ranking Greek families in Constantinople to send their boys to the College. The effect was as one might have predicted. Some of these young Greeks became Roman Catholics; many more of them (probably the great majority) returned to the Orthodox East as firm friends of Rome, to lead a Romanising

---

[11]   See previous Chapter, section 2.

movement within the theology and spirituality of Orthodoxy. The Jesuits themselves set up their own schools in various parts of the Ottoman Empire, at Pera, Thessalonica, Smyrna, Constantinople itself. Again these schools were centres of the highest academic excellence, and again many of the Greek boys who studied there either became Roman Catholics or pro-Roman Orthodox. Here was the (from an Orthodox viewpoint) cruel legacy of Orthodoxy's own intellectual and cultural decline after the Islamic conquest. Unable to provide education for its own people, it had to see the cream of its youth being captured by the superior resources and services offered by Rome.

4. Greek Orthodoxy and Lutheranism

The story of the contacts between Orthodoxy and Lutheranism forms one of the most intriguing chapters in 16th century religious history. The Lutherans hoped to gain a theological ally against the papacy, which would show that Lutherans could claim the heritage of the ancient Church more truly than Roman Catholics could. After all, one half of the Christian world had never admitted the claims of the papacy. If the new Protestant Churches of the West could strike up a harmonious relationship with these long-standing Eastern foes of the pope, it would add immense prestige to the Reformation. A further impulse, it must be admitted, was the desire of at least some Lutherans to gain a hearing within Orthodoxy for the Lutheran faith, hoping (in effect) to make Orthodox territory into a mission field for Lutheran propaganda.

Philip Melanchthon was the first Lutheran to conceive the idea of ecumenical contact with Orthodoxy, and in 1542 he sent a letter to Antony, the "eparch" (governor) of Corfu and professor of Greek at Milan university in northern Italy, sounding him out about the possibility of Lutheran-Orthodox dialogue. Antony, however, responded unfavourably in 1543. His negativity did not stem so much from religious hostility to Lutherans, as from political hostility: the Lutherans had wickedly divided the Holy Roman

Empire at a time when Western political unity was needed to fight off the Ottoman advance into Eastern Europe. Antony's criticism was rather unfair, given that France, Venice, and the papacy were also allied against the Holy Roman Empire at this juncture, without any taint of Lutheranism!

The next stage in the Lutheran approach to Orthodoxy came in 1558, when a certain *Demetrius Mysos*, an elderly and learned Orthodox deacon from Montenegro, turned up in Wittenberg and charmed everyone. He had come at the bidding of patriarch Joasaph II to investigate the Lutheran faith and take back a report to Constantinople. Melanchthon translated the Augsburg Confession into Greek,[12] adapting its language into a more Orthodox tone, and wrote a letter to patriarch Joasaph, suggesting that Lutherans and Orthodox had much in common. In late 1559 Demetrius returned to Constantinople, carrying with him the Greek version of the Augsburg Confession. Patriarch Joasaph and his advisors were thrown into a quandary by this overture. They wanted friendship with the German Lutheran princes for political reasons (any external ally was welcome who could act as a curb on Ottoman ill-treatment of Greek Christians), but they thought that the Augsburg Confession contained anti-Orthodox heresies. So, in accordance with the time-honoured ways of Eastern diplomacy, they "lost" both the Confession and Melanchthon's letter. The second attempt at establishing Lutheran-Orthodox dialogue thus fizzled out. Demetrius himself embraced Lutheranism, and evangelised the villages of Transylvania and the Slavic territories of the Habsburgs.

The third attempt was more successful. In 1570 the Holy Roman emperor Maximilian II sent as his ambassador to Constantinople a Lutheran named David von Ungnad, who in turn took with him a Lutheran chaplain, Stephen Gerlach. Gerlach struck up a friendship with the young "protonotary" *Theodore Zygomelas* (1544-1614), an official in the patriarchal court, who introduced him to patriarch *Jeremias II* (1572-95). Jeremias, a native of Anchialos on the

---

[12] Some historians think it was the German scholar Paul Dolscius of Plauen who translated the Augsburg Confession into Greek.

shores of the Black Sea, was a learned man, and one of the great patriarchs of our period; he staunchly resisted the Protestant and Roman Catholic influences that were making inroads into Orthodoxy, and played a crucial role in the development of Russian Orthodox Church life (see section 5).

Gerlach put Jeremias in touch with the Lutheran theologian *Martin Crusius* (1526-1607) of Tubingen, Germany's most distinguished teacher of the Greek language. Tubingen university itself was now one of the leading centres of Lutheran theology in Germany. A correspondence ensued, and in 1574 Crusius, acting in concert with *Jacob Andreae* (1528-90), the chancellor of Tubingen university, sent six copies of the Augsburg Confession in Greek to Jeremias. This time, Constantinople could not diplomatically lose the Lutheran letters and Confession, as Joasaph had done in 1559; the imperial ambassador, von Ungnad, and his chaplain Gerlach, were right there in Constantinople awaiting and urging a response. It was still some time in coming; but at last, in 1576, Jeremias wrote back to Crusius and Andreae. His reply was not a private effort, but was drafted in collaboration with Zygomelas and several members of the holy synod, and so had a quasi-official status.

Jeremias went through the Augsburg Confession point by point, affirming what he believed was in harmony with Orthodox teaching, but rejecting what he believed were Lutheran errors. If we limit ourselves to what Jeremias rejected, we find that he had the following problems with Lutheran theology as summarised in Augsburg. He could not endorse the Lutheran principle that the Holy Spirit spoke bindingly through Scripture alone; the Spirit had also spoken through the Councils and the fathers. He objected to the filioque clause in the Lutheran form of the Nicene Creed. He criticised Lutheran baptismal practice: baptism must be by triple immersion, he said, followed by chrismation (anointing with oil). He repudiated justification by faith alone; God will bestow no grace on those who fail to live holy lives, and good works have a parallel importance alongside faith. He disapproved of the Lutherans' Augustinian view of predestination. He insisted that there were seven sacraments, not just two (baptism and eucharist) as the Lutherans said. He maintained that leavened bread must be used in the eucharist, as against the Lutheran preference for unleavened. He disallowed the Lutheran doctrine of Christ's presence in the eucharist; it was weak and inadequate (Jeremias's view was virtually identical with transubstantiation). He disputed the Lutheran notion that many of the Church's rites and ceremonies were indifferent in nature. He condemned the Lutheran concept of the bondage of the fallen will, quoting John Chrysostom against it at some length. He also took the Lutherans to task for denying the invocation of the saints: all the angels and saints in heaven, Jeremias averred, are our mediators and intercessors with God.

After this fairly full-blooded criticism of Lutheran theology, Jeremias went on to make some further points of his own, including the necessity of sacramental confession to a priest if a believer is to make true progress in the spiritual life, and the exalted value of monastic life as the superior pathway to holiness.

When Jeremias's reply arrived in Tubingen, the Lutherans must have been disappointed by its critical nature. However, it was written in an amicable style, and did not dissuade them from continuing the dialogue. Crusius and Lucius Osiander (1534-1604) drafted a response to Jeremias in June 1577. The chief points they made were as follows. The Lutheran view of justification by faith was not in reality very different from Jeremias's; the two sides were using different language but were not teaching incompatible truths. They affirmed the Lutheran belief in the real presence of Christ in the eucharist, although also stating that there was no material change in the bread and wine, which retained their proper nature. They argued that there were only two biblical sacraments; and they persevered in rejecting the invocation of saints.

Jeremias eventually responded in May 1579. This time he was more forthright in his language to the Lutherans. Jeremias set out plainly that Lutheranism taught a number of unOrthodox errors which he could by no means accept. He rejected their belief in the

filioque clause, their view of the bondage of the will and justification by faith, their notion that there were only two sacraments, and
their denial of the invocation of saints and the veneration of icons
and relics. He exhorted the Lutherans to stop introducing novelties
into the faith, and to conform to the interpretation of Scripture that
had been given by "holy tradition" through the Councils and the
fathers.

One must admire the doggedness of the Lutherans. Crusius,
Andreae, Osiander, and Gerlach wrote back to the patriarch in June
1580, determined to pursue the dialogue. They went through the
various controverted points, offering defences of the Lutheran
position on the authority of Scripture, the *filioque* clause (at huge
length), free will, justification by faith, the sacraments, invocation
of saints, and monasticism, quoting where possible not only
Scripture but the fathers in support. It is difficult to see what they
hoped to achieve, except a glaring clarity about Lutheranism's
disagreement with Orthodoxy. Jeremias's reply this time was
relatively brief and brusque. After restating the Orthodox view on
the disputed matters, he said:

> "We ask that from now on you give us no more grief, nor
> write to us on these subjects. In your words you honour and
> exalt the theologians who gave light to the Church, but in
> your deeds you reject them. For you try to prove that our
> weapons are useless, namely, holy and divine works, about
> which we have written to you, exhorting you. Please give us
> rest from these burdens. Go your own way. Do not write to
> us any more about doctrines. If you do write, let it be only
> for friendship's sake. Farewell."

Amazingly, the Lutherans wrote yet again to Jeremias, once more
going over the theological issues that divided them. This time,
Jeremias ignored it. The dialogue was over.

Lutheranism had found that Orthodoxy was neither Roman Catholic
nor Protestant. It was genuinely a third force, a spiritual entity in its

own right, which shared some things in common with the Reformation (notably the rejection of the papacy and of the whole indulgence system), some things in common with Rome (notably the monastic-ascetic impulse and the place of saints, icons, and relics in Christian piety), but could not be assimilated to either. Or could it? The testing time for Orthodoxy in this regard would come in the 17th century.

5. Russian Orthodoxy

While Greek Orthodoxy groaned under the Ottoman yoke, Russian Orthodoxy occupied a vast geographical area eventually matching that of the Ottoman Empire, and here the Orthodox faith flourished, free from Muslim or Catholic domination. Indeed, this freedom gave Russian Orthodox an increasingly exalted view of their place and destiny in God's providential scheme of things. They were convinced that Constantinople, the "New Rome", had fallen to the Turks because of its infidelity to the apostolic faith, as it had flirted with heretical Old Rome in pursuit of military assistance against the might of Islam, instead of trusting in God. And so with the Islamic conquest of Constantinople in 1453, and the end of the Byzantine Empire, it seemed that God's purposes had moved to Russia, and that Moscow was the "Third Rome". This almost messianic sense of Russian Christian identity, however, brought its own problems, as we shall see.[13]

As the 16th century dawned, tension was beginning to simmer within Russian Orthodoxy between two conflicting visions of what the Russian Church ought to be. The two men in whom these visions were embodied were Nilus of Sora and Joseph of Volokolamsk.

---

[13] For the way that Russia under the tsars inherited the mission and symbols of Byzantium, see below.

Nilus of Sora (1433-1508), or Nil Sorsky, belonged to the nobility
of Moscow, but had renounced worldly life, becoming a monk in
the convent of Saint Cyril at White Lake (Belozersk), in northern
Russia (the region above lake Rybinskoye). Nilus became deeply
disenchanted, however, with the White Lake monastery, and
resolved on going to live on Mount Athos.

> "My departure from the White Lake monastery was for my
> own spiritual benefit. Yes, for my spiritual benefit, for I did
> not see that the way of life at White Lake was being
> preserved in accord with God's law and the traditions of
> the fathers. Rather, it was a life in accord with one's own
> will and human notions. There were many people there who
> acted wickedly and yet imagined they were living a godly
> life."

On Athos, Nilus became a hesychast (practising the prayer-
discipline that found its focus in the "Jesus prayer", so ably
expounded and vindicated in the 14th century by Gregory Palamas).[14] He also visited Constantinople, and made a study of the
different types of monasticism, especially the "skete" type which,
until then, he had not come across. A skete (from the Skete region
of Egypt) was a sort of cross between the hermit's way of life and
cenobitic (community) monasticism. A small group of up to 12
monks would live together with a more experienced monk, who
acted as their spiritual director; they would meet together with other
local sketes for joint-services on Sundays and other holy days.
Back on Athos, Nilus conceived it as his mission in life to introduce
sketes into his native Russia.

Nilus's true place in history began, then, when he returned to
Russia, to the area of his old monastic home at White Lake, where
he soon began founding sketes along the Sora or Sorka river – from
which he derived his name "Nilus of Sora" (or "Sorsky"). Nilus
and his monks built monastic cells in the forest, around a central

---

[14]   For Gregory Palamas and hesychasm, see Part Two, Chapter 9, section 3.

church. Each cell housed no more than three men. The monks gathered together in the church on Saturdays, Sundays, and festival days; on the other days, each worked and prayed in his own cell. Nilus drew up a strict rule for skete life (see end of Chapter), which expressed his devotion to puritan simplicity of life and worship: there must be no adornments made of silver in church, he declared, even for the eucharistic vessels, and the healthy monk must wear himself out with fasting, thirst, and manual labour. By the time of his death in 1508 at the age of 76, Nilus had become widely known as a holy man and spiritual leader, deeply revered by many Russian bishops.

Nilus and his monks emerged as champions of a school of thought in Russian Orthodoxy called the "Non-Possessors" (or "Transvolgans", from their location north of the river Volga). Their ideal was a Church free of the materialistic burdens of property and unsullied by any entanglement with politics or the state. In some ways they remind us of the Franciscans.[15] They especially disliked the monastic ownership of land (one third of all Russian land) and of villages, where peasants worked like slaves on behalf of the monks. As one prominent Non-Possessor, **Vassian Patrikeev**, put it:

> "Where in the traditions of the Gospels, apostles, and fathers are monks ordered to acquire populous villages and enslave peasants to the brotherhood? We look into the hands of the rich, grovel slavishly, and flatter them, in order to get some little village from them. We harm and rob and sell Christians, our brothers [the peasants]. We torture them with scourges like wild beasts."

Nilus was also passionately opposed to state interference in Church affairs. He was equally insistent that false religion and heresy were the concern of the Church, not the state. Religious coercion and persecution were always wrong; the Church must meet the claims and the advocates of wrong belief with the purely spiritual weapons of persuasion and education.

---

[15] See Part Two, Chapter 8, section 4.

Nilus's great opponent was **Joseph of Volokolamsk** (1439-1515).
Named after the monastery he founded, he had a completely
different conception of Church and state from Nilus. Joseph
regarded the state as a religious body, with Moscow as the Third
Rome, and the tsar of Moscow as a sacred king, Christ's representative, the supreme judge in all spiritual matters; he saw the Church
as the state's intimate ally and partner, working to build Christ's
kingdom on earth, and needing to be wealthy and endowed with
property in order to carry out this calling. How could the Church or
its monasteries run hospitals, schools, orphanages, or give relief to
the poor, if they had no wealth or property? Joseph was also
sceptical about Nilus's skete movement; to Joseph, this was an
innovation that smacked of insubordination. Joseph remained
committed to the traditional conception of cenobitic monasticism.
Joseph's supporter, archbishop Gennady of Novgorod, further
argued that it was the state's duty to punish religious nonconform-
ists. It is said that Joseph fully approved when tsar **Vassily III**
(1505-33) gave the command, "Cut off the tongues of some
heretics, and deliver others to the fire."

The outlook embodied in these attitudes was called the "Possessor"
(or "Josephite") school of thought. The successors of Joseph in the
Possessor school, however, seem to have compromised his original
vision, for his ideals of "sacred kingship" provided no justification
for dictatorship in the tsar or subservience in his subjects. Joseph
was quite clear that the tsar could rule only within the constraints of
God's law. A tsar who trampled on God's law was no tsar at all but
a devil and a tyrant to whom no one owed obedience. Joseph even
made tentative approaches towards the possibility of tyrannicide –
the righteous killing of a tsar who wickedly abused his power. This
radical note was soon lost, as we shall see when we come to the
reign of Ivan the Terrible.

At the heart of the dispute between the Non-Possessors and the
Possessors lay ultimately a conflict of spiritual ethos. Nilus and the
Non-Possessors were more deeply grounded in the old ideals of the
desert fathers of Egypt, and they saw the Church as a pilgrim body

in an alien land; her wellsprings were in the heavenly Jerusalem, and she must always place (at the very least) a question mark over the things of this perishing world, even its beauty – Nilus's puritanical hostility to adorning churches was based on his conviction that even the beauty of an icon or of church music could become an idol. Joseph and the Possessors were more rooted in the theocratic Byzantine vision, translated into Russian terms; for them, the Church on earth was a genuine embodiment of God's kingdom, and they were therefore much more world-affirming in their attitude. In the setting of Moscow under the tsars, this could easily mean the sanctification of nationalism.

Despite Nilus's high reputation as a holy man, he fell into disfavour in the court of tsar **Ivan III** (1462-1505), especially on account of his denial of Ivan's spiritual authority. Ivan had fairly exalted views of his own status. In 1472 he had married the niece of the last Byzantine emperor, establishing a blood-link between the ruling families of old Orthodox Byzantium and its successor, new Orthodox Moscow. Ivan also adopted the Byzantine sign of the double eagle, the symbol of Byzantine imperial power; Ivan made it the official emblem of Russian power too, thus proclaiming that Moscow had inherited the Christian empire of the Byzantines. To underline this he took the title of "tsar" (Caesar). Naturally, therefore, he was more inclined to listen to the arguments of Joseph and the Possessors, rather than Nilus and the Non-Possessors.

Other great Russian monastic saints of this period included **Alexander of Svir** (1449-1533), who built a monastery beside the river Svir in response to a famous vision of the Trinity instructing him to do this. Alexander really preferred the life of a solitary hermit, feeling too sinful to guide others; he had several visions telling him to found a monastery and a church at Svir, but ignored them all – his life story reads as though the whole Trinity had to appear to him to get him over the otherwise invincible barrier of his sense of unworthiness! After founding the monastery in 1508, he became a spiritual mentor to a large body of disciples who then made their own mark in Russian monastic life.

After Nilus's death, the Non-Possessors found a new leader in a Greek theologian who had settled in Russia, known usually as **Maximus the Greek** (1480-1556), or sometimes Maximus the Hagiorite. A native of Arta in Epirus, Maximus became a man of the Renaissance who had drunk deeply of the new learning in Paris and Florence. At Florence he had fallen under the enchanting spell of the great Savonarola, admiring him so much that he joined the Dominican order to follow in his master's footsteps.[16] However, Maximus returned to Greece after Savonarola's death (and returned to Greek Orthodoxy). He then spent some time at the Vatopedi monastery on Athos, where he became a devoted librarian, caring for many of Athos's manuscript treasures.

In 1518, patriarch Theoleptus I sent Maximus to Moscow at the request of tsar Vassily III, who had asked for a learned Greek monk to translate the great works of Greek Orthodox religion into Slavonic. Maximus at first translated these works into Latin (as he did not yet know Slavonic), and his Latin versions were then translated into Slavonic by other scholars who knew Latin (but not Greek). However, Maximus learned Slavonic, and began making his own direct translations. His output was astonishing: he produced Slavonic renderings of Greek liturgy, biblical exegesis, lives of saints, history, controversial writings against pagans, astrologers, Jews, Muslims, Catholics, and (eventually) Lutherans. Indeed Maximus has been called "the father of later Russian theology". His translations of Greek anti-Catholic treatises ensured that a powerful hostility to Rome became a constant factor in Russian Orthodoxy. The Russians needed little encouragement in this direction; they were always far more antagonistic to Rome than the Greeks were. For the Russians, Roman Catholicism meant the invading hosts of Teutonic Knights and other eastern Catholic Europeans who had ravaged Russia since the 13th century.

Maximus's career soon took a troubled turn when he became caught up in the Non-Possessor movement. A friendship sprang up

---

[16] For Savonarola, see Chapter 1, section 5.

between Maximus and Vassian Patrikeev, an ardent disciple of Nilus of Sora. Maximus now became a thorn in tsar Vassily's side, denying his authority in Church affairs. Finally in 1525, Maximus and Patrikeev went too far when they protested against Vassily's second marriage as contrary to Church law. Vassily divorced his wife Solomonia because she was childless; metropolitan Daniel of Moscow, a staunch Possessor, fell in with Vassily's plans, compelled Solomonia to enter a nunnery, and married Vassily to Elena Glinski (the mother of the next tsar, Ivan the Terrible). Because Maximus had opposed the divorce and remarriage, Daniel had Maximus arrested. A Church synod accused the Greek of exalting the authority of the patriarch of Constantinople over the Russian Church, denying Vassily's rightful spiritual authority, altering liturgies in translation, and other offences. He was imprisoned in the Volokolamsk monastery (the power-centre of his Possessor enemies) where he spent the next 25 years. During this time, however, he was allowed to continue his literary activity. As often happens, his long captivity as a prisoner of conscience ultimately enhanced Maximus's prestige; when he was finally freed in 1551, he was a figure of awesome sanctity and repute.

While Maximus languished in prison, the Possessors found a great new champion in **Macarius of Luzhetski**, archbishop of Novgorod and then metropolitan of Moscow. Tsar **Ivan IV** (1547-84), better known to history as "Ivan the Terrible", placed complete reliance on Macarius, who used his power as metropolitan to crush the Non-Possessor movement. Since the smaller, poorer monasteries were the strongholds of the Non-Possessors, Macarius simply closed them down, or amalgamated them into larger monasteries with stricter control from the top. He also ensured that monasteries were made more accountable to the bishops, who were themselves under the final authority of the tsar as "sacred king". In this way he succeeded in driving the Non-Possessor movement "underground"; its impact on Russian Church life was severely curtailed, and the Possessors largely won the day. Macarius was in addition quite a Church reformer. He convened two synods in Moscow in 1547 and 1549 to incorporate officially into the Russian liturgy many saints

who, until then, had enjoyed only a local significance. The action of
the synods of course made these saints into national figures for all
Russia. Macarius also wrote a very important, detailed 12 volume
"Menologion", lives of the saints arranged according their festival
days in the Church year, together with many of the saints' own
writings. The compiling of the Menologion was a labour of love
which cost Macarius 20 years.

The programme of Church life promoted by the Possessors led to
an important controversy over icons. Beginning in Novgorod and
Pskov, and spreading from there to Moscow, a new style of iconography (icon painting) was flourishing. Influenced by the icons of
Byzantium in its last years, and by Western Latin art, this new style
was less concerned with depicting a saint, more with telling a story,
creating an illustrated allegory (*e.g.* of a biblical text). Among other
things, it led to depictions of Christ in symbolic and allegorical
form (*e.g.* as an angel) rather than as a human being in the context
of the incarnation. The Possessors encouraged the new iconography, but others found it disturbing. One prominent person who was
disturbed was Ivan Viskovaty, chancellor of the tsar's foreign
office. When many of the Moscow churches were renovated after a
great fire in 1547, Viskovaty protested against the new icons that
adorned their interiors. His immediate criticism was the figurative
portrayals of Christ, arguing that they undermined the reality of the
incarnation, and appealing (correctly) to canon 82 of the Quinisext
Council of 692, which had decreed that Christ was to be depicted in
human form.[17] He was soon quarrelling mightily with metropolitan
Macarius, who as usual triumphed over anyone who opposed him:
Viskovaty was condemned for heresy and innovation and excommunicated for three years. This was an ironic sentence, since it was
the new iconography that was historically the innovation. But
Macarius's victory ensured that the new iconography secured its
permanent place in Russian religious art.

---

[17]   For the Quinisext Council, see Part One, Chapter 12, section 5.

The forward march of the messianic "Third Rome" view of Moscow reached another milestone in 1547, when Ivan the Terrible underwent a coronation ceremony which imitated the enthronement rituals of Byzantium. (Ivan's reign is usually dated from this coronation. After Vassily III's death in 1533, Ivan was only three years old, and Russia experienced a decade of faction-ridden government by its aristocracy.) Previous rulers of Moscow had claimed the title "tsar", but none before had been crowned as tsar according to Byzantine royal ritual. It involved the anointing of Ivan with holy oil by metropolitan Macarius, and a kind of liturgy of ordination setting Ivan apart as a sacred king.

Even more significant, in 1551 Ivan summoned another Moscow synod, again imitating in this the Byzantine emperors from Constantine onwards, who had always taken the initiative in calling Church councils. Macarius presided at the synod. Its aim was to settle the question of the differences that had developed between Russian and Greek Church practice. The synod affirmed that Russian practice was correct at every point! This did not go down too well among the Greek Orthodox; even the Russian monks on Athos disowned the synod as schismatic. This did not trouble Ivan and Macarius. The synod passed a number of important decrees known as the Stoglav ("hundred chapters") relating to Church organisation, monasteries, education of the clergy, and other administrative matters. Ominously for the future, the synod's pro-Russian programme led it to assert that two alleluias were to be sung in the liturgy before the hymn "Glory to You, O Lord," and that the sign of the cross was to be made with two fingers. The rest of the Orthodox world sang three alleluias and made the sign of the cross with three fingers. Given the Orthodox reverence for the liturgy as an icon of heaven's worship, this unilateral declaration by the Russian synod was pregnant with problems for the future; in the 17th century, these liturgical differences between Russian and Greek Orthodoxy would produce the most bitter dispute in Russian Orthodox history, the schism of the Old Believers.[18]

---

[18]   See Part Four for the Old Believers.

The Possessor vision of an intimate alliance between Church and state with the tsar as sacred king could work in a fruitful way if the tsar was a pious ruler. Ivan the Terrible ruled quite benevolently and effectively from 1547 to 1553. But in 1553 he suffered a grave illness which (he believed) laid him at death's door, and he became infuriated by the reluctance or refusal of many of his advisors and nobles to swear allegiance to his young son Dmitry (they preferred Ivan's cousin Vladimir as the new tsar). When Ivan recovered from the illness, his reign degenerated into a bloody reign of terror, especially after the death of his beloved wife Anastasia in 1560. The reign of terror was carried out through a special military force called the *oprichniki*, who wore black and rode on black horses; their sole purpose was to destroy anyone whom Ivan believed to be his enemy. Entire communities were sometimes annihilated, especially the great historic city of Novgorod in 1570. When metropolitan Philip of Moscow dared to protest against Ivan's tyranny in 1569, Ivan had him thrown in prison, where the *oprichniki* killed him. It has been said that Philip's protest was the last time the Russian Church stood up against the Russian state: "I am a stranger upon the earth and am ready to suffer for the truth. Where is my faith if I am silent?" After Philip's martyrdom, the Church hierarchy fell silent. One of Ivan's most famous political opponents, prince Andrew Kurbsky, a one-time servant of Ivan who had fled to Lithuania, gave an eloquent witness to this silence from his Lithuanian exile: "Where are the faces of the prophets who could accuse the kings of injustice? Where is Ambrose who restrained Theodosius? Where is John Chrysostom who exposed the greedy empress? Who defends his offended brother?"[19]

One last matter deserves consideration. It seemed wrong to the Possessors and the tsars that their Church had no patriarch of its own. If Moscow really was the Third Rome, how could its bishop be a mere metropolitan? Should he not be a patriarch, of the same status (at least!) as the bishops of Constantinople, Alexandria, Antioch, and Jerusalem? Ivan the Terrible began to press for this;

---

[19] For Ambrose and Theodosius, see Part One, Chapter 7, section 2. For John Chrysostom and the empress Eudoxia, see Part One, Chapter 9, section 1.

but the most he could get, in 1561, was confirmation of his title of tsar from patriarch Joasaph II. Constantinople was hesitant because it disliked and distrusted what it considered Russian Orthodox arrogance, so egregiously displayed (in the Greek view) at the Moscow synod of 1551. However, the logic of relationships pushed the two sides inexorably together. The tsars needed the approval of Constantinople's patriarch for the elevation of Moscow's metropolitan – such an act could not be undertaken unilaterally: the patriarch of Constantinople was still the "ecumenical patriarch", the first among equals throughout the Orthodox world. And on their part, the patriarchs of Constantinople could hardly ignore the greatest Orthodox political power in the world, mighty Russia. Just as the Middle Eastern Orthodox under the Muslim yoke had once looked to the Byzantine emperors to champion their cause, so the Greek Orthodox, now under the same yoke, looked increasingly to the tsars of Russia to champion *their* cause.

Affairs came to fruition at last under Ivan the Terrible's successor **Fyodor I** (1584-98). Fyodor was almost the exact opposite of his father. Ivan had been a cruel tyrant; Fyodor's only interests were praying and visiting monasteries and churches. His piety verged on simple-mindedness, but since the "fool for Christ" was an accepted and admired figure in Russia, this endeared him to his subjects. He was soon being nicknamed "the sanctified Tsar", and also "the Bellringer" (from his habit of ringing church bells to summon the faithful to worship). Not surprisingly, the patriarchs of Constantinople found it a lot easier to deal with Fyodor than they had with Ivan. So when 1587 Fyodor asked Constantinople if the metropolitan of Moscow might be raised to patriarchal rank, there was a more positive response. Patriarch Jeremias II of Constantinople (he who had corresponded with the Lutherans) visited Moscow in 1588 while touring Russia to collect charitable gifts for the Ottoman Greeks, and officially bestowed the rank of patriarch on metropolitan Job of Moscow. During the ceremony, Jeremias acknowledged the Third Rome ideology of Moscow by addressing tsar Fyodor thus:

"Since the first Rome fell through the Apollinarian heresy,[20] and the second Rome, which is Constantinople, is held by the unbelieving Turks, so your great Russian tsardom, O pious tsar, which is more pious than previous kingdoms, is the Third Rome. You alone under heaven are now called Christian emperor for all Christians in the whole world. Therefore our act in establishing the [Moscow] patriarchate will be accomplished according to God's will, the prayers of the Russian saints, your own prayer to God, and according to your counsel."

The patriarch of Moscow was to rank last in order of precedence among the Eastern patriarchs, after Constantinople, Alexandria, Antioch, and Jerusalem. But that mattered little compared to his position next to the tsars of the Third Rome. Ironically, the Moscow patriarchate was to have a short life of little more than 100 years; it was abolished under tsar Peter the Great (1682-1725), to be revived only in the 20th century. But for those 100 years the patriarchs of Moscow took their place in the Orthodox world as the fifth member of the "pentarchy", the five leaders – Constantinople, Alexandria, Antioch, Jerusalem, Moscow – who jointly guided the destinies of Orthodoxy.

---

[20] Jeremias had his theological wires crossed here. The heresy of the "first Rome" in Eastern eyes was the *filioque* clause, not Apollinarianism (the denial that Christ had a human soul or spirit).

Important people

The Church	*Political and military*
Orthodox	Sultan Mehmet II (1451-81)
Patriarch Gennadius II (born 1405;	Tsar Ivan III (1462-1505)
Reigned 1454-56, 1463, and	Tsar Vassily III (1505-33)
1464-65; died 1472)	Tsar Ivan IV "the Terrible"
Nilus of Sora (1433-1508)	1439-1515)
Joseph of Volokolamsk (1547-84)	Tsar Fyodor I (1584-98)
Alexander of Svir (1449-1533)	
Manuel of Corinth (died 1551)	
Pachomius of Rhus (died 1553)	
Maximus the Greek (1480-1556)	
Vassian Patrikeev (flourished early 16th century)	
Joannes Kartanos (flourished mid-16th century)	
Macarius of Luzhetski (flourished mid-16th century)	
Demetrius Mysos (flourished mid-16th century)[21]	
Patriarch Jeremias II (1572-95)	
Theodore Zygomelas (1544-1614)	

Lutherans
Jacob Andreae (1528-90)
Martin Crusius (1526-1607)

Orthodox martyrs under the Ottoman Empire

The martyrdom of Macarius

This blessed soul was truly a powerful wrestler in the athletic school of Christ. He was a monk who strictly kept the precepts of monastic life, and ardently imitated all the noble qualities of his mentor, Saint Niphon [patriarch of Constantinople in the late 1490s]. He arrived at such a pitch of godliness and the love of God that he became utterly consumed with a profound desire to finish

---

21 Demetrius ended his life as a Lutheran.

his race with a martyr's death. He went to Saint Niphon, then
residing on the Holy Mountain [Athos] for the second time, at the
holy monastery of Vatopedi, and told him about his desire and his
holy motive. As Saint Niphon listened to Macarius and his wish, he
discerned that it was in accord with God's will. So he encouraged
Macarius with these words:

> "Go, my child, on the path of martyrdom. In accordance
> with your fervour you will receive from heaven the crown of
> your struggle and rejoice for ever with the martyrs and
> saints."

Saint Niphon then added a prayer, and sealed Macarius with the
sign of the venerable and life-giving cross. Then he embraced him
and dismissed him in peace.

The blessed Macarius, armed with Saint Niphon's blessing, left
Mount Athos with joy, and made haste to enter the arena of martyrdom all the sooner. He went to Thessalonica and noticed a large
crowd of Ottomans. Immediately Macarius began preaching to
them, without any reserve, that Christ is the Son of God, who
dwells in the heart of the Father, and became man, and so on. He
set forth in great detail the economy of Christ's incarnation.[22] When
the Ottomans within hearing range heard this sermon, they all
attacked Macarius violently with knives and clubs. They struck his
body on every side and wounded him so that blood flowed from his
injuries like a river. Then he was thrown in prison. In the morning
they gathered together and brought the martyr before their tribunal.
They flattered him at first in ever way, promising him precious gifts
if only he would renounce the faith of Christ and accept their
religion. Christ's martyr, however, replied boldly:

> "May God grant that you will come to know the true and
> blameless faith of Christians, and that you will be baptised in
> the name of the Father, the Son, and the Holy Spirit, and be

---

[22] "Economy" is the Orthodox term for what God does outside Himself in the
      sphere of creation.

rescued from your false religion by the holy Trinity of one essence."

On hearing this, the Turks lost all restraint and rushed upon the martyr, beating him, stabbing and goading his flesh with knives, causing many wounds. At last they cut off his venerable head on the 14th of September 1527. So the saint received the unconquerable crown of martyrdom. At that moment the Holy Spirit informed Saint Niphon at Vatopedi of Macarius's martyrdom, and Saint Niphon revealed it to another of his disciples, Joasaph:

> "My child, understand that today your brother Macarius has ended his course as a martyr; he is already in heaven, rejoicing with the glorious choir of the saints and martyrs."

By the intercessions of Macarius, may we too be made worthy of heaven's blessedness. Amen.

The martyrdom of Damian

Christ's new athlete Damian was born in Arahova, or Parakabulion of Eurytania, as it used to be. He was the child of pious parents. In his boyhood he longed to become a monk; so he said farewell to the world and all its affairs, and went to the Holy Mountain [Athos], to the monastery of Philotheou, where he received the monk's tonsure.[23] He remained a short time there, growing in monastic virtue. But then he left so that he could advance still further in spirituality by becoming a disciple of Dometian, a champion of the ascetic life. They lived together for three years, working hard at godliness with fervour and strictness. Then Damian was made worthy to hear the voice of God:

> "Damian, you should not just seek your own welfare, but the welfare of others."

---

[23] In Orthodoxy, the tonsure is the cutting of four strands of hair from the head in the form of a cross when one embraces the monastic life.

So Damian left Mount Athos immediately and went to the villages around Mount Olympus. There he preached God's Word energetically, exhorting and warning the Christians to repent and to give up deeds of unrighteousness and all other forms of wickedness, to keep God's commands, and to work towards goodness and the deeds that please God. Many of these people, however, were Christians in name alone; in life, they were ungodly. So the devil, who hates the human race, stirred them up to slander the saint, accusing him of being a deluded imposter. Some persecuted him, even trying to kill him. Damian followed the example of Christ and left the place in order to keep his peace of mind. He went to Kissavon and Larisa, where once more he preached God's Word, and once more underwent the same trials. So he set off again and went to the mountains of Agrafa, where he taught the Christians to stand firm in the faith and to keep the Lord's commands. But the devil never sleeps; he aroused the irreverent and the ungodly against the saint, and they made his life a misery, accusing him of being deceived and a false monk. So Damian departed and went back to Kissavon so that he could find peace. He built a monastery there, and lived in it together with other monks, offering his prayers to God every day. Many people came flocking to Kissavon in order to receive blessing for their souls from Damian's health-giving teachings, for he had a good knowledge and was full of God's gifts.

One day he went to the village of Bulgarene to obtain certain necessary items for the monastery, but more particularly for the benefit of the Christians of Kissavon. A group of Muslims arrested him and handed him over to the authorities in Larisa. They testified that Damian forbade Christians from buying and selling on Sundays, and persuaded them to stand firm in the faith of Christ. The authorities therefore ordered that he receive a severe beating, and put heavy chains round his neck and feet, throwing him in prison.

Damian spent 15 days in prison, where he suffered all kinds of harsh tortures. At times the Muslims spoke ominous threats to him, at times they spoke flattery and promises, all designed to make

Damian forsake the faith of Christ. The local magistrate, however, was quite unable to prevail upon the saint. Indeed, Damian with an intrepid spirit demonstrated the falsehood of the Muslims' religion and their prophet, and declared without reserve that Christ is the true God. He made it clear that he was ready to undergo ten thousand tortures. Those present burned with anger, and they condemned Damian instantly to be hanged, and then to be thrown into the fire. The magistrate took Damian and hanged him; but when they cut the rope with an axe (which grazed the martyr's head), Damian fell down to the ground half-dead. While the breath of life was still in him, they snatched him up and threw him in the flames. Afterwards they gathered his ashes and cast them into the river Pinios. So the blessed Damian received his crown, in the year 1568.

By the intercessions of Saint Damian, may we be set free from the snares of the enemy and made worthy of the kingdom of heaven. Amen.

The skete rule of Nilus of Sora

1. The monks should earn their own living by working with their hands. They should not, however, become involved in agriculture; its complicated nature makes it unsuitable for hermits.
2. They should not accept charitable gifts except when they are ill or in extreme need. They should never accept any gifts that might be a cause of scandal to anyone.
3. They should not leave the skete.
4. In the church there should be not be any adornments made of silver, not even for the holy vessels [for celebrating the eucharist]. Everything should be simple.
5. The young and healthy monks should exhaust their bodies with fasts, thirst, and manual labour. Some relaxation of this requirement is allowed for the old and the infirm.
6. No women whatsoever must enter the skete.

The last testament of Nilus of Sora

In the name of the Father, the Son, and the Holy Spirit. This is my testament to you, my faithful masters and brothers who share my way of life. I entreat you to throw my body into the wilderness so that beasts and birds may eat it. It has sinned against God so much that it is unworthy of a burial. If you fail to do this, please bury me without honour; just dig a hole in the place where we live. Revere the words that the great Arsenius gave as a testament to his disciples: I will stand in judgment on you if you give my body to anyone. My whole business, as far as I was able, was to refuse to be accounted worthy of any of this world's glory or honour. Since this was my aim in life, let it be so in death too. I entreat you to pray for my sinful soul, and I myself entreat everyone to forgive me. And may I forgive for my own part. May God forgive us all.

To my masters and brothers who will carry on the work on these grounds, I bequeath the large cross containing the passion-stone [a black opal], together with the little books I've written. I sincerely and humbly ask that you offer prayers for me until the fortieth day after I have died. I also bequeath the small volumes of John of Damascus, the breviary, and the irmologion.[24] Send to the Kirillov monastery the psalm book copied out by Ignatius. Also give back all other books and items which belong to that monastery and were given to me for the sake of God's love. Distribute the rest to the poor, to other monasteries, and to laypeople. Let everything be given back to those to whom it belongs.

Alexander of Svir's vision of the Trinity

In the year 1508, 23 years after the saint settled in the wilderness, Saint Alexander was standing one night in his solitary hermitage, praying to God according to his habit, when suddenly there

---

[24] A breviary is a book containing the daily prayers for the seven "canonical hours" of worship (matins and lauds, the first, third, sixth, and ninth hours, vespers, and compline). An irmologion is a liturgical book with prayers for singing rather than reading.

appeared a great light in the cabin where he stood. The saint was amazed. He thought to himself, "What does this mean?" Suddenly he saw three men coming towards him. They wore bright garments, being clothed in white, whose purity was beautiful. They shone brighter than the sun, lighting the cabin with unspeakable heavenly glory. Each held a staff in his hand. Seeing them, the Saint trembled all over; fear and terror had gripped him. Then, coming somewhat to his senses, he understood what was happening, and he tried to bow down before them to the ground. But they took him by the hand and lifted him up. They said: "Let your heart be filled with hope, blessed one. Don't be afraid." The saint replied: "My lords, if I have found favour in your sight, tell me who you are. You shine with such glory and brightness, yet you have condescended to visit me, your slave. I have never seen anyone clothed with such glory as you." They answered him: "Don't be afraid, O man of strong desires, for the Holy Spirit has been pleased to dwell in you, because your heart is pure. Just as I have previously said to you on many occasions, so now I say again, you shall build a church, gather together a band of brothers, and establish a monastery. For it is My good pleasure to save many souls through you, bringing them to a knowledge of the truth."

When he heard this, the saint once more bowed down. He was flooded with tears. He said: "O my Lord, who am I – a sinner, the worst person alive – who am I to be counted worthy of what You have spoken concerning me? I am not worthy to receive such a calling. I came to this place as an unworthy man, not to do what you have just commanded, but to weep over my sins." The saint said this, lying prostrate. But the Lord again took his hand and lifted him up, saying, "Stand on your feet. Be enabled; be strong. Do everything that I have commanded." The saint replied: "O my Lord, do not be angry with me, that I have dared to speak in Your presence. This church that Your love for humanity wishes to build here, tell me what it shall be called." The Lord said to the saint: "Beloved, just as you see the One speaking to you in three persons, build the church in the name of Father, Son, and Holy Spirit, the Trinity, One in essence." Then He also said: "My peace I leave with

you; My peace I give to you." And suddenly the Saint saw the Lord
with outspread wings, going upon the ground as though with feet;
and then He vanished. And Saint Alexander was overwhelmed with
great joy and fear, and he gave great thanks to God the Lover of
humanity.

Lutheran-Orthodox dialogue: The Lutheran critique of invoking the saints

No one should doubt that we ought to think and speak with honour
toward the saints. So we encourage our people, as opportunity
arises, to imitate their faith, self-control, patience, piety, and the
other virtues that have made them illustrious. This is indeed good.
But we do not think it necessary to invoke them so that they may be
our mediators and intercede with God, either for us or for the dead.
Likewise we do not approve of worshipping the saints or their
icons, nor honouring them by dedicating churches and votive
offerings to them. We do not give to created beings the honour that
God alone deserves. For the same reason we do not worship the
holy angels. Why not? Even if one were to seek an academic
distinction between worship (which is owed to God) and the state
and service assigned to the saints, yet in reality we see people
attributing to the saints what belongs only to God. When people
invoke the saints, they believe the saints know and hear our
thoughts, sorrows, and cries. But only God can do this. Indeed the
prophet Isaiah shows that the saints do not know the specific things
done here on earth, for he says: "You are our Father, though
Abraham does not know us and Israel [Jacob] does not acknowledge us" [Isaiah 63:16]. Also Elijah, before God took him up to
heaven, said to Elisha: "Ask me what I shall do for you before I am
taken from you" [2 Kings 2:9], which implies that in the future life
he would not be able to know Elisha's requests. And if the God-
loving patriarchs and prophets were ignorant of what happened on
earth at that time, they do not know today how things go among us,
nor do they hear our prayers. For although they are in a general
sense favourably disposed towards God's Church, and intercede
with Him (in accordance with the prevailing conditions of the time)

that the Lord will take care of His Church, it does not follow from this that we should worship or pray to them so that they will take care of each of us or pray to the Lord for us. We therefore have no basis for calling them mediators.

Paul says, "There is one Mediator between God and humanity – the man Christ Jesus" [1 Timothy 2:5]. This Mediator is sufficient for us. The Holy Scriptures nowhere encourage us to invoke saints or angels, nor to worship them and their icons. Even the angels would not allow themselves to be worshipped, saying that they are our fellow servants [Revelation 22:8-9], and Peter refused to let Cornelius worship him [Acts 10:26]…[The Lutherans quote Epiphanius of Salamis, Basil of Caesarea, and John Chrysostom against invocation of saints]

Further, we find no promise anywhere in the Scriptures that such invocation or worship would bring us any benefit. Indeed there is no example in the Scriptures of any godly man who invoked any saint. Nor do we need any mediator to reconcile Christ to us, since in truth the Son of God became man for this very reason, to reconcile us as His brothers to His Father. Christ is so kindly disposed towards us that He says, "Come to Me, all you labour and are heavy laden, and I will give you rest" [Matthew 11:28]. Again, "whoever comes to Me I will never cast out" [John 6:37]. And Christ is our Mediator not just in salvation, as some say, but also in the matter of intercession. Paul says: "He is at the right hand of God interceding for us" [Romans 8:34]. Christ commands us as we pray to go to God simply and directly, saying: "our Father in heaven" [Matthew 6:10]. And He promises we will be heard. For He says: "Truly, truly I say to you, if you ask anything of the Father, He will give it to you in my name" [John 16:23]. No one should think there is any saint or angel who has a concern and a love for us so great as God's. "For God so loved the world that He gave His only Son, that whoever believes in Him should not perish but have eternal life" [John 3:16]. Paul adds: "What shall we say to this? If God is for us, who is against us? He Who did not spare His own Son, but offered Him up for us all, how will He not along with

Him freely give us all things?" [Romans 8:31-32]. Why then do we need any other mediators when the Father Himself loves us so much?

The response of the Lutherans of Tubingen to patriarch Jeremias's first critique of the Augsburg Confession, June 1577

Lutheran-Orthodox dialogue: The Orthodox defence of invoking the saints

As for the fifth article about the invocation of the saints, you claim that you imitate their faith, patience, and all other things that work salvation. And yet you deny that we should invoke them or that they intercede with God, and you will not venerate them or their icons, or honour them in churches, offering them spiritual commemorations, because you are concerned that you may transfer to created beings what belongs to God alone.

Regarding this, we say it is necessary to invoke the saints, since they can help us. Many things prove this. First of all, consider God's Word in Job chapter 42:

> "After the Lord had spoken these words to Job, the Lord said to Eliphaz the Temanite, 'You and your two friends have sinned, for you have not spoken what is right concerning Me, as My servant Job has. Now, therefore, take seven bulls and seven rams, and go to My servant Job, and offer for yourselves a burnt offering, and My servant Job will pray for you."

This teaches us that the righteous intercede and pray for us, not for the living only, but also for the dead, as in the case of the dead man who was thrown on Elisha's grave in 2 Kings. Again, the Church of Christ refers to the saints as alive and in God's hand, and to their death as a sleep; for they laboured on earth, and will live until the end of time. God is life, and those who are in His hand are alive. The holy apostle underlines the fact that God has dwelt in them, through their minds and in their bodies, when he says, "Do you not know that your body is the temple of the Holy Spirit?" [1 Corinthians 6:19). Why should we not honour the living temples of God? When they were living, the saints openly testified to God [by their works]. Christ has opened up many sources of redemption for us. By invoking the saints, demons are driven out, illnesses are expelled, temptations are warded off. God also bestows His gift from above through our invocation of the blessed angels, whom He immediately sends to those who invoke their names...

Although we say, "O Saint John, intercede for us," and, "all-holy Theotokos [Mother of God], intercede for us," and, "holy angels, intercede for us," yet in the presence of all we cry out, "O Lord of hosts, be with us, for besides You we have no other helper in time of trouble. Have mercy on us, O Lord of hosts." You see the most true and perfect purpose of the Church, that it prays to God that He will come as a help, and calls on His mercy? As it is written, He is the blessed and only Master...

Cyril, great in wisdom, in his interpretation of Daniel's prophecy, says that intercession will also take place at the Lord's coming. Angels will intercede for some, and the Lady [Mary] will intercede for the world, as will the saints too. But they will not intercede for absolutely everyone, nor for those who died in a sinful condition. Not at all! God has finally shut the door of mercy on them. For God has spoken out against them in these words: "Even if Noah, Daniel, and Job were among them, they would save neither their sons nor their daughters" [Ezekiel 14:20]. The saints will intercede only for those on whose behalf intercession will be accepted, namely, those who have been able to change their life through repentance, but who could not entirely wipe out the stains of sin.

The response of patriarch Jeremias to the June 1577 letter of the Tubingen theologians, May 1579

GLOSSARY

Anabaptism, Anabaptist
That form of the Radical Reformation which was (ultimately) distinguished by its commitment to the New Testament as the supreme rule of faith and practice; believers' baptism; a rigorous approach to the excommunication of the unworthy – or the "ban", as Anabaptists called it; the Lord's Supper as an ordinance that belongs only to those baptised as believers; the complete separation of true believers from unbelievers in all religious and political matters; the high importance of the pastoral office; total pacifism and non-violence, and hence the rejection of politics as a Christian calling, since rulers have to use force to uphold the law; and the total rejection of oaths.

Augsburg confession
The confession of faith submitted by Protestants to the Holy Roman emperor Charles V at the diet of Augsburg in 1530. It became the basic Lutheran doctrinal statement.

Aristotelianism
The system of philosophy derived from the pagan Greek philosopher Aristotle (384-22 BC). Its view of knowledge was influential – that the mind's knowledge of everything (apart from the laws of reason) is mediated to the mind from the external world through the senses.

Augustinian
(i) Relating to the theology of the early Church father Augustine of Hippo (354-430), especially his understanding of sin and salvation. We can sum it up like this: (a) the whole human race fell in Adam; (b) the fallen human will is in helpless bondage to sin and Satan; (c) God's sovereign grace alone can liberate the fallen will and

cause it to repent and believe in Christ; (d) those whom Christ liberates are eternally chosen for this destiny in the mystery of unconditional election. Most of the great Western medieval theologians and reformers – Anselm of Canterbury, Bernard of Clairvaux, Peter Lombard, Thomas Aquinas, Gregory of Rimini, John Wyclif, John Huss – moved within an Augustinian spectrum of thought. The Protestant Reformers were Augustinians; the Radical Reformers were anti-Augustinian; Roman Catholics varied (cardinal Contarini, a leading figure in Rome in the 1520s and 1530s, was strongly Augustinian, whereas the Jesuit order became notable for its anti-Augustinianism).

(ii) The Augustinians were an order of friars which emerged in the 13th Century, living according to the monastic rule of Augustine of Hippo. Martin Luther was an Augustinian friar.

Bull

A papal edict. It comes from the Latin *bulla*, "seal", referring to the wax seal by which a pope impressed the sign of his authority on the edict. Bulls were known by their opening words in Latin, e.g. the bull *Exsurge domine* ("Rise up, O Lord") which condemned Luther.

Byzantine Empire

The Eastern Roman Empire with its capital in Constantinople. "Byzantine" comes from Byzantium, the site on which Constantinople was built. Historians call them Byzantines, but the Byzantines called themselves "Romans", and we should remember that the Byzantine Empire was a direct continuation of the Roman Empire which did not "fall" in the East until 1453.

Calvinist

See Reformed.

Cardinal

Originally a title for the deacons and priests of Rome, and the bishops of Rome's suburban churches. Later, bishops who were geographically remote from Rome began to be nominated as cardinals to act as the pope's representatives. The Hildebrandine reform movement of the 11th century placed the election of new popes in the hands of the cardinals.

Christendom

"The Christian domain". The nations and territories of Eastern and Western Europe, which – despite political and cultural differences – were united by the fact that Christianity was the public faith in each of them. People often use the word today to refer to the idea of a society publicly committed to the Christian religion. From the reign of Roman emperor Theodosius the Great in the 4th Century up to the French Revolution in the 18th, it also meant the political union of Church and state, whichever of the two was the dominant partner.

Conciliarism

From the Latin *concilium*, "council". A movement in the Western Church in response to the Great Schism of 1378, when there were two (later three) rival popes. The conciliarists wanted to restore the unity of the Church by making the papacy subject to the higher authority of a general or ecumenical Council of the Church. Conciliarism remained a force to be reckoned with in the 16th century.

Deification

"Becoming divine". This was the accepted understanding of salvation in the Eastern Orthodox Church. It does not mean that human beings are gods by nature or become God by nature. It means that through union with Christ, believers share by grace in the glory and immortality of God, and in that sense become divine – "partakers of the divine nature" (2 Peter 1:4). In many ways, "deification" in Eastern theology is the equivalent of "sanctification" and "glorification" in Western theology.

Devotio Moderna

"The modern way of serving God". A spiritual movement beginning in the mid-14th Century in the Netherlands. It was marked by a sense of God's closeness to the individual believer, and a focusing of the mind on Christ's life and sufferings as recorded in the Gospels. It inspired the creation of communities of Christian men and Christian women ("brotherhoods" and "sisterhoods") who would live, pray and follow Christ together, but without becoming monks or nuns; they would work for a living "in the world" and take no monastic vows. The most influential and well-known writing to emerge from the *devotio moderna* was *The Imitation of Christ*, written by Thomas a Kempis (1380-1471).

Disputation
A public educational event in a university, in which a teacher and a student would set out to solve a problem. The problem would take the form of two statements which appeared to contradict each other, but which were both found in authoritative texts. The student would have to give all the arguments for and against each statement, by quoting passages from the Bible and great theologians, and offering his own comments on these passages. The teacher would then make remarks on what the student had said, and would offer a solution to the problem. Lecturers also engaged in disputations over debated subjects; they would draw up a set of statements or "theses", announce that they were going to defend them in debate, and challenge anyone to argue with them and disprove the theses.

Dominican
An order of friars founded in 1214 by Dominic (1171-1221). The order devoted itself especially to the study of theology, producing great theologians like Albertus Magnus and Thomas Aquinas. Dominicans ran the inquisition, which made them unpopular with the other monastic orders. They had the unique right to preach anywhere and everywhere.

Eastern Orthodoxy
A title often given to the Eastern Greek-speaking Church of the Byzantine Empire, and its daughter Churches in Russia, the Balkans, and elsewhere. Strictly speaking, we should only refer to it

in this way after the great East-West schism of 1054; it was only at
that point that East and West separated into two mutually hostile
Churches.

Ecumenical Council
A conference of bishops from all parts of the Christian world to
decide questions of doctrine and discipline. There were seven
ecumenical Councils recognised by both East and West – Nicaea
(325), Constantinople (381), Ephesus (431), Chalcedon (451),
Second Constantinople (553), Third Constantinople (680-81), and
Second Nicaea (787). The Western Church had other Councils it
regarded as ecumenical after 787, but these were not recognised by
the East. Most Protestants have not accepted the 2nd Council of
Nicaea for theological reasons (rejecting its doctrine of the veneration of icons). The Council of Trent was an ecumenical Council in
Roman Catholic eyes. "Ecumenical" comes from the Greek for
"the inhabited world"; when used in the phrase "ecumenical
Council", it has nothing to do with the modern "ecumenical
movement".

Eucharist
The Lord's supper or holy communion. From the Greek *eucharis-
teo*, "to give thanks".

Filioque clause
Filioque is Latin for "and from the Son". This phrase was added to
the Nicene Creed by the Western Church, first by Spanish Christians at the council of Toledo in 589, and at length by the papacy in
the early 11th Century. The addition altered the Creed's teaching
about the Holy Spirit; it originally said that the Spirit "proceeds
from the Father", but after the insertion of the *filioque* clause,
Western versions of the Creed now said that the Spirit "proceeds
from the Father and from the Son". This generated fierce controversy between East and West. The East protested that (a) the West
had no right to alter an ecumenical Creed by unilateral action, and
(b) this particular alteration was theologically incorrect – in the
eternal relationships of the Trinity, the Spirit proceeds from the

Father alone. The *filioque* clause was the chief theological difference between East and West which led to the great schism of 1054.
It remained a divisive East-West issue in the 16th century. Protestants did not question the *filioque* clause when they broke with
Rome, so that it divided them too from the East.

Franciscans
An order of friars founded in 1209 by Francis of Assisi. They were
originally committed to absolute poverty – no ownership of any
property – but this was modified in various ways as the order
developed. Many great medieval thinkers were Franciscans, e.g.
Duns Scotus and William of Ockham.

Holy Roman Empire
The political and religious entity created by pope Leo III on
Christmas day 800, when he crowned the Frankish king Charlemagne as "emperor of the Romans". The Holy Roman Empire
claimed that it, not Byzantium, was the true successor to Constantine and the Christian Roman Empire in the West. Its territories
constantly shrank and grew under different emperors; at its greatest,
the Empire embraced Germany, the Netherlands, Bohemia, Austria,
Switzerland, much of Italy, and parts of eastern France. It was
marked by prolonged conflict between popes and emperors over
which of them held the supreme authority in the Empire. In the 16th
century, the emperors were Roman Catholic in religion, but often at
loggerheads with the popes politically.

Humanism
The general outlook fostered by the Renaissance. Its basic thrust
was to insist that life in this present world had its own proper worth
and beauty, that the "secular" sphere was as valuable as the
"sacred", and that no knowledge was profitable unless its relevance
to human well-being could be demonstrated. Renaissance humanism should not be confused with current humanism. The term is
now employed to refer a philosophy that excludes the supernatural.
Most Renaissance humanists, however, were committed to a
Christian worldview.

Hussites
The most successful dissenting movement in the Western medieval world. Hussites were followers of the 15th century Bohemian reformer John Huss. Eventually they separated into two parties, the Utraquists and the United Bohemian Brotherhood. The Utraquists remained within the Catholic Church but with their own Hussite practices – preaching from the Bible in Czech (the language of Bohemia), the wine as well as the bread served to the laity in communion. The United Bohemian Brotherhood broke away from the Catholic Church and was doctrinally more radical (rejecting transubstantiation, prayers for the dead, the invocation of saints). In the 16th century, Hussites allied themselves with the Reformation and became part of the larger Protestant world.

Hutterites
After Jacob Hutter (died 1536). An Anabaptist group in Bohemia distinguished by their practice of living in communes where all property was held in common.

Icon
A pictorial representation of Christ, saints or angels. The word is Greek for "image" and usually restricted to the Eastern Church's use of such images. In the East, icons are two-dimensional (not statues), and regarded not as works of human art but God-given points of contact with the spiritual world. In the West, icons or images can also be three-dimensional.

Imperialism, imperialist
The view that the emperor, not the pope, was the supreme authority in the Holy Roman Empire.

Indulgence
A pardon which released a sinner from the obligation to pay the "temporal penalties" of sin. Temporal penalties included penitential acts of Church discipline and sufferings in purgatory. Only the pope could issue an indulgence. His right to do so stemmed from his power over the "treasury of merits" – the merits of the saints by

which they had performed acts of obedience above and beyond the call of duty. Such merits the pope could transfer to sinful souls on earth and even in purgatory. The sale of indulgences produced several indignant protests in the late Middle Ages, and were the spark which finally ignited the Reformation.

Inquisition

The "holy office", a separate organisation within the Western Catholic Church, free from episcopal control, subject only to the pope, dedicated to the forcible suppression of heresy and dissent. Pope Innocent III (1198-1216) laid the basis for the inquisition. In 1227 Innocent's system was consolidated as the "holy office". Staffed by Dominicans, the inquisition became the most feared organisation in the Middle Ages. It was reinvigorated by the popes of the Catholic Counter-Reformation. (The notorious Spanish inquisition was only the branch of the inquisition that operated in Spain.)

Justification

The key doctrine of the Magisterial Reformation in the sphere of soteriology (the theology of salvation). For the Protestant Reformers, justification meant God's forensic (law-court) declaration that the believer was righteous, not on account of his own righteousness, but through Christ's righteousness reckoned (imputed) to his account. Since, for the Reformers, Christ was received by faith alone, justification became "justification by faith alone".

Laity, laypeople

From the Greek *laos*, "the people". All Church members who are not clergy. This includes most monks, the majority of whom are not priests.

Legate

An ambassador or representative of the pope.

Lollards, Lollardy
The followers of the English reformer John Wyclif (1330-84). It is uncertain what "Lollard" means – possibly "one who mumbles or mutters". Wyclif anticipated many of the views of the Protestant Reformers, *e.g.* his rejection of the papacy and transubstantiation, his conviction that preaching, not the sacraments, lay at the heart of the ministry, and his championing of the Bible as supreme authority in the Church, with the right and duty of all believers to study it in their native language. In the 16th century, Lollards were the first to welcome the Reformation in England, and entered the mainstream of English Protestantism.

Lutheran
The form of the Magisterial Reformation that took its impetus from the life and teaching of Martin Luther, primarily, but also of Philip Melanchthon. It was distinguished from the Reformed wing of the Magisterial Reformation by its more conservative approach to the reform of worship, its doctrine of the bodily presence of Christ in the eucharistic bread and wine, its willingness to see the Church effectively controlled by the state, and its less emphatic emphasis on predestination.

Magisterial Reformation
Sometimes called "the conservative Reformation", comprising Lutherans, Anglicans, and Reformed. They were united in accepting an Augustinian theology, justification by faith, and infant baptism, and in being committed to a positive working relationship between Church and state (hence "magisterial", from "magistrate" – political ruler). Opposed to the Radical Reformation (see below).

Medieval
Pertaining to the Middle Ages.

Mennonites
After Menno Simons (1496-1561). An Anabaptist group in Germany and the Netherlands, marked by a strong biblicism

(rejection of private revelations), ardent pacifism, and stringent use of the ban (excommunication) and shunning.

Merit

(i) Often used in Latin theology to mean "virtue", "goodness", without any idea of earning salvation.

(ii) More specifically, the obedience of the saints above and beyond what God strictly required of them, sometimes called their "works of supererogation". According to the later Western medieval theory, the pope could transfer these merits to sinners on earth and in purgatory by means of an indulgence.

Middle Ages

The period of history "in the middle" between the patristic age and the Renaissance and Reformation. I have taken this period as beginning around about the late 7th Century (after the sixth ecumenical Council of Constantinople in 681) and ending with the Hussites in the mid-15th Century.

Mysticism

This has always been a hard term to define. Mysticism is rooted in the belief that a person can enter into a state of spiritual "union" with God, and that this union – the ultimate experience – can be pursued by certain disciplines or techniques. But there are seemingly endless varieties of mysticism: Christian, Muslim, pagan, and others.

Neo-Pelagian, neo-Pelagianism

A term sometimes applied to the teaching of William of Ockham (1285-1349) and his disciples, that God grants saving grace to those who "do their best" by their own natural powers. Ockham's opponents condemned this as a revival of the Pelagian heresy. Luther and Calvin were both reared on this teaching, which helps explain their hostility to medieval theology.

Neoplatonists, Neoplatonism

Neoplatonism means "the new Platonism", and is the name given to the philosophy of the great 3rd Century pagan thinker Plotinus (205-70), a more vigorous form of Platonism which became a religious faith. It had a huge impact on the Church, providing a philosophical backdrop for much theology. Partially eclipsed by the Aristotelian revival of the 12th century, Neoplatonism came back into its own with the Renaissance.

Nestorianism

After Nestorius (381-451), patriarch of Constantinople from 428 to 431. Nestorians believed that in the incarnation, Christ not only had two distinct natures, but was two distinct persons – a divine Son of God indwelling a human Son of Mary. The Council of Ephesus in 431 condemned Nestorianism as a heresy.

Nicene creed

Confusingly, this is the Creed drawn up by the Council of *Constantinople* in 381. The Creed which the Council of Nicaea formulated in 325 is not called the Nicene Creed, but "the Creed of Nicaea". The Nicene Creed was recited during the eucharist. The Western addition of the *filioque* clause to the Creed was the major cause of the great East-West schism of 1054.

Oratory

In Roman Catholicism, a chapel where mass may be celebrated.

Orthodoxy

Literally "right glory", the correct way of praising God. A term applied to the Eastern Chalcedonian Churches after the great East-West schism of 1054.

Ottoman Empire

The Islamic Empire under the leadership of the Ottoman Turks. It reached its high point of power and splendour under Suleiman the Magnificent, who ruled from 1520 to 1566. It was arguably the greatest empire in the world at that time, and constantly threatened central Europe from its territories in Eastern Europe (Greece and the Balkans). Suleiman conquered Egypt, Syria, Iraq, North Africa, and Eastern Europe as far as Hungary.

Papacy

From the Latin *papa*, "father". The office of Roman bishop, understood as being founded by the apostle Peter and enjoying first place of honour and dignity above all other bishops. The claims of the Roman bishops became ever more exalted, but the papacy as we know it today, claiming to be the "vicar of Christ" on earth, came to its maturity only in the Middle Ages, in the reign of pope Innocent III (1198-1216).

Papalism, papalist

The view that the pope, not the emperor, was the supreme authority in the Holy Roman Empire.

Patriarch, patriarchate

From the Greek for "fatherly ruler". The title of patriarch was given from the end of the 4th Century to the bishops of Rome, Constantinople, Alexandria and Antioch, and then in the 5th Century to the bishop of Jerusalem too. All other bishops were subject to the authority of the patriarch in whose territory their church was situated. A "patriarchate" is the office and jurisdiction of a patriarch.

Patristic

Relating to the early Church fathers. From the Greek and Latin *pater*, "father". There are various ways of defining the patristic period; I take it as covering the first six centuries of Church history (roughly the period of the first six ecumenical Councils).

Pelagianism

Named after Pelagius (active 383-417). Pelagius held that all human beings were born into the world as sinless as Adam was before he fell; the apostasy of Adam had not corrupted humanity's nature, but had merely set a fatally bad example, which most of Adam's sons and daughters had freely followed. Pelagius defined

God's grace, not in terms of the inner renewing power of the Holy Spirit, but as the moral law, the example of Christ, and the persuasive power of rewards and punishments. Human free-will therefore became the chief source of salvation in the Pelagian scheme. Pelagianism was fought vigorously by Augustine of Hippo (354-430) and condemned by the ecumenical Council of Ephesus in 431.

Platonism
The philosophy of the Greek thinker Plato (427-347 BC) – in terms of influence, the world's greatest philosopher. The heart of Platonism is often held to be its view that everything that exists in the visible world is based on "ideas" that have a higher existence in a higher spiritual world. These ideas were later (*e.g.* by Neoplatonists, both pagan and Christian) identified with the thoughts of God.

Purgatory
A place between heaven and hell where Christians are purified from sins which they failed to wash away on earth through holy communion and works of love. Some of the early Church fathers teach a form of this doctrine, but not in any developed way; it was Gregory the Great (540-604) who brought the idea to its maturity in the Western Church. The East rejected it.

Radical Reformation
The Radical Reformation was an alternative movement to the Magisterial Reformation. Historians call them "Radicals" because they departed from the Catholicism of the Middle Ages much more "radically" (in a more thoroughgoing way) than the other Reformers did, especially in rejecting infant baptism and the Church-state alliance. More fundamentally, they abandoned the ideal of Christianising society and culture, rejected the notion of a Christian state, and saw the Church as an alternative society living in an irredeemably wicked and hostile world. Not a unified movement, the Radicals embodied three tendencies – the Anabaptist, the Rationalist (or anti-Trinitarian), and the Spiritualist. These were not three separate, rigidly defined parties, but one of these tendencies would

generally assume a dominant influence in the mind of a Radical or local grouping of Radicals, although the other two tendencies might also be present in a more muted form.

Rationalist

One form of the Radical Reformation, in which "right reason" was accepted as the supreme authority, and most of the basic doctrines derived from the patristic era, especially the Trinity, were rejected as irrational.

Reformed

Often (less accurately) called "Calvinism". The non-Lutheran form of the Magisterial Reformation. Its leading Continental theologians were Martin Bucer, Heinrich Bullinger, John Calvin, Peter Martyr, and Ulrich Zwingli. It was distinguished from the Lutheran Reformation by its more iconoclastic approach to the reform of worship, its eucharistic doctrine (Christ is present in the Holy Spirit, but is received by believers only, and through faith rather than orally), its high view of the Church's independence from all state control, and its stronger emphasis on predestination.

Sacrament

A Western Latin word meaning "an oath of allegiance". It was applied by the Reformers to baptism and holy communion. Roman Catholics also applied the term to confirmation, penance, marriage, ordination, and extreme unction (the last rites). In the East, sacraments were called "the mysteries".

Sanctification

In Reformation theology, the work of the Holy Spirit in the life of believers, whereby they are personally and spiritually transformed by degrees into the likeness of Christ. The Reformers distinguished sanctification from justification, but insisted that the two always went together as inseparable twin graces.

Schmalkaldic League
An alliance of German Protestant princes and cities formed in December 1531 (named after the town of Schmalkalden in Saxony, where the League was constituted). The League embraced eight princes and 11 cities, mostly Lutheran, but including Strasbourg and other southern cities that leaned to a more Swiss Reformed outlook

Scholasticism
The type of theology that developed in Western universities during the later Middle Ages. It was marked by a commitment to explore and state rationally the full content of individual Christian doctrines, and a desire to fit them together in a comprehensive system of truth. Scholasticism also tended to include the questions of philosophy within its quest for a system of truth – questions about the nature of space, time, matter, causality, *etc*. Later scholasticism was also marked by its increasing reliance on the philosophical concepts and methods of Aristotle.

Schoolmen
The scholastic theologians.

Semi-Pelagians, Semi-Pelagianism
A theological position midway between Pelagianism and the teachings of Augustine of Hippo regarding the origins of the experience of salvation. Pelagianism placed salvation in the power of human free-will; Augustine ascribed salvation (regeneration, the new birth) wholly to God's grace; the Semi-Pelagians held that salvation was empowered by God's grace, but depended for its effect on human cooperation which could always be withheld.

Skete
A small group of up to 12 monks who lived under the spiritual direction of a more experienced monk and met with other sketes for worship on holy days. Named after the Skete region of Egypt.

Sola Scriptura
The key doctrine of the Magisterial Reformation in the sphere of authority. Sola Scriptura (Latin for "Scripture alone") meant for the Reformers that canonical Scripture (excluding the apocrypha) was the only infallible source of teaching in the Church. Other sources of teaching (patristic creeds, Protestant confessions, the preaching ministry) were valid and helpful, but they were not infallible, and their role was to expound Scripture.

Spiritualist
One form of the Radical Reformation. Its distinctive feature was a subordinating of all external authorities – Scripture, tradition, the Church – to the living voice of God speaking directly in the individual's own heart. For the Spiritualists, inward personal experience became the supreme factor in their understanding of God and practice of Christianity. (Not to be confused with Spiritualism in the sense of contacting the dead through mediums.)

Thomism
The theology of Thomas Aquinas, a synthesis of medieval Augustinianism with Aristotelian philosophy.

Treasury of merit
The merits of the saints, which the pope has power to transfer to souls on earth and in purgatory.

Ubiquity
From the Latin *ubique*, "everywhere". The distinctive Lutheran view that Christ is mysteriously present everywhere, not only in His deity, but in His humanity, so that His body and blood are present in the bread and wine of every eucharist.

Universalism
The belief that all human beings, and perhaps the demons too, will finally be saved.

Via antiqua

The "ancient way": the older type of scholastic theology prior to William of Ockham (1285-1349). The via antiqua was more Augustinian theologically, and more committed to "realism" philosophically (the view that the "idea" of a tree, a cat, a human, has independent reality in the mind of God).

Via Moderna

The "modern way": the newer type of scholastic theology, deriving from William of Ockham (1285-1349). The via moderna was neo-Pelagian in its understanding of salvation, and philosophically committed to "nominalism" (the view that the "idea" of a tree, a cat, a human, is simply a deduction made by the human mind from the various examples of actual trees, cats, and humans in the world).

Vulgate

Jerome's Latin translation of the Bible. "Vulgate" comes from the Latin word for "common" – the common Bible, *i.e.* the one in common use. Variations developed, and the Council of Trent authorised a new definitive edition as the authoritative form of Scripture, superior to the Hebrew and Greek originals.

Waldensians

One of the great dissenting movements of Western Christendom. Originated by a certain Valdes or Waldes in Lyons sometime between 1173 and 1176, they were scattered across much of Western Europe, although their stronghold came to be in the Alpine valleys of northern Italy. In many ways they anticipated the views of the Protestant Reformers, e.g. in rejecting the papacy, transubstantiation, purgatory, prayers for the dead and indulgences, and in upholding the supreme authority of Scripture and the right and duty of all believers to study it in their native language. In the 16th century, Waldensians allied themselves with the Reformation and became part of the larger Protestant world.

Western Catholic

I use this term to describe (especially after the great East-West schism of 1054) the Church of Western Europe, which used Latin as its theological and liturgical language, and looked to the Roman papacy for spiritual leadership, although Western Churchmen did not necessarily accept all the increasingly lofty claims that the popes made for themselves. The term *Roman* Catholic is, arguably, best applied to the branch of the Western Catholic Church that rejected the Protestant Reformation of the 16th Century.

Zwinglian

A term often used to describe a doctrine of the Lord's Supper which sees in it little or nothing more than a badge of Christian discipleship and a commemoration of Christ's death. The Swiss Reformer Zwingli held a view similar to this for the bulk of his career.

BIBLIOGRAPHY

Once again I offer here a selection of the books I used in writing this volume,[1] and which the enthusiastic non-specialist should be able to enjoy and profit from. I have highlighted a few of the books in bold print; these, I think, are especially helpful for those coming to Renaissance and Reformation studies for the first time.

I feel obliged to say that many of the general treatments of 16th century Europe, while strong on the political *etc.* dimensions of events, are often woefully inadequate or downright misleading when they deal with theological issues.

General works that have sections on this period

John Baillie, John McNeill, and Henry Van Dusen (editors), *The Library of Christian Classics* (26 volumes) (London: SCM, 1954-)

Geoffrey Barraclough (editor), *The Christian World* (London: Thames and Hudson, 1981)

Henry Bettenson and Chris Maunder, *Documents of the Christian Church* (Oxford University Press, 1999)

Louis Berkhof, *The History of Christian Doctrines* (Edinburgh: Banner of Truth, 1996)

Thomas Bokenkotter, *A Concise History of the Catholic Church* (New York: Image Books, 1990)

Henry Chadwick and G. R. Evans, *Atlas of the Christian Church* (Amsterdam: Time-Life Books, 1991)

F. L. Cross and E. A. Livingstone, *The Oxford Dictionary of the Christian Church* (Oxford: Oxford University Press, 1997)

---

[1] Other good books have been pointed out to me, which I have not included here. Their non-inclusion is simply because I don't know them well enough to justify a recommendation. It is not a reflection on their quality.

J. D. Douglas (editor), *The New International Dictionary of the Christian Church* **(Grand Rapids: Zondervan, 1978)**

Tim Dowley (editor), *The History of Christianity* **(Oxford: Lion, 1990)**

R. S. Franks, *The Work of Christ* (Edinburgh: Thomas Nelson, 1962)

J. Derek Holmes and Bernard W. Bickers, *A Short History of the Catholic Church* (Tunbridge Wells: Burnes and Oates, 1992)

J. N. D. Kelly, *The Oxford Dictionary of Popes* (Oxford University Press, 1988)

Tony Lane, *The Lion, Concise Book of Christian Thought* **(Oxford: Lion, 1996)**

Kenneth Scott Latourette, *History of Christianity* (2 volumes) (San Francisco: Harper, 1986)

Bernard Lohse, *A Short History of Christian Doctrine* (Philadelphia: Fortress Press, 1985)

Alister McGrath, *Iustitia Dei: A History of the Christian Doctrine of Justification* (Cambridge: CUP, 1998)

John McManners (editor), *The Oxford History of Christianity* (Oxford University Press, 1993)

Stephen Neill, *A History of Christian Missions* (Harmondsworth: Penguin, 1964)

J. Neuner and J. Dupuis, *The Christian Faith in the Doctrinal Documents of the Catholic Church* (London: Collins, 1983)

James Orr, *The Progress of Dogma* (London: Hodder and Stoughton, 1901)

Jaroslav Pelikan, *The Christian Tradition: A History of the Development of Doctrine* (5 volumes) (Chicago: University of Chicago Press, 1971-)

Philip Schaff, *History of the Christian Church* (8 volumes) (Grand Rapids: Eerdmans, 1994)

---------*Creeds of Christendom* (3 volumes) (Grand Rapids: Baker, 1996)

Williston Walker, *A History of the Christian Church* (4th edition, revised, Edinburgh: T. & T. Clark, 1986)

Books on worship that deal in whole or in part with this period

Charles Baird, *A Chapter on Liturgies: Historical Sketches* (London: Knight & Son, 1856)

Andrew Wilson-Dickson, *A Brief History of Christian Music* (Oxford: Lion, 1997)

Horton Davies, *Worship and Theology in England: From Cranmer to Baxter and Fox* (Grand Rapids: Eerdmans, 1996)

Gregory Dix, *The Shape of the Liturgy* (London: Continuum International, 2001)

Alasdair Heron, *Table and Tradition* (Edinburgh: The Handsel Press, 1983)

Cheslyn Jones *et al* (eds.), *The Study of Liturgy* (London: SPCK, 1992)

Gary Macy, *The Banquet's Wisdom: A Short History of the Theologies of the Lord's Supper* (New York: Paulist Press, 1992)

Keith Mathison, *Given For You: Reclaiming Calvin's Doctrine of the Lord's Supper* (Phillipsburg: Presbyterian and Reformed, 2002)

William D. Maxwell, *An Outline of Christian Worship, its Development and Forms* (London: Oxford University Press, 1949)

William D. Maxwell, *The Liturgical Portions of the Genevan Service Book* (Westminster: Faith Press, 1965)

John W. Nevin, *The Mystical Presence: A Vindication of the Reformed or Calvinistic Doctrine of the Holy Eucharist* (Eugene, Oregon: Wipf and Stock, 2000)

Hughes Oliphant Old, *Guides to the Reformed Tradition: Worship* (Atlanta: John Knox Press, 1984)

Hermann Sasse, *This Is My Body* (Eugene, Oregon: Wipf and Stock, 2001)

Robert M. Stevenson, *Patterns of Protestant Church Music* (Duke University Press, 1953)

Gordon Wakefield, *An Outline of Christian Worship* (Edinburgh: T&T.Clark, 1998)

Books on the Renaissance and/or Reformation

~~~Studies of individuals~~~

There are excellent studies of Martin Luther, Ulrich Zwingli, John Calvin, and Menno Simons, in **Timothy George, *Theology of the Reformers* (Leicester: Apollos, 1988).**

Erasmus

Roland Bainton, *Erasmus of Christendom* (London: Collins, 1969)
A. G. Dickens and Whitney R. D. Jones, *Erasmus the Reformer* (London: Methuen, 2000)
Basil Hall, 'Erasmus: Biblical Scholar and Catholic Reformer', in *Humanists and Protestants* (Edinburgh: T. & T. Clark, 1990)
Erika Rummel (ed.), *The Erasmus Reader* (Toronto: University of Toronto Press, 1990)

Martin Luther

James Atkinson, *Martin Luther and the Birth of Protestantism* (London: Marshall Morgan and Scott, 1968)
Roland Bainton, *Here I Stand: A Life of Martin Luther* (Nashville: Abingdon Press, 1950)
A. G. Dickens, *The German Nation and Martin Luther* (Fontana, 1974)
Lowell C. Green, *How Melanchthon Helped Luther Discover the Gospel* (Fallbrook: Verdict Publications, 1980)
T. M. Lindsay, *Luther and the German Reformation* (Edinburgh: T&T. Clark, 1900)
Jaroslav Pelikan, *Obedient Rebels: Catholic Substance and Protestant Principle in Luther's Reformation* (London: SCM, 1964)
E. G. Rupp and Benjamin Drewery, *Martin Luther* (London: Edward Arnold, 1970)
Gordon Rupp, *Luther's Progress to the Diet of Worms 1521* (London: SCM, 951)

John M. Todd, *Martin Luther* (London: Burns and Oates, 1964)

George Yule (ed.), *Luther: Theologian for Catholics and Protestants* (Edinburgh: T. & T. Clark, 1985)

Ulrich Zwingli

Jaques Courvoisier, *Zwingli: A Reformed Theologian* (Richmond: John Knox Press, 1963)

Ulrich Gabler, *Huldrych Zwingli: His Life and Work* (Edinburgh: T. & T. Clark, 1987)

G. R. Potter, *Huldrych Zwingli* (London: Edward Arnold, 1978)

---------*Zwingli* (Cambridge: CUP, 1976)

Jean Rilliet, *Zwingli: Third Man of the Reformation* (London: Lutterworth, 1964)

John Calvin

William Bouwsma, *John Calvin: A Sixteenth Century Portrait* (Oxford: OUP, 1989)

Alexandre Ganoczy, *The Young Calvin* (Philadelphia: Westminster Press, 1987)

John T. McNeill, *The History and Character of Calvinism* (New York: OUP, 1954)

T. H. L. Parker, *John Calvin: A Biography* (Philadelphia: Westminster Press, 1975)

---------*Portrait of Calvin* (London: SCM, 1954)

David C. Steinmetz, *Calvin in Context* (Oxford: OUP, 1995)

Emanuel Stickelberger, *John Calvin* (Cambridge: James Clarke, 1959)

Ronald Wallace, *Calvin's Doctrine of Word and Sacrament* (Edinburgh: Oliver and Boyd, 1953)

Francois Wendel, *Calvin* (Collins, 1963)

Other persons

M. W. Anderson, *Peter Martyr* (Nieuwkoop: B. de Graaf, 1975)

Walter Besant, *Gaspard de Coligny* (London: Chatto and Windus, 1905)

David Daniell, *William Tyndale: A Biography* (New Haven: Yale University Press, 1994)

Marcus Loane, *Masters of the English Reformation* (London: Church Book Room Press, 1954)

J. C. McLelland, *The Visible Words of God: An Exposition of the Sacramental Theology of Peter Martyr Vermigli* (Grand Rapids: Eerdmans, 1957)

Philip McNair, *Peter Martyr in Italy* (Oxford: Clarendon, 1967)

Rosalind K. Marshall, *John Knox* (Edinburgh: Birlin, 2000)

J. E. Neale, *Queen Elizabeth I* (St Albans: Panther, 1979)

Hesketh Pearson, *Henry of Navarre* (London: Heinemann, 1963)

Gordon Rupp, *Six Makers of English Religion* (London: Hodder and Stoughton, 1957)

David Steinmetz, *Reformers in the Wings* (Oxford: OUP, 2001)

Pasquale Villari, *Life and Times of Savonarola* (London: T. Fisher Unwin, 1889)

C. V. Wedgwood, *William the Silent* (London: Methuen, 1960)

David Wright (ed.), *Martin Bucer: Reforming Church and Community* (Cambridge: CUP, 1994)

--------- (ed.), *The Common Places of Martin Bucer* (Sutton Courtenay Press, 1972)

~~~More general studies~~~

H. G. Alexander, *Religion in England 1558-1662* (London: Hodder and Stoughton,1968)

C. F. Black et al, *Atlas of the Renaissance* (Amsterdam: Time-Life, 1993)

Nigel Cameron (ed.), *Dictionary of Scottish Church History and Theology* (Edinburgh: T. & T. Clark, 1993)

Owen Chadwick, *The Reformation* (Harmondsworth: Penguin, 1972)

Claire Cross, *Church and People 1450-1660* (Fontana, 1976)

Merle D'Aubigné, *The Reformation in England* (London: Banner of Truth, 1962)

C. S. L. Davies, *Peace, Print and Protestantism 1450-1558* (St Albans: Paladin, 1977)

A. G. Dickens, *The Counter Reformation* (London: Thames and Hudson, 1968)

---------*The English Reformation* (Fontana, 1967)

---------*Reformation and Society in Sixteenth-Century Europe* (London: Thames and Hudson, 1966)

W. A. Dunning, *A History of Political Theories: From Luther to Montesquieu* (New York: MacMillan, 1905)

J. H. Elliot, *Europe Divided 1559-98* (Fontana, 1968)

G. R. Elton, *England Under the Tudors* (London: Methuen, 1974)

---------*Reform and Reformation* (London: Edward Arnold, 1977)

---------*Reformation Europe* (Fontana, 1963)

B. A. Gerrish, *Continuing the Reformation* (Chicago: University of Chicago, 1993)

Pieter Geyl, *The Revolt of the Netherlands* (London: Ernest Benn, 1958)

Janet Glenn Gray, *The French Huguenots* (Grand Rapids: Baker, 1981)

V. H. H. Green, *Renaissance and Reformation* (London: Edward Arnold, 1964)

John Hale, *The Civilisation of Europe in the Renaissance* (London: Harper Collins, 1993)

Basil Hall, *Humanists and Protestants* (Edinburgh: T. & T. Clark, 1990)

Hans Hillerbrand (editor), *The Reformation* (Grand Rapids: Baker, 1978)

---------*The Protestant Reformation* **(New York: Harper Torch-books, 1968)**

Kenneth Hylson-Smith, *Christianity in England from Roman Times to the Reformation. Volume III: 1384-1558* (London: SCM, 2001)

Pierre Janelle, *The Catholic Reformation* (Milwaukee: Bruce, 1963)

David R. Janz, *A Reformation Reader* (Minneapolis: Fortress Press, 1999)

R. Tudur Jones, ***The Great Reformation*** **(Bryntirion: Gwasg Bryntirion Press, 1997)**

H. G. Koenigsberger and G. L. Mosse, *Europe in the Sixteenth Century* (London: Longman, 1968)

C. S. Lewis, *English Literature in the Sixteenth Century* (London: OUP, 1973)

Daniel Liechty (ed.), *Early Anabaptist Spirituality* (New York: Paulist Press, 1994)

Carter Lindberg (ed.), ***The European Reformations Sourcebook*** **(Oxford: Blackwell, 2000)**

---------*The Third Reformation?* (Macon: Mercer University Press, 1983)

T. M. Lindsay, ***History of the Reformation*** **(2 vols.) (Edinburgh: T&T. Clark, 1907)**

J. D. Mackie, ***A History of the Scottish Reformation*** **(Edinburgh: Church of Scotland Youth Committee, 1960)**

Alister McGrath, *Intellectual Origins of the European Reformation* (Oxford: Blackwell, 1987)

John T. McNeill, ***The History and Character of Calvinism*** **(New York: OUP, 1954)**

Keith Mathison, *The Shape of Sola Scriptura* (Moscow, Idaho: Canon Press, 2001)

J. L. Motley, *The Rise of the Dutch Republic* (London: George Allen, 1912)

Ronald Musto, *Catholic Peacemakers. Volume II: From the Renaissance to the Twentieth Century, Part I* (New York: Garland, 1996)

Stephen Neill, *A History of Christian Missions* (Harmondsworth: Penguin, 1964)

Heiko Oberman, *Forerunners of the Reformation* (Philadelphia: Fortress Press, 1981)

Thomas Oden, *The Justification Reader* (Grand Rapids: Eerdmans, 2002)

Maurice Powicke, *The Reformation in England* (London: OUP, 1961)

Keith Randall, *The Catholic and Counter Reformations* (London: Hodder and Stoughton, 1990)

Bernard Reardon, *Religious Thought in the Reformation* **(London: Longman, 1995)**

Jasper Ridley, *Bloody Mary's Martyrs* (London: Constable, 2001)

Gordon Rupp, *The English Protestant Tradition* (Cambridge: CUP, 1947)

George Tavard, *Holy Writ or Holy Church: The Crisis of the Protestant Reformation* (New York: Harper, 1959)

Leonard Verduin, *The Reformers and Their Stepchildren* (Grand Rapids: Eerdmans, 1964)

G. H. Williams, *The Radical Reformation* (Kirksville: Sixteenth Century Journal Publishers, 1992)

G. H. Williams and A. M. Mergal (eds.), *Spiritual and Anabaptist Writers* (London: SCM, 1957)

~~~*Internet resources*~~~

Renaissance
http://www.learner.org/exhibits/renaissance/
A useful "guided tour" of the Renaissance.

La Renaissance
http://www.ibiblio.org/wm/paint/glo/renaissance/
Another useful guide.

Renaissance
http://www.dieu-soleil.net/renaissance.html
This site is devoted to Renaissance art and artists.

Schaff's History of the Christian Church
http://www.ccel.org/s/schaff/history/About.htm
One of the most brilliant histories of the Church ever written: all 8 volumes are online. Volumes 7-8 cover our period.

The Hall of Church History
http://www.gty.org/~phil/hallmap.htm
The Hall of Church History (also known, more colourfully, as "Theology From A Bunch Of Dead Guys"!) covers the whole 2000

years of Christianity, but it has a section on the Church of the Reformation era.

The Reformation Guide
http://www.educ.msu.edu/homepages/laurence/reformation/index.htm
An excellent guide to Reformation material on the internet.

The Protestant Reformation
http://history.hanover.edu/early/prot.html
Another excellent guide.

Reformation Europe
http://www.fordham.edu/halsall/mod/modsbook02.html
From the Internet Modern History Sourcebook. Very good.

Project Wittenberg
http://www.iclnet.org/pub/resources/text/wittenberg/wittenberg-home.html
A superb site for materials relating to the Lutheran Reformation.

Lutheran Theology Website
http://www.angelfire.com/ny4/djw/lutherantheology.html
A comprehensive Lutheran website. A lot is not strictly related to the Lutheran Reformation in the 16th century, but it will help the student to understand the distinctives of Lutheran theology.

John Calvin
http://www.educ.msu.edu/homepages/laurence/reformation/Calvin/Calvin.Htm
This site provides links to sites on the life and work of Calvin, including his writings online.

Anabaptist Mennonite History
http://anabaptists.org/history/
A good Mennonite site for Anabaptist history.

Our Unitarian Heritage
http://online.sksm.edu/ouh/
This site has chapters covering the history of the Rationalist, anti-Trinitarian wing of the Radical Reformation. Very informative.

The Eastern Orthodox world

Richard Charques, *A Short History of Russia* (London: English Universities Press Ltd., 1959)
G. P. Fedotov, *A Treasury of Russian Spirituality* (Gloucester, Mass.: Peter Smith, 1969)
George A. Maloney, *A History of Orthodox Theology since 1453* (Belmont: Nordland, 1976)
George Mastrantontis, *Augsburg and Constantinople* (Brookline: Holy Cross Orthodox Press, 1982)
Nicholas Riasanovsky, *A History of Russia* (Oxford: OUP, 1993)
Seraphim Rose and Herman Podmoshensky (compilers and translators), *The Northern Thebaid: Monastic Saints of the Russian North* (Platina: St Herman of Alaska Brotherhood, 1995)
Sir Steven Runciman, *The Great Church in Captivity* (Cambridge: CUP, 1968)
Alexander Schmemann, *The Historical Road of Eastern Orthodoxy* (London: Harvill Press, 1963)
Robert Wallace, *The Rise of Russia* (Netherlands: Time/Life, 1967)
Timothy Ware, *The Orthodox Church* (London: Penguin, 1997)
Nicolas Zernov, *Eastern Christendom* (London: Weidenfeld and Nicolson, 1963)

INDEX to NAMES

INDEX to SUBJECTS